THE ART OF SUBVERSION IN INQUISITORIAL SPAIN

Purdue Studies in Romance Literatures

Editorial Board

Floyd Merrell, Series Editor
Jeanette Beer
Paul B. Dixon

Benjamin Lawton
Howard Mancing
Allen G. Wood

Associate Editors

French
Paul Benhamou
Willard Bohn
Gerard J. Brault
Mary Ann Caws
Gérard Defaux
Milorad R. Margitić
Glyn P. Norton
Allan H. Pasco
Gerald Prince
David Lee Rubin
Roseann Runte
Ursula Tidd

Italian
Fiora A. Bassanese
Peter Carravetta
Franco Masciandaro
Anthony Julian Tamburri

Luso-Brazilian
Fred M. Clark
Marta Peixoto
Ricardo da Silveira Lobo Sternberg

Spanish and Spanish American
Maryellen Bieder
Catherine Connor
Ivy A. Corfis
Frederick A. de Armas
Edward Friedman
Charles Ganelin
David T. Gies
Roberto González Echevarría
Patricia Hart
David K. Herzberger
Emily Hicks
Djelal Kadir
Amy Kaminsky
Lucille Kerr
Alberto Moreiras
Randolph D. Pope
Francisco Ruiz Ramón
Elżbieta Skłodowska
Mario Valdés
Howard Young

 volume 30

THE ART OF SUBVERSION IN INQUISITORIAL SPAIN

Rojas

and

Delicado

Manuel da Costa Fontes

Purdue University Press
West Lafayette, Indiana

Copyright ©2005 by Purdue University. All rights reserved.

09   08   07   06   05   5   4   3   2   1

∞The paper used in this book meets the minimum requirements of
American National Standard for Information Sciences—Permanence of
Paper for Printed Library Materials, ANSI Z39.48-1992.

Printed in the United States of America
Design by Anita Noble

Library of Congress Cataloging-in-Publication Data

Fontes, Manuel da Costa.
    The art of subversion in inquisitorial Spain : Rojas and Delicado /
Manuel da Costa Fontes.
      p.   cm. — (Purdue studies in Romance literatures ; v. 30)
    Includes bibliographical references and index.
    ISBN 1-55753-348-2 (pbk.)
    1. Rojas, Fernando de, d. 1541. Celestina. 2. Delicado, Francisco, 16th
cent. Retrato de la Loçana andaluza. 3. Religion and literature—Spain.
4. Christianity in literature. 5. Marranos—Spain—Intellectual life. I. Title.
II. Series.

PQ6428.F56 2004
862'.2—dc22   2004011669

For Maria-João

Contents

- *ix* **Preface**
- 1 **Chapter One**
  The Converso Problem
- 33 **Chapter Two**
  Repression and Artistic Expression
- 79 **Chapter Three**
  The Idea of "Limpieza" in *Celestina, La Lozana andaluza,* and Other Literary Works
- 101 **Chapter Four**
  Celestina as an Antithesis of the Blessed Mother
- 142 **Chapter Five**
  Christian Prayer and Dogma in *Celestina:* The Polemic Continues
- 171 **Chapter Six**
  "Sailing," Renaissance Rome, and Exile in *La Lozana andaluza:* An Allegorical Reading
- 202 **Chapter Seven**
  The Holy Trinity and the Annunciation in *La Lozana andaluza*
- 231 **Chapter Eight**
  Rojas, Delicado, and the Art of Subversion
- 259 **Appendix**
  English Translations
- 273 **Notes**
- 303 **Abbreviations**
- 305 **Works Cited**
- 339 **Index**

Preface

Unlike other European countries, by the end of the Middle Ages Spain had a large number of *conversos*, Jews or descendants of Jews who, in most instances, had been forced to embrace Christianity. The problem started in 1391, when numerous pogroms devastated the country. Christian mobs invaded the Jewish quarters of numerous towns, and the Jews they caught were given two choices: to accept Christianity at once, or to die. There were thousands of martyrs, but, understandably, many more chose to live. During the first two decades of the fifteenth century, Christian propaganda and intimidation led to thousands of additional, "voluntary" conversions.

Although the Church recognized that conversion ought to be a matter of conviction, there was no turning back for those who had been baptized. Besides being known as *conversos* or New Christians, people also called them *marranos* ("little pigs"), and these names continued to be applied to their descendants, generation after generation, even when a person only had a remote Jewish ancestor.

These conversos were a very small proportion of the population, but, since many of them were highly educated, they formed an important sector of the intelligentsia of late medieval and Renaissance Spain. The conversion had opened many doors previously closed to them. Resenting the competition, most Old Christians continued to regard them as Jews, claimed that they followed the law of Moses secretly, betraying Christianity, and looked for ways to prevent them from assimilating and becoming full-fledged members of society. In other words, the populace was anti-Semitic, and wanted the former Jews to be kept in their place.

To a large extent, they got what they wanted. By the middle of the fifteenth century, laws of "blood purity" excluded conversos from many official honors and positions. After 1481, the ever vigilant Inquisition tried very hard to ensure the "purity" of their faith, and they lived in terror until the 1520s, when the Inquisition felt that it had essentially achieved its aims. There continued to exist a climate of fear and suspicion afterward, however. Since anonymous denunciations were encouraged, people watched their New Christian neighbors carefully, including their dietary habits, in order to detect the smallest sign of Judaism. Thus, conversos found themselves living "on the margin of two societies, from one of which they could not fully escape and the other of which they could not fully enter" (Silverman 1971b, 147).

The victims of this unrelenting discrimination reacted in different ways. Some remained truly Jewish in their hearts, practicing the faith of their ancestors as best they could, in great secrecy, while others joined the Church as monks, nuns, and priests. A few even became bishops and cardinals. There were also inquisitors of converso extraction, and some, such as St. Theresa

Preface

and St. John of the Cross, were recognized as saints. Others found refuge in literature, and, by virtue of their education, made an important, disproportionate contribution to the development of Spanish letters.

At one time, poets such as Antón de Montoro were able to express freely their bitterness at the discrimination that they continued to suffer as New Christians. Using folly as a very thin disguise, some of the converts writing in the *Cancionero de Baena* (1445) displayed their doubts concerning the central dogmas of their new faith—the Virgin Birth, the Incarnation, and the Holy Trinity. One of them, Nicolás de Valencia, even dared to ask in one of his poems if the birth of Christ did not constitute divine sanction for adultery, in the sense that God had begotten a Son by someone else's wife. Such freedom disappeared with the establishment of the Inquisition in 1481. Afterward, the only relatively safe way for those conversos who wished to exercise their human need to express their feelings and doubts was in a covert, indirect manner.

Fernando de Rojas and Francisco Delicado participated in this type of counterdiscourse. Rojas published *Celestina* in 1499, in Burgos, and Delicado, who spent many years of his life as an exile, published *La Lozana andaluza* in 1530, in Venice, two years after being forced to leave Rome, because of the sack of that city by the imperial army of Charles V in 1527. Rojas uses metaphor, irony, parody, and allegory to protest against the situation in which he had to live and to attack Christian dogma, but in such an indirect, ambiguous manner that many scholars dispute that he attempted to do so at all. A like-minded converso, Delicado understood this aspect of *Celestina* quite well and set out to surpass it, shedding important light on Rojas's ambiguity in the process, since, after all, he could hardly imitate and compete with something unless it were already there. But whereas *Celestina* is extremely ambiguous and, as Rojas himself cautiously points out, susceptible to various interpretations, Delicado, no doubt because he felt much safer in Venice, is much less worried about deniability. He attacks Christian dogma in a more daring, open manner, and even parodies and mocks the precautions of his unnamed predecessor, with whom he also conducts good-natured banter.

Notwithstanding his daring, however, Delicado was not suicidal, and so he also encoded his message, allowing himself some room for deniability. Writers have done this frequently in order to express their disagreement with official ideology under dangerous, repressive circumstances, addressing this aspect of their works to readers with similar ideas. It goes without saying, however, that a proper understanding of such views depends on interpretation, and, since the authors themselves encoded their subversion for the sake of their own personal safety, such interpretations can never be definitely proven.

Preface

On the Iberian Peninsula, the latest examples of this type of writing occurred in Franco's Spain. Now that Spain is free, it is possible to speak with some authors and confirm that they did indeed encode messages against the establishment in works that they managed to publish and even to stage. Unfortunately, it is not possible to go back to the Middle Ages and the Renaissance in order to do the same, and there has been a strong reaction against the investigators who detected a subversive converso component in many distinguished Spanish writers. Scholars such as Américo Castro and Stephen Gilman were accused of inventing or overemphasizing a Semitic, non-Western element in Spanish literature, and of attributing a converso background to many writers without sufficient proof. They were also criticized for trying to explain the whole work of an author through this particular lens, and for developing fanciful, surrealistic interpretations in order to justify preconceived theories. Although some errors were made, this does not justify an a priori, automatic dismissal of that type of research and of all the new evidence that might be brought forward. Such an attitude is most unfair, for it is tantamount to an anachronistic, retroactive censorship of the past, silencing the voices of the authors involved.

The existence of many important converso writers, some of whom protested against the situation in which they had to live, is undeniable, and, rather than detracting from Spanish literature, their encoded messages contributed to enriching it even more. As the late Joseph H. Silverman perceptively pointed out, the unenviable situation of the converso, paradoxically, also provided him with a unique, privileged perspective: "He lived on the margin: he observed from without or from a precarious position within; he had a perspective and a capacity for cynical evaluation of motives that were unlikely in persons born to full membership in their society" (1971b, 147). In addition, this unique perspective enabled converso writers to envision new, previously unexplored regions, and to contribute to the development of genres such as the picaresque, Moorish, and pastoral novels.

As generally recognized, *Celestina* and *La Lozana andaluza* are the two most important precursors of the picaresque novel. In the pages that follow, I will attempt to show, with more concrete evidence than presented before, that Rojas and Delicado's situation as conversos must be taken into account in order to gain a fuller understanding of their works. Although the converso element is but one component of their rich, multifaceted character, it is also a crucial one, for it contributes considerably to an even better understanding of Rojas and Delicado's artistic genius.

For quotations from the two works under discussion, I have chosen carefully from the available editions. Because of its widespread use in American classrooms, for *Celestina* I have used Dorothy S. Severin's edition of Zaragoza 1507 (Rojas 1987), noting the few instances in which it differs

Preface

slightly from others. For *La Lozana andaluza*, I have selected Claude Allaigre's edition (Delicado 1985), which is in the same series.

The English translations of the longer quotations are located in the appendix. For the English version of quotations from *Celestina* and *La Lozana andaluza*, I have followed translations by Mack Hendricks Singleton (Rojas 1975 [1958]) and Bruno M. Damiani (Delicado 1987), respectively, but I have modified them considerably in the process. For English translations of quotations from Cervantes, I have also added some modifications to the translations I had at hand,[1] but, unless otherwise indicated, the other translations are completely mine.

Portions of this book were published as articles,[2] and it has benefited much from the help of several friends and colleagues. Samuel G. Armistead discussed many ideas with me over the years, read an earlier version of Chapter 7, and offered numerous, valuable suggestions. Joseph H. Silverman talked with me repeatedly about conversos, an exchange that began shortly after my graduation from U.C.L.A., and the offprints that he sent me were an early, crucial source of inspiration. Francisco Márquez Villanueva read drafts of the articles on exile and the Holy Trinity in *La Lozana andaluza*, discussed conversos and the *Cárcel de amor* with me, and offered invaluable suggestions. A perusal of the bibliography will give a better idea of my indebtedness to him. Albert A. Sicroff, the top expert on the statutes of blood purity and their consequences, also shared his wisdom with me. Joseph T. Snow provided important bibliographical information, read drafts of three of the articles used here, and saved me from some grievous mistakes. Richard M. Berrong, Daniel Eisenberg, Maria Eugenia Lacarra, Joseph V. Ricapito, Charlotte M. Stern, Mercedes Vaquero, and Louise O. Vasvari also read drafts of some of the articles used here. My heartfelt gratitude to each and every one of them. Javier E. Cattapan, Rosa Commisso, Jerry Craddock, Radd Ehrman, William H. González, José Labrador, Jennifer Larson, and Jack Weiner also helped to clarify various questions. My daughter Natacha read the translations and made several important suggestions. I would also like to thank three former students: To Frances Rocafort, I owe an accurate count of the number of times that the name of Jesus appears in *Celestina*; Robert E. Sitler noticed the similarity between the names of Calisto and Cristo; Elizabeth Strbik pointed out that the sixty-six *mamotretos* in *La Lozana andaluza* correspond to the number of books in the Protestant Bible. Through Mediber, the listserv on Medieval Iberia, Miriam T. Shadis and Beth Quitslund confirmed that St. Jerome's Vulgate also contained sixty-six canonical books, and thirteen deuterocanonical ones as well. I am also grateful to the numerous persons in Mediber and the listserv entitled Jewish-Languages for answering my query regarding Jewish and Christian polemics in Spain. One of the anonymous readers improved the manuscript with

Preface

numerous stylistic observations, offering invaluable insights and additional bibliography as well. The Kent State University Research Council provided a Research Appointment that enabled me to devote the spring of 1999 to this project.

Finally, I would like to thank my wife, Maria-João, for her patience in listening to the gradual, often repeated reading of every page in this book, for playing devil's advocate, and for her unabashed criticism. It was only as I was reading to her the first half of the last chapter that I realized that she had been an invaluable critic for me for no fewer than twenty-seven years.

Chapter One

The Converso Problem

According to Islamic tradition, Christians and Jews are "people of the book" because they are mentioned in the Koran, which includes Jewish and Christian figures such as Abraham, Isaac, Mary, and Jesus. Since Muslims believe that the angel Gabriel transported to heaven the founder of Islam, Mohammed, from the very rock on which Abraham almost slew his son Ishmael (rather than Isaac) in obedience to God on the summit of Mount Moriah, Jerusalem is almost as important to Islam as to followers of the other two faiths.

After the Islamic conquest of Spain in 711, this syncretism laid the foundation for a period of tolerance, in which Christians, Muslims, and Jews lived together in peaceful co-existence.[1] This practice did not stop in the lands that were slowly reconquered by the Christians. People of different faiths continued to live in the same towns, to show a measure of tolerance for each other's beliefs and cultures, and were even able to work together.[2]

The best example of this multicultural collaboration, however, is perhaps the scholarly activity that went on in the city of Toledo, reconquered in 1085. Since the Muslims had developed a brilliant civilization, far more advanced than anything that existed in contemporary Europe, Christians and Jews worked together in the translation of numerous books written in Arabic, particularly during the twelfth and thirteenth centuries.[3] These works, which dealt with philosophy, astronomy, mathematics, geometry, botany, and medicine, had a considerable, often unacknowledged amount of influence in the development of the European mini-Renaissance of the thirteenth century.[4]

Unfortunately, this peaceful co-existence, subsequently designated as *convivencia*,[5] began to change as the Christians gained the upper hand. It became clear that the completion of the Reconquest was only a matter of time after Ferdinand III conquered Córdoba (1236) and Seville (1248), and the small kingdom of Granada remained the last Muslim stronghold in the Peninsula.[6]

Christian resentment toward the Jews who lived in their midst, mostly in Jewish quarters known as *aljamas* or *juderías*, increased during the fourteenth century. Thanks to their tradition of learning and superior education,

1

Chapter One

at a time when most Christians were illiterate, some Jews had achieved positions of importance in the royal courts of Castile, Aragon, and Portugal. Jews served as tax collectors and moneylenders,[7] administered the properties of the great nobles, and prospered in business and trade. Many dedicated themselves to medicine.

The common people hated the opulent merchants, the tax collectors who served as front for their Christian masters,[8] and the moneylenders. The vulgar anti-Semitism previously developed in other European countries—the Jews had been banished from England in 1290 and were expelled from France and Germany in the fourteenth century—spread throughout the land. People accused Jews of having poisoned the wells during the Black Plague (1348),[9] of blaspheming against Christianity, of stealing and desecrating the Host, and there were intermittent reports that they kidnapped and killed children so as to use their blood in satanic, anti-Christian rituals. In the opinion of most people, the only solution was conversion. Some preachers wanted to achieve this through proselytizing activity, claiming that the very presence of Jews brought about divine punishment and all sorts of calamities; others thought that violence should be used to convert them. Whether they advocated conversion by persuasion or by force, however, both groups agreed that it was necessary to put an end to Judaism in Spain (Suárez 1992,182).

In Castile, the situation became even worse because of the wars between Peter I (1350–69), son of Alfonso XI and María de Portugal, and his illegitimate brother Henry, Count of Trastámara, whose mother was Alfonso's mistress, Leonor de Guzmán. Peter I favored the Jews, who occupied important administrative positions at court, and, in order to gather popular support, Henry claimed that his brother had placed the realm in their hands. The English and the French, who were engaged in the Hundred Years' War, intervened. Led by Bertrand du Guesclin, the French came to the aid of Henry. Commanded by Edward, the Black Prince, the English fought on the side of Peter. There were anti-Jewish outbreaks in several towns. When Henry assumed the throne, after assassinating his brother by his own hand (1369)—some said that du Guesclin helped him with the murder—he argued that the government could not be run without the Jews, but there was great opposition. The seeds of hatred, which had always been there, had grown much stronger (Beinart 1993, 166–73).

In 1378, a rabid anti-Semite, Ferrant Martínez, archdeacon of Écija, began to preach in Seville against the Jews. He encouraged his listeners to cease all contact with them and to destroy their twenty-three synagogues, where the devil allegedly held sway. The archbishop of the city, Pedro Gómez Barroso, tried to use his influence at court to put a stop to the archdeacon, warning that the situation was becoming dangerous. The Jews were regarded as the personal property of the king, Henry II—they were under his jurisdiction

The Converso Problem

and their taxes went directly to the royal treasury. In spite of this, Henry II's response, a letter sent out on March 3, 1378, was so meek that Ferrant Martínez ignored it and began to make recruits among the rabble and the most fanatical individuals in the city, promising them eternal salvation if they destroyed the Jews. Further efforts on the part of Henry's successor, John I, to make him desist from his crusade came to naught. On July 7, 1390, the archbishop died and Ferrant Martínez became administrator of the diocese. Three months later (October 9) the king also died, after a fall from his horse. His son, Henry III, was too young to govern, and a large, ineffectual regency council consisting of seventeen persons was put in place (Suárez 1992, 187–89).

Ferrant Martínez took the opportunity to unleash his rabble on the Jewish quarter of Seville on June 6, 1391. Many so-called good people joined the crowd, including some nobles, certain that they would profit richly from the booty. Those who were unable to flee or hide and refused to be baptized were invariably put to death. The rioters reportedly murdered 4,000 people, but the number of those who accepted baptism in order to escape was even greater. Incited by outside agitators from Seville, the disturbances spread like wildfire to neighboring towns and from there to the rest of Castile and also to Aragon, including Valencia, Catalonia, and the Balearic Islands. Members of the clergy, some nobles, and city councilmen participated practically everywhere. The number of converts always exceeded the dead. In Madrid, all the Jews reportedly asked to be baptized. In Burgos, there were so many converts that they came to occupy an important section in the city.

The feeble attempts of the authorities to impose order and stop the carnage failed in most instances. Unlike Castile, Aragon had a mature king, John I. He and his queen were in Zaragoza when the disturbances began, and they tried to prevent the destruction by sending out letters with instructions to governors and city councils. In several towns, Jews found protection within castle walls, but some of those castles fell to the fury of the masses. In Valencia and Barcelona, the destruction was so thorough that the Jewish quarters ceased to exist. In Majorca, the old Jewish quarter became a New Christian neighborhood practically overnight. Thanks to the reaction of their monarchs, however, the Jews of Aragon fared slightly better than those in Castile. The communities of Zaragoza and a few other towns escaped.

The only part of Christian Spain that seems to have been completely unaffected by the riots was the tiny kingdom of Navarre, governed by Charles III (Baer 1992, 2: 118–19). When the disturbances finally ended, most Jewish communities lay in ruins. Fearing to concentrate in large cities as they had done before, because they realized that this made it easier for them to be attacked, many Jews decided to settle in small towns and villages, where they could have better personal relations with their Christian neighbors and feel a greater measure of security. In the fifteenth century,

3

there were no fewer than 216 communities in Castile and 35 in Aragon. This dispersion, however, also had devastating effects. Besides stifling intellectual and religious life (Suárez 1992, 204), it made recovery much more difficult.

Once a person had been baptized, there was no turning back. According to Christian doctrine, a sacrament is not valid unless it is freely and willingly received. Although those who converted had done so in order to save their lives, Christian theologians and experts in canon law maintained that their baptism could not be revoked; the fact that many other Jews had refused conversion, they asserted, showed that they had accepted it of their own free will (Suárez 1992, 202). But perhaps there was a better, more human explanation. In the words of Renée Levine Melammed, "the possibility of permitting so many newly baptized individuals to revert to their former religion was unthinkable, for it would make a mockery of the Catholic Church and its dogma" (1999, 4).

This is how the converso problem in Spain began. Thousands of people found themselves turned into Christians from one moment to the next, with little or no knowledge of the new faith that had been so cruelly imposed upon them. Numerous families were divided, for whereas many of those who were caught accepted baptism, those who had been able to hide or flee remained Jewish. In some cases, even husbands and wives ended up with separate religions (Baer 1992, 2: 132–33). The so-called converts, also known as New Christians and *marranos* ("pigs"),[10] had to attend Mass, marry and bury their dead in the Church, and act publicly as Christians. Naturally, most of them maintained close relationships with their Jewish relatives and friends, and, as their Old Christian neighbors well knew, they continued to practice the faith of their ancestors secretly, passing it on to their children.

Though much diminished, at least as far as official numbers were concerned, Judaism continued to exist, but both the civil authorities and the clergy wanted it to disappear completely from Spanish soil. The Papacy intervened in their favor. This was the period of the great schism of the Western Church (1378–1417), when there were two rival popes, one in Rome and another in Avignon, and the latter decided to undertake the conversion of the Jews of Spain in order to draw the Christian world to his side (Netanyahu 1995, 182–83). He was Benedict XIII, a Spaniard, formerly Cardinal Pedro de Luna, and he entrusted the mission to Vincent Ferrer (c. 1350–1419). Already in his sixties, Ferrer, a Dominican friar from Valencia, was subsequently canonized. Although St. Vincent did not approve of violence and stated that only conversion by persuasion was valid, he either encouraged or failed to oppose the anti-Semitic laws of 1412, enacted in Ayllón, under the direction of the Castilian co-regent, the Queen Mother Catalina of Lancaster, Henry III's widow.

The Converso Problem

These provisions were so harsh that they isolated Jews from Christians and practically reduced them to misery, depriving them of the means to make a decent living. Those with homes and businesses in Christian areas were directed to move within eight days and were forbidden to exercise most professions. They could not serve Christians as physicians, pharmacists, smiths, carpenters, tailors, clothiers, butchers, shoemakers, or merchants (Suárez 1992, 214–17; Netanyahu 1995, 191–96). Clearly, these restrictions were designed to speed up the process of conversion, suggesting that it was God Himself who was punishing them for their obstinacy (Suárez 1992, 214). However, the effect of the new laws was probably mostly psychological. As Luis Suárez pointed out, had they been strictly applied, the survival of the Jewish community would have been rendered impossible (217), but that was not the case. Henry Kamen came to the same conclusion. Since the legislation of 1412 was unenforceable in practice, it must have been either ignored or revoked (1998, 14).

Through lengthy sermons, St. Vincent sought to convert everyone, including Muslims and bad Christians. He began his campaign in southwestern Castile in 1411, one year before the publication of the laws of Ayllón or Catalina's laws, as they were also called, and traveled north, entering Toledo on May 30, 1411. St. Vincent continued to preach throughout Castile and Aragon for several years. Jews were forced to attend his sermons under the threat of severe fines. If they tried to oppose him with their arguments, they were fined for proffering insults against the Christian faith (Suárez 1992, 219). In several localities, St. Vincent entered synagogues, expelled the Jews, and dedicated them as churches (Baer 1992, 2: 166). Crowds of pious people, beggars, vagabonds, fanatics, and flagellants, who whipped themselves bloody with chains, followed him everywhere, terrifying the Jews, who feared that what had happened in 1391 could start again at any moment. People converted by the thousands, but it goes without saying that, in most cases, such conversions were as sincere as those that had taken place two decades before.

St. Vincent's preaching lasted until 1416, when Benedict XIII was deprived of his authority (Baer 1992, 2: 231–32), just before the end of the schism of the Western Church (1417). Still in 1416, St. Vincent took his campaign north, to France (Kamen 1998, 14).

In the middle of all this, the Disputation of Tortosa, which lasted almost two years (Feb. 1413–Nov. 1414), dealt yet another blow to Judaism. The former Joshua ha-Lorqui, who took the name of Jerónimo de Santa Fe ("Jerome of the Holy Faith") upon his conversion by St. Vincent in 1412, being named physician to the Pope in the same year, proposed to convince the Jews of their error by proving to them that, according to the Talmud, the Messiah had already come. Benedict XIII, who had taken up residence in his native Aragon, "invited" each Jewish community in that kingdom and

Chapter One

Catalonia to send two to four representatives to his papal court, in Tortosa (Baer 1992, 2: 171–72; Maccoby 1993, 82–94).

The meetings were held in a large auditorium. On the Christian side there were seventy chairs for cardinals, archbishops, and bishops; many nobles and burghers were in attendance as well (Gerber 1992, 125). The Pope himself was present, with Santa Fe serving as the chief spokesman for Christianity.

Contrary to what its title indicated, this so-called disputation was not really a debate, since the purpose of the twenty-four theses formulated by Santa Fe was to prove the tenets of Christianity through the Talmud and to convert the Jewish scholars, who were severely limited in the manner in which they could reply. The intimidating, one-sided affair was regarded as a great Christian victory, even though the number of converts—about 3,000, according to the Pope himself—was relatively small. On the other hand, this included the well-educated members of several prominent families (Baer 1992, 2: 210–12), fourteen rabbis (Suárez 1992, 224), and, notwithstanding the intimidating circumstances, these conversions could be claimed to have been effected by "persuasion" rather than by force.[11]

The riots of 1391, St. Vincent's campaign (1411–16), the laws of 1412, and the Disputation of Tortosa (1413–14), then, led to thousands of conversions. Since medieval numbers are incredibly inflated, varying considerably from writer to writer, it is impossible to come up with precise figures. For example, contemporary estimates for the conversions made by St. Vincent Ferrer, which included Jews, Muslims, and reformed Christians, range anywhere between 15,000 and 100,000 (Netanyahu 1995, 1098). Modern scholars have not been able to agree regarding the number of conversions effected between 1391 and 1416, either. Netanyahu, in whose opinion the unenforceable laws of 1412 were implemented with the desired effect, came up with no fewer than 400,000 (1995, 1102). Jane S. Gerber arrived at a much lower figure, estimating that there were 100,000 conversions in 1391 and as many as 50,000 more by 1415, which brings the total to 150,000 (1992, 113, 117). Antonio Domínguez Ortiz, in whose opinion there were about 250,000 Jews in Spain at the time, estimated that there were 150,000 converts as well (1992, 41–43).

Popular anti-Semitism was such that the relatively small number of persons who converted prior to this period were never well accepted. The *Siete partidas*, the famous legal compilation completed in 1265 during the reign of Alfonso X "The Wise," reveals that people called them *tornadizos* ("turncoats") and "reproached them in many other evil and insulting manners." This attitude prevented many who wished to become Christian from doing so, and a fine was prescribed for those who proffered such insults. By 1380, during the reign of John I of Castile, the word *marrano* ("pig") had already

The Converso Problem

been added to the insulting vocabulary (Netanyahu 1995, 260–65). Although both Church and State encouraged conversion and all Christians agreed that this was desirable, the masses did not want to see them in their midst.

Given this bigotry, the sudden admission of thousands of newcomers into the Christian fold provoked a strong reaction: "The idea of too many former Jews unabashedly assimilating into their midst was simply intolerable to many Spanish Christians" (Melammed 1999, 6). The former Jews were now able to compete for numerous public offices that were previously closed to them and even to join the ranks of the Church. Thanks to their superior education, the conversos soon occupied a great number of administrative positions, ranging from city councils to the royal courts. Many entered into the religious orders, and there were converso bishops, archbishops, and even cardinals. The Old Christian majority, which continued to despise and regard them as Jews, was outraged, perceiving this as a takeover. Feeling that public and Church offices rightfully belonged to them, the Old Christians soon began to take steps in order to retain control and exclude the New Christians. Who did they think they were, anyway? To put it bluntly, everything ought to be done to keep those outsiders in their place.

That was the origin of the racist idea of "limpieza de sangre" ("purity of the blood"),[12] which limited access to public offices and institutions to persons without Jews or Moors among their ancestors. Attempts to exclude converts from offices in which they could exercise control over Old Christians had been made as far back as the twelfth century (Netanyahu 1995, 256–60). Shortly after 1391, Diego de Anaya, the bishop who founded the College (student residence) of San Bartolomé at the University of Salamanca, stipulated in the statutes (1414) that persons of Jewish stock, "whether the grade or origin is remote or near," could not be admitted, even though he knew that, according to Catholic doctrine, the sacrament of baptism made all Christians one in the body of Christ (272–75).[13] As Netanyahu demonstrated, this anti-Semitism served as a prelude to the anti-marrano disturbances that broke out in Toledo in 1449, after a supposed period of goodwill toward New Christians.

John II reigned in Castile at that time. His favorite, Alvaro de Luna, had created an efficient administration by placing a great number of marranos at court and in city councils. Pedro Sarmiento, commander of the castle of Toledo, decided to initiate a rebellion against the powerful favorite and, to obtain the support of the common people in the city, he unleashed them against the hated conversos. Accusing the latter of siding with Alvaro de Luna and of being secret Jews, Sarmiento established a court, burned in the city's plazas several people suspected of Judaizing, and then proceeded to confiscate their property. In June of the same year, the rebels promulgated the *Sentencia-Estatuto* ("Judgment and Statute"), which constitutes a bench

7

Chapter One

mark on blood purity. It declared that conversos were evil by virtue of their ancestry and excluded them from any public or Church office in the city of Toledo and the surrounding area, thus creating by law an unredeemable and inassimilable new class that, in fact, was neither Jewish nor Christian (Gerber 1992, 127):

> We declare the so-called *conversos*, offspring of perverse Jewish ancestors, must be held by law to be infamous and ignominious, unfit, and unworthy to hold any public office or any benefice within the city of Toledo, or land within its jurisdiction, or to be commissioners for oaths or notaries, or to have any authority over the true Christians of the Holy Catholic Church. (Gerber 1992, 127)

Although this racist statute was a local development, it did in fact express the feeling of the masses throughout the country. Pope Nicholas V banned it as un-Christian, but King John II felt pressured to approve it in 1451. Other city councils soon followed suit.

The anti-converso disturbances continued. In 1467 there were riots in Toledo, Ciudad Real, and Burgos. In 1473–74 even bloodier disturbances took place in Córdoba, Jaén, and other Andalusian cities. In Córdoba, the riots began because of a procession, when a ten-year-old girl accidentally emptied from a window a jug of water on top of a statue of the Blessed Mother. The house where the girl happened to be belonged to a New Christian. A rumor spread that the jug was full of urine, and people began to kill conversos and burn their homes (Caro Baroja 1986, 1: 143).

The reaction against New Christians initiated by the *Sentencia-Estatuto* also spread to several cathedral chapters, religious and military orders, and university colleges, which eventually adopted their own statutes of blood purity. The first cathedral chapter was that of Badajoz (1511); it was followed by those of Seville (1515), Córdoba (1530), and others. Among the religious orders the first were the Jeronimites, embarrassed by the discovery that some monks were Judaizing within the protection afforded by the walls of their monasteries. In 1485 the Inquisition burned Brother Diego Marchena, from the mother house at Guadalupe.[14] During torture, he confessed that he never consecrated the Host during Mass (Domínguez Ortiz 1992, 149–50).[15] In 1486–87, five monks from the monastery of La Sisla were burned at the stake. Instead of consecrating the Host during the elevation, the prior, García de Zapata, would say instead: "¡Sus, periquete, que mira la gente!" ("Look out, little Pete, people are watching!"; Caro Baroja 1986, 2: 300). The scandal led the Jeronimites to adopt a statute in 1486. Although the Catholic Monarchs revoked it after a special appeal (Kamen 1998, 235), Pope Alexander VI approved it in 1495 (Domínguez Ortiz 1992, 150).

The Converso Problem

The Franciscans had a statute by 1525. The Jesuits, who befriended the meek, the persecuted, and the poor, had admitted many conversos with open arms—the successor of St. Ignatius as general of the order, Diego Laínez, was a New Christian—and resisted the pressure to adopt one until 1592 (Sicroff 1960, 270–90).[16] Among the prestigious military orders, Santiago de Alcántara was the first one to have a statute of *limpieza*; Pope Sixtus IV sanctioned it in 1483. The University College of San Bartolomé at the University of Salamanca, which, as we have seen, was the first to have a statute of exclusion (1414), was followed by others during the first half of the sixteenth century. These university colleges took great pride in the strict manner in which they applied their statutes (Domínguez Ortiz 1992, 162). In 1522 the Inquisition took matters even further, barring conversos, their children, and grandchildren from obtaining degrees at the universities of Salamanca, Valladolid, and Toledo, but it seems that the ruling was never implemented (161).

The statute enacted by the Cathedral of Toledo two decades later had greater impact because, besides being the most important and prestigious city in Castile, Toledo also was the see of the Church in Spain. The process was set in motion by Juan Martínez Guijeño ('pebble-like'), a man of humble peasant stock who Latinized his nonaristocratic-sounding name to Silíceo. He studied for six years at the Sorbonne, taught there, and was admitted to the University College of San Bartolomé upon returning to Spain (144–45). Charles V chose him as tutor for his son, the future Philip II, a post in which he served for ten years, and appointed him archbishop of Toledo in 1546, when the see became vacant. Finding many conversos among the canons of the cathedral chapter, Silíceo succeeded in refusing admission to Dr. Hernán Ximénez, on the ground that his father had been penanced by the Inquisition, even though Ximénez had been appointed by Rome (Caro Baroja 1986, 2: 295). In 1547, Silíceo proposed a statute limiting future membership to Old Christians. The chapter voted 24 to 10 for approval, but the conversos fought back. The archbishop eventually won, obtaining the sanction of Rome in 1555, and his former pupil, Philip II, ratified the statute in 1556 (Kamen 1998, 238).

There was considerable resistance to such statutes on the part of New Christians, and some Old Christians opposed them as well. The Jews of Spain thought of themselves as being noble, tracing their lineage back to aristocratic families, and some even thought that they descended from King David (Gerber 1992, x). This pride was transmitted to their converso descendants. In the face of the widespread discrimination, they insisted that, if nobility depended on antiquity, they could trace their families further back in time than anybody else, and that Christ himself had been born a Jew. Proud

9

Chapter One

of the cultural achievements of their forebears in Spain, learned conversos scorned the backward peasants for their supposed *limpieza*, which was based on the claim that their ancestors had never mixed with either Moors or Jews. After all, many Jews and conversos had married into the nobility, which, being better educated, was little affected by the rabid anti-Semitism of the masses; the pride of the ignorant, illiterate peasants was simply risible to them.

Some Old Christians objected to the statutes as well. The founder of the Company of Jesus, St. Ignatius, a Basque nobleman, was heard to say that God would have granted him a great privilege if God had granted him Jewish ancestors, for this would have made St. Ignatius a blood relative of Christ (Sicroff 1960, 282). In his *Apologías sobre ciertas materias morales en que hay opinión*, the Dominican Domingo de Baltanás, citing St. Paul's exhortation to unity amongst Christians (1 Cor. 1.10), "condamne l'injustice qu'il y a dans l'exclusion des Judéo-Chrétiens des charges ecclésiastiques" ("condemns the injustice of excluding Christians of Jewish extraction from ecclesiastic positions"; Sicroff 1960, 145), but thought that the descendants of a person who had been either Jewish or condemned by the Inquisition ought to be excluded for three or four succeeding generations (145). Thus, despite his defense of conversos, Brother Domingo still favored racism, with the caveat that it should not last forever. St. Ignatius, on the other hand, always rejected such strictures.

In any case, Old Christians such as these were very few, and with good reason. Anyone who dared to oppose the statutes in writing would have been accused of being a converso or even a Jew, "plaidant une cause qui l'intéressait personnellement" ("pleading a cause that affected him personally"; Sicroff 1960, 144). Although *limpieza* never became completely accepted, and "numerous prominent intellectuals from the mid-sixteenth-century onwards questioned it and attacked it" (Kamen 1998, 252), most of them happened to be New Christians.

One such individual was Fray Luis de León (1527–91), a noted Augustinian poet and writer who taught at the University of Salamanca. While jailed by the Inquisition for nearly five years, he wrote *De los nombres de Cristo*, in which he explains the various names given to Christ in the Holy Scriptures. In the section on Jesus's title as King, one of the interlocutors, Marcello, explains that everyone is equal and noble in the Kingdom of God; all Christians are brothers, for they are the children of Christ. Turning to Juliano, Sabino observes that, in this world, kings sometimes have to punish their vassals by disgracing them, and asks what he thinks of those sovereigns who make provisions for this shame to spread from generation to generation, so as to last forever. Julian replies that such rulers do not deserve to be called kings, for their duty is to ensure the well-being of their vassals, and not "hazerlos apocados y viles" ("to make them despised and humiliated"; León 1966–69, 2: 113).[17] The attack against "limpieza de sangre" is perfectly clear.

Fray Luis had been dead for eighteen years when a Dr. Alvaro Piçario de Palacios noticed the passage and denounced it as an attack against the Inquisition and the king, asserting that such opinions were current among people of impure origin. As Sicroff pointed out, Fray Luis would probably have had the opportunity to enrich his experience with the tribunals of the Holy Office if he were still living (1960, 265).

Although writers such as Fray Domingo de Baltanás proposed that the laws of blood purity apply for only three or four generations, the situation was more like Fray Luis described it. The shame was transmitted from generation to generation, and affected families with any Jewish ancestry, no matter how remote. Some writers even maintained that the milk of "Jewish" (read "converso") wet-nurses could transmit a tendency to Judaize and cause all sorts of mischief (Caro Baroja 1986, 2: 326; Rivera 2002). In other words, the mere presence of Jewish blood in a person "was seen as creating a proclivity to undermine the Church and its dogma" (Melammed 1999, 7).

The effects of such discrimination were devastating. Since the New Christians continued to exercise the same professions as their forebears, physicians, lawyers, clerks, and merchants came to be regarded as conversos, and this implied that they were suspicious in matters of faith. Everyone who applied for posts in organizations with statutes had to present genealogies in order to prove the purity of their lineage, being required to pay for the concomitant investigations. The rejection of an application for membership in one of the military orders meant disgrace to the candidate and to all of his relatives. As profusely documented in the literature of the period, *limpieza* became a national obsession (see Chapter 3); even the illiterate peasants made good use of it, boasting of their supposed purity at every turn. A good example is Sancho Panza, in the *Quijote*, for the squire takes pleasure in stressing his Old Christian roots on many occasions (see Eisenberg 1987, 148–50n164). To make matters worse, people had long memories and were well aware of the background of their neighbors, as they are still today in some villages of northeastern Portugal.[18] Given such a stifling environment, conversos made every effort to hide their origins. To escape discrimination, a few moved to towns where they were not known; some even hid their ancestry from their children (Shepard 1982, 46).[19]

Nevertheless, as Francisco de Quevedo put it in one of his *letrillas*, "Poderoso caballero / es don Dinero" ("Lord Money / is a powerful knight"; Blecua 1984–87, 2: 201), and the conversos who had it were often able to circumvent the statutes, obtaining certificates of nobility and blood purity. Although the nobles were reputed to be impure, a certificate meant exemption from taxes and provided a certain amount of protection. One frequent ploy was to remove an ancestor from the family tree, replacing him or her with some other name. Some changed their own names. It was also convenient to claim that the family originated in La Montaña—the mountainous region comprising the northern provinces of León, Asturias, and Santander— or in the Basque country, because those areas supposedly had never been inhabited by Moors or Jews. In sum, the need for the certificates led to a considerable amount of corruption, since applicants paid off officials and also the witnesses in the towns to which they traveled during the course of their investigations.[20] One interesting example is that of the father of St. Theresa of Avila. In 1485, her grandfather, Juan Sánchez de Toledo, had been lightly penanced by the Toledo Inquisition, together with seven of his eight children. He moved to Avila, where he continued to work as a merchant, and changed his name to Juan Sánchez de Cepeda. The saint's father, Alonso de Cepeda, and his three brothers decided to obtain a certificate of nobility. When the family's background was discovered they were turned down, but, nevertheless, they succeeded in 1520 (Tomás Alvarez 1995, 609–11).

Even the royal family itself was affected. Since Ferdinand the Catholic had inherited Jewish blood from his mother, Doña Juana Enríquez (Castro 1971, 49), Charles V, Philip II, and their successors could also have been regarded as conversos (Domínguez Ortiz 1992, 40). This did not keep them from supporting the statutes, however. Charles V tolerated the presence of conversos in some public positions, but vetoed their access to the highest posts (51). We have already seen how Philip II ratified Silíceo's statute for the cathedral of Toledo in 1556. When he decided to create a militia in 1596, just two years before his death, Philip took care to charge the recruiters to enlist only Old Christians (58).

Nevertheless, it is important not to generalize and to keep in mind that the statutes of *limpieza* were not enacted everywhere. Kamen maintains that "the statutes could be found only in Castile and only in a very small number of bodies there" (1996, 21), and goes on to stress that "their number does not add up to an epidemic. Of the 35 sees in sixteenth-century Castile, for example, possibly only ten ever had them; and in some . . . the clergy refused to observe the statute" (Kamen 1996, 21).[21] But there were statutes in Navarre and Valencia (Caro Baroja 1986, 2: 310–11), and also in Aragon, even though they seem to have become rare in that kingdom before the late sixteenth century (Kamen 1996, 21). In the Basque country, in 1483 the province of Guipúzcoa forbade New Christians from marrying and settling in the area (Sicroff 1960, 89). In 1511, the province of Vizcaya ordered the conversos who had sought refuge from the Inquisition to leave within six months. In 1564, the city of Bilbao required outsiders who intended to become residents to pay for the expenses of an investigation of their blood

The Converso Problem

purity (Domínguez Ortiz 1992, 163-64). Whereas the statutes limited access to some posts, these laws were even worse, for they aimed at the complete exclusion of conversos from the region. Proud of their supposed purity—contrary to popular opinion, Jews had resided in the area before—the Basques wanted to ensure that they kept it.

Although the statutes never became Spain's official law, they were the law for many institutions, some parts of the country, and cannot be regarded as mere membership rules "adopted by private societies" (Kamen 1996, 21). Since the university colleges were student associations, it is perhaps possible to regard them as being private, but this certainly does not apply to municipal councils, cathedral chapters, religious and military orders, the militia created by Philip II, not to say anything about whole Basque provinces.

The national government hesitated. At times it attempted to put a stop to the insanity, but it also gave its seal of approval to many statutes, and there is no question that it tolerated *de facto* discrimination (Domínguez Ortiz 1992, 48). Laws such as these did not have to be observed rigorously or even enacted everywhere in order to have profound, insidious effects. As we shall see, the literature of the period testifies to the widespread preoccupation with *limpieza*, and so does the strong opposition of so many individuals, most of whom happened to be conversos. But although *limpieza* constituted a grave, insulting handicap, it did not threaten anybody's life. The Inquisition would pose a far more serious danger.

Since thousands of people had been forced to convert suddenly, from one moment to the next, and continued to live in the same communities as their Jewish friends and relatives, it is only logical that, notwithstanding some exceptions, the vast majority should continue to practice their former faith in secrecy and to transmit it to their children and grandchildren, even though they had to live publicly as Christians. Their Old Christian neighbors knew this perfectly well, continued to regard all of them as Jews, and accused them of betraying and endangering the Christian faith.[22] Such heresy would surely provoke the wrath of God.

The Catholic Monarchs could not fail to know this, but they became more aware of the extent of the situation in Andalusia, where there had been a greater number of forced conversions, when they visited the region in 1478. The persons who apprised them of this appealed to their consciences, stressing that the failure to punish and put an end to the Judaizing would cause great harm to Christianity:

> Algunos clérigos e personas religiosas e otros seglares, informaron al Rey y a la Reyna, que en sus Reynos e señorios habia muchos christianos del linage de los judios, que tornaban a judayzar, e facer

13

> ritos judaycos secretamente en sus casas; e ni creian en la fe christiana, ni facían las obras que catholicos christianos debian facer. E sobre este caso les encargaban las consciencias, requiriéndoles, que pues eran principes catholicos, castigasen aquel error detestable; porque si lo dexasen sin castigo, e no se atajaba, podria crecer de tal manera, que nuestra santa fe catholica recibiese gran detrimento. (Pulgar 1953, 331 [1])

Alonso de Espina, confessor of Henry IV, Isabella's brother, had already fought for an inquisition, but Henry rejected his advice. A rabid anti-Semite, Espina, who may have been himself a converso,[23] put forth his views in *Fortalitium Fidei* (Fortress of the Faith; 1460), a book in which he dealt with heretics, Jews, Muslims, and demons. Besides starting a campaign against the crypto-Jews, this book full of hatred also provided the blueprint for an inquisition (Beinart 1981, 10–20; Ginio 1996; Netanyahu 1995, 814–47).

Ferdinand and Isabella concluded that they could not follow the same path as Henry IV. Realizing that the strong anti-converso reaction in Andalusia could cause serious disturbances, they decided to ask Rome for permission to institute an inquisition. Their main advisor was Tomás de Torquemada, possibly a converso,[24] who possessed the dynamism and organizational skills needed to implement and develop the blueprint that Espina had already provided. Torquemada became the first inquisitor general in 1482 (Beinart 1981, 35, 45–47).[25]

Sixtus IV agreed quickly to the request of the Monarchs, issuing the bull that authorized the creation of the Castilian Inquisition in November 1478, but they hesitated for another two years. The first inquisitors that they named, two Dominican friars, arrived in Seville in November 1480 (Domínguez Ortiz 1992, 21–24). The first auto-da-fé took place in that city on February 6, 1481, when six people were burned at the stake (Kamen 1998, 47). Since the Inquisition was particularly ferocious during the first years of its existence, many more were to follow.

Upon arriving in a town, the inquisitors would preach a sermon that included a list of heresies and practices that suggested the observance of Jewish rites, and proclaim an edict of grace,[26] giving people thirty to forty days to come forward and discharge their consciences by confessing their sins. The suspicious practices ranged from circumcision and praying in Hebrew to wearing clean clothes on Saturdays, a dislike for pork, and various dietary customs. Ignorance of Christian prayers and lack of devotion constituted signs of suspicion as well (Domínguez Ortiz 1992, 27–28).[27] Those who came forward during the period of grace were also required to denounce others (Kamen 1998, 57). Since the penalties were spiritual in nature, thousands of people took advantage of the opportunity to become reconciled to the Church, but there were also thousands, who, fearing the consequences,

The Converso Problem

preferred to abandon their homes and flee to other parts of Spain or abroad. Many went to Portugal, North Africa, and even to Rome (Domínguez Ortiz 1992, 28).

Anonymous denunciations were encouraged and became the norm, since the inquisitors did not consider it prudent to reveal the names of the accusers; it could subject them to acts of revenge. When discovered, some were murdered. Witnesses were sworn to secrecy, and it was a crime to discuss the affairs of the Inquisition. If the charges appeared to be credible, the accused were brought in, imprisoned in secret jails, and isolated, without any contact with the outside world. Contrary to common belief, they were not held in filthy, inhumane conditions. These jails were usually better than the public ones. Prisoners who could afford it were allowed to eat what they wanted, and those who could not discovered that the food was good and often better than in their own homes (Blázquez Miguel 1988, 87).

Three days after arriving, prisoners were asked to confess without being told what the accusation was, for the inquisitors felt that they ought to know it. Those who denied guilt or did not seem to tell the truth were sent to the torture chamber, but not in a systematic manner. Since the inquisitors did not have their own torturers, it was necessary to hire them from civil justice, and they could be very expensive. Then came the charges, which a secretary read to the accused in the presence of the inquisitors. If they wished to make a defense, the Holy Office, as the Inquisition was also called, provided lawyers from its own personnel. To prevent false accusations, defendants were asked for a list of enemies and to enumerate the reasons why they regarded them as such. If they named some of their anonymous accusers, those witnesses were brought in, interrogated, and often dismissed from the case (Blázquez Miguel 1988, 88–89). Since the accused were required to denounce others in their turn, many named family members and friends. Thus, one "single charge might produce scores of suspects" (Shepard 1982, 19). The sentences were announced during the autos-da-fé, which were public affairs attended by great crowds.

Being extremely thorough, the inquisitors kept careful records of everything, including the depositions of the witnesses and the interrogations. They transcribed some of the crypto-Jewish prayers extracted from their victims, and occasionally even noted gestures. The documentation was so extensive that the trial of one person is sometimes enough to fill a thick volume.

Few defendants were found innocent. Most were "reconciled," that is, accepted back into the Church after the imposition of penalties that varied according to the offense. For light, first-time infractions, people were required to say a certain number of prayers, pay small fines, or attend church on specified days. Some were condemned to house arrest (Gitlitz 1996, 21), or to wear the sanbenito or penitential garb of the Inquisition publicly for a

Chapter One

certain amount of time.[28] For other offenders there were heavy fines, flogging, jail terms, and confiscation of goods (Domínguez Ortiz 1992, 29). Life in prison was frequently imposed, but the sentences were usually commuted when prisoners petitioned to go free after two or three years (Blázquez Miguel 1988, 90). People found guilty of relapsing and extremely serious offenses were "relaxed," which meant that they were handed over to the civil authorities in order to be burned at the stake. Those who showed contrition were garroted first, but the ones that did not were burned alive. When persons who had already died were found guilty of having Judaized, their bones were exhumed and consigned to the bonfires. Their property was also confiscated, which often condemned their children and grandchildren to misery. People who could not be caught or managed to flee were burned in effigy.

The sanbenitos, or scapular-like garments that the penanced wore during the autos-da-fé, were usually yellow and displayed St. Andrew's cross. Devils and flames were added to the black ones worn by those scheduled to be "relaxed." These sanbenitos were then placed on the walls of parish churches and labeled with the names of the victims, thus perpetuating the infamy that they had transmitted to their respective families. When time caused the sanbenitos to decay, the authorities took good care to replace them, lest anyone forget. In this manner, they made certain that the infamy lasted for generations, multiplying as the descendants of the victims grew in number. The only escape was to change the family name and move elsewhere (Lea 1922, 3: 162–72).[29]

We have already seen how some Jeronimite monks were burned at the stake between 1485 and 1487 for Judaizing. Priests and other clergymen were also burned, and bishops of converso stock came under suspicion as well. Sixtus IV deprived of his position Pedro de Aranda, bishop of Calahorra, for suspicion of heresy, and Juan Darias Davila, bishop of Segovia, fled to Rome with the bones of his father to prevent the Inquisition from exhuming and burning them (Domínguez Ortiz 1992, 23–24). The Inquisition also burned some powerful merchants, doctors, and municipal officers, but most of its victims were small businessmen and artisans, such as weavers, shoemakers, and tailors, not to mention their mothers, wives, daughters, and unmarried sisters. In his study of the Valencia Inquisition, Stephen Haliczer realized that women were often responsible for keeping alive the flame of Jewish faith among conversos and that "Judaizing was one of the few offenses tried by the Valencia tribunal in which there was a rough equality between the sexes" (1990, 213). It would not be surprising if the proportion of women turned out to be similar elsewhere.[30]

Since the Inquisition was created to deal with crimes against the faith, generally it did not have jurisdiction in cases involving Jews and Muslims. At first it focused almost exclusively on Judaizers, but it eventually came to

The Converso Problem

concern itself with other types of heresy. Because of the Reformation, Illuminists (*alumbrados*) and Protestants received special attention. Both were few in number, however. The Illuminists sought an interior, pure religion that stressed personal illumination, i.e., direct contact with God, thereby minimizing the role of the clergy. Some claimed to have visions, which the Church viewed with suspicion. Even worse, they rejected the veneration of the saints and the worship of the cross as idolatry.[31]

The Protestants were usually foreign. The first one to be burned (1539) was John Tack, a young Englishman. Some Flemings were also persecuted, but most of the foreign victims were French. Between 1560 and 1600, the Inquisition executed eighty Frenchmen, burned one hundred in effigy, and condemned nearly four hundred to serve as galley slaves (Kamen 1998, 100).

As the number of crypto-Jews dwindled—after 1515 fewer and fewer people were found guilty of Judaizing (Domínguez Ortiz 1992, 47)—the Inquisition sought to justify its existence by shifting its attention to blasphemy, heretical propositions, crimes against the Holy Office, bigamy, unaccepted sexual behavior, and superstition (Henningsen 1987, 220). Superstition included witchcraft, but, fortunately for those accused of it, the inquisitors were learned men and regarded the deeds attributed to witches as delusions. In the words of Gustav Henningsen, who, together with Jaime Contreras, examined 44,000 trial summaries for the period 1540–1700: "Spain had just as many witch trials as other countries; the difference lies only in the fact that the Spaniards—thanks to the Inquisition—were rarely allowed to burn their witches" (1987, 226).[32]

By 1540, crypto-Judaism had practically disappeared from southern Castile, where it had been strongest (Domínguez Ortiz 1992, 36). The problem did not resurface until the 1580s, after the crowns of Spain and Portugal became united under Philip II. The union was to last for sixty years (1580–1640). Thousands of Portuguese, including numerous merchants, took the opportunity to emigrate to Spain and its American colonies. The Spanish authorities soon realized that many of them Judaized. The word *portugués* became synonymous with crypto-Jew, and the Inquisition restarted its activities against conversos. In fact, a good portion of these immigrants descended from Spaniards who had sought refuge in Portugal. Crypto-Judaism was rampant in that country, because, unlike Spain, which had allowed the Jews who did not wish to convert to leave the country in 1492, the so-called Portuguese expulsion of 1497 was really a forced, mass conversion.[33] The ferocious persecution that took place in Majorca during the late seventeenth century (1675–95) was a different case, for it did not involve any Portuguese.[34]

Besides the court that began to function in Seville in 1480, the Inquisition established eleven tribunals under the crown of Castile, four under the jurisdiction of Aragon, and there were also tribunals in Sicily, Sardinia, Mexico, Lima, and Cartagena de las Indias (Lea 1922, 1: 541), which brings the total to twenty-one. They were overseen by an inquisitor general. The first one, Tomás de Torquemada, we recall, may have been a converso of Jewish extraction (Caro Baroja 1986, 1: 154); there seems to be no doubt regarding his successor, Diego de Deza (Lea 1922, 1: 120).

As we saw in the case of Jerónimo de Santa Fe, conversos were often among the most ferocious persecutors of Jews. They also played key roles in the hunt for Judaizers. During the 1480s, when at least one New Christian served as inquisitor general, the Jews, who were in an excellent position to know the identity of the Judaizers, were required to denounce them, and great numbers served as witnesses against conversos until their expulsion in 1492 (Blázquez Miguel 1988, 86). For motives that ranged from religious conviction to personal resentment, grudges, and quarrels, conversos known as *malsines* ("back biters") also denounced other conversos (Shepard 1982, 72–76). There existed a climate of great fear, for the Old Christian majority knew only too well who their New Christian neighbors were, and suspicious behavior was often brought to the attention of the inquisitors (see Haliczer 1990, 219–21). Moreover, the Inquisition counted on the support of lay officials known as *familiares*, which it appointed. According to Caro Baroja, these were spies, and their job was to watch over the religious behavior of their neighbors (1986, 1: 325). Kamen, on the other hand, maintains that although the *familiares* had to be ready to serve the Holy Office at all times in a variety of manners and to protect the inquisitors, their real purpose was never to act as informers (1998, 145; see also note 36, below). In any case, there were thousands of *familiares* throughout the country.[35]

In the early years, the number of victims in Seville was such that a spacious, elevated square *quemadero* ("burning area") had to be built outside the city, with holes for the posts to which the victims were chained (Domínguez Ortiz 1992, 31). Hundreds perished in other Andalusian towns. Since a number of records were lost, it is difficult to determine the precise number of victims during the early period, when the Inquisition was particularly cruel. Using the fragmentary evidence available, which excludes Seville, Domínguez Ortiz estimated that about 4,000 persons had been burned by 1520, and that perhaps 20,000 had received lighter penalties (1992, 43). Although most New Christians were not directly affected by the Inquisition, the number of people who suffered as a result of these trials was much higher. The thousands who fled abroad seldom returned, numerous families were ruined because of confiscations, and all the descendants of those penanced by the Inquisition were subject to the infamy perpetuated by the sanbenitos on the walls of their parish churches. These sanbenitos, of course, also meant that the extended families to which they belonged lacked *limpieza*.

The Converso Problem

Between 1540 and 1700 there were 44,000 trials in nineteen of the twenty-one tribunals, but the focus shifted to Old Christians, who made up 58 percent of the total. The remaining 42 percent were "Jews" (i.e., conversos), Moriscos (baptized descendants of Moors), Protestants, and Illuminists. The sentences became less severe, since the number of victims put to death decreased considerably: 826 persons were burned alive and 778 in effigy (Henningsen 1987, 220, 230).

To their credit, many Spaniards opposed the Inquisition from its very beginning. Fernando del Pulgar and others pointed out that evangelization had hardly been tried. They recommended instruction in the Christian faith and objected to capital punishment. The opposition was particularly bitter in Aragon, where the Inquisition was regarded as a Castilian institution, and as a means of undermining local laws and privileges in order to impose central control (Bennassar 1994, 25). In 1484, the city of Teruel refused entry to two inquisitors sent to establish a tribunal, but it was forced to submit the year after. In Barcelona, so many conversos began to flee that in 1485 the councilmen complained to Ferdinand that the introduction of the Inquisition would ruin the city. The King did not listen, and when it was implemented in 1487, most conversos had already fled.

On September 15, 1485, the inquisitor Pedro de Arbués was murdered as he knelt in prayer at the cathedral of Zaragoza. Public opinion changed when it was discovered that the assassins were conversos. Although these assassins belonged to important families, they were hunted down and paid for their crime in autos-da-fé. One of them was the son of Jerónimo de Santa Fe, Francisco, who committed suicide. The Inquisition burned his corpse. Another was Luis Santangel. Because John II had knighted him for bravery, he was beheaded before being consigned to the bonfire (Kamen 1998, 50–55). These conversos paid with their lives for the murder of Pedro de Arbués, rather than for Judaizing, but that was not the case of Santangel's homonymous cousin, who was Columbus's chief sponsor. In July 1491, he had to wear a sanbenito during a procession (55).

In the sixteenth century, the Jesuit historian Juan de Mariana summed up what a number of his contemporaries thought about the Inquisition: defendants were not allowed to confront their accusers, whose names were unfairly kept from them; secrecy robbed people of free speech, depriving them of their freedom; children were made to pay for the crimes of their parents; and anyway, sins of that sort should not be punished by death (Kamen 1998, 67).

The main opponents of the Inquisition were, however, New Christians. Old Christians began to show their discontent "only when the officers of the tribunal in Castile began to extend their activities to non-conversos" (Kamen 1998, 72), but they were few in number. As Juan Blázquez Miguel pointed out, the rabidly anti-Semitic masses could not agree more with the persecutions:

Chapter One

"pensar que el entramado social del pueblo español se pudo oponer a un Tribunal que venía a hacer justicia, a descubrir y castigar a unos malvados judaizantes de los que todo el mundo sabía sus nombres y que hasta el momento habían gozado de total impunidad, es, pienso yo, un deseo de modernos historiadores, preocupados en intentar justificar un hecho poco agradable, más que una auténtica realidad histórica" ("to think that the social fabric of the Spanish people could oppose a Tribunal whose purpose was to carry out justice, to uncover and punish those wicked Judaizers whose names everyone knew and who had enjoyed complete impunity until then, constitutes, I think, a whim of the modern historians preoccupied with an attempt to justify a disagreeable event, rather than true historical fact"; 1988, 84–85).

Spain was to pay dearly for this popular prejudice. As the Inquisition extended its domain to Old Christians, common people were brought before its tribunals for incredibly blasphemous oaths (Kamen 1998, 40; Bennassar 1987, 178), heterodox ideas, such as the belief that simple fornication was not a sin, and other infractions. To ensure conformity, the Holy Office pursued a deliberate policy of instilling fear in everybody, and admitted it frankly. In 1578, an inquisitor wrote: "we must remember that the essential aim of the trial and death sentence is not saving the soul of the defendant but furthering the public good and terrorizing the people" (qtd. in Bennassar 1987, 178). There is no question that it worked. People were afraid to say what was on their minds, and the expression "Beware of what you say" became commonplace. Even in Galicia, where the Inquisition had less influence than in other areas, "the very words 'familiar' or 'official of the Holy Office' were sufficient to produce terror" (Bennassar 1987, 179).[36]

There were serious consequences abroad as well. Because of their deliberate publicity, the shocking trials left a lasting impression. Foreigners generalized and soon began to think that all Spaniards were marranos. To justify their jealousy and plunder of the Spanish empire—Spain had become the most powerful nation in the world—rival countries developed the black legend, which, among other charges, asserted that Spaniards were cruel fanatics, and that the Inquisition tortured and burned most of its victims. At least between 1540 and 1700, however, 90 percent of the accused were never tortured (Henningsen 1987, 230) and, as we have seen, the proportion of the defendants who were put to death was relatively small. These facts are by no means intended to justify the activities of the Inquisition, but, to be fair, it must be evaluated within the context of the period. Almost without exception, people were cruel and intolerant everywhere, and Spain avoided the barbarous witch hunts and the devastating religious wars that produced far more victims in several European countries (see Costa Fontes 1994, 59–60).

Fernando del Pulgar, chronicler of the Catholic Monarchs and himself a converso, understood only too well that the Inquisition was a religious insti-

The Converso Problem

tution designed to extirpate crypto-Judaism. Other fifteenth- and sixteenth-century writers agreed. As the Inquisition was coming to an end, however—it was finally abolished on July 15, 1834—other views began to emerge. Agreeing with what many victims used to claim, some critics asserted that the main reason for the Inquisition was economic: the Catholic Monarchs needed to find a way "to lay their hands on the conversos' wealth and property" (Beinart 1981, 22). Others maintained that it was a secular, state institution, established for political rather than religious motives. During the last forty years, some scholars even denied or minimized the existence of crypto-Judaism, arguing that the conversos assimilated very quickly.[37] If I am not mistaken, the idea was first set forth by António José Saraiva, a Marxist. Because of his quest to explain the Portuguese Inquisition in class and economic terms, he needed to exclude the religious factor. By doing so, Saraiva was able to demonstrate to his own satisfaction the notion that the Inquisition was a political tool designed to perpetuate the control of the ruling aristocracy against the threat posed by the growing economic power of the bourgeoisie. Since businessmen and conversos were regarded as being one and the same, the Inquisition accused this wealthy class of heresy in order to keep it in its place, "fabricating" Jews where there were none (Saraiva 1956; 1969).[38]

This denial of crypto-Judaism contradicts those historians who witnessed the events and the Catholic Monarchs themselves. Other modern historians have come up with other reasons for the creation of the Inquisition, including racism (Netanyahu 1995), but the racism that lay behind the desire to prevent the infiltration of conversos into Christian society certainly was not the main factor. Ferdinand himself was a converso on his mother's side, and neither he nor Isabella shared the anti-Semitism of the masses. Many conversos held important positions at court. In 1484, a Polish traveler observed that the Queen seemed to have more confidence in baptized Jews than in Old Christians (Carrete 1992, 41). For several years, her confessor and one of her most trusted advisors was the saintly Fray Hernando de Talavera, a converso who was named bishop of Granada in 1492 (Márquez Villanueva 1960, 105–09). Ferdinand was also surrounded by conversos until the end of his life (Domínguez Ortiz 1992, 44–45). Racism, therefore, must be excluded as one of their motivations.

The desire for religious unity may have played a role, but it probably did not constitute one of the main motivations. After all, there was still a large Jewish community in the country, and Muslim Granada was not conquered until 1492, twelve years after the implementation of the Inquisition.

The strong anti-converso reaction that Ferdinand and Isabella discovered in Andalusia and the fear of the disturbances to which it could lead constitute a much more compelling motive. It probably seemed more prudent to go along with public opinion. Even more important, the Monarchs happened

Chapter One

to be Christian, and the widespread practice of crypto-Judaism must have been as offensive to them as it was to others.

According to Fernando del Pulgar, who was in a position to know the Queen extremely well—he was her secretary before assuming the post of royal chronicler—Isabella was a profoundly religious woman. Seeing how whole towns and regions had become ruined and desolated because of the Inquisition, she assumed responsibility, stating in her correspondence that she had done this only out of her devotion for Our Lord and His Mother. Those who claimed that she intended to accumulate wealth from the confiscations, the Queen maintained, were liars. In fact, the Queen went on to say, she had used part of the confiscated money to establish dowries for the children of the victims.

Although far from being as religious as his wife, Ferdinand's motives were the same. When the city council of Barcelona begged him not to allow the introduction of the Inquisition, protesting that the flight of conversos would ruin the city, the King replied that he was well aware of the losses to the city and to the royal revenues, but that he had placed the service of Our Lord above his own interests (Beinart 1981, 28–29).

In a nutshell, like all their contemporaries, including prominent New Christians who were sincere Catholics, Isabella and Ferdinand knew for a fact that thousands of conversos Judaized and wished to return to their Jewish faith. Instead of favoring the advice of those who pointed out that the humane, Christian remedy was to use reason, educating the Judaizers in the Christian doctrine, the Monarchs accepted the counsel of the party that believed punishment to be the only effective solution, and obtained the Papacy's permission to institute the Inquisition in Castile.

The scholars who maintain that crypto-Judaism did not exist seem to feel that, since they had chosen conversion over martyrdom, the thousands of Jews who were forced to turn Christian between 1391 and 1416 lacked faith and therefore must have assimilated very quickly into Christian society.[39] If they had been good Jews, they would have preferred to die. Such scholars forget that most Jews lived pious, religious lives, that the skeptics among them constituted a small, intellectual minority, and that Jews were as human as anybody else. Although martyrs were numerous, it is only natural that the majority should have chosen to live. Once the terror and the coercive, life-threatening conditions were over, their only desire was to return to their ancestral faith. They did not wish to assimilate, and the masses did not want them to infiltrate into Christian society, either.

Besides being illogical, the notion that the instant Christians made at sword point could become sincere Catholics and transmit the faith thus imposed on them to their children constitutes a grievous offense to their memory. The words of Blázquez Miguel regarding this point are well worth quoting:

The Converso Problem

¿Y qué pensar de esas masas de convertidos bajo la amenaza de la espada sobre sus cabezas, con sus hogares saqueados o quemados a sus espaldas, con la ruina de su hacienda al frente, hasta qué extremo podían ser sinceros cristianos? El plantearse siquiera la duda ofende. Ellos no pudieron ser nunca verdaderos cristianos; su generación en ningún momento pudo olvidar lo que significó abrazar esa nueva fe y, por tanto, malamente podrían haber inculcado sus creencias a sus hijos. Esa primera generación debió ser Judaizante en su plena totalidad y los hijos nacidos de ella vivieron, desde el momento de abrir los ojos, inmersos en un mundo judaizante dentro de su hogar. (1988, 51 [2])

Unfortunately for the conversos, there was no going back. Once baptized, they had to remain Christian. Thus, they lived between two worlds, being neither fully Jewish nor fully Christian. Except for the wealthy and the learned, who were readily admitted into high class circles, the conversos who eventually realized that they had no choice but to become a part of Christian society met with all sorts of barriers. In part, this was because there were simply too many of them. Haim Beinart understood the situation well: "since neither the religious nor the secular authorities were able to create the conditions necessary to facilitate their integration into Christian society, or indeed made any effort to do so, many years were to pass before those *anusim* [forced converts] and Conversos who wished to enter Christian circles by their own efforts actually succeeded" (1981, 1; see also Beinart 1992d, 348).

As more and more managed to do so, there was a violent Old Christian reaction. The chronicler Andrés Bernáldez echoes popular feeling when he alleges that the aim of the conversos was to increase and multiply in order to destroy Christianity from within (Beinart 1981, 21). Everything ought to be done to keep them out. Hence the bloody anti-converso riots, the statutes of blood purity, and the hanging of sanbenitos on the walls of parish churches.

It would be utter nonsense to claim that subsequent generations consisted exclusively of Judaizers, as the ignorant, prejudiced masses thought. There were conversos everywhere, "desde judaizantes a inquisidores" ("from Judaizers to inquisitors"; Márquez Villanueva 1996–97, 171). Their religious identity depended on self-concept. Some thought of themselves as Jews, others vacillated between the two religions, many were sincere Catholics, a number ended up without any religious beliefs (Gitlitz 1996–97, 164), and a few even followed both faiths simultaneously, failing to see any incompatibility between them (Haliczer 1990, 214).[40] The insightful manner in which Melammed sums up the problem is well worth quoting:

> The reactions of the converts themselves were as varied as they could possibly be, and any given converso might alter his or her path more than once. A convert might make a serious attempt to live as a devout Catholic, genuinely hoping to assimilate; as society became less

tolerant of converso presence, this same individual was apt to encounter discrimination and decide that all efforts to gain acceptance had been in vain. Many of the conversos fluctuated during their lifetimes, uncertain which religious group was more appropriate, expedient, or comfortable for them; often the reality was that neither would ever provide a perfect fit. (1999, 5–6)

On the other side of the spectrum, as Netanyahu emphasized, there were also conversos who sought "full amalgamation with the Old Christians (when possible, by means of intermarriage), did not wish to be reminded of their Jewish origin, and held the Jews, as the Hebrew sources tell us, in derision and contempt" (2000, 547–48). Unfortunately, Netanyahu, in whose opinion the former Jews assimilated practically overnight, insists that this was true of all conversos, even though the inquisitorial trials document that many of them preferred the law of Moses.

Whether steadfastly or only at certain times in their lives, there can be no question that many individuals Judaized. According to some of the scholars interested in denying or minimizing crypto-Judaism, the conversos themselves insisted to the inquisitors that they were truly Christian, even though a few of them admitted to some religious confusion. It did not take long for the rabbis, who regarded the first victims as *anusim* ("forced converts"), to classify them as *meshumadim* ("renegades").[41] Inquisitorial documents cannot be taken seriously, since the trials were used in order to influence public opinion.

For those who Judaized, however, it would have been sheer insanity if, when brought before the Inquisition, they readily admitted it rather than insisting that they were truly Christian. What was at stake was nothing less than their lives, their property, and the security of their families. Only the most inveterate positivism would take such insistence at face value.

The rabbis who, in time, maintained that all conversos were *meshumadim* ("renegades") rather than forced converts were not completely wrong; although those who had been forced to convert had lived as Jews, their descendants had been born officially Christian. As Márquez Villanueva has pointed out, "from a technical or rabbinical viewpoint it is obvious that they simply were not Jews. It could be ridiculous to label as such people who were separated by three or more generations from their ancestors in the *aljamas* [Jewish quarters]" (2000a, 17–18). Although this may be technically true, what really mattered was what the Judaizers felt, and they insisted on regarding themselves as Jews. The clashing conclusions constitute a good example of the difference between a conservative and a liberal attitude, that is, the letter and the spirit of the law. Literally, the conversos who Judaized were no longer Jews; spiritually, that is exactly what they were, even though, as the years passed, their knowledge and observance of their faith became more and more deficient.

These crypto-Jews sometimes identified "with the Jews in Egypt, oppressed and surrounded by idolatry (i.e., Catholicism)" (Bodian 1997, 15). Being a despised minority, their faith provided them "with an affirmative sense of inner self and group" (15), enabling them to preserve their sense of dignity (16). The Iberian monarchs corresponded to Pharaoh and "identification with the Israelites in slavery reassured crypto-Jews that God was on their side despite their apparent helplessness, that their suffering was part of a divine plan, that deliverance would come at the appointed hour and the enemy would be humiliated, destroyed, and exposed as fraudulent" (17).[42]

Nevertheless, some scholars insist on denying or minimizing all of this. A few even claim that inquisitorial files cannot be trusted as evidence because they were used as propaganda, which is simply absurd. Secrecy was strictly enforced, failure to keep silent constituted a crime against the Holy Office, and no inquisitor ever dreamed that those files would eventually be read by outsiders. As Blázquez Miguel put it, the effort to dismiss automatically such massive, trustworthy evidence, is nothing less than preposterous (1988, 50–51).

Scholars who deny the existence of crypto-Judaism maintain that offenses involving customs and diet habits, such as a dislike for pork and pork products, were cultural rather than religious. Although this was probably true in many instances—an aversion to pork, rabbit, and shellfish does not necessarily have anything to do with religion—the same cannot be said about the *adafina*, a meal prepared ahead of time so as not to have to cook on Saturday, the avoidance of work on that day, the baking of unleavened bread around Easter, and a variety of practices well documented in numerous trials (see Blázquez Miguel 1988, 53–66; Gitlitz 1996, 531–61).[43] By modern standards, the Inquisition was truly monstrous, but, according to the standards of the time, most inquisitors were people of conscience. They were religious men, and most of them sincerely believed that they were saving souls. The voluminous files that they compiled on each individual demonstrate that they usually made a great effort to be just, and did not penance or relegate their victims to the secular arm indiscriminately, for mere trifles. As Beinart pointed out, "it was the intention underlying the deed or precept that the Inquisition interpreted as a design on the part of the Conversos to judaize" (1992b, 62).

A few scholars also maintain that the heterodox ideas attributed to some defendants, including skepticism about the afterlife, existed among the general population as well, and that Old Christians also had the habit of proffering blasphemous oaths involving the Virgin, Christ, and the Mass. The blasphemous oaths proffered by Old Christians, however, were—and still are—quite different from the assertions that some New Christians had the imprudence to make in front of the wrong people. They were no doubt repeating what they had heard from their Jewish ancestors, who saw the dogma of the Incarnation in human terms, regarding the Virgin Mary as an immoral, unfaithful woman, and her Son, Jesus, as illegitimate. Whenever they could, they avoided mentioning his name, and when angry, they often did so in the most disrespectful terms (Gitlitz 1996, 141). At the end of the fifteenth century, some conversos processed by the Inquisition stated that Christ was the product of an illicit relationship (Caro Baroja 1986, 2: 459). At the beginning of the fifteenth century, a converso mocked Christians for believing that Jesus was the Messiah and Mary a Virgin (Caro Baroja 1986, 1: 456). In 1521, Juan Beltrán was heard to say before the Holy Sacrament: "Adórote, carpintero; adórote, carpintero" ("I worship you, carpenter; I worship you, carpenter"; 454), implying that Christ was a carpenter's and not God's son. In 1571, Gonçalo Vaz, a Portuguese student in Granada, said that Jesus was a scourge sent by God to punish humankind. Many stated that his miracles were nothing but tricks. In 1511, a witness testified that, during the Passion, Juan de Teva would spit whenever the name of Jesus was mentioned (Gitlitz 1996, 140–41). In 1484, Catalina de Zamora was accused of saying "que era Nuestra Señora vna puta judihuela" ("that Our Lady was a little Jewish whore"; Beinart 1974–77, 1: 389). Similar blasphemous statements can also be documented in the Americas. In 1617, in Mexico, Juan Treviño de Sobremonte told his son Rafael, who subsequently testified against his father: "God has no mother; if He created us, how could He be born? All that is nonsense; there is only one God who created the heaven and the earth and everything the Church believes is nonsense" (Gitlitz 1996, 144). In 1626, Francisco Maldonado de Silva told the Lima Inquisition that "it was a lie to say that Mary was a virgin when she gave birth to Our Lord, because she was only a woman married to an old man and she went out somewhere and got pregnant and was not a virgin" (143).

In addition, some conversos mistreated Christian images and the Host, probably unaware that, as David Gitlitz pointed out, this implied a tacit acceptance of the Christian belief that they were holy (1996, 137). In 1515, the licentiate Diego Alonso was accused of taking a consecrated Host and burning it (Caro Baroja 1986, 1: 457). In 1623, Benito Ferrer, a defrocked monk, took the Host from the hands of a priest and stomped on it (1: 191–92). In the 1630s, a man with a devout Christian wife used to get up in the middle of the night and profane a crucifix that he had hidden in a barn. Before being put to death, he praised Judaism and declared himself a martyr (1: 188–89). Many other such examples could be culled from inquisitorial trials (see Gitlitz 1996, 135–82).

The Converso Problem

The aversion to Jesus and the Blessed Mother has survived into modern times. The Sephardic versions of the ballad *El idólatra de María* refer to the Virgin in insulting terms, and some even call her "puta María" ("Mary the Whore"; Costa Fontes 1994–95a, 259). Other Sephardic ballads document a clear aversion to the names of Mary and Christ (Armistead and Silverman 1982, 137–38). Earlier in the present century, in the town of Argozelo, located in the district of Bragança, in northern Portugal, some old crypto-Jewish women were reported to attach a crucifix to the hem of their skirts during the week of Easter in order to drag it on the ground, saying: "quanto mais te arrasto, mais vontade tenho de te arrastar" ("the more I drag you, the more I feel like dragging you"; Paulo 1971, 49).

Of course not every converso investigated for practicing Judaism was guilty. Many were falsely accused by their enemies, or for trivial, baseless suspicions (Márquez Villanueva 2000b, 525–27). The most outrageous example is the process against Fray Hernando de Talavera, archbishop of Granada. Fray Hernando respected freedom of conscience, thought that only conversions made out of conviction were valid, and that the proper, Christian way to achieve them was by preaching and example (Márquez Villanueva 1960, 115–16). As former confessor and trusted advisor of the Queen, his was one of the strongest voices against the Inquisition and its methods. In 1505, the merciless Diego Rodríguez Lucero, chief inquisitor in Córdoba since 1499, accused Fray Hernando, his relatives, and his closest collaborators of Judaizing. On May 21, 1507, the bishop of Burgos, who defended Fray Hernando, wrote him a letter announcing that he had been found innocent and his relatives set free, but the saintly octogenarian archbishop had died in complete poverty a few days before, on May 14 (131–39). It was his custom to give everything he owned to the poor, and he had even gone to the point of selling at auction every object that was unessential in his household.

As he was expiring, Fray Hernando wrote a letter addressed to the Pope, the College of Cardinals, the King and the Queen, and the Grandees of Spain, in which he proclaimed his innocence and that of his family, servants, and dependents, and denounced Lucero and his accomplices for their hatred of conversos. He also pointed out that their actions went against the Christian faith, which, according to St. Paul, does not authorize any distinction between Jew and Greek. Fray Hernando then asked for the last rites, held a cross and a candle in his hands, and died (Márquez Villanueva 1960, 153–54). Not surprisingly, no effort has been made to canonize him, but perhaps justice will eventually come. He was a saint.

Although there is no question that many falsely accused, innocent people suffered, the vast majority of those who were actually charged during the first decades of the Inquisition were crypto-Jews. Generally speaking, the inquisitors were educated men, and knew what they were doing. As Blázquez

Chapter One

Miguel, who took the trouble to read thousands of trials and other inquisitorial documents, explains, there were numerous denunciations, but the inquisitors could see that most of them were based on trifles, and the proportion of those charged was relatively small: "No hay más que ver las visitas de distrito que realizaban los inquisidores, en las que recibían multitud de denuncias y en cambio pocos eran los procesados, pues veían claramente que muchas se fundaban en puerilidades" ("All one has to do is to check the visits that the inquisitors made to the districts for, although they received numerous accusations, the defendants were very few. They could clearly see that many of the accusations were based on trifles"; 1988, 52).

In sum, it is indisputable that many conversos wished to revert to Judaism. These crypto-Jews maintained that salvation was possible only through the law of Moses, saw themselves as being superior, denounced Christianity as a false religion, and mocked Christians, regarding them as dupes for believing that the illegitimate son of an unfaithful woman was the Son of God. As Sanford Shepard explains, "the medieval Jews and later their converso descendants did not hesitate to use their sharp wit and skeptical bent of mind to ridicule Christian belief and practice. Transubstantiation, virgin birth, resurrection were, then as they are today, burdensome to credulity and objects of sarcastic banter" (1982, 74). Christians were aware of this, and it caused them to hate the crypto-Jews even more.

Notwithstanding the horrible persecutions of the first decade, crypto-Judaism continued to thrive. Many thought that the very presence of a Jewish minority retarded assimilation, because Jews and conversos were related to each other, usually lived in the same communities, and had numerous contacts. The Jews did everything they could to help and encourage those who wished to return to their faith: "*Conversos* and Jews were one people, united by bonds of religion, destiny and messianic hope" (Baer 1992, 2: 424).[44] Realizing this, the Inquisition resolved to separate them and began to banish the Jews from several communities in Andalusia (1483). One year later they all had left that region. Thus, this was a prelude to the general expulsion that would come soon after (Beinart 1992c, 20).

When Ferdinand and Isabella decided to resume the war against the last Muslim stronghold in the Peninsula (1481), the Jewish community was heavily taxed in order to help with the expenses. Ironically, the Catholic Monarchs were still in Granada, which had fallen on January 2, 1492, when, on March 31, they issued the edict that gave the Jews until July 31 to leave the country. Since the decree was not made public until May 1, that left only three months to prepare for exile.

Contemporaries attempted to explain the decision in a variety of ways. Some thought that Torquemada had intimidated the Kings, and that they themselves had never intended to oust the Jews. Others claimed that

Ferdinand wanted to avoid paying the large sums he had borrowed from some rich Jews because of the war, and to confiscate their property to boot. A few blamed the Queen. According to one account, Ferdinand did not agree with her. During an argument, Isabella screamed that he loved the Jews because he was of their flesh and blood, and the enraged King took off his shoe and threw it at her. One chronicle goes so far as to place the responsibility on converso self-hatred, claiming that some highly placed New Christians at court had encouraged the King (Gerber 1992, 135–36). However, the main thrust came from the Inquisition (Kamen 1998, 20–21) and, as Gerber points out, "the best explanation for the expulsion can be derived from the decree itself" (1992, 137). The edict justifies the decision as follows: "Bien sabedes o deuedes saber que . . . nos fuemos ynformados que en nuestros reynos auia algunos malos christianos que judaysauan e apostotauan de nuestra santa fe catolica, de lo qual era mucha cabsa la comunicaçion de los judios con los christianos" ("You must know or ought to know that . . . we were informed that in our kingdoms there were some bad Christians who Judaized and committed apostasy against our holy Catholic faith, and that to a great extent this was caused by the contact between Jews and [New] Christians"; Beinart 1993, 224).[45]

Clearly, the main motive for the expulsion was religious, and Isabella and Ferdinand agreed with each other, as usual. Both signed the edict. In a letter sent to the Count of Aranda, Ferdinand explained that their only motive was a question of faith, and that he realized that there would be significant financial consequences for the crown: "The Holy Office of the Inquisition, seeing how some Christians are endangered by contact and communication with the Jews, has provided that the Jews be expelled from all our realms and territories, and has persuaded us to give our support and agreement to this, which we now do . . . despite the great harm to ourselves, seeking and preferring the salvation of souls above our own profit and that of individuals" (qtd. and trans. in Kamen 1998, 21).[46] Together with the conquest of Granada, this decision would earn Isabella and Ferdinand the title of Catholic Monarchs. Pope Alexander VI bestowed it on them the very same year.[47]

It is not difficult to imagine the reaction of the people affected by the cruel decree. In Isaac Abrabanel's moving description, "wherever word of the decree reached, there was great mourning among the Jews. There was great trembling and sorrow the likes of which had not been experienced since the days of the exile of the Jews from their land to the land of foreigners. The Jews encouraged each other: Let us strengthen ourselves on behalf of our faith, on behalf of the Torah of our God" (qtd. in Gerber 1992, 138).

Although the decree did not give a choice between conversion and expulsion, everything indicates that "the edict did not seek to expel a people, but to eliminate a religion" (Kamen 1998, 22). As soon as it was published, the

Chapter One

clergy launched a campaign to convert the Jews (Baer 1992, 2: 435–36; Bernáldez 1962, 252). When the rabbis went among the people, encouraging them to remain steadfast in their faith, the authorities forbade them from doing so. Many chose conversion, but great numbers prepared themselves for exile. One of those who became a Christian was Abraham Seneor, head judge of the Jewish communities of Castile and royal treasurer, who changed his name to Fernán Núñez Coronel. He was baptized in a great ceremony in Guadalupe, with Ferdinand and Isabella as sponsors, but two of his daughters and his youngest brother refused to convert (Beinart 1992c, 32–35; 1993, 231).[48]

Last minute efforts to make the Kings change their minds were of no avail. Because of the short amount of time that they had been given, people had to sell their homes and the land that they owned for ridiculous prices (Bernáldez 1962, 255). Since they were forbidden to take gold and silver out of the country,[49] the value of the goods they were allowed to carry increased astronomically. Some buried their valuables, hoping to return. Common property such as synagogues and cemeteries were confiscated by the crown. A few synagogues became churches; the cemeteries were turned into pastures and the headstones were sold to be used for construction purposes by order of the Queen (Beinart 1993, 229).

Since everyone had to be out of the country by the end of July, the exodus started at the beginning of the month. To prevent disturbances, the exiles were provided with army escorts, a few of which robbed them (Beinart 1993, 230 and n9). Even the anti-Semitic chronicler-priest Andrés Bernáldez seems to have been moved by their plight:

> en la prostera[50] semana del mes de jullio . . . se metieron al trabajo del camino; e salieron de las tierras de su nascimiento, chicos e grandes e viejos e niños, a pie e cavalleros en asnos e en otras bestias e en carretas; e continuaron su viage, cada uno a los puertos que avían de ir. E ivan por los caminos e canpos por donde ivan con mucho trabajo e fortuna, unos cayendo, otros levantando, unos muriendo, otros nasciendo, otros enfermando, que no avía cristiano que no oviese dolor dellos; e sienpre por donde ivan los conbidavan al bautismo, e algunos con la cuita se convertían e quedavan, enpero muy pocos; e los rabíes los ivan esforçando e hazían cantar a las mugeres e mancebos, e tañer panderos e adufes, por alegrar la gente. E así salieron de Castilla e llegaron a los puertos donde enbarcaron, los unos, e los otros a Portugal. (1962, 256, 258 [3])

Some of the exiles gave up, however. They returned to their towns, asked to be baptized, begged to have their property returned for the price they had sold it, and it was often restored to them (Caro Baroja 1986, 1: 196). After great hardships, many of their surviving brethren reached Portugal, where they had to pay a head toll upon crossing the border. Others settled in Navarre, which resisted pressure to issue a decree of expulsion until 1498. A good number went to North Africa, the papal estates in Avignon, the kingdom of Naples, and the Eastern Mediterranean. Many eventually settled in the Ottoman Empire, and some reached the Holy Land (Beinart 1993, 233).

Although the edict of expulsion threatened with the death penalty anyone who, having left the country, dared to return (Beinart 1993, 226, 228), many came back, asking to be baptized. Slightly over a month after the expulsion, on November 10, "the queen issued an order permitting all those who had returned and converted to purchase their property at the price they sold it for, with the addition of an added value payment if the asset had appreciated" (Beinart 1992c, 38). Thus, their property was restored to them. It is impossible to determine how many people were involved, but it must have been a good number. We know that in one town, Torrelaguna, most of the exiles decided to return (Domínguez Ortiz 1992, 42).

On September 5, 1499, the Catholic Monarchs "issued a second edict, permitting expelled Jews to return to Spain provided that they accepted Christian baptism at their ports of re-entry into the country and remained faithful to their conversion" (Sicroff 2000, 602). Albert Sicroff, in his response to Netanyahu (1995; 2000), uses the term "religious racism" to characterize the official attitude in order to show that religion constituted the primary factor for both the establishment of the Inquisition and the expulsion. He goes on to ask: "Was that a manifestation of official racial hatred of Jews?" (2000, 602).

In any case, the number of Jews in Spain at the time of the expulsion is difficult to estimate. Contemporary figures, as usual, are greatly exaggerated, and vary considerably. Andrés Bernáldez calculates 335,000 persons, excluding Aragon (Caro Baroja 1986, 1: 199). Writing over a century later, Juan de Mariana says that most authors reckoned that there were 170,000 families, and that some put the total figure at 800,000 souls (Kamen 1998, 23). Also over a century later, Zurita vacillates between 170,000 and 400,000 people (Suárez 1992, 336).

The number of exiles varies as well. Some sources speak of 200,000, but Isaac Abrabanel says that 300,000 persons left (Beinart 1993, 232–33). Others raise the number to 400,000 (Caro Baroja 1986, 1: 199).

Using tax records, modern scholars have been able to come up with more reliable figures recently. There were 80,000 (Kamen 1998, 23) to 100,000 (Suárez 1992, 338) Jews in Spain in 1492. The evidence is too scanty to determine how many converted or returned and how many remained in exile. Kamen estimates that possibly half opted for conversion (1998, 24). Domínguez Ortiz speaks of 20,000 or 30,000. Taking into account the demographic growth of the 150,000, who, according to his calculations, had converted several generations before, he estimates that the total number of conversos came to nearly 250,000, that is, about 4 percent of the population (1992, 43).

Kamen was certainly right when he concluded that the purpose of the edict of expulsion was not to eliminate a people, but a religion. Since everything was done to convert the Jews, the official policy was to keep them, albeit as Christians. As far as the crown was concerned, they constituted an asset, and their departure would only impoverish the country. In fact, the edict was a last effort to convert them. Faced with a choice between conversion and emigration, the government hoped, most Jews would probably embrace Christianity in order to keep their homes and property, and avoid the heartlessness of exile. Thus, the purpose of the edict was twofold: to keep as many Jews as possible by turning them into Christians, and to extirpate the Judaizing problem. There could be no compromise on this point, and, if everyone became Christian, the problem would certainly disappear. Ironically, since the thousands who embraced Christianity did so only to avoid exile, the Judaizing problem became even worse.

Although the crown regarded the conversos as an important asset, the racist masses did not. Official policy clashed with popular feeling. Seeing the suffering of the Jews on their way to exile, many Christians felt sorry and pleaded with them to be baptized. This sympathetic, human reaction was only momentary, however. The masses continued to regard conversos as Jews and were jealous of their success, supporting the Inquisition and the laws of blood purity meant to exclude them from mainstream society. In short, they wished to be rid of them.

Chapter Two

Repression and Artistic Expression

This was the suffocating environment in which Fernando de Rojas and Francisco Delicado had to live. Being conversos, they belonged to a repressed, unwanted minority. Rojas published *Celestina* anonymously in Burgos, in 1499, seven years after the conquest of Granada, the expulsion of the Jews, another wave of mass conversions, and the arrival of Columbus in the Americas.[1] He revealed his name through eleven preliminary acrostic stanzas added to the second edition of his book (Toledo, 1500). Delicado published *La Lozana andaluza* in Venice, also anonymously, in 1530. He disclosed his authorship four years later, in the introduction to his Venetian edition of a Spanish chivalry romance, the *Primaleón* (1534).

Celestina tells the story of two ill-fated young lovers, Calisto and Melibea, who meet with tragic deaths soon after being brought together by an old procuress, Celestina. The force of the bawd's character is such that, even though Rojas had entitled the first version of his work, written in sixteen acts, *Comedia de Calisto y Melibea*, changing it to *Tragicomedia de Calisto y Melibea* in a subsequent edition expanded to twenty-one acts by popular demand (1502), readers soon began to call it *Celestina*. Delicado entitled his book *Retrato de la Loçana andaluza*, but everyone refers to it as *La Lozana andaluza*. Since it tells the adventures of a young girl from Córdoba who ends up living in Rome, it may be said that both works have women as protagonists. Unlike Rojas, Delicado combines dialogue with narration and divides his book into sixty-six chapters or sketches entitled *mamotretos* ("bundles of papers"), but *Celestina* inspired him to such an extent that he purports to compete with it, boasting in the subtitle: "El qual Retrato demuestra lo que en Roma passaua y contiene munchas mas cosas que la Celestina" ("A portrait that shows what was happening in Rome and contains many more things than *Celestina*"; 1985, 165).[2] This marketing strategy—if that is what it really was—did not work, however. Whereas *Celestina* continued to be the subject of numerous editions (listed in Marciales 1985, 1: 5–13)—Delicado himself oversaw the publication of one in Venice (1531)—*La Lozana andaluza* disappeared from circulation. It

33

Chapter Two

seems to have been unknown to other writers, and was not rediscovered until 1845, when Ferdinand J. Wolf mentioned the single surviving copy, which he found at the Imperial Library, in Vienna.

Little is known about either author. There is not enough data to determine the date of Rojas's birth accurately. In the acrostic verses, he says that he is a Bachelor of Law from Puebla de Montalbán, which is fourteen miles west of Toledo. The nucleus of the town had been a Jewish settlement, and a substantial number of the inhabitants were conversos (Gilman 1972, 222, 233). Thanks to an annotated family tree printed by the Chancery Court of Valladolid when a distant cousin of Rojas's, Hernán Suárez Franco, attempted to obtain a certificate of nobility in 1606,[3] we know that Rojas had many relatives in Toledo and that the family was of Jewish origin. As we have seen, other conversos, such as St. Theresa's father, had been able to obtain such certificates.

Each name in the family tree is numbered, and the corresponding notes, which are written in a hurried, telegraphic style, contain information culled from inquisitorial documents. Suárez Franco claimed that the family was originally from Asturias, descending from Pedro González, a notary with three sons, two of whom had moved. Pedro Franco had settled in Toledo, and his brother, Garcí González de Rojas, had gone to live in Puebla de Montalbán, where he fathered the Bachelor Fernando de Rojas. The note that corresponds to Rojas's name recalls that he wrote *Celestina*, and states that Garcí González's real name was the same as his son's, Fernando de Rojas. This Rojas had been condemned as a Judaizer in 1488, and his descendants had replaced him with an Asturian great-grandfather: "El Bachiller Rojas que compuso a Celestina la vieja. El señor Fiscal pretende que fue hijo de Hernando de Rojas condenado por judayzante año de 88 y que deste deciende el Licenciado Rojas abogado que fue de Valladolid letrado de Hernán Suárez para quien también pretendieron traer visaguelo de Asturias" ("The Bachelor Rojas, who wrote *Celestina*, the old one. The prosecutor claims that he was the son of Hernando de Rojas, condemned as a Judaizer in '88, and that from him descends the Licentiate Rojas, who was a lawyer in Valladolid, learned [ancestor] of Hernán Suárez, for whom they also tried to invent a great-grandfather from Asturias"; Gilman 1972, 502). Conversos who sought such certificates often changed or replaced the names of ancestors who figured in inquisitorial archives, and Asturian origins, we recall, were practically regarded as a guarantee of nobility and blood purity.

Disagreeing violently with Gilman's assertion that Rojas's father had been burned at the stake—in fact, the word *condenado* could merely mean "penanced" in the context—Miguel Marciales disputed this documentation, pointing out that the name Fernando de Rojas was current in the area of Toledo, and that it was very uncommon for father and son to bear the same name (1985, 1: 272–73). In the rare instances in which this happened, *el viejo* ("the Elder") was added to the father's name, and *el moço* ("the Younger") to the son's. There was no reason to make such a distinction in the hurried, telegraphic note just quoted, however. Furthermore, the family tree in question mentions plenty of relatives connected with crypto-Judaism. For example, the note on Pedro Franco, Rojas's uncle, states that he was married to María Alvarez, who, in 1485, together with four of her six children, took advantage of the customary Edict of Grace (the Toledo Inquisition had been established the year before) in order to become reconciled without incurring major penalties: "Pedro Franco, arrendador y trapero, que casó con María Alvarez, reconciliada, año 1485, la qual dize son sus hijos, Alonso Franco, Juan Franco, Mencía, muger de Alonso de San Pedro, y Catalina Alvarez, muger de Antonio de San Pedro, y dize fueron reconciliados en tiempo de gracia por judayzantes" ("Pedro Franco, contractor and clothes merchant, who married María Alvarez, reconciled in 1485. She says that Alonso Franco, Juan Franco, Mencía, Alonso de San Pedro's wife, and Catalina Alvarez, Antonio de San Pedro's wife, are her children and were reconciled during the period of grace for Judaizing"; Gilman 1972, 498). These four children were Rojas's first cousins.

Since the last person involved with the Inquisition is the writer's homonymous father, the family seems to have been able to avoid the Holy Office after 1488. Hernán Suárez Franco and the relatives who petitioned with him were condemned to pay court costs and to keep "perpetual silence," i.e., to desist from future claims to nobility. According to Gilman, the petition was made in 1606 (1972, 35), but the last date given here is 1593: "están condenados en vista de la propiedad y en costas personales y procesales y puesto perpetuo silencio, año 1593" ("as shown [?], they are condemned to property, personal, and court costs, and to perpetual silence, 1593"; 503).

Rojas says that he wrote *Celestina* during a two-week vacation, and this has led most scholars to believe that he was then a student at the University of Salamanca, even though he refers to himself as "jurista" (1987, 70), which can mean both law student and lawyer. If Rojas was still in school when he wrote his masterpiece, some of his fellow students were Francisco López de Villalobos, later court physician to King Ferdinand and to Charles V; Juan de Cervantes, Cervantes's grandfather; and Hernán Cortés, conqueror of Mexico (Gilman 1972, 272). Since students began their university education between the ages of fourteen and sixteen, and it took six years to complete the degree of Bachelor of Laws, scholars have deduced that Rojas was born in 1475 or 1476 (Dunn 1975, 14). Marciales, on the other hand, thought that Rojas was already a lawyer when he wrote *Celestina*, and surmised that he was ten years older, placing the date of his birth between 1465 and 1466 (1985, 1: 270–73).

Chapter Two

In any case, Rojas returned to Puebla de Montalbán and resided there for some time before moving in 1507 to Talavera de la Reina, a larger town twenty-five miles away. The population included a high proportion of conversos whose ancestors had been baptized in 1391, and a good number of more recent New Christians, who had accepted baptism in order to avoid exile in 1492 (Gilman 1972, 415–16). Rojas lived there until he died in 1541. Still in 1507 or shortly after, he married a local girl, Leonor Alvarez, daughter of Alvaro de Montalbán (207–11), a wealthy businessman who gave her 80,000 *maravedís* as dowry (421). They had six children.

Rojas was a fairly prosperous, well-respected lawyer, and served as Lord Mayor of Talavera on several occasions (Gilman 1972, 126). Overall, he seems to have lived a fairly undisturbed life. Around 1517, he testified before the Inquisition on behalf of Diego de Oropesa, a tax farmer arrested and charged with crimes such as a dislike for paying tithes, a propensity to wear clean shirts on Saturday, and reluctance to eat bacon. Oropesa had been denounced by two village women at the instigation of their local priest, probably because he was having an affair with the priest's sister. The result is unknown, for the record of the trial is incomplete (468–71).

The imprisonment of Alvaro de Montalbán by the Toledo Inquisition in 1525 and the impoundment of his goods must have been far more shocking to Rojas. His father-in-law had been reconciled about forty years before, around 1485, during the same period when the author's aunt and cousins had taken advantage of the Edict of Grace. Apparently in his mid-thirties back then, the old man was now seventy-five years old. When interrogated in 1485, he had broken down, accusing many relatives. The remains of his parents had been burned publicly in an auto-da-fé. Since it was far more dangerous to appear before the Inquisition a second time, the family had to be extremely worried. If found guilty, Alvaro could be classified as relapsed, burned, and have all of his property confiscated. As it was, his dishonor already affected all of his relatives.

This time, the old man could not think of anything he had done and held his peace, without denouncing anyone else. Under interrogation he revealed that, although his grandfather was already Christian, the family purchased meat from the Jewish butcher, and that he himself went on occasion to the synagogue. Alvaro could no longer remember whether he did this "con yntincion de judayzar" ("with the intention of Judaizing"; Gilman 1972, 73). Since Christian and Jewish children played together, it is clear that in Puebla de Montalbán the conversos continued to maintain good relations with their Jewish brethren.

Unable to extract anything useful from the old man, the inquisitors had to inform him of the charges. While visiting his daughter Constança Núñez and her prosperous husband, Pero de Montalbán, at their home in Madrid, he had accompanied them and two guests on an outing to a country property that they owned. The guests were Iñigo de Monçón and Father Alonso Ruiz, parish priest of San Ginés. As they were returning after a picnic, Iñigo commented that they had a good time, and Alvaro replied: "Here let me be well off, since I know nothing about what lies beyond" (Gilman 1972, 83). Iñigo took this as a denial of the immortality of the soul and the afterlife, and denounced him. The priest went along, serving as second witness.

Either because of agnosticism or mere skepticism, some Christians used to proffer similar statements (Kamen 1998, 40), but Alvaro's words expressed the same idea as "no hay que nascer e morir" ("There is nothing more to life than to live and die"; Shepard 1982, 91), which used to be attributed to Jews. This skepticism was current among highly educated Jewish and Muslim aristocrats who followed the rationalistic philosophy, which denied the immortality of the soul (Márquez Villanueva 1994c; Shepard 1982, 91–95). This doctrine, which contradicts Jewish belief as well, seems to have persisted among some conversos.

At first Alvaro refused a lawyer, but changed his mind a few days later. He would like to be defended by his son-in-law, Fernando de Rojas, who, he said, was also a converso. Since the Inquisition apparently drew the lawyers from its own, pre-approved list, the request was denied.

Just for this imprudent statement, Alvaro was condemned to life in prison and to wear a sanbenito for the rest of his life, but the sentence was commuted to house arrest (Gilman 1972, 67–83). Everything he had acquired since 1480 was confiscated (480),[4] and Rojas and his brother-in-law were required to surrender half of their wives' dowries. Fernando's share came to 40,000 *maravedís*, Pedro's to 37,500. Both appealed, and it seems that Pedro got his money back. It is not clear whether Rojas paid or succeeded in having his money returned, but he mentions his wife's dowry in his will, leaving her the full amount (Redondo 1965). As for Alvaro, he was eventually eliminated from the family tree, being replaced by a less notorious Dr. Juan Alvarez (Gilman 1972, 49–50).

Rojas's will is dated April 3, 1541.[5] He died shortly after, for, on April 8, his wife commissioned an inventory of his possessions. In the will, Rojas reaffirms his belief in the Holy Trinity and his wish to die in the bosom of the Church, in which he has always lived, and asks to be dressed in the habit of St. Francis and buried in the convent of La Madre de Dios ("Mother of God"; Gilman 1972, 484–86).[6]

A very Christian death, indeed. For some scholars, this proves that Rojas was a convinced, orthodox Catholic. For those who perceive unorthodox ideas in *Celestina*, Rojas's last-minute protestations of faith and request for a Christian burial are not necessarily sincere. Gilman stressed that he could be attempting to protect his family, shielding their inheritance from postmortem confiscations. Moreover, as Francisco Márquez Villanueva's study of the convents founded by St. Theresa of Avila demonstrates, certified Christian burial in a religious institution was of the utmost importance to wealthy, albeit insecure conversos (1968, 169–70).

Rojas's dying profession of faith in the Holy Trinity is most intriguing. As we will see in Chapter 7, that dogma presented more difficulty to conversos than accepting that Christ was the Messiah. This was so well known to contemporary Italians, who had many converso refugees in their midst, that they referred to it ironically as *il peccadiglio di Spagna* ("the little sin from Spain"; Caro Baroja 1986, 1: 315; Pérez 1981, 100). It would be interesting to examine other wills of the period in order to see if Rojas's profession of faith in the Holy Trinity was customary or not, but, even it was not, we will never know whether he was motivated by religious conviction or prudence.

What is certain is that danger was always present, and a person of Rojas's background had good reason to be extremely careful. As we have seen, his father was penanced and perhaps even burned by the Inquisition in 1488, and some of his relatives had been punished in 1485 for Judaizing. Later, we recall, the Inquisition demanded half of the dowry that his wife had brought into the marriage. In a nutshell, it is extremely difficult to see how these circumstances could have failed to have had a profound effect on Rojas's worldview.

The biographical information on Francisco Delicado is also scanty. The little that we know about him is what he tells us about himself in *La Lozana andaluza* (Venice, 1530); *El modo de adoperare el legno de India Occidentale* (2nd ed. Venice, 1529; reed. 1970–71), a short medical treatise about syphilis; the *Spechio vulgare per li Sacerdoti* (Rome, 1525; see Ugolini 1974–75), a succinct manual designed to help Spanish parish priests in Rome; and in the editions of several Spanish works that he supervised in Venice between 1531 and 1534 (Gallina 1962). In the first of the appendices to *La Lozana andaluza* (485), he states that he also wrote a treatise for the sick, *De consolatione infirmorum*. This book seems to have been published either in Rome or in Venice in 1549, but it has been lost.[7]

Delicado's name is an Italianized form of the Spanish Delgado. He seems to take great pride in his hometown, stressing frequently that he is from Peña de Martos (province of Jaén),[8] but he was born in the vicinity of Córdoba. He identifies more with Peña de Martos because his mother raised him there, which suggests that his father either died or abandoned the family. In *La Lozana andaluza*, Lozana asks Silvano, a friend of the author (spelled both "Auctor" and "Autor") who is fictionalized and depicted in the process of writing her story: "Señor Silvano, ¿qué quiere decir que el autor de mi retrato no se llama cordobés, pues su padre lo fue, y él nació en la diócesi?" ("My Lord Silvano, why doesn't the author of my portrait call himself a Cordoban, since his father was one and he himself was born in the diocese of Córdoba?"; 399). To which Silvano replies: "Porque su castísima madre y su cuna fue en Martos, y como dicen: no donde naces, sino con quien paces" ("Because his very chaste mother was from Martos and he was raised there, and, as the saying goes, what matters is not where you are born, but with whom you live"; 399).

Delicado's date of birth is unknown. There is not enough data to determine it even tentatively, and, as Tatiana Bubnova indicated (1987, 59), the dates that have been postulated, 1480 (Allegra 1983, 46; Vilanova 1952b, xii) and 1488 or 1489 (Ugolini 1974–75, 491), are purely speculative.[9] Despite the lack of clear, indisputable documentation, there is no doubt that Delicado was a New Christian. As we will see in Chapter 6, he had an intimate knowledge of converso gastronomy, empathized with their inherited dislike for pork, ridiculed the idea of "limpieza de sangre" ("purity of the blood"), knew the exiled converso and Sephardic communities in Rome extremely well, was proud of the learning of Spanish Jews, lived in Italy for many years without returning to his native Spain, and denounced "voluntary" exile in *La Lozana andaluza*. Perhaps all of this could be attributed to any Spaniard, but, as we shall also see, there is further reason to think that an Old Christian could not possibly have written such a book.

Some scholars have hypothesized that Delicado left Spain at the time of the expulsion of the Jews, in 1492 (Serrano Poncela 1962, 126; Bubnova 1987, 59; Vilanova 1952b, xiii–xv), but there is no evidence for this. Being a converso rather than a Jew, he did not have to go into exile at that time. On the contrary, many Jews converted so as not to have to leave their country. Thousands of conversos began to flee from Spain in 1481, but that was because they feared the Inquisition, which conducted the first auto-da-fé that year, in Seville. Delicado was probably a refugee from the Inquisition himself, but the chances are that he arrived in Italy much later.

The two possible dates given in *La Lozana andaluza* do not prove anything; after all, they appear in a work of fiction. The first date occurs when an Andalusian conversa, Beatriz, says that she has been in Rome since the beginning of the Inquisition, i.e., 1481 (202). Delicado probably did not come then, however. If we were to suppose that he was about twenty years old in 1481, he would have been born around 1461, and, therefore, would have to be seventy-three years old when we last hear of him in 1534. This is an unlikely ripe old age for a sixteenth-century man who suffered from syphilis for many years. In its later stages, the disease attacks vital organs such as the heart and the liver.

The second date is Lozana's arrival when Leo X was about to be crowned pope (191), i.e., 1513. Since there is a strong identification between the fictionalized Auctor and his protagonist—among other coincidences, Lozana is depicted as a syphilitic conversa from Córdoba—it is possible that Delicado also arrived in Rome at that date or shortly before. At one point the Auctor asks Lozana's companion, Rampín, if they had not first met "en tiempo de Julio segundo en plaza Nagona, cuando sirviédes al señor canónigo" ("during the time of Julius II, in Nagona Square, when you were in the service of the Lord Canon"; 252). Julius II was pope between 1503 and 1513, but this does not necessarily imply a contradiction, for the Auctor could have been referring to the end of Julius's pontificate. In any case, although more likely, this approximate date of arrival still constitutes an hypothesis.

On November 2, 1525, Delicado published the *Spechio vulgare per li Sacerdoti,* in Rome. A short, succinct manual in Italian with information about local religious customs, advice, and Italian expressions for newly arrived Spanish priests, the booklet is permeated with numerous Latinisms and Hispanisms that show that it must have been difficult for Delicado to write in Italian (Ugolini 1974–75, 465). He recalls the example of Fray Hernando de Talavera, bishop of Granada, who realized that it was necessary to communicate with the Moriscos in his diocese in Arabic in order to evangelize them (466), informs his readers that he himself was in a situation similar to theirs when he arrived in Italy—which suggests that he was already ordained—and that he had learned from some old priests in Santa Maria della Pace how to understand and make himself understood by his parishioners: "el quale modo et documento vulgare io imperai in santa Maria della Pace de uno curato et anticho sacerdoto et anche da li sacerdoti antichi li quali concurrevano innella prima fundatione della compagnia, sacrosanta societatte de li sacerdoti in santa Maria in Aquiro" ("I learned that manner of common speech in Santa Maria della Pace, from an old parish priest and also from some of the old priests who shared in the foundation of the Company of the Holy Society of Priests of Santa Maria in Aquiro"; 469).

Delicado's name does not figure in the frontispiece, which, below the title, displays an engraving of six kneeling priests hearing another one celebrate Mass before the altar, but rather in the *explicit,* where he identifies himself as "Frencesco Delicato, Hispano" ("Francisco Delicado, a Spaniard"), priest in the church of "Sancte Maria in Posterule de Urbe" (449–50). This suggests that much of the material in *La Lozana andaluza,* which depicts a world of prostitution, is taken from life, for the front of Delicado's church was next to "d'ell'Orso" street, well known for harboring a great number of courtesans. While showing Lozana the city, Rampín informs her that "Por esta calle hallaremos tanta[s] cortesanas juntas como colmenas" ("Down this street the courtesans are as thick as bees in beehives"), and adds: "Aquí se dice el Urso" ("This is called Urso [Bear] Street"; 213). As Francesco Ugolini indicated, the laundrywomen and shirtmakers mentioned in *La*

Lozana andaluza also lived near Delicado's church, and some of the names he uses happen to be historical (1974–75, 452–55). The "Tregus hebreus," the "Teresa Spagnola" and the "Marina spagnola" listed in the Roman census of 1526 correspond to the "jodío Trigo" (240), Teresa de Córdoba, and Marina Hernández (191). Recalling Marcelino Menéndez y Pelayo's insight about the courtesans in Delicado's book—he had surmised: "todos estos nombres tienen traza de ser históricos" ("all of these names look historical"; 1961, 59)—Alfonso Reyes (1945, 94–95) pointed out that another character, the beautiful Garza Montesina (Forest Heron), whose house Lozana visits at one point (448–51), may be the same "Garza montesina" mentioned in a *villancico* by another priest, Juan del Encina, a poet and playwright who is regarded as the father of modern Spanish theater. Encina had visited Rome at the beginning of the century.

The *Spechio* contains an additional nugget of biographical information when the author explains that his Spanish colleagues had asked him for this book, and that he had taken the opportunity to write it while interned at the hospital of St. James with an incurable illness that had made him unworthy to exercise his duties as parish priest: "essendo io in lo Archihospitale de santo Jacobo in Augusta infirmo incurabile . . . essendo stato indeigno curato in la parrochia supraditta" ("I was in the great hospital of St. James in Augusta, with an incurable illness . . . I was the unworthy priest of the aforesaid parish"; Ugolini 1974–75, 468–69). The hospital in question is San Giacomo degli Incurabili (St. James of the Incurable), and Delicado is referring to the syphilis that was going to cause him to write his next work, *El modo de adoperare el legno de India Occidentale*.

This is a booklet. According to the colophon, it was published in Venice on February 10, 1529, but, within the text, Delicado refers to an earlier edition, promising a third: "no puse en esta segunda estampa la composición del lectuario, no por auaricia mas por la excellentia de la cosa en la tercera estampa lo diré" ("it is not for the sake of gain that I did not write down the formula in this second printing, but because of its excellence; I will give it in the third one"; 1970–71, 265). Since the left bottom corner of the large engraving on the frontispiece has two lines stating that "francisc.º delicado composuit / .ī alma urbe anno.1525" ("Francisco Delicado wrote this / in the illustrious city [Rome], in 1525"; 253), Ugolini deduced that the booklet was probably first published in Rome in 1525–26 (1974–75, 462–63n40), and that Delicado took the printing block with him to Venice. Below the engraving in the frontispiece, however, we read: "Con gratia & priuilegio: per diece anni" ("with copyright for ten years"). This copyright, which is placed after the colophon, where Clement VII refers to the author as "dilectus filius Franciscus Delgado, presbyter giennen[sis] dioc[esis]" ("our beloved son Francisco Delicado, priest in the diocese of Jaén"; 270), concludes with

Chapter Two

the formula: "Datum Rome apud sanctum Petrum sub annulo piscatoris. Die iiij Decembris MDXXVI, Pontif[icati] nostri anno quarto" ("Given in Rome at St. Peter's under the ring of the Fisherman. December 4, 1526, fourth year of our Pontificate"; 271). Since the frontispiece claims this copyright, the booklet could not have been published in 1525–26, as Ugolini surmised. What the date of 1525 on the left corner of the engraving indicates, then, is when *El modo* was written. Since the copyright was granted in December of 1526, Damiani is probably correct in suggesting that the booklet was first published in Rome in 1527 (1969b, 13).

The booklet has sections in Latin, Italian, and Spanish. The author states that he has suffered from syphilis for twenty-three years (1970–71, 255) and believes himself cured thanks to the properties of the "palo santo" ("holy wood") or guaiacum wood, from some small islands near Santo Domingo, which he explains how to use. Nevertheless, he also attributes his cure to St. James, and seems to have vowed to go to Santiago on a pilgrimage. After promising a third edition, he writes: "Deo dante et diuo Jacobo, cuyo peregrino so al presente por la gratia recebida en Roma" ("God and the divine St. James willing; I have vowed a pilgrimage to the latter because of the grace received in Rome"; 265). The Pope also refers to the miraculous intervention of the Apostle in the copyright: "ac Dei benignitate apostoloque ipso favente magna omnium admiratione ad pristinam salutem restitutus" ("with the goodness of God and the apostle himself showing favor, restored to his former health"; 270).

Besides showing that this second edition was published in Venice in 1529, the colophon indicates that Delicado had been named Vicar of Valle de Cabezuela, a village in the province of Cáceres: "Impressum Venetiis sumptibus vene[rabilis] presbiteri Francisci Delicati, hyspani de opido Martos, Vicarij vallis loci de Cabeçuela" ("Printed in the great Venice by the venerable priest Francisco Delicado, a Spaniard from the town of Martos, Vicar of Valle de Cabezuela"; 270). He must have enjoyed the proceeds of this benefice in absentia, for he never returned to Spain.

The engraving on the frontispiece (253) presents Our Lady of Consolation on top of the guaiacum tree, in the center. The tree divides the composition in two halves. St. James the Elder is on the left, holding a staff, and stands in front of the kneeling Delicado, who also holds a staff between his chest and his right arm. Dressed as a priest, Delicado has a small stature, wears a beard, and his hairline is beginning to recede. He holds his hands together in prayer. On the ground, there are four books and a staff similar to the one he is holding. Below, we find the aforementioned two-line legend with his name and the date of 1525. The right half portrays St. Martha with the palm of martyrdom in one hand and an aspersorium in the other. The hand with the palm also holds a rope tied to a dragon in the form of a large serpent, which is identified as Tarascurus. The water on which the saint stands represents the "flumen Rodanus" (the "Rhone River").[10]

St. Martha, sister of Lazarus and St. Mary Magdalene, was known as Christ's hostess, because she had received him in her home. According to legend, she ended up in Provence, converted the people, and subdued a dragon called Tarasconus that lurked in the Rhone, near the town of Norluc. The grateful inhabitants changed the name of the town to Tarascon in order to commemorate the event. This legend eventually migrated to Spain, becoming associated with the Peña de Martos, where Delicado was raised.[11]

The presence of St. James, of course, alludes to Delicado's internment in the hospital of that name. According to Ugolini, this curious mix of devotion and legend also suggests that Delicado regarded his apparent cure as a miracle and had vowed to go on a pilgrimage to Santiago de Compostela, in Galicia: "La rappresentazione è allusiva alla guarigione miracolosa dell'autore e al voto fatto del pellegrinaggio a Compostella" ("The figure alludes to the author's miraculous cure and to the vow regarding the pilgrimage to Compostela"; 1974–75, 462). Allegra agreed with this hypothesis, interpreting the engraving as follows: "gracias al guayco y bajo la protección de la Virgen, el autor se ha curado; pasando por Francia, donde Santa Marta, que también es protectora de Martos, tiene su santuario (Tarascón), pretende cumplir su peregrinación a Compostela y dar gracias al Apóstol" ("the author has been cured thanks to the guaiacum wood and the protection of the Virgin; passing through France, where St. Martha, who is the patroness of Martos, has her sanctuary, he intends to realize his pilgrimage to Compostela and give thanks to the Apostle"; 1983, 53). Thus, the engraving would seem to indicate that Delicado is a good priest, devoted to the Blessed Mother, St. James, and St. Martha.

El modo includes a second engraving, also divided in two halves. It alludes to the author's origins, for the left side depicts the Peña de Martos, and the right the city of Córdoba, where he and his father were born.

It is almost certain that Delicado was already a priest when he left Spain. His poor Italian helps to confirm this. Had he studied for the priesthood in Italy, the chances are that it would have been much better. Moreover, as we have seen, he also informs the newly arrived Spanish priests for whom he wrote the *Spechio* that he was in a similar situation when he first arrived in Italy. In other words, he was already a priest.

Since it is in 1525 that Delicado declares that he has suffered from syphilis for twenty-three years, he must have caught it in 1502 or 1503. Curiously, the picture of the third priest in the *Spechio* is the same as the one in the frontispiece of *El modo*. Thus, rather than constituting a generic priest, what we have here is probably an actual portrait of Delicado (Ugolini 1974–75, 464). The priest has a small stature, and, in the first of the appendices to

Chapter Two

La Lozana andaluza, the narrator states that, unlike so many others, he was unable to reach the branches and leaves of the tree of folly because he was so short, and so had to content himself with sitting next to it: "como vi coger los ramos y las hojas del árbor de la vanidad a tantos, yo que soy de chica estatura, no alcancé más alto: asénteme al pie hasta pasar, como pasé, mi enfermedad" ("I saw many people pick the branches and the leaves of the tree of folly, but, being short in stature, I could not reach high enough, and so I sat near it until my illness would pass, which indeed it did"; 485).

The dates when Delicado wrote and published *La Lozana andaluza* have posed some problems. This work consists of sixty-six *mamotretos* ("bundles of papers") divided into three parts. In the epigraph to Part I, the narrator says that his "retrato" (i.e., the book) was written in Rome on June 30, 1524: "Comienza la historia o retrato sacado del jure cevil natural de la señora Lozana, compuesto el año mil y quinientos y veinte e cuatro, a treinta días del mes de junio, en Roma, alma cibdad" ("Here begins the story or portrait taken from the natural civil register of Lady Lozana; composed on June 30, 1524, in the illustrious city of Rome"; 175). As he ends the last *mamotreto*, he seems to contradict himself, stating that he finished the book on December 1, 1524: "Fenezca la historia compuesta en retrato, el más natural que el autor pudo, y acabóse hoy primo de diciembre, año de mil quinientos e veinte e cuatro a laude y honra de Dios trino y uno" ("Let us finish the story written as a portrait, in the most faithful manner that the author was able to compose it. It was completed today, December 1, 1524, in praise and honor of the one and triune God"; 481). The apparent contradiction can be easily reconciled if we assume that the first date refers to the time when he began writing *La Lozana andaluza*, and that he finished six months later. The first appendix, where the Auctor excuses himself for having written such a book, seems to confirm this. He explains that he was in the middle of a serious, long-lasting illness, and that such nonsense cheered him up: "siendo atormentado de una grande y prolija enfermedad, parecía que me espaciaba con estas vanidades" ("suffering from a long and troublesome illness, it seemed that I amused myself with these trifles"; 485). Then he mentions his lost *De consolatione infirmorum*, which also seems to have been written during an illness. Although there is no way to determine how long Delicado spent at San Giacomo degli Incurabili, he seems to have written *El modo* shortly afterward, and, therefore, he could have been interned in 1524. On the other hand, *La Lozana andaluza* includes prophetic references to the brutal sack of Rome by the army of Charles V, which began on May 6, 1527, and the appended materials make it clear that Delicado witnessed the catastrophe. In the sixth and last appendix, entitled "Digresión que cuenta el Autor en Venecia" (Digression written by the Author in Venice; 507), the narrator explains that he and others left Rome on February 10 of the following year together with the invading army, "por no esperar las crueldades vindicativas de naturales" ("so as to avoid the cruel revenge of the inhabitants"; 508).

Most scholars have taken the Auctor at his word, accepting that *La Lozana andaluza* was written in 1524, and explain the prophecies as interpolations added shortly before it was supposedly published in 1528, in Venice. Bubnova has even attempted to show that those prophecies do not fit properly (1987, 128–52). Lilia Ferrara de Orduna, on the other hand, believed that the book was written after February, 1528 (1973, 109).

I also fail to see any dissonance between the text and the prophecies. As most scholars will agree, the narrator is utterly unreliable (see Allaigre 1985b, 18–26). Because of the notorious corruption of Rome, a series of predictions foretold that a horrible punishment would soon fall upon the city, and works such as Torquato's *Pronosticon*, published in 1534 but supposedly written in 1480, presented prophecies a posteriori in order to reinforce the idea that the calamity had been sent by God (Chastel 1983, 81; García-Verdugo 1994, 59–60). Delicado could well have been using the same technique. As we will see in Chapter 6, the idea of exile constitutes the core of the work, and, therefore, it was probably Delicado's second exile, as a result of the sack, from the city that had become a second home to him, that triggered the writing of *La Lozana andaluza*. Of course Delicado could also have written the book about his earlier exile from his native Spain, adding references to the sack that caused his exile from Rome afterward. Nevertheless, the shock and injustice of this second exile seem to constitute a much more likely reason. As we will see in Chapters 6 and 7, notwithstanding its bawdiness and apparent *joie de vivre*, *La Lozana andaluza* is a very angry book.

The generally accepted publication date of 1528 poses a serious obstacle to this hypothesis, since it hardly allows enough time for the voyage from Rome to Venice, and to write and publish the book the very same year. The unreliable narrator suggests this date by claiming that he published *La Lozana andaluza* right away because he found himself alone in Venice without any financial resources, and that it earned him more than other works of his that he considered legitimate. Otherwise, he would have waited to publish it posthumously, and only after someone who knew more than he did had corrected it: "esta necesidad me compelió a dar este retrato a un estampador por remediar mi no tener ni poder, el cual retrato me valió más que otros cartapacios que yo tenía por mis legítimas obras, y éste, que no era ligítimo, por ser cosas ridiculosas, me valió a tiempo, que de otra manera no lo publicara hasta después de mis días, y hasta que otrie que más supiera lo emendara" ("this necessity forced me to give this portrait to a printer, so as to remedy my poverty, and to me it was worth more than some batches of papers that I regarded as being legitimate. And this batch, which was not,

Chapter Two

because it consists of funny things, helped me just in time. Were it not for this, I would not have published it until I was dead, when someone who knows more than I do had corrected it"; 508).

Since the narrator contradicts himself several times, it would be very unwise to take him at his word. In the initial summary, which must have been written at the same time as the addenda—such matters are usually left until the end—he states that he does not want anyone to add or take anything away from his work: "y porque no le pude dar mejor matiz, no quiero que ninguno añada ni quite; que se miran en ello, lo que al principio falta se hallará al fin" ("and since I did my best, I don't want anyone to add or subtract anything from it. And if you pay attention, you will see that what is missing at the beginning will be found at the end"; 173). Now he would like others to correct the book. In fact, he also invites his readers to do so twice in the third appendix: "cada día queda facultad para borrar y tornar a perfilarlo, según lo que cada uno mejor verá" ("it is always possible to erase and make changes, according to what each person prefers"; 491); "Ruego a quien tomare este retrato que lo enmiende antes que vaya en público, porque yo lo escrebí para enmendallo" ("I beg anyone who looks at this portrait to correct it before it becomes public, for I wrote it for the sake of correction"; 492). Besides contradicting what had been stated earlier, these words constitute a contradiction in themselves. Delicado could have addressed them to readers of his manuscript, but, since they appear when it is already published, the speaker is the unreliable narrator, and he is having fun with another of his tricks. The book had already been published and, therefore, there was no way to correct it before it became available to the public.

Since the author regards *La Lozana andaluza* as a funny book designed to make people laugh—the expression "cosas ridiculosas" meant "comical things" in the sixteenth century (Allaigre 1985b, 19n3)—it is not easy to fathom why he should care to publish it after his death. That is, unless it contained something important and too dangerous to say while he was still living, in which case the characterization of the book as "cosas ridiculosas" would represent yet another contradiction. Moreover, Delicado could not fail to be aware of the sexual, arguably pornographic character of what he had written, and that such a legacy could not possibly be of benefit to the soul of any deceased Christian.

There are still more contradictions. Although arrangements could be made to have the book corrected and published posthumously, it is difficult to see how Delicado could have done it himself, but, by speaking in the first person, he implies that this is exactly what he plans to do (Allaigre 1985b, 19). Once dead, however, he would not have been able to publish anything.

Last but not least, it is also doubtful that Delicado was able to sell the manuscript for as handsome a profit as he claims. Being anonymous and without a date of publication in the frontispiece, *La Lozana andaluza* bears the earmarks of a clandestine edition (Ugolini 1974–75, 448). Delicado's contemporaries would no doubt have had something to say about such a scandalous book, but they seem to have been completely unaware of its existence. The indices of forbidden books do not mention it, and the survival of one single copy implies that either this was a very small, limited edition or that little effort was made to distribute it. Taken together, all of this suggests that no publisher in his right mind would have paid a good sum for such a book. In all probability, it was a limited, privately printed author's edition, and Delicado distributed the few copies he had to his friends. Since no attempt was made to distribute the book—after all, there was no scandal—Delicado could hardly have made any money on it. In fact, as Allegra hypothesized, "no parece arriesgado suponer una destrucción deliberada y escrupulosa de los ejemplares localizables" ("it does not seem risky to suppose that there was a deliberate, scrupulous destruction of the copies that could be found"; 1983, 12).

Clearly, the unreliable narrator cannot be trusted when he leads his readers to think that he published *La Lozana andaluza* for economic reasons in 1528, shortly after his arrival in Venice. Furthermore, there is evidence that it appeared later. Ugolini maintained that there exists a clear, undeniable relationship between the second edition of *El modo* and *La Lozana andaluza*. Though dated February 10, 1529, the former did not appear until February 10, 1530, because Venetian printers used to pre-date their books by one year on a routine basis. The chances are that *La Lozana andaluza* began to be printed right after, and it would take a few months to finish such a large, richly illustrated work. At the earliest, then, *La Lozana andaluza* was published in 1530 (Ugolini 1974–75, 458–59), which means that Delicado had enough time to write it in Venice. Since, in all probability, the anger caused by his second exile is what triggered the idea of writing such a book, the date of 1524 found in the text must be intended to justify the "prophetic" allusions to the catastrophe that occurred three years later, in 1527.

Besides publishing the second edition of *El modo* and *La Lozana andaluza* in 1530 under the auspices of Giovan Battista Pederzano, known as Pedrazano da Beschia as well, Delicado also found employment in Venice with that publisher. Working together with Pedrazano's printers, Giovanni Antonio and Stefano Nicolini da Sabio (Ugolini 1974–75, 458–59 and n30), he proofread, corrected, and supervised editions of *Celestina* (Oct. 14, 1531; 2nd ed., 1534), *Cárcel de amor* (Nov. 20, 1531), *Amadís de Gaula* (Sept. 7, 1533), and the *Primaleón* (Feb. 1, 1534). José Hernández Ortiz (1974, 20) and Bubnova (1987, 61) added to this list an edition of *Questión de amor de dos enamorados* (1533), "Correta de las letras que trastrocadas estavanse" ("With the letters that were transposed corrected").

Chapter Two

In his editions of *Celestina* and *Primaleón*, the author offers an essay on comparative Italo-Hispano pronunciation entitled "Introducción que muestra el Delicado a pronunciar la lengua española" (Introduction in which Delicado shows how to pronounce the Spanish language), destined for Italian readers who wished to read Spanish works out loud (Damiani 1974, 16–17).[12] As Delicado explains in the note placed after *Celestina*'s title—still given as *Tragicomedia de Calisto y Melibea*—numerous Italians and other foreigners knew Spanish, and there was a good market for Spanish books in Italy. Pedrazano had decided to publish Rojas's work "apeticion y Ruego de muy muchos magnificos señores desta prudentissima señoria. Y de otros / munchos forasteros los quales como que el su muy d / licado y polido estilo les agrade y munchos mucho la / tal comedia amēn maxime enla nuestra lengua Roman/ce Castellana q̃ ellos llaman española q̃ cassi pocos la ygnoran" ("as a response to the petition of many magnificent lords of this judicious city, many foreigners who enjoy its polished and delicate style, and many people who prefer the said play in our Castilian language, which they call Spanish, for there are few who do not know it"; Gallina 1962, 78–79). Since Spain was the most powerful country in Europe, Spanish had become a truly international language.

In his editions of *Amadís* and *Primaleón*, Delicado identifies himself as Vicar of Valle de Cabezuela and states that he is from Peña de Martos, which he also mentions in his edition of *Celestina*. This implies that he was very proud of Martos, but, in Ugolini's opinion, such repeated references suggest that he also missed Spain (1974–75, 461–62). Interestingly, he always refers to himself as Delicado, which shows that he preferred the Italian form of his name. The original Delgado appears only once, in Clement VII's copyright of 1526.

The extent of the author's formal education is difficult to determine. The narrator says that he is "andaluz y no letrado" ("Andalusian and not learned"), repeating shortly after: "Si me dicen por qué no fui más elegante, digo que soy iñorane, y no bachiller" ("And if they ask me why I was not more elegant, I will reply that I am ignorant and do not have a bachelor's degree"; 485). Since false modesty was a tactic used by many authors, the unreliable narrator's protests of ignorance are probably a mere topos.[13] On the other hand, there was no reason for him to hide a degree, and, therefore, if Delicado ever attended a university, the chances are that he did not complete his studies. In his introduction to Book I of *Primaleón*, while defending chivalric romances against some "bachilleres remendados" ("poorly educated people with bachelor's degrees"), who regard them as pure nonsense, he refers to Antonio de Nebrija, the great humanist who taught at the University of Salamanca and later at Alcalá, as if Nebrija had been his teacher: "como dezía mi preceptor Antonio de Librixa, quien menos vale se endereza en las puntillas por parecer más de lo que es" ("as my teacher Antonio de Nebrija used to say, those who are worth little raise themselves on their tiptoes in order to appear more worthy"; E. Asensio 1960–63, 110). In *La Lozana andaluza*, one of the characters praises Nebrija as he speaks with Lozana: "sabéis lo que está en las honduras, y Lebrija lo que está en las alturas" ("you know about what is in the depths, and Nebrija knows about what there is in the highest places"; 424–25). Perhaps Delicado was Nebrija's student and heard the words quoted above directly from him (Guitarte 1979, 158), but he could also have heard them from somebody else. In any case, he admired the author of the first Spanish grammar and considered himself his disciple.[14]

According to Damiani, Delicado "shows a significant knowledge of classical letters, scriptural material, and contemporary linguistic and literary currents." As a Renaissance man, "his own intellectual activity reflects a wide range of interests: novelistic, editorial, and scientific" (1974, 13). Having surveyed the works mentioned by the author in *La Lozana andaluza*, Allegra also concluded that he was a fairly well-read man (1983, 32–40). Angel Chiclana, on the other hand, regards Delicado as "un representante del nivel cultural del bajo clero de su época" ("a representative of the cultural level of the low clergy of his time"; 1988, 23), accepts the narrator's claims of ignorance literally, says that his Latin is poor, and that only two of his Latin citations can be traced to classical authors. Perhaps the best solution to these two diametrically opposed views is a middle ground. Delicado had a wide range of interests, and, although he was not a great humanist, he was well-read and far above the average, ignorant clergy of the time. As *La Lozana andaluza* unequivocally demonstrates, he was also an artist of great genius.

All traces of Delicado disappear after the publication of *Primaleón* on February 1, 1534 (see note 21, below). Basing himself on the author's apparent vow to go to Santiago and his homesickness, Ugolini admits the hypothesis that he could have returned to Spain (1974–75, 461).[15] In fact, at the end of *La Lozana andaluza* the narrator states that he is the only one of his group who went to Venice, and plans to visit Santiago: "de los que con el felicísimo ejército salimos, hombres pacíficos, no se halla salvo yo en Venecia, esperando la paz, quien me acompañe a visitar nuestro santísimo protetor, defensor fortísimo de una tanta nación, gloriosísimo abogado de mis antecesores, Santiago y a ellos, el cual siempre me ha ayudado, que no hallé otro español en esta ínclita cibdá" ("of the men of peace who left with the victorious army, I am the only one in Venice, where I am hoping for peace, for someone to accompany me on a visit to our holy protector, strong defender of such a great nation, glorious intercessor on behalf of my ancestors, 'St. James, let's get them!' He has always helped me, for I did not find another Spaniard in this illustrious city"; 508).

Chapter Two

Delicado did not plan to go to Spain, however. The Inquisition that had caused him to flee was still alive and well. As for Santiago, the apostle was regarded as the protector of Old Christians, not of Delicado's Jewish ancestors.[16] The assertion that the saint is "defensor fortísimo de una tanta nación" ("strong defender of such a great nation") is ironical, for the expression "gente de nación" ("people of nation") was used to designate conversos.[17] It could also apply to the Moriscos, whose ancestors Old Christians had fought for centuries, attacking them with the battle cry "Santiago y a ellos" ("St. James, let's get them!") or something similar[18] until Granada had fallen. Spaniards used the same battle cry when fighting against other Christians, and, since he resided in Rome, Delicado probably had the opportunity to hear it when they assaulted and savagely sacked that city in 1527.[19] Thus, they were ultimately responsible for his exile in Venice. The implied contrast between the narrator and the other men of peace with him and the brutal retreating army is not a matter of coincidence. Just before, in the previous appendix, Lozana summed up the sad events that had taken place as follows: "sucedió en Roma que entraron y nos castigaron y atormentaron catorce mil teutónicos bárbaros, siete mil españoles sin armas, sin zapatos, con hambre y sed, italianos mil y quinientos, napolitanos reamistas dos mil, todos éstos infantes" ("there entered Rome, punishing and tormenting us, 14,000 Teutonic barbarians, 7,000 unarmed, shoeless, hungry, and thirsty Spaniards, 1,500 Italians, and 2,000 [?] Neapolitans, all of them infantrymen"; 503).

Of the 7,000 Spaniards ironically described as being unarmed, shoeless, hungry, and thirsty, the vast majority belonged to the infantry that had been placed under the command of Gian d'Urbina (J. Hook 1972, 125). As they broke into Rome, enraged by a wound that d'Urbina "had sustained in the face from a Swiss pike, [they] swept through the Leonine city and killed all those who crossed their path" (166). According to a contemporary account, "every person, even if unarmed, was cut to pieces in those places which formerly Attila and Genseric, although the cruellest of men, had treated with religious respect" (qtd. in J. Hook 1972, 166).[20] Clearly, the narrator is being ironical when he maintains that Santiago has always helped him. Even *El modo*, where he apparently attributes his cure from syphilis to the saint, as if it were a miracle, is really a book about what he believed to be the real remedy—the guaiacum.

No, Delicado had no plans to return to Spain and go to Santiago on a pilgrimage. Once again, the unreliable narrator plays with his readers, but now the game is dangerous and deadly serious. Probably the only sentence that can be taken at face value is the hope that he will be able to find in Venice the peace that his less pacific countrymen had denied him, first in his native Spain and then in Rome. Given the circumstances, it would not be

Repression and Artistic Expression

surprising if, contrary to what he seems to indicate, the author, in actuality, had been happy at not encountering another Spaniard in Venice.

Delicado probably found the peace for which he searched so desperately. Since the guaiacum only relieved the symptoms of syphilis, perhaps the ravages of the illness from which he had suffered for over thirty years finally caught up with him. Whatever the cause, he must have died in Venice soon after February 1534.[21]

According to some critics, *Celestina* and *La Lozana andaluza* reflect Rojas's and Delicado's converso background. Both were able to transmute what they felt about their situations into art. Other scholars prefer to think that literature and life are separate, and refuse to accept such psychological deductions as evidence. After all, they are based on the interpretation of creative rather than historical works. This position has been recently buttressed by historians who claim that conversos assimilated into Old Christian society very quickly, that the Inquisition was a political instrument designed to exclude them, and that crypto-Judaism soon ceased to exist. As we have seen, that was not the case. In the chapters that follow, I will attempt to show, hopefully in a more precise manner than has been done before, that both *Celestina* and *La Lozana andaluza* reflect the bitterness of Rojas and Delicado against the society that insisted on marginalizing and persecuting New Christians, especially in matters of conscience. Before doing so, however, it is necessary to survey the contribution of conversos to Spanish letters, and the techniques that some of them used in order to express themselves freely before the establishment of the Inquisition and afterward, that is, in extremely repressive, dangerous conditions.

* * *

As we have seen, conversos constituted a relatively small minority. At the very most, they formed about 4 percent of the total population, but, thanks to the tradition of learning inherited from their Jewish ancestors, many of them were much better educated than the average Old Christian. This explains why they made such an important, disproportionate contribution to the development of Spanish culture during the fifteenth, sixteenth, and seventeenth centuries. There were numerous physicians, theologians, philosophers, historians, and creative writers of converso background.[22]

The *Cancionero de Baena* (1445), which is named after Juan Alfonso de Baena, secretary of John II, gathers together nearly 600 poems by 56 authors from four successive generations, with the earliest going back to 1370. These poets were associated with the royal court. The compiler of their work, which is crucial to our knowledge of fifteenth- and sixteenth-century Castilian

Chapter Two

poetry, was born Jewish (Alborg 1992, 329), and so were several of the poets in his *Cancionero*, including Ferrant Manuel de Lando and Ferrant Sánchez Calavera (Cantera Burgos 1967).

Other fifteenth-century converso poets are Juan Alvarez Gato (died c. 1510), Antón de Montoro (c. 1404–c. 1480), Juan de Mena (1411–56), Rodrigo Cota (died after 1504), and Fray Iñigo de Mendoza (c. 1425–c. 1507). Mosén Diego de Valera (1412–c. 1488) and Diego de San Pedro are remembered especially for their prose.[23] Américo Castro, who mentioned many other writers of converso extraction from this period, emphasized their importance to Spanish letters as follows: "sin la obra de los hispano-hebreos, la literatura del siglo XV aparecería bastante desmantelada" ("without the contribution of persons of Jewish extraction, fifteenth-century Spanish literature would be rather poor"; 1963, 207). In their reaction against Castro, several scholars sought to deny that there was any Semitic influence in the development of Spanish culture, as if, somehow, this would impoverish rather than enrich it, but, as Kenneth Scholberg pointed out, "niéguelo quien quiera, o sea cual fuere la interpretación, es un hecho el que los conversos figuran visiblemente entre los literatos de los reinos de Juan II y sus hijos, Enrique IV e Isabel I" ("no matter who denies it, or how the fact is interpreted, the truth of the matter is that converts figure prominently among the writers during the reigns of John II and his children, Henry IV and Isabella I"; 1971, 305).

During the sixteenth century, numerous religious writers, including Fray Luis de León (1527–91), St. Theresa of Avila (1515–82), and St. John of the Cross (1542–91) were also of converso extraction.[24] The playwrights include Juan del Encina (1468?–1529?), "father of modern Spanish theater," Bartolomé de Torres Naharro (d. 1520),[25] Juan Ruiz de Alarcón (c. 1580–1639), and Antonio Enríquez Gómez (1600–63).[26] Other important figures were Alonso Núñez de Reinoso, whose Byzantine novel, *Historia de los amores de Clareo y Florisea*, was published in Venice in 1552,[27] and Mateo Alemán (1547–after 1613), author of the picaresque *Guzmán de Alfarache* (1599–1604), which was one the most popular books of the time.[28]

A good number of writers of certain or nearly certain converso backgrounds could be added to this list, but it is often difficult to document whether a writer was a converso or not, because, after the establishment of the Inquisition, people seldom claimed converso ancestry. Given the discrimination that existed, it was more prudent for them to keep it to themselves; most sought to hide it. Nevertheless, at times a writer may exhibit in his works certain ideas and attitudes that suggest that he is a converso. That is the case with Diego de San Pedro's *Cárcel de amor* (1492) and two anonymous works that constitute the first of their respective genres: *El Abencerraje y la hermosa Jarifa* (c. 1550), a Moorish novel, and the first picaresque novel, *La vida de Lazarillo de Tormes* (1554). We will discuss *Cárcel de amor* at the end of this chapter, and will examine some aspects of *El Abencerraje* and the *Lazarillo* in Chapter 3, where we will also see that, in all probability, Cervantes was a converso as well.

These conversos frequently managed to express what they felt. In an essay on Fray Luis de León and the *Lazarillo de Tormes*, Fernando Lázaro Carreter pointed out that, in a repressive environment, people tend to find refuge in either external or internal exile. When exile is external, they perceive the circumstances as unbearable, and prefer to leave their country; when it must remain internal—and most people cannot simply leave everything and emigrate—they seek refuge within themselves. This sensation of exile constitutes a particularly strong incentive for artists, whose awareness and need for self-expression is sharper than that of the average individual, and they often find ways to show what they feel about the repressive environment in which they have to live. They fight. Besides constituting a weapon, this kind of exile, which also relieves anger, can take various forms. Unlike external exiles, who, feeling free from persecution, often go to extremes, those whose exile is internal cannot afford to do so. Unless they are suicidal, they search for other, subtler ways to express their dissent (Lázaro Carreter 1986, 10–13). There are many such artists wherever repression is found. In Spain, the most recent examples occurred during Franco's long-lasting dictatorship (1939–75; see Paul Ilie's fundamental *Literature and Inner Exile* [1994]). One only has to think of playwrights such as Antonio Buero Vallejo and Alejandro Casona, who managed to elude the censors, publish, and even stage plays in which they criticized the regime right under its nose.[29] As Lázaro Carreter stresses in his thought-provoking essay, "la falta de vista y de olfacto ha constituido siempre el único encanto de la censura" ("The inability to see and to smell has always been the only good thing about censorship"; 1986, 32).

Many fifteenth-century writers did not have to face such tribulations, however. The statutes of *limpieza* did not begin to influence public opinion until after the second half of the century, and the Inquisition did not begin to instill the fear of being accused of heresy until 1481. Before its existence, conversos still felt free to express openly what they thought about discrimination and also their questions and doubts regarding their new faith.

The *Cancionero de Baena* includes several such examples. As already pointed out, Jews and many of their converso descendants found the dogma of the Holy Trinity even more difficult to accept than the coming of the Messiah. In a question to Fray Alfonso de la Monja, Ferrant Manuel de Lando inquires if the Trinity already existed before Creation, for the Second Person,

Chapter Two

the Son, had not yet been incarnated. If the answer is affirmative, how could Christ become a man, and, therefore, separate himself from the other two Persons?:

    Maestro esçelente, sotil graduado
    en altas çiençias, jurista discreto,
    el alto profundo de aqueste secreto
    querría de vos saber esplanado:
5   enante qu'el mundo fuesse criado,
    quando eran tinieblas e confusidat,
    si era Dios bivo ya en Trenidat,
    pues que non era el Fijo encarnado.

    E, si me dezides que siempre ayuntado
10 fue trino el Señor en simple unidat,
    ¿cómo vistió la umanidad
    dexando los dos al uno apartado?
                             (Baena 1993, no. 281 [4])

As Charles Fraker pointed out, the same query appears in a fifteenth-century poem included in a polemical handbook dedicated to Jewish arguments against Christianity (1966, 11).

In a similar question to Fray Diego de Valera, Ferrant Sánchez Calavera presents an additional caveat. Since the Holy Trinity is indivisible, how could the Son possibly father himself and still remain one with the other two Persons, without becoming a separate entity?:

    Maestro señor, quiérovos preguntar,
    pues es indivisa la Trenidat,
    de cómo pudo el Fijo encarnar
    e tomar Él en sí la umanidat,
5   ser engendrado el engendrador,
    sallir d'ellos amos el Consolador,
    todos tres eguales, non mayor nin menor,
    en una sustançia, sin se apartar.
                                   (No. 526 [5])

Sánchez Calavera goes on to ask why, after Adam's Fall, God had to be so vilely crucified. Because this seems to be impossible to him, the author is in fact questioning the doctrine of Original Sin and Christ's Redemption of humanity through his Passion:

25 E porque Adán la gloria perdiesse
     por su culpa e fuesse a infierno levado,
     ¿qué meresçió Dios por que assí fuesse

por él tan vilmente muy cruçificado?
Demás, que paresçe por muy imposible
30   que Dios padesçiesse seyendo impassible. [6]

Sánchez Calavera's doubts reflect the Jewish notion that, rather than going to hell and transmitting his guilt to humankind, Adam himself paid for his sin by being cast from the Garden of Eden and having to enjoy the fruits of the earth through the sweat of his brow (Fraker 1966, 16). This implies that there is no Original Sin and that, therefore, Christ's Passion was not necessary. The poet hastens to say, however, that he believes everything the Church requires, and that he merely intends to test the mettle of Fray Diego's knowledge:

Segunt la Iglesia lo manda creer,
yo creo esto todo muy simplemente,
35   e mi entençión de a vos comover
fue por provar vuestro buen ungüente. [7]

Fray Diego replies not once but twice. In the first poem, he explains the questions that had been posed to him (no. 527); in the second one, he advises his interlocutor to stay away from theology, and to avoid making the mistake of the king who had caused great confusion and a schism by questioning the dogma of the Holy Trinity:

10   que vos alongués de la theología,
ca es muy más fonda que la poetría
e caos es su nombre e lago profundo;
catad non sigades al rey segundo
que, con sotileza del su coraçón
15   en las tres personas puso confusión,
quebrando grant çisma por parte del mundo.
                                    (No. 528 [8])

The last four verses probably refer to Arianism, a heresy introduced in the fourth century by Arius, a priest from Alexandria, who denied that Jesus was God because he had to have been younger than the Father. Arianism was subsequently brought to Spain by the Visigoths. Fray Diego is warning Sánchez Calavera that his questions border on heresy, but his words probably did not carry a threat. After all, Fray Diego was himself a converso (Solà-Solé and Rose 1976–77).

Sánchez Calavera's insinuation that, being one with the Holy Spirit, the Son would have had to father himself, comes very close to insulting Christ and His Mother. Nicolás de Valencia goes even further when he tells Fray Diego de Valencia openly that a wife whose husband fails to satisfy her does

Chapter Two

not really sin if she has sex with another man. Since God had done precisely that to St. Joseph by begetting a son by his wife, Mary, anyone who did the same with somebody else's wife did not really deserve to be punished:

      Señor, nos avemos que muger casada
10   que tenga marido, maguera cuitado,
      que biva con él muy desconsolada,
      si quier' tomar a otro, que faze pecado;
      e yo sobre esto tengo maginado
      que non faz' pecado nin comete error,
15   pues que lo fizo Dios Nuestro Señor
      al Santo Joseph, que era desposado

      con Sancta María, segunt que sabedes,
      que será fallado en la su letura,
      e vos, señor noble, assí lo leedes
20   siempre de cote en la Santa Escriptura.
      E pues plogo a Dios e fue su mesura
      de fazer su Fijo en muger ajena,
      non me paresçe que meresçe pena
      el que en tal peca en toda figura.
                  (No. 485 [9])

While disguising his poem as a question, the author is really making a statement that combines the medieval concept that St. Joseph was an old man incapable of fulfilling his marital obligations (see Vasvari 1995) and the Jewish charge that Mary was an immoral, unfaithful wife, who sought elsewhere what she was lacking at home. Nicolás then concludes that the Incarnation constitutes divine sanction for adultery and that, therefore, men ought to take one woman after another, having children with as many as possible:

      Assí que concluyo que todo qualquier
      non deve muger ninguna guardar,
      sinon dexar una e otra tomar,
40   faziendo sus fijos por onde pudier. [10]

Despite the liberty with which Christians themselves parodied the sacred during the fifteenth century (Lida de Malkiel 1946), Nicolás de Valencia is going too far. Although he could probably claim that he was merely joking, his Christianity seems to be nominal, for he continues to mock it as if he were still a Jew.

Clearly, most converso poets in the *Cancionero de Baena* did not feel a need to hide or be silent about their background. Since they had either converted or were descended from people who had become Christian in 1391 or during the proselytizing activities undertaken between 1411 and 1416, there was not any point in doing so. In fact, many converso poets mocked their own Jewishness and that of others. Old Christians became involved as well. The apparent purpose was to entertain, eliciting laughter. This type of poetry had its origin in earlier courts, where the fool or jester, who inherited the role previously attributed to the jongleur, made himself the subject of laughter in order to amuse his patrons. The phenomenon is pan-European, but, as Márquez Villanueva demonstrated (1979, 1982, 1985–86), in Spain the role was frequently played by converted Jews and their descendants. With the notable exception of Alfonso Alvarez Villasandino, an impoverished Old Christian nobleman, practically all the jesters in the *Cancionero de Baena* are conversos who, besides mocking themselves, heap incredible abuse upon each other.

Since this type of abuse constituted banter designed to amuse the court, it should not be taken at face value, even if one of the participants happened to be an Old Christian. In a poem against the buffoon Alfonso Ferrandes Semuel, whom Baena describes in his epigraph as "el mas donoso loco que ovo en el mundo" ("the wittiest madman in the world"; 1993, no. 140), Villasandino reminds him that he had been a Jew "bien quarenta años o más" ("at least forty years or more"; v. 18). After Semuel's death, Villasandino composed a mock will where, after some perfunctory Christian bequests, the deceased asks to have the Cross placed at his feet, the Koran on his chest, and the Torah, which is his life and light, on top of his head. Although Semuel seems to have doubts regarding his religious identity and "makes a bow to the three religions" (Márquez Villanueva 1982, 389), according to Villasandino there is no doubt that he favors Judaism:

>   Manda a la Trenidat
>   un cornado de los nuevos,
>   a la cruzada dos huevos
> 20   en señal de christiandat;
>   e, por mayor caridat,
>   manda çient maravedís
>   para judíos avís
>   que non labren en sabad.
> 25   Manda que l' pongan la cruz,
>   a los pies, ¡ved que locura!,
>   el Alcorán, nesçia escriptura,
>   en los pechos al marfuz;
>   el Atora, su vida e luz,
> 30   en la cabeça la quiere;
>   d'estas leys quien más podiere,
>   éssa lieve este avestruz.

(No. 142 [11])

Chapter Two

Villasandino writes in a similar vein when he asks for help against Davihuelo, another buffoon, because Davihuelo was slandering him mercilessly:

> 5 mas guardatme del maldito,
> lengua suzia, vil, maldita,
> Davihuelo, pues que grita
> muchas vilezas en grito,
> como dañado e preçito.
>
> (No. 183 [12])

As he continues, Villasandino says that, in his opinion, Davihuelo is but a gluttonous, fornicating, vile, and dirty Hebrew who does not fear God or believe in the Gospels:

> A Dios non teme nin creo
> qu'en sus Evangelios crea;
> 30 gula e luxuria desea,
> nunca pierde este deseo.
> Este suzio e vil hebreo,
> fijo de una suzia ebrea. [13]

Contrary to what has been asserted (i.e., Rodríguez-Puértolas 1986, 107), these insults are part of the customary banter and, therefore, do not necessarily constitute a sign of anti-Semitism.[30] Conversos did the same to each other.

One good example is a debate between Juan Alfonso de Baena and Ferrant Manuel de Lando, whose difficulties with Christian dogmas we have already observed. Lando, who had arrived recently from Seville, was a new courtier. When Lando threatens to teach Baena another lesson if he fails to sue for peace right away, Baena retorts that, although Lando may have succeeded against some people in Seville or some Galicians, his boasting talk does not frighten him a bit:

> Fernand Manuel, a los de Çadique
> o del Açuaica d'allá de Sevilla,
> o algunos gallegos de la Costanilla,
> porniedes vos miedo con vuestro replique;
> 5 mas a mi lengua de fierro de Vique,
> polida, graçiosa, que assí vos atiesta,
> non le pornedes parlando de gesta
> miedo tan grande que le terrifique.
>
> (1993, no. 361 [14])

The Seville locations mentioned in the first two verses were probably Jewish or converso areas, the word *gallego* ("Galician") in the third verse was a euphemism for marrano—like their northern *asturiano* ("Asturian"), *montañés* ("from La Montaña"), or *vizcaíno* ("Basque") brethren, *gallegos* ("Galicians") were supposed to be Old Christians of Gothic origin (Shepard 1982, 57–58)—and the Costanilla that follows probably refers to Costanilla de Valladolid, whose inhabitants were reputed to be of Jewish ancestry (Shepard 1982, 36–39).[31] Thus, Baena is saying that Lando can only scare Jews, which implies that Lando himself is one.

As the debate continues, Baena mocks Lando's learning, calling him a "puríﬁco, casto, muy alto poeta" ("purifying, chaste, very high poet") and "lindo fidalgo" ("genteel nobleman"; no. 369.6–7). The word *puríﬁco* ("purifying") may refer to purity of the blood, and *lindo* ("genteel") was used to designate Old Christians, serving as the opposite of marrano and *puto* ("homosexual"; Shepard 1982, 71–72). Here the word is employed ironically, in order to call Lando a Jew. On the other hand, Lando may also have been a *fidalgo* ("nobleman"), for he probably descended from Pedro de Lando, a French knight, one of the mercenaries commanded by Bertrand du Guesclin, who, we recall, fought on the side of Prince Henry during the Trastámara wars (Gerli 1994, 153).

Lando replies by reminding Baena that he, too, is a converted Jew, being an expert on the use of syllogisms as well:

> Al noble, esmerado, ardit e constante,
> bañado de agua de santo bautismo,
> al sabio profundo que por silogismo
> penetra los çentros del çírculo estante,
> 5   al puro jurista qu'el curso formante
> dotó perfecçiones de abto profeta,
> al digno de alta e rica planeta,
> presento respuesta e só replicante.
>
> (No. 370 [15])

Baena may have been brave and cunning, but, since he had been bathed in the water of holy baptism (vv. 1–2), he was anything but constant, for, in so doing, he had abandoned the Law of Moses in order to embrace the Law of Christ. Baptism, of course, also alludes to the doctrine of Original Sin, which, we recall, according to Judaism, affected only our first parents. Since their sin was not transmitted to their descendants, there was no need for the Redemption brought about by the Passion, that, according to Christian doctrine, atoned for Adam's sin, enabling humankind to regain access to a spiritual heaven that was quite different from the earthly paradise from which

Chapter Two

Adam and Eve had been cast. Thus, the sacrament of Baptism was unnecessary, for the sin which it purported to erase did not really exist. In this respect, Baena's constancy was as constant as the supposed relationship between the Old and the New Laws.[32]

Baena's expertise in the use of syllogisms to penetrate the centers of the fixed, unmoving circle (vv. 3–4) encloses additional religious implications. The "çírculo estante" ("motionless circle") is heaven, which, being round, should have only one center, as in Dante's Paradise, which consists of seven concentric circles, in the center of which we find God. This circle, however, has several centers, i.e., more than one god. The "syllogisms" that Baena expertly uses in order to penetrate the mysteries of this apparently pluralistic heaven refer to a code word previously used by Jews in order to mock the Holy Trinity. This was possible because, like the Trinity, the Aristotelian syllogism consists of three parts (major premise, minor premise, conclusion). Thus, one was three and three was one. It is because of this special connotation that the rabbis summoned to the Disputation of Tortosa "entreated to be excused from the controversy, as they could not argue by *sophistry* and *syllogisms*" (Lindo 1970, 211; emphasis mine). According to two Jewish polemicists, Profit Duran and Joseph ben Shem Tov, syllogistic reasoning, being the basis of scientific knowledge, also sufficed to demonstrate that the dogma of the Holy Trinity was illogical, and, therefore, could not possibly be true (Lasker 1977, 90–93).

Baena replies to Lando in a similar vein:

> Lindo fidalgo, en la luna menguante
> leístes poetas, segunt que sofismo;
> por ende, avisatvos por el inforismo
> del alto poeta retórico, Dante,
> 5 e luego veredes que andades errante,
> assí como anda estrella cometa
> quando recursa al sol que someta
> sus rayos distintos por ser igualante.
>
> (No. 371 [16])

Baena continues to joke with Lando about the purity of his blood by calling him a "lindo fidalgo" ("genteel nobleman"; v. 1). As Dutton and González Cuenca explain in their edition, the expression "luna menguante" ("waning moon") meant "en período de mal agüero" ("at an unlucky time"), but, at a more literal level, Baena could also be comparing Lando's nobility with a crescent, rather than with a full moon. If so, this lends additional humor to the first verse, for it implies that Lando's nobility is as partial as his blood purity, while pointing to his Eastern origin, for the crescent was emblematic of Islam. At the time, the East included Palestine, which also happened to be under Islamic control.

Baena then goes on to say that he "imagines" that Lando has read poets, using the word *sofismo* (v. 2), which also means "sophism," as a verb. Through alliteration, the "poetas" in Baena's second verse echo the "profeta" in Lando's preceding poem (no. 370.6), and, as a noun, the accompanying *sofismo* refers to an argument that, though correct in form and appearance, is actually invalid, being designed to deceive. Consequently, the verse in question may be read as an allusion to false prophets, i.e., prophets who deceive through sophistry. While professing to correct Lando's statement that he, his opponent, employs syllogisms to penetrate the mysteries of heaven (v. 5), Baena is in fact agreeing with Lando, for he suggests that the syllogisms in question amount to sophistry. On the other hand, Lando will never match Baena's skills as a poet. Like a comet, he tries to equal the sun in its brilliance (vv. 6–8), but, of course, he will never be able to do so.

Clearly, both poets concur that the Holy Trinity is a syllogism, and a sophistic one at that. Their good-humored banter was probably impenetrable to their Old Christian audience. Together with the references to the Costanilla, *lindo fidalgo* ("genteel nobleman"), the pluralistic heavenly circles, and the crescent moon, these syllogisms and sophisms are tantamount to a code, an in-house language that enabled conversos to communicate openly with each other while excluding their Old Christian audience.[33]

On another occasion, in a question addressed to all the troubadours and poets who may care to answer him, Baena asks if the art of poetry depends on knowledge, genius, audacity, and wisdom, or if it borders on folly and could lead to destruction:

> Dezidme, señores, por vuestra mesura,
> 10 el arte de trobas si es por çiençia
> o es por engenio o es por femencia
> o es por audaçia o es por cordura;
> o el arte gayosa si toca en locura,
> o aquel que la sigue si sube en el peso
> 15 de ser estruido su cuerpo con sceso,
> si non lo mampara quien fizo Natura.
>
> (No. 429 [17])

Rodrigo de Arana takes up the challenge, telling Baena that he will soon see who really masters the science that he considers to be so impenetrable: "e luego veredes quién tiene apreso / aquesta çiençia que avéis por escura" ("and you will soon see who has learned / this science that you regard as difficult"; no. 430.15–16). Baena retorts that he will make him eat salt pork

Chapter Two

as if it were a tasty bird ("yo vos faré qu'el puerco salpreso / comades por ave de mucha dulçura" ["I will make you eat salt pork / as if it were a very sweet bird"; no. 431.15–16]), which, of course, suggests that the very idea of having to eat pork is repugnant to his opponent because of his Jewish background. Not to be outdone, Arana threatens to do to Baena what happened to Lucifer when he tried to be three in essence and was consigned to the depths of hell for his audacity:

>   El ángel Luzbel sobido en altura
> 10   quiso paresçer a tres en esençia,
>   pero non se pudo levar en paçiençia,
>   que luego lançado non fue en la fondura;
>   e bien se demuestra vuestra catadura
>   seguir las passadas de aqueste sahueso,
> 15   con furia e con piedra, fablando muy teso,
>   e devaneando con la calentura.
>   (No. 432 [18])

Besides comparing his opponent to Satan, Arana mocks the Holy Trinity by designating God as "three in essence," rather than just calling him by his name.

When Baena refuses to take the bait to become involved in an argument about the Holy Trinity, professing that he is a truly religious man ("pues só religioso, de vida muy neta" ["I am religious, and lead a very clean life"; no. 433.18]), Arana threatens to punish him if he fails to appear before his tribunal. Since he is an apostate without any religion, he will be condemned to life in jail and flogged for trying to behave like Don Bueso, a prototypical Christian knight in Spanish balladry:

>   Yo proçederé por toda censura,
> 10   si non paresçedes en mi audiençia,
>   a vos, que andades sin obediençia,
>   apóstata fecho con mucha blandura,
>   e a cárçel perpetua so mi çerradura
>   seréis condenado, sin dubda, don Bueso;
> 15   entonçe sabredes cómo yo baldreso
>   con mi diçiplina la vuestra çintura.
>   (No. 434 [19])

The implication, of course, is that, by avoiding the debate on the Holy Trinity and professing to be a truly religious man, Baena is trying to pass for an Old Christian. That is why Arana threatens to punish him as one, for the cat-o'-nine-tails with which he plans to scourge his waist recalls the harsh ropes that some devout Christians wore around their waists as penance.

Antón de Montoro, a wealthy, talented, and highly connected poet and businessman from Córdoba who assumed the pose of a tailor and became known as El Ropero ("Clothes Merchant"), as if he were a mere merchant of used clothes (Gerli 1994–95, 268–75), also engaged in this type of banter. When he offers advice to Juan de Valladolid, also known as Juan Poeta, he claims to be doing a favor to a fellow Jew: "por ser vos y yo judíos / vuestros enojos son míos / y mis daños también vuestros" ("since you and I are Jews / your troubles are mine / and my injuries are also yours"; Montoro 1990, no. 65a.8–10). Valladolid replies angrily, calling Montoro a fat converso and a marrano: "Podéis llamarme nemigo / de vos, confeso marrano, / redondo como bodigo, / non vos precio mas que un figo" ("You may call me your enemy, / you self-avowed marrano, / as round as a loaf of church bread; / I don't care a fig for you"; no. 65b.1–4).

A quarrel between Montoro and Román appears to be much worse. It begins when Montoro tells Román that some verses he had sent to a lady are so bad that he should pretend someone else had written them (no. 69a). Apparently furious, Román calls him a "vil escopido marrano, / muy anín, / del todo punto judío / circuncidado por mano / del rabín" ("vile, spit-upon marrano, / very plaintive, / a Jew in everything, / circumcised by the hand / of the rabbi"; no. 69b.80–84). Montoro replies that Román's mother is a Moor ("Vuestra madre no será / menos cristiana que mora" ["I suppose your mother is / more Moorish than Christian"; no. 69c.61–62]), and then calls him Hamete (v. 73), as if he were a Muslim, adding that he is a dirty, ugly Arab: "vuestra mancilla m'echáis / vos, alárabe probado, / sucio y feo" ("you cast your blemish on me, / you, a proven, / dirty and ugly Arab"; vv. 91–93). Striving to outdo his rival, Román advises Montoro to confess his sins, because he is about to kill him, and adds:

> catá que salen de juego
> 15 estas coplas que a vos van,
> que mis trobas llevan fuego
> qu'es peor que d'alquitrán,
> con que luego os quemarán.
>
> (No. 69d [20])

Román's threat brings to mind the Inquisition, but he could not have been thinking of it, since it did not yet exist. More probably, Román is referring to the burning of Jewish and converso homes during popular riots. Although his threat has been taken seriously (Márquez Villanueva 1982, 397), it is more likely that he is clowning around, and, if so, what we have here is yet another example of the banter that characterizes the poetry of court jesters. The dispute, we recall, began when Montoro accused Román of penning some poor verses—hardly a reason to have someone killed, much less burned alive. Román's concluding advice for Montoro to quit writing poetry and to restrict himself to his mending ("que dexés este trobar / y que os váys a remendar" ["stop making those verses / and go back to your darning"; no. 69d.170–71]) cannot be taken at face value, for, as we know, his rival was really a prosperous businessman. In other words, Román is addressing himself to the poetic persona, rather than to the real Montoro. Last but not least, whether of Moorish or Jewish background, Román was himself a converso.[34]

Román's threat to burn Montoro, then, was in jest. The Inquisition would come afterward, shortly after Montoro's death in 1477. It burned Montoro's wife, Teresa, about ten years later (Márquez Villanueva 1982, 397).[35]

During the first three quarters of the fifteenth century, conversos also felt free to protest against the persecution and the discrimination to which they were subjected. Montoro stands out here as well, for he was not afraid to address himself to the most powerful in the land. As Julio Rodríguez-Puértolas emphasized, "in the world of the *cancioneros*, it is the Cordobese *converso* Antón de Montoro whose tragicomic verse most keenly reveals his tormented personal life and the mistreatment of the ethnic and social group to which he belongs" (1998, 192).

When the previously mentioned anti-converso riots broke out in Córdoba in 1473, triggered by the little girl who supposedly threw urine on a statue of the Virgin from a window, the crowds killed many conversos, burning those whose homes they set on fire. The leading noble in the city, Alonso de Aguilar, defended them with great difficulty, killing the blacksmith who led the rioters. Probably to prevent further disturbances, Aguilar then banished the conversos from the city, and many sought temporary refuge in Seville. In a poem addressed to Don Alonso, Montoro asks him what he thinks of the calamity that had fallen upon the conversos, and then does not fear to state that they would have been better off if they had remained Jewish:

>   Buen cavallero leal
> que los defetos olvida,
> de sangre pura real,
> ¿qué os ha pareçido el mal
> 85   desta gente convertida?
> Digno de mill señoríos,
> de corazón y de manos,
> muy más por sus desvaríos
> les valiera ser judíos
> 90   que cristianos.
>
> (Montoro 1990, no. 97 [21])

The riots to which Montoro refers, we recall, spread to other cities. In a poem addressed to Queen Isabella, the poet reminds her that Our Lord does not wish sinners to die, but to live and repent; as he was dying on the Cross, he asked God the Father to forgive those who had crucified him. Therefore, as a defender of the faith, the Queen ought to put an end to the riots,[36] at least until Christmas, when, no doubt because of the winter cold, the heat of fire is more appreciated.[37] Since the Inquisition did not begin to function until 1481, the fire ironically mentioned here alludes to the burning of the homes of conversos during the disturbances:

>   30 pues Reyna de gran valor,
>   que la santa fee creçienta,
>   no quiere Nuestro Señor
>   con furor
>   la muerte del pecador,
>   35 mas que biva y se arrepienta.
>   Pues Reyna de gran estado,
>   hija de angélica madre,
>   aquel Dios crucificado,
>   muy abierto su costado,
>   40 con vituperios bordado
>   e ynclinado,
>   dixo: "Perdónalos, Padre."
>   Pues Reyna de auctoridad,
>   esta muerte sin sosiego
>   45 çese ya por tu piedad
>   y bondad
>   hasta allá por Navidad,
>   quando save bien el fuego.
>   (No. 14 [22])

Montoro was then in his seventies. At the beginning of the same poem, he does not hesitate to complain against personal discrimination. He had always believed in Mary's virginity, said the Creed, worshiped stew pots of salt pork, heard Mass after Mass, but still could not get rid of the scent of a converso. Although he had prayed on his knees and made the sign of the cross, worshiping Christ, God, and Man, who had wiped him clean of his sins, people still looked upon him as an old, Jewish fag.[38] This last insult was one of the charges commonly made against Jews, who, in addition to the libels already seen, were also accused of sexual perversions:[39]

>   ¡O Ropero amargo, triste,
>   que no sientes tu dolor!
>   ¡Setenta años que naçiste
>   y en todos siempre dixiste
>   5   *ynviolata permansiste*
>   y nunca juré al Criador!

65

Chapter Two

>   Hize el *Credo* y adorar
>   ollas de toçino grueso,
>   torreznos a medio asar,
> 10   oyr misas y rezar,
>   santiguar y persignar
>   y nunca pude matar
>   este rastro de confeso.
>   Los ynojos encorvados
> 15   y con muy gran devoçión
>   en los días señalados
>   con gran devoçión contados
>   y rezados
>   los nudos de la Passión,
> 20   adorando a Dios y Hombre
>   por muy alto Señor mío,
>   por do mi culpa se escombre,
>   no pude perder el nombre
>   de viejo, puto y judío. [23]

In other words, the Old Christian majority refused to accept the old man because of his Jewish background, even though, at least according to what he himself claims, he seems always to have been a Christian (see vv. 3–6, above).

It is important to observe that, despite its obvious bitterness, Montoro's poem to the Queen is also burlesque. The failure of his Christian toils and the salt pork and bacon that he had to swallow, even though they were repugnant to him, in order to remove the stigma of being a "viejo, puto y judío" ("an old, Jewish fag") are designed to elicit laughter, just like his preference for the heat of fire around Christmas, when it is cold. By mocking himself, Montoro is also playing the role of the fool, thus minimizing the offense that his daring in proffering advice to the Queen could cause by making her laugh. Indeed, buffoonery was the price that had to be paid "for the sake of unbridled expression and the liberty to speak the bitter truth" (Márquez Villanueva 1982, 399). At the same time, Montoro's self-deprecating humor and talent enabled him and others in similar circumstances to gain access to court circles, "often securing not only the business but the personal recognition and protection of their noble clients" (Gerli 1994–95, 272). Thus, Montoro's self-representation as a marginalized, impoverished old converso clothes merchant was in fact a literary strategy, as well as a vehicle for "his own social and economic advancement" (274).

Although Montoro claims that he has always been a Christian, it has been suggested that he may have converted at an early age (Rodríguez-Puértolas 1990, 13). In a burlesque poem in which he speaks to his horse, Montoro declares that his parents, a sister, and several of his children and grandchildren have never been baptized:

> que tengo hijos y nietos
> 65 y padre pobre muy viejo
> y madre doña Jamila[40]
> y hija moça y ermana,
> que nunca entraron en pila.
>
> (No. 31 [24])

However, it is difficult to see how, as a Christian, Montoro could have failed to baptize his children. In all probability, he is exaggerating in order to make his poem seem even funnier, and it would not be surprising if his family had been converted generations before, as in the case of the Juan Marmolejo whom he describes as a drunkard in one of his poems (no. 100), and who also figures as a thieving, Judaizing, and cuckolded pimp in one of Baena's pieces (see Ciceri's and Rodríguez-Puértolas's note to the aforesaid poem [1990, 306]). In reality, Marmolejo belonged to a powerful family from Seville that had converted to Christianity a century before, and was a member of the elite (Gerli 1994–95, 271–72).

These poets used laughter in order to question their new faith, to mock each other about their Jewish background, and, in the case of Montoro, to complain bitterly about discrimination. On the surface, the self-deprecating banter with which they perpetuated the role of the court jesters amused their Old Christian masters, who occasionally joined them in the game, but, at another level, it was far more serious, for it covered a great deal of pain. As Kenneth Scholberg well understood, their self-mockery was but a mask, forming part of a defensive mechanism against a hostile world: "Las minorías oprimidas, y especialmente la judía, siempre se han refugiado en la risa, para no caer por completo en la desesperación. Este humorismo amargo, dirigido contra sí mismo, es a la vez una máscara para ocultar los verdaderos sentimientos ante los ojos hostiles y un mecanismo defensivo para mantener el equilibrio mental en un mundo perverso y enemigo" ("Oppressed minorities—and this is especially true of Jews—have always found refuge in laughter, so as not to fall into complete despair. This bitter, self-addressed humor constitutes both a mask designed to hide one's true feelings before enemy eyes, and a defense mechanism designed to preserve one's mental health in a perverse, hostile world"; 1971, 320). According to Scholberg, Montoro seems to poke fun at himself and his people in the poem addressed to the Queen, but "el verdadero ataque y la sátira van dirigidos contra el mundo externo" ("the true aim of the attack and the satire is the outside world"; 1971, 320). Ultimately, these words apply to most of the poems just examined. In the final analysis, these writers are complaining about a world that encouraged conversion only to place them in such a humiliating situation.

Baena himself once referred to the verbal dueling we have seen, with its coded words and intentions, as an "arte confessa" ("a converso art"; no. 395.11). As Márquez Villanueva pointed out, "it was just that" (1982, 395). By mocking themselves individually, as well as each other, through the language of folly and the liberating power of laughter, conversos were able to neutralize "the social constraints under which they were suffocating," finding in literature "the only avenue for the affirmation of human dignity and intellectual freedom" (408). At the same time, their poetic talent gained them further acceptance as well as a voice in higher social circles. Except for Antón de Montoro, the conversos discussed lived at court, formed an integral part of the administration, and, as far as common people were concerned, they practically belonged to the ruling class.

Of course, not all high-ranking conversos engaged in self-deprecating counterdiscourse. Many, such as Juan Alvarez Gato and Fray Iñigo de Mendoza (Scholberg 1971, 329–31), kept to themselves what they thought about their ethnic background, accepted the dominant ideology, and managed to assimilate to a much higher degree. Another good example is Mosén Diego de Valera, son of Alonso Chirino, John II's converso physician, who chose his mother's instead of his father's name, probably because the latter sounded too Jewish. John II appointed him ambassador to Denmark, France, and England, and he served Henry IV and the Catholic Monarchs as chief steward. Having written the *Espejo de verdadera nobleza* and the *Ceremonial de príncipes*, Valera became acknowledged as "the ultimate authority in questions of nobility, ruling-class honors, and courtly protocol" (Gerli 1996–97, 22). Well-integrated conversos who were sincere Christians even joined Old Christians in attacking those whose Christianity was in doubt, and felt particularly threatened by newcomers (Solà-Solé and Rose 1976–77, 374–75). If the formidable Torquemada himself was not a New Christian, he was very close to them, for the Cardinal Juan de Torquemada, an uncle on his father's side, in fact, was *ex-illis*. Another inquisitor general, Diego de Deza, also was of Jewish extraction. Thus, "there is no such a thing as a typical *converso*" (Gerli 1996–97, 33). No matter how well assimilated, however, those persons could never completely efface the Jewish past of their ancestors and forget that they were conversos.[41]

The freedom to express doubts in matters of dogma disappeared toward the end of the century, with the establishment of the Inquisition. If Valencia had once dared to joke about God having a son with another man's wife, there is no question that, at that later time, he would have been burned at the stake. Even the self-deprecating banter came to an end: "The slightest allusion could have grave results for the supposed converso" (S. E. Rose 1983, 8; see also Arbós 1985, 82). As Scholberg pointed out, "el sentimiento anticonverso y la escrupulosidad por la limpieza de sangre se arraigaron tan fuertemente en la vida española que tal proceder habría sido del todo imposible. Lo único que deseaba todo el mundo era ocultar cualquier indicación de impureza" ("anti-converso feeling and the preoccupation with blood purity became so strongly entrenched in Spanish life that it would have been impossible to act in that manner. The only thing that people wanted was to hide the slightest sign of impurity"; 1971, 360).

Besides worrying about discrimination and the Inquisition, disaffected converso writers eventually had to be concerned about official censorship as well. It came about at the beginning of the sixteenth century, because of the centralization of state and church power, the religious conflicts that arose because of Protestantism, and the invention of the printing press, which permitted dissidents to disseminate their ideas much more quickly and efficiently than before (Pinto 1987, 303). At first, the religious authorities required licensing prior to publication. This began in the diocese of Metz in 1485. In Castile, where the process was controlled by the civil authorities, a royal ordinance of the Catholic Kings made licensing mandatory in 1502 (309). The Inquisition soon took over the activity. Books could be censured, with offensive phrases and passages expurgated, or prohibited by edict, and those who possessed them could be prosecuted. However, the Inquisition did not issue an index of forbidden books, the Valdés index, until 1559. Although several other indices were to follow and some books were lost to subsequent generations because of censorship (Alcalá 1987a, 333–50), the number of literary works that were published increased and their quality was such that the period became known as the Golden Age of Spanish letters. This was possible thanks to self-censorship, since, obviously, the threat of having a book prohibited was a serious threat to writers (Pinto 1987, 311).

Nevertheless, some disaffected authors, those inner exiles whom Lázaro Carreter discussed, still found ways to say what they wanted. The code that began to be developed in the *Cancionero de Baena*, enabling less integrated New Christians to communicate openly and yet secretly with each other,[42] expressing ideas that, for obvious reasons, they did not care to share with Old Christians, would eventually serve succeeding generations well, when censorship and the Inquisition posed a serious, dangerous threat to freedom of conscience and free expression. Such writers had to become far more subtle, camouflaging their ideas so as to leave them open to interpretation and hopefully accessible only to like-minded readers. Fortunately, sixteenth- and seventeenth-century censors were no better than modern ones, and writers often found ways to deceive them. Paradoxically, inquisitorial control contributed to enriching the literature of the time.

Chapter Two

Let us look at one example. Diego de San Pedro's sentimental novel *Cárcel de amor* (1492) opens with an allegory. Traveling through the Sierra Morena on his way home after having served in one of the wars of the ten-year campaign against Granada (1482–92), the dramatized Auctor (henceforth, the Author), who figures in the work as narrator, observer, and intermediary,[43] runs into a wild man, Deseo ("Desire"), followed by a prisoner who asks him for help. Both disappear, but, continuing his journey, the Author sees an elaborate, three-cornered tower that turns out to be an allegorical Prison of Love. There he finds Leriano, son of a duke, imprisoned because of his love for Laureola, daughter of Gaulo, King of Macedonia. Somehow, the traveler has found himself in that country.

The Author goes to court and intercedes with the princess, who, although extremely worried about her honor, eventually writes to Leriano, saying that she is doing so only out of pity, for she does not love him. Exhilarated by her letter, Leriano travels to court, where the jealous Persio, suspecting something, tells the king that Leriano and Laureola are in love and see each other every night. Gaulo jails his daughter at once, instructing Persio to accuse Leriano of treason and to challenge him to a trial by ordeal. When Leriano is about to kill the defeated Persio for refusing to take back his lie, the latter's relatives convince the king to stop the combat. Feeling wronged, Leriano asks the king to restore his honor, but Gaulo tells him to go to Susa in order to avoid quarrels between his relatives and Persio's.

Meanwhile, Persio arranges for three of his friends, whom he pays off handsomely, to confirm the lie. Believing the false witnesses, Gaulo keeps his daughter in jail and plans to have her executed. The cardinal of Gausa, together with all the great lords who are present at court, begs him to spare her, but he will do so only if a witness comes forth to testify to her innocence. The queen and her ladies beg for Laureola's life as well, but to no avail. As a last resort, Leriano, allied with Galio, the queen's brother, attacks Suria. Leriano orders one of his captains to kill Persio, liberates Laureola, and hands her over immediately to her uncle, who takes her to a fortress that he owns. Furious, the king follows Leriano to Susa and lays siege to the city. Leriano makes a sortie, takes one of the false witnesses prisoner, and the man confesses the truth under torture. The king accepts this evidence, as he had promised, orders the execution of the three witnesses, but then asks Leriano to stay away from court until he appeases Persio's relatives.

Laureola, however, does not wish him to return. Fearing for her honor, she thinks it best not to see Leriano again. Leriano falls ill, refuses all food and drink, and when a friend, Tefeo, tries to restore his health by berating all women, Leriano defends them at length. He reprimands those who speak ill of women, lists twenty reasons why men are obliged to them, and gives examples of virtuous women from classical antiquity, the Old Testament, and Spain. With his mother by his bedside, Leriano tears into pieces all the letters that he had received from Laureola in order to protect her, places them in a cup of water, and drinks it. Then he dies. Grieving, the Author decides to leave and, still crying, he arrives in Peñafiel.

The central, obvious theme of this novel is courtly love. Obliged to obey each and every wish of his lady, the lover, who has been deprived of reason, being left with nothing but emotion, dies when it becomes clear that she never wants to see him again. However, Leriano's fate is uncommon. Generally, the spurned courtly lover merely suffers, and his suffering is supposed to be an ennobling source of virtue, not death (see Gili Gaya 1967, xi–xiv).

Something is definitely wrong here. Laureola's refusal to see Leriano has been attributed to an irreconcilable opposition between the medieval codes of love and honor (Wardropper 1953a, 189), but these codes were not that rigid in real life (Whinnom 1984, 37n51; Márquez Villanueva 1976, 147). The courtly poetry of the period, which is decidedly erotic (Whinnom 1981b), testifies to a far more relaxed attitude. Nevertheless, although Leriano is a high ranking noble, the slightest suspicion of a relationship with him could ruin the princess's reputation. The king's role poses problems as well. His interruption of the judicial combat that he himself had instigated prevents Leriano from proving his innocence, and he requires his imprisoned daughter to demonstrate hers by proving a negative, which is essentially impossible. All of this suggests that, despite its indisputable literary merit, *Cárcel de amor* may not be a mere literary exercise. It could well include more than what meets the eye.

Márquez Villanueva confirmed this when he examined *Cárcel de amor* as a political work (1966; 1976). The cardinal of Gausa, the nobles, the queen, the ladies at court, and Laureola herself warn the king against hasty decisions made in anger, lack of moderation, and cruelty, but he refuses to listen to anyone. Although he is wrong, his power is absolute. This forces Leriano and his subjects, including a member of the king's family, the queen's brother, to rebel against him. Since the Catholic Monarchs were approaching the zenith of their power at the time, Diego de San Pedro is warning against the centralized, absolute monarchy that they are forging. This type of monarchy, of course, constituted the basis for the modern state. Instead, Márquez Villanueva argues, San Pedro seems to prefer the medieval model, where the king's power is tempered and limited by the feudal nobles and the Church (1966, 188–93).

Besides questioning the authoritarian, absolute power of the king, Diego de San Pedro, a converso, also protests against "limpieza de sangre" and the Inquisition. The king tells his daughter and those who defend her that "sola una mácula en el linage cunde toda la generación" ("a single stain in one's lineage spreads to the whole progeny"; San Pedro 1984, 132).[44] Obviously,

Chapter Two

it does not make any sense to interpret these words solely in terms of chastity. They refer to "limpieza de sangre," for the slightest suspicion could cause an indelible stain in an entire family and their descendants. While in prison, Laureola is tortured and the only person who is allowed to visit her, and then only once, is the queen. In a letter that she manages to get out to Leriano through the Author, by tossing it from a window in her cell, she complains: "con gruesas cadenas estoy atada; con ásperos tormentos me lastiman; con grandes guardas me guardan, como si tuviese fuerças para poderme salir" ("I am bound with thick chains; they hurt me with harsh torments; they guard me with powerful guards, as if I were strong enough to escape"; 127). Since there is no logical reason for such torture, what we have here is a subtle reference to the Inquisition. Moreover, "semejante insistencia en el detalle de la incomunicación, rasgo privativo y temidísimo del proceso inquisitorial, viene a constituirse en una alusión transparente" ("such insistence on the detail of solitary confinement, which was extremely feared and exclusive to inquisitorial processes, becomes a transparent allusion"; Márquez Villanueva 1966, 195).

Laureola suffers these tribulations because of a false denunciation, which, of course, also brings to mind the Inquisition. The central problem does not lie in a rarefied, inhuman, and illogical opposition between honor and love, but in the incompatibility between honor and "limpieza de sangre." The mere suspicion of a relationship with Leriano and the *mácula* ("stain") that this could bring to her whole family suggests that he is a converso, and there is a strong identification between the hero, the Author, and Diego de San Pedro, who, as we know, was not "limpio."

The novel is framed in the first person. As it opens, the Author states that he is on his way back from the wars against Granada, and Diego de San Pedro probably participated in one of the campaigns (Whinnom 1985, 25). As the novel ends, the grieving Author tells Don Diego Hernández, to whom he has dedicated his book, that "con tales pasatienpos llegué aquí a Peñafiel, donde quedo besando las manos de vuestra merced" ("with such pastimes I arrived here in Peñafiel, where I remain, kissing your lordship's hands"; 176). San Pedro lived in Peñafiel, where he was probably born (see Whinnom 1985, 15–17). Since there is a sudden, unexplained shift from the Sierra Morena to Macedonia, and then from Macedonia to Peñafiel, the story itself constitutes either a vision or a dream, i.e., an extension of the initial allegory (Wardropper 1952, 42). While it is true that the Author should not be identified directly with San Pedro, but rather with San Pedro's dream representation of himself (44), this projected narrator is also part of San Pedro.

Leriano and the Author are more clearly differentiated. Besides being a foreigner, the latter returns home, leaving his dead friend behind. Nevertheless, the two characters also have much in common, for the Author is

Leriano's closest friend, representing him before his beloved Laureola throughout most of the novel. Scholars have hypothesized that the vision may be a passing review of a love experience in San Pedro's life, with Leriano representing the Author at an earlier period (Wardropper 1952, 44), and the evidence that follows suggests that, at one level at least, Leriano and the Author are indeed one and the same.

As the vision begins, with Leriano being dragged behind a savage knight, he moans painfully once in a while: "En mi fe se sufre todo" ("In my faith, one suffers everything"; 81). The word "faith" could refer to the religion of love, in the courtly sense, but, since just before dying, after drinking the cup of water containing the torn letters that echoes the bile and vinegar that Christ drank on the cross, Leriano also echoes Jesus's dying words ("Acabados son mis males" ["My suffering is finished"; 176], corresponds to Jesus's "Consumatum est" ["It is finished"]), the word *faith* can also be read in a religious sense. As the vision continues, we discover that the Prison of Love in which Leriano endures so much suffering (i.e., martyrdom) on account of his faith is described as follows: "El cimiento sobre que estava fundada era una piedra tan fuerte de su condición y tan clara de su natural cual nunca otra tal jamás había visto" ("The foundation on which it lay was such a naturally strong, clear rock, that he had never seen another like it"; 84–85). What we have here is an allusion to the rock of St. Peter, the one on which Christ said that he would build his Church. Since the author's family name is San Pedro, the connection is clear. The characterization of the rock as exceedingly "clara de su natural" ("naturally clear [pure, illustrious]"), of course, amounts to a rejection of "limpieza de sangre."

The Author, Leriano, and Diego de San Pedro, therefore, are one and the same. Besides being framed in the first person, the novel is also framed in faith, and this, of course, suggests that the narrative in between has to do with faith as well (Prieto 1975, 305). Since San Pedro was a New Christian, this faith, besides referring to the courtly religion of love and to Christian faith in general, also refers to the faith of a converso (307).

And it is precisely because Leriano is a converso, I repeat, that the slightest hint of a relationship with him would cause an irreparable stain in the royal lineage. The action is ostensibly set in a foreign land, but this is an illusion. Without really leaving Spain, somehow the Author finds himself in Macedonia, a country whose name echoes "Babilonia," and, therefore, the exile of the biblical Jews. Since the city of Susa was connected with the Babylonian empire (*Encyclopædia Judaica*, s.v. "Shushan"), there is no question that San Pedro had Babylon in mind.[45] Consequently, the Author is also an exile, a foreigner of sorts in his country. That is why, while protesting to the king about the manner in which he favored Persio and his relatives by interrupting the combat, Leriano says: "si por ventura lo consentiste por verte aquexado de la suplicación de sus parientes, cuando les otorgaste la merced devieras acordarte de los servicios que los míos te hizieron, pues sabes con cuánta costança de coraçón cuántos dellos en muchas batallas y conbates perdieron por tu servicio las vidas" ("if by chance you allowed it because you became tired with the supplication of his relatives, when you granted them the favor you should have remembered the service of my relatives, for you know well how many of them courageously gave their lives for your sake in numerous battles and engagements"; 120).[46] Then he reminds the king that everyone ought to be equal before the law: "eres obligado a ser igual en derecho" ("it is your duty to dispense justice equally"; 120).

Leriano and "los suyos" (his clan) are not, however, treated equally. Being New Christians, they are regarded as outsiders, rather than as full-fledged citizens of the land of their birth. Spain is indeed another "Babilonia." As Gregory Kaplan pointed out, "by creating a distinction between Persio's 'parientes' and his own, Leriano evokes the concept of a discriminatory justice that randomly favors the lineage of Persio over his own bloodline" (2002, 113). It is also because of this discrimination that, while addressing his men as they are about to attack Susa in order to free Laureola, Leriano tells them that they are fighting for future generations, so as to deliver them from shame and humiliation: "agora se nos ofrece causa para dexar la bondad que heredamos a los que nos han de heredar, que malaventurados seríamos si por flaqueza en nosotros se acabasse la heredad; assí pelead que libréis de vergüença vuestra sangre y mi nonbre" ("now we have good reason to bequeath the excellence we inherited to our own heirs, for we would be unfortunate if it were to end through our weakness; and so, fight in such a manner as to preserve your blood and mine from shame"; 146).

Rather than standing for a specific woman in San Pedro's life, then, Laureola, whose name is related to *laurel*, in the sense of "triumph," represents the desire of conversos to be accepted and treated as equals. Since Leriano and his clan, like contemporary New Christians, can count on important allies in the Church and among the nobility, including some members of the royal family, there is still reason for hope. Laureola is freed. But her refusal to see and have anything to do with Leriano afterward—although the logical outcome would be for the hero to win her hand in marriage, she knew only too well what the consequences could be—puts an end to the dream. And so he dies. Here the message is one of failure and despair.

It is also tempting to search for a specific religious message in *Cárcel de amor*, for the work is framed within the idea of faith, and Leriano's figure has much in common with Christ's. While he is in the Prison of Love, yearning for Laureola, the Author observes how "dos dueñas lastimeras con rostros llorosos y tristes le servían y adornavan, poniéndole con crueza en la cabeça una corona de unas puntas de hierro sin ninguna piedad, que le traspasavan todo el celebro" ("two grieving ladies with sad faces covered with tears served and adorned him, and placed on his head a crown of iron spikes, harshly and without any mercy, for the spikes pierced through his whole head"; 86). Albeit only partial—Jesus suffered at the hands of Roman soldiers, not of women—the parallel with the crown of thorns placed on his head is obvious. Right after this, the Author recalls how "un negro vestido de color amarilla venía diversas vezes a echalle una visarma" ("a black man dressed in yellow came to hit him with a halberd") and that the prisoner "recebía los golpes en un escudo que súpitamente le salía de la cabeça y le cobría hasta los pies" ("received the blows on a shield that suddenly came out of his head and covered him from head to toe"; 86–88). Despite great differences, these blows recall the flogging of Christ. The visit of Leriano's mother just before his death brings to mind the presence of the Blessed Mother before the cross, as her Son is about to expire. As already pointed out, the cup of water that Leriano drinks containing the torn letters of Laureola corresponds to the bile and vinegar that the Roman soldier gives to Jesus on the cross, and Leriano's last words, "Acabados son mis males" ("My suffering is finished"; 176), are essentially the same as Our Lord's "Consumatum est" ("It is finished"; Wardropper 1953a, 176).

Although the parallels between the suffering of a lover and the Passion of Christ are heretical (comparisons of the sort are one of the reasons why the Church denounced courtly love, which it practically viewed as a rival religion), such abuses were common enough and, therefore, cannot be used as evidence that San Pedro was not an orthodox Christian.[47] Buried among the virtuous women whose example Leriano recalls just before dying, the first of the Jewish heroines is described as follows:

> De las judías, Sarra, muger del padre Abraham, como fuese presa en poder del rey Faraón, defendiendo su castidad con las armas de la oración rogó a Nuestro Señor la librase de sus manos, el cual como quisiese acometer con ella toda maldad, oída en el cielo su petición enfermó el rey, y conocido que por su mal pensamiento adolecía, sin ninguna manzilla la mandó librar. (168–69 [25])

The story is in the Old Testament. Because of a famine in Canaan, Abraham sought refuge in Egypt and, suspecting that the Egyptians would lust after his wife, Sarah, who was extraordinarily beautiful, he instructed her to say that she was his sister; if they knew he was her husband, they would probably kill him. Sarah was taken to the house of Pharaoh, who heaped flocks, herds, and servants upon Abraham on her account. Then God punished Pharaoh and his household with great plagues. When Pharaoh realized that Sarah was already married, he called Abraham and said: "Why have you done this to me? Why did you not tell me she was your wife? Why did you say she

Chapter Two

was your sister and let me marry her? Here now is your wife; take her and go" (Gen. 12.18–19).

Although San Pedro abbreviates the story considerably, he includes two details absent from the version in the Old Testament: Sarah's prayer and the unequivocal assurance that Pharaoh did not have sexual relations with her.[48] The prayer derives from the legendary, post-biblical Jewish tradition according to which Sarah prays to God to deliver her from the Egyptian monarch: "We came hither to save our people from starvation, and now hath this terrible misfortune befallen. O Lord, help me and save me from the hand of this enemy, and for the sake of Thy grace show me good" (Ginzberg 1967–69, 1: 223). Pharaoh makes Abraham, whom he believes to be Sarah's brother, extremely rich, and then marries her. On the wedding night, an angel who is visible only to the bride strikes Pharaoh with a stick on the hand whenever he attempts to touch her. Horrified by a plague, Pharaoh consults his priests, who tell him that Sarah is already married. At this point he sends for Abraham, returning his wife to him "pure and untouched" (224).

Since the Old Testament says nothing about Sarah's prayer and fails to specify that she was delivered from Pharaoh "sin mancilla" ("without blemish"), San Pedro is using a legendary Jewish version probably unknown to most Old Christians. The chances are that he learned it from his own family, as a child. Note that, in his version, Pharaoh alone is punished, with an illness. There is no plague. Was San Pedro aware that his version differed from the biblical account and, therefore, from the version that was readily available to Old Christians? If so, his summary could well embody a message to other conversos, subtly reminding them of their Jewish roots. But there is more, for Sarah addresses her prayer to "Nuestro Señor" ("Our Lord"). As we know, in Spanish the expression refers exclusively to Christ, rather than to God the Father, who is designated as "el Señor" ("the Lord").[49] Thus, Sarah prays to Christ, centuries before he was born. Since, according to Christian dogma, the Son is one with the Father, he is equally eternal. He always existed. However, Sarah did not know this. In the Old Testament, prayers are invariably addressed to God the Father, and even a Christian would not think of an Old Testament character praying to Christ. By attributing such a prayer to Sarah, San Pedro is making an ironical allusion to the Holy Trinity, and his converso readers were far more likely to apprehend it.

In fact, the allusion embodies questions that recent conversos were not afraid to ask openly during the first half of the century, before the Inquisition, whose establishment San Pedro had witnessed in 1481. We have already seen examples of these questions in poems written by Ferrant Manuel de Lando and Ferrant Sánchez Calavera, which were subsequently included in the *Cancionero de Baena* (c. 1445). Did the Son always exist? If so, how could he be born, becoming separate from the Father, and still remain one with him? Did this mean that Christ also fathered himself?

Of course, these questions do not necessarily mean that Ferrant Manuel de Lando and Ferrant Sánchez Calavera were crypto-Jews. They could have been making an effort to gain a better understanding of their new faith. Although San Pedro's brilliantly laconic, ironical allusion to the Holy Trinity encapsulates the very same questions, this alone does not necessarily mean that he was a crypto-Jew, either. However, the very fact that he poses such questions in a work that he deliberately frames on the idea of faith certainly provides us with grounds to wonder.

In sum, *Cárcel de amor* portrays the vicissitudes of courtly love so well that it was enormously successful, but this did not prevent San Pedro from dealing with other subjects as well. By participating in the campaign against Granada and returning to Peñafiel, the Author is closely identified with San Pedro himself. Leriano, whose Prison of Love is founded on a rock that recalls the rock of St. Peter, is also identified with San Pedro. Thus, this tripartite San Pedro is writing about himself and his converso background, for the work is framed on faith. Within this frame, he expresses his dislike for the repressive, absolute monarchy that the Catholic Monarchs were forging, the Inquisition, "limpieza de sangre," and the persecution and discrimination that they caused. The vision is set in Macedonia, which echoes "Babilonia," a land of exile for his Jewish ancestors, because, like the Author who sees himself transported from one moment to the next to that country, San Pedro himself is a foreigner of sorts, an outsider in the land of his birth. The city of Susa, we recall, was associated with Babylon, and was nowhere near Macedonia. Laureola represents the desire for acceptance. For a moment, Leriano hopes that he can have her, but his dream is shattered. And so he returns, at least emotionally, to the Prison of Love found at the beginning of the work, and dies. Thus, the Prison of Love turns out to be Spain. With Leriano's demise, the part of San Pedro that still held some hope for acceptance dies as well, but the grieving Author who also represents him returns to reality and goes on living. Nothing has changed.

The Prison of Love that represents Spain is also a Prison of Faith. The ironical attribution of Sarah's prayer to a Christ who had not yet been born, which embodies several questions regarding the dogma of the Holy Trinity, may indicate that, whether a crypto-Jew or not, San Pedro held some profound doubts regarding Christianity. Whatever the case may have been, through this allusion, which is somewhat hidden, being strategically placed among the lengthy list of virtuous women from the past, where it was least likely to be noticed, the writer is communicating surreptitiously with his fellow conversos, for they were far more likely to apprehend what it meant.

Chapter Two

With the centralization of royal power and the advent of the Inquisition, the freedom that earlier conversos had to ask questions regarding their new faith and even to protest against the discrimination to which they were subjected—Antón de Montoro is an excellent example—no longer existed. The tolerance that still prevailed during the first part of the century was completely gone. Theirs was indeed another Spain. Although they or their ancestors had been either forced or encouraged to convert, they were still persecuted and treated as outsiders in the land that they loved. Their Spain had indeed become a *Cárcel de amor*; even the freedom to complain had disappeared. Nevertheless, San Pedro could not remain silent. That is probably why, in his dedication to Don Diego Hernández, his very first words are: "me falta sufrimiento para callar" ("I lack the patience to be silent"; 79). And so he dealt with these subjects in the only way that was still possible: indirectly, in an artistic manner that depended on interpretation, leaving room for denial, if necessary. Artists have always used similar techniques when they had to work under repressive circumstances. Not long ago, there were examples of this in Franco's Spain, in the former Soviet Union, and in some Latin American countries. We will continue to find them wherever tyranny and censorship exist.[50]

Chapter Three

The Idea of "Limpieza" in *Celestina*, *La Lozana andaluza*, and Other Literary Works

"Limpieza de sangre" was particularly vexing to learned conversos, who took inordinate pride in their Jewish ancestry, tending to regard themselves as noble. In the Iberian Peninsula, Judaism reached the greatest heights ever achieved in the history of the Diaspora, to such an extent that medieval Spain came to be regarded as the Golden Age of the Jewish spirit (Papo 1987, 4). Thanks to their learning, success in various enterprises, and close relationship with the governing classes who employed them, many Jews also occupied positions of great importance. In the words of Américo Castro, "los judíos se preciaban de ser judíos, y con más intensidad que en ninguna otra parte, pues sólo en España tuvieron tan altos motivos para hacerlo" ("the Jews took pride in being Jewish, and more so than anywhere else, for it was only in Spain that they had such a good reason for this"; 1963, 156).

Around 1420, Rabbi Mosé Arragel de Guadalajara made this very clear to Luis de Guzmán, Grand Master of the Order of Calatrava, at whose request he translated and glossed the Hebrew Bible, now known as *Biblia de Alba*, because the dukes of Alba have owned it for two centuries (see Lazar 2000; Sicroff 1988). According to the rabbi, Castilian kings and great nobles were lucky to have such subjects, for they were the best and most knowledgeable Jews of the Diaspora: "Esta preheminencia ovieron los reyes e señores de Castilla: que los sus judíos súbditos, memorando la magnificencia de los sus señores, fueron los más sabios, los más honrados ['ilustres'] judíos que quantos fueron en todos los regnos de la su transmig[r]ación, en quatro preheminencias: en linaje, en riqueza, en bondades, en sciencia" ("The kings and lords of Castile had this distinction: their Jewish subjects, who recorded the magnificence of their masters, were the most illustrious of all the Jews throughout the reigns of the diaspora, surpassing them in four things: lineage, wealth, grace, and knowledge"; Castro 1963, 158).

Some conversos continued to show the same pride. Solomon ha-Levi, learned rabbi of Burgos, converted to Christianity with his family in 1391, just before the pogroms that had started in Seville reached that city (Netanyahu 1995, 168–71), changing his name to Pablo de Santa María (Paul of the Holy Mary). He was later ordained bishop of Burgos, became

Chapter Three

chancellor of Castile, and boasted about his descent from the tribe of Levi (Caro Baroja 1986, 1: 422), that he belonged to the line of David, and that, therefore, he was a kinsman of the Virgin Mary (Shepard 1982, 136).[1]

Some New Christians went further, and regarded themselves as vastly superior. Addressing himself to those who had been recently penanced by the Inquisition of Seville, Pérez de Prado, one of the inquisitors, told them that he knew perfectly well how they taught their children to despise their Old Christian counterparts: "Apenas llegan vuestros hijos a la edad de alguna discreción, bastante a guardar secreto, quando los retiráis aparte y ostentando un gran misterio les dezís: que sepan que son descendientes del patriarca Abraham y por esto de muy alto linaje, incitándolos al desprecio de quantos no vengan de esta generación, y aun entre vosotros os apellidáis Vizcaínos para denotar con disimulo esta antigüedad" ("Your children hardly reached the age of some discretion sufficient to keep the secret when you take them aside and with a display of great mystery tell them that they must now know that they are descendants of the ancient and illustrious patriarch Abraham and therefore of very noble lineage. You teach them to despise all who are not thus descended. And among yourselves your refer to each other as *Vizcaínos* in order to emphasize surreptitiously your antique genealogy"; Domínguez Ortiz 1955, 185n66; trans. Shepard 1982, 136).

Aware of this imprudent attitude, some Old Christians resented it tremendously. After mentioning the fortunes that many Jews managed to accumulate, Andrés Bernáldez, priest of Palacios (1488–1513), near Seville, complains in his *Memorias del reinado de los Reyes Católicos*:

> E así tenían presunción de soberbia, que en el mundo no avía mejor gente, ni más discreta ni aguda, ni más honrrada que ellos, por ser del linage de las tribus e medio de Isrrael. En cuanto podían adquirir honrra, oficios reales, favores de reyes e señores, eran muy diligentes. Algunos se mezclaron con fijos e fijas de cavalleros cristianos con la sobra de riquezas, e halláronse bienaventurados por ello, porque los casamientos que así ficieron quedaron en la Inquisición por buenos cristianos e con mucha honra. (1962, 98 [26])

Although Bernáldez is talking about both Jews and conversos, he fails to distinguish between the two groups. As far as he is concerned, they are all the same, and equally proud. Conversos, however, were no longer Jews, and the prejudice of the Old Christian majority toward them had already began to affect their self-confidence when he wrote these words, probably in the 1480s, soon after the establishment of the Inquisition.[2]

When the inhabitants of the Basque province of Guipúzcoa forbade New Christians from marrying and settling in the area in 1483, so as to preserve their vaunted blood purity, Fernando del Pulgar ridiculed them in a letter that he wrote to Pedro González de Mendoza, Cardinal of Spain. The Cardinal, who belonged to the distinguished family of the Marquis of Santillana, sympathized with the conversos (Márquez Villanueva 1960, 127 and n86*bis*). According to Pulgar, their land was so poor that no one would want to settle there anyway and, although they enacted such laws, the Basques sent their children to serve conversos in Castile in order to learn trades and how to read and write. On the other hand, Pulgar also felt deeply hurt. His letter is worth quoting in full:

> Ilustre y reuerendísimo señor: sabido aurá V. S. aquel nueuo istatuto fecho en Guipúzcoa, en que ordenaron que no fuésemos allá a casar ni morar etc., como si no estouiera ya sino en ir a poblar aquella fertilidad de Axarafe, y aquella abundancia de canpiña. Un poco paresce a la ordenança que ficieron los pedreros de Toledo de no mostrar su oficio a confeso ninguno. Así me vala Dios, señor, bien considerado no vi cosa más de reir para el que conosce la calidad de la tierra y la condición de la gente. ¿No es de reír que todos o los más enbían acá sus fijos que nos siruan, y muchos dellos por moços d'espuelas, y que no quieran ser consuegros de los que desean ser seruidores? No sé yo por cierto, señor, cómo ésto se pueda proporcionar: desecharnos por parientes y escogernos por señores; ni menos entiendo cómo se puede conpadecer de la una parte prohibir nuestra comunicación, e de la otra fenchir las casas de los mercaderes y escriuanos de acá de los fijos de allá, y estatuir los padres ordenanças injuriosas contra los que les crían los fijos y les dan oficios e cabdales e dieron a ellos cuando moços. Cuanto yo, señor, más dellos vi en casa del relator aprendiendo escreuir que en casa del marqués Iñigo Lopez aprendiendo justar. Tanbién seguro a vuestra señoría que fallen agora más guipuzes en casa de Fernand Aluraes [*sic*] e de Alfonso de Auila, secretarios, que en vuestra casa, ni del condestable, aunque sois de su tierra. En mi fe, señor, cuatro dellos crío agora en mi casa mientras sus padres ordenan esto que vedes, y más de cuarenta omnes honrados y casados están en aquella tierra que crié y mostré, pero no por cierto a facer aquellas ordenanças. (Pulgar 1958, 137–38 [27])

While continuing to take pride in their ancestors, some New Christians soon felt a need to defend their background. Because of a sly remark about his ancestors, Alonso de Cartagena, son of Pablo de Santa María, who also became bishop of Burgos, replied that his Jewish lineage was older and therefore nobler than others, and went on to complain that past greatness was now being turned into infamy: "Do not think that you put me to shame by calling my fathers Hebrews. Indeed they are, and I am proud of this. Because if antiquity is nobility, where would one more ancient be found? ... O eternal God! Every opprobrium is now transformed into glory, and glory is made into infamy!" (trans. in Faur 1992, 32).

Chapter Three

Diego de Burgos, one of the Jeronimite monks from Guadalupe who came to the attention of the Inquisition in the 1480s, reacted even more strongly: "mas le plazia venir del linaje de los Judios donde venia nuestro señor Jesucristo que no del linaje del demonio, donde venian los gentiles" ("it pleases me more to stem from the lineage of Jews whence stemmed our Lord Jesus Christ than from the lineage of the devil whence the gentiles stem"; qtd. in Sicroff 1965, 113; trans. in Faur 1992, 35). Writing much later, in 1599, Agustín Salucio, another monk, protested in his *Discurso* against the notion that all peasants were *limpios* and that anyone with a drop of Jewish blood was "unclean," emphasizing that peasants ignored who their ancestors were anyway, even though some of them could have been Jewish: "Es recia cosa pensar, que vn hijo de un herrador, o de otro más baxo oficio se deve estimar por mas onrado y de mejor casta que un nobilissimo cauallero, aunque sea nieto de un grãde, si por algun lado tiene alguna raça . . . para ser Cristiano viejo basta ser ombre baxo, y no saberse de sus abuelos, aũque uviessen sido judios" ("It is a difficult thing to think that a farrier's son or the son of someone with an even lower occupation should regard himself as being more honorable and of a better caste than a very noble gentleman, even if the latter were the grandson of a grandee, but happened to have a drop of non-Christian blood . . . all that is necessary to be an Old Christian is to be a man of low rank, and not to know who one's ancestors are, even if they were Jewish"; 1975, 13).[3]

Because conversos were automatically at a disadvantage just for being who they were, others minimized the idea of lineage, saying that what really mattered was to live a virtuous life. One of the monks in the Jeronimite monastery of Guadalupe put it this way: "beuir el hombre virtuosamente, ora sea de linaje de acá o de acullá, éste es de loar" ("for one to live virtuously, whether from this or that lineage, this is worthy of praise"; qtd. in Sicroff 1965, 113; trans. in Faur 1992, 35). There is nothing un-Christian here. Since all Christians, including conversos, were one in the body of Christ, lineage had nothing to do with religion. As Sicroff points out, however, these were dangerous words, for the majority did not see things that way: "To place virtue of one's personal deeds above the value of Christian 'blood purity' was indeed to subvert the society envisaged by Spanish Old Christians" (1965, 113).

In time, most conversos did not dare to make statements such as we have just seen. Because of the discrimination that they suffered, they did what they could in order to efface their origins, and it was very imprudent to mock "limpieza de sangre" or to make sly remarks about the value of being a "Cristiano Viejo" ("Old Christian"), which meant essentially the same thing: "To dare question the idea of purity of blood, the corner stone of honor, was equivalent to rejecting a basic principle held dear by the preponderant majority of Spanish society" (Silverman 1971b, 143). However, some writers could not resist the temptation: "la literatura de los cristianos nuevos (llamados conversos o confesos, aunque su cristiandad datara de varias generaciones), no reconocía valor a la limpieza de sangre, la rechaza, la desdeña o la ironiza" ("the literature produced by New Christians—they were called conversos or 'confessed' even if their Christianity went back for several generations—did not recognize the value of blood purity, which it rejected, despised, and mocked"; Castro 1967, 22). These authors often expressed their opinion in ambiguous, oblique ways susceptible to various interpretations, because this allowed them to preserve deniability. A fairly frequent manner was through the use of the adjective *limpio*. Although the word simply means "clean," it was enough in itself to conjure up the idea of lineage. As defined by Covarrubias, "Limpio de dize comúnmente el hombre christiano viejo, sin raza de moro ni de judío" ("'Clean' usually designates Old Christians, those without any drop of Moorish or Jewish blood"; 1994).[4] Thus, the word also came to mean "pure," and when applied to morals, it could mean "chaste" as well.

Since this variety of meanings makes it difficult to determine an author's intentions, the danger of seeing an ironical reference to "limpieza de sangre" when it is not really there is always present. Even when there is no doubt that "limpieza" is being ridiculed through a particular narrator or one of his or her characters, modern critics can claim that the attack is being perpetrated for artistic reasons, and has nothing to do with the author's personal background. However, this fine distinction was not made during the late fifteenth or the sixteenth and seventeenth centuries. A writer who dared to challenge openly the opinion of the majority in the matter risked raising the suspicion that he himself was not "limpio," and there was a time when it would have been utter folly to do so. Throughout most of the sixteenth century, even conversos who could not resist the temptation to mock "limpieza," I repeat, usually did so in a veiled manner.

Probably because he was living in Italy, Francisco Delicado did not care to take any such precautions. In *La Lozana andaluza* (1530), the protagonist, while earning her living as a prostitute in Rome, runs into Sagüeso, a bum who "tenía por oficio jugar y cabalgar de balde" ("whose job was to gamble and to get laid for free"; 417). When Sagüeso tries to convince Lozana to have sex with him by claiming that another prostitute, the wealthy Celidonia, surpasses her in everything, Lozana replies: "en dinero y en riquezas me pueden llevar, mas no en linaje ni en sangre" ("people can beat me in money and riches, but not in lineage or bloodlines"; 418). Sagüeso counters: "Voto a mí que tenéis razón; mas para saber lo cierto, será menester sangrar a todas dos, para ver cuál es mejor sangre" ("I swear you're right but, to be sure, it will be necessary to bleed both of you, so as to see which one has the best blood"; 418). Shortly after, the old, syphilitic Divicia informs Lozana that prostitutes have their own union, and that it includes "de todos los linajes buenos que hay en el mundo" ("all the good lineages found in the world"; 429). The fact that Lozana and Divicia are of converso extraction makes their words even funnier and would, no doubt, cause readers to laugh even more heartily. Nevertheless, this laughter does not eliminate the subversion entailed by what they said. Clearly, prostitution is being used in order to mock blood purity and lineage.[5]

Unlike Delicado, Fernando de Rojas was living in Spain. He wrote *Celestina* (1499) in very dangerous times, when the Inquisition was particularly ferocious, and his attack against "limpieza" is so ambiguous that it is extremely difficult to demonstrate. The discussions about the presence of "limpieza de sangre" in that work have hinged on the fact that neither of the protagonists, Calisto or Melibea, ever thinks of legitimizing their love through marriage. According to some critics, they could not marry because Calisto was a converso; his Jewish blood rendered him unacceptable either to Melibea or to her parents. Others concluded the opposite, despite Calisto's apparent belief in Melibea's "limpieza de sangre."[6] A third group, which includes scholars such as Américo Castro and Stephen Gilman, declared the whole controversy to be irrelevant. Referring specifically to Melibea, Castro wrote that "el que ... resultara ser cristiana o judía carecería de interés estructural, funcional, dentro de la obra" ("whether ... she turned out to be Christian or Jewish would not have any functional or structural interest in the work"; 1965, 107). Gilman went even further. After recalling the popularity of Rojas's work among his fellow converts and "his artful rapport with them," he stated that "the proposition that *Celestina* contains a secret message about racial prejudice and matrimonial discrimination seems dubious" (1972, 366). Both scholars agreed that only a convert could have written such a book, but they maintained that this is to be seen especially in Rojas's destructive attack against the social, religious, and literary values of his time.

For conversos, however, the most vexing of those values was the Old Christian obsession with the "limpieza de sangre," which condemned them to perpetual marginalization. If it is true that Rojas perpetrates such a corrosive attack against the society of his time, it is difficult to see how he could fail to include the subject. In the pages that follow, I will attempt to show that he also attacks blood purity through the word *limpio*, albeit in a careful, rather ambiguous manner.

According to my count, forms of this word (noun, adjective, verb, and adverb) appear twenty-two times in *Celestina*, and no less than four are found in the prefatory and concluding verses, where the author addresses his readers in a more direct manner. Since the word is common, it would be unreasonable to expect it to be employed ironically in every instance, but, within the *Tragicomedia* itself, it is used in hypocritical, ironical, and incongruous ways at least thirteen out of the eighteen instances in which it appears.[7]

Let us look at the first thirteen examples. When the lovesick Calisto asks a servant, Sempronio, to accompany him in order to get a present for Celestina, because she promised to help him to conquer Melibea, Sempronio agrees that the old bawd must be rewarded at once, for suspicion ought to be "cleansed" from the heart of friends with good works: "Bien harás, y luego vamos, que no se deve dexar crescer la yerva entre los panes, ni la sospecha en los coraçones de los amigos, sino limpiarla luego con el escardilla de las buenas obras" ("It will be well for you to do it. Let's go at once, for it is not right to let the weeds grow in the wheat or for suspicion to rise in the hearts of friends, but to *clean* it right away with the weed-hook of good works"; 1987, 117). Obviously, there is nothing "clean" in rewarding the procuress for the kind of service that Calisto expects from her. Since Sempronio plans to share in the profits, he is really being false to his master. Thus, it is rather ironical that Calisto himself should praise the faithfulness and "limpieza" of Sempronio's services later on: "Sempronio, mi fiel criado, mi buen consejero, mi leal servidor, sea como a ti te parece. Porque cierto tengo, según tu limpieza de servicio, quieres tanto mi vida como la tuya" ("Sempronio, my faithful protégé, my good adviser, my loyal servant, it will be as you say, for I can tell from your devotion [*cleanliness*] to my service that you care as much about my life as about your own"; 221). The reader knows how disloyal Sempronio is, but Calisto is unaware of it.

Beginning with the corruption of the younger Pármeno, a servant who is still faithful to his master—and this corruption would eventually lead to his violent death—the word here in question is often used by Celestina. At one point she tells the boy how happy she is that he is beginning to see the wisdom of her advice with these words: "por ende, gózome, Pármeno, que ayas limpiado las turbias telas de tus ojos" ("I'm therefore glad, Pármeno, that you have cleared away [*cleaned*] the dark webs from your eyes"; 128). Rather than opening his eyes, Pármeno is doing precisely the opposite, thereby falling into her corrupt hands. Later on, Celestina insists to the boy that her advice to befriend Sempronio is given with the "pure desire" to see him gain some honor ("Toma mi consejo, pues sale con limpio desseo de verte en alguna honrra" ["Take my advice, for I am giving it with the sincere [*clean*] desire to see you achieve some prosperity"; 195]), but the reader knows that she is really interested in her own profit, not his. There is nothing "clean" or "pure" about Celestina's motivations.

The idea of "limpieza" is used in an even more deceptive manner during Celestina's first visit to Melibea's house. When she excuses herself to Alisa for not having paid her a visit sooner, she says: "mas Dios conoce mis

Chapter Three

limpias entrañas, mi verdadero amor, que la distancia de las moradas no despega el amor de los coraçones" ("but God knows my pure [*clean*] heart, my true love, for the distance between houses does not remove love from people's hearts"; 153). As we know, what Celestina really wanted was to seduce Alisa's daughter. While appeasing the angry Melibea a little later, Celestina refers to her "limpio motivo" ("pure [*clean*] motive"; 164) for seeking her out, and then goes on to describe her profession as a "clean business" ("Una sola soy en este limpio trato" ["I am the only one in this *clean* (respectable) business"; 165]), even though the irony of the words that follow undermines the respectability that she claims for her affairs: "en toda la cibdad, pocos tengo descontentos. Con todos cumplo . . . " ("there are few in this whole town who are dissatisfied with me. I fulfill my obligations to all . . ."; 165). What cleanliness could there possibly be in the treacherous procuress's "limpias entrañas" ("pure [*clean*] heart"), "limpio motivo" ("pure [*clean*] motive"), and "limpio trato" ("*clean* [respectable] business")?

Celestina displays the same high regard for her dishonorable profession while trying to deceive Sempronio when he demands his share of a gold chain that Calisto had given her, as if her job were the same as any other: "Bivo de mi officio, como cada official del suyo, muy limpiamente" ("I live from my profession, as other professional people do, and very respectably [*cleanly*] too"; 273).

The idea of "limpieza" is also used to praise another procuress, Pármeno's deceased mother, in the following manner: "¡O qué graciosa era, o qué desembuelta, limpia, varonil!" ("Oh, how graceful, deft, *clean*, and spirited [manlike] she was!"; 196). The fact that the gracefulness and cleanliness of Pármeno's mother means precisely the opposite is emphasized by the adjective "varonil," which suggests that she was endowed with masculine qualities (so much for her gracefulness), even though Celestina goes on to modify this meaning with a reference to Claudina's fearlessness (i.e., *varonil* in the sense of "valor," "courage") in going from cemetery to cemetery at night: "Tan sin pena ni temor se andava a media noche de cimiterio en cimiterio buscando aparejos para nuestro officio, como de día" ("At midnight she used to go from cemetery to cemetery without anxiety or fear, looking for stuff for our profession, as if it were broad daylight"; 196).[8]

The word under scrutiny is connected with deceit in the nine examples just examined. The two examples that follow may be the most incongruous seen so far, for "limpieza" is associated with the beds of two prostitutes. While trying to convince Areúsa to sleep with Pármeno, who is waiting outside, without any further preliminaries—the girl is already in bed—Celestina exclaims: "¡Ay cómo huele toda la ropa en bulléndote! ¡Aosadas, que está todo a punto; siempre me pagué de tus cosas y hechos, de tu limpieza y atavío; fresca que estás! ¡Bendígate Dios, qué sávanas y colcha, qué almohadas y qué blancura!" ("Oh, how sweetly the bedclothes smell when you move about! I can see that everything is ready. I have always taken pleasure in your things and deeds, your *cleanliness*, and finery. You look so fresh! May God bless you. What sheets and bedspread, what pillows, and how white everything is!"; 201–02). After Celestina's death, Elicia, a prostitute who lived in her house, having resolved to put an end to her mourning, decides to make the bed in which she earns her living "porque la limpieza alegra el coraçón" ("because *cleanliness* brightens up the heart"; 308).

So far, we have examined eleven instances of the use of the word *limpio*. Since cleanliness is most commendable on the part of everyone, including prostitutes (if not more so, given the nature of their commerce), it is certainly possible to read these passages as mere praise for that saintly virtue. It could also be argued that the fashion in which *limpieza* has been used so far has nothing to do with "limpieza de sangre," and that Rojas's frequent ironical attribution of that quality to what is mostly unclean constitutes an integral part of his art, for antitheses abound in *Celestina*.

The next two examples, also found within the *Tragicomedia* itself, are not as easy to dismiss. The first one is the only explicit reference to "limpieza de sangre" in the whole work. Calisto makes it during his first tryst with Melibea, when he doubts his good fortune with the following words: "Pero como soy cierto de tu limpieza de sangre y hechos, me estoy remirando si soy yo Calisto a quien tanto bien se le hace" ("But since I am certain about the purity of your blood and of your deeds, I am examining myself to see if I am really the Calisto to whom such favor is being shown"; 261).[9] As Gilman pointed out, there was nothing pure in Melibea's decision to meet a young man secretly in her garden during the middle of the night, and, therefore, "the real ironical dig here may be at the meaningless purity of her *sangre*, given what we know about the impurity of her *fechos* [deeds]" (1972, 366). This is true, but there is yet another, simpler level of irony: Since what Calisto wanted so desperately was to make love to Melibea, her supposed blood purity did not matter in the least. A pretty girl is a pretty girl, and it would be ridiculous for a man to worry about her bloodlines before taking her to bed. This was but a matter of common sense for contemporary readers and listeners, as it ought be for readers today, and, therefore, this passage would cause them to laugh their heads off. When the chips were down, so to speak, "limpieza de sangre" did not really matter.

Another dig at "limpieza" is probably present when Melibea's father, Pleberio, tells his wife that there is nothing like early marriage to preserve the "clean reputation" of virgins, for he could have easily said "good reputation" instead: "no ay cosa con que mejor se conserve la limpia fama en las vírgenes que con temprano casamiento" (302). The difference between Pleberio's earnestness and what the reader already knows involves irony as well. Since Melibea has already lost her virginity, she is no longer "pure." Alisa's utilization of the word *sangre* in her reply to Pleberio ("antes pienso que faltará ygual a nuestra hija, según [tu][10] virtud y tu noble sangre" ["I rather think that there will not be anyone equal to our daughter, given your virtue and noble *blood*"; 303]) confirms this interpretation. Since other writers used the technique of disjunction in order to suggest matters that could not be discussed openly, what we have here is probably another mocking reference to "limpieza de sangre." The anonymous author of *El Abencerraje* and Cervantes availed themselves of the same technique (see below), and, as we will see in Chapter 5 (pp. 162–63), Rojas himself repeated it, albeit with a different purpose, in another part of *Celestina*.

Let us now examine the prefatory and concluding verses, where Rojas uses the word on no less than four occasions—nearly 20 percent of the total of twenty-two occurrences—while addressing his readers more directly, rather than through his characters. The disproportion, I think, is simply too great to be justified as pure coincidence.

In the fourth stanza of the prefatory verses, Rojas insists on the "clean motive" that led him to write *Celestina*:

>Si bien queréys ver mi *limpio motivo*,
>buscad bien el fin de aquesto que escrivo,
>...............................
>o del principio leed su argumento.

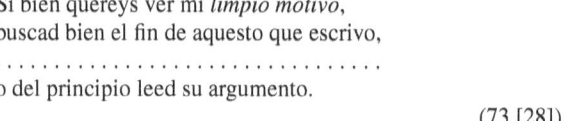

Besides insisting on his "pure motive" with the same expression that Celestina uses in order to disguise her true reason for visiting Melibea, Rojas tells his readers that they can see it for themselves by "searching" (looking for, understanding) the "fin" (ending, purpose) of what he has written or read the initial "argumento" (probably the summary attributed to the printers). The summary in question tells us about Calisto's and Melibea's lineages and how they and two of Calisto's servants come to a bad end because of Celestina's machinations (82–83). The brief description of the lineages of the two protagonists does not embody a clear reference to "limpieza," but if we look at the first of three possible endings, the final stanza of the introductory verses, we will find the following admonition: "*Limpiad* ya los ojos, los ciegos errados" ("Clear [*clean*] your eyes, you blind sinners"; 75). This does not seem to have anything to do with blood purity, either.

A second possible *fin* are the very last words of the *Tragicomedia*, which conclude Pleberio's lament before the body of his daughter. Since the work ends with his disconsolate "¿Por qué me dexaste triste y solo in hac lacrimarum valle?" ("Why did you leave me, sad and alone, in this vale of tears?"; 343), the idea of "limpieza" is not present here.

The Idea of "Limpieza"

Thirdly, *fin* could also refer to the three stanzas appended afterward, entitled "Concluye el autor" (The author concludes), which contain Rojas's final observations on the purpose of his work and some additional exculpations. He begins the very last stanza by protesting

> Y assí no me juzgues por esso liviano
> mas antes celoso de *limpio bivir*,

and concludes:

> dexa las burlas, qu'es paja y grançones,
> sacando *muy limpio* dentrellas el grano.
> (344 [29])

Having told his readers to search for his "limpio motivo" ("pure [clean] motive") either at the beginning or the end "de aquesto que escrivo" ("of this that I write"), Rojas reiterates the idea of "limpieza" twice in the prefatory verses and then goes on to repeat it another two times in the very last of the three stanzas he appends to *Celestina*, where the word *limpio* is present in the second verse as well as in the very last verse to issue from his pen.

Of course, each of these four references to "limpieza" could be read in straightforward, unambiguous ways. Nevertheless, Rojas's "limpio motivo" ("pure [clean] motive") for writing the *Tragicomedia*, the admonition to lovers, "limpiad ya los ojos" ("clear [clean] your eyes right away"), and the claim to a personal desire for a "limpio vivir" ("pure [clean] life") after his portrayal of a world of prostitution and the seduction of an innocent young girl like Melibea can certainly be questioned. If *Celestina* were such a moral work, there would be fewer "jests" ("burlas") and less of a need to "clean" or "glean" the moral ("grano") from all the straw and chaff ("paja y grançones"). Rojas is perfectly aware of this; hence his repeated protestations concerning his moral intentions. If his purposes had been clearly and indisputably didactic, however, there would have been no need for such caution. Furthermore, Rojas's protestations are rendered even more ambiguous by the fact that they are couched within the idea of "limpieza" on no less than four occasions in only eleven stanzas.

In sum, the utilization of "limpieza" in order to affirm the didacticism of a work like *Celestina* is truly ironical, especially in view of the fact that, within the *Tragicomedia*, "limpieza" is mercilessly ridiculed through procuresses such as Celestina and Claudina, servants such as Sempronio and Pármeno, prostitutes such as Elicia and Areúsa, and even highly placed characters whose lineages were supposedly pure, such as Melibea. Some of these examples could be dismissed as part of Celestina's strategies of persuasion, and others could be cast aside as constituting an integral part of the

Chapter Three

antithetical technique through which so many time-honored and even religiously sanctioned precepts are mischievously reversed. In other words, they could also be justified as plain, inoffensive irony without any ulterior motivations. But that is not the case when Calisto mentions Melibea's "limpieza de sangre" as he is trying desperately to get her into bed, as if it mattered in the least, or with the oblique, ironical reference to "limpieza de sangre" through Pleberio's and Alisa's conversation, when their daughter was no longer "pure." The double utilization of the word in the last of the appended strophes, including the very last verse to issue from Rojas's pen, confirms, once again, that he also had "limpieza de sangre" in mind. At this point, the repetition of the word *limpio* twice, in quick succession, is particularly telling. During that time, books were often read out loud in front of audiences, and, since the word was enough in itself to conjure up the idea of blood purity, converso listeners, and especially those who were aware of Rojas's background, could hardly fail to make the connection. Here Rojas was writing especially for them, and they probably got the message.

The existence of other works where the word *limpio* is used to attack "limpieza de sangre" in a clearer, albeit still ambiguous manner, supports this interpretation. Despite his anonymity, the author of *La vida de Lazarillo de Tormes* (1554) still felt it necessary to be careful. In the *Lazarillo*, the eponymous protagonist's mother gives him as guide to a blind man, because she herself cannot afford to support him. After being fired by his second master, a miserly priest who almost starved him to death, the boy is hired by a proud, penniless squire who had moved recently to Toledo, and soon discovers that he is the one who has to feed his master.

As soon as they arrive in the house that the squire had rented, the man ensures that the boy's hands are clean before folding and putting away his cape: "Desque fuimos entrados, quita de sobre sí su capa, y preguntando si tenía las manos *limpias* la sacudimos y doblamos, y muy *limpiamente* soplando un poyo que allí estaba, la puso en él" ("As soon as we entered, he took off his cape, and asking if my hands were *clean* we shook and folded it, and blowing very *cleanly* on a stone bench that was there, he laid the cape on it"; 1976, 152). These two successive references to "limpieza" are sufficient in themselves to arouse suspicions, which become confirmed when, taking the largest of the three pieces of bread that Lázaro had obtained as alms, the squire asks if it had been kneaded by clean hands: "¿Si es amasado de manos *limpias*?" ("Was it kneaded by *clean* hands?"; 154). The boy replies that he does not know, but, nevertheless, the squire eats the bread. Since he is hungry, "limpieza" does not really matter.

The morning after, as soon as he gets up, the squire cleans his clothes carefully before putting them on: "La mañana venida, levantámonos y comienza a *limpiar* y sacudir sus calzas y jubón y sayo y capa" ("When morning came, he got up and began to *clean* and shake his pants and doublet and coat and cape"; 157). In other words, "limpieza" is really a matter of appearances. As Lázaro goes on to ponder, after seeing his master leave the house all dressed up, "¿A quién no engañará aquella buena disposición y razonable capa y sayo? ¿Y quién pensará que aquel gentilhombre se pasó ayer todo el día sin comer, con aquel mendrugo de pan que su criado Lázaro trujo un día y una noche en el arca de su seno, do no se le podía pegar mucha *limpieza*, y hoy, lavándose las manos y la cara, a falta de paño de manos, se hacía servir de la halda del sayo?" ("Who will not be deceived by that good disposition and reasonable cape and coat? And who will imagine that yesterday that gentleman went all day without eating, with nothing but the crumb of bread that his servant Lázaro carried one day and one night in the coffer of his bosom, where it could not catch much *cleanliness*, and that today, while washing his hands and face, he used the rim of his coat for lack of a hand towel?"; 158).

Lázaro clearly perceives the squire's preoccupation with "limpieza." Although the text never says so explicitly, his obsession does not really have to do with cleanliness, but rather with blood purity. In other words, the squire's "limpieza de sangre" is questionable. Given the charged meaning that the word *limpio* had acquired, no further proof is necessary, but the squire himself provides it later, when he reveals to Lázaro that he was born in Costanilla de Valladolid (174), which was well known for the Jewish ancestry of its inhabitants (McGrady 1970, 562; Shepard 1982, 36–39). He had moved only to avoid having to doff his hat to greet a neighbor: "díjome ser de Castilla la Vieja y que había dejado su tierra no más de por no quitar el bonete a un caballero su vecino" ("he told me that he was from Old Castile and that he had left home for no reason other than having to doff his hat to a gentleman neighbor"; 172). The man greeted him back, but he usually forced the squire to doff his hat first: "Mas de cuantas veces yo se le quitaba primero, no fuera malo comedirse él alguna y ganarme por la mano" ("But given the number of times I doffed it to him first, it would not have been a bad idea for him to be obliging for once and to beat me to it"; 172). Although this seems to be a very poor reason for the squire to take the drastic step of moving to another town, it becomes more compelling when we understand that a grave insult was involved. As McGrady pointed out, making a man wait was a favorite method of calling him a converso, because it implied that he was still waiting for the Messiah (1970, 562; see also Shepard 1982, 46–51). Unable to stand the situation any longer, the squire moved to Toledo, where no one knew him.

Clearly, the squire's excessive preoccupation with "limpieza" reflects his obsessive desire to assimilate into mainstream society by hiding his "impure" origins. In the last analysis, his quest is utterly meaningless, for "limpieza"

Chapter Three

is shown to be nothing but a matter of appearances, and can be easily set aside when hunger strikes.

Manuel Ferrer Chivite discovered other details that point to the squire's converso background (1996). Although they do not include the word *limpio*, they are worth noting because they are related to the idea of "limpieza." The straw that the squire uses to clean his teeth by the front door in order to make people think that he had eaten recalls the silver and ebony toothpicks that crypto-Jews used publicly in their days of fasting (179–80). When he takes his sword from the scabbard and checks the edge with his fingers, this brings to mind the Jewish ritual of ensuring that the knives used to slaughter animals did not have any dents (182). We could have a mere coincidence here, of course, but when the squire girths his sword afterward, he takes care to place "un sartal de cuentas gruesas en el talabarte" ("a string of thick beads in his sword-belt"; 157). As Ferrer Chivite emphasized, none of the boy's other masters felt the need to display their piety in such manner, and, therefore, he is "el más obsesionado por aparecer frente a los demás como auténtico cristiano viejo" ("the one most obsessed to appear before others as an authentic Old Christian"; 184). Why? Because he is not "limpio."[11]

Only a converso writer, who was intimately familiar with the various ways in which the contemporary obsession with blood purity influenced people's lives, because he felt it in his own flesh, could have drawn the figure of this squire in such fine detail. The author probably vents his anger at the situation of conversos in the previous treatise as well, when the miserly priest who nearly starves Lázaro to death, believing that his bread has been spoiled by mice, tells him to eat it, anyway, for "el ratón cosa limpia es" ("mice are clean things"; 140). The assertion is so preposterous that the anonymous author must have had "limpieza de sangre" in mind (Gilman 1966, 165n67).[12]

The anonymous author of *El Abencerraje y la hermosa Jarifa* (1561), the first Moorish novel, attacks "limpieza de sangre" as well. The action is set in the fifteenth century, when the Muslims still held the kingdom of Granada and there were numerous border skirmiches with Christians. Traveling from Cártama to Coín in order to see his beloved Jarifa, the valiant Abindarráez runs into a five-man Christian patrol and defeats them. The Christian commander, Rodrigo de Nárvaez, comes to the rescue of his soldiers with another patrol, fights with Abindarráez in a single combat and takes him prisoner with some difficulty, even though the Moor and his horse are already tired and wounded. Rodrigo then allows Abindarráez to visit Jarifa, provided that he gives his word to return to captivity within three days, which he does. The mutual respect and religious tolerance depicted between Muslims and Christians contrast sharply with the situation during the 1550s, when *El Abencerraje* was written. The Jews had been expelled in 1492, and both the conversos and the Moriscos, who had also been forced to convert, suffered great discrimination and were persecuted by the Inquisition.[13] Consequently, the novel's idealized vision of the past embodies an implicit criticism of the present. As Claudio Guillén observed, "una novela puede muy bien narrar sucesos pretéritos sin cesar de aludir aún más significantemente al momento en que se escribe y lee" ("a novel can very well narrate past events while alluding even more significantly to the time in which it is written and read"; 1988, 118).

Only a converso could have written such a work. The model of tolerance and coexistence that it proposes was of special interest to conversos, for it could benefit them as well.[14] *El Abencerraje* is dedicated to Don Jerónimo Jiménez de Enbún, an Aragonese noble of converso extraction on his mother's side, who defended from the Inquisition the industrious, hard-working Moriscos who cultivated his lands (Lapesa 1987, 48–49). The portrayal of a Moor as being as noble and valiant as any Christian contradicts the Old Christian majority. They hated and despised the Moriscos, as the conquered and converted Moors came to be called.

Abindarráez is one of the last of the Abencerrajes, a family that had been falsely accused of conspiring against the king of Granada, who "had all of them beheaded in one night" ("los hizo a todos una noche degollar"; *El Abencerraje* 1987, 114). While telling the story to Rodrigo, Abindarráez refers to this lineage as being illustrious, and, despite their beheading, goes on to describe their demise with allusions to fire and burning that recall an auto-da-fé: "Vees aquí en lo que acabó tan *esclarecido linaje* y tan principales caballeros como en él había; considera cuánto tarda la fortuna en subir un hombre, y cuán presto le derriba; cuánto tarda en crescer un árbol, y cuán presto va al *fuego*; con cuánta dificultad se edifica una casa, y con cuánta brevedad *se quema*" ("Here you see how such an *illustrious lineage* and the numerous distinguished noblemen in it ended up; ponder on how long fate takes to raise a man, and how quickly it demolishes him; on how long a tree takes to grow, and how quickly it goes into the *fire*; on the hardship with which a house is built, and how quickly it is *burned*"; 115).

As far as the Old Christian majority was concerned, no Moor could possibly belong to a distinguished lineage; quite the contrary, for a drop of Moorish blood sufficed to disgrace a family. Clearly, the anonymous author is attacking "limpieza de sangre," and, since the Inquisition focused especially on persons of Jewish extraction, he is thinking of conversos as well.

But then the author does not use here the word *limpio*, which is the focus of the present chapter. However, there is one example toward the end of the novel, when Abindarráez, who had been freed without a ransom, writes to Rodrigo in order to thank him for the manner in which he had treated him. Having received his and Jarifa's freedom as a present from Rodrigo, who decided to forgo the usual ransom, Abindarráez wants to be equally

Chapter Three

generous, so as to resemble his ancestors "y no degenerar de la alta *sangre* de los Abencerrajes" ("not to degenerate the illustrious *blood* of the Abencerrajes"; 136). Abindarráez then concludes his brief letter with the following words: "Rescibirás de ese breve presente la voluntad de quien le envía, que es muy grande, y de mi Jarifa, otra tan *limpia* y leal que me contento yo de ella" ("This modest present represents the goodwill of the one who sends it, which is very great, and also of my Jarifa, whose goodwill is so *pure* [clean] and loyal that it pleases me"; 136). Through the technique of disjunction, an example of which we have already seen in Rojas, the anonymous author mocks "limpieza de sangre" once again, by attributing it to those who were regarded as anything but "pure." But since, generally speaking, the Moriscos made little or no effort to assimilate—most of them had been poorly catechized, and, unlike the Jews, who had no country of their own, they knew that there were powerful Muslim nations (Barkaï 1994b, 29)—the author is thinking especially of the conversos who had nowhere else to go.

El Abencerraje is a masterpiece, and, as Rafael Lapesa warned, "valerse sólo de una de las interpretaciones puede conducir a una visión parcial del caso" ("to avail oneself of only one of the interpretations can lead to a partial vision of the work"; 1987, 51). David Darst's dislike for the interpretation just presented was such that, after examining the literary and artistic conventions that hold the novel together, he maintained that *El Abencerraje* has nothing to do with contemporary society: "Literature, in this case, is self-expressing, drawing on the literary world for its information rather than on the real world" (1983, 272). In other words, here art exists in a vacuum, totally disconnected from life. However, that is not the case, and, although the *Abencerraje* is unquestionably a literary masterpiece, one interpretation does not invalidate the other.[15] On the contrary, the brilliant, necessarily ambiguous manner in which the prudently anonymous author portrays real life through an idealized, tolerant past that constitutes an antithesis of the intolerant period in which he wrote makes his work even greater.[16]

Although the attacks of the anonymous authors of the *Lazarillo* and the *Abencerraje* against "limpieza de sangre" are clearer than Rojas's, they remain somewhat ambiguous, and it is certainly possible for those who insist on understanding both texts literally, without reading between the lines, to dispute the interpretations just presented. This suggests that both authors still felt it necessary to exercise some caution, but the situation seems to have changed by the beginning of the seventeenth century, when some writers apparently threw all precautions to the winds, for they attack blood purity in a much clearer fashion.

An excellent example of this can be found in Cervantes's playlet *El retablo de las maravillas*, which deals with a puppet theater whose invisible wonders can be seen only by those without a trace of Moorish or Jewish blood who also happen to be legitimate children of their fathers. All peasants were supposedly "pure," but the spectators in the village where the play is represented are so insecure that everyone pretends to see the invisible wonders, and the women panic when the narrator, La Chirinos, describes a nonexistent drove of mice in the following terms: "Esa manada de ratones que allá va, deciende por línea recta de aquellos que fueron criados en el arca de Noé; dellos son blancos, dellos albarazados, dellos jaspeados, y dellos azules; y, finalmente, todos son ratones" ("That drove of mice over there descends in a direct line from those that were raised in Noah's Ark. Some are white, some are marbled, some are spotted, and some are blue. In a word, all are mice"; 1976, 177).

The obsession with "limpieza de sangre" is ridiculed through the fact that the mice are descended from those supposedly saved (just like all the humans who survived the deluge) in Noah's Ark. An ancient, pure, and noble lineage, indeed, despite their striking differences: some are white, some marbled, some streaked, and some blue, but this mythical "limpieza" does not really matter, for, after all, they are but mice. They are all the same. And so are men. Note that, if the only survivors from the deluge were those in Noah's Ark, everyone in the world would have to be ultimately Jewish, anyway.

To add insult to injury, these "Jewish mice" also happen to be phallic (Vasvari 1995).[17] That is why the panicky Juana Castrada ("Joanne Castrated") warns her friend Teresa Repolla ("Theresa Cabbage") to tighten her skirts: "Amiga, apriétate las faldas, y mira no te muerdan" ("Friend, tighten up that skirt around your legs, and watch out, lest they bite you"; 177–78). All precautions are in vain, however. As Teresa explains to her friend, "se me entran sin reparo ninguno; un ratón morenico me tiene asida de una rodilla; ¡socorro me venga del cielo, pues en la tierra me falta!" ("they are climbing up my skirt without any shame. A swarthy mouse has me fast by the knee. May the Heavens help me, for no one on this earth does!"; 178). So much for the mythical blood purity of the simple country folk.

With this adaptation of the international folktale known as *The King's New Clothes* (Aarne and Thompson 1973, no. 1620),[18] Cervantes also attacks the manner in which his contemporary Lope de Vega glorified the peasants in his plays because of their much-vaunted "limpieza" by suggesting that the existence of many cuckolds and illegitimate children in town made it impossible for them to be too certain about their ancestry, anyway (Gerli 1989a; 1995b, 95–109).[19] As if this daring, insulting attack on those who valued "limpieza" were not yet enough, a close reading reveals that the most intelligent villagers are depicted as conversos, while their Old Christian counterparts are invariably portrayed as ignorant and dumb (Martínez-López 1992, 90–93).[20]

Chapter Three

Joseph H. Silverman emphasized another passage where Cervantes questions blood purity with less derision, on moral grounds, by using the word *limpio*. In *El coloquio de los perros*, where the protagonists are two dogs, Cipión and Berganza, the former tells his companion that it is much easier for an honest man ("hombre de bien") to serve the Lord in heaven than a master on this earth (contemporary Spain), for God merely requires a pure heart:

> Muy diferentes son los señores de la tierra del Señor del cielo: aquéllos, para recibir un criado, primero *le espulgan el linaje*, examinan la habilidad, le marcan la apostura, y aun quieren saber los vestidos que tienen; pero para entrar a servir a Dios, el más pobre es el más rico; el más humilde, *de mejor linaje*; y con sólo que se disponga de LIMPIEZA [no de sangre sino] *de corazón* a querer servirle, luego le manda poner en el libro de sus gajes, señalándoselos tan aventajados que, de muchos y de grandes, apenas pueden caber en su deseo.[21] [30]

In other words, the very idea of "limpieza de sangre" is ridiculous. If God could not care less for it, why should men?

Berganza reprimands Cipión for digressing from the main purpose of their conversation by moralizing, but, as Silverman explained, Cipión's sermon reflects the anguished existence of many marginalized souls in sixteenth- and seventeenth-century Spain, as well as their hope for an open, less cruel society: "Pero es un sermón que perros-moros ladraban, que marranos chillaban, que cristianos nuevos y algunos cristianos viejos predicaban, con la esperanza de lograr en España una sociedad abierta" ("But this is a sermon that Moorish dogs barked, marranos shrieked, New Christians and some Old Christians preached, with the hope of attaining an open society in Spain"; 1978, 202).

Another, albeit more ambiguous attack on "limpieza" can be found in *Don Quijote*. In the inserted novella of "El curioso impertinente" (The man who couldn't keep from prying), Anselmo's wife, Camila, who is having an affair with his best friend, Lotario, protests her innocence with the following words: "*Limpia* entré en poder del que el cielo me dio por mío; *limpia* he de salir dél, y, cuando mucho, saldré bañada en mi casta *sangre*, y en la *impura* del más falso amigo que vio la amistad en el mundo" ("I was *pure* [clean] when Heaven entrusted me to Anselmo, and I must leave him *pure* [clean]; at the worst, I will leave him bathed both in my own chaste *blood* and in the *impure* blood of the falsest friend that the world has ever seen"; 1978, 1: 431). Although "limpieza de sangre" has nothing to do with the Florentine characters—the obsession was uniquely Spanish—the utilization of the words *limpia, sangre,* and *impura* makes it perfectly clear that the narrator is also referring ironically to blood purity, for Camila's actions had been anything but "pure." This manner of alluding to the concept by separating the words *limpia* and *sangre* recalls Pleberio's decision to marry off his daughter soon in order to preserve her "limpia fama" ("clean reputation") and Alisa's reference to his "noble sangre" ("noble blood") in her reply because the technique of disjunction, which we also saw in *El Abencerraje*, is being used here as well.

Cervantes often derides blood purity and other Old Christian values elsewhere (see Castro 1974a, 9–143). Although he had physicians, lawyers, and merchants among his ancestors, and was himself a tax collector (Cannavagio 1990, 19–25)—these professions were typically Jewish and continued to be favored by New Christians—there is no definite proof that he was a converso. Nevertheless, it is difficult to imagine how seventeenth-century Old Christian could possibly ridicule the values of the majority so mercilessly.[22]

Mateo Alemán, whose converso background was apparently common knowledge, could not resist the temptation to ridicule blood purity, either. In the *Guzmán de Alfarache*, the eponymous hero, who is still a boy, travels in the company of a muleteer he has met on the road. They stop at an inn whose owner had to kill a mule criminally engendered by the donkey and the Galician mare that he carelessly kept together, for there were severe laws forbidding such mixtures in southern Spain (1981, 1: 169n8). Since mules are sterile, "limpieza de sangre" had been extended to those poor animals for obvious economic reasons.

To minimize his loss, the innkeeper decided to serve the hybrid, "impure" meat of the mule to his guests. Notwithstanding his unquestionable "limpieza," the rustic muleteer does not even dream that something is wrong. Being born of low, coarse parents, such people can seldom tell the difference, anyway, for they have very poor taste: "De mi compañero no hay que tratar dél, porque nació entre salvajes, de padres brutos y lo paladearon con un diente de ajo; y la gente rústica, grosera, no tocando a su bondad y *limpieza*, en materia de gusto pocas veces distingue lo malo de lo bueno" ("There is no need to speak about my companion, because he was born among savages, of brutish parents who rubbed his palate with a clove of garlic. Except for their goodness and [blood] *purity* [cleanliness], when it comes to good taste these rustic, gross people seldom distinguish good from bad"; 1981, 1: 171–72).[23] The muleteer's "limpieza" is worthless when it comes to detecting the nauseating "impurity" of the meat that he has been fed; he liked it so much that he could not get enough. It is the young Guzmán who, after eating a little, despite the self-avowed "impurity"of his blood, realizes that something is not quite right, as he should have right away, for he had been raised by civilized parents: "Mas que yo, criado con regalo, de padres políticos y curiosos, no sintiese el engaño, grande fue mi hambre y esta excusa me desculpa" ("But it is only because of my great hunger that I, having been raised by courteous and attentive parents, did not realize the deceit, and this excuse exonerates me"; 1: 172). It would be difficult to come up with a more ingenious and devastating way to ridicule the common belief in the genetically inherited "purity" of peasants and the idea of "limpieza de sangre" in general.

If there are any doubts regarding this interpretation, note that afterward, when the dishonest innkeeper learns from the stupid muleteer about a woman who had served semi-hatched eggs to her clients, he swears up and down that he himself is irreproachably honest with the following words: "¡Loada sea la *limpieza* de la Virgen María, que con toda mi pobreza no hay en mi casa mal trato! Cada cosa se vende por lo que es; no gato por conejo, ni oveja por carnero. *Limpieza* de vida es lo que importa y la cara sin vergüenza descubierta por todo el mundo. Lleve cada uno lo que fuere suyo y no engañar a nadie" ("Blessed be the *purity* [cleanliness] of the Virgin Mary for, despite my poverty, people aren't badly cared for in this house! Everything is sold for what it is; no cat for rabbit, nor lamb for ram. What matters is a *pure* [clean] life and to be able to show one's face without shame to the whole world. Let each one take what is his without deceiving anyone"; 1: 176). Although the word *sangre* is never used, the emphasis on "limpieza" makes it perfectly clear that he is referring to "limpieza de sangre." In relation to the Virgin, of course, the word also means "purity," but, since the Blessed Mother was Jewish, another level of irony is probably present in the attribution of that quality to her.[24]

Little is known about Francisco López de Úbeda, who wrote another picaresque novel, *La pícara Justina* (1605), but the chances are that he was one of those self-mocking conversos who, rather than hiding their background, did not hesitate to proclaim it in his book: "La ironía multiforme de López de Úbeda (toledano originario de la Andalucía, donde imperaba también la mezcla de sangres), dirigida contra *leoneses, montañeses y asturianos*, es la de un hombre que se ríe de su propia *impureza* en las mismas barbas de una minoría seudo selecta que reivindica el monopolio de la *pureza* para monopolizar honores y prebendas" ("The multiform irony of López de Úbeda—he was an inhabitant of Toledo with origins in Andalusia, where mixed blood also prevailed—which is addressed against *Leonese, people from La Montaña,* and *Asturians,* is the irony of a man who mocks his own *lack of purity* in the face of a pseudo-select minority that claims the monopoly of *purity* in order to monopolize privileges and benefices"; Bataillon 1982b, 34). Thus, López de Úbeda does not feel any need for ambiguity in his attacks against "limpieza." One of the best examples is found when, upon setting up their home as an inn, Justina's father instructs his family in the manner in which the business ought to be run: "Nunca digáis que vuestra ropa no es *limpia,* que en España es cosa afrentosa. Y para vencer tretas de huéspedes que, para ver si la sábana está *limpia*, miran si está tiesa o sin arrugas, si cruje o no (como si hubiéramos de almidonar las sábanas), para esto, lo que habéis de hacer es rociarlas y emprensarlas, que con esto podréis hacer información que son *limpias* de todos los cuatro costados" ("Never say that your bedding is not *clean*, for this is an insulting thing in Spain. And to beat the ruses of those guests who, in order to see if a sheet is *clean*, check whether it is stiff or without wrinkles, and whether it crackles or not [as if we were supposed to starch the sheets], what you must do is to sprinkle and press them, for, with this, you can tell them that they are *clean* on all four sides"; López de Úbeda 1982, 126). There is no question that blood purity is being mocked through its association with clean sheets, which brings to mind, once again, the question of conjugal fidelity.[25] A faithless wife was not likely to investigate the bloodlines of her lovers. Sheets, of course, have only two sides, and it would be ridiculous to certify that they were clean on all four. This certification alludes to the contemporary "probanzas" ("depositions") and the expression "por los cuatro costados" ("on all four sides") refers to people, for it was used to designate the four grandparents of a person. Should one of them have a drop of Jewish or Moorish blood, the person could not possibly be "clean."

Except for Delicado's and Cervantes's mockery of "limpieza de sangre" through the lineages of prostitutes and mice, respectively, and the *Abencerraje*'s attribution of noble lineage to a Moor, the examples that we have seen achieve their aim through the use of the word *limpio*. Writers mocked blood purity in other ways, such as poking fun at peasants who took great pride in being "Cristianos Viejos," or emphasizing that virtue ought to be more important than lineage, but we focused on the aforesaid examples because Rojas uses the word *limpio* as well.

The repeated use of that word in the last of his appended strophes, including the very last verse to issue from his pen, we recall, is particularly significant. In the verses that follow, Alonso de Proaza, the "corrector de la impresión" ("editor"), after stating that the name of the author whom he obviously admires must not remain anonymous ("cubierto de olvido" ["covered with forgetfulness"]), tells readers to put together the first letter of each of the prefatory verses in order to discover "su nombre, su tierra, su clara nación" ("his name, his hometown, his illustrious nation [people]"; Rojas 1987, 239).[26] This lends a renewed significance to the acrostic where Rojas reveals that he was born in Puebla de Montalbán, a town that was notorious for the Jewish ancestry of its inhabitants. Since "nación" was another way to designate converts, the "clara nación" is the Jewish background that Rojas proudly proclaims to the world despite the fact that, as far as the Old Christian majority was concerned, being from Puebla de Montalbán amounted to an indelible, dishonorable stain in itself. As Gilman pointed out, "what

Chapter Three

Proaza and Rojas are up to in their calculated and ironical game of hide-and-seek is precisely the reversal of that evaluation. For them, Puebla and the *conversos* who inhabited it together constitute a 'nación' which, far from dishonored, is 'clear' by definition" (1972, 237). The word *clara* can mean both "famous" and "pure" in the context. But there is more. Since the prefatory and concluding verses place an inordinate emphasis on the idea of "limpieza," Rojas's revelation of the place of his birth, besides constituting a proclamation of pride in his origins, embodies a specific challenge to the concept that would deny such pride.

Américo Castro felt that Rojas's protestations concerning the didactic purpose of *Celestina* were motivated by fear: "el autor se precave contra quienes juzguen 'mi limpio motivo,' porque él mismo se siente 'cercado de dudas y antojos.' No caben más titubeos y no pedidas excusas" ("the author takes precautions against those who may doubt 'my pure motive' because he himself feels 'full of doubts and fancies.' There could not be more hesitations and unrequested excuses"; 1965, 78). However, there is much more than an abject fear in the profuse exculpations found in Rojas's verses. Other converts could not fail to understand that his proclamation of pride in his origins was tantamount to a challenge, to a reaffirmation of his and their integrity as human beings. This is one of the reasons for what Gilman has called Rojas's "artful rapport with them" (1972, 366). Thus, the exculpations and protestations couched by Fernando de Rojas within the idea of "limpieza" constitute a shield that is used to hide a wonderfully ambiguous, double-edged sword. This shield reflects the controlled fear of a man of courage who is taking a calculated risk, the wise precaution of the warrior who knows that he must protect himself while ridiculing and demolishing the "limpieza de sangre" that had been jealously imposed by mediocre persons who, besides fearing the competition of better qualified New Christians, wanted to keep them "in their place." As we shall see in the next chapter, Rojas still had much more to say about the oppressive society in which he had to live.

Chapter Four

Celestina as an Antithesis of the Blessed Mother

First published anonymously, *Celestina* was a controversial work from the very beginning.[1] In the preliminary letter to an unnamed friend, Rojas says that he found the equally anonymous first act, which some attributed to Juan de Mena and others to Rodrigo Cota, already written, and that he decided to continue it during a two-week vacation (69–70). In the prologue, Rojas points out that his readers quarreled with each other about the quality of the work: "esta presente obra ha seýdo instrumento de lid o contienda a sus lectores para ponerlos en differencias, dando cada uno sentencia sobre ella a sabor de su voluntad. Unos dezían que era prolixa, otros breve, otros agradable, otros escura" ("this present work has been the cause of conflicts and disputes among its readers, for it has led them to disagreements, and each one has passed judgment as he pleased. Some said that it was long-winded, others too short; some found it enjoyable, others unclear"; 80). Rojas also points out that people argued about the meaning of *Celestina*, and alerts readers to the fact that it can be interpreted in different ways: "¿quién negará que aya contienda en cosa que de tantas maneras se entienda?" ("who will deny that disputes will arise about something that can be understood in so many different ways?"; 81). After indicating that the printers insisted on adding summaries of their own at the beginning of each act, even though he himself did not agree,[2] Rojas goes on to tell us that some people argued that *Celestina* ought to be called a tragedy rather than a comedy, since it ended with sadness, and that this had caused him to compromise, classifying it as a tragicomedy instead. Then he reveals that many readers insisted that he should expand the section that dwelt on "el proceso de su deleyte destos amantes" ("the progress of the pleasure of these two lovers"; 81), and that he decided to oblige them even though it was against his will, thus increasing the original comedy of sixteen acts to the present tragicomedy, with twenty-one.

These early controversies continue unabated. Scholars are still arguing whether Rojas really found the first act already written, or whether this was a mere literary ruse on his part.[3] If we suppose that two writers were indeed

Chapter Four

involved and take both into account,[4] the problems of interpretation become even more intricate, but, as Ciriaco Morón Arroyo pointed out, it is best to regard the first act as belonging to Rojas and to consider the work as a whole, since, after all, he appropriated it (1984, 42). The question of genre now focuses especially on whether *Celestina*, given its length and factors that are not relevant to the present discussion, ought to be classified as a play or as a novel.[5] But what has caused rivers of ink to run is the question regarding the author's intentions and the message of his work.[6] The ensuing interpretations can be broadly divided into two groups. According to some scholars, *Celestina*'s corrosive view of contemporary society, a rationalist perspective that replaces Divine Providence with a chain of cause and effect, and its radical pessimism reflect Rojas's situation as a semioutsider. Only a converso, they argue, could have written such a work. Other scholars maintain that *Celestina* is indeed a Christian, didactic work penned as a warning against lust and deceit, as the author proclaims it to be.[7] The controversy rages on. In the words of Joseph T. Snow, "after almost five centuries of textual life, and after one hundred years of critical commentary on the *Tragicomedia*, we still have no consensus as to its meaning" (1995, 256).

Since few if any literary works have provoked as many fundamentally, diametrically opposed interpretations, it is difficult to imagine that the author did not deliberately set out to create an ambiguous work.[8] His awareness of the controversial nature of what he had written can be seen clearly in the prologue, and then he goes on to take unusual precautions in the apparently pious preliminary and postliminary verses, which were absent from the first, anonymous edition, thus supplementing the lengthy *incipit*, where he had already claimed that *Celestina* was written "en reprehensión de los locos enamorados" ("as a reprimand to unchaste lovers"; 82). Despite this apparently clear, straightforward purpose, Rojas still finds it necessary to explain his intentions further. In the preliminary verses, which he purports to have written in order to excuse himself "de su yerro en esta obra que escrivió" ("for his error in this work that he wrote"; 71), he praises the anonymous author to whom he attributes the first act, and hopes that he is in heaven with the only meaningful reference to the name of Christ found in the whole work:[9] "al qual Jesuchristo reciba en su gloria / por su passión sancta que a todos nos sana" ("may Jesus Christ receive him in his glory, / for the sake of his holy Passion, which heals all of us"; 75).[10] As he concludes the postliminary verses, Rojas takes the precaution of warning readers to take good care to understand his true intentions:

> Y assí no me juzgues por esso liviano
> mas antes zeloso de *limpio* bivir;
> zeloso de amar, temer y servir

Celestina as an Antithesis of the Blessed Mother

>   al alto Señor y Dios soberano;
>   por ende si vieres turbada mi mano
>   turvias con claras mezclando razones,
>   dexa las burlas, qu'es paja y grançones
>   sacando muy *limpio* dentrellas el grano.
>
>   (344 [31])

Rojas was obviously afraid of something. If the book in which he portrays a world of prostitution and the seduction of a young girl of good family like Melibea with few explicit, valid moral arguments were really the Christian, didactic work he claimed, I repeat, there would probably be fewer "jests" ("burlas") and less of a need to "clean" or "glean" the moral ("grano") from all the straw and chaff ("paja y grançones"). Rojas was worried because he knew what he had done. In fact, it is difficult to read these words in any other manner. As Dorothy Severin states in her introduction, "la última estrofa escrita por Rojas antes de que su voz enmudeciera para siempre, transparenta un innegable tono nervioso" ("the last strophe written by Rojas before his voice became forever silent betrays an undeniable nervous tone"; 1987, 20). Américo Castro, we recall, puts it this way: "el autor se precave contra quienes juzguen 'mi limpio motivo,' porque él mismo se siente 'cercado de dudas y antojos.' No caben más titubeos y no pedidas excusas" ("the author takes precautions against those who may doubt 'my pure motive' because he himself feels 'full of doubts and fancies.' There could not be more hesitations and unrequested excuses"; 1965, 78). In sum, Rojas found it necessary to take such extraordinary precautions because he was perfectly aware of the ambiguous, deliberately controversial nature of his book.

According to Snow, the controversy lies in the portrayal of a world with few signs of redemption, and the preliminary materials had the desired effect: "Rojas was busy creating a subtly subversive work at a time when the Inquisition was gathering force. It was in his interest to ward off those readers who might accurately condemn it as a subversive work. *Celestina* secured a long exemption from the *Index* [1640], because—I suspect—of the success these preliminary materials achieved in deflecting the stronger criticisms" (1995, 254–55).

I could not agree more. However, the subversive character of Rojas's work goes far beyond the portrayal of a world with few signs of redemption. As we will see in the pages that follow, *Celestina* includes a multipronged attack against Christian prayer and the central dogmas of Christianity. We will begin by examining the manner in which Rojas created Celestina's figure as a deliberate antithesis of the Virgin Mary, but first, a brief summary of *Celestina* and an examination of the first scene ought to prove helpful to students and readers who are not thoroughly familiar with the work.

Chapter Four

The initial summary, which was no doubt written by Rojas, must be read as an integral part of the text, for it includes information that is necessary in order to understand the beginning of Act 1. Calisto follows his falcon into Melibea's garden (this is in the summary), falls suddenly in love with her, and the irate Melibea tells him to get out when he says that he would like to show her his "secreto dolor" ("secret suffering [pain]"; 86). The lovesick Calisto goes home, where his servant Sempronio advises him to engage the services of an old procuress, Celestina. Sempronio's girlfriend, Elicia, lives with her, but he ignores that she has sex with other men for money, and Celestina has to warn her to hide a customer in a broom closet when her boyfriend arrives. When Sempronio returns with Celestina, another of Calisto's servants, the younger Pármeno, warns his master about her: Besides having been an insatiable, shameless prostitute, Celestina is a dangerous woman who used to run a very popular whorehouse, caused many girls to lose their virginity, and dabbled in witchcraft. However, Calisto refuses to listen.

Celestina and Sempronio had agreed to divide whatever she managed to extract from his master. Seeing that Pármeno is an obstacle, the old bawd decides to bribe him, and discovers that he is the son of a deceased friend, Claudina, who had lived with her as a little boy. The reluctant Pármeno gives in when Celestina promises to get him into bed with Elicia's cousin, Areúsa, an independent prostitute who owns her own home.

Before visiting Melibea, Celestina, who has a veritable laboratory in the house, sends Elicia to fetch snake oil, bat and goat's blood, and other ingredients for a ceremony in which she conjures the devil, commanding him to get into the yarn that she plans to sell as an excuse to get into Melibea's home. Although the maid who comes to the door, Lucrecia, is also Elicia's cousin, Celestina's reputation is so bad that she is embarrassed to say her name to Alisa, Melibea's mother. Laughing, Alisa tells her to invite the old woman in and leaves her daughter alone with her shortly afterward, explaining that she has to visit her sister, who is ill with a backache.

When Celestina mentions Calisto's name, Melibea flies into a rage, but calms down as soon as the procuress informs her that Calisto is sick with a bad toothache, and that she only intended to ask Melibea for a folk spell that she knew for the effect, the prayer to Saint Appolonia, and for her rope belt,[11] which was reputed to have touched all the holy relics in Rome and Jerusalem. Melibea gives the belt to Celestina right away, but asks her to return for the prayer very secretly the day after, since there was probably not enough time for her to write it down before her mother came back.

Calisto goes into a frenzy as soon as he touches the rope belt. Sickened by his fetishism, Sempronio says that if he keeps having fun with it he will probably no longer need Melibea. Calisto rewards Celestina, who takes back the belt, stating that she needs it, and Calisto then orders Pármeno to accompany her home. Noticing that the boy's loyalty to his master is causing him to waver, Celestina takes him to Areúsa's house and watches while they make love.

A few days later, Melibea sends for Celestina, saying that she is not feeling well. The bawd gets her to admit that she is in love with Calisto and suggests a tryst in the garden that very evening, at midnight. Delighted with the news, Calisto rewards Celestina with a heavy gold chain. When he meets Melibea by the door of the garden, which now appears surrounded with tall walls, he is unable to enter, but Melibea asks him to return the day after, ready to scale them. Then Sempronio and Pármeno go to Celestina's house in order to get their share of the gold chain. When the old woman refuses to give them anything, claiming that the chain is lost and could have been stolen, they kill her. Attracted by the noise, the constable and his men arrive on the scene. Pármeno and Sempronio jump out of a window, get badly hurt, and a judge orders them to be swiftly beheaded publicly, in the plaza.

Nevertheless, Calisto decides to keep his tryst with Melibea, taking along two younger servants, Sosia and Tristán. Using a ladder, Calisto climbs the wall of the garden and makes love to Melibea while Lucrecia and the two boys listen to what is going on. Crying, Elicia informs Areúsa of what has happened, and then both decide to take revenge. Areúsa sends for Sosia, finds out from him when Calisto and Melibea are going to meet again, and tries to enlist the help of a lazy ruffian whom she supports, Centurio. Since he is a coward, Centurio gets the lame Traso and his companions to do the job. Hearing the noise that they make, Calisto tries to climb down the ladder, falls, and dies. Melibea goes to the top of a tower in the garden, tells her father, Pleberio, what has happened, and jumps. With Alisa passed out on top of the body of their only daughter, the disconsolate Pleberio proffers a heartbreaking lament before her corpse.

A proper understanding of the language is crucial to the interpretation of any literary work, and *Celestina* abounds in the use of euphemisms and metaphors whose meaning is no longer clear to us. For example, the opening words of the summary, "Entrando Calisto una huerta empos dun falcon suyo halló ý a Melibea, de cuyo amor preso, començóle de hablar" ("Entering a garden in pursuit of his falcon, Calisto found Melibea there and, falling in love, began to speak to her"; 85), indicate that, besides being a hunter, Calisto is wealthy; since falcons were very expensive, only aristocrats could afford to own them. The sudden love that he feels for Melibea as soon as he sees her confirms that what is involved here is the hunt of love,[12] for love used to be described in terms of both hunting and war. Although Melibea tells Calisto to leave, the text suggests that he will eventually succeed, because, at another level, the falcon was a phallic symbol (Gerli 1983), and the garden could also designate the female genitalia (see Chapter 5, p. 155).

Calisto tries to behave as a courtly lover, for he addresses Melibea as if she were a goddess when he tells her that "los gloriosos santos que se

Chapter Four

deleytan en la visión divina no gozan más que yo agora en el acatamiento tuyo" ("the glorious saints who delight before the Vision Divine don't enjoy themselves more than I do in seeing you"; 86). As we know, courtly love transformed women into goddesses, and their lovers, besides worshiping them, also had to behave as their vassals, serving them and obeying their every command. Melibea becomes extremely angry with Calisto, however. Some scholars believed that this was because, by addressing her in such a direct manner, without any preliminaries, Calisto was not behaving as a proper courtly lover (Green 1953; see also Lacarra 1990, 53–56), but now that we understand the language of the time better, we know that there was yet another, more compelling reason. As soon as he sees Melibea, Calisto tells her that she reminds him of the greatness of God ("En esto veo, Melibea, la grandeza de Dios" ["In this, Melibea, I see the greatness of God"; 85]), and when she asks him why, he replies: "En dar poder a natura que de tan perfecta hermosura te dotasse, y hazer a mí, inmérito, tanta merced que verte alcançasse, y en tan conveniente lugar, que mi secreto dolor manifestarte pudiesse" ("In empowering nature to endow you with such beauty, and in granting me, albeit unworthy, the great favor of being able to see you, and in such a convenient place, where I can show you my secret suffering"; 86). On the surface, the word *dolor* means "pain," and, therefore, Calisto seems to be saying that the love that he is feeling for Melibea causes him to suffer. At another level, the word *dolor*, being associated with a toothache, which was a metaphor for sexual desire (West 1979; Herrero 1986), also meant "erection."[13] Since *Celestina* was supposed to be acted out, with the intonation and the expressions required for each part—Alonso de Proaza advises readers to do so in the postliminary verses[14]—one can only imagine the gesture that Calisto probably made when telling Melibea that he wishes to show her his "pain." That is why she flies into a rage and tells him to get out right away: "¡Vete, vete de a ý, torpe! Que no puede mi paciencia tolerar que aya subido en coraçón humano conmigo el ilícito amor comunicar su deleyte" ("Get out, get out, you idiot! My patience is too thin to allow a man whose heart is filled with lust to show me how I delight him"; 87). Besides confirming the interpretation just presented, these irate words show that Melibea understands perfectly well what Calisto wants, and is not quite the guileless, innocent little girl that some critics liked to envision.

Many modern readers will no doubt find all of this offensive, but, to judge from the numerous examples of sexual metaphors present in *Celestina* and other early works—i.e., the *cantigas d'escarnho e de mal dizer* ("songs of mockery and slander") from medieval courts, Juan Ruiz's *Libro de buen amor*, and some courtly poetry[15]—our ancestors were far more earthy than we are, and probably saw it as mere humor.

The examples just examined show how a proper understanding of this sort of language is indispensable to a proper interpretation of *Celestina*. As

Celestina as an Antithesis of the Blessed Mother

María Eugenia Lacarra emphasized, "el humor afecta a la construcción de los personajes y al significado de la trama, por lo que silenciarlo altera nuestra percepción de la obra" ("humor affects the characterization of the characters and the meaning of the plot; therefore, silencing it alters our understanding of the work"; 1996, 431).

There is also humor in the language that Calisto uses in order to present himself to Melibea as a courtly lover, and understanding this is crucial to the interpretation of *Celestina* as well. By coupling the language of courtly love with his rude behavior—later on, Calisto's servant, Sempronio, will use similar language with his girlfriend, Elicia, who is a prostitute[16]—the author is in fact mocking courtly love. Since this type of love first developed among the aristocracy at court—hence its name[17]—Rojas's book could also be an expression of resentment toward the upper classes, incorporating an attack on the nobility (van Beysterveldt 1977, 102–13; see also Whinnom 1981a, 61–67). On the other hand, since courtly love, including its language, had descended from its lofty origins, being widely imitated in lower circles (Mackay 1989; rpt. in Macpherson and Mackay 1998, 140–56), Rojas could simply be reflecting reality. In any case, humor, including metaphor and parody, plays a key role in *Celestina*, but no matter how it is interpreted, the undeniable parody of courtly love does not exclude other interpretations. *Celestina* is a rich, multifaceted, complex work, and Rojas did not have a one-track mind.

Despite the central position of the love affair—after giving in to the readers who preferred to call his work a tragicomedy, we recall, Rojas referred to it as "la Comedia o Tragicomedia de Calisto y Melibea" ("the Comedy or Tragicomedy of Calisto and Melibea"; 82)—the power exercised by the procuress who brings the two lovers together is such that their names were soon banished from the title, being replaced by hers instead. That is why readers today still know Rojas's immortal work as *Celestina*.[18] As Morón Arroyo pointed out, this constitutes a splendid example "of how a text and its reception impose their own logic over and above the intention of the author" (1994, 4).

The various ways in which scholars have interpreted the old bawd's figure help to explain this phenomenon. To Weinberg, she constitutes an archetypal, primordial force that represents both Mother Earth and the Great Mother. Since at one point Pármeno describes her as "la más antigua y puta tierra, que fregaron sus espaldas en todos los burdeles" ("the oldest and biggest whore, Earth, for she has been on her back in every brothel"; 116), the boy "clearly sees the connection between Celestina, arch whore, and that greatest whore of all, Mother Earth, who provides a tolerant bed for all the coupling creatures within the universal 'brothel,'" the "indifferently productive earth . . . archetypally . . . identified as the Great Mother" (Weinberg 1971, 149). To Everett Hesse, on the other hand, Celestina represents no less than

Chapter Four

five different concepts: "la Gran Madre, la Vieja Sabia, la Madre Naturaleza, la Curandera y la Hipócrita" ("Great Mother, Sage Old Woman, Mother Nature, Folk Healer, and Hypocrite"; 1966, 87). Other scholars have seen Celestina as an embodiment of pure evil, an antithesis of Christ, and as high priestess of an anti-Christian religion. Since Calisto equates her with the Messiah when he asks God to lead Sempronio to her as he had guided the Three Wise Men to Bethlehem with the star, Celestina is much more than a mere "sacerdotisa de la carne" ("priestess of the flesh"; Anderson Imbert 1949, 304), for she exercises "un magisterio satánico (parodia del magisterio de Jesús) en el que es Maestra irremplazable y Madre solícita" ("a satanic teaching [parody of the ministry of Jesus] in which she is both an Irreplaceable Teacher and a Caring Mother"; Gurza 1977, 167).[19]

Far from being mutually exclusive, these interpretations supplement each other because Celestina is a rich, multidimensional character, a spider whose web either dooms or radically affects the lives of everyone who has anything to do with her.[20] The power of her figure is such that she overwhelms all the other characters, including the two ill-fated lovers after whom the "comedia" or "tragicomedia" was originally named. It is only fitting, therefore, that it should be known as *Celestina*.

In his *Sentido y forma de La Celestina*, Morón Arroyo suggested that the text also equates Celestina with the Blessed Mother. Calisto adores her "como si fuera la Virgen medianera" ("as if she were the Virgin as Mediatrix"), and "en un momento en boca de Melibea, Celestina nos aparece como la Virgen a la cual se pide que nos presente a Cristo" ("at one point, Celestina appears in Melibea's mouth as the Virgin whom one asks to show us Christ"; 1984, 50). In the first edition of this book (1974), after stating that this interpretation is supported by a great number of religious parallelisms and parodies of the kind, Morón Arroyo, who has seen this aspect of *Celestina* better than anyone else, makes a hasty retreat. If, rather than depicting the consequences of illicit love, Rojas really intended to mock Christian theology in such a manner, he was not, Morón Arroyo argued, a Christian but a crypto-Jew, and the chances are that he would have been promptly unmasked: "o Rojas el buen cristiano quiso efectivamente apartar a los locos enamorados de sus sacrilegios, o Rojas el criptojudío quiso hacer una burla sangrienta de la teología cristiana. Ahora bien, en este último caso ¿no hubiera sido desenmascarado?" ("either Rojas, as a good Christian, really wanted to influence unchaste lovers to mend their ways, or Rojas, as a crypto-Jew, really wanted to effect a horrible mockery of Christian theology. Well, now, had the latter been the case, wouldn't he have been unmasked?"; 1974, 71).

These words have been removed from the second edition, but Morón Arroyo repeated the idea elsewhere, with the difference that, instead of speaking only about the relationship between Celestina and the Blessed Mother, the author now applies it to Catholic dogma in general: "la cantidad de alusiones sacrílegas es tal en la *Celestina*, que todo el texto podría leerse como una parodia de los dogmas más sagrados del catolicismo" ("the quantity of sacrilegious allusions in *Celestina* is so great that the whole text could be read as parody of the most sacred dogmas of Catholicism"; 1984, 109). Then Morón Arroyo goes on to say that, if that was the case, Rojas managed to hide his assault against Catholicism in such a manner that even his first readers failed to understand it: "Si él, como converso resentido, tuvo esa intención, logró expresarla y al mismo tiempo ocultarla de tal manera que hasta sus primeros lectores habían perdido la clave; o sea, en el fondo no supo decir lo que quería decir" ("If Rojas, as a resentful converso, had such an intention, he managed both to express it and at the same time hide it in such a manner that even his first readers couldn't find the clue; in other words, in the last analysis he did not know how to say what he wanted"; 1984, 109). The implication, then, is that, notwithstanding all the indications to the contrary, Rojas did not attempt to do such a thing.

It would have been suicidal, however, for Rojas to make his position any clearer. Given the repression that existed, it was crucial to preserve deniability, and, as we have seen, Rojas knew perfectly well that his work could be interpreted in various ways. Moreover, the readers that were most likely to understand this particular aspect were like-minded conversos, and they could be expected to keep the matter to themselves.

For Christians, the very thought of equating a woman like Celestina with the Virgin Mary is extremely disquieting, to say the least. The immediate reaction of many of the Catholic readers to whom the idea occurs is to banish it completely from their minds in order to eliminate the guilt felt for having had it in the first place, as if the sacrilegious notion were originally theirs. Even if such readers realized they were not at fault, they would then probably fear that, by disseminating their knowledge, they would somehow repeat the horrible sin time and again by the very act of propagating it. That is what I have felt for the past twenty-five years while teaching this particular aspect of *La Celestina* to my students.

In all probability, Fernando de Rojas wanted to effect such a reaction, for he knew that he had created a rich, complex character whose multiple roles could be viewed in a variety of ways. In the pages that follow we will do exactly the opposite and suggest the unimaginable, bringing together a number of religious parallelisms and parodies that show that Rojas created the figure of Celestina as a deliberate antithesis of the Blessed Mother.

This unthinkable blasphemy is first indicated by Celestina's name. Sebastián de Covarrubias claimed that it was related to the Latin for "wicked" ("Nombre de una mala vieja, que le dio a la tragicomedia española

Chapter Four

tan celebrada. Díjose así cuasi *Scelestina, a* SCELERE, por ser malvada alcahueta embustidora" ["Name of a bad old woman, who gave it (her name) to the famous Spanish tragicomedy. It sounds almost like *Scelestina*, from SCELERE, because she was an evil, deceitful bawd"; 1994, 294]).[21] Some attempts have also been made to link Rojas's choice of name to previous sources.[22] The name, however, speaks for itself; it is really derived from *caelestis* ("celestial"; see Corominas's entry for *cielo* ["heaven"]). And any speaker of Spanish knows, even without the benefit of Latin, that "Celestina" means "little celestial one."[23] Her very name, then, suggests, ironically, that she is some sort of heavenly figure, although she is precisely the opposite.[24]

The analogy becomes clearer when the text applies titles commonly used to designate the Virgin to Celestina. As Jane Hawking emphasized (1967), practically everyone calls her "mother," and on one occasion Sempronio, as if in ecstasy upon seeing her, exclaims: "Madre bendita, ¡qué deseo traigo! Gracias a Dios que te me dexó ver" ("Blessed mother, I'm glad to come! Thanks be to God for letting me see you"; 104).[25] Even more awed when he first meets her, Calisto addresses and adores Celestina as if she were a goddess. Not daring to kiss her healing hands, he humbly kisses the ground upon which she walks:

> ¿Qué hazes, llave de mi vida? Abre. ¡O Pármeno, ya la veo; sano soy, bivo soy! ¡Miras qué reverenda persona, qué acatamiento! . . . ¡O gloriosa esperança de mi desseado fin! ¡O fin de mi deleytosa esperança! ¡O salud de mi passión, reparo de mi tormento, regeneración mía, vivificación de mi vida, resurrección de mi muerte! Desseo llegar a ti, cobdicio besar essas manos llenas de remedio. La indignidad de mi persona lo enbarga. Dende aquí adoro la tierra que huellas y en reverencia tuya la beso. (116 [32])

As if this were not enough, Calisto goes on to call her "señora y madre mía" ("my lady and mother"; 176), "reyna y señora mía" ("my queen and mother"; 178), the rarest of jewels, succor of his sufferings, mirror of his sight, and his glory and repose: "O joya del mundo, acorro[26] de mis pasiones, spejo de mi vista" ("Oh rarest of jewels, succor of my sufferings, mirror of my sight!"; 249); "¿Qué dizes, gloria y descanso mío?" ("What are you saying, my glory and repose?"; 249).

Like Celestina in her community, the Virgin was regarded as Mother by all Catholics. Her litany, which Fernando de Rojas must have heard many times in church,[27] hailed her as "Mater purissima" ("Mother most pure"), "Mater castissima" ("Mother most chaste"), and "Mater inviolata" ("Mother inviolate"). Being a whore and procuress, Celestina is an antithesis of all these qualities. Sempronio's "madre bendita" means precisely "blessed mother," and Calisto's designation of the old bawd as "reina y señora mía" ("my queen and lady") also parallels the litany, where Mary is hailed several times as queen, including "Regina Virginum" ("Queen of Virgins"), i.e., queen of the very virgins that Celestina, whose reign consists of lechery and prostitution, labors to undo. Calisto had sought her out in order to cure his infirmity, for love was considered a serious illness during the Middle Ages. Hence his reference to her healing hands, a reference that brings to mind other epithets applied to Mary: "Salus infirmorum" ("Health of the sick"), "Refugium peccatorum" ("Refuge of sinners"), and "Consolatrix afflictorum" ("Comfort of the afflicted"). Celestina is also a healer, refuge and comfort to lovers, sinners, and the afflicted who seek her assistance, but she "redeems" them by leading them into more sin. Calisto's "espejo de mi vista" ("mirror of my sight") could echo "Speculum justitiae" ("Mirror of justice"), another of the Blessed Mother's epithets. The parallels are so many that Rojas must have had a similar litany in mind; they cannot be dismissed as a matter of pure coincidence. Rojas, however, was familiar with epithets applied to the Virgin in other sources. When Calisto refers to Celestina as "gloriosa esperança de mi desseado fin" ("Glorious hope of my desired goal"; 116), for example, the reader recalls that "La Gloriosa" ("the Glorious one") was one of Berceo's favorite epithets. Calisto's "reina y señora mía" ("my lady and queen") and "joya del mundo" ("rarest of jewels") echo Alfonso X's "Santa Reynna" ("Holy Queen"; 1986–89, no. 105.7) and "mui Preciosa" ("very Precious"; no. 106.15). It is possible to find other parallels of this type, but these suffice to make the point clear.[28]

Thus, Celestina is much more than a mere woman. Calisto is so gratified by her presence when he first meets her, that he kisses the ground on which she walks. Later he kneels before the old bawd when she brings him news of her successful "intercession" before his other goddess, Melibea: "Sube, sube, sube, y assiéntate, señora, que de rodillas quiero escuchar tu suave respuesta" ("Come up, come up, come up and sit down, my Lady, for I want to listen to your sweet report on my knees"; 180). Calisto's love infirmity and the madness associated with it help to explain his bizarre behavior,[29] but such manifestations of devotion are not usually rendered to other human beings. On one occasion, Calisto even tells Celestina that "en todo me pareces más que muger" ("in everything you do you seem to be more than a mere woman to me"; 183). Melibea implies something similar when she addresses her as "muger bien sabia y maestra grande" ("extremely wise woman and great teacher"; 241). Note that the litany also invokes the Virgin Mary as "Sedes sapientiae" ("Seat of wisdom"). Furthermore, when Calisto invites the procuress to his room to hear the tidings in detail, Pármeno complains about his master's intimate association with her by making the first of only three overt mentions of the name of the Blessed Mother in the entire work: "¡O santa María, y qué rodeos busca este loco por huyr de nosotros, para poder

Chapter Four

llorar a su plazer con Celestina de gozo, y por descubrirle mil secretos de su liviano y desvariado apetito . . . !" ("Oh, Holy Mary, how this madman beats around the bush in order to get away from us, so as to be able to weep for pleasure with Celestina as much as he wants, and to reveal a thousand secrets of his lascivious and raving appetite to her . . . !"; 180). As Calisto tells Celestina, Pármeno makes the sign of the cross over and over while uttering these words: "Mira, señora, qué hablar trae Pármeno, cómo se viene santiguando de oýr lo que has hecho de tu gran diligencia" ("Look, Madam, how Pármeno speaks and how much he crosses himself because he heard about what you have done with your great diligence!"; 180). Whatever the boy's real reason for performing this gesture may have been—rather than being astonished by the success of the old woman, as Calisto surmises, Pármeno may feel that he is in the presence of pure evil—Catholics also perform the same gesture before statues of St. Mary, whose name he had just pronounced, and Calisto goes on to kneel before her antithesis, Celestina. As Morón Arroyo indicated, "el caballero enamorado adora a la vieja como si fuera la Virgen" ("the enamored gentleman worships the old hag as if she were the Virgin"; 1984, 20).

Like the Blessed Mother, Celestina is also linked to the rosary. When the already corrupted Pármeno suggests to Sempronio that they look for the procuress in church before going to the great banquet that they had planned in her house, largely at the expense of their unwitting master, Sempronio replies that she could not possibly be there. According to him, Celestina goes to church only when there is not enough to eat in her house; she uses the rosary not to pray, but to count the maidens and lovers with whom she carries on her depraved dealings:

> Quando ay que roer en casa, sanos están los santos; quando va a la yglesia con sus cuentas en la mano, no sobra el comer en casa. Aunque ella te crió, mejor conozco yo sus proprietades que tú. Lo que en sus cuentas reza es los virgos que tiene a cargo y quántos enamorados ay en la cibdad, y quántas moças tiene encomendadas, y qué despenseros le dan ración y quál mejor, y cómo los llaman por nombre, porque quando los encontrare no hable como estraña, y qué canónigo es más moço y franco. (223 [33])

Anxious to show Pármeno, who was raised by Celestina, that he knew her very well himself, Sempronio exaggerates; in fact, she spends much time in churches, convents, and monasteries, where she conducts a great portion of her business. Nevertheless, a rosary in the hands of such an unrepentant old whore and procuress—there is no need to rely on Sempronio alone at this point, for Celestina herself had already mentioned it to Alisa (154)—

constitutes a profanation of the rosary, which is emblematic of the Blessed Mother. As Michael Ruggerio emphasized, "the go-between keeps track of virgins on her rosary beads. Since the rosary is a form of special devotion to the Virgin Mary, Rojas's point is clear" (1970, 57).

But the daring of Fernando de Rojas goes much further. Since many churches are especially dedicated to the Blessed Mother, bearing her name in one form or another—St. Mary's, Our Blessed Lady, Immaculate Conception, Our Lady of Sorrows, etc.—he decided that Celestina's house should also be the shrine of a cult where anti-Marian and anti-Christian rites are performed. The congregation is composed of the servant girls who apparently go there to practice their sewing under the direction of Celestina, the high priestess who uses her ability as master seamstress to cover her less honorable professions: "Era el primero officio cobertura de los otros, so color del qual muchas moças destas sirvientes entravan en su casa a labrarse y a labrar camisas y gorgueras y otras muchas cosas" ("Her first trade served as cover for the others, and because of it many of these young servant girls came to her house in order to get sewed and to sew nightshirts, ruffs, and many other things"; 110).

A seamstress uses the needle, a phallic symbol, in her profession. Celestina is a *labrandera* ("seamstress"), and the young girls who come to her house *a labrarse* ("to get sewed") go there in order to give up the virginity that the Blessed Mother represents and defends as "Mater purissima" ("Mother most pure"), "Mater castissima" ("Mother most chaste"), "Mater inviolata" ("Mother inviolate"), and especially as "Regina Virginum" ("Queen of Virgins"). Note that *labrar* also means "to plough," i. e., "to fornicate." The term was already used with identical meaning in ancient Greece.[30] "Labrar camisas" ("to sew shifts") alludes to the blood shed by the girls while losing their virginity, for "la camisa" ("the shift") also constitutes a reference to menstruation: "Estar la mujer con su camisa" ("a woman on her shift") is defined by Covarrubias as "estar con su regla o menstruo, porque no la ha de mudar hasta que de todo se le aya acabado la purgación; y las que por muy limpias lo han hecho, les ha costado caro y a muchas la vida" ("being with her period or menstruating, because she must not change it [her shift] until the bleeding has stopped. Many women did this because they were very clean, but it cost them dearly, and many paid for it with their lives"; 1994, 246).

The rest of the congregation is formed by the students, stewards, and clergymen's servants to whom she sells the virginity of the servant girls: "Assaz era amiga de studiantes y despenseros y moços de abades. A éstos vendía ella aquella sangre innocente de las cuytadillas, la cual ligeramente aventuravan en esfuerço de la restitución que ella les prometía" ("She was a very good friend of students, stewards, and clergymen's servants. To these she sold the innocent blood of the poor girls, who ventured it easily because she promised to restore their virginity"; 110).

The reference to the "sangre innocente" ("innocent blood") shed by Celestina's apprentices while being deflowered implies a sacrificial offering involving blood, an offering tantamount to an anti-Marian rite. This phrase also brings to mind the slaughter of the innocents by order of King Herod, who, hoping to catch the recently born Jesus, slew all the boys two years old and under in Bethlehem. Celestina is like him in a way, for she keeps a registry of all the girls who are born in her town (141). Unlike King Herod, however, she is not after a specific victim; the registry in question merely lets her know how many prospective followers escape from her net. In other words, she is after them all. Whereas the Blessed Mother would like each and every one of those maidens to remain pure, Celestina, her antithesis, does everything in her power to make sure they will not.

Celestina's apprentices, then, shed their innocent blood while being deflowered, a rite that is equivalent to the loss of their innocence and a simultaneous initiation into the anti-Marian cult presided over by Celestina. In their turn, these neophytes enable the high priestess to make new converts, attracting other girls—more closely guarded ones—to her flock; the latter are able to come to her shrine less frequently, however, because they can get away only late at night, a time that Rojas ironically designates as "tiempo honesto" ("a decent hour"; 110). They must have come in great numbers, for there were enough of them to hold stations, night processions, midnight and early morning masses, and other "secret devotions": "Subió su hecho a más: que por medio de aquellas, comunicava con las más encerradas, hasta traer a execución su propósito, y aquestas en tiempo honesto, como estaciones, processiones de noche, missas del gallo, missas del alva, y otras secretas devociones" ("But she went even further, for by means of these girls she communicated with others who were more closely guarded, and then she was able to execute her plans. They came at a decent hour, such as the time for the stations of the cross, night processions, midnight and early morning masses, and other secret devotions"; 110).

While it can be argued that the rituals being mocked used to occur in church rather than in Celestina's house, it seems to me that those ceremonies are characterized as "secret devotions" because they constitute metaphors for erotic activities that are unlikely to be held in church (see also Lacarra 1996, 426). Perhaps the girls involved here were more closely guarded because they belonged to a higher social class, and could escape only at night, when their parents slept. That is precisely what Melibea does later on, even though she does not need to go beyond her garden. The reference to "las más encerradas" ("those who were more closely guarded"), however, could also embody an allusion to the nuns who, imprisoned by watchful mother superiors, the walls of their convents, and the rules of their orders, could manage to escape only in the middle of the night.[31] If that is the case (and, as we shall see, there are other reasons to think that it could be), the heresy of the passage is compounded by the fact that nuns, while imitating the Blessed Mother in their virginity, are also considered to be brides of Christ.

Rojas seems to be expressing more than anti-Marian sentiments here. My interpretation is reinforced by Pármeno's claim, right after enumerating the ceremonies in question, to have seen many "encubiertas" ("covered women") enter Celestina's house. The sequence indicates that they are the more closely guarded young ladies whose secret affairs Pármeno had just mentioned.[32] Moreover, besides applying to girls who covered their faces so as not to be recognized, the term could also describe the habit worn by nuns, a habit that also covers their faces at least to some extent: "Muchas encubiertas vi entrar en su casa; tras ellas hombres descalços, contritos, y reboçados, desatacados, que entravan allí a llorar sus peccados" ("I saw many covered women enter her house, followed by barefoot, contrite men with their breeches open, who went there to weep their sins"; 110–11). The fact that the "encubiertas" are followed by monks who covered themselves up in a similar manner reinforces this interpretation even more. Note that "hombres descalzos" means not just barefooted men, for "descalzos" was also used to refer to monks who belonged to "órdenes de religiones que profesan andar descalzos" ("religious orders that vow to go barefoot"; Covarrubias 1994, 410). These monks pulled up the hoods of their habits in order to cover their faces ("rebozados"), so as not to be recognized, rather than as a sign of contrition, for they entered with their breeches already unfastened, eager to "weep"[33] for their "sins."[34] Although they had vowed chastity just like the nuns, their vows could not withstand the magnetic attraction of the lecherous cult headed by Celestina, who parodies the Virgin Mary's role as "Refugium peccatorum" ("Refuge of sinners") and "Consolatrix afflictorum" ("Comfort of the afflicted") in this context. Therefore, it would seem that the status of nuns, the brides of Christ who imitate the Blessed Mother in their purity, and the celibacy equally demanded of monks, who, in turn, imitate the chastity of Christ in this respect,[35] here become the object of a corrosive, systematic attack.

Unsatisfied with the size of her flock, which includes laity and clergy alike, Celestina labors constantly to attract more followers to her cult. That is why she is always visiting churches, convents, and monasteries. As Pármeno informs Calisto, "Con todos estos affanes, nunca passava sin missa ni bíspras ni dexaba monasterios de frayles ni de monjas; esto porque allí hazía ella sus aleluyas y conciertos" ("Despite all of these toils, she never

Chapter Four

went without Mass or Vespers services, or stayed away from monasteries or nunneries, because this is where she made arrangements for her merrymaking and trysts"; 111).[36]

This redoubles Celestina's heresy, for she focuses her attack precisely on the places of prayer of her rival religion, thereby insinuating that its members were only too ripe to fall into her clutches. Moreover, this activity brings to mind the fact that, although the Blessed Mother—"Virgo veneranda" ("Virgin most venerable") and "Vas insignis devotionis" ("Singular vessel of devotion") in her litany—has churches especially dedicated to her, she is also revered in all other churches as well as in convents and monasteries. Similarly, as high priestess of an antithetical cult, Celestina is able to inspire an inordinate amount of devotion in those very places. When Alisa asks her to pray for her sister, who is not feeling well, Celestina promises to charge the monks who are "devoted" to her to do so: "Yo te prometo, señora, en yendo de aquí me vaya por estos monesterios, donde tengo frayles devotos míos y les dé el mismo cargo que tú me das" ("I promise you, Madam, that when I leave here I will go from monastery to monastery, where I have friars devoted to me, and I will charge them with the same request"; 154). Thus, Celestina deceives Alisa with the truth, for the procuress did indeed visit those monasteries frequently.

Celestina does not claim that all the monks in the various monasteries are devoted to her, but she is obviously characterizing herself as a religious figure with a following of her own, for she has authority over her "devotos," i.e., those who belong to her cult. The analogy with the Blessed Mother becomes clearer when Celestina goes on to promise to give four turns to her own rosary: "Y demás desto, ante que me desayune, dé quatro bueltas a mis cuentas" ("Besides this, I will say my rosary four times over before breakfast"; 154).

Of course the procuress is being hypocritical in order to ingratiate herself with Alisa, whose daughter she intends to corrupt. As high priestess of an anti-Christian cult, she certainly does not plan to tell the monks to say the kind of prayers that Alisa hopes for, and even less to repeat them herself with the rosary that she uses as cover. Celestina's hypocrisy, however, does not detract from the interpretation posited here. She is able to inspire inordinate devotion on the part of many monks in various monasteries because those monks are also hypocrites of the same order, whose miracle worker is Celestina.

Consequently, it is not surprising that Celestina should be accorded equal devotion elsewhere, in a perverse parallel of the reverence of Christians for the Blessed Mother. Note how much havoc she could provoke upon entering church a few years earlier, when she was even more powerful:[37]

> En entrando por la yglesia, vía derrocar bonetes en mi honor como si yo fuera una duquesa. El que menos avía que negociar conmigo, por más ruyn se tenía. De media legua que me viessen dexavan las horas; uno a uno y dos a dos venían a donde yo estava, a ver si mandava algo, a preguntarme cada uno por la suya. Que hombre avía, que estando diziendo missa, en viéndome entrar se turbavan, que no hazían ni dezían cosa a derechas. Unos me llamaban señora, otros tía, otros enamorada, otros vieja honrrada. Allí[38] se concertavan sus venidas a mi casa, allí las ydas a la suya. Allí se me offrescían dineros, allí promessas, allí otras dádivas, besando el cabo de mi manto, y aun algunos en la cara por me tener más contenta. (235 [34])

As is so often the case in *La Celestina*, this passage can be read on more than one level. The procuress compares herself to a duchess when, though already old, she was still in her golden days, because her influence was at its zenith. As she herself had stated before, her power derived from the fact that the great number of girls under her command paid her total obedience, sleeping with whomever she dictated: "no escogían más de lo que les mandava: coxo o tuerto o manco, aquél avían por sano que más dinero me dava" ("they chose only as I told them—lame, one-eyed, or maimed. To them, the healthiest was the one who brought me more profit"; 235). Every man wanted to be in her good graces because of her role as mediator. This explanation, however, is not enough to justify all the havoc that her entrance caused. When she came in, men forgot that church is a place of worship, focusing all of their attention on her. She became the main object of their devotion, displacing God in his own house. The rapture that she provoked therefore elevated her into the category of a divine, anti-Christian figure. Promises were made to her, and some "devotos" even went to the point of kissing the hem of her mantle. It goes without saying that such manifestations of devotion could be equally directed to the Virgin Mary.

Celestina's power, then, extended far beyond the whorehouse that Rojas depicts as a shrine, the main temple of a cult with numerous lay and clerical followers drawn from the churches, convents, and monasteries in the whole city. That is why, when she returned home, the clergy hurried to bring her part of the tithes paid to their churches—chickens and hens, geese and ducks, etc.—so that she and the girls with whom she served them could eat well: "Cada qual como lo recibía de aquellos diezmos de Dios, assí lo venían luego a registrar para que comiesse yo y aquellas sus devotas" ("As they received those blessed tithes, they brought them to my house, so that I and their lasses could eat well"; 236). Priests who could not afford to be as generous never failed to send her loaves of votive bread as soon as they received it: "Pues otros curas sin renta, no era offreçido el bodigo quando en besando el feligrés

Chapter Four

la stola era de primero boleo en mi casa" ("Other priests, without income, upon receiving a loaf of church bread and the parishioners who offered it had kissed their stole, brought it to my house as soon as they could"; 236).

Celestina regretfully admits that, now that she is older, she is no longer capable of commanding such devotion. Her business no longer prospers. Some might object that if she were really being portrayed as a divine figure, her power would never decline. Despite everything that the antithetical nature of her character implies, however, Celestina remains a mere human being. If Rojas had carried the analogy to its ultimate consequences, he would have had to make her immortal.

Notwithstanding her painful decline, Celestina's powers are still formidable, for she is implicitly rendered into a goddess of sorts on no less than three additional occasions. When Sempronio leaves to call her for the first time, Calisto compares her to the Messiah, asking God to lead his servant to her as he had guided the Three Wise Men to Bethlehem with the star: "¡O todopoderoso, perdurable Dios, tú que guías los perdidos, y los reyes orientales por el estrella precedente a Bethleén truxiste y en su patria los reduxiste, húmilmente te ruego que guíes a mi Sempronio, en manera que convierta mi pena y tristeza en gozo, y yo indigno meresca venir en el desseado fin" ("Oh almighty and perdurable God, Thee who guides the steps of lost souls and guided the Eastern kings to Bethlehem with the star, leading them back to their countries, I humbly beg you to guide my Sempronio so that he may turn my suffering and sadness into joy, and bring me, albeit unworthy, to my desired goal"; 104).

The heresy of this prayer[39] is compounded by Calisto's reference to the fact that God helps "los perdidos," but God guides lost souls away from sin, not in ways that would lead them to sin even more, and Calisto, who lusts for Melibea, hopes to cure his "illness" with the assistance of Celestina. Thus, Calisto sees Celestina as his "Savior." Christ redeemed humanity from sin through his death on the cross; Celestina, on the other hand, will "cure" Calisto's sin of lust by making Melibea available to him. Although this passage depicts the old bawd like another messiah, being a woman, she is more like a goddess. In Catholicism, the figure who comes closest to such an entity is the Virgin Mary. Rojas may therefore have been suggesting that the cult of the Blessed Mother had reached such proportions that it had come to rival that of her Son, the Messiah, in Catholic devotion. I have not been able to find any contemporary Christian documents that support this deduction, but Erasmus suggests as much in *The Praise of Folly*, written just a few years later (1509): "Some saints have a variety of powers, especially the virgin mother of God, to whom the ordinary run of men attribute more almost than to her son" (1979, 65).

Celestina as an Antithesis of the Blessed Mother

The text also implies the elevation of Celestina to divine status when Pármeno informs Calisto that every person, animal, instrument, rock, or anything capable of producing a sound by which she passes calls her an old whore:

> Si entre cient mugeres va y alguno dize "¡Puta vieja!," sin ningún empacho luego vuelve la cabeça y responde con alegre cara. En los combites, en las fiestas, en las bodas, en las confadrías, en los mortuorios, en todos los ayuntamientos de gentes, con ella passan tiempo. Si passa por los perros, aquello suena su ladrido; si está cerca las aves, otra cosa no cantan; si cerca los ganados, balando lo pregonan; si cerca las bestias, rebuznando dizen: "¡Puta vieja!"; las ranas de los charcos otra cosa no suelen mentar. Si va entre los herreros, aquello dizen sus martillos; carpinteros y armeros, herradores, caldereros, arcadores, todo officio de instrumento forma en el ayre su nombre. Cántanla los carpinteros, péynanla los peynadores, texedores; labradores en las huertas, en las aradas, en las viñas, en las segadas con ella passan el afán cotidiano; al perder en los tableros, luego suenan sus loores. Todas cosas que son hazen, a doquiera que ella está, el tal nombre representan. ¡O qué comedor de huevos assados era su marido! Qué quieres más, sino que, si una piedra topa con otra, luego suena "¡Puta vieja!" (108–09 [35])

According to Gustavo Correa, this portrait of Celestina constitutes a parody of the song of nature and all creatures to their Creator. Correa goes on to give the following selections from Psalm 19 as examples: "Los cielos pregonan la gloria de Dios y el firmamento anuncia la obra de sus manos . . . su pregón sale por la tierra toda y sus palabras llegan a los confines del orbe y de la tierra . . . " ("The Heavens declare the glory of God and the firmament proclaims his handiwork . . . through all the earth, their voice resounds, and to the ends of the world, their message"; 1962, 11–12n18). But since what is being celebrated here is the glory of God as proclaimed by the heavens, Pármeno's portrait is much closer to Psalm 148, where everything in Creation, including the animals and birds missing in Psalm 19, is exhorted to praise the name of the Lord, just as everyone or everything capable of making a sound called Celestina an "old whore":

I

1 Praise the Lord from the heavens,
 praise him in the heights;
2 Praise him, all you his angels,
 praise him, all you his hosts.
3 Praise him, sun and moon;
 praise him, all you shining stars.

Chapter Four

> 4 Praise him, you highest heavens,
>   and you waters above the heavens.
> 5 Let them praise the name of the LORD,
>   for he commanded and they were created;
> 6 He established them forever and ever;
>   he gave them a duty which shall not pass away.
>
> II
>
> 7 Praise the LORD from the earth,
>   you sea monsters and all depths;
> 8 Fire and hail, snow and mist,
>   storm winds that fulfill his word;
> 9 You mountains and you hills,
>   you fruit trees and all you cedars;
> 10 You wild beasts and all tame animals,
>   you creeping things and you winged fowl.
>
> III
>
> 11 Let the kings of the earth and all peoples,
>   the princes and all the judges of the earth,
> 12 Young men too, and maidens,
>   old men and boys,
> 13 Praise the name of the LORD,
>   for his name alone is exalted;
> 14 His majesty is above earth and heaven,
>   and he has lifted up the horn of his people.
>   Be this praise from all his faithful ones,
>   from the children of Israel, the people
>   close to him. Alleluia.

Whatever the specific source for Pármeno's discourse might be, if there is one, his characterization of Celestina certainly has the earmarks of a song of praise. It would seem that, through the utilization of what amounts to a psalm to sing the "praises" of Celestina—according to Pármeno, she loved to be called "¡Puta vieja!" ("Old whore"), taking it as a compliment—Rojas perversely compared her wide appeal to that of a divinity. Once again, Rojas was thinking of the Blessed Mother, implicitly suggesting that her cult, besides rivaling the devotion to her Son, also competed with the cult to God the Father, the God of the Old Testament.

Rojas compounded these blasphemies by the manner in which he emphasized the great popularity that Celestina enjoyed. Men gathered at banquets, parties, weddings, brotherhoods, and funerals "con ella passan tiempo" ("spend time with her"; 108), and farmers otherwise occupied in gardens and fields, vineyards or the harvest "con ella passan el afán cotidiano" ("pass their daily toil with her"; 109). There is much more involved here than just calling her an old whore. Notwithstanding all of this incredible, superhuman activity, she is so insatiable that her now deceased husband had to rebuild his strength constantly by eating many "huevos asados" ("roasted bull's testicles") in order to keep up with her.[40] Nowadays, we would describe such a woman as an insatiable nymphomaniac. Rojas had the audacity to create her as an antithesis of the Blessed Mother.

The text compares Celestina to a divinity on a third occasion. Overwhelmed by the news that Melibea has agreed to an interview with him in her garden at midnight—a propitious, revealing timing, not to say anything about what her "garden" implies in itself—Calisto declares himself unworthy of such good fortune, and Celestina brags that, even if he happened to lack everything that is required in a lover, she would have surmounted every obstacle on his behalf with the following words: "Mira, mira, que está Celestina de tu parte, y que aunque todo te faltasse lo que en un enamorado se requiere, te vendería por el más acabado galán del mundo, que te[41] haría llanas las peñas para andar; que te haría las más creçidas aguas corrientes passar sin mojarte. Mal conoces a quien das tu[42] dinero" ("Look, look, Celestina is on your side, and even if you lacked everything that a lover ought to have, she could still sell you as the most accomplished beau in the world. She would smooth the crags before your step, and cause swollen waters to flow by you without your becoming wet. You do not know well to whom you are giving your money"; 252).

This constitutes a clear reference to the parting of the Red Sea, a miracle performed by God. In this instance, Celestina is claiming divine power for herself. This may be seen as an exaggeration on her part, a product of the great pride that she feels for having succeeded with Melibea,[43] but, as the analogies previously made by Calisto and Pármeno demonstrate, this choice of words is hardly a matter of pure coincidence. There is no question that Celestina is implicitly equating her powers to God's and that, being a woman, her closest parallel is the Virgin.

According to Catholic theology, the Blessed Mother remained pure despite the fact that she gave birth to Christ: *ante partum*, *in partu*, and *post partum* (before, during, and after giving birth; see the *New Catholic Encyclopedia* [1967], 9: 223*b*). Hence her promotion of chastity. This is mirrored in two of her titles, "Sancta Virgo virginum" ("Holy Virgin of virgins") and "Regina virginum" ("Queen of virgins"). As her antithesis, Celestina is an arch whore whose main purpose is to destroy virginity. According to Sempronio, we recall, "Lo que en sus cuentas reza es los virgos que tiene a cargo" ("What she prays with her beads is the number of virgins in her charge"; 223). Her house is really a shrine, a temple of lust where her young apprentices, besides giving up their "innocent blood," attract others to the cult over which she presides.

Celestina, who is capable of provoking lust even in rocks, has been extremely successful in that capacity. According to Sempronio, she is responsible for the defloration and subsequent "restoration" of more than

Chapter Four

five thousand virgins in the city in which she lives: "passan de cinco mil virgos los que se han hecho y deshecho por su autoridad en esta cibdad. A las duras peñas promeverá y provocará a luxuria, si quiere" ("the number of virgins that have been made and unmade thanks to her in this city surpasses five thousand. If she wishes, she can cause rocks and crags to melt with lust"; 103). As she boasts to Sempronio, she is the broker for practically every girl who "opens up shop," i.e., for maidens who have reached an age appropriate to engage in sex; as soon as a girl is born, Celestina has her name inscribed in her registry so as to keep track of the few who escape from her net: "Pocas virgines, a Dios gracias, has tú visto en esta ciudad que hayan abierto tienda a vender, de quien yo no haya sido corredora de su primer hilado. En nasciendo la mochacha, la hago scrivir en mi registro, y esto para que yo sepa quántas se me salen de la red" ("Few virgins, thank God, have opened up shop in this town without me brokering their first yarn. As soon as a baby girl is born, I have her name written in my register, so as to know how many escape my net"; 141).

Although Celestina needs to earn her way, this would also seem to constitute a determined, systematic attack on the virginity simultaneously represented and promoted by the figure of the Blessed Mother. As Esperanza Gurza perceived, "Celestina, la descendida del cielo, la angélica, produce siempre efectos contrarios: arruina doncellas empujándolas a la prostitución y las lleva a ellas y a sus amantes a una esclavitud de la cual nunca podrán redimirse" ("Celestina, though descended from Heaven and angelical, always causes the opposite: she ruins young girls by pushing them into prostitution, and leads them and their lovers to a bondage from which they can never be redeemed"; 1977, 294).

The parody of the Marian cult, then, is really multifaceted. Celestina's role as an arch whore is a direct, blasphemous parody of Mary's perpetual virginity as defined by the Catholic Church; her amazing success in the systematic defloration of the maidens in town constitutes a reversal of the chastity encouraged as an imitation of the Blessed Mother. Rojas ridicules the idea of virginity even more through Celestina's technical ability to restore deflowered maidens to their original status: "Esto de los virgos, unos hazía de bexiga y otros curava de punto" ("Regarding maidenheads, some she made of bladder, others she sewed up"; 112). There is a second level of irony even here, for the stitches ("puntos") are also made with the yarn (semen) that she sells as an excuse to get into other people's homes, conveniently rolled up into "madejas" ("testicles"), and the needle (phallus).[44] Celestina is so proficient in this capacity of "maestra . . . de hazer virgos" ("expert . . . in making virgins"; 110) that she was able to deceive a high ranking specialist like the French ambassador no fewer than three times with the same girl, selling her to him as a virgin on each occasion: "quando vino por aquí el embaxador francés, tres vezes vendió por virgen una criada que tenía" ("when the French ambassador was here, she sold him the same maid as a virgin three times"; 112).

The implication is that virginity does not really matter, for it can be easily "restored." Once lost, however, the virginity with which the maidens parallel the Blessed Mother's exalted status can never be regained. That is why Melibea complains to Calisto that he has caused her to lose "el nombre y corona de virgen por tan breve deleyte" ("the name and crown of a virgin for such a brief pleasure"; 286). At this point, Rojas is also alluding to the Holy Virgin, because, as Queen of Heaven, Mary was already portrayed with a crown in medieval iconography (see Pelikan 1978, 168–69).

Celestina's role as a procuress constitutes another perversion of the Marian cult. As Mediatrix and Coredemptrix, the Blessed Mother helps souls to reach heaven; Celestina, on the other hand, "exists because men create paradises of their fantasies and require them to be made of flesh; she is their 'celestial' broker" (Dunn 1976b, 414). As Calisto informs Pármeno, he needs an "intercessor o medianero" ("intercessor or mediator"; 134) in order to reach his objective. At one point, Melibea also refers to Celestina as "medianera de mi salud" ("mediator of my health"; 238). Thus, the old bawd "tiene en el texto la función de la Virgen en la salvación del cristiano" ("has in the text the same function as the Virgin in the salvation of the Christian world"; Morón Arroyo 1984, 19).

It could be argued here that any procuress is a mediator because of the very nature of her profession, and that this is probably the most important factor in the creation of Celestina as an antithesis of the Virgin Mary. This central coincidence, however, does not detract from my thesis, for Rojas adorned the old bawd with many additional correspondences that are not essential to her role as a procuress. Some of those parodic parallelisms have already been indicated, but there are even more. Once they are examined, there should remain little or no doubt that this crucial, coincidental aspect of Celestina's figure is rendered into a deliberate parody of the role of the Virgin as Mediatrix.

Catholic theologians emphasize that Mary's mediation is "wholly dependent on Christ's" (*New Catholic Encyclopedia* 1967, 9: 359). In other words, she intercedes for men before her Son. As stated by Gonzalo de Berceo in plain, uncomplicated language for the sake of the layman,

> Como es la Gloriosa   plena de bendición,
> es plena de gracia,   e quïta de dición;
> no.l seríe negada   ninguna petición,
> no li diçríe tal Fijo   a tal Madre de non.

(1987, c. 181 [36])

Chapter Four

Celestina does precisely the opposite, for she uses the devil in order to help her customers reach the carnal paradise that they desire. As priestess of her own cult, she conjures him through the Black Mass that she celebrates in the whorehouse that, as we have seen, in Pármeno's eyes also represents a kind of church.

While preparing for this diabolical perversion of the central part of the Christian Mass, Celestina orders Elicia to bring her "la sangre del cabrón, y unas poquitas de las barvas que tú le cortaste" ("blood of the he-goat and some of the whiskers you cut from him"; 147). As Mac Barrick showed in a splendid article, the goat, being one of the most incontinent animals in nature, symbolizes lust as well as the devil. The possession of the clippings from its beard "implies a magic power over the animal from which they came and over the Devil which he represents" (1977, 12), and the blood of the goat parodies the wine that, through Transubstantiation, according to Catholic doctrine, is transformed into the blood of Christ during Mass. Note that Catholicism stresses a real rather than a symbolic or spiritual presence in the Eucharist. Through this blood Celestina conjures the devil instead, commanding him, as if he were physically there, to get into the yarn that she plans to use as an excuse to enter into Melibea's house. This diabolical ceremony, which parodies part of the Christian Mass, could also embody a simultaneous attack on and denial of the doctrine of transubstantiation, a central dogma in Catholicism.

Celestina certainly believes in the effectiveness of the rite that she has performed, for she concludes it with the following words: "assí confiando en mi mucho poder, me parto para allá con mi hilado, donde creo te llevo ya embuelto" ("and so, very confident in my great power, I shall leave for that place with the yarn where I think, [oh Devil,] I've already got you entangled"; 148). When Melibea becomes angry with her upon hearing Calisto's name, Celestina exhorts the devil in the yarn to do the job that he is supposed to perform: "¡Ce, hermano, que se va todo a perder!" ("Come on, brother, or everything is lost!"; 162). Upon leaving, she credits him with her success: "¡O diablo a quien yo conjuré, cómo compliste tu palabra en todo lo que te pedí!" ("Oh Devil whom I conjured up, you kept your word in everything I asked of you!"; 171). And when Sempronio sees her on the way back, he makes the sign of the cross, for, despite all of his previous dealings with Celestina, he senses now the presence of something truly evil. Rather than taking offense at his reaction, Celestina understands it perfectly well: "¿De qué te santiguas, Sempronio? Creo que en verme" ("What are you crossing yourself for, Sempronio? I think it's because you see me"; 172). As already indicated, Pármeno makes the same gesture over and over when Calisto invites Celestina to his room in order to receive the news of her successful intervention in great detail.

Celestina as an Antithesis of the Blessed Mother

The devil had indeed performed the task for which he had been summoned. When Celestina arrives at her destination, Alisa decides to visit her sister who was ill with a mere backache as soon as she touches the yarn, imprudently leaving her daughter alone with the old bawd, despite the fact that Celestina's reputation was well known. As Alan Deyermond pointed out, "the only possible explanation . . . is that the Devil was in the skein and that at the slightest contact he has taken possession of Alisa's judgement and will" (1977, 7).[45] The devil also takes possession of Melibea, "inflaming her with desire for Calisto" (1977, 7). Although the rope belt was reputed to have touched "todas las reliquias que ay en Roma y Hierusalem" ("all the relics in Rome and Jerusalem"; 164), Celestina's persuasion combined with the power of her helper are much greater than those holy relics, for the belt fails to protect Melibea. The relics in which medieval Christians placed so much faith turn out to be utterly useless. Thus, when Melibea surrenders the belt to Celestina as a cure for Calisto's "toothache" ("a metaphor for sexual arousal, we recall), she is also surrendering the chastity that it represents (see Weinberg 1971, 136, and Dunn 1976b, 414).[46] As Deyermond suggested, the devil may have indeed passed from Melibea's body to her rope belt (1977, 8). Celestina addresses it as if it possessed an independent life of its own ("¡Ay cordón, cordón! yo te haré traer por fuerça, si bivo, a la que no quiso darme su buena habla de grado" [Oh rope belt, rope belt! If I live I will force you to bring me that silly girl who refused to speak civilly with me"; 172]), and Calisto does the same thing ("O cordón, cordón, ¿fuísteme tú enemigo? Dilo cierto . . . . Conjúrote me respondas por la virtud del gran poder que aquella señora sobre mí tiene" ["Oh, rope belt, rope belt! Were you my enemy? Tell me for sure . . . . I conjure you to answer by virtue of the great power that lady has over me"; 187), going into a frenzy as soon as he touches it. Sickened by this fetichism, Celestina tells him to control himself, and Sempronio goes on to say that Calisto is enjoying the rope belt so much that he probably will no longer need Melibea: "Señor, por holgar con el cordón, no querrás gozar de Melibea" ("Sir, you are having so much fun with the rope belt that you will no longer want to enjoy Melibea"; 188). Love was believed to induce madness in the lover, but the rapture that Calisto feels upon touching an object that had hugged Melibea's body so intimately is insufficient to explain such a reaction. The devil's work had indeed gone far beyond the specific task for which he had been summoned.[47]

The Blessed Mother endeavors to take the faithful to heaven with the help of her Son; one of her titles is "Janua coeli" ("Gate of Heaven"). Celestina, besides parodying her role as Mediatrix, assists those who fall into her clutches to reach a carnal paradise with the assistance of the antithesis of Christ, the devil, whom she summons in cases that are especially difficult, such as Melibea's.

Chapter Four

The idea of paradise is put forth through the polysemous nature of the garden where Calisto and Melibea make love. Melibea describes it to him in the following manner:

> Mira la luna, quán clara se nos muestra. Mira las nuves cómo huyen. Oye la corriente agua desta fontesica, quánto más suave murmurio y zurrío lleva por entre las frescas yervas. Escucha los altos cipresses, cómo se dan paz unos ramos con otros por intercessión de un templadico viento que los menea. Mira sus quietas sombras, quán escuras están y aparejadas para encobrir nuestro deleyte. (322–23 [37])

This idealized description first brings to mind the topical *locus amoenus*.[48] Since it is a garden, it also evokes paradise, because gardens were often used as symbols of paradise in medieval literature: "essendo il Paradiso un giardino, un giardino poteva essere denominato paradiso" ("since Paradise was a garden, a garden could also be called paradise"; Del Monte 1970, 110). Note that Calisto had already referred to that garden as a paradise: "De día estaré en mi cámara, de noche en aquel paraýso dulce, en aquel alegre vergel, entre aquellas suaves plantas y fresca verdura" ("By day I'll stay in my room, by night in that sweet paradise, that happy garden, among those gentle plants and that cool verdure"; 292). Calisto could be using "paraýso" as a metaphor for "great happiness" or something of the sort, but there is no doubt that Melibea's "huerto" is another Garden of Eden, for it is the place where she and Calisto taste of the forbidden fruit, i.e., sex without the sanction of marriage. Morón Arroyo saw this clearly as well: "El amor se consuma en el paraíso" ("Love is consummated in paradise"; 1984, 49).

The walls that surround the garden suggest several additional meanings. Besides "serving as a moral obstacle ("ignored") to both Melibea's and Calisto's lust for one another" (Barbera 1970, 8), the wall renders the garden into a fortress to be besieged, a *hortus conclusus* ("enclosed garden") that represents the chastity (Del Monte 1970, 112) or virginity that Melibea still shares with the Blessed Mother. Furthermore, in medieval Christian art the enclosed garden was also emblematic of the Virgin Mary (Weinberg 1971, 143), standing for her perpetual virginity.[49] The idea was that, in her purity, Mary was like a fortress, a garden whose walls had not been breached despite the fact that she had conceived Christ, thus retaining her virginity. Since Calisto manages to penetrate this garden, the blasphemy is clear.

The ladder that Calisto must use to scale the walls conveys yet another symbolic meaning, for it is an antithesis of the ladder whose rungs represented the virtues needed to reach heaven in medieval iconography (Barbera 1970, 11–12).[50] Therefore, this garden is also an allegory of the spiritual Christian heaven for which the terrestrial Garden of Eden stood in the first place. Notwithstanding the moral obstacle and the chastity represented by its walls, Calisto simultaneously penetrates the "huerto" that constitutes "a widespread euphemism for the female sexual organs" (Weinberg 1971, 138), the Garden of Eden, and the Christian heaven inhabited by the Christian God and his saints, as well as by the Blessed Mother, whose perpetual virginity the *hortus conclusus* ("enclosed garden") also represents. The penetration of Melibea's "huerto" would therefore seem to embody another inversion of the values of the Marian cult.

Celestina, who is both associated with and described as a snake, makes possible Calisto's and Melibea's initial tryst in the garden. Together with coals of foals and babies and ropes from hanged men, vipers tongues, "a substance associated with uncontrollable sexual desire" (Weiner 1969, 394), constitute one of the many revolting ingredients that she stores for her witchcraft (112). The serpent, of course, also represents the devil, being associated with lust as well.[51] After Celestina conjures him in the Black Mass, commanding him to get into the yarn, she proceeds to anoint it with snake's oil, a poisonous liquid believed to be endowed "de fuerza diabólica especial debido a la tradicional afición del demonio a disfrazarse de serpiente" ("with special diabolic power due to the devil's special inclination to disguise himself as a serpent"; Russell 1978, 260). Its effectiveness is confirmed when Melibea, already inflamed with lust for Calisto, complains to Celestina, from whom she seeks a cure for her affliction, "que me comen este coraçón serpientes dentro de mi cuerpo" ("vipers within my body devour my heart"; 239). Besides being linked with this oil, Celestina herself is described as a serpent by Sempronio, who, while realizing how dangerous she really is, fails to heed his own advice to stay away from her: "Mala vieja, falsa es ésta; el diablo me metió con ella. Más seguro me fuera huyr desta venenosa bívora que tomalla" ("This old crone is false and evil; the devil mixed me up with her. It would be safer for me to run away from this poisonous snake than to try to control her"; 174). Thanks to her viper's tongue she is also a temptress (see Ayerbe-Chaux 1978), just like the devil who, disguised as a serpent, caused Adam and Eve to taste the forbidden fruit in the Garden of Eden. Ironically, it is Celestina herself who, while tempting Melibea, alludes to that very role of the devil, a role that she is in the very process of duplicating: "¿y no sabes que por la divina boca fue dicho, contra aquel infernal tentador, que no de sólo pan biviriemos?" ("and don't you know what that divine mouth said against that tempting devil, that man shall not live by bread alone?"; 158). Obviously, these words of Christ are being placed in a distorted, perverse context, for Celestina uses them in order to convince Melibea to make love with Calisto.

Although the serpent represents the devil, the antithesis of Christ, it is an antipathy of the Blessed Mother as well. The Virgin has been viewed in Catholic theology as a New Eve "who repaired by her obedience what the first Eve had devastated by her disobedience" (*New Catholic Encyclopedia* [1967], 9: 355). This analogy was common enough in Spain. As Gerli indicated, the "tipología que ligaba la Virgen a Eva era tan difundida durante la Edad Media que llegó a constituirse en torno a ella una especie de paronomasia anagramática entre la clerecía. Sabemos que la dualidad Ave/ Eva, Eva/Ave se conocía en la España del siglo XIII" ("typology that connected the Virgin to Eve was so current during the Middle Ages that a sort of anagram-like play on words related to it came to develop among the clergy. We know that the dualism Ave/Eva and Eva/Ave was known in thirteenth-century Spain"; 1985, 8). Together with her Son, the New Adam, she crushed the head of Satan (the serpent), enabling man to enter paradise once again (*New Catholic Encyclopedia* [1967], 9: 353). Celestina is her antithesis in this context because she also represents the snake whose head Mary crushed.

The forbidden fruit is Melibea who, notwithstanding her impure thoughts, resembles the Blessed Mother in her virginity, and is placed within the walls of the *hortus conclusus* ("enclosed garden"), which, as we have seen, stands for Mary's perpetual virginity, the Garden of Eden, as well as for heaven itself.

The pleasures available to Calisto and Melibea in their carnal paradise parallel the glory that the souls of the redeemed experience in heaven. When Melibea tells Lucrecia to move aside before surrendering to Calisto, he protests that he would like others to witness his "glory": "Bien me huelgo que estén semejantes testigos de mi gloria" ("I am glad to have such witnesses to my glory"; 285).[52] Rojas was merely following tradition in the sense that this "glory," which also stands for the orgasm that Calisto achieves by penetrating another sort of paradise, Melibea's "huerto," was a widely used metaphor in the love poetry of the period (Whinnom 1981b, 41–43).[53] Pármeno's reaction after sleeping with Areúsa thanks to the mediation of Celestina,[54] however, suggests that the very act of sexual intercourse enables one to achieve such glory: "Quál hombre es ni ha sido más bienaventurado que yo . . . O alto Dios, ¿a quién contaría yo este gozo? . . . ¿A quién daré parte de mi gloria?" ("What man is or has ever been more blessed than I? . . . Almighty God, to whom could I recount this joy? . . . with whom shall I share my glory?"; 212). Although Melibea's garden, being an allegory, constitutes the most complete representation of paradise, the implication is that paradise can be replicated wherever the forbidden fruit, copulation without the sanction of marriage, is enjoyed. Obviously, there are many such paradises; only the resulting "gozo" ("pleasure") and "gloria" ("glory") remain constant. As an antithesis of the Blessed Mother, Celestina specializes in leading her followers to those perverted paradises.

Since Melibea's garden is more specifically designed as a paradise, it is particularly fitting that Calisto should reenact Adam's fall as a punishment for his transgression. During one of his trysts with Melibea, he hears a noise and decides to leave momentarily in order to assist Sosia and Tristán, the two young servants who had accompanied him after Pármeno's and Sempronio's demise, falling to his death from the top of the ladder that, having been used to sin, can be safely presumed to possess "rungs of the vices rather than the virtues" (Barbera 1970, 12).

According to Jack Weiner's splendid article, Calisto's fall concludes the allegorical parallels between Melibea's garden and the Garden of Eden: "Having transgressed God's law, he falls from his garden of paradise, literally and figuratively" (1969, 396). Those parallels, however, will come to an end only when Melibea is equally cast out of paradise.

Unwilling to go on living without her lover, Melibea commits suicide by jumping off a tower before her father's eyes. This tower "duplicates the symbolism of the garden surrounded by a high wall. . . . Like the enclosed garden, it is emblematic of the Virgin Mary" (Weinberg 1971, 143), i.e., of her perpetual virginity. In her litany, Mary is called "Turris Davitica" ("Tower of David") and "Turris eburnea" ("Tower of Ivory"). In a way, then, Melibea's suicide represents a rejection of the Blessed Mother. Chastity had become meaningless to her, and she prefers to follow her lover even in death. Note that, notwithstanding their phallic symbolism (Deyermond 1991, 104–05), towers are associated with chastity and enforced marital fidelity in literature and folklore (D. Hook 1978, 29). Finally, the tower parallels the ladder that caused Calisto's accidental death, for towers "expressed the same symbolism as the ladder—linking earth and heaven" (Cirlot 1972, 345). Melibea's suicide, therefore, also represents her fall from paradise.[55] The parallels with the Garden of Eden are now complete.

Calisto dies with the following words on his lips: "¡O válame Santa María, muerto soy! ¡Confessión!" ("Oh, may the Holy Mary help me! I'm dying! Confession!"; 326). Ironically, he calls upon the Virgin while falling from the garden where he had taken Melibea's virginity, the profaned *hortus conclusus* ("enclosed garden") that is also emblematic of Mary's perpetual virginity. Having sinned, he does not belong in paradise, and reenacts the fate of Adam by falling to his death. His cry for confession seems to be more motivated by fear than by any real contrition. From a Christian point of view, Calisto's dying words could also be interpreted as evidence of last minute repentance for the sin of fornication that he was committing just before the accident, leading to the argument that it is impossible for the reader to determine God's judgment in the matter (see Deyermond 1984). The opinion of the other characters, however—and their reaction is all we have to go by— would seem to indicate otherwise. Tristán exclaims: "O triste muerte y sin confessión!" ("Oh, what a sad death, and without confession"; 327),[56] and Melibea also emphasizes that Calisto's life was cut short, without confession:

Chapter Four

"Cortaron las hadas sus hilos, cortáranle sin confessión su vida" ("Fate cut through his thread, his life was cut without confession"; 334). As Anne Eesley stated, such a death meant "a sure descent into hell" (1983, 19). Consequently, there can be no doubt as to the fate Rojas assigned to his hero in the afterlife. Since confession is a Christian sacrament, Calisto is thrown into a Christian hell.[57]

Before committing suicide, Melibea compounds her sin by falling into the blasphemy of trying to justify herself before God, as if attempting to convince him to change his law in order to forgive her for taking her own life. She deems herself helpless, unable to proceed in any other manner, because her physical love for her deceased Calisto is stronger than the love that she feels for the parents whom she is about to abandon so cruelly: "Tú, Señor, que de mi habla eres testigo, ves mi poco poder, ves quán cativa tengo mi libertad, quán presos mis sentidos de tan poderoso amor del muerto cavallero, que priva al que tengo con los bivos padres" ("Lord, Thou who are witness to my words can see my frailty, how captive is my will, how my senses are imprisoned by such a powerful love for the dead gentleman, and how this deprives me of my sense of duty to my parents, who are alive"; 332). As she jumps from the tower, she offers her soul to God ("A Él offrezco mi alma" ["To Him I offer my soul"; 335]), committing an additional blasphemy in the process, for Christianity teaches that only God has the right to take away the life that he gives. As a suicide, she is automatically condemned to the Christian hell to which Calisto has already gone (Rodríguez Puértolas 1996, 44–45).

A summary of the main points made thus far is needed to demonstrate that the parallels brought together do not constitute a matter of pure coincidence. The very meaning of the old bawd's name, "little celestial one," suggests that she is some sort of heavenly figure. Practically everyone who addresses her in the text calls her mother, and many of the titles used by the Catholic Church to designate the Virgin are applied to Celestina, who is also associated with the rosary. Calisto goes to the point of kneeling before her. Like a church especially dedicated to the Virgin, her house is designed as the shrine of a cult where many maidens give up their virginity under her direction as high priestess, shedding their innocent, virginal blood in initiations that amount to anti-Marian rites. This shrine is also attended by monks, who thus betray the chastity that they had vowed to maintain. To enlarge her flock even more, Celestina is always visiting churches, convents and monasteries, focusing her attack precisely on the consecrated places of prayer of a rival religion that placed such a premium on virginity, chastity, and celibacy, elevating them into its highest virtues. Like the Blessed Mother, she is revered everywhere. Upon entering church during the peak of her power, she provoked such rapture that she became the main object of the reverence of the faithful, displacing God in their devotion. To make the analogy of her house as a special shrine even more complete, Celestina received part of the tithes paid to the churches in the city. Clergymen are among her best customers.[58]

The exalted status of the Blessed Mother in the Catholic Church causes the old bawd to be more specifically linked with God on three additional occasions. Calisto refers to her as another messiah, God the Son, when he prays to God the Father to lead Sempronio to her as he had guided the Magi to Bethlehem with the star; Pármeno reports how everyone and everything that is capable of making a sound calls her an old whore in a passage that brings to mind one of the psalms where everything in nature praises the name of the Creator, thus rendering her into an antipathy of God the Father; Celestina herself repeats the same comparison by bragging to Calisto that, if necessary, she would have made the waters part for him to pass without getting wet, paralleling the parting of the Red Sea. This transformation of Celestina into a goddess corresponds to Erasmus's nearly contemporary objections to the exalted status of the Blessed Mother in the devotion of Catholics. Note that "Mariology" is still frequently termed "Mariolatry" by many of the Christians whose ancestors chose to separate themselves from Rome during the Reformation.

Celestina's systematic attack against the virginity exemplified by the Blessed Mother extends beyond those who are directly enticed into her cult. She is responsible for the defloration of more than five thousand maidens in the town where she lives, and has the name of every girl born there inscribed into her registry, so as to keep track of those who manage to escape from her net. Given her great power and expertise, this does not amount to too many, it would seem. If that were not the case, what would be the point of keeping such a registry? The Christian emphasis on virginity is therefore dealt with as a ridiculous, unnatural pretension. Virginity does not really matter that much for, after all, Celestina is able to restore it through her technical ability, as if she could also perform her own "miracles"; no one seems to be able to detect the difference, anyway.

Celestina's main role as a procuress, a mediator, parallels the most important aspect of the Marian cult in the Middle Ages. In her capacity as Mediatrix, the Blessed Mother saves souls by interceding for them before her Son, Christ; her antithesis, Celestina, uses the devil as a helper by conjuring him through the Black Mass that she celebrates in the whorehouse turned into a temple. She commands him to get into the yarn that she uses as an excuse to enter the house of her prospective victim, then depends on him to inflame her with desire for Calisto. Like the serpent whose head had been crushed by the Blessed Mother—and the procuress is both associated with and referred to as a serpent—Celestina leads Calisto and Melibea toward a carnal paradise that is the opposite of the heaven to which the Blessed Mother endeavors to take the faithful. In an apparently Christian solution—the two sinners do not seem to be warned or given much of an opportunity to repent—Calisto and Melibea are cast out of this paradise, being punished for their sin with death and eternal damnation.

Of course any go-between parodies the Blessed Mother's central role as Mediatrix because of the very nature of her profession. Many of the parallelisms just summarized could also apply to other procuresses. In his useful summary of Adolfo Bonilla's (1906), Norman Spector's (1956), and María Rosa Lida de Malkiel's (1962, 534–72) studies on the evolution of the go-between from the Roman *lena* ("procuress") to the Renaissance, Ruggerio emphasizes that the type is usually an old woman who feigns a saintly life, a convent-trotter who peddles items such as make-up and thread in order to get into the homes of her prospective victims, using sorcery to further her aims (1966, 4–5). This sorcery is not the same as witchcraft, for it is "an attempt to control nature, to produce good or evil results, generally by the aid of evil spirits";[59] the witch embraces this tradition, but she takes a step further by allying herself with the devil. Consequently, "the witch has abandoned Christianity, has renounced her baptism, has worshipped Satan as her God, has surrendered herself to him, body and soul,[60] and exists only to be his instrument in working the evil to her fellow-creatures, which he cannot accomplish without a human agent" (Lea 1922, 4: 206, qtd. in Ruggerio 1966, 6). According to Ruggerio, this is the main ingredient added by Rojas to the type (1966, 53), but, as we shall see, there are others.

Celestina's figure does indeed embody all the characteristics piled upon the figure of the go-between throughout the centuries. Previous *alcahuetas* ("procuresses") could be equally viewed as antitheses of the Blessed Mother because of the mediating aspect of their profession, the resulting offensive against virginity and chastity, and the association with convents and other places of prayer added to the type during the Middle Ages. Alfonso Martínez de Toledo had already denounced such women as "unas viejas matronas, malditas de Dios e de sus santos, enemigas de la Virgen Santa María" ("some old matrons, cursed by God and his saints, and enemies of the Holy Virgin Mary"; 1992, 197) more than half a century before (1438). The new facets added by Rojas to Celestina's character, however, render the possibility of a mere coincidence most implausible. The choice of her name, "little celestial one," could be dismissed as pure irony, but why should Rojas have gone on to give her an extensive number of titles that are usually reserved for the Blessed Mother and make Calisto kneel before her? Why should the old bawd have been transformed into the high priestess of a cult and her house into a shrine where countless maidens give up their virginity? Why should Celestina claim the authority to command the monks who are devoted to her to pray for what she wishes, displace the Deity in the devotion of the faithful upon entering church in her golden days, and be practically turned into a goddess in three additional instances? Why should the evil mediator have the power to summon the devil's assistance in order to take Calisto and Melibea to a carnal paradise? Finally, why should this paradise be so deliberately created as the opposite of heaven, leading to hell instead? Any *alcahueta* ("procuress"), I repeat, is an antithesis of the Blessed Mother by virtue of her profession, but Fernando de Rojas adorned Celestina with so many additional antithetical parallelisms that the possibility of an easy or traditional coincidence must be discarded.

Rather than contradicting what has been put forth in these pages, the three overt references to the name of Mary in *Celestina* confirm it. Her name is first mentioned by Pármeno when he complains about the fact that Calisto has invited Celestina to his room in order to hear the news of her first meeting with Melibea: "¡O santa María, y qué rodeos busca este loco por huyr de nosotros . . . !" ("Oh, Blessed Mary, how this madman beats around the bush in order to get away from us"; 180). Pármeno makes the sign of the cross while saying these words, Catholics perform the same gesture in front of a statue of the Blessed Mother, and Calisto goes on to kneel before Celestina, as if she were another Virgin. Whether Pármeno's reaction is motivated by amazement at Celestina's success, revulsion, or perhaps even fear, the sequence and the analogy that it embodies, I repeat, perversely make us see her as a parodic parallel to the Virgin. Note that Pármeno's exclamation does not indicate any real devotion to the Blessed Mother or anything that she represents; another religious name, even an expletive, could have been easily substituted for it.

The name of the Blessed Mother appears for the second time in an expression used by Tristán to chastise Sosia for mentioning Melibea's name in a manner that could be overheard, while advising silence and caution when both were on their way to her house: "Pues tan sotil y discreto eres, no me dirás en qué mes cae Santa María de agosto, porque sepamos si ay harta paja en casa que comas ogaño" ("You are so very sharp and smart, I bet you can't tell me in what month falls the feast of Holy Mary in August, so we'll know if there is enough straw in the house for you to eat this year, [you ass]"; 288). In this instance, Mary's name constitutes a simple allusion to a particular time of the year.

The third and final reference to the Blessed Mother is found in Calisto's anguished cry as he falls to his death: "¡O válame Santa María, muerto soy! ¡Confessión!" ("Oh, may the Holy Mary help me! I'm dying! Confession!"; 326). Once again, her name is not associated with true devotion. Since Calisto's cry does not seem to constitute a real sign of devotion, it is an exclamation that could have been easily replaced by another one. Moreover,

Chapter Four

it is ironical that Calisto should call precisely on the Virgin while falling from the walls of the very garden where he had deflowered Melibea, the *hortus conclusus* ("enclosed garden") that also stands for Mary's perpetual virginity, especially now that her antithesis, Celestina, no longer walks the earth.

The three appearances of the name of the Blessed Mother in *Celestina*, then, are not indicative of any genuine devotion to the Virgin or anything she represents. Its first occurrence may be part of a deliberate, sacrilegious analogy between her figure and Celestina's; the second is embodied within an expression used to call someone else an ass; the third is truly ironical, in that it is placed on Calisto's lips right after he has been fornicating.

The manner in which the name of the Blessed Mother is used parallels the fashion in which Rojas deals with the name of Christ. There are five (or eight, depending on how you count them) references to the name of the Savior throughout the *Tragicomedia* itself.[61] During her first meeting with Celestina, Melibea, furious with her for daring to mention Calisto, shouts: "Quemada seas, alcahueta falsa, hechizera, enemiga de honestidad, causadora de secretos yerros. ¡Jesú, Jesú, quítamela, Lucrecia, de delante, que me fino, que no me ha dexado gota de sangre en el cuerpo!" ("May you be burned, you false procuress, witch, enemy of decency, and cause of secret errors. Jesus, Jesus! Take her out of my sight, Lucrecia, for she will kill me. She hasn't left me a drop of blood!"; 161). A little later, Melibea warns Celestina not to repeat Calisto's name to her with the following words: "¡Jesú, no oyga yo mentar más esse loco saltaparedes, fantasma de noche, luengo como cigüeña, figura de paramento mal pintado, sino aquí me caeré muerta!" ("Jesus! Never mention that lecher to me again, that spook, as long as a stork, that badly painted picture on a hanging, or I'll drop dead right here!"; 162). Angry with Sempronio for praising Melibea's beauty, his girlfriend Elicia protests: "¡Jesú, Jesú, y qué hastío y enojo es ver tu poca vergüença! ¿A quién gentil?" ("Jesus, Jesus, and how disgusting and exasperating it is to see how shameless you are! What's so lovely about her?"; 226). When Pármeno and Sempronio tell Celestina of the supposed dangers that they had suffered while accompanying Calisto to Melibea's garden as a pretext to demand their share of the gold chain that Calisto had given her, the procuress exclaims: "¡Jesú! ¿Que en tanta afrenta os avés visto? Cuéntamelo, por Dios" ("Jesus! Were you in so much trouble? Tell me about it, by God"; 269). And Areúsa, upon seeing the grieving Elicia at her door, says: "¡Ay, triste yo! ¿eres tú mi Elicia? ¡Jesú, Jesú, no lo puedo creer!" ("Oh, poor me! Is that you, Elicia dear? Jesus! Jesus! I can't believe my eyes"; 295).

It should be noted here that, whereas the name of Mary is invariably placed in the mouth of men (Pármeno, Tristán, Calisto), the name of Jesus is always used by women (Melibea, Elicia, Celestina, Areúsa). Since Catholic men and women are as likely to invoke Christ as the Blessed Mother, without favoring one exclusively over the other, Rojas could well be implying that the Marian cult had led to a form of polytheism, suggesting that there was a female goddess for men and a male god for women. This idea, however, must remain a mere hypothesis, for it is impossible to show that Rojas's apparent choice is not a matter of simple coincidence.

Whatever the case, there is no question that Christ's name is reduced to a mere expletive in all of the instances examined. This formulaic utilization is tantamount to a virtual absence, an absence that some critics have attempted to explain in relation to *Celestina* or *Lazarillo de Tormes* (where the two names in question do not even appear), as a result of Rojas's classical, pagan sources (Mancing 1976, 51) or the subsequent influence of the "alumbrado" ("Illuminist") movement (M. Asensio 1959, 91–92). Reacting against Castro's observation that the absence of the names of Christ and Mary in the *Lazarillo* supports the hypothesis that the anonymous author was a converso (1967, 154–55), Víctor García de la Concha counted the numerous instances in which the name of God is used (see also Rank 1980–81), and concluded that "el lenguaje coloquial de aquella época estaba punteado a cada paso por referencias a la Divinidad" ("the colloquial speech of that time was frequently punctuated by references to the Deity"; 1972, 248). In order to prove that Castro was wrong, García de la Concha then examined three works— *Celestina*, *La Lozana andaluza*, and Torres Naharro's *Propalladia*—which either omit or seldom mention the names of Mary and Christ, and deduced that this was customary during the period (259–61). These three writers were conversos, however. Consequently, without realizing it, García de la Concha succeeded in undermining his own argument, adding further evidence to Castro's thesis.

If it was customary to mention God's name so frequently, why should the other two names be omitted, anyway? Moreover, Rojas and the anonymous author of the *Lazarillo* availed themselves of a great number of additional sources, including the folk tradition in which both names appear over and over, being evoked in meaningful, devout ways.

On the other hand, Jews came to loathe the very names of Jesus and Mary, and, although they were originally Jewish, they fell into such disuse that it would probably be impossible to find a Jewish person with either one. Maimonides expressed this aversion in the *Mishnah Torah* (Codification of laws) while discussing the signs of the Messiah. In a censored edition printed in Rome c. 1480, Maimonides refers to Jesus without mentioning his name, but in a subsequent, uncensored manuscript from 1564, he calls him "Yeshua' ha.Noṣri" ("Jesus the Nazarene") twice, adding each time: "¡borrado sea su nombre y su recuerdo!" ("May his name and his memory be erased!"; Del

Valle Rodríguez 1992, 33–34). This attitude is understandable, for Jews had suffered much in the name of Christ. It was also under his name that many Spanish Jews were forced to convert in 1391 and after, and, therefore, it is not surprising that their dislike for the names of Jesus and his Mother should have been passed on to succeeding generations. Consequently, Gilman's explanation makes much more sense to me. In his opinion, "it would seem that Rojas shared the hateful reluctance of certain of his fellow *conversos* to name directly an imposed and spurious messiah. Perhaps he too used such evasions (recorded in numerous Inquisitional transcripts) as 'Otohays' (meaning 'that fellow'), 'aquel enforcadillo' ('that strung-up wretch'), or 'barbillas' ('Mr. Beard') whenever in appropriate company it was necessary to speak of Christ" (1972, 363).

But since hell is the real paradise to which Celestina leads her followers with the assistance of the devil, on the surface *Celestina* is indeed the moral work announced by Rojas in the lengthy title: "Síguese la comedia o Tragicomedia de Calisto y Melibea, compuesta en reprehensión de los locos enamorados que, vencidos en su desordenado apetito, a sus amigas llaman y dizen ser su dios. Assimismo hecha en aviso de los engaños de las alcahuetas y malos y lisonjeros sirvientes" ("There follows now the comedy or Tragicomedy of Calisto and Melibea, composed as a reprimand to unchaste lovers who, overcome by their excessive appetite, call their ladies God. The play was also written as a warning against the wiles of procuresses and bad, flattering servants"; 82). This title stresses Calisto and Melibea's folly in giving in to lust, and the two lovers are indeed punished with death for transgressing God's law.

Because of this apparently Christian solution, many scholars sustain that *Celestina* is in fact the moral work that Rojas claims it to be. Since the creation of Celestina as an antithesis of the Blessed Mother constitutes a parody, and religious figures, ceremonies, and teachings such as Christ and the Virgin, the Mass, and the commandments were often used in an irreverent, arguably sacrilegious way,[62] it could be easily assumed that Rojas merely echoes that tradition in order to show how evil the procuresses mentioned in the title can really be. After all, such women are the opposite of everything the Blessed Mother stands for.

On the other hand, there is nothing covert in the tradition that inspired Rojas; being undertaken for comic effect, religious parodies were usually transparent.[63] By creating Celestina, who is characterized as an insatiable whore, as a covert antithesis of the Blessed Mother, Rojas, a converso, also suggested that the Virgin Mary was a prostitute. To a convinced Catholic, this amounts to an unthinkable blasphemy. As perceived by Morón Arroyo, such a man would have to be a crypto-Jew. Morón Arroyo assumed that if Rojas had really dared to perpetrate that sacrilege, his contemporaries would have unmasked him, but this deduction is incorrect. As Rojas calculated, his Old Christian contemporaries were not literary critics, and, although they could not fail to see some of the parallels between Celestina and the Blessed Mother, they were unlikely to assemble all the coincidences into a meaningful whole.

Rojas's transformation of Mary into a prostitute is far from an isolated case. In fact, he is repeating, in a covert, artistic way, what a few other converts used to say. Though officially Christian, some converts did not accept the dogma of Mary's virginity. The two passages that follow are taken from the previously cited trial brought by the Inquisition of Ciudad Real against Catalina de Zamora, a conversa, in 1484.[64] She and her daughter were complaining that a woman was being unjustly burned when someone arrived and explained "que la quemauan por que avi(a) dicho que Nuestra Señora la Virgen Santa Maria era vna muger comun" ("that they were burning her because she had said that Our Lady, the Holy Virgin Mary, was just a common woman"). Catalina allegedly confirmed the assertion of the sacrificed woman by stating: "¡Qué marauilla! ¿Nunca oyestes vos desir que era vna ensangrentada?" ("Little wonder! Haven't you ever heard that she menstruated?"; Beinart 1974–77, 1: 388). The implication is that, since the Virgin Mary menstruated, she was a woman like any other. Another witness reported that, besides performing an obscene gesture while at a window from which a structure (a convent?) dedicated to the Blessed Mother could be seen ("la casa de Nuestra Señora Santa Maria de Alarcos" ["the house of Our Lady Holy Mary of Alarcos"]), Catalina had also referred to the Virgin in blasphemous terms: "e le vido dar higas a Nuestra Señora la Virgen Maria; e le dixo la moça por que lo haçia; e le dixo que duelos la diese Dios, que era Nuestra Señora vna puta judihuela" ("and seeing her put down Our Lady, the Virgin Mary, she asked the girl why she was doing that. And the girl cursed her, saying that Our Lady was a little Jewish whore"; Beinart 1974–77, 1: 389).

The records of the Portuguese Inquisition document similar occurrences. In Oporto, where "a descrença na virgindade de Maria era motivo de denúncias frequentes" ("the disbelief in the virginity of Mary was a motive for frequent accusations"), a witness testified that "as cristãs-novas tinham tal ódio a quem invocasse o nome de Maria ou de Jesus que chegavam a maltratar duramente quem o fizesse" ("New Christian women so hated those who invoked the names of Mary or Jesus that they at times harshly mistreated whoever did it"). When Tovar, a New Christian, passed by a woman who was praying before "Nossa Senhora da Ribeira" ("Our Lady of the Stream; an image?"), he told her: "asy he ella vyrgem como he a may que me pario" ("she is as much a virgin as the mother who bore me"; Tavares 1987, 94; other examples: pp. 149, 156).

Chapter Four

Earlier in the fifteenth century, we recall, the converso Nicolás de Valencia, one of the poets represented in the *Cancionero de Baena* (c. 1444), "cynically asks if the birth of Christ is not a sanction for adultery, in that God 'begot' a Son by someone else's wife" (Fraker 1966, 31). Nicolás de Valencia could ask such a question openly in one of his poems because he was writing before the establishment of the Inquisition in Spain (1481). If that institution had already existed, the only way for Valencia to avoid the fate of individuals such as those mentioned above would have been to express his thoughts in a covert manner.

That is precisely what Francisco Delicado, who knew *Celestina* quite well, does in *La Lozana andaluza* (1528).[65] Although the passage that follows will be re-examined in Chapter 7, it needs to be mentioned here as well. While speaking with her friend Imperia, Lozana, who earns her living as a prostitute in Rome, asks the last of four things that she would like to know with the following words: "Y la cuarta que *pénitus* iñoro es de quién me tengo de empreñar cuando alguno m'empreñe" ("And the fourth thing that I completely ignore is by whom I ought to get pregnant when someone impregnates me"; 1985, 466). Although the Latinism *pénitus* means "absolutely," there is no doubt that it is also being used in a comical way, in order to designate the penis. Prostitutes surely know what penises are, and any pregnant woman who claimed not to know what one was would have to be lying. The language of folly is operative here—there is no doubt that Lozana's outrageous claim would elicit much laughter—but this does not detract from the heresy of her query, since it echoes the words of the Virgin to the Angel Gabriel when he told her that she was to conceive and bear a son: "How shall this happen, since I do not know man?" (Luke 1.34).[66] Delicado attributes a similar query to a whore because, in the eyes of nonbelievers, a woman who made the preposterous claim that she had become pregnant by the grace of the Holy Spirit (Luke 1.35) was exactly that, thus paralleling what Catalina de Zamora and other poorly converted conversos thought: "que era Nuestra Señora vna puta judihuela" ("that Our Lady was a little Jewish whore"; Beinart 1974–77, 1: 389).

Such conversos were really crypto-Jews, and they hated Mary because, without her, there would be no Christ. She had literally given birth to the religion in whose name they were persecuted. What Catalina, Tovar, and the other marranos were merely stating in an open, foolish manner is precisely what Rojas more cautiously implies in a brilliant, artistic fashion, by creating Celestina as an antithesis of the Blessed Mother. A few years later, Delicado also dares to imply that the Blessed Mother was a prostitute by attributing the query just examined to his protagonist.

Aversion toward Mary is still echoed in the folklore of the Sephardim, the descendants of the Jews who were forced to leave Spain (1492) and Portugal (1497) in order to preserve their faith.[67] In *El idólatra de María*, a ballad that the Sephardic tradition preserves as an anti-Marian poem (she fails to assist the captain or the sailor[s] who ask for her help because only God can perform miracles), the Blessed Mother is addressed as "hadolla" ("imagen religiosa" ["religious image"]), "Fedionda" ("stinking woman"), "puta María" ("Mary the Whore"), and "falsa y mentirosa" ("false and deceitful"; see Catalán 1970, 271–73).[68] Samuel Armistead and Joseph Silverman have documented additional examples of this aversion in other Sephardic ballads, but none are as drastic. In a version of *Leonisio de Salamanca*, the initial invocation to Jesus and Mary, "En el nombre de Jesús / y la Virgen Soberana" ("In the name of Jesus / and the Sovereign Lady") becomes "En el nombre dilo tú / y su madre soberana" ("In the name of you say it / and his sovereign mother"); and in the answer of Delgadina to her father's incestuous advances in the ballad of the same title, "No lo permita Dios Padre, / ni la Virgen Soberana" ("May God the Father not allow it, / nor the Sovereign Virgin"), the name of the Blessed Mother is replaced by verses such as "No lo permita Dios, padre; / ni tal quiera, ni tal haga" ("May God not allow such a thing, father; / may He not want it or do it"), or "ni mi madre la honrada" ("nor my chaste mother"; Armistead and Silverman 1982, 137). Although there still exists a Christian substratum in Judeo-Spanish balladry (147), it is only logical to surmise that the process of de-Christianization so brilliantly demonstrated by Armistead and Silverman began in Spain itself before the expulsion, particularly during the fifteenth century, in the days when the confrontation between the two religions reached its peak, becoming openly hostile in the Muslim or Muslim-controlled territories where the vast majority of the Sephardim found refuge.

Rojas transmuted this aversion to the Blessed Mother into art through Celestina's character. The three overt references to Mary in the *Tragicomedia*, which, as we recall, always appear in the mouth of men, are not indicative of any genuine devotion to the Virgin or anything she represents. Nevertheless, Rojas closed his work with an indirect reference to her. This happens when the disconsolate Pleberio ends the *Tragicomedia* by asking the corpse of his daughter, as if she were still alive: "¿Por qué me dexaste triste y solo *in hac lacrimarum valle?*" ("Why have you left me so sad and alone in this vale of tears?"; 343). These words are taken from the *Salve, Regina* (Hail, holy Queen), a prayer still commonly addressed to the Blessed Mother today, in which the faithful, poor banished children of Eve, mourning and weeping in this vale of tears, beg her as Queen, Mother of Mercy, and their most gracious advocate to show them the blessed fruit of her womb, Jesus, at the end of the exile that life on this earth represents:

> Salve, Regína, Mater misericórdiæ; vita, dulcédo et spes nostra, salve. Ad te clamámus, éxsules fílii Evæ. Ad te suspirámus geméntes et flentes in hac lacrimárum valle. Eia ergo, advocáta nostra, illos tuos

> misercórdes óculos ad nos convérte. Et Jesum, benedíctum fructum ventris tui, nobis, post hoc exsílium, osténde. O clemens, o pia, o dulcis Virgo María! Ora pro nobis, sancta Dei Génitrix. Ut digni efficiámur promissiónibus Christi. (*Saint Andrew Daily Missal* 1953, 942 [38])

Pleberio's allusion to this beautiful prayer constitutes a fit ending in more than one way. To begin with, the *Salve, Regina* "was sung after Compline in all the Latin rites from the fourteenth century on . . . while the lights [were] being put out and the church [was] left in darkness" (Dunn 1976b, 417). The last words of *Celestina*, then, coincide with the seventh and last of the canonical hours and with the closing of churches throughout Western Christendom. Secondly, the world had indeed become a vale of tears for the disconsolate Pleberio. The prayer from which his words are taken, however, also combines several key aspects of the Marian cult that had been so carefully parodied through the figure of Celestina, for it alludes to the Blessed Mother as Queen of Heaven, Mediatrix, and the New Eve who had made it possible for Christians to return to the lost paradise by giving birth to the New Adam, Jesus. In a word, the utilization of a phrase taken from the *Salve, Regina* to conclude *Celestina* is no mere accident, pointing to the parody of the Marian cult throughout the *Tragicomedia* by virtue of its position at the close.[69]

Rojas's multipronged attack is centered on the doctrine of Mary's perpetual virginity. The Blessed Mother is allegorically transformed into a prostitute through parodic associations with Celestina, thus bringing to mind the constant denial of her virginity on the part of many converts, as well as the blasphemous libel for which Catalina de Zamora was denounced to the Inquisition of Ciudad Real in 1484. Since it was felt that Mary was not a virgin but an unfaithful wife to begin with, the dogmas of the Virgin Birth and the Incarnation were equally false. To believe that God, who was pure spirit, would choose to be incarnated through a son born of a mortal woman seemed to defy all logic. So much for the Divinity of Christ, and what it implies regarding the dogma of the Holy Trinity. The exalted rank of the Blessed Mother in the Catholic faith is also ridiculed by the comparison of her antithesis, Celestina, to God the Son and God the Father.

Rojas got away with this because the correspondences between Celestina and the Blessed Mother are dispersed throughout his book. Read in isolation, many of them are extremely funny, and probably caused readers and listeners to laugh heartily. Thus, humor is used as cover. It is only after putting all the correspondences together that it is possible to realize that they are not merely isolated examples of parody and irony, but an allegory. As Rojas realized, most readers were not capable of doing this, and the few who could understand it were like-minded, educated conversos.

Celestina as an Antithesis of the Blessed Mother

It goes without saying that anyone capable of doing these things could not possibly be a true Catholic. It could be argued that the expulsion of 1492 and the suffering of his fellow converts as a result of discrimination and the ubiquitous, ever vigilant Inquisition caused Rojas to lose faith in any God, Jewish or Christian, who allowed such great injustices to come to pass,[70] but, although he asked to be buried in the convent of La Madre de Dios ("The Mother of God"), dressed in the habit of St. Francis, he may well have been a crypto-Jew.[71] As documented in the Jewish medieval polemics against Christian dogmas (see Lasker 1977, 105–34, 153–59), as well as in numerous inquisitorial trials, Rojas was merely echoing objections and doubts that were common enough among both Jews and conversos in fifteenth-century Spain (and after). In this respect, his originality lies in his ability to transmute those charges into art in the least dangerous form possible—in a covert, ambiguous, polysemous manner—a transmutation that allowed him to realize the human need to express what he (and many others) felt concerning the situation in which conversos had to live.

Chapter Five

Christian Prayer and Dogma in *Celestina*
The Polemic Continues

In a work entitled *The Refutation of Christian Principles* (c. 1398), Hasdai ben Judah Crescas (c. 1340–1410 or 1411), chief rabbi of Zaragoza, whose son had been killed in the riots of 1391, listed his philosophical arguments against the principal beliefs of Christianity as follows: "(1) The original, universal sin of Adam; (2) Redemption from this sin; (3) Trinity; (4) Incarnation; (5) Virgin birth; (6) Transubstantiation; (7) Baptism; (8) Messiah; (9) A new Torah; (10) Demons" (Crescas 1992, 24). This list encapsulates the main objections of Jews against Christianity, but there were others, such as the belief in saints and the veneration of images.

Crescas addressed his book to a learned audience, for he assumed that his readers knew the philosophy of Aristotle (Lasker 1992, 9), but common, unlearned Jews were familiar with the basic arguments against the Christian beliefs that he outlined. Living in a Christian environment in which their faith was extremely detested, it was only natural that they should express objections against the religion of the majority among each other. Moreover, since Judaism was under assault and the pressure to convert was extremely great, they also needed to know how to defend their faith.

The highly polished, philosophical arguments found in Crescas's *Refutation* and other polemical works were far too intellectual for common people, however. Among unlearned Jews, those objections probably took a coarse, rather vulgar form, more along the lines of the *Toledot Yeshu* (Heb. "The Life of Jesus"), a pseudo-historical, violently anti-Christian retelling of the story of Jesus from a Jewish perpective.[1]

Whatever the case, many of those who were forced to accept baptism in 1391 and after transmitted similar arguments to their children and grandchildren. We know this because some conversos were imprudent enough to express them publicly, being subsequently denounced to the authorities. As Eleazar Gutwirth pointed out in an excellent article profusely documented with passages drawn from inquisitorial trials (1996), such vulgar objections against Christian belief often reflected topics that had been previously discussed in various polemics.

Far more prudently, other resentful conversos preferred to transmute their objections against Christianity into art, in a manner that could not be easily detected by the authorities or the Old Christian majority. As we saw in the previous chapter, Rojas attacked the dogma about the virginity of the Blessed Mother by creating the figure of Celestina as her antithesis, thus reflecting the charge that Mary was a shameless prostitute. This attack, of course, embodies a denial of the Incarnation and the Holy Trinity, for it implies that Jesus was really an illegitimate child. As we will see in the present chapter, Rojas also misused the Scriptures and attacked Christian prayer and dogma in other ways.

The material drawn from the Scriptures is turned upside down, for, instead of being used to teach moral values, it becomes part of a strategy of corruption and deception. Therefore, it is not surprising that several references to the Scriptures should be placed in Celestina's mouth when, in her role as "priestess," she attempts to corrupt Pármeno and Melibea, thus "converting" them to her cult. At the same time, the old bawd mimics the role of the devil, for she is in fact tempting both.

Since Pármeno knows what kind of woman she is, his loyalty to Calisto constitutes an obstacle that she needs to remove in order to conduct her business. At first the boy resists, and Celestina warns him with words taken from the proverbs attributed to Solomon: "Al varón que con dura cerviz al que le castiga menosprecia, arrebatado quebrantamiento le verná, y sanidad nunca conseguirá" ("The man who proudly disdains counsel will be crushed suddenly and will never be healthy"; 127). The biblical passage reads as follows: "The man who remains stiff-necked and hates rebuke will be crushed suddenly beyond care" (Prov. 29.1).[2] Since these words apply to sinners, and Celestina is trying to get Pármeno to betray his master, the passage in question is really being reversed. Later on, Celestina does essentially the same by telling the boy that "Dios no pide más del pecador, de arrepentirse y emendarse" ("all that God asks from sinners is to repent and mend their ways"; 193), thus twisting God's words regarding salvation: "As I live, says the Lord God, I swear I take no pleasure in the death of the wicked man, but rather in the wicked man's conversion, that he may live" (Ezek. 33.11).[3] The sort of conversion that Celestina proposes to the boy, however, leads not to salvation, but to damnation.

Celestina repeats the same technique in her corruption or "psychological defloration" of Melibea (Handy 1983). As soon as she arrives in her house, she greets the maid, Lucrecia, by saying "Paz sea en esta casa" ("May there be peace in this house"; 151), thus echoing the advice of Jesus to the Apostles ("As you enter the house, salute it. If then that house be worthy, your peace will come upon it"; Matt. 10.12–13),[4] as well as the greeting of Christians to each other after saying the Lord's Prayer during Mass: "May

Chapter Five

the peace of the Lord be with you." But what Celestina is bringing into that home, of course, is precisely the opposite.

When Melibea suggests that Celestina ought to leave because it seems that she has not yet eaten, the woman paraphrases the words used by Christ to reject the devil's temptation to turn a stone into a loaf of bread during his forty-day fast in the desert: "¿y no sabes que por la divina boca fue dicho, contra aquel infernal tentador, que no de sólo pan biviriemos?" ("and don't you know what that divine mouth said against that tempting devil, that man shall not live by bread alone?"; 158).[5] Nevertheless, the procuress's role here is the opposite of Christ's, for, like the devil, she also intends to tempt Melibea.

When the girl becomes furious after discovering that the purpose of Celestina's visit is not just to sell yarn, the old bawd explains that she is really seeking help to remedy Calisto's "toothache"; if he had offended Melibea before, the fault was his, not hers: "No paguen justos por pecadores. Imita la divina justicia que dixo: El ánima que pecare, aquella misma muera; a la humana, que jamás condena al padre por el delicto del hijo, ni al hijo por el del padre" ("Let not the just pay the debts of sinners. Imitate divine justice, which says: 'The soul that sins shall be the one to die.' Imitate also human justice, which never condemns the father for the sins of the son, nor the son for the sins of the father"; 165). In the Bible, God does indeed say: "Only the one who sins shall die. The son shall not be charged with the guilt of his father, nor shall the father be charged with the guilt of his son" (Ezek. 18.20).[6] Once again, the biblical words are being used in reverse, for Celestina is anything but innocent.

The most sacrilegious reference to the Scriptures may be found when, thinking about the deaths of Pármeno, Sempronio, and Celestina, because the old bawd had refused to share the gold chain with them, Calisto says to himself: "La vieja era mala y falsa, según paresce que hazía trato con ellos, y assí que riñeron sobre la capa del justo" ("The old woman was evil and false, as the manner in which she did business with them seems to show, and so they fought over the cape of the just man"; 281–82). Covarrubias defines the proverbial expression "sobre la capa del justo" ("over the cape of the just man") as "cuando paga el que no tiene culpa" ("when the innocent one pays"; 1994, 693, s.v. "Justo"), which brings to mind the figure of Christ, but the chain also recalls the division of Jesus's clothes among the Roman soldiers after his crucifixion. St. Matthew (27.35) and St. Mark (15.24) mention the event, but St. John describes it in greater detail: "The soldiers therefore, when they had crucified him, took his garments and made of them four parts, to each soldier a part, and also the tunic. Now the tunic was without seam, woven in one piece from the top. They therefore said to one another, 'Let us not tear it, but let us cast lots for it, to see whose it shall be'" (19.23–

24).[7] Being of one piece, the gold chain was indivisible, thus corresponding to Jesus's tunic, but the allusion under scrutiny is so laconic that it is impossible to be absolutely certain that this is what Rojas had in mind. Just before, Sosia told Calisto that he had seen Celestina's corpse with "más de treynta stocadas" ("more than thirty stabs"; 280), which recalls the thirty coins for which Judas reportedly sold Christ, but this, of course, does not prove anything, either.

In any case, the systematic reversal of scriptural material is undeniable. While Celestina's reversals can be justified in terms of characterization—in her role as temptress, she parallels the devil—the utilization of Christian prayer will reveal a pattern that may be more difficult to explain. As we have already seen, Celestina's house is the antithesis of a shrine, the ceremonies held there in her glory days involved prayers and rituals that amounted to various types of sexual activity, and the Black Mass that she celebrates is an antithesis of the Christian Mass. In addition to the avoidance of the names of Jesus and Mary, which often appear in prayers, there are numerous, invariably ironical references to prayer in general, and most of the specific prayers proffered by the characters are nothing less than heretical.

Let us begin with the references. As Pármeno had informed Calisto, Celestina "nunca passava sin missa ni bispras" ("she never went without Mass or vespers services"; 111), but her constant presence in places of prayer such as churches, convents, and monasteries was motivated by her business. When Alisa asks the bawd to remember her sister in her devotions, she promises to charge the monks who are "devoted" to her in various monasteries with the same request, and says that she will do so herself right away: "Y demás desto, ante que me desayune, dé quatro bueltas a mis cuentas" ("Moreover, before I have breakfast, I will say my rosary four times over"; 154). Of course Celestina is lying, and, as already pointed out, it is ironical that she should be portrayed with a rosary, which is emblematic of the Blessed Mother. Moreover, as Sempronio informs Pármeno, "lo que en sus cuentas reza es los virgos que tiene a cargo, y quántos enamorados ay en la cibdad, y quántas moças tiene encomendadas" ("what she prays with her beads is the number of virgins in her charge, how many lovers there are in the city, and how many girls are entrusted to her"; 223). Thus, Celestina uses prayer as a cover for her illegitimate activities.

When Celestina discovers that Pármeno is the son of her old friend Claudina, she suggests that she had been praying constantly in order to find him: "hasta agora ha plazido a Aquel que todos los cuytados tiene y remedia las justas peticiones y las piadosas obras endereça, que te hallasse aquí donde solos ha tres días que sé que moras" ("it is only now that it has pleased him who sustains all the wretched, listens to just petitions, and oversees works of piety, for me to find you here. It was only three days ago that I found out

Chapter Five

where you live"; 121).[8] Obviously, she had been doing nothing of the sort; her pretension is designed to deceive Pármeno. That is also why, later on, Celestina informs the boy that girls prayed constantly for his mother's well-being, even though she had just made it clear that Claudina was also a powerful witch and a procuress: "Pues moças y donzellas, assí rogavan a Dios por su vida como de sus mismos padres" ("Girls and young ladies prayed for her well-being as much as they prayed for their own parents"; 197). These girls clearly found Claudina's services indispensable and feared losing her, but it goes without saying that Christians do not pray to God for the means to sin even more.

Generally speaking, the greetings and farewells that are tantamount to prayers of sorts are also hypocritical. Upon leaving Calisto's house after promising to help him with Melibea, Celestina says "Quede Dios contigo" ("May God stay with you"), to which he replies: "Y él te me guarde" ("And, for my sake, may he watch over you"; 129). Given the nature of their business, these words are not appropriate. Although Celestina visits Melibea's house with the yarn into which she has conjured the devil in order to corrupt her, her first words to Alisa are "Señora buena, la gracia de Dios sea contigo y con la noble hija" ("Good lady, may the grace of God be with you and your noble daughter"; 153). When Celestina leaves Areúsa's house after watching her make love with Pármeno, Areúsa tells her "Dios vaya contigo" ("God go with you"), and the old bawd replies to her and to the boy "acompáñeos Dios" ("and may God be in your company"; 209), even though they were in the process of committing a mortal sin.

In all of these references and prayer-like greetings and farewells, then, prayer is turned upside down, being used as cover, to deceive, and to ask for help in order to sin. The specific prayers parodied, mentioned, or proffered in the text have equally outrageous purposes. As we saw in the previous chapter, Calisto's prayer for God to lead Sempronio to Celestina as he had guided the Three Wise Men to Bethlehem with the star (104) is nothing less than heretical, for he wants the old bawd to make it possible for him to get Melibea into bed. Then Pármeno goes on to parody Psalm 148, in which everything in Creation praises the name of the Lord, in order to tell his master how everyone and everything capable of making a sound called Celestina an old whore (108–09). This is enormously sacrilegious. Calisto practically prays to the old bawd when he kisses the ground on which she walks, addresses her with titles that parallel the litanies of the Blessed Mother (116, 178, 249), and also kneels before her, as if she were a goddess: "de rodillas quiero escuchar tu suave respuesta" ("I want to listen to your sweet report on my knees"; 180).

Although the Sermon on the Mount is biblical, Jesus's lesson, subsequently known as the Beatitudes, has been treated as a prayer. When

Christian Prayer and Dogma

Pármeno begins to capitulate to Celestina, who wants him to be friends with Sempronio, he says to himself in an aside: "La paz no se deve negar, que bienaventurados son los pacíficos, que hijos de Dios serán llamados" ("Peace should not be refused, since 'Blessed are the peacemakers, for they shall be called children of God'"; 127), thus misapplying the words attributed to Jesus in the Gospel of St. Matthew (5.9).[9] When Celestina tells Pármeno how his mother was punished as a witch—she had been placed in the middle of the plaza for half a day with a painted miter ("rocadero pintado," 198), which suggests that the Inquisition was involved (Severin 1997, 421–22)— the procuress states that the priest who came to comfort Claudina had told her that "bienaventurados eran los que padecían persecución por la justicia y que aquéllos poseerían el reyno de los cielos" ("blessed were they who suffered persecution for justice's sake, and that the kingdom of heaven would be theirs"; 199). In this instance, it is a priest who reportedly misapplies one of the Beatitudes (Matt. 5.10).[10] Celestina then goes on to proclaim Claudina's innocence, saying that she had been accused by false witnesses and forced to confess under torture ("con falsos testigos y rezios tormentos la hizieron aquella vez confessar lo que no era" ["with false witnesses and severe torture, that time they made her confess what she was not"; 199]), but she had made it perfectly clear to the boy that his mother was an accomplished witch shortly before: "Pues entrar en un cerco, mejor que yo, y con más esfuerço. . . . ¿Qué más quieres? Sino que los mismos diablos la avían miedo. . . . Tumbando venían unos sobre otros a su llamado" ("She could enter into a witch's circle much better than I, and with less effort . . . What else can I tell you? The very devils were afraid of her . . . They came tumbling one over another when she called them"; 196–97). Thus, Claudina may have been innocent only in the sense that, in that particular instance, she had not been practicing witchcraft. Since there is no doubt that she was a witch,[11] Celestina herself misapplies the Beatitude just quoted when she goes on to tell Pármeno that Claudina must be in heaven: "Assí que todo eso passó tu madre acá, devemos creer que le dará Dios buen pago allá" ("And since your mother suffered all that in this world, we must believe that God will reward her in the other"; 199–200). Having sold their souls to the devil, however, witches presumably went straight to hell.

As the plot develops, Calisto spends a whole day in church, proffering sacrilegious prayers, but it is necessary to put together several dispersed passages in order to realize this fully. Having brought Melibea's rope belt to Calisto after her first interview with her, Celestina leaves his house when it is already dark, promising to see the girl again the day after. When his servants awaken him, Calisto believes that it is already light outside only when he hears the bells calling for Mass, and decides to go to St. Mary Magdalene's in order to pray for Celestina to succeed: "Dacá mis ropas; yré

Chapter Five

a la Madalena; rogaré a Dios aderece a Celestina y ponga en coraçón a Melibea mi remedio, o dé fin en breve a mis tristes días" ("Hand me my clothes. I'm going to the Church of the Magdalene to beg God to guide Celestina and to put the manner of my cure in Melibea's heart, or to put an end to my sad life"; 219). The crazed lover then says that he will not leave church or eat anything until he receives good news: "Yo me voy solo a missa y no tornaré a casa hasta que me llaméys, pidiéndome las albricias de mi gozo con la buena venida de Celestina. Ni comeré hasta entonce" ("I'm going to Mass alone and won't come home until you call me and ask for a reward for the joy you will give me when you bring news of Celestina's success. I won't eat anything until then"; 220–21). Obviously, one does not pray to God for illicit sex.

Calisto keeps his word. During a banquet held at Celestina's house with food that Pármeno and Sempronio had stolen from Calisto, Celestina inquires after their master, to which Pármeno replies: "Allá fue a la maldición, echando huego, desesperado, perdido, medio loco, a missa a la Madalena a rogar a Dios que te dé gracia, que puedas bien roer los huessos destos pollos, y protestando de no bolver a casa hasta oýr que eres venida con Melibea en tu arremango" ("He took off cursing, all afire, desperate, lost, half-crazed, to hear Mass at the Magdalene and to beg God to give you grace, so that you could pick the bones of this chicken well. He was also vowing that he wouldn't return home until he heard that you had come back with Melibea up your sleeve"; 230).

As the table is being cleared, Lucrecia arrives, saying that her mistress is ill and needs to see Celestina right away. When Melibea admits that she is in love with Calisto, the procuress arranges for her to meet him in her garden that very evening, at midnight. On her way back, Celestina sees Pármeno and Sempronio on their way to St. Mary Magdalene's, follows them there, and asks Calisto to step outside in order to give him the good news. Ecstatic, Calisto can hardly believe his good luck, and addresses the following prayer to God: "O Señor Dios, Padre celestial, ruégote que esto no sea sueño" ("Oh Lord God, my Father in Heaven, please don't let this be a dream"; 251). What we have here is another prayer in reverse.

It is important to note that Melibea's capitulation occurs while Calisto is praying fervently for her surrender in a church dedicated to a former sinner, St. Mary Magdalene, for he is there when Melibea sends Lucrecia to fetch Celestina. And there he stays, praying with all of his heart, until Celestina returns with the good tidings. Since the references to this are dispersed throughout three acts (8, 9, 11), it is easy enough for the reader to miss the point, but, as Marciales indicated, Rojas takes good care to provide a reminder (1985, 1: 90). During the first tryst, desperate because the doors of the garden prevent him from getting closer to Melibea, Calisto proffers yet another sacrilegious prayer, asking God for them to burn down: "¡O molestas y enojosas puertas, ruego a Dios que tal huego os abrase como a mí da guerra, que con la tercia parte seríades en un punto quemadas!" ("Oh annoying and frustrating doors, I pray God that you be burned with a fire such as the one that is devouring me. A third of it would be enough to incinerate you in a minute!"; 262; Act 12). Then Calisto requests Melibea's permission to have his servants tear the doors down, but she reminds him that the noise would cause her father to become aware of the grave sin she is committing. Calisto denies that a sin is involved by recalling how hard he had been praying in church: "O mi señora y mi bien todo, ¿por qué llamas yerro a aquello que por los santos de Dios me fue concedido? Rezando hoy ante el altar de la Madalena me vino con tu mensaje alegre aquella solícita mujer" ("Oh my Lady and my treasure, why do you call a mistake what was granted to me through all the saints of God? Today, while I was praying before the altar of the Magdalene, that diligent woman brought me your message"; 263).

Since it was through the intercession of the saints and, in particular, St. Mary Magdalene, that Calisto had been granted the favor for which he prayed so fervently, Melibea could not possibly be committing any sin. Although Calisto is out of his wits because of his love for Melibea, his prayers and his deduction are incredibly sacrilegious. Once again, Christian prayer is being turned upside down.

Having heard his master's last statement, Pármeno stresses that Calisto's attribution of his success to the saints is un-Christian, and credits Celestina's witchcraft instead: "¡Desvariar, Calisto, desvariar! Por fe tengo, hermano, que no es cristiano; lo que la vieja traydora con sus pestíferos hechizos ha rodeado y hecho, dize que los santos de Dios se lo han concedido y impetrado" ("You rave, Calisto, you rave! It seems to me, brother, that he is not a Christian. According to him, what the old treacherous woman has concocted and done was granted by all of God's saints"; 263). This retraction, however, does not change the heresy of what Calisto had done and said.

The equally lovesick Melibea had made a prayer of this kind earlier, when, anxious for Celestina to arrive after sending Lucrecia to fetch her, she asks God to help her to hide the true cause of her malady and to pretend that something else ails her:

> O soberano Dios, a ti que todos los atribulados llaman, los passionados piden remedio, los llagados medicina, a ti que los cielos, mar y tierra, con los infernales centros obedescen, a ti el qual todas las cosas a los hombres sojuzgaste, humilmente suplico: des a mi herido coraçón sofrimiento y paciencia, con que mi terrible passión pueda dissimular, no se desdore aquella hoja de castidad que tengo assentada sobre este amoroso desseo, publicando ser otro mi dolor que no el que me atormenta. (238 [39])

Chapter Five

Although Melibea, like Calisto, is out of her wits because of the madness that love was supposed to induce, this does not excuse the sacrilege of asking God for help in deceiving anyone.

Incidentally, saints are seldom mentioned, and when they are, it is either in a neutral manner or without any respect. We have already seen how the text deals with the Blessed Mother, St. Mary Magdalene, and how Calisto attributes his luck with Melibea to Mary Madgalene and the intercession of the saints. Since the prayer to St. Appolonia that Celestina requests from Melibea (164) is a paraliturgical, folkloric spell for real toothaches, its use in order to cure Calisto's metaphorically ailing "tooth" is hilarious, and can hardly be classified as heretical. On the other hand, this disrespects that poor saint, whose martyrdom included having all of her teeth knocked out. There are other examples of the sort. Centurio, the bragging rogue kept by Areúsa, swears to do everything in his power for his mistress "por el santo martilogio de pe a pa" ("by all the holy martyrs, from beginning to end"; 315), as if the poor martyrs had something to do with their unsavory business. When Celestina arrives at Areúsa's house in order to arrange for her to sleep with Pármeno, who is waiting outside, she greets her as follows: "¡Bendígate Dios y el señor Sant Miguel Ángel, y qué gorda y fresca que estás; qué pechos y qué gentileza!" ("May God and St. Michael, the Angel, bless you. How chubby and fresh you look! What breasts and loveliness!"; 202). Invoking God and the supposedly handsome St. Michael to praise the beauty of a prostitute may have been flattering to Areúsa, but it was hardly respectful to the Archangel, not to say anything about God. Realizing that he can count on Pármeno as an ally after the boy has spent the night with Areúsa, Sempronio shows his satisfaction with an allusion to St. John: "Sea lo passado questión de Sant Juan, y assí paz para todo el año" ("Let what happened in the past be one of those quarrels that take place around St. John's, and let's have peace from now on"; 217). There is no sign of disrespect here, for Sempronio is paraphrasing a well-known proverb ("Las riñas de por San Juan son paz para todo el año" ["Quarrels during St. John's bring peace for the rest of the year"; Correas 1992, 264]),[12] but the point is that not a single saint is named with any sign of devotion. Celestina's comparison of Calisto to a St. George in full armor is not quite as neutral: "Pues verle armado, un sant Jorge" ("When he is armed, he looks like another St. George"; 167). Since Celestina is trying to corrupt Melibea, and Calisto was suffering from a grievous "toothache," the word *armado* is probably used here in the sense of *rigidus*, as it often appeared in openly erotic poetry (Alzieu et al. 1984, s.v. "armar," "armado").

This entails a lack of respect that brings to mind the vulgar things that some contemporary conversos used to say about the saints. In 1502, for example, a few people were denounced in Soria for saying that St. Peter was

Christian Prayer and Dogma

a male whore (Gutwirth 1996, 269). María Alvarez, who had converted in 1482, stated that the saints were nothing but pieces of wood (272). This is probably what a conversa from Zaragoza had in mind when, in 1487, she denounced Christianity to an Old Christian *beata* ("pious woman") in the following terms: "You are idolaters who worship dogs and cats, you and your families" (271). In 1665, in Mexico, María de Zárate took matters a little further, for she was reported to have said that "all Christians were going to hell, for being idolaters and adoring images and the image of Jesus Christ and of wooden saints" (Gitlitz 1996, 146).

In sum, there is no question that the Scriptures, Christian prayer, and the saints are systematically turned upside down, being used in sacrilegious and heretical ways. Of course it is always possible to explain these reversals in artistic terms. Celestina's distortion of scriptural material, we recall, may be justified as part of her characterization, for she does so as a temptress, while mimicking the role of the devil. Some will say that her misuse of Christian prayer and St. Michael's name are not surprising, since, after all, she is a witch. Calisto and Melibea's sacrilegious prayers can be dismissed as symptoms of the lovesickness that affects their minds, and also as a reflection of the religious parody found in the courtly poetry of the period. Even Pármeno's blasphemous parody of Psalm 148 may be explained away as part of the characterization of Celestina. According to Miguel Martínez, who surveyed the use of prayer and the Scriptures in *Celestina* extremely well (1996, 100–17), albeit in conjunction with an examination of the effects of magic or witchcraft, which he anachronically denies, as if modern ideas on the subject already applied during the Middle Ages, the author simply disliked superhuman intervention of any kind. Therefore, what we have just seen amounts to nothing more than "un testimonio fehaciente y crítico de Rojas respecto a supercherías de uno y otro signo, groseramente arraigadas en sus personajes" ("a reliable and critical statement on Rojas's part regarding the mumbo-jumbo of all sorts rudely entrenched in his characters"; 112).

I disagree, for the simple reason that prayer, the Scriptures, and the saints are consistently used in negative ways, without a single exception to the contrary,[13] and because, despite numerous prayers, the names of Jesus and Mary are systematically avoided. As we know, those two names, along with references to the Holy Trinity, appear very often in most Catholic prayers. In a nutshell, at times the blasphemy is so monstrous that it is not likely to be a matter of simple literary parody, but rather the contrary—shameless blasphemy in the guise of parody.

The attack that Rojas perpetrates against the Virginity of Mary and, by implication, against related Christian dogmas, supports this interpretation. Moreover, as we will see, Rojas also attacks Christian dogmas by relating Calisto and Melibea to Adam and Eve.

Chapter Five

Jack Weiner (1969) was the first scholar to demonstrate systematically, I believe, that Adam and Eve imagery plays an important role in *Celestina*. Let us begin with Melibea's paradisiacal garden. The idyllic description that she makes to Calisto is related to the topical *locus amoenus* ("pleasant location") that writers used as a meeting place for lovers in general: "Mira la luna, quán clara se nos muestra. Mira las nuves, cómo huyen. Oye la corriente agua desta fontesica, quánto más suave murmurio y zurrío lleva por entre las frescas yervas. Escucha los altos cipresses, cómo se dan paz unos ramos con otros por intercessión de un templadico viento que los menea. Mira sus quietas sombras, quán escuras están y aparejadas para encobrir nuestro deleyte" ("Behold the moon, and how clear it is. Behold the clouds, and how they move. Hear the rippling water of this little fountain, and its soft murmur and buzz as it goes through the green grass. Listen to the tall cypresses, and how some of their branches kiss each other thanks to the soft breeze that sways them. Behold their silent shades, how dark and fit they are to conceal our pleasure"; 322–23). Note, however, that Calisto had previously referred to this garden as a paradise, thus linking it clearly to the Garden of Eden: "de día estaré en mi cámara, de noche en aquel *paraýso* dulce, en aquel alegre vergel entre aquellas suaves plantas y fresca verdura" ("By day I'll stay in my room, by night in that sweet paradise, among those gentle plants and that cool verdure"; 292).

While it is true that any garden could represent paradise in medieval literature (Del Monte 1970, 110), Rojas took matters further, for he deliberately associated Calisto not only with the Garden of Eden, but also with Adam. When Sempronio realizes that what ails his raving master is his love for Melibea, he promises to cure him of his "limp" with the following words: "bien sé de qué pie coxqueas; yo te sanaré" ("I know only too well which foot is causing you to limp; I'll cure you"; 93). As Weiner indicated, this image, which was commonplace during the Middle Ages, "also refers to the limp which Adam is thought to have suffered as a result of his Fall" (1969, 392).[14]

Making fun of Calisto for placing Melibea above God—Calisto had just proffered the famous "¿Yo? Melibeo só, y a Melibea adoro, y en Melibea creo, y a Melibea amo" ("Me? I am a Melibean, I worship Melibea, I believe in Melibea, and Melibea I love"; 93)—Sempronio further associates Calisto with Adam by alluding to his master's delirium with the same words that appear in Genesis 2.24, right after the creation of Eve: "*Mandaste al hombre por la mujer dexar el padre y la madre.* Agora no sólo aquello, mas a ti y a tu ley desamparan, como agora Calisto" ("[Lord], you commanded man to leave father and mother for the sake of a woman. Now they do not only that, but they also abandon you and your Law, as Calisto does now"; 94).[15]

In his ensuing diatribe against women, Sempronio again brings up Adam, warning Calisto that it was because of a woman that Adam was cast from

Paradise: "Por ellas es dicho: arma del diablo, cabeça de peccado, destrución de *paraýso*. ¿No has rezado en la festividad de San Juan, do dize: las mugeres y el vino hazen a los hombres renegar do dize: ésta es la mujer, antigua malicia que a *Adam* echó de los deleytes de *paraýso* . . . ?" ("It is said of them: 'Weapon of the devil, origin of sin, destruction.' Haven't you prayed during the feast of St. John, where they say: 'Women and wine make men renounce their faith; this is woman, the ancient malice that caused Adam to be cast from the delights of Paradise . . . ?'"; 97–98). Just before, Sempronio had reminded Calisto of the fate of famous men at the hands of women with words that are reminiscent of Adam's Fall: "Lee los yestoriales, estudia los filósofos, mira los poetas. Llenos están los libros de sus viles y malos enxemplos y de las *caýdas* que levaron los que en algo, como tú, las reputaron" ("Read the historians, study the philosophers, look at the poets. Their books are full of vile and evil examples of women and of the falls that befell those who, like you, have regarded them as being worthy"; 96).

Since these various allusions make Calisto an Adam of sorts, Melibea also becomes another Eve, at least implicitly. It is not surprising, therefore, that at one point Melibea's genitalia should be identified, through Greek mythology, with an apple (see Weiner 1969, 394–95). Calisto describes her vertically from head to toe—she is a green-eyed blonde—and concludes as follows: "Aquella proporción que veer yo no pude, no sin dubda por el bulto de fuera juzgo incomparablemente ser mejor que la que Paris juzgó entre las tres diesas" ("To guess from its outer shape, that part that I wasn't able to see must be incomparably superior to the one Paris judged among the three goddesses"; 101).

Calisto relates Melibea to the Apple of Discord once again while praising her beauty to Pármeno: "Si ella se hallara presente en aquel debate de la mançana con las tres diosas, nunca sobrenombre de discordia le pusieran, porque sin contrariar ninguna todas concedieran y vivieran conformes en que la llevara Melibea. Assí que se llamara mançana de concordia" ("Had she been present in that dispute about the apple with the three goddesses, it would never have been known as the Apple of Discord, since without objecting all would have agreed to let Melibea win it, and so it would have been called the Apple of Concord"; 190). Calisto's comparison of Melibea's "apple" to the Apple of Discord, however, suggests the forbidden fruit as well as the discord that led to God's expulsion of Adam and Eve from the earthly paradise.

Even Melibea associates herself with a fruit when she asks Calisto not to go too far just before they first make love in her garden: "Bástete, pues ya soy tuya, gozar de lo esterior, desto que es propio *fruto* de amadores; no me quieras robar *el mayor don* que la natura me ha dado" ("Since I am already yours, let it be enough to enjoy looking at me, for that is the *fruit* proper to lovers; do not seek to rob me of the *greatest gift* that nature has given me"; 285).

Chapter Five

Thus, the text doubly identifies Melibea with Eve and with the forbidden apple of the Tree of Knowledge. Since Eve and the apple were two different things, the final transgression comes about when both Calisto and Melibea taste the forbidden fruit—sex without the sanction of marriage.

Rojas's text further reinforces this analogy to the Garden of Eden by having Celestina, another serpent, make possible Calisto's and Melibea's tryst in the garden. Engaged by Calisto at Sempronio's suggestion after Melibea's angry initial rejection of him, the old bawd replicates the role of the devil disguised as a snake by tempting Melibea, who agrees to meet Calisto only after the procuress's intervention (see Ayerbe-Chaux). As we have seen, while playing this role, Celestina ironically repeats the very words that Christ had said to the devil in similar circumstances, when she asks Melibea: "¿y no sabes que por la divina boca fue dicho, contra aquel infernal tentador, que no de sólo pan biviriemos?" ("and don't you know what that divine mouth said against that tempting devil, that man shall not live by bread alone?"; 158).[16]

The text associates Celestina with the snake and the devil that it represents in other ways as well. Among the numerous ingredients that she stores for her witchcraft, we recall, there are vipers' tongues (112), an ingredient "associated with uncontrollable sexual desire" (Weiner 1969, 394). Moreover, Celestina owns a "bote del azeyte serpentino" ("container of snake oil"; 146), and anoints with snake oil the yarn that she pretends to sell as an excuse to enter into Melibea's house (148). The text is clearly connecting the procuress to a serpent in both of these instances, but, as we have seen, at one point Sempronio makes the analogy even clearer by referring to her as such: "el diablo me metió con ella. Más seguro me fuera huyr desta *venenosa bívora* que tomalla" ("the devil mixed me up with her. It would be safer for me to run away from this *poisonous snake* than to try to control her"; 174).

The parallels with the Garden of Eden come to an end when Calisto, like another Adam, falls to his death from the top of the ladder that he had used in order to scale the walls of Melibea's garden. Melibea is also cast out of this second paradise when, either unable or unwilling to go on living after Calisto's death, she commits suicide by jumping from a tower before the eyes of her father. Unlike Calisto, she undertakes her exit from the garden willingly but, nevertheless, her death also results from a fall. Elicia's curse upon discovering that Celestina had been killed has come true, for that prostitute had wished that the very grass of the earthly paradise where Calisto and Melibea took their pleasure would turn into snakes: "las yervas deleytosas donde tomáys los hurtados solazes se conviertan *en culebras*; los cantares se os tornen lloro; los sombrosos árboles del huerto se sequen con vuestra vista; sus flores olorosas se tornen de negra color" ("I hope that the delightful grass of the paradise where you have your hidden pleasure turns into snakes; may your songs become cries, the shady trees of the garden dry up before your eyes, and its sweet-smelling flowers turn black"; 298).

At another level, Melibea's garden also alludes to her sexual organs. This metaphor, which was very common during the Golden Age (Alzieu et al. 1984, 16, 138–39, 160–61, 280), still survives in modern folk poetry. In some modern versions of the ballad *La princesa y el segador*, for example, when the harvester asks the princess for the location of the crop that she wishes him to reap, she replies that it is "numa hortica funda / debaixo de mia enágua" ("in a deep garden / under my petticoat"; Costa Fontes 1987, no. 685).[17] Therefore, the "argumento" placed before the first act of *Celestina* effectively summarizes much of the action that follows because, besides mentioning Melibea's "huerta," it also refers to Calisto's "falcón," a hunting bird that, as we saw, constitutes a phallic metaphor: "Entrando Calisto una huerta empos dun falcon suyo, halló ý a Melibea, de cuyo amor preso, començóle de hablar" ("Entering a garden in pursuit of his falcon, Calisto found Melibea there and, falling in love, began to speak to her"; 85).

To medieval readers, the fact that Calisto later manages to enter into Melibea's garden, thus breaching its apparently impenetrable walls, conveyed exactly the same meaning. Consequently, it is easy to imagine their mirth when the enamored Calisto says: "de día estaré en mi cámara, *de noche en aquel paraýso dulce*, en aquel *alegre vergel* entre aquellas *suaves plantas y fresca verdura*" ("by day I'll stay in my room, *by night* in that *sweet paradise*, that *happy garden*, among those *gentle plants* and that *cool verdure*"; 292). To them, the paradise that Calisto mentions here was probably the same one that a young girl promised to a prospective lover in a Golden Age poem: "—Tú sí que gozarás mi paraíso" ("You are the one who will enjoy my paradise"; Alzieu et al. 1984, 213).

Another sexual connotation is involved when Calisto objects to Melibea that he would prefer Lucrecia, whom she has sent away, to remain in order to witness his "gloria" (285). The word was widely used in the poetry of the time as a euphemism for orgasm, which Calisto was about to achieve by penetrating Melibea's "paradise" (Whinnom 1981b, 41–43).

At still another level, Melibea's polysemous garden also stands for heaven itself, that is, the spiritual paradise that the earthly Garden of Eden represented. The tall walls that encircle it transform it into the unbreached *hortus conclusus* ("enclosed garden"), which in medieval Christian art was emblematic of the Virgin Mary because of the dogma concerning her perpetual virginity (Weinberg 1971, 143). Within this garden there is a tower that, besides linking heaven and earth, could also be taken to represent the Blessed Mother's perpetual virginity; one of her titles was "Turris Davitica" ("Tower of David").[18] Moreover, the ladder that Calisto uses to scale the walls of this garden corresponds to the biblical ladder of Jacob; besides also linking heaven and earth, the latter's rungs represent the virtues needed to reach heaven in medieval iconography (Barbera 1970, 11–12). Consequently, the "glory" that Calisto experiences in this garden also stands for the glory of the redeemed in heaven.

Since other, devoutly Christian writers used potentially religious words such as *huerto* ("garden"), *paraíso* ("paradise"), *gloria* ("glory"), and so on, as erotic metaphors in their own works, one cannot accuse Rojas of heresy on these grounds alone. At the time, we recall, numerous authors of unquestionable orthodoxy even used key words related to the Passion of Christ, like *muerte* ("death"), *pasión* ("passion"), and *resucitar* ("to resuscitate") as sexual metaphors (see Tillier 1985). As we shall see, however, Rojas took matters much further.

Through their trysts in the "huerto," which also represents the Garden of Eden, where they taste the forbidden fruit with the help of a serpent, and their apparent punishment by dying in two separate falls, Calisto and Melibea reenact the drama of our first parents, thereby being transformed into another Adam and another Eve.

Any garden could suggest paradise, but these parallels are too numerous for all of this to be a matter of pure coincidence, and, as we have just seen, the author also linked Calisto and Melibea with Adam and Eve in other ways. Moreover, the text purposely equates this garden, which is portrayed as Calisto's "paradise," with the spiritual Christian heaven as well. The garden's depiction as an *hortus conclusus* brings to mind "Mary's little garden," and the Virgin Mary was also known as Queen of Heaven. The correspondence between Calisto's and Jacob's ladders and the "glory" experienced by Calisto and Melibea recall heaven rather than the earthly paradise. In all probability, rather than constituting subconscious artistic parallels that came about as Rojas was writing, the correspondences between Melibea's garden, the Garden of Eden, and the spiritual Christian heaven were quite deliberate on the author's part.

There is further evidence to support this interpretation. Besides reenacting the drama of our first parents, the transformation of Calisto and Melibea into another Adam and another Eve brings to mind the Christian dogma concerning the New Adam and the New Eve. According to Christian doctrine, the Virgin Mary was a new Eve "who repaired by her obedience what the first Eve had devastated by her disobedience" (*New Catholic Encyclopedia* [1967], 9: 355). Whereas Eve had disobeyed God by eating the fruit of the Tree of the Knowledge of Good and Evil, inducing Adam to follow her example, Mary's obedience consisted of her acceptance of God's will, as portrayed in the Annunciation. When the Angel Gabriel told her that she would bear the Son of God by the grace of the Holy Spirit, she replied: "Behold the handmaiden of the Lord; be it done to me according to thy word" (Luke 1.38).[19] On the other hand, Christianity viewed Christ as the New or Second Adam. Together, Mother and Son reenacted the story of the Fall in reverse, for it was thanks to the birth of Christ that it became possible for humanity to regain the paradise lost by Adam and Eve, with the difference that the original earthly Garden of Eden now became transformed into a spiritual paradise to be attained only after death: "As mediatrix, Mary was also the Second Eve, just as Christ was the Second Adam. As it had been through a woman that the earth had come under the curse of sin and death, so it would be through a woman that blessing would be restored to the earth" (Pelikan 1978, 167).

This doctrine was well known in medieval Spain. In his *Milagros de Nuestra Señora*, Berceo stated that

> Los que por Eva fuemos   en perdición caídos,
> por ella recombramos   los solares perdidos;
> si por ella non fuesse   iazriémos amortidos,
> mas el so sancto fructo   nos ovo redemidos.
>
> Por el so sancto fructo   que ella concibió,
> que por salud del mundo   passión e muert sufrió,
> issiemos de la foya   que Adán nos abrió,
> quando sobre deviedo   del mal muesso mordió.
>
>   (1987, cc. 621–22 [40])

As Gerli indicated, the "tipología que ligaba la Virgen a Eva era tan difundida durante la Edad Media que llegó a constituirse en torno a ella una especie de paranomasia anagramática entre la clerecía. Sabemos que la dualidad Ave/Eva, Eva/Ave se conocía en la España del siglo XIII" ("typology that connected the Virgin to Eve was so current during the Middle Ages that a sort of anagram-like play on words related to it came to develop among the clergy. We know that the dualism Ave/Eva and Eva/Ave was known in thirteenth-century Spain"; 1985, 8). The following song of praise in Alfonso X's *Cantigas de Santa María* constitutes an excellent example of this duality:

> *Entre Av' e Eva*
> *gran departiment'á.*
>
> Ca Eva nos tolleu
> o Parays' e Deus,
> Ave nos y meteu;
> porend', amigos meus:
> *entre Av' e Eva*
> *gran departiment'á.*
>
>   (1986–89, no. 60 [41])

Chapter Five

The *villancico* ("Christmas carol") that follows documents that the dogma that viewed Christ and his Mother as a New Adam and a New Eve was still well known in seventeenth-century Spain:

> Albricias, zagales;
> Que nacido ha
> El mas bello niño
> 10   De nuestro lugar;
> El que al hombre preso
> Viene á libertar,
> Y este es paraíso
> Del *segundo Adan*.
> 15   El soldado fuerte,
> Diestro capitan,
> Que de los abismos,
> Muerto, triunfará;
> Por quien *Eva en Ave*
> 20   Se pudo mudar. . . .
> (Sancha 1950, 195*b* [no. 477] [42])

It is pointless to belabor the analogy with additional examples; today, it remains as crucial to Christian doctrine as it did in the past.

In the pages that follow, I will show that Rojas's artistic creation of Calisto and Melibea as another Adam and Eve is probably related to this essential dogma, for the text also links Calisto deliberately with Christ, and Melibea with the Virgin Mary. From a Christian perspective, the idea is incredibly blasphemous, and it is difficult to understand how Rojas could possibly dare to do such a thing, but the evidence that follows will show that this is probably what he had in mind.

The text portrays Melibea as a virgin. In her virginity, she parallels the Blessed Mother. Rojas places her in an *hortus conclusus* that, besides recalling Mary's perpetual virginity, also suggests the Garden of Eden as well as the Christian heaven. As we know, medieval Christianity placed a premium on chastity and virginity: "Christ had not only remained a virgin himself and chosen to be born of a virgin, but he had even selected as his guardian and putative father one who was also a virgin. . . . Christian virgins shared in Mary's reversal of the victory that the 'ancient foe' had achieved over Eve in the fall" (Pelikan 1978, 164). Because of this emphasis, the Blessed Mother, besides being known as Queen of Heaven, was also given the title of "Regina Virginum" ("Queen of Virgins").

Melibea's complaint to Calisto, right after making love, that he has caused her to lose "el nombre y corona de virgen por tan breve deleyte" ("the name and crown of a virgin for such a brief pleasure"; 286) would seem to link her even more directly with the Blessed Mother. Medieval iconography portrayed the Virgin Mary, as Queen of Heaven, with a crown (Pelikan 1978, 168–69).

Obviously, "el nombre y corona de virgen" ("the name and crown of a virgin") constitutes "una frase hecha" ("a standard expression"), a mere commonplace without any necessarily ulterior ramifications. Through his utilization of this commonplace, however, Rojas also meant to say something else, for, by making Melibea refer to her lost "crown," he also linked her, once more, with the Blessed Mother, the Queen of Virgins, right after the girl loses her virginity. Moreover, besides depicting Calisto as another Adam in Melibea's paradise, he also portrayed him as a Christ of sorts.

Since Christianity also viewed Jesus as a new Adam—as Gerli pointed out, "el advenimiento de Cristo no solamente marca la salvación del hombre y cumple con las profecías del Antiguo Testamento, sino que simboliza la repetición invertida de la historia de Adán" ("the coming of Christ not only marks the salvation of humankind, fulfilling the prophecies of the Old Testament; it also symbolizes the repetition of the story of Adam in reverse"; 1985, 7–8)—it is not surprising to find that, at one point, Celestina describes Calisto to Melibea as being like another Christ who will redeem her from the "wound" that afflicts her: "No desconfíe, señora, tu noble juventud de salud; que quando el alto Dios da la llaga, tras ella embía el remedio. Mayormente que sé yo *al mundo nascida una flor* que de todo esto te delibre" ("Do not allow, my Lady, your noble youth to despair of gaining health for, when the mighty God sends the wound, he sends the remedy for it afterward. Moreover, I know of a *flower born unto the world* who will deliver you from all this"; 244).[20]

Medieval Christians believed that "flor" ("flower") was one of the names given to Christ in the Old Testament. According to Fray Luis de León, "si en el capítulo treinta y cuatro de Ezequiel es llamado *planta nombrada*, y si Esaías en el capítulo onze le llama unas vezes *rama*, y otra *flor*, y en el capítulo cincuenta y tres, *tallo* y *rayz*, todo es dezirnos lo que el nombre de PIMPOLLO o de fructo nos dize" ("if in chapter thirty-four of Ezekiel he is called *plant*, and Isaiah sometimes calls him *branch*, and another *flower*, and in chapter fifty-three *stalk* and *root*, all of this is meant to tell us what the name of BUD or *fruit* tells us"; 1966–69, 1: 58–59). The Blessed Alonso de Orozco said exactly the same thing, but more succinctly: "Ezequiel le llamó *Planta nombrada* y Esaías unas veces le llama *Rama*, y otras veces *Flor*, *Tallo* y *Raíz*; que es decirnos lo que el nombre de Pimpollo" ("Ezekiel called him *plant* and Isaiah at times calls him *branch*, and other times *Flower*, *Stalk*, and *Root*; which tells us the same as the name BUD"; 1966, 260). Christ's name as "flower" is also common enough in poetry. In some verses on the

Chapter Five

flight to Egypt by Fray Ambrosio de Montesino, who was very active in the court of the Catholic Kings, the Blessed Mother tells her Son not to cry with the following words:

> Callad vos, mi luz é aviso,
> Pues que vuestro Padre quiso
> Que seais del paraíso
> F*lor* que nunca *se desflora*
> Y llora.
>
> (Sancha 1950, 459*a* [43])

Gil Vicente used the same metaphor twice in a beautiful song included in his *Auto da Feira* (c. 1527):

> Branca estais, colorada,
> Virgem sagrada.
> Em Belém, vila do amor,
> da rosa naceu *a flor*,
> Virgem sagrada.
> Em Belém, vila do amor,
> naceo a rosa do rosal,
> Virgem sagrada.
> Da rosa naceo *a flor*,
> pera nosso Salvador,
> Virgem sagrada.
> Naceo a rosa do rosal,
> Deos e homem natural,
> Virgem sagrada.
>
> (1979, 138 [44])

Alonso de Bonilla opened a poem published in 1617 by referring to Christ as a flower that was born without being seeded, an evident allusion to Mary's perpetual virginity:

> *Flor* sin sembrar producida,
> ¿Por qué en pesebre á luz sales?
> ¿Quieres que esos animales
> Te pazcan recien nacida?
>
> (Sancha 1950, 223 [no. 594] [45])

There are many other examples, but these suffice to establish that "flor" was one of the names traditionally used to designate Christ. Rojas applied it to the lovesick Calisto and decided to compound the heresy, making it even greater, by suggesting that God had sent the cure for Melibea's infirmity, just as God the Father had sent Christ to redeem humanity from Original

Sin. Furthermore, Rojas made God responsible for the wound from which Melibea suffers, a wound that, besides bringing to mind the wounds of Christ, also happens to be a metaphor for sexual desire as well as for her vagina.[21] Since Calisto is another new Adam and Melibea another new Eve, the monstrosity of what Rojas did becomes readily apparent.

So far, besides his possible standing as a New Adam of sorts, all that Calisto has in common with Christ is the fact that Celestina, the serpent who makes Melibea, depicted as another "manzana" ("apple"), available to him, refers to her young, apparently inexperienced client as "una flor al mundo nacida" ("a flower born unto the world") who will deliver her from her "infirmity." And besides her virginity, the identification of Melibea with an *hortus conclusus* is all that links her with the Virgin Mary.

Further textual evidence, however, supports the thesis presented here. When Calisto arrives at the door of her garden for the first tryst, Melibea asks who told him to come, and he replies: "Es la que tiene mereçimiento de mandar a todo el mundo" ("It was the one who is worthy to command the whole world"; 259). These words could have been addressed to the Virgin as well. Right after, when Melibea says that she came only to tell him to forget about her, Calisto protests, stating that she holds "las llaves de mi perdición y gloria" ("the keys to my perdition or my glory"; 260), as if he could achieve salvation only through her, and this, of course, brings to mind the role of the Virgin as Mediatrix. Mollified, Melibea calls him "mi señor y mi bien todo" ("my lord and my whole love"; 261), as if he were another Christ, and the ecstatic Calisto thanks her with words that could apply to the Blessed Mother as well: "¡O señora mía, esperança de mi gloria, descanso y alivio de mi pena,[22] alegría de mi corazón!" ("Oh my Lady, hope of my glory, repose and relief of my sorrow, joy of my heart!"; 261). Then he declares himself unworthy of her love, and treats the whole event as a miracle, addressing Melibea as if she were a goddess: "Pues, ¡o alto Dios!, ¿cómo te podré ser ingrato, que tan milagrosamente as obrado conmigo tus suaves maravillas?" ("How then, oh God in the Highest, can I ever be ungrateful to you, since you have worked your soft wonders so miraculously upon me?"; 261) These words do not necessarily involve a contradiction, for, as we know, even some Christians thought that the proportions that the cult of the Blessed Mother had reached were transforming her into a goddess.

Rojas then goes on to make the relationship between Calisto and Melibea with Jesus and the Virgin Mary even clearer. During the second tryst, Melibea begins by calling herself Calisto's "sierva" ("servant") and "cativa" ("captive"; 284), thus behaving like a mystic nun in the throes of a divine vision. Calisto, who already has her in his arms, replies with epithets that are transparently sacrilegious, and the rapture that he describes is anything but mystical: "O *angélica ymagen*, o *preciosa perla*, ante quien el mundo es

Chapter Five

feo. O *mi señora* y *mi gloria*, en mis braços te tengo y no lo creo. Mora en mi persona tanta turbación de plazer que me haze no sentir todo el gozo que posseo" ("Oh *angelic image*, oh *precious pearl* before whom the whole world is ugly! Oh *my Lady and glory*, I hold you in my arms and yet I can't believe it. The pleasure I feel perturbs me so much that I cannot comprehend all the joy that is mine"; 284). But then, when Melibea at first denies him the heavenly "glory" he seeks, Calisto protests that it is unjust for her to refuse him "sweet harbor" after all he has suffered on her account: "No me pides tal covardía; no es hazer tal cosa de ninguno que hombre sea, mayormente como yo, nadando por este huego de tu desseo toda mi vida. ¿No quieres que me arrime al *dulce puerto* a descansar de mis passados trabajos?" ("Don't ask me for such cowardliness; no man would do such a thing, especially loving as I do, since I have been drowning in the fire of this desire for you all of my life. Don't you want me to snuggle up into the *sweet harbor* in order to rest from my past suffering?"; 285).

Besides its erotic connotations, Calisto's reference to Melibea as "dulce puerto" ("sweet harbor") is related to one of Mary's titles because of a linguistic pun on her name: "One [title] was the identification of the Virgin as 'Mary, the star of the sea [Maria maris stella],' a name that was said to have been given her from on high" (Pelikan 1978, 162).

In the thirteenth century, Berceo referred to the Blessed Mother as "Estrella de los mares, güiona deseada" ("Star of the Sea, desired guide"; 1987, 32*b*) and "La Virgen glorïosa, estrella de la mar" ("The Glorious Virgin, Star of the Sea"; 73*a*). In two of the refrains of his *Cantigas*, Alfonso X called her "a Virgen, estrela do mar" ("The Virgin, Star of the Sea"; 1986–89, no. 112) and "Strela do Dia, / ca assi pelo mar grande / come pela terra guia" ("Star of the Day / who thus through the vastness of the sea / guides as she does on land"; no. 325). That is why "Ella es dicha *puerto* a qui todos corremos" ("She is called *harbor* to which we all hasten"; Berceo 1987, 35*c*). As patron of sailors, the Blessed Mother guides them to a good, safe harbor, and, since all human beings were regarded as sailors in this life, "the image of Mary as the star guiding the ship of faith was an especially attractive one" (Pelikan 1978, 162).

Calisto's reference to Melibea as "buen puerto" ("safe harbor") does not necessarily indicate anything in itself, of course, but Melibea's reply—notice the disjunction—suggests otherwise. She begs Calisto to keep still, to refrain from taking the greatest gift (i.e., "the apple") that nature has given her, for, though the good shepherd shears his ewes, he should not despoil and render them useless: "Bástete, pues ya soy tuya, gozar de lo esterior, desto que es propio fruto de amadores; no me quieras robar el mayor don que la natura me ha dado; cata que del *buen pastor* es propio tresquilar sus ovejas y ganado, pero no destruyrlo y estragallo" ("Since I am already yours, let it be

Christian Prayer and Dogma

enough to enjoy looking at me, for that is the fruit proper to lovers; do not seek to rob me of the greatest gift that nature has given me. Look that it is proper for the *good shepherd* to sheer his sheep and stock, but not to destroy and ruin them"; 285).

The good shepherd is none other than Christ, of course. The expression was so current in medieval European literature that there is no point in documenting it. Moreover, the fact that Melibea refers to Calisto as "buen pastor" ("good shepherd") right after he had addressed her as "buen puerto" ("safe harbor") cannot be discarded as a mere coincidence. Notwithstanding the humor that is present in the utilization of the two expressions—Melibea's "buen puerto" ("safe harbor") also stands for her vagina,[23] and Calisto, unlike a good shepherd, intends to do more than just to "shear" her[24]—the two comparisons are simply heretical. Since Calisto and Melibea make love shortly afterward, what is being artistically projected here is an incestuous relationship between Mother and Son.

The religious imagery continues. After returning home at dawn, Calisto worries for a few moments about the dishonor that the execution of his servants has brought him, since he failed to avenge them as he should, and, in the same breath, he decides to spend the days in his room, and the nights "en aquel paraýso dulce" ("in that sweet paradise"; 292). Afterward, as if Melibea were a divine figure, he tries to envision "la presencia angélica de aquella ymagen luziente" ("the angelical presence of that luminous image"; 292). During the third tryst narrated in the text—there were others—Calisto begins to speak to Melibea, once again, as if she were more than a mere mortal: "O mi señora y mi bien todo, ¿quál mujer podría aver nascida que desprivasse tu gran merescimiento?" ("Oh my Lady and all my love, how could a born woman possibly detract from you?"; 322). In her turn, Melibea, once again, addresses Calisto as if he were Christ, and she herself a mystic in the throes of the divine vision: "O sabrosa trayción, o dulçe sobresalto, ¿es mi señor y mi alma, es él? No lo puedo creer. ¿Dónde estavas, luziente sol? ¿Dónde me tenías tu claridad escondida?" ("Oh pleasant treason, oh sweet surprise! Is it my Lord and my soul, is it? I can't believe it. Where were you, shining sun? Where were you hiding your brightness from me?"; 322).

But this idyllic tone changes when Melibea asks Calisto to leave her clothes alone, suggesting that they should tarry and enjoy each other's company in other ways. Calisto refuses to waste any time with preliminaries, however, and replies with incredible vulgarity and rudeness: "Señora, el que quiere comer el ave, quita primero las plumas" ("Madam, he who wishes to eat a bird must first pluck out its feathers"; 324). Thus, Calisto compares coitus with food, a comparison that, as Lacarra pointed out, was frequent enough "en la lírica cortesana y popular de sátiras y burlas" ("in the courtly and in the popular lyric dealing with satire and jests"; Rojas 1995, 174n565; see also Alzieu et al. 1984, s.v. "comer [*futuere, futui*]"). This sudden, unexpected change in tone, besides constituting a parody of the courtly lover, suggests that Rojas may be up to something else.

Still trying to slow down Calisto, Melibea asks if he would like Lucrecia to fetch him a drink. He replies: "No ay otra colación para mí sino tener tu cuerpo y belleza en mi poder; comer y bever dondequiera se da por dinero y cada tiempo se puede aver y qualquiera lo puede alcançar, pero lo no vendible, lo que en toda la tierra no ay igual que en este huerto, ¿cómo mandas que se me passe ningún momento que no goze?" ("I wish no refreshment other than your body and your beauty in my power. Food and drink can be bought anywhere for money, can be had at any time, and anyone can get it. But what money cannot buy and has no equal in all the world other than in this garden, how can you tell me to spend even one moment without enjoying it?"; 324).

These words enclose pornographic and religious levels of meaning. On the surface, Calisto refuses a drink from Lucrecia because, at least for the moment, the only food and drink in which he is interested is Melibea. There is no woman like her in the whole earth. She is priceless, nothing at all like prostitutes, who can be had for money at any time (see Lacarra's interpretation in Rojas 1995, 174n569). At another level, there is a comparison between coitus and Communion, for the Eucharist consists of food (bread) and drink (wine). Morón Arroyo interpreted the episode as follows: "En el momento del goce Melibea pregunta si Calisto desea una colación. Por la respuesta, parece como si Calisto viera la fusión sexual con Melibea como una comunión profanada" ("In the moment of pleasure, Melibea asks Calisto if he wants a refreshment. From his answer, it seems as if Calisto viewed his sexual union with Melibea as a profaned Communion"; 1984, 49).

This metamorphosis of coitus into a Communion of sorts also brings to mind the Jewish objections to the doctrine of Transubstantiation, which teaches that either the Host or a piece of bread, together with wine, are transformed into the body and blood of Christ. According to Rabbi Crescas, Christians make God for themselves every day, and "there is no difference between making him by hand or by word, since their priests believe that they make God by word when they say, 'This is my body; this is my blood'" (1992, 61). Later on, some conversos maintained that the Eucharist was just a piece of bread or dough. In 1526, a converso from Las Palmas remembered having heard his father say to his mother that "God being present in the Host was nonsense" (Gitlitz 1996, 150). In 1549, João Manuel, a Portuguese converso, complained that "they want me to believe that the Host that the priest is kneading at night with his mistress the next day becomes the true and complete God!" (151). Others complained that, if that was indeed the case, Communion was really a form of cannibalism (150).[25]

Christian Prayer and Dogma

In a way, then, Rojas transforms the sex act between Calisto and Melibea into another form of Communion, with Melibea serving as the Host, while turning Calisto into a cannibal of sorts. After all, he had compared Melibea to a bird shortly before, telling her that she had to be plucked so that he could proceed to devour her. Since Melibea represents the Virgin Mary and Calisto stands for Christ, the blasphemy is monstrous.

But Rojas is not yet satisfied, for he does not stop at this. As they are making love for the third time (the aroused Lucrecia, who is listening, remarks that "a tres me parece que va la vencida" ["it seems to me they are on the third round"; 324]), Calisto tells Melibea: "Jamás, querría, señora, que amanesciesse, según la gloria y descanso que mi sentido recibe de la noble conversación de tus delicados miembros" ("I only wish, Madam, that daylight would never break, considering the glory and peace that my senses receive from this noble communion with your delicate flesh"; 324). Melibea reacts as follows: "*Señor*, yo soy la que gozo, yo la que gano; tú, señor, el que me hazes con tu *visitación* incomparable *merced*" ("*My Lord*, I am the one who rejoices most, it is I who profit. You, my Lord, are the one who bestows upon me an incomparable *favor* with your *visitation*"; 324).

As Severin observed, this passage "features angelic imagery. Calisto now becomes Melibea's god, an angel who visits her in her garden" (1995, 42). Here Calisto is indeed portrayed as being both an angel and a god, and Melibea's gratitude to him for "visiting" her brings to mind the Annunciation, where an angel visits and tells the Virgin Mary that she has found grace with God, and will conceive and bear a son by the grace of the Holy Spirit: "The Holy Spirit shall come upon thee and the power of the most High shall overshadow thee; and therefore the Holy One to be born shall be called the Son of God" (Luke 1.35).[26]

The Blessed Mother then visits her cousin, St. Elizabeth, who was pregnant with St. John the Baptist, whom she had miraculously conceived despite her old age, and proffers the *Magnificat*, the beautiful prayer in which she thanks the Lord for having chosen her (Luke 1.46–55). Note that Melibea's gratitude to Calisto for the "incomparable merced" ("incomparable favor") that he is bestowing upon her recalls the Blessed Mother's prayer.

Up to this point, Calisto has been portrayed as another Christ, i.e., as the Second Person of the Holy Trinity. Now he is related to the First Person, God the Father, for it is to him that the *Magnificat* is addressed. Given the context—Calisto and Melibea were in the process of making love for the third time when these words are spoken—the use of this imagery is incredibly blasphemous, and even more so on the part of a converso.

According to Morón Arroyo, who was the first one to notice the sacrilegious manner in which the Eucharist is demystified, "en todas estas alusiones, a mi parecer indiscutibles, debemos evitar ver alegorías" ("all of these allusions seem indisputable to me, but we must avoid seeing allegories in them"; 1984, 49). In his opinion, paradise and Communion are mere images, and he goes on to say that Calisto adores Celestina as if she were the Virgin in her role as Mediatrix (49–50). In other words, if Celestina is like the Virgin, Melibea could not possibly be another Virgin as well. Unrestricted by such logic, Rojas does exactly that, however, thereby creating two monstrous allegories. Celestina represents the Blessed Mother as Mediatrix, as well as what those who saw her as a common, unfaithful wife thought of her. Melibea represents the Virgin Mary as daughter, wife, and mother of God, which, according to logic, constitutes an impossibility. That is why, when Calisto and Melibea make love, what is being artistically projected is an incestuous relationship between Mother and Son. In order for the Son to be one with the Father and the Holy Spirit, as Christians maintained, he would have to sleep with his own mother, fathering himself in the process. It is only in such a manner, albeit illogical, that the Virgin could simultaneously be mother and wife of God, as well as his daughter.

This vulgar charge is closely related to the view that the Christian dogmas of the Incarnation and the Virgin Birth were illogical and therefore preposterous (Lasker 1977, 105–34, 153–59). In his *Refutation of Christian Principles*, we recall, Rabbi Crescas dedicated separate chapters to each of those dogmas. Regarding the dogma of the Incarnation, Jews and some conversos argued that it was ridiculous to believe that God, who was pure spirit, should choose to be born of a mortal woman. Around 1478, Jehuda Gargonia, a converso, told a friend: "I hold it is very impossible that our Lord God had to take on human flesh and it is very hard [to believe] that God should command the Jews to do one thing and command the contrary thing to the Christians and this is a great marvel to me" (Gutwirth 1996, 261). In 1541, Simão Vaz said in Lisbon that God "had no need of putting himself into the womb of a woman and that the Messiah was not God" (Gitlitz 1996, 138). In 1686, Pedro Onofre Cortés, of Majorca, pleaded guilty to having said that "although the Christians say that Christ is God, it cannot be, because he was born and died, and God is infinite, and is not born and cannot die, because He is the creator, and His greatness does not fit in a man" (139).

As documented in numerous inquisitorial trials, many conversos also refused to believe that the Blessed Mother remained a Virgin after conceiving and giving birth to Jesus. As far as they were concerned, since she had deceived her husband, she was no better than a prostitute. We already saw some examples of this disrespectful attitude in Chapter 1 (pp. 26–27), but I will add a couple more in order to illustrate the point. Around 1465, Salvadora Salvat, a conversa with three children, told them by the fire that "while Joseph had gone from home an iron-monger came into the house where Joseph had left St. Mary and that iron-monger did it with St. Mary and from that came out Jesus Christ, son of the iron-monger" (Gutwirth 1996, 272). Once again the Blessed Mother is depicted as anything but a virgin, and a faithless wife to boot. During the 1480s, Fray Alonso de Nogales, one of the Jeronimite monks in Guadalupe, "speculated about the channel by which Jesus was conceived and born" (Sicroff 2000, 600). When someone suggested to him that Jesus had been conceived when the word of the Annunciation entered Mary's ear, and that Jesus had emerged from her the same way, Fray Alonso walked away, repeating scornfully: "Through the ear? Through the ear?" (600).

The dogma of the Holy Trinity did not fare any better. To uncompromising monotheists, Trinitarian Christians were in fact polytheists, even though they regarded the Father, the Son, and the Holy Spirit to be three in one. As we have already seen, the difficulty that the numerous conversos who sought refuge in Italy after the establishment of the Inquisition (1481) had in accepting the dogma of the Holy Trinity was so well known to their Italian hosts that they referred to it as the *peccadiglio di Spagna* ("the little sin from Spain"; Pérez 1981, 100). What Pedro, a silversmith from Catalayud, told a Christian neighbor around 1486 reflected the opinion of many others: "The Trinity is a joke and if Jesus Christ was God why did he have to call his father [when he was on the Cross] and since he was the Lord why did he have to say *Pater maior me est*?" ("My Father is greater than me"; Gutwirth 1996, 261–62).

In one of the medieval debates between rabbis and Christian theologians, Profit Duran, a rabbi, referred to this dogma as a mere syllogism. He wrote the following in a letter to a recently converted friend:

> God forbid that you should believe that the conclusions of the first mood of the first figure of the figures of the syllogisms, which is the foundation of the whole science of logic, will follow from the conditional predicated on the universal. You will be led into a denial of the faith if you should say (A) The Father is God; (B) God is the Son; this should not "generate" the result that (C) The Father is the Son. (Lasker 1977, 90)[27]

According to Lasker's interpretation, "Duran was saying that, despite Christian teaching that the Father was God and God was the Son, the Christians did not draw the logical inference that the Father was the Son" (1977, 219n323). In other words, what Duran implied is that the Son would have had to have had an incestuous relationship with his mother in order to be one, or the same as, his own father, even though this was equally illogical. A contemporary rabbi appears to agree with this interpretation for, in his opinion, Duran was merely joking: "As Joseph ben Shem Tov commented, Duran wrote in jest, since the conclusion would obviously follow from the premises" (Lasker 1977, 90). Fraker also seems to have understood the third part of the "witty" syllogism in a similar manner. Comparing Duran's objections to the Holy Trinity with those of another rabbi, Joseph Albó, who participated in the famous Judeo-Christian Disputation of Tortosa (1413–14), he writes: "Profit Duran expresses the same 'philosophical' bias in much cruder and simpler terms" (Fraker 1966, 37). From a Christian perspective, however, the slightest suggestion of an incestuous relationship between Our Lord and his mother exceeded mere crudity by far; such a blasphemous, unthinkable idea constituted a heresy of the worst sort.

Rojas implied precisely this, however, in associating Calisto with Christ, and Melibea with the Virgin. Notwithstanding the Greek origin and appropriateness of their respective names,[28] phonetically, "Calisto" happens to be suspiciously close to "Cristo,"[29] and "Melibea," though distant from "María," begins and ends with the same letters. This could be a mere coincidence, and it will never be possible to prove otherwise. Given what we know now, however, the chances are that it is not.

The Christian belief in the Holy Trinity was expressed in poems where Mary was called Wife and Mother of God, as well as Virgin, as in the following *canción* ("song") by Juan del Encina: "Esposa y Madre de Dios, / sagrada Virgen bendita" ("Wife and Mother of God / sacred, blessed Virgin"; 1972, no. 101). In another of his poems, Encina wrote that the Virgin is both daughter and mother of her Creator, who, in turn, is her father and son as well:

> Vos sois *hija*, vos sois *madre*
> de Aquél mesmo que os crió.
> Él es vuestro *hijo* y *padre*
> y por madre a vos nos dio.
>
> (1972, no. 54 [46])[30]

Like his Jewish ancestors and many of his fellow conversos, Rojas was unable to fathom such reasoning. The artistically projected incestuous relationship he presented reflects the thought of those who, unable to accept the central dogmas of Christianity, insisted on viewing the illogical wonders that it proposes in human terms. It did not make any sense to them that a mortal woman could simultaneously be daughter, wife, and mother of God, and that her son could be her son and father, as well as his own father.

Calisto's penetration of Melibea's *hortus conclusus*, then, reflects the objections of those who could not accept the dogmas of the Incarnation, the Virgin Birth, Transubstantiation, the Holy Trinity, and everything that they

Christian Prayer and Dogma

implied. The relationship of Calisto and Melibea as New Adam and New Eve corrosively illustrates the consequences of God the Son begetting himself as a result of being one with the Father.

While falling from the top of the ladder that he had used to enter his carnal paradise—a ladder whose rungs, since they had been used to sin, can be presumed to represent vices rather than the virtues depicted in medieval iconography as needed to reach heaven (Barbera 1970, 12)—Calisto calls on the Blessed Mother whose *hortus conclusus* he has defiled. His last words are: "¡O válame Santa María, muerto soy! ¡Confessión!" ("Oh, may the Holy Mary help me! I'm dying! Confession!"; 326). Melibea commits suicide a few days later by jumping from the tower in her father's garden.

At the time of his death, Calisto had committed a mortal sin; he had just fornicated with Melibea. Since he asked for confession, it could be surmised that God's decision in the matter is inscrutable, and that the Lord could have forgiven him (Deyermond 1984). Both Tristán (327) and Melibea (334), however, lament that Calisto died without confession because such a death meant "sure descent into hell" (Eesley 1983, 19). Today, at least in the rural, unsophisticated Catholic societies that tend to hold on to old, conservative ideas, death in a state of mortal sin still carries the same penalty. As we saw in the previous chapter, since confession is a Christian sacrament, Calisto is thrown into a Christian hell.

Although Melibea commends her soul to God before jumping from the tower, according to Christianity, both medieval and modern, only God can take away the life that he gives. As a suicide, Melibea is automatically condemned to the Christian hell to which Calisto had already gone.[31] Such a death is only fitting, for, after all, Melibea's purpose was to rejoin her deceased lover, who had died in a state of sin without the benefit of any sacraments. Consequently, it is not too far-fetched to deduce that Rojas, besides the blasphemy of suggesting an incestuous relationship between Our Lord and his Mother, was also perversely throwing them out of heaven.

The fate that Rojas assigned to his protagonists in the afterlife further demonstrates his hatred of Christianity. In the Old Testament, Adam and Eve are exiled from the Garden of Eden after eating the forbidden fruit, being commanded to multiply while living elsewhere on earth. According to St. Paul, their sin is transmitted from generation to generation,[32] barring their children and the children of their children not just from the Garden of Eden, but also from heaven. This is the Original Sin from which Christ and his Mother free mankind. As the New Eve, Mary crushes the head of the serpent by giving birth to Christ, the New Adam whose death on the cross enables Christians to reverse the inherited guilt derived from humankind's first parents through the sacrament of Baptism. His sacrifice makes it possible for

Chapter Five

Christians to return to paradise, with the difference that the earthly Garden of Eden is transformed into a spiritual paradise (see the *New Catholic Encyclopedia* 1967, 9: 354–55).

In *Celestina*, Melibea's garden offers an allegorical representation of this paradise. As mediator, the serpentine, diabolic Celestina enables Calisto to penetrate it, but the incestuous glory that the lovers experience as a result leads to their eternal damnation, as well as to the damnation of the false religion that they represent.

For, according to Judaism, there is no such thing as Original Sin: "Adam's bequest to his descendants consists only in physical death and the necessity of 'eating bread in the sweat of one's brow'; there is no question of inherited guilt and none of the abandonment to Hell on account of his sin" (Fraker 1966, 16). Since there was no Original Sin, there was no need to be redeemed from anything, and Christ's role as Savior was nothing but a hoax. From this perspective, then, Christianity could be viewed as an abomination, for it perverted the word of God as handed down in the Torah; hence the systematic perversion of Christian prayer and the Scriptures in *Celestina*. That is also why, whereas Adam and Eve are merely exiled from the Garden of Eden for their transgression, Calisto, Melibea, and the Christianity that they come to represent—a religion that, after all, would never have existed without the New Adam and the New Eve for which they stand—are mercilessly thrown into a Christian hell.

In sum, Rojas's apparently didactic purpose constitutes a clever, indispensable cover for a bitter, multipronged attack on Christianity. Through his characters, he mocked the Christian interpretation of the Old Testament, the New Testament, Christian prayer, the Virginity of Mary, the Incarnation, Transubstantiation, and the Holy Trinity. Since he could not possibly have written such things openly during his time, he exercised his human need to express what he thought in a covert, ambiguous, artistic manner. Although Rojas knew that his book could be interpreted in various ways, he still felt a need for the profuse, precautionary exculpations found in the preliminary and postliminary materials added after 1499, where he referred to Christ in an open, apparently pious manner. As Snow pointed out, these materials probably succeeded in deflecting criticism, for *Celestina* did not figure in the index until 1640 (1995, 254–55). I would like to add that these materials also helped Rojas to hide his attack against the central dogmas of Christianity. Since he was unlikely to go to all of this trouble for himself alone, he also did it for the sake of the learned, like-minded conversos who were more likely to understand this aspect of his work. As we will see in the next chapters, one of them was Francisco Delicado, an exiled Andalusian who tried to compete with Rojas in this and in other respects as well.

Chapter Six

"Sailing," Renaissance Rome, and Exile in *La Lozana andaluza*

An Allegorical Reading

Written by Francisco Delicado, an Andalusian priest who lived in Rome for many years, *La Lozana andaluza* (Venice, 1530) opens with a prologue (167–70) where the author dedicates his book to an unidentified "Ilustre Señor" ("Illustrious Lord"),[1] claiming that he is merely describing what he saw and heard, and that, after all, a letter does not blush. In the summary that follows (171–73), the author says that his book will be enjoyed only by those who read it from beginning to end, and that not a single word ought to changed, for, as anyone who has met the protagonist will realize, it constitutes a faithful portrait. Then there begins the story of the beautiful Andalusian woman, which consists of sixty-six sketchlike "mamotretos" that combine both narrative and dialogue. The book is divided into three parts. The word *mamotreto* can mean several things, including "notebook" or "bundle of papers" (see Allaigre 1985b, 26–45), but, since it starts with the first person singular of *mamar* ("to suck"), it has erotic connotations as well. Corominas indicated that it also means "el que mama por mucho tiempo" ("the one who sucks for a long time") or "mamón" ("big sucker"; 1954, 3: 212*b*), and it is obvious that the suffix -*treto* recalls the word *teta* ("tit").

The story that follows is that of a sharp, sexually precocious young lady from Córdoba named Aldonza—"desde chiquita me comía lo mío" ("my private parts itched since I was little"; 1985, 193),[2] she says—who loses her virginity at a very tender age when, "saltando una pared sin licencia de su madre, se le derramó la primera sangre que del natural tenía" ("jumping over a wall without her mother's permission, she spilled blood from her nature for the first time"; 176).[3] After the death of her father, Aldonza and her mother leave Córdoba, apparently for economic reasons, and they travel throughout southern Spain, moving constantly from place to place—Granada, Jerez, Carmona, and so on.

When her mother dies, Aldonza ends up in Seville, where she finds "una su parienta" ("a relative of hers") whom she calls "aunt." Bereft of any worldly goods other than her wits, the young lady soon meets an Italian merchant from Ravenna, Diomedes, and elopes with him. They travel extensively

Chapter Six

in the Levant ("the Eastern Mediterranean"), and seem to be happy together. Wherever they happen to be, their house is always full of guests who, seeing Aldonza's *lozanía* ("beauty"), begin to call her Lozana instead. She and Diomedes have an unspecified number of children. When his father orders him to visit, Diomedes sends his children ahead to him, in Italy. He plans to leave Lozana in Marseilles and to marry her in Spain after visiting his father, but the father, who intends to marry Diomedes to another woman, has him imprisoned before he is able to depart from that French city. The distraught Lozana is abducted and taken, "en camisa" ("in her shift"), to a boatman, with no possessions other than a ring hidden in her mouth, in order to be drowned at sea. Realizing that the victim is a woman, the boatman feels sorry for her and puts her on land instead.

Lozana's grief upon finding herself alone and poor is such that she repeatedly strikes her head, until she acquires a great migraine and a wound that the text describes as a star on her forehead. She makes her way to Rome, where she comes upon the Spanish colony in that city, meeting Rampín, a young man who becomes her companion. Tired of being a prostitute and of going in and out of the houses of other prostitutes, for whom she performs a variety of services, the heroine eventually chooses to earn her living primarily as a beautician, an art of which she had learned a great deal during her travels. She also works as a quack or physician of sorts, and continues to dabble in prostitution. Finally, she decides to retire to the island of Lipari together with her inseparable Rampín, just before the sack of Rome by the multinational army of Charles V in 1527. In Lipari, she changes her name to La Vellida.

The book concludes with no less than six appendices: (1) an apology ("Cómo se escusa el autor" [How the author excuses himself]; 483); (2) an explanation; (3) a letter added by the author in 1527, because of the destruction of Rome; (4) a versified letter of excommunication against a prostitute; (5) a letter from Lozana to the prostitutes who have stayed in Rome; and (6) a letter penned by the author in Venice. In the explicit, after claiming that his book has 125 characters, Delicado states that the word *mamotreto* means "libro que contiene diversas razones o copilaciones ayuntadas" ("book with various arguments or collected materials brought together"; 487), and then goes on to say that in secular works such as his "no se debe poner nombre ni palabra que se apertenga a los libros de sana y santa dotrina" ("should not be written names or words pertaining to the books of healthy and holy doctrine"; 487). Thus, Delicado seems to be suggesting that his intention was to avoid the word *capítulo*, for the Bible is divided into chapters, but, nevertheless, the sixty-six *mamotretos* bring to mind the sixty-six books of the Christian Bible in the Vulgate, as well as in the Protestant tradition, which divides the Old Testament into thirty-nine books, and the New Testament into twenty-seven (Metzger and Coogan 1993, 79). The coincidence—if that is what it is—is interesting. On the other hand, given the manner in which, as we will see in Chapter 7, Delicado attacks Christianity, those sixty-six *mamotretos* and their "trinitarian" organization could well be part of the assault. Unfortunately, we will never know for certain.

In any case, since *La Lozana andaluza* focuses on a woman with a healthy, unabashed sexual appetite, who earns her living as a prostitute in Rome and manages to retire, without experiencing any punishment, together with the companion who also happens to be her favorite sex partner, there would seem to be little point in discussing the work's didactic merits. Throughout the text, which he claims to have written in 1524 (175), however, Delicado includes a series of prophetic warnings regarding the disaster of 1527,[4] and there is some moralizing, albeit ambiguous, in the preliminary as well as in the profuse end materials.[5]

This has led some critics to view *La Lozana andaluza* as a moral, didactic work.[6] According to Bruno Damiani, Delicado exposes the corruption of Rome in order to justify the sack of that city by the forces of Charles V; thus, Rome is punished for its collective sins.[7] In the opinion of Hernández Ortiz, the protagonist eventually learns that this world is pure fantasy, nothing but deceit, and that the only truth lies in God (1974, 38). Therefore, despite *La Lozana andaluza*'s Renaissance celebration of the pleasures available in this worldly life and its apparent de-emphasis of the afterlife, its moral lesson would be a medieval one. Augusta Espantoso-Foley argues that "the amoral content matter gradually becomes secondary—or even forgotten at times" (1977, 7), suggesting that there is a strong possibility that "Delicado presented the accumulation of exaggerated sexual activities in order to create a sense of disgust in the reader and eventually detract from his interest in this type of material" (20). This would have caused readers to concentrate "on the moral aim, aesthetic value and technique" (7) of the book instead. But because the text is permeated with abundant, exuberant sexual activity, and the protagonist is able to retire peacefully, without punishment, other critics have regarded the work as being completely immoral and even pornographic.

Fortunately, modern scholars have been able to read *La Lozana andaluza* without the nineteenth-century Victorian strictures that imposed "el rigor de un gusto vestido de traje y corbata" ("the sternness of a taste garbed in suit and tie"; Bubnova 1995, 27), and this enabled them to offer more interesting interpretations. Whereas Pamela Brakhage (1986) stressed theological aspects, Ronald Surtz (1982) saw *La Lozana andaluza* as a parody of hagiographic narratives. Among other parallels, the fictionalized eyewitness narrator is portrayed in the act of writing Lozana's story in a manner that recalls how the first biographers of some female saints followed them around with the purpose of recording their every word and action. As Peter Dunn stressed, the heroine, who seems to repent, "re-writes her life on the pattern of St. Mary of Egypt: she retires to an island and becomes a pious recluse" (1976a, 356). Ruth Pike (1969), Márquez Villanueva (1973), Juan Goytisolo (1977), Angus Mackay (1992), and John Edwards (1996) emphasized that the protagonist is portrayed as a conversa and that the underworld in which she lives after her arrival in Rome is largely composed of conversos who had fled from the Inquisition. According to John B. Hughes, Delicado condemns the abuse of the meek at the hands of the powerful and all forms of violence, with emphasis on the brutal sack that forced him and others to flee from the refuge that they had found in their exile, just like his main character (1979, 333). To Mackay, *La Lozana andaluza* is much more than a bawdy account of life in Rome; Delicado is concerned with the fate of the Andalusian New Christian girls who, as predicted by Pulgar, had fled abroad for fear of the Inquisition; by far and large, Mackay observes, the characters are Andalusians, conversos, and females (1992, 226). Shepard (1975) would probably agree, for, recalling the Old Testament's image of faithless Israel as a harlot and that some Jewish writers used it to characterize the communities of Burgos and Barcelona after their forced conversion in 1391, he sees a parallel with Lozana, who is both a harlot and a conversa. In the opinion of Espantoso-Foley (1977, 27), Damiani (1970), and other proponents of a moral interpretation, however, Delicado is more preoccupied in showing that the sack of Rome was a result of divine wrath because of its notorious corruption. Some even held that Delicado's purpose was to justify the sack, much like Juan de Valdés in his *Diálogo de las cosas ocurridas en Roma* (Damiani 1970, 242; Ferrara de Orduna 1973, 115).

To others, *La Lozana andaluza* is more of an amusement. Segundo Serrano Poncela found it to be a happy, refreshingly shameless book: "es, sobre todo, un libro escrito con alegría" ("more than anything else, it is a book written with joy"; 1962, 117; see also Damiani and Imperiale 1991, 24). Chiclana concurred, stating that it was written "como mero pasatiempo, como pura diversión" ("as a mere pastime, as pure entertainment"; 1988, 41). In Louis Imperiale's opinion, except for Aretino, "[no] nos parece que ningún autor se haya divertido tanto como Francisco Delicado" ("it does not seem that any author had as much fun as Francisco Delicado"; 1994, 321). Reyes (1960–63) saw the book as a hymn to easy, uncomplicated sex without any hang-ups. Edward Friedman emphasized the artistic aspect: "morality and didacticism are at the service of art, an art that establishes an order for quotidian reality" (1987, 74). Bubnova provided a Bakhtinian reading, stressing the carnivalesque content (1987). Other critics maintained that it is either a feminist (cf. García-Verdugo 1994, 35–36; Goytisolo 1977, 49–50) or a misogynistic book (Cruz 1989, 144–48; Paglialunga de Tuma 1973, 143).[8] Since *La Lozana andaluza* is an extremely rich, polysemous work, all of these interpretations may be valid to some extent.

"Sailing," Renaissance Rome, and Exile

Because of the vivacity and "naturalism" of Delicado's vignettes, most scholars stressed the concept of "realism," which they equated with "veracity," as if the graphic, uncompromisingly "true" portrayal of a world of prostitution and a corrupt Rome, in a detached, "documentary," almost photographic or cinematic manner, somehow constituted a moral lesson in itself.[9] Wardropper imagined that Delicado based himself on a real character (1953b, 476), and Damiani even suggested that she was the woman who gave him the syphilis from which he suffered for so many years (1974, 89, 119).[10] The lesson here, it would seem, would be to stay away from such women, even if for no other reason than to preserve one's health.

La Lozana andaluza is far from being a realistic work, however. In the pages that follow, we will see how, despite its apparently "realistic" vignettes, Delicado (1) uses sex as part of a sailing allegory designed to establish the identity of the protagonist as a syphilitic, marginalized conversa, who, (2) besides eventually incarnating or representing Rome, (3) constitutes an alter ego for the author, and that sex constitutes a springboard for (4) an allegory dealing with exile as well. The last point is probably the most important one, for, at its core, *La Lozana andaluza* is an allegorical work created as a protest against the "voluntary" exile sought by many Spaniards of converso background after the implementation of the Inquisition in their country (1481).

As an examination of Lozana's and Diomedes's extensive travels in the Levant will demonstrate, Delicado's apparent realism must be taken with great caution, for it often covers much more than what meets the eye. As we have seen, the precocious Lozana engages in sex willingly at a very early age, while her mother is still alive, and she decides to elope with Diomedes after being introduced to him by the aunt with whom she was staying in Seville (181–82). They embark in Cádiz, and their extensive travels in the Levant are condensed in the fourth of the sixty-six *mamotretos* ("bundles of papers") that make up the book. On the surface, the couple lives very happily together, and Diomedes even plans to marry Lozana. According to Antonio Vilanova, Lozana is completely loyal to him: "ha guardado el recato y la honestidad que corresponde a una esposa legítima" ("she has behaved with the modesty and honesty that corresponds to a legitimate wife"; 1952b, xli). In Espantoso-Foley's opinion, "their relationship, though not legalized by a marriage contract, is surrounded by an atmosphere of stability, deep love, and mutual admiration" (1977, 23; see also Paglialunga de Tuma 1973, 124).

This apparently idyllic situation is not what it seems to be, however, for it serves as cover for illegitimate commerce. Being a merchant from Ravenna, a city whose name was associated with "rabo" ("tail") in the burlesque geography of the time, Diomedes is really a "mercader del rabo" ("merchant of tail"), that is, a pimp. Lozana is very happy with him because "nature"

175

has endowed him abundantly with its goods: "y ella muy contenta, viendo en su caro amador Diomedes todos los géneros y partes de gentilhombre, y de hermosura en todos sus miembros, que le parecía a ella que la natura no se había reservado nada que en su caro amante no hubiese puesto" ("and she was very happy, seeing in her beloved Diomedes all the manners and parts of a gentleman, and that all of his limbs were handsome. It seemed to her that nature had not failed to endow her dear lover with anything"; 183–84). For this reason, the lusty young lady always obeys him willingly, receiving numerous guests who, in their turn, have ample opportunity to see that their hostess was not lacking in anything "ansí en la cara como en todos sus miembros" ("in the face or in any of her members"; 184), and that her "lozanía era de su natural" ("beauty was from her nature"; 184). She does her job so well that "no había otra en aquellas partes que en más fuese tenida" ("no woman was held in higher esteem in those parts"; 184). Diomedes's voyages and mercantile activities consist in selling her charms. The area chosen for these activities reflects more than mere geography, for, being a form of the verb *levantar* ("to raise"), "Levante" also means "erection" (see Allaigre 1985b, 102–03, 120–22).[11]

Although the text never says so explicitly, sailing was the only way to travel so extensively in the Levant in those days, but the literary and folkloric evidence that follows shows that "sailing" constituted a euphemism for intercourse just in itself, and that, at another level, Lozana's and Diomedes's Levantine voyages are as real as their apparently idyllic relationship. In fact, all of the fourth *mamotreto*, including Lozana's attempted drowning off the coast of Marseilles after her forced separation from Diomedes and the concluding voyages that she undertakes to Liorna (Leghorn) and Rome, constitutes an allegory based on sailing.

Since water represents fertility, it appears in some form or other in many early love songs. Lovers often meet next to a body of water, and in some songs a maiden also brings up the sea in order to lament the absence of her beloved. The number of medieval Galician-Portuguese *cantigas de amigo* ("songs about a friend") that refer to fountains, lakes, rivers, and the sea is so great that the last two form a subcategory known as *barcarolas* ("boat songs") or *marinas* ("sailing songs").[12] In one example, a maiden tells her mother that seeing the boats on the sea is causing her to die of love, thus suggesting that her beloved is aboard one of them, and that she misses him very much:

> Vi eu, mia madr', andar
> as barcas eno mar
> e moiro-me d'amor.
> (Nunes 1926–28, 2: no. 79 [47])[13]

Many popular Castilian *villancicos* ("peasant songs") from the fifteenth and sixteenth centuries mention the sea as well. In Gil Vicente's appropriately entitled *Nau de Amores* (Boat of love), the caulkers say that the sea is calm and tell the oarsmen to start rowing with the following popular song:

> muy serena está la mar,
> a los remos, remadores,
> esta es la nave d'amores.
>
> (1979, 291 [48])[14]

In another *villancico* ("peasant song"), the maiden implies that her lover is leaving her alone when she tells her mother that the ships are on their way to the Levant:

> Ya se parten los navíos, madre,
> van para Levante.
>
> (Frenk 1987, no. 938 [49])

In the following poem, the maiden says that she would like to embark with her beloved, so that he will not be all alone:

> Por la mar abajo
> ban los mis ojos:
> quiérome ir con ellos,
> no baian solos.
>
> (Frenk 1987, no. 177B [50])

These examples make it clear that these songs establish a relationship between lovers and the sea. At the literal level, the eroticism that the songs encode is very light, but that is not necessarily the case at another level. Without any further documentation, it may seem far-fetched to surmise that the girl in the *barcarola* is also telling her mother that seeing the boats in the ocean makes her feel like making love, that the oarsmen in the popular *villancico* will do the same as soon as they begin to row the ship of love, and that the maiden in the third example is referring to the Levant with the same meaning that we find in *La Lozana andaluza*. It would also seem to be very far-fetched to conclude that, by stating that she would like to embark with her lover, the girl in the last example is also saying that she wants to make love with him. Nevertheless, as an openly erotic version of that poem demonstrates, these songs encode both levels of meaning, and the singer, listener, or reader is free to interpret them as he or she wishes:

Chapter Six

> Por la mar abajo,
> va Catalina,
> las piernas de fuera,
> un fraile encima.
> (Alzieu et al. 1984, no. 135 [51])

The implied singer, who was no doubt a young girl in the veiled, decorous example, is now a male. Since the two lovers are depicted at sea, Catalina represents a ship, the monk is the mariner, and "sailing" becomes a metaphor for lovemaking. These implied images were common enough, as can be seen in a burlesque poem where Lucrece stands simultaneously for a ship and the gulf that Tarquin penetrates in his role as mariner:

> Sobre los muslos de marfil Tarquino
> embarcó su deseo y, con tormenta,
> de la mar de Lucrecia el golfo tienta,
> que para todo un rey halla camino.
> (Alzieu et al. 1984, no. 104 [52])

The depiction of the woman as a ship is clearer in a poem in which Diogo Fogaça berated a fat lady who had the misfortune to fall on top of him. Since this poem, which Garcia de Resende included in his *Cancioneiro Geral* (1973, 1: no. 184), is too long to be quoted here, I will cite Mário Martins's effective synthesis. According to Fogaça, the woman was like a heavy, poorly mended boat with a leak on the bottom: "Tudo, nela, é *cu e mamas* / e *barriga*. Aquilo parecia uma barca a meter água pelo fundo, gordura *sobresalente* e a quilha podre remendada com um odre" ("She is all *ass*, *tits*, / and *belly*. She looked like a boat taking in water through the bottom, / *way too fat*, her rotten keel mended with a wineskin"; Martins 1978, 74).

The *cantiga de amigo* ("song of a friend") and the *villancicos* ("peasant songs") quoted above are both folkloric and literary, for they constitute popular songs that were either used or adapted by learned poets. Despite their learned character, the openly erotic examples and Diogo Fogaça's poem help to confirm that the early tradition also enclosed secondary, obscene levels of meaning, for they use the same metaphors.[15]

The modern oral tradition has perpetuated some of those early metaphors as well. In the following poem, the impassioned lover describes how he used his five senses on a young girl after promising to marry her. When he gets to the fourth and fifth senses, which he mistakenly identifies with the first ("to see"), the lover refers to the girl as a boat, and asks her to raise her sails so that he can navigate. The voyage lasts all night long:

E o quarto é ver   quando o barco se faz de vela;
24 corri-lhe a mão pelos peitos   e cheguei o meu corpo ao dela.
     O quinto é ver   q'ando o barco se deita ao mar.
26 —Menina, levantai panos,   quero agora navegar.
     Toda a noite naveguei   sem nunca poder dormir;
28 quando foi pela manhã   'tava em estados de cair.
                    (Costa Fontes 1983, no. 359 [53])[16]

Since this poem belongs to the *literatura de cordel* ("chapbook literature"), it may be semilearned, but I recorded a folktale that confirms that the images under scrutiny are still part of the oral tradition.[17] Since that story is too long to be printed here, I will summarize the relevant passages. A prostitute puts a sign under her window, challenging those who know how to sail for a bet. She places a basin full of water in her room, saying that she is the boat, and that she must be guided so as not to hit land. If she overturns the basin, the customer loses one gold eagle; if she does not, the customer wins one gold eagle and gets to have sex with her. A sea captain loses the bet, but one of his sailors, António, is luckier. When the prostitute begins to swirl and sways toward the basin, António yells out: "Leeward!" When she swings from the other direction, he shouts: "Windward!" This goes on for some time. All of a sudden, the sailor commands: "Pull down the big sail!" She takes off her dress. Then he orders her to pull down the other sails, one by one. Finally, he says: "Now it's time to put the rudder on the boat!" and guides her to bed, winning the bet.

It would be possible to present several additional examples, both early and modern, but these suffice to show that sailing constituted a traditional metaphor for lovemaking in the past, and that it has survived until the present. The woman was often depicted as "the boat," her partner as "the sailor." Being familiar with this tradition, Delicado's contemporaries would have realized immediately that, since Lozana and Diomedes were lovers, their Levantine travels represented intercourse, without any need for the confirmation later provided in the text. As Rampín, Lozana's lover and consenting companion after her arrival in Rome tells her during one of their "sailing trips," "Parecéis barqueta sobre las ondas con mal tiempo" ("You look like a boat struggling with the waves during a storm"; 280).

There is no doubt, then, that Lozana's travels in the Levant with Diomedes, a merchant from Ravenna, combine several metaphors, constituting an allegory for prostitution. Diomedes is Lozana's lover, as well as her pimp. Although this does not necessarily mean that their maritime adventures cannot be simultaneously understood on a literal level as well, there is evidence that the text was meant to be read primarily as an allegory, for several contradictions suggest that those voyages do not really take place.

At a literal level, the couple is already in Rhodes when Diomedes informs Lozana that his father had commanded him to travel extensively throughout the Levant and all of Barbary, presenting her with the following list: "tengo de estar años, y no meses, como será en Alejandría, . . . en el Caire, y en el Chío, en Constantinópoli, en Corintio, en Tesalia, en Boecia, en Candía, a Venecia y Flandes" ("I have to be gone for several years, not just months, in Alexandria, . . . Cairo, Khíos, Constantinople, Corinth, Thessaly, Boeotia, Crete, Venice, and Flanders"; 184–85). As Claude Allaigre indicated, besides recalling the constant voyages found in the chivalry romances, these maritime adventures bring to mind "las perpetuas mudanzas de las prostitutas, históricamente comprobadas" ("the constant moves of prostitutes, which have been historically verified"; 1985b, 122).[18] Given the nature of Lozana's and Diomedes's commerce, some of the place names in the list could also lend themselves to related interpretations. For example, in an erotic context, "Chipre" also meant "pudendas femeninas" ("the female organs"; Delicado 1985, 184n15), "Caire" or "Cairo" could mean "lo que gana la mujer con su cuerpo" ("what a woman earns with her body"; 184n16), and "Tesalia" may also refer to "tieso" ("with a hard on"; 185n17). Such double-entendres do not contradict the story being told, but enrich it by giving it yet another dimension. Rather than ending in Venice as one might logically expect, however, these voyages conclude in Flanders, a country whose name was also used to mean "el colmo del deleite" ("the height of pleasure," i.e., an orgasm; Allaigre 1985b, 122 and n137).[19] Since Flanders is nowhere near the Levant, its inclusion at the end of this list suggests that the couple's voyages do not correspond to geographic reality.

There is further evidence to support this hypothesis. While in Candía (Crete), Diomedes informs Lozana that he has sent her children to his father, who wants to see him in Italy. Rather than taking the most direct route to Ravenna, which would be to sail up the Adriatic, Diomedes decides to go to Marseilles, planning to leave Lozana there while he goes on alone to Italy in order to obtain his father's permission to marry her. The need for this apparently unnecessary detour becomes clear only after Lozana's forced separation from her lover. Finding herself destitute, she reportedly strikes her head until she acquires a "star" (186) that turns out to be the first manifestation of the syphilis that would eventually cause her nose to disappear. Seeing this, an old woman makes her very angry by identifying it as "greñimón" ("grunting [?]"; 192), i.e., a syphilitic lesion. Later on, another woman refers to syphilis as "el mal del Francia" ("the disease from France"; 218). That is the reason for the illogical detour to Marseilles. What better place to catch the disease commonly known at the time as "el mal francés" ("the French disease) than in France itself? In other words, geographic verisimilitude is irrelevant because the detour is undertaken for symbolic reasons, thus forming yet another component of the allegory presented in the fourth *mamotreto*.

Lozana's attempted drowning does not correspond to reality in a conventional sense, either. Without Diomedes's knowledge, his father comes to Marseilles and visits Lozana secretly, threatening her. The father then has his son imprisoned. Lozana is kidnapped in the middle of the night, wearing nothing but a shift, and is able to salvage only a ring, which she hides in her mouth: "no salvó sino un anillo en la boca" ("she was able to save only a ring, in her mouth"; 186). Then she is taken to a boatman in order to be drowned at sea: "Y así fue dada a un barquero que la echase en la mar, al cual dio cien ducados el padre de Diomedes, porque ella no pareciese; el cual, visto que era mujer, la echó en tierra y, movido a piedad, le dio un su vestido con que se cubriese" ("In this state, she was handed over to a boatman in order to be thrown into the sea. Diomedes's father paid him a hundred ducats to make her disappear. Seeing that she was a woman, however, the boatman threw her ashore ["on land"; "on the ground"] and, overcome with pity, he gave her some of his clothes so she could cover herself"; 186).

As we know, sailing was a metaphor for intercourse, with the woman depicted as the boat, the lover as sailor. The expression "la echase en la mar" ("to be thrown into the sea") suggests a sexual encounter, recalling the erotic poem that begins "Por la mar abajo va Catalina" ("Down the seas goes Catalina). The corresponding expression, according to which the boatman "la echó en tierra" ("threw her on the ground), giving her "un su vestido con que se cubriese" ("some of his clothes so she could cover herself) confirms this interpretation. He puts Lozana on the ground and gets on top of her, "covering" her with his own body. Since the boatman is another lover, Lozana's attempted drowning does not correspond to conventional reality, forming part of the allegory as well.

After this incident, Lozana travels to Leghorn and eventually makes her way to Rome: "Finalmente, su fortuna fue tal que vido venir una nao que venía a Liorna y, siendo en Liorna, vendió su anillo, y con él fue hasta que entró en Roma" ("Finally, her luck was such that she saw a ship that was coming to Leghorn, and once in Leghorn, she sold her ring, and with it she went until she entered Rome"; 187).

Lozana sails to Leghorn on a ship that, paradoxically, was coming ("venía") rather than going to that city, thus undertaking another "sea voyage" with a different, unspecified customer. This confirms that the ring that she is selling is her vagina (see Allaigre 1980b, 137 and 172–73n44),[20] and that the last two voyages are symbolic. At a literal level, however, Lozana's sojourn in Leghorn makes perfect sense, for that city is on the way to Rome, which she reaches in the following chapter. The narrative is now consistent

Chapter Six

on both levels, for one does not undermine or contradict the other. Nevertheless, the relationship between sailing and sexual intercourse in the last two voyages connects them to the earlier Levantine travels, making them part of the allegory.

In sum, since sailing was the only way to travel extensively in the Levant, including visits to islands such as Rhodes and Crete, and "Levante" also meant "erection," Lozana's "voyages" with Diomedes indicate that she is having sex with him. Lozana has sex with others as well. Being a merchant from Ravenna, a city whose name also meant "rabo" ("tail") in the burlesque geography of the time, Diomedes is also a pimp, selling his mistress to the customers—"levantados" ("erect"), no doubt—who visit their home constantly, and appreciate their hostess's charms and hospitality so much that they change her name from Aldonza to Lozana ("beautiful," "healthy looking," "lush").

The allegorical character of these travels and commerce does not necessarily indicate that the text cannot be simultaneously read at a literal level. On the other hand, Diomedes's reference to Flanders ("orgasm") in a "Levantine" context, suggests that the text is supposed to be read primarily as an allegory, for Flanders is nowhere near the Levant. This is also true of Diomedes's projected voyage from Crete to Ravenna. Rather than sailing up the Adriatic, he and Lozana go to Marseilles, so that Lozana can acquire in France the syphilis that used to be known as "el mal francés" ("the French disease"). Thus, these two instances of geographical inconsistency relegate the literal meaning of the text to a secondary level.

Although Lozana's attempted sea drowning in French waters and her subsequent sea voyages to Leghorn and Rome can be logically understood at a literal level, the sexual implications involved conclude the transformation of the fourth *mamotreto* into a sailing allegory designed to portray the heroine as a prostitute.

Besides being a euphemism for a syphilitic lesion, the "star" that Lozana acquires by striking her head repeatedly at the end of the French episode refers to her Jewish ancestry. Lozana is a Christian but since, as we will see, she is also a conversa, the star of David will mark her for as long as she lives.

It goes without saying that at another, more realistic level, Lozana acquires that "star," which is inextricably related to her fate, upon being born. The indelible Jewishness of her background is what brings her so many misfortunes. The discrimination on the part of the Old Christian majority causes her to be constantly screwed; hence the Levantine "sailing voyages" designed to establish her identity as a prostitute.

In sum, there is no question that, despite the Levantine voyages and the mercantile activities that it depicts, the fourth *mamotreto* is meant to be read primarily as an allegory. Notwithstanding the apparent realism of its vignettes, this applies to Lozana's career as a prostitute in Rome as well. As we will see in the pages that follow, sex is really a cover for a protest against the "voluntary" exile that many conversos were forced to undertake from their native Spain, and later, from the city that had become a second home to them.

As Márquez Villanueva emphasized, the protagonist of Delicado's book is a New Christian, "y sólo tomando esto en cuenta se aclaran muchos pasajes y se desentrañan ciertas intenciones profundas de *La Lozana andaluza*" ("and it is only by taking this into account that many passages can be clarified and certain deep intentions of *La Lozana andaluza* can be figured out"; 1973, 88). Lozana's identity as a conversa is established at the very beginning, when the narrator informs us that "fue muy querida de sus padres por ser aguda" ("she was dearly beloved by her parents for being sharp"; 175). This "agudeza" ("sharpness"), which becomes an integral part of her character, was a characteristic generally attributed to conversos.[21] When she tells her aunt about the culinary abilities of her grandmother, from whom she had learned how to cook, Lozana says that one of her dishes was so good that "cuantos traperos había en la cal de la Heria querían proballo" ("all the clothes merchants in Market Street wanted to taste it"; 177).[22] The profession of *trapero* ("clothes merchant") was associated with conversos, and so was the merchant's street of Seville known as la calle de la Feria (Market Street; see Delicado 1975, 81n4). Moreover, Lozana stresses that her grandmother prepared "nabos sin tocino y con comino" ("turnips without salt pork, but rather with cumin"; 178),[23] and the ancestral dislike of conversos for pork was a well-established fact (Castro 1974b, 25–32; Silverman 1971a, 706–07n37). Lozana herself detests it. Should other prostitutes be imprudent enough to upset her, her tongue was such that "diría peor d'ellas que de carne de puerco" ("she would talk about them even worse than about pork"; 292). Note that pork is completely absent from the lengthy catalogue presented at this point. As Márquez Villanueva indicated, the numerous dishes that Lozana describes constitute a true "enciclopedia de la gastronomía conversa" ("encyclopedia of converso gastronomy"; 1973, 91).[24] Moreover, the text identifies her as "parienta del Ropero" ("related to Ropero [The Clothes Merchant]"; 348), i.e., Antón de Montoro, the famous converso poet from Córdoba (1990).[25]

There are many other conversos in Rome. The Spaniards in Pozo Blanco are portrayed as New Christian refugees for, when Lozana speaks with some women upon arriving, one of them, Beatriz, states: "No querría sino saber d'ella si es confesa, porque hablaríamos sin miedo" ("I would only like to know whether she is a conversa; if so, we could speak openly"; 196). The kinds of food that people ate and the manner in which they prepared it was

Chapter Six

extremely important from a social point of view, and it is precisely through food that the Spanish *conversas* whom the protagonist meets in the area of Pozo Blanco are able to identify her as one of their own. One of them, Teresa, tests her by stating that they are planning to make "hormigos" ("sweet fritters"), and, when they find out that Lozana prepares them with olive oil rather than "water,"[26] another woman, Beatriz, exclaims to Teresa in an aside: "¡Por tu vida, que es *de nostris!*" ("By golly, she is one of us!"; 200). These women are shirtmakers, a profession associated with *conversos*, and the professions of their husbands—a tanner *(cortidor)*, a money changer *(cambiador)*, a linen merchant *(lencero)*, a shoemaker or shoe salesman *(borceguinero)*, and a clothes merchant *(trapero)*—indicate that they are *conversos* as well (Márquez Villanueva 1973, 90). Lozana then asks Beatriz how long she has been in Rome, and she replies: "Señora mía, desde el año que se puso la Inquisición" ("Ma'am, since the year the Inquisition began"; 202). That was in 1481.[27] Clearly, Beatriz and her family had left Spain "voluntarily" in order to escape from the Inquisition, and so had many of the other Spaniards in Rome. Lozana herself had arrived in March, 1513, when a new pope, Leo X, "iba a encoronarse" ("was about to be crowned"; 191).

Despite what she had endured, Lozana remains optimistic. Being alone and destitute, she does not even attempt to find a decent job. Once a prostitute, always a prostitute. There was no turning back, i.e., a *conversa* was marked for life. Nevertheless, Lozana decides that she must make the best of the situation, and find a way "para ser siempre libre y no sujeta a ninguno" ("to be always free and not subjected to anyone"; 187). In other words, since her freedom is so precious to her, she does not intend to live in a bordello or to work for a pimp, as many prostitutes had to. Nevertheless, she either cannot or does not attempt to escape her past, for the base for her activities remains the *converso* community.

Having a gift for gab, Lozana is never at a loss for words. When four Spaniards ask her to make them all happy, she quickly replies: "Hermanos, no hay cebada para tantos asnos" ("Buddies, there isn't enough barley for so many asses"; 195). Soon after, a woman from Naples married to a Spaniard, Jumilla, introduces her to her teenage son, Rampín, who shows her the city. They end up at the house of the boy's aunt, and sleep together. At first Lozana pretends to resist his advances, but then gives him instructions, making it absolutely clear that she is the one in control: "Pasico, bonico, quedico, no me ahinquéis. Andá comigo: ¡por ahí van allá! ¡Ay, qué priesa os dais, y no miráis que está otrie en pasamiento sino vos! Catá que no soy de aquellas que se quedan atrás. Esperá, vezaros he: ¡ansí, ansí, por ahí seréis maestro! ¿Veis como va bien? Esto no sabiedes vos; pues que no se os olvide . . . Caminá, que la liebre está echada. ¡Aquí va la honra!" ("Slow down, take it easy, stay still, don't rush me. Move with me: that's the way. Oh, how you hurry and forget that you are not the only one! Watch out, I'm not one of those who lag behind. Wait a minute, I will show you how. This way, this way you will soon be an expert! See how good it is? That's something you didn't know. Well, don't you forget it . . . Keep going, for I'm [the hare is] almost there. Here I come [goes my honor]!"; 232).[28] Lozana and Rampín continue to make love all night long, and then sleep until noon. This is the most detailed description of the sex act in *La Lozana andaluza*, but other passages confirm that, although Lozana uses her body as merchandise, she also enjoys her profession tremendously. As Imperiale pointed out, "esta mujer está dominada por el deseo de gozar sexualmente" ("this woman thinks of nothing but sexual pleasure"; 1989, 78). Given the profuse erotic descriptions, it would seem that sex is the main focus of Delicado's work, but, as we will see, that is not really the case.

Because of his valiant performance, the red-bearded Rampín becomes Lozana's favorite sex partner. He is half-Spanish, and the color of his beard suggests that, like Lozana, he is of converso extraction himself, for Jews were popularly believed to have inherited red hair from Judas.[29] When, later on, Rampín is forced to eat bacon as a prank—he tried to refuse, but had to agree because he had been put on the spot publicly—his revulsion is such that he vomits in front of everyone,[30] and the appropriately named Falillo,[31] one of the boys who had put him through the ordeal, voices what everyone really thinks of bacon: "¡Quemado sea el venerable tocino!" ("May the venerable bacon be burned!"; 342). This confirms that Rampín is a converso, just like Lozana.

Though representing a group apart from the Spanish Jews in the city, the conversos maintain close relations with them, which makes perfect sense, for they were often related to each other. When Lozana asks Beatriz if there are Jews in Rome, she replies: "Munchos, y amigos nuestros; si hubiéredes menester algo d'ellos, por amor de nosotras os harán honra y cortesía" ("Many, and they are friends of ours. If you need anything from them, they will treat you with honor and courtesy for our sake"; 202). As Rampín and Lozana pass by a Catalan synagogue, he is quick to point out that Spaniards are far more learned than other Jews: "Más saben los nuestros españoles que todos" ("Our Spaniards know more than all the others"; 245). And it is precisely to one of those Jews, Trigo, who swears by "el Dío" (246), rather than by the supposedly plural "Dios" ("God"), that Rampín takes Lozana for help in getting started the day after. Trigo refers to the boy as "pariente" ("kinsman"; 246), which suggests that they are related. Seeing the "ring" that Lozana had been able to keep when abducted back in Marseilles, he rents her a house for six months, gets her some furniture, and provides her with her first paying clients—no fewer than three.

When the third one leaves, Lozana informs Rampín that, henceforth, she does not wish to spend the nights with anyone but him. Then they make love. Once again, the heroine tells Rampín not to hurry, for she also wishes

Chapter Six

to climax: "¡A la par, a la par lleguemos a Jodar!" ("Together, let's arrive in Jodar [Fuckland] together!"; 280). Afterward, they become inseparable, but, since Lozana is perfectly capable of making her business arrangements on her own, Rampín is not really a pimp. To a great extent, he is more of a kept man, a consenting companion, and the situation fails to change even after their apparent marriage.[32]

A conversa, Lozana joins other conversos upon reaching Rome, takes a converso as lover and companion, and is set up in business by a Jew. Although most of her customers are probably Christian, she becomes a member of the Spanish community of Pozo Blanco, a good portion of which was of converso extraction, just as she is.

There would seem to be no question that this crucial factor must be taken into account in order to arrive at a proper understanding of Delicado's book, for it is through the eyes of the conversa that he is supposedly portraying in his *Retrato* that Delicado, himself a converso, paints his supposedly "realistic" portrait of the capital of contemporary Christendom.

The narrator deliberately fostered this feeling of realism by claiming to tell only "lo que oí y vi" ("what I heard and saw"; 169), a strategy that embodies a specific denial of responsibility for the immoral contents of his work. This technique succeeds because he "presents the moral degradation of the city as a reality" (Espantoso-Foley 1977, 21)[33] through the apparently photographic or cinematic vignettes that arise from a dialogue thanks to which "we are able to see, touch, hear and at times even smell" (54). Delicado, then, seems to be merely portraying what he heard and saw. This apparent verisimilitude and the absence of explicit moral comments other than the sporadic references to the punishment that was to come in 1527 enhance the appearance of objectivity,[34] thus reinforcing the impression of "realism." Even Menéndez y Pelayo, for whom *La Lozana andaluza* was a thoroughly immoral work without any redeeming qualities, thought that Delicado's source was life itself (1961, 57). As we have already seen in regard to Lozana's and Diomedes's Levantine voyages, that was not the case, however. Although apparently realistic, those voyages constitute an allegory for prostitution.

The realism of Lozana's activities in Rome is equally questionable. As we have seen, Lozana's grief upon finding herself alone and poor causes her to strike her head time and time again until she acquires an "estrellica" ("a euphemism for a scar or syphilitic lesion") on her forehead in the process. When she arrives in Rome, an old woman identifies that so-called "star" as "greñimón" ("grunting [?]"; 192), i.e., a syphilitic lesion. Notwithstanding Lozana's vehement denials, Beatriz comes to a similar conclusion, pointing out that the illness has even eaten away her nose: "Hermana, ¿vistes tal hermosura de cara y tez? ¡Si tuviese asiento para los antojos! Mas creo que si se cura que sanará" ("Sister, have you seen such a beautiful face and complexion before? It's too bad she doesn't have a bridge for her glasses. Nevertheless, I imagine that her nose will get better if she is cured"; 195). Teresa Hernández does not believe that such a cure is possible: "Súbele más de mitad de la frente; quedará señalada para cuanto viviere" ("It covers more than half of her forehead; she will remain marked for as long as she lives";195–96). And marked she remained for, a few years later, the Auctor himself, who becomes one of the characters, being portrayed while writing his own book, observes that Lozana "no tiene chimenea, ni tiene do poner antojos" ("doesn't have a chimney, nor a place for eyeglasses"; 295).

Although people are very much aware of syphilis and its symptoms throughout the text, Lozana, who bears such an obvious mark, is able to work as a prostitute in Rome. Being "roma," a noseless or flat-nosed prostitute, the heroine comes to be identified with the "Roma putana" ("Harlot Rome") in which she exercises her profession. Here we may take the unreliable narrator at his word when he states in the argumento: "quise retraer munchas cosas retrayendo una" ("I wanted to condemn many things through just one"; 171). As Wardropper observes, his technique "consiste en pintar el detalle para retratar el todo, en pintar a Lozana para retratar a Roma" ("consists in focusing on one detail in order to depict the whole, in painting Lozana in order to portray Rome"; 1953b, 485). Lozana does indeed represent Rome itself (Allaigre 1985b, 127–31). Contrary to what some critics have surmised, however, she does not constitute a woman known to Delicado (i.e., Damiani 1974, 89, 119; Wardropper 1953b, 476). Despite the seducing "realism" of her adventures, her syphilis is so obvious that no one fails to notice it, and a woman in such a condition could not possibly earn a living as a prostitute. That would defy all logic. Since people catch syphilis inadvertently, not on purpose, a man would have to be insane to touch her with a ten-foot pole. Consequently, Lozana's career is as "real" as her Levantine voyages with Diomedes, and the narrator is being less than truthful when he claims to depict "sólo lo que oí y vi" ("only what I heard and saw") and that his portrait is so "natural" that "no hay persona que haya conocido la señora Lozana, en Roma o fuera de Roma, que no vea claro ser sacado de sus actos y meneos y palabras" ("there is no one who met Lozana, either in Rome or elsewhere, who will not clearly realize that it is based on her actions, mannerisms, and words"; 172). Once again, sex is really an illusion, constituting a cover for something else.

Since *La Lozana andaluza* is a highly allegorical work, the objectivity of the supposedly realistic portraits of Rome also becomes very suspect. Moreover, as already pointed out, Delicado, a converso, paints most of his vignettes as seen through the eyes of a conversa who lives in a Spanish community partly created by the exile that many conversos had to seek because

Chapter Six

of the intolerance of their fellow Christians. Since the "roma" ("flat-nosed") Lozana, a whore, is designed to represent the city of Rome, also known as a whore, Delicado's portrait would seem to constitute a strong indictment of the capital of Christendom.

The city is in fact portrayed as being completely immoral, without any redeeming qualities. Perhaps partly because of the Renaissance celebration of the body, which came to be regarded as a source of beauty and pleasure (Buendía López 1994, 375; Damiani and Imperiale 1991, 33), more in accordance with a classical, pagan worldview, the idea of sin never seems to occur to Lozana or the other characters. Like Lozana, the prostitutes use their bodies readily as merchandise, take great pleasure in sex, and stop practicing prostitution only when they are too old and ugly. There is no shame. Right in front of Lozana, Divicia, an old woman who had come to visit her, pretends to fall asleep on top of the legs of another guest, Sagüeso, who proceeds to have sex with her. When Divicia wakes up and asks what had happened, he says that she had slept only from the waist up, to which she replies: "La usanza es casi ley; soy usada a mover las partes inferiores en sintiendo una pulga" ("The habit is practically automatic; I'm used to moving my lower parts whenever I feel a flea"; 426). Then she offers him a pair of jackknives to repeat what he had just done.[35] These prostitutes, including the higher ranking courtesans,[36] live by selling their bodies, and perhaps should be expected to feel little or no guilt. But they belong to an underworld. This is not the case of most of their customers, who represent practically every social class, ranging from stableboys (312), pages (303), and squires (335), all the way to the knight commander of a military order (310) and an ambassador (349). Among the clergy, there is a friar (281), a canon who gets both his mistress and Lozana pregnant (283), and a monsignor (328). They do not feel any guilt, either. Sex is exclusively physical. The act of love does not require any preliminaries, and women are as ready to engage in it as men (Wardropper 1953b, 481).

Prostitution seems to pervade the whole city. A letter carrier that Lozana meets shortly after her arrival describes numerous kinds of prostitutes (270–72), and the lengthy list that he makes of their nationalities when Lozana asks him if they are all from Rome indicates that they come from practically everywhere:

> Señora, no, hay de todas naciones: hay españolas, castellanas, vizcaínas, montañesas, galicianas, asturianas, toledanas, andaluzas, granadinas, portuguesas, navarras, catalanas y valencianas, aragonesas, mayorquinas, sardas, corsas, secilianas, napolitanas, bruzesas, pullesas, calabresas, romanescas, aquilanas, senesas, florentinas, pisanas, luquesas, boloñesas, venecianas, milanesas, lombardas, ferraresas,

> modonesas, brecianas, mantuanas, raveñanas, pesauranas, urbinesas, paduanas, veronesas, vicentinas, perusinas, novaresas, cremonesas, alejandrinas, vercelesas, bergamascas, trevisanas, piedemontesas, saboyanas, provenzanas, bretonas, gasconas, francesas, borgoñas, inglesas, flamencas, tudescas, esclavonas y albanesas, candiotas, bohemias, húngaras, polacas, tramontanas y griegas. (275 [54])

Rome is indeed a gigantic bordello, and this portrayal of the capital of Christendom reflects contemporary opinion. Attracted by the presence of armies of clergymen imbued with the immorality of the period, prostitutes flocked to the city in droves. Without taking into account the numerous "concubine e meretrici secrete" ("concubines and secret harlots"; Alberti 1941, 67), the census taken in 1490 lists no fewer than 6,800 courtesans out of a total population of 50,000.

But although *La Lozana andaluza* seems to be a celebration of free, uninhibited sex, the text also points out important drawbacks. Since they usually fail to provide for their old age, former prostitutes often end up living in poverty, like the laundrywoman that Lozana meets shortly after her arrival (218), or the formerly famous and rich Portuguese courtesan who begs for alms in the street (408). When Lozana asks the letter carrier whether the prostitutes have lovers from their own countries, he replies that they take them as they come, but that the very last one, who is always French (syphilis), stays with them until they die: "Señora, al principio y al medio, cada una le toma como le viene; al último, francés, porque no las deja hasta la muerte" ("Ma'am, at first and in the middle, each one takes them as they come; the last one is French, for he stays with them until they die"; 277). In fact, people are very much aware of syphilis and its symptoms. The old laundrywoman, who has lost her hair because of it, disguises her condition with forelocks made of tar, and explains to Lozana that she had come to Rome "cuando vino el mal del Francia" ("when the French disease began"; 218). Divicia describes how the illness supposedly got started in 1488 (421), in Genoa, during a French invasion (431).[37]

Note that the negative consequences of illicit sex described here are exclusively a matter of cause and effect, and have nothing to do with Divine Providence. God seems to be absent from the capital of Christendom, for, in addition to its immorality, the idea of sin appears to be completely irrelevant.

Nevertheless, what Delicado is portraying even here is not exactly what he heard and saw, as he claims. What he presents is a deliberately distorted picture, created in order to serve his purposes. In one of his appendices, the author betrays the truth once more when he claims that "Ansimismo porque en semejantes obras seculares no se debe poner nombre ni palabra que se apertenga a los libros de sana y santa dotrina, por tanto, en todo este retrato no hay cosa ninguna que hable de religiosos, ni de santidad, ni con iglesias, ni eclesiásticos, ni otras cosas que se hacen que no son de decir" ("Because such secular works ought not to include names or words pertaining to the books of healthy and holy doctrine, in all of this portrait there is not anything about members of the religious orders, saintliness, churches, clergymen, or other things that people do but are not to be said"; 487). He has done precisely the opposite. To begin with, his protagonist, Lozana, a prostitute, is identified with Rome, the capital of Christendom. As if that were not enough, Rome is explicitly denounced as being completely corrupt and a gigantic bordello. According to Rampín, people referred to that city by saying: "Roma, triunfo de grandes señores, paraíso de putanas, purgatorio de jóvenes, infierno de todos, fatiga de bestias, engaño de pobres, pecigüería de bellacos" ("Rome is a triumph for great lords, a paradise for whores, a purgatory for young people, hell for everyone, hard labor for beasts of burden, a hoax for the poor, and a shop for swindlers"; 242). On another occasion, Rampín claims that "Es la mayor parte de Roma burdel, y le dicen: Roma putana" ("Most of Rome is a bordello, and people call it 'Harlot Rome'"; 216).[38] And, although the narrator states that his book does not say anything about either religion or the clergy, that is not really the case. In Rome, cardinals are depicted as ridiculously proud, "como los mamelucos" ("like the Mamelukes"; 213); it seems that it is a clergyman who gets Lozana pregnant at one point (283); according to the Auctor, a sexton took the virginity of a baker woman's daughter with "el cirio pascual" ("the Easter Candle"; 251); Rampín paraphrases the words of Christ when he tells one of Lozana's customers who brings a partner along: "Dice que no podéis servir a dos señores" ("She says that you cannot serve two masters [at the same time]"; 264); and when Rampín is imprisoned for stealing four eggplants, Lozana, who thinks that he has killed four men, suggests that she is able to intercede for him, albeit indirectly, before the Pope himself (328). The final assertion that the book avoids other things that ought not to be said is equally false, for the comical but nevertheless erotic, graphic portrayals of several sexual encounters definitely represent "cosas que no son de decir" ("things that are not to be said"), at least as far as generally accepted standards of morality were concerned.

Obviously, the narrator has not refrained from touching upon words taken from books of "santa dotrina" ("holy doctrine") at least in a Christian sense, the church, the clergy, and the other sensitive issues which he claims to have avoided. In other words, he cannot be taken at his word. As already stated, the Rome that he knew did indeed suffer from many of the evils portrayed; a good number of his contemporaries would probably have agreed with him, accepting his vignettes as "realistic." On the other hand, the fact that the narrator does precisely the contrary of what he says also renders his portrayal suspicious. Since his allegorical portrait of Rome constitutes a caricature—he manages to present the restricted world of a prostitute as if it represented the city as a whole—there is no question that he exaggerates a great deal. Moreover, as we have seen, that prostitute comes to represent Rome itself.

Perhaps that is why sex comes constantly into play, even when the text attempts to moralize. The third of the six appendices, where Delicado describes the sack, bears the following epigraph: "Esta epístola añadió el autor el año de mil e quinientos e veinte e siete, vista la destruición de Roma, y la gran pestilencia que sucedió, dando gracias a Dios que le dejó ver el castigo que méritamente Dios premitió [sic] a un tanto pueblo" ("The author added this epistle in 1527, having seen the destruction of Rome and the great pestilence that followed, and thanks God for letting him see the just punishment that he wrought upon such a great city"; 489). Then the narrator contradicts the date just mentioned, referring to a flood of the Tiber on January 12, 1528 (490). Notwithstanding the seriousness of the subject and the conclusion that the disaster was a punishment sent by God, the addenda continue to deal with illicit sex without any display of contrition. The fourth appendix, in verse, is a letter where Cupid, vicar of the god of love, excommunicates a cruel "doncella de sanidad" ("health maiden," i.e., a prostitute) for refusing her services to a lovesick customer who is euphemistically designated as her "lover" (495–501; see Dunn 1976a). In the appendix that follows, Lozana writes a letter assuring her fellow prostitutes that, despite the cruelty of the 14,000 barbaric Germans, 7,000 "unarmed" Spaniards, and the Italian troops in Charles V's army, they will be able to conduct their business for many years to come with the following words: "Por ende, sosegad que, sin duda por munchos años, podéis hilar velas largas luengas" ("Therefore, don't worry, for, no doubt, you will be able to spin big, long candles for many years to come"; 505). Were it not for fear, Lozana continues, she certainly would have preferred to stay in Rome with them.

In a nutshell, the moralizing cannot be taken seriously, for this supposedly Christian work appears to celebrate sin constantly, and lacks any hint of guilt or true repentance. This suggests that, although many Catholics also decried the immorality of Rome at the time without in any way attacking Christianity, the case may have been different with Delicado. As we shall see, he was a justifiably bitter individual, a Spaniard of Jewish background who had to flee from Rome to Venice after the sack. To someone in his circumstances, Rome could easily have represented Christianity itself.

Paradoxically, besides representing Rome, the protagonist also has much in common with the author. The little that we know about Delicado, we recall, is what he tells us about himself in *La Lozana andaluza*, in *El modo de adoperare el legno de India Occidentale*, in the *Spechio vulgare per li*

Chapter Six

Sacerdoti, and in the editions of several Spanish works that he supervised in Venice between 1531 and 1534. Born in the diocese of Córdoba, his name was Francisco Delgado, but he seems to have preferred the Italian form of his name, Delicado, and used the Latinized form Delicato as well. He was in Rome by 1513, perhaps even earlier, referred to himself in 1525 as priest of Santa Maria in Posterule, a Roman neighborhood inhabited by courtesans and artisans, stated in 1529 that he had suffered from syphilis for 23 years, and left Rome on February 10, 1528. We know that he was in Venice between 1528 and 1534, but ignore what happened to him afterward. There is no doubt that he was a New Christian. Delicado had an intimate knowledge of converso gastronomy, empathized with their inherited dislike for pork, ridiculed the idea of "limpieza de sangre" ("purity of the blood"), knew the exiled converso and Sephardic communities in Rome extremely well, was proud of the learning of Spanish Jews, lived in Italy for many years without returning to his native Spain, and, as we will soon see, denounced "voluntary" exile in *La Lozana andaluza*. Perhaps all of this could be attributed to any Spaniard, but, in Chapter 7, we will present further reason to think that an Old Christian could not have possibly written such a book.

The two allegorical aspects of *La Lozana andaluza* examined so far, sailing as an allegory for prostitution and marginalization, and the creation of Lozana as an allegory of Rome, can certainly be accounted for in nothing but artistic, literary terms, but there is more. In this instance—and in many others, I suspect—caricature and allegory do not constitute mere literary exercises, an end unto themselves, without any ulterior implications. Like Lozana, Delicado is a converso, an *andaluz* (Andalusian), and a *cordobés* (Cordoban), even though he identifies himself more with Martos, in Jaén, because his mother had raised him there (399).[39] It is not by chance that La Peña de Martos is depicted right next to Córdoba in one of the engravings, with the name "Lozano" inscribed below one of the houses (174). After the death of her father, we recall, Lozana had also left her native Córdoba, being raised elsewhere by her mother. She spends most of her life in Rome, as does Delicado. Whereas the protagonist bears three different names throughout her life—Aldonza, Lozana, and La Vellida—the author's original name was Delgado; Delicado constitutes an Italianized form, and he signed one of his books, the *Specchio vulgare per li Sacerdoti* (1525), as Delicato (Ugolini 1974–75, 449). Both Lozana and Delicado are syphilitic (Damiani 1974, 14–15; Ugolini 1974–75, 451–52), and both spend the last part of their lives on islands. Lozana seems to escape from Rome to Lipari, which is off the coast of Sicily, just before the sack of Rome; she goes there seeking peace. Delicado takes off to Venice, another island, in February of 1528, fearing that the inhabitants of Rome will seek revenge: "por no esperar las

"Sailing," Renaissance Rome, and Exile

crueldades vindicativas de naturales" ("so as to avoid the cruel revenge of the inhabitants"; 508).

The narrator explains the name of Lipari by stating that "antiguamente aquella ínsula fue poblada de personas que no había sus pares, d'adonde se dijeron li pari: los pares; y dicen en italiano: li pari loro non si trovano, que quiere decir: no se hallan sus pares" ("long ago that island was settled by people who had no equals, and so they called themselves *li pari*, i.e., 'the equals.' And people say in Italian; *li pari loro non si trovano*, which means: 'their equals are not to be found'"; 487). He then goes on to say that "cuando un hombre hacía un insigne delito, no le daban la muerte, mas condenábanlo a la ínsula de Lipari" ("when a man committed a big crime, they did not put him to death, but exiled him to Lipari instead"; 487). When Delicado arrives in Venice, he does not find his "pares," either, in the sense that there were not any other Spaniards in the city: "no hallé otro español en esta ínclita cibdá" ("I did not find another Spaniard in this illustrious city"; 508).

Another interesting connection between Lozana and Delicado is the love boat or boat of folly placed on the frontispiece, just below the title (165). Lozana sits at the bow, below a banner with the twice-repeated motto "A Venetia" ("To Venice"); Rampín is in the rear, next to a banner with the words "De Roma" ("From Rome"). The passengers are prostitutes, two of whom are identified as Divitia and Celidonia.[40] Since Lozana and Rampín appear to retire in Lipari, scholars have taken the unreliable narrator at his word, interpreting the boat as a representation of the book itself on its way to Venice.[41] I disagree. Lozana goes to Venice rather than Lipari because Delicado created her as an alter ego.[42] The identification between them is such that, speaking of how much she likes the fictionalized "Auctor" ("Author") who is writing her story, the heroine states that he depicts her so faithfully that she herself could have mistaken his portrait for her real self: "Quiérolo yo muncho, porque me contrahace tan natural mis meneos y autos ... cuando yo lo vi contrahacerme, me parecía que yo era ... me contrahizo, que quedé espantada" ("I like him a lot, because he imitates my mannerisms and actions so naturally ... when I saw him imitating me, it seemed that I was looking at myself ... he imitated me so well that I was astonished"; 394–95). This is no wonder, for, artistically, they are one and the same. The parallels between Lozana and her creator are far too many to be a matter of pure coincidence. Through Lozana, Delicado was able to express what he and others in the same situation felt about the times in which they lived, transmuting his and their suffering into art.

Since Venice corresponds to Lipari, it is implied that his exile to that city is as "voluntary" as the exile of those sent to Lipari, with the difference that he was merely a victim of circumstances, for he had not committed any crimes. In sum, there is no question but that, in a way, Delicado is really writing about himself.

Last but not least, the beginning and concluding references to exile in a book whose protagonist, like its author, whether "voluntarily" or not, besides living in exile, finds it necessary to seek refuge elsewhere on a second occasion, acquire a special significance. The very first allusion to exile may be found at the very beginning of the book, in the prologue, for the narrator purports to write in order to forget his grief, just like Fernando del Pulgar, to whom he attributes the phrase "así daré olvido al dolor" ("I shall forget sorrow in this manner"; 170).

At first sight, this grief seems to consist of the syphilis that had afflicted Delicado for so many years; in the apology that follows the last *mamotreto*, the author claims to have written his book as a distraction during a serious illness, and goes on to refer to his now lost *De consolatione infirmorum* and his treatise on *El modo de adoperare el legno de India Occidentale* (see Damiani 1969b), the miraculous remedy that, he believed, had cured him of that infection (485).

This explanation for composing the narration of his sorrow is less than convincing, however, since, right after stating that he is writing to forget his personal grief, the author explains that he also has the much broader purpose of reminding his readers of the less than exemplary events of his time: "y también por traer a la memoria munchas cosas que en nuestros tiempos pasan, que no son laude a los presentes ni espejo a los a venir" ("and also to remind people of many things that are taking place in our times; they reflect poorly on the present, and cannot serve as an example for the future"; 170).

In Wardropper's opinion, Delicado is addressing the Spanish refugees who mourn the sack of Rome, blaming themselves for the disaster: "Quienes van a leer su libro ("publicado en Venecia en 1528") están de luto: son refugiados españoles que han huído de la ira de los romanos y se han cubierto—metafóricamente—de cilicio y ceniza por el Saco de Roma, por la podredumbre que los rodea, por su responsabilidad en el desastre" ("Those who are going to read his book [published in Venice, 1528] are in mourning: they are Spanish refugees who have escaped to avoid the anger of the Romans and have covered themselves—metaphorically, that is—with hair shirts and ashes because of the sack of Rome, the corruption that surrounded them, and their responsibility in the disaster"; 1953b, 477).

Although it is logical to surmise that the Spanish refugees from Rome mourned their exile—as I intend to substantiate even further, the idea of exile is extremely important in *La Lozana andaluza*—it does not make sense to attribute feelings of guilt to them. After all, the sack of the city that had also become theirs certainly was not their fault. If anything, they had been doubly victimized, for, besides suffering as a result of the sack, they had to flee afterward because the Romans blamed the marranos in their midst for the catastrophe (Pérez 1981, 100). Moreover, as we shall see, Delicado had a much broader audience in mind.

According to Damiani and Allegra, Delicado attributes the phrase "así daré olvido al dolor" ("I shall forget sorrow in this manner") to Pulgar because he is thinking of the "Letra de Fernando del Pulgar contra los males de la vejez" ("Letter of Fernando del Pulgar against the ailments of old age"), where that author expresses almost the very same idea (Delicado 1975, 70–71n9). *La Lozana andaluza* does not constitute an apostrophe against the evils of old age, however. Moreover, it should be kept in mind that Pulgar, besides being another converso, also happened to be the chronicler of Ferdinand and Isabella, the monarchs who were ultimately responsible for the establishment of the Inquisition that caused so many conversos to exile themselves "voluntarily" from Spain and for the expulsion of the Jews in 1492.

Perhaps this is what the narrator, unreliable as usual—the phrase in question does not even seem to belong to Pulgar—really had in mind.[43] Whatever the case, that historian, whose chronicle does not cover the events of 1492, certainly explains why so many Spaniards, like the Spanish characters in *La Lozana andaluza*, were living in countries other than their own.

In the chapter of his chronicle on the Inquisition, Pulgar states that that institution was established because the Catholic Kings had been informed of the existence of numerous crypto-Jews among the conversos. Having witnessed the manner in which the Inquisition dealt with them—a great number of the accused were burnt at the stake and even the dead were exhumed and their bones equally condemned to the bonfires—many conversos felt such fear that they preferred to abandon their homes and property, seeking refuge abroad, rather than to risk a similar fate. Note that Pulgar does not designate those individuals as crypto-Jews; it is as if their guilt consisted of their "lineage" more than of any other factor: "Vista esta manera de proceder, *muchos de los de aquel linage*, temiendo aquellas execuciones, desampararon sus casas e bienes, e se fueron al Reyno de Portogal, e a tierra de Italia, e a Francia, e a otros Reynos" ("Seeing how [the Inquisition] went about its business, many people of that lineage, fearing these executions, abandoned their homes and property, and went to Portugal, Italy, France, and other countries"; 1953, 332). The author then goes on to say that most of the refugees were from Andalusia, with greater emphasis on Córdoba and Seville: "Falláronse especialmente en Sevilla, e Córdoba, y en las cibdades e villas del Andalucía en aquel tiempo quatro mil casas, e más, do moraban muchos de los de aquel linage; los quales se absentaron de la tierra con sus mugeres e fijos" ("At that time, especially in Seville, Córdoba, and other cities and towns of Andalusia, there were over four thousand [empty] homes belonging

Chapter Six

to people of that lineage who had left the country with their wives and children"; 332–33).

All the Spanish women that Lozana had met upon arriving in Rome were from Andalusia, and one of them, we recall, told her that she had been in Rome "desde el año que se puso la Inquisición" ("since the year the Inquisition began"; 202). Although Lozana and Delicado had come at a later date, both were conversos from Córdoba.

In the final analysis, it is ultimately impossible to prove that Delicado had this part of Pulgar's chronicle in mind while attributing to him the words "así daré olvido al dolor" ("I shall forget sorrow in this manner"). Nevertheless, the connection established between that expression and the unfortunate events of the time, together with the fact that Delicado is writing from Venice soon after his unwilling departure from Rome, leaves little doubt that he is thinking about his second exile.

There is a clear, prophetic reference to that very exile elsewhere. When Rampín mentions the bronze statue of a "Rodriguillo español" ("little Spanish Rodrigo") believed to have been in Rome a long time ago, Lozana exclaims: "¡Por mi vida, que es cosa de saber y ver, que dicen que en aquel tiempo no había dos españoles en Roma, y agora hay tantos! Verná tiempo que no habrá ninguno, y dirán Roma mísera, como dicen España mísera" ("By my life, it is really something to know and see, for they say that there were scarcely two Spaniards in Rome at that time, and now there are so many. There will come a time when there won't be any, and they will say 'wretched Rome,' just as they say 'wretched Spain' today"; 216). The implication here is that most Spaniards in Rome are there involuntarily (i.e., they are either conversos or Jews); that is why they refer to their country as "España mísera" ("wretched Spain"). In time they will say exactly the same thing about Rome, for they will be forced to leave it, just as they had to leave Spain. As the narrator will state toward the end of the book, although it is good to learn what is happening elsewhere, it is much better to live in one's own country: "Ansimismo, por este sabrán munchas cosas que deseaban ver y oír, estándose cada uno en su patria, que cierto es una grande felicidad no estimada" ("Likewise, through this [book] they will learn many things they wished to see and hear, while each one remains in his own country, which is certainly a great, unappreciated boon"; 485–86).[44] Delicado and Lozana, whose lives have so much in common, do not seem to have had such a choice. The same is true of most of the large Spanish community of Rome, which is largely composed of conversos and Jews. In time, Rome becomes their "segunda patria" ("second homeland") but, unfortunately, they are forced to seek exile once again after the imperial army sacks that city in 1527.

"Sailing," Renaissance Rome, and Exile

In the last analysis, Lozana's departure from Spain constitutes an exile of sorts. It is almost tempting to say that being a poor, unfortunate "orphan," she must seek her fortune elsewhere, just like the author who created her story. Interpreted in this manner, the protagonist's status as an orphan does not necessarily correspond to any sort of reality, either. Her biological parents could have been very much alive. In a way, Lozana had really been orphaned twice. In a literal sense, the God of the Old Testament, the natural father of her ancestors, had been exchanged for the God of the New Testament, who thus became a stepfather of sorts. On another level, Lozana, like all conversos, was an orphan because her motherland, the country where she was born, did not really want her. These concepts, which will no doubt seem to be extremely far-fetched to many readers, could provide a new, interesting insight concerning the birth of the picaresque novel, of which *La Lozana andaluza* constitutes an important precursor,[45] for, in that type of novel, the protagonist is usually an orphan.

Since *La Lozana andaluza* begins and ends with exile and its protagonist and main characters are conversos, it would seem that the idea of exile constitutes the core of the book. Furthermore, the parallels between Lozana's and Delicado's lives are undeniable. Consequently, the chances are that *La Lozana andaluza* was not first written in 1524, as stated in the epigraph to Part I (175) and elsewhere, and finalized with some interpolated references to the sack of 1527 added in Venice soon after the narrator's departure from Rome in 1528, "a diez días de febrero por no esperar las crueldades vindicativas de naturales" ("on February 10, so as to avoid the cruel revenge of the inhabitants"; 508). Since the sorrow that led Delicado to write *La Lozana andaluza* consists of this second exile, the book was more probably planned and written after February of 1528. Therefore, it is very unlikely that it was published in that very same year, as often believed. In all probability, it did not appear until 1530.[46]

Since Delicado's book has a female protagonist, scholars have sought to determine his attitude toward women. Some stressed the importance of heredity in Lozana's career. Edward Friedman saw her position as "genetically and socially determined, a testimony to the importance of bloodlines for social respectability and responsibility" (1987, 83). These words seem to imply that Delicado sympathizes with Lozana, portraying her as a victim. María Luisa García-Verdugo arrived at a similar conclusion. Since poverty is what made Lozana a prostitute, Delicado cannot be regarded as a misogynist; his intention was "dejar constancia de un mundo cuyos males determinan el destino de mujeres y hombres, incluido el mismo autor" ("to portray a world whose ills determine the destiny of women and men, including the author himself"; 1994, 36).

Chapter Six

Other scholars saw Delicado as a feminist. Focusing on Lozana's sensuality, Goytisolo emphasized that, rather than being a passive object of male pleasure, the heroine usually takes the initiative, and is the dominant partner in her relationship with Rampín (1977, 49–50). Thus, Delicado created her as a strong, independent character. Diego Martínez Torrón went further, maintaining that Delicado thought very highly of women: "El autor tiene un alto concepto de la mujer, contrariamente a la misoginia frecuente en algunas obras de la época precedente" ("The author has a high concept of women, contrary to the misogyny which is frequent in some works of the preceding period"; 1979, 111). According to Imperiale, Delicado is really a feminist *avant la lettre*: "aboga por la emancipación de la mujer, liberada completamente del yugo de una sociedad misógina" ("he advocates the emancipation of women, completely freed from the yoke of a misogynic society"; 1991, 94n63). Imperiale was even more emphatic in 1995: "Lozana será una de las primeras mujeres del 'arroyo' capaces de 'tomar conciencia' de su condición femenina y rebelarse abiertamente contra la tiranía paternalista de una intransigente y autoritaria cultura falologocéntrica" ("Lozana seems to be one of the first women from 'the gutter' capable of 'assuming an awareness' of their female condition and to rebel openly against the paternalistic tyranny of an intransigent, authoritarian phallologocentric culture"; 151–52).

Bubnova's analysis (1995) was more balanced. While stressing Delicado's recognition of female sensuality (31) and his surprising ability to describe it from a female perspective (20), she also suggested that the book was probably written for a male audience (23), and that, according to male folklore, women who enjoy sex were and are still automatically regarded as prostitutes (30).

Then there are those who concluded that Delicado was a misogynist. In the opinion of Mercedes Paglialunga de Tuma, the freedom that Delicado gives Lozana is far from being positive: "Libertad no tenía otro sinónimo que libertinaje" ("The only synonym for freedom was licence"; 1973, 126); therefore, *La Lozana andaluza* "sigue la línea antifeminista en boga durante la Edad Media" ("follows the antifeminist trend that was in fashion during the Middle Ages"; 143). Finally, Anne Cruz (1989) thought that Lozana was badly mistreated. Delicado restricts her to the role of a prostitute and marginalizes her, separating her from decent, mainstream society (144–45). Because of the ravages of syphilis on her forehead and her nose, the beauty that the text attributes to her is false.[47] Given the "idealization" of her life, she can hardly be considered a real woman (146).

In my opinion, there is no question that the autonomy that Delicado attributes to his character is merely apparent. Lozana is clearly the product of a background that provides her with the strong sexual appetite that first manifests itself when she is still a child. Her mother's character is as questionable as her aunt's (Imperiale 1995, 153–54), and, although Lozana is poor, nothing forces her to elope with Diomedes from one moment to the next.[48] There is no indication that their "Levantine" activities displease her in the least. Since Lozana was practically born a prostitute, it is not surprising that she should choose to remain one after her arrival in Rome, without even attempting to explore other alternatives. It is true that she plays an active role and manages to retain a certain amount of independence, but, nevertheless, she remains a prostitute. She is totally shameless, and acts more like a predatory male on the hunt. Her manner and speech do not correspond to a real woman. As Imperiale pointed out in an earlier piece, while comparing Lozana with the Nanna of Pietro Aretino's *I ragiomenti*, "El retrato de la Lozana andaluza va a 'deleitar a todo hombre,' porque Lozana (y luego Nanna) no habla como una mujer, sino como les gustaría a los hombres que hablase la mujer. Nuestras dos protagonistas son puros objetos sexuales" ("The portrait of the Andalusian Lozana will 'delight every man' because Lozana [and Nanna afterward] does not speak like a woman, but the way men would like women to speak. Both heroines are pure sex objects"; 1989, 77; see also Imperiale 1997, 158).

To sum up, although *La Lozana andaluza* puts the generally perceived immorality of the Rome of the time to good use, its supposed "realism" is a mere illusion. Delicado did not intend to create a real woman. Sex serves as a cover for marginality, and, underneath its apparent joy of life and exuberant sensuality, *La Lozana andaluza* is a very angry book.

There are several allegories. Lozana's travels with her lover, Diomedes el Raveñano, throughout the Levant, do not really take place. Being a merchant from Ravenna, Diomedes's trade consists of the "rabo" ("tail") in which he specializes. He sells Lozana to his "levantados" ("erect") customers. The purpose of this initial allegory, we recall, is to establish the conversa that Delicado creates as protagonist as a syphilitic, marginalized prostitute. Lozana's business as a prostitute in Rome, which occupies the rest of the book, does not correspond to any reality either, at least in the conventional sense of that word. Thus, it constitutes a second allegory. As Cruz observed, Lozana's beauty is really false. Since she is clearly marked by the syphilis that supposedly left her without a "chimney," she could not possibly have earned her living as a prostitute. Having lost her nose to syphilis, she becomes "roma," flat-nosed," thus coming to represent the Roma in which she lives, a city whose name, when reversed, becomes "amor," the very profession that she supposedly exercises.

There is a reference to exile at the very beginning of the book, in the prologue, when the narrator says that he is writing in order to forget his grief and to remind his readers of the less than exemplary events of his time (170). These words are no doubt addressed to other fellow refugees from Rome. As

Chapter Six

the story begins, Lozana, who descends from converts, leaves Spain, reaches Rome, and immediately becomes integrated into the Spanish community settled in Pozo Blanco. This community, we recall, was largely composed of self-exiled conversos who felt they could no longer live in their beloved "España mísera" ("wretched Spain"). The sack of Rome forces the whole community to go into exile once again, and it is in the last of the six appendices, at the very end of his book, that the author explains how he and others had to leave the city on February 10, 1528 (508). These two exiles and the impossibility of living in peace, especially for a converso, constitute the core of the book that they frame. Significantly, Lozana's very "retirement" to the island of Lipari constitutes a search for peace. As she informs Rampín, "haré como hace la Paz, que huye a las islas" ("I will do like peace, which flees to the islands"; 481).

Of course the star in Lozana's forehead, the very lesion that supposedly represented the first sign of the syphilis that caused her to lose her nose, is equally symbolic. Although she is a Christian—perhaps only a nominal one, but, nevertheless, a Christian—it stands for the Judaism of her ancestors, and will mark her for as long as she lives, rendering her impure and untouchable, as if she were really syphilitic.

The fact that the author, Francisco Delicado, has a great deal in common with Lozana suggests that he created her as some sort of alter ego; perhaps Delicado felt that, in reality, he was also prostituting himself by living a life quite different from the one that he would have chosen for himself had he been given a choice. We know that he was a Catholic priest, and a syphilitic one at that. Moreover, contemporary society marginalized conversos as effectively as if they were prostitutes.

This may be going too far, especially for those who maintain that there is no point in trying to understand an author's innermost thoughts and feelings through an interpretation of his or her writings, as if an author's writings and his life were two completely separate, unrelated phenomena. Such critics would never deny that literature ultimately springs from life, of course. Nevertheless, their emphasis on precedents and literary technique, besides blurring and obstructing the message that an author such as Delicado is trying to convey, would seem to negate the existence of such a connection.

At any rate, one thing is fairly certain: had he been able to, chances are that Delicado would have remained in Spain in the first place. As he tells his readers in the apology—and it is quite clear that he is not addressing only his fellow exiles—thanks to his portrait of Lozana, they will learn about many things that they craved to see and hear, "estándose cada uno en su patria, que cierto es una grande felicidad no estimada" ("while each one remains in his own country, which is certainly a great, unappreciated boon"; 486). The ability to live in one's own country constitutes a boon insufficiently appreciated by those who never have to leave it. It is obvious that, while addressing *all* of his fellow Spaniards, Delicado is really thinking of people who did not have such good fortune, of conversos like himself who, as implied by Fernando del Pulgar, sought refuge abroad with good reason, for they felt their lives threatened by the Inquisition for no reason other than their ethnic and religious background.

In this first exile in search of a country where they could live in peace, those New Christians had been victimized because of the circumstances of their birth and the intolerance of their fellow Christians. Ironically, the second exile, from the city that had become their "segunda patria" ("second homeland"), is caused by a Spanish invasion and the fact that, as far as the native Romans were concerned, they were Spaniards, even though the Old Christian majority of Spain refused to accept them fully as such. Since they also happened to be marranos, in its turn the Roman majority decided that, somehow, that made them even more likely to have caused the disaster. A very sad, paradoxical situation indeed. There was no way out; a lasting peace could not be found anywhere; hence Delicado's decision to attempt to forget his great personal grief by writing a book in which he reminded his readers of the calamities of his time: "así daré olvido al dolor" ("I shall forget sorrow in this manner"; 170). It goes without saying that, even from Venice, Delicado may have felt that he could not have said all of these things with impunity, expressing what he felt about the injustice of his two "voluntary" exiles in a clear, straightforward manner. One never knew what the future could bring. And so he chose to say them allegorically, through his narrator, his characters, and an alter ego, the protagonist of *La Lozana andaluza*.

Chapter Seven

The Holy Trinity and the Annunciation in *La Lozana andaluza*

By presenting the capital of Christendom as a whore, Delicado coincided with those Christians who also decried the immorality of Rome and sought to reform the Church. Although they disagreed with Rome, their Christianity was not in doubt. Delicado was not one of those reformers. As we will see in the pages that follow, he avoids the names of Mary and Christ, shows no respect for saints, and the only Christian prayers proffered in the text are superstitious, paraliturgical incantations. Furthermore, Delicado also decided to attack the Annunciation and the dogma of the Holy Trinity, which constitute the core of the religion of the Old Christian persecutors ultimately responsible for both of his "voluntary" exiles.

Whereas God is invoked well over one hundred times, Christ's name seldom appears (Mackay 1992, 234–35n9; see also Macpherson and Mackay 1998, 181–82 and 182n5). The first reference to him is made by Silvano, a friend of Lozana, when he describes to her Peña de Martos, where the "Auctor" had been raised. After associating the town with the god Mars—it had been first called Peña de Marte—Silvano goes on to relate Martos to St. Martha, sister of Lazarus and St. Mary Magdalene, whose house Christ had visited in Bethany, stating that the church in the plaza was dedicated to the "solícita y fortísima y santísima Marta, huéspeda de Cristo" ("most diligent, strong and holy Martha, hostess of Christ"; 397). Silvano then associates the saint with the French legend of the dragon Tarascon, transferring it to Martos, where the dragon slain by St. Martha is turned into "un ferocísimo serpiente, el cual devoraba los habitadores de la cibdad de Marte, y ésta fue la principal causa de su despoblación" ("an extremely ferocious serpent that was devouring the inhabitants of the city of Mars, and this was the main reason for its depopulation"; 398). There is an allusion to this legend, we recall, in the frontispiece of *El modo de adoperare el legno de India Occidentale*, which is about the miraculous guaiacum wood that had supposedly delivered Delicado from the syphilis whose cure he attributes simultaneously to St. James (see Chapter 2, pp. 42–43). Since the engraving portrays St. Martha standing on the Rhone, Delicado should have known better than to transfer

The Holy Trinity and the Annunciation

it to Spain. In other words, what we have here is a joke. Moreover, St. Martha is placed on the same level as the god Mars: Martos, Marte, Marta, they are all the same.

Still within the same speech, Silvano states that outsiders envy Peña de Martos because of its prosperity and the matchless hospitality that he attributes to St. Martha, mentioning Christ's name a second time: "que en todo el mundo no haya tanta caridad, hospitalidad y amor projimal cuanta en aquel lugar, y cáusalo la caritativa huéspeda de Cristo" ("there is no other place in the world with so much charity, hospitality, and love toward one's neighbors, and all of this is caused by the kind hostess of Christ"; 398).

Delicado seems to take great pride in Peña de Martos, which he mentions frequently, but this praise is ridiculously excessive, and, therefore, extremely suspicious. It could very well signal the opposite. The appearance of Christ's name is incidental, for it is secondary to St. Martha's in both instances. Moreover, right after mentioning Christ for the second time, Silvano states that "Allí poco lejos está la sierra de Ailló, antes de Alcaudete" ("Not far from there stand the mountains of Ailló, previously known as Alcaudete"; 398), to which Lozana replies: "Alcaudete, el que hace los cornudos a ojos vistas [sic]" ("Alcaudete, the one who turns men into cuckolds"; 398).

These references to a pimp and to cuckolds right after the name of Christ are hardly respectful, for they bring to mind the Jewish charge that St. Joseph had been cuckolded by the Virgin Mary. Christ also appears as "el Salvador" ("the Savior"; 442) at the end of an incantation (quoted below), and as "nuestro Señor" ("Our Lord"), when Delicado wishes health and prosperity to the captain of the imperial army to whom he dedicates his book: "deseo ... a vuestra merced servir y darle solacio, la cual [merced] nuestro Señor, próspero, sano y alegre conserve munchos y felicísimos tiempos" ("I wish ... to serve and amuse Your Lordship, and may Our Lord keep you prosperous, healthy, and happy, for many happy years to come"; 492). The last example constitutes the only one in which Christ appears to be invoked with any meaning, but, since this is done in order to bless a captain in the army that had sacked Rome, the blessing in question may be really a curse. In fact, Delicado seems to detest the name of Jesus, for its virtual absence from his portrait of the city, which, despite its immorality, was still the capital of Christendom, is very strange.

Another way of referring to Christ was through his words, but the two examples of words attributed to him do not indicate any devotion. Upon entering the house of a courtesan whose property is administered by a monsignor, Lozana says, "Paz sea en esta casa" ("May there be peace in this house"; 283), thus repeating Christ's advice to his disciples: "Whatever house you enter, first say, 'Peace to this house'" (Luke 10.5).[1] At the very least,

Chapter Seven

Lozana's use of these words is ironical, for the monsignor, who is afflicted with a venereal disease, gets her pregnant afterward. And when Rampín informs a mace-bearer (a euphemism for "phallus") who wishes to visit Lozana together with a "valijero" or letter carrier (as we will see below, the word is used as a euphemism for "testicles") that Lozana cannot see both of them at the same time—"Dice que no podéis servir a dos señores" ("She says that you cannot serve two masters [at the same time]"; 264)—the words chosen for her reply are nothing less than sacrilegious, for they echo one of the teachings of Jesus during the Sermon on the Mount: "No man can serve two masters" (Matt. 6.24).[2]

Another way of alluding to Christ was by mentioning the Holy Eucharist, at times called "cuerpo de Dios" ("Body of God"; Kasten and Cody 2001, 204*b*, s.v. "cuerpo"), because, contrary to Jews, who maintained that God was pure spirit, i.e., incorporeal, Christians claimed that the Father had been incarnated, that is, had become human through the Son, and that they received the body of Christ whenever they had Communion. The expression "cuerpo de Dios" is used in strange situations twice. While helping Lozana to look for Rampín, Trinchante discovers that he has fallen into a latrine, where he is apparently in danger of drowning, and exclaims: "¡Mirá, cuerpo de Dios, está en la privada y andámoslo a buscar!" ("Look, Body of God, he is in the latrine and we're looking for him!"; 332). Although any Christian could have used the expression being examined under the circumstances, given what we already know about Delicado, it is certainly justified to wonder if he meant to establish a parallel between Rampín's predicament and the sacrament of Communion.

A second example appears in a similar, albeit somewhat less revolting situation, when Rampín starts to vomit after being forced to eat a piece of bacon publicly. The aptly named Falillo, one of the boys who had forced him to eat it, describes what happens as follows: "¿Y las tripas echas? ¡Sal de allá, que no es atriaca! ¡Ve d'aquí, oh cuerpo de Dios,[3] con quien te bautizó, que no te ahogó por grande que fueras!" ("And you are vomiting your guts out? Get out of here, it's not an antidote. Get out of here, oh Body of God, and go to whoever baptized and failed to drown you, no matter how big [a baby] you were"; 341). Rampín vomits because, although he is a converso, he still feels the ancestral Jewish revulsion for pork. Although the reference to God's body, i.e., to Christ, functions here as a common interjection, it may also establish a parallel between Rampín's reaction to the bacon and the Communion through which Christians receive the body of Christ. Jews and unconvinced conversos, we recall, looked upon this as illogical nonsense. Some argued that it did not make any sense for God to divide himself and to be present in heaven and in many churches at the same time (Crescas 1992, 60), and that, in a way, Communion was also a form of cannibalism.

The Holy Trinity and the Annunciation

In any case, whether with ulterior motives or not, thanks to the expression "el cuerpo de Dios" ("the Body of God"), Delicado is able to refer to Christ without having to mention his name.

According to Allaigre, Falillo's wish that Rampín had been drowned by whoever baptized him, no matter how big he was, alludes to the fact that "bautizaron al judío a la fuerza, cuando ya era grande" ("they baptized Jews by force, when they were already grown up"; 341n24). Since Rampín is the son of baptized parents—as Lozana points out, tasting bacon once had made his father sick for seven years (341)[4]—and there were no forced conversions after 1391 and the early fifteenth century, that could not have been the case. Rampín was probably baptized as a baby, according to custom. Therefore, what Falillo probably means is that whoever baptized him should have drowned him in the small amount of water normally used in baptismal fonts, even if he happened to be a big baby; as his reaction to the pork clearly demonstrated, the baptism had not done him any good.

From a positivistic perspective, this episode can certainly be interpreted as being anti-Semitic. One possible reading is that, once a Jew, always a Jew, for Judaism is inherited through bloodlines, and, therefore, all conversos are false Christians. But read literally, in such a manner, the self-mocking conversos studied in Chapter 2 would turn out to be anti-Semitic as well. In fact, what we have here is a converso, in-house joke. Lozana goes along with the prank, but, as we know, she herself hates pork. The main instigator, Falillo, is also a converso. That is why, when the whole thing is over, he exclaims: "¡Quemado sea el venerable tocino!" ("May the venerable bacon be burned!"; 342). Bacon is "venerable" in the sense of "old," because it eventually came to represent "Old" Christians. If Falillo himself had to eat such a thing, there is no question that his reaction would have been the same as Rampín's.[5]

In sum, although Christ's name is virtually absent, Delicado still manages to refer to him in unflattering ways, without having to mention him directly.[6] The name of the Blessed Mother is practically absent as well, for it is mentioned only as a place name, the "villa de Santa María" ("town of Holy Mary"; 397), which is reportedly near Martos. But there are veiled references to the Virgin. While describing to Lozana the numerous types of whores found in Rome, the letter carrier informs her that there are "putas con virgo, putas sin virgo, putas el día del domingo, putas que guardan el sábado hasta que han jabonado" ("virgin whores, whores without virginity, Sunday whores, and whores who keep the Sabbath until they have used the soap"; 271), as if it were possible for whores to remain virgin, which brings to mind the Jewish charge that Mary was really a prostitute who got pregnant and then claimed to be a virgin. To make the inference even clearer, the letter carrier then goes on to establish a difference between Christian and

205

Chapter Seven

Jewish whores, with the Christian ones taking Sundays off, and the Jewish ones abstaining from work on Saturdays until they have used the "soap," whatever that might mean. Clearly, Delicado calls attention to Christian and Jewish whores in order to make like-minded readers stop and think about what he had just said about virgin whores. In other words, he wanted to make sure that they savored the oxymoron.

But there is more. The bed-ridden, syphilitic Trujillo, who had arrived from Spain recently, sends a servant to fetch Lozana, hoping that she can cure him, and says to her as soon as she arrives: "Señora Lozana, vuestra merced me perdone, que yo había de ir a homillarme delante de vuestra real persona y la pasión corporal es tanta que puedo decir que es interlineal. Y por eso me atreví a suplicalla me visitase malo porque yo la visite a ella cuando sea bueno, y con su visitación sane" ("Lady Lozana, pray forgive me, for I was going to humble myself before your royal person, and my corporal passion is so great I can say it's in between the lines. And so I dared to beg you to visit me now that I'm sick, so that I can visit you when I'm well, and recover my health with your visitation"; 410). As Allaigre explained (Delicado 1985, 410n4), these words enclose a sacrilegious reference to the Annunciation, when the Angel Gabriel visits the Blessed Mother and tells her that she will bear the Son of God (Luke 1.26–33). Since Lozana is the one who visits Trujillo, what we have here may be seen as an Annunciation in reverse, with the Virgin visiting the angel. Trujillo hopes that the visitation will cure him, and then promises to reciprocate. According to Allaigre, Trujillo calls Lozana "real persona" ("royal person") in order to flatter her (410n1), but the title probably reflects the fact that Christians regard Mary as Queen of Heaven. Lozana's reply, "¡Nunca en tal me vi!" ("I've never been in such straits before"; 410), is a verse from a popular song, *La niña de Gómez Arias* (see Allaigre's note on p. 265), but, all the same, it embodies an allusion to the Blessed Mother's reaction to Gabriel's initial salutation: "When she had heard him she was troubled at his word" (Luke 1.29).[7] To make the sacrilege even worse, after Lozana feels his parts, Trujillo asks to see hers, suggesting that this will suffice to cure his affliction, as if by miracle ("Señora, yo he oído que tenéis vos muy lindo lo vuestro, y quiérolo ver por sanar" ["My Lady, I've heard you've got a very pretty pussy, and I'd like to see it in order to be cured"; 412]), and then tricks her into having sex with him for free, which embarrasses Lozana tremendously: "Éste fue el mayor aprieto que en mi vida pasé; no querría que se supiese por mi honra" ("This is the greatest predicament I've ever been through; I hope no one finds out, for the sake of my reputation"; 413–14).[8]

Despite the apparent absence of her name from *La Lozana andaluza*, then, the Virgin Mary is also present in Delicado's mind. As we will see later in

The Holy Trinity and the Annunciation

this chapter, the author will find yet another mean, pornographic way in order to attack her.

Naturally, the saints do not fare well in Delicado's work, either. Mackay counted some twenty-eight references, but, as he pointed out, "many of these are grotesque" (1992, 234n9). Angry at a woman from Majorca, Lozana swears, in Catalan, by St. Arnold's ass: "¡Cul de Sant Arnau, som segurs! ¡Quina gent de Déu!" ("By the ass of St. Arnold, we're sure! What creatures of God!"; 205). A grocer from whom Rampín tries to steal some eggplants, saying that he had brought them with him, yells back: "¡Pota de Santa Nula; tú ne mente per la cana de la gola!" ("By St. Nula's cunt, you're lying through your beard"; 325). This St. Nula (cf. It. *nulla*, "nothing") seems to be a non-existent saint invented by Delicado, and so is probably the most badly treated of them all, the poor St. Nefija,[9] who was so charitable "que daba a todos de cabalgar en limosna" ("that she let everyone mount her, as charity"; 414; see also 284), and who, according to Trujillo, must have suffered an unusual martyrdom, for she is the saint who "murió de amor suave" ("died of sweet love"; 412).

Because of the references to Martos, St. Martha and St. Mary Magdalene receive more attention. The fact that St. Martha's fountain is next to a place called "Bad Neighbor" and happens to be the same one where Mars used to water his horses is strange: "tiene otra [fuente] al pie de Malvecino, donde Marte abrevaba sus caballos, que agora se nombra la fuente Santa Marta, salutífera contra la fiebre" ("there is another fountain near Malvecino [Bad Neighbor], where Mars used to water his horses; now it's called St. Martha's Fountain, and the water is good for fever"; 398). This places the pagan god on the same footing as the Christian saint, but, nevertheless, people still think that the water of the fountain has miraculous properties. In the plaza, there is an altar dedicated to St. Mary Magdalene, St. Martha's sister, who is called the "hairy one," no doubt because she used her tears to wash the feet of Jesus, drying them with her hair afterward: "La mañana de San Juan sale en ella la cabelluda, que quiere decir que allí munchas veces apareció la Madalena" ("On St. John's morn the hairy one comes out of it [the fountain], and this means that the Magdalene appeared there many times"; 398). Note that the appearances of St. Mary Magdalene are described in terms of scary, evil apparitions. Right after, we discover that "el templo lapídeo y fortísima ara de Marte" ("the stone temple and very sturdy altar of Mars"; 398) are presently consecrated "a la fortísima Santa Marta" ("to the very strong St. Martha"; 398), no doubt because of her prowess in killing the "ferocísimo serpiente" ("extremely ferocious serpent"; 398). Thus, the saint is described in martial terms, which, of course, can be viewed as a contradiction in itself. Since all of this is part of Silvano's description of Delicado's supposedly

Chapter Seven

beloved Peña de Martos, it makes you wonder whether Delicado really loved the place or not.

In the last analysis, Delicado is mocking St. Martha and St. Mary Magdalene. Although he appears to be devoted to Santiago in *El modo*, claiming that he had vowed to go to Compostela on a pilgrimage—the hospital where he had stayed, San Giacomo degli Incurabili (St. James of the Incurable), bore his name—this may constitute a pose. *El modo*, we recall, is about guaiacum wood, which, according to Delicado, is what had really cured his syphilis. Although it was certainly possible for the author to believe that both the guaiacum and the saint had a hand in the affair, the manner in which he deals with St. James in *La Lozana andaluza* suggests that he is as devoted to him as to St. Martha, St. Mary Magdalene, or any other saint. St. James is called "Santiago de las Carretas" ("St. James of the Carts"; 393) because, in Rome, those with incurable illnesses were taken to San Giacomo, and people with syphilis looked as if they had been run over by a cart: "Al que está contrecho del mal francés, decimos haberle tomado la carreta, porque parece haber pasado sobre él alguna rueda de carreta que le ha dejado lisiado" ("We say that those crippled by the French disease have the cart because they seem to have been run over and injured by the wheels of a cart"; Covarrubias 1994, 277). Those who had been in the Roman hospital are said to have stayed "en la posada del señor don Diego" ("at the inn of Lord St. James"; 406, 415). These two references, together with the constant association of St. James, Patron of Spain, with syphilis, are anything but respectful. Moreover, as we saw in Chapter 2 (pp. 49–50), Delicado mentions the saint's name at the very end of his book, as part of the battle cry "¡Santiago y a ellos!" ("St. James, let's get them!"; 508), as he explains how he had to leave the city that had become a second home to him together with the army that had sacked it, thus causing his second exile.

All of this suggests that Delicado has no use for saints, and this is also probably true of Christian prayer, since the only examples he gives, which he invents, mock those superstitious, paraliturgical folk spells in which some people were foolish enough to believe. The first one, an incantation against syphilis, will be examined when we see how Delicado deals with the Holy Trinity, for it mocks the idea that three can be one and vice-versa. Lozana proffers the second incantation in order to cure a child from the evil eye: "Si te dio en la cabeza, válate Santa Elena; si te dio en los hombros, válante los apóstolos todos; si te dio en el corazón, válgate el Salvador" ("If it struck you on the head, may St. Helen help you; if it struck you on the shoulders, may all the Apostles help you; if it struck you in the heart, may the Savior help you"; 441–42). The third and last example is for the benefit of a stableboy named Sarracin, whose "hidalguía" ("nobility") Lozana verifies after feeling the erection he has. Lozana pretends to cure the venereal dis-

The Holy Trinity and the Annunciation

ease from which he suffers with the following words: "Santo Ensalmo se salió, y contigo se encontró, y su vista te sanó; ansí como esto es verdad, ansí sanes d'este mal, amén" ("Holy spell went out, ran into you, and his sight cured you; as this is true, may you be cured of this illness, amen"; 473). Then she adds, encouragingly: "Andá que no será nada; que pecado es que tengáis mal en tal mandragulón" ("Go on; it is probably nothing. It's a pity that such a big cock is sick"; 473).

Since these are merely parodies of folk spells, perhaps the best indication of what the author really thinks of Christian prayer has to do with the rosary, which, as we know, is emblematic of the Virgin Mary. Angry at a bearded old woman who apparently can no longer work as a prostitute, Lozana suggests that the rosary that she carries is merely for the sake of appearances: "¡Nunca yo medre si vos decís todas esas cuentas!" ("May I never prosper if you ever pray all of those beads!"; 258). The old woman replies: "No lo digáis, hija, que cada día los [*sic*] paso siete y siete, con su gloria al cabo" ("Don't say that, my daughter; I pray them seven times over each day, with the *Gloria* at the end"; 258).

The woman claims that she prays the rosary over and over, all day long, maintaining that she concludes each recitation with the *Gloria*. The last statement suggests that she is lying, for the rosary ends with the *Salve, Regina*, not with the *Gloria*, which is repeated, together with the *Pater Noster*, between each set of ten Hail Mary's. Therefore, the old woman's need to stress that she says the *Gloria* at the end of each recitation suggests that she does not really know the rosary, and that the prayer in question bothers her more than most. And the truth of the matter is that insincere conversos made every effort to avoid saying the *Gloria*, for the words "In the name of the Father, the Son, and the Holy Ghost" constitute an affirmation of faith in the Holy Trinity, cornerstone of the Christianity that they could not possibly accept (Gitlitz 1996, 464). Needless to say, the prayer in question does not appear anywhere in Delicado's work.

Jews and Muslims have always considered Trinitarian Christians to be polytheists because of their belief in the Father, the Son, and the Holy Ghost, even though such Christians regard the three as being only one. Contrary to what might be expected, it was not the question concerning the coming of the Messiah but the doctrines of the Holy Trinity and the Incarnation, both of which are basic to Christianity, that troubled Jews most, zealous as they were "in affirming the unity and incorporeity of God" (Fraker 1966, 12–13). That is why these two doctrines occupy a central position in the medieval debates between rabbis and Christian theologians. As historians have pointed out (i.e., J. Friedman 1978, 18; Bainton 1962, 135), the mystery of the Holy Trinity was particularly problematic to Jews, constituting the main stumbling block in converting them.

Chapter Seven

One of the Jewish arguments against the Trinity was that, besides denying the unity and incorporeity of God, such a dogma was contrary to reason itself. According to Joseph Albó, a scholar who participated in the famous Disputation of Tortosa, the doctrine of the Holy Trinity was not even prefigured in the Old Testament, as Christians claimed.[10] In his opinion, since it also defied all logic, it was patently false: "The law of Moses says nothing about trinity because it is not true from the point of view of reason, and the Torah does not inculcate an idea that is not true, such as that *one is three and three are one*, while remaining separate and distinct, as they say" (Albo 1946, 3: 224; emphasis mine).

Not surprisingly, the Jewish apologists refer to the concept of three in one and one in three time and again. In the twelfth century, Maimonides "cited the Christians who employed the trinitarian formula, 'God is *one*, but also *three*, and the *three* are *one*,' as an example of people who say one thing but must believe something quite different" (Lasker 1977, 46), because the statement is contradictory in itself. Also in the twelfth century, another Cordoban, Averroes, mentioned the same concept: "Therefore they say that the *three* are *one*, i.e. *one* in act and *three* in potency" (65). In the thirteenth century, Moses ben Solomon of Salerno "argued that if there were *three* Persons and they were *one*, then there must be something which united them and something else which distinguished them into three" (67). Around 1263, Nahmanides, a native of Gerona, protested that "even if these were accidents in God, the thing which is the Godhead was not *three* but *one*, bearing three accidents" (68). In the fourteenth century, Hasdai Crescas pointed out that "since God's essence is one in all aspects, if the attributes were His essence or part of His essence, it would be like the doctrine of those who say that He is *one* but He is *three* and the *three* are *one*" (70). Still in the fourteenth century, Moses Narboni stated that "As for us, when we say that God, may He be blessed, is the thinker, the thinking, and the thought, and they all are one, we are not saying He has in Him these *three* things and they are *one*" (80). Simon Duran, who lived during the fourteenth and fifteenth centuries (1361–1444), wrote that though the Christians "verbally negate multiplicity in God, they actually do assume it since they believe that He is both *one* and *three*" (79). In the fifteenth century, while clarifying some aspects of Hasdai Crescas's philosophy, Joseph ben Shem Tov explained that Crescas's doctrine "is not liable to any of the difficulties necessitated by the Christian belief, nor does he believe that they [the attributes] are both *three* and *one*" (74). Also in the fifteenth century, the already mentioned Joseph Albo returns to the charge with these words: "But that there should be in Him *three* distinct things, each one existing by itself, *distintos en personas* [of distinct Persons] as they say, and that they should nevertheless be *one*,

The Holy Trinity and the Annunciation

this is impossible, unless two contradictories can be true at the same time, which is opposed to the primary axioms and inconceivable by the mind" (81).

The point in citing all of these examples is to show that the concept of three in one and one in three was sufficient in itself to designate the dogma of the Holy Trinity without naming it directly, for, as we will see, Delicado took advantage of this.

Since even Christians had trouble with the concept of the Holy Trinity—hence its designation as a dogma, because the mystery cannot be logically explained—it is not surprising to see that this doctrine was particularly problematic for the early conversos, who were familiar with the Jewish objections to that dogma, even when they made a sincere effort to believe in all the tenets of their new faith.[11] As Fraker demonstrated (1966, esp. pp. 11–20; see also Chapter 2, pp. 53–62), the mystery in question continued to plague many of the conversos represented in the *Cancionero de Baena* (1445). Some of the poems that they wrote make this quite clear. These New Christians passed on their doubts to their children, who, in many instances, continued to transmit them to their descendants (Fraker 1966, 61–62).

Scholars have not determined whether Delicado was a first, second, or third generation converso, but, as we shall see, the dogma of the Holy Trinity greatly troubled him. Many of his fellow exiles shared the same problem. As already pointed out, his perceptive Italian contemporaries, who had received a great number of New Christian refugees in their country, soon realized that many of their Spanish guests did not believe in the Holy Trinity, a major difficulty which the Italians ironically designated with a diminutive, as if it could be easily dismissed as a venial, unimportant little sin: "El italiano veía muchas veces al español como un marrano, un cristiano semitizado. *Peccadiglio di Spagna*, así hablaban los italianos para señalar que uno no creía en el dogma de la Santa Trinidad" ("Italians often regarded all Spaniards as marranos, Christians with a strong Semitic influence. They used the expression *little sin of Spain* in order to indicate that one did not believe in the dogma of the Holy Trinity"; Pérez 1981, 100; see also Bataillon 1982a, 60).

Delicado's protagonist, we recall, goes by no less than three names. The narrator himself calls attention to this in the *escusa* ("excuse") placed after the very last *mamotreto*. His heroine "gozó de tres nombres: en España, Aldonza, y en Roma, la Lozana, y en Lípari, la Vellida" ("enjoyed three names: Aldonza in Spain, Lozana in Rome, and La Vellida in Lipari"; 484). In the section that follows, he says: "Item, ¿por qué más la llamé Lozana que otro nombre? Porque Lozana es nombre más común y comprehende su nombre primero Aldonza, o Alaroza en lengua arábica, y Vellida lo mismo, de manera que Lozana significa lo que cada un nombre d'estos otros significan" ("Also, why did I call her 'Lozana' more than some other name? Because 'Lozana' is more common and includes her first name, 'Aldonza,' which is 'Alaroza' in Arabic, and 'Vellida' means the same thing, so that 'Lozana' means the same as each one of these other names"; 487).[12]

In other words, Lozana is an almost perfect anagram for Aldonza, and Vellida means the same as Lozana, so that, even though his protagonist seems to have three names, she really has only one. Delicado alludes to the concept of three in one and one in three while explaining the name of a prostitute. This unquestionably planned onomastic equivalence therefore seems to constitute a deliberate mockery of the dogma of the Holy Trinity all by itself. Further evidence supports the fact that this is not just an isolated, meaningless coincidence.

Significantly, *La Lozana andaluza* is divided into three parts, and Delicado frequently mocks the idea of three in one and one in three in a tripartite manner, no fewer than three times in a row, often in obscene terms. Moreover, Delicado concentrates most of his invective in the third part of a book that is itself divided in three parts.

The first example is particularly important, because Delicado uses it in order to alert like-minded readers that there is a hidden message in his book. It occurs shortly after Lozana's arrival in Rome, when Rampín takes her to Trigo, who agrees to rent for her the house in which she is to live. This takes place in *mamotreto* xvi. Then the narrator intercalates a *mamotreto* (no. xvii) entitled "Información que interpone el autor para que se entienda lo que adelante ha de seguir" (Information that the author interpolates, so that what follows can be understood; 250), in which Rampín visits the "Auctor," who is in the process of writing Lozana's story, and falls down the stairs as he is leaving the house. The concerned "Auctor" offers the boy a piece of cloth to put around his head, which he refuses, replying that he will ask Lozana to cure him with the following incantation for the "mal francorum":

> Eran tres cortesanas
> y tenían tres amigos
> pajes de Franquilano,
> la una lo tiene público.
> 5 y la otra muy callado;
> a la otra le vuelta con el lunario.
> Quien esta oración dijere
> tres veces a rimano,
> cuando nace sea sano, amén.
>
> (256 [55])[13]

According to Bruno M. Damiani and Giovanni Allegra, the Franquilano of the incantation could have some connection with "francorum," but it could

The Holy Trinity and the Annunciation

also be an allusion to a previously mentioned prostitute named "Franquilana" (Delicado 1975, 171n44). Claude Allaigre agrees with their interpretation (Delicado 1985, 256n38). Rather than referring to any specific character, however, "Franquilano" is another name for syphilis, the "mal francorum" that the spell is supposed to cure. In other words, Rampín is syphilitic, just like Lozana. As we saw in the last chapter, the purpose of Lozana's syphilis, which first manifests itself through a "star" on her forehead, eventually causing her to become flat-nosed ("roma"), is to point to her Jewish background and to identify her with the "Roma putana" ("Harlot Rome") where she lives. Since such an obviously syphilitic woman would have been able to attract few if any customers, Lozana's disease, as indeed her career in Rome, constitutes an allegory. Consequently, it is not too far-fetched to surmise that Rampín's syphilis is as "real"; in all probability, the illness serves to emphasize his converso extraction as well.

The three friends or companions of the three courtesans refer to the manner in which the syphilis that afflicts these three women affects each of them. Everyone knows that the first one is infected: "la una lo tiene público" ("one has hers publicly"). The second one has managed to hide her condition thus far, which would seem to indicate that she was trying very hard not to scare away customers: "y la otra muy callado" ("another very secretly"). The third lady seems to have been in the early stages of the disease, for the symptoms only appear when she is having a period: "a la otra le vuelta con el lunario" ("the third's returns with each moon"). The three friends of the three courtesans, then, are really one. They are "pajes de Franquilano" ("pages of Franquilano") because they refer to the manner in which syphilis afflicts the three women. Thus, the three pages stand for one single entity, which manifests itself though the three of them. Since the three pages are one, syphilis, and the three women really have the same "friend," rather than three separate lovers, three is one and one, three. As is often the case, here Delicado mocks the doctrine of the Holy Trinity no less than three times in a row, that is, in a tripartite manner: there are *three* courtesans, *three* pages, and the prayer must be said no less than *three* times in a row: "tres veces a rimano." Since it parodies similar Christian folk spells for a variety of ills that amount to nothing but superstitious nonsense,[14] Delicado probably also meant to imply that the dogma of the Trinity was as nonsensical.

The Jews knew better, however. In their strict, uncompromising monotheism, they could not possibly accept the logically untenable idea that three are one and one, three. That is why, in the previous *mamotreto*, Trigo, a Spaniard, swears by "el Dio" (246), rather than by the supposedly plural "Dios" (God) that Christians use. Given its position just before such an attack on Trinitarianism, Trigo's oath was probably meant to contrast the concept of a single, indivisible God, with the idea of a triune God.

Chapter Seven

As Allaigre indicates (250n1), the *mamotreto* under scrutiny appears out of chronological sequence. Rampín invites the "Auctor" to go to Lozana's house, where he could find "más de diez putas" ("more than ten whores"; 251), as if she already were well established in business. It is only in the next *mamotreto*, however, that Lozana finally arrives in the house that Trigo has rented for her. This obviously intentional lack of temporal sequence suggests a folly alluded to by the engraving of a ship of fools in the frontispiece of the book. Besides its surprising transformation of the narrator into one of the characters, the break in narrative sequence has the undeniable effect of jolting the reader. Through this break, the text becomes unexpectedly self-reflexive, calling attention to itself. The principle of folly is even more evident toward the end of the *mamotreto*. To begin with, it was undoubtedly foolish for Rampín to prefer the spell to a piece of cloth with which to make a bandage for his apparently broken head. Given the nature of its veiled message, the foolish spell also constitutes an act of folly in itself. Thus, Delicado meant to alert knowing readers already familiar with similar codes, that is, conversos like himself, that there was a "secret message" encoded throughout his book. The title of the *mamotreto* suggests that it contains information needed to understand what follows, and, as we have seen, the incantation itself suggests that the work deals with the question of a triune God. This first attack on Trinitarianism is then repeated time and again throughout the rest of the book.

The next example appears shortly afterward. Not long after accompanying Lozana to the house that he has rented for her, Trigo, who, as we have seen, swears by the one "Dio" rather than by the supposedly plural "Dios," sends Lozana her first paying customers—no more or less than three. One woman with three men, and vice-versa. This constitutes another graphic, obscene mockery of the idea of three in one and one in three, but there is more. As Allaigre pointed out (261n1), these three clients, with whom Lozana begins to earn her living, in no place other than Rome, capital of the contemporary Trinitarian faith, were not chosen by chance. The first customer is a *mastresala*, the chief waiter who tasted what was served at the table of his master so as to protect him from being poisoned. The second client is a *macero*, "mace bearer," "el que lleva la maza delante de los cuerpos o personas autorizadas que usan esta señal de dignidad" ("the one who carries the mace in front of his body or of important persons who use it as a sign of their rank"; Real Academia de la Lengua, *Diccionario*). The third customer is a *valijero*, "letter carrier," who informs Lozana that his *valija* ("bag") happens to be "full" (266). Since the *mastresala* ("taster") evokes the tongue and mouth, the *macero* ("mace bearer") stands for the phallus, and the *valijero* ("letter carrier") with the full bag represents the testicles,

The Holy Trinity and the Annunciation

the three men could well stand for just one man, here represented by the parts used in sexual activity. Once again, three is really one.

As we have already seen, the *macero* ("mace bearer") and the *valijero* ("letter carrier") arrive together after the *mastresala*'s ("taster"'s) departure, and Rampín paraphrases Christ's Sermon on the Mount when he repeats Lozana's reply to the two men's request: "Dice que no podéis servir a dos señores" ("She says that you cannot serve two masters [at the same time]"; 264; cf. Matt. 6.24). The *valijero*, whom the text logically identifies as a servant of the *macero* (266), is told to return in the evening. Nevertheless, although the three men are really one, at another level Lozana ends up sleeping not just with two, but with "tres señores" ("three gentlemen"), at three different times. Since these three men stand for the mouth, penis, and testicles, it is obvious that this constitutes another extremely violent, obscene attack on the dogma of the Holy Trinity. As if this were not already more than enough in itself, Delicado's attack is, once again, tripartite: Lozana has three clients, the three men are really one, but, at another level, they take three separate turns. The implication, of course, is that the situation is as illogical and paradoxical as the dogma of the Holy Trinity.

As already stated, the references to the concept of three in one increase in Part III and the appended materials. The first of these occurs when, after the departure of some women who had come to Lozana's house in order to avail themselves of her services as a beautician, Lozana reflects on how hard their husbands work to support them, making three needles out of one, whereas their wives do precisely the opposite: "y de *una* aguja hacen *tres* y ellas al revés" ("from *one* needle they make *three*, and they do the opposite"; 404).

Again, one becomes three and three, one. Obviously, Lozana also means to say that, although their husbands stretch their hard-earned money as much as possible, the women do not even think twice about spending it, but her choice of words, which suggests another trivializing allusion to the Holy Trinity, hardly appears to be another simple coincidence.

The two additional references to the number three that follow immediately after reinforce this interpretation. In an apparently disconnected discourse—her words do not seem to have anything to do with what she had just said—Lozana recalls that, in the Levant where she had supposedly traveled, the Moors used to chide Christians for three things, one of which consisted of dedicating no less than one third of the year to festivities:

> Yo me recuerdo haber oído en Levante a los cristianos de la cintura, que contaban cómo los moros reprendían a los cristianos en *tres* cosas: la primera, que sabían escrebir y daban dineros a notarios y a quien escribiese sus secretos, y la otra, que daban a guardar sus dineros y hacían ricos a los cambiadores; la otra, que hacían fiesta la tercia parte

del año, las cuales son para hacer al hombre siempre en pobreza, y enriquecer a otrie que se ríe de gozar lo ajeno. (404 [56])

Although the Muslims could very well have disapproved of the three Christian practices enumerated, their main objection to Christians was the polytheism that they perceived to be a result of their belief in the Holy Trinity (see Cardaillac 1977, 225–55).

Immediately after this monologue, a young man recently arrived from Spain, Herjeto, whose master would like Lozana to pay him a visit, informs her that on the ship in which he had traveled there were some women who were coming to Rome to be present during the Holy Year because "según dicen, han visto dos, y con éste serán *tres*" ("according to what they say, they have seen two, and this one would make it *three*"; 405). Once again, three such successive references to the number, beginning with an allusion to the concept of one in three and three in one, are very unlikely to be a matter of pure coincidence.

In the example that follows, Delicado contrasts the monotheism of Jerusalem with the alleged polytheism of Rome. When Sagüeso, a vagrant who "tenía por oficio jugar y cabalgar de balde" ("whose job was to gamble and to get laid for free"; 417), tries to seduce Lozana by stating that another prostitute, Celidonia, surpasses her in almost everything, Lozana, who is too astute not to realize that Sagüeso is hoping that she will attempt to prove the contrary to him, free of charge, merely replies: "¿Sabes con qué me consuelo? Con lo que dijo Rampín, mi criado: que en dinero y en riquezas me pueden llevar, mas no en linaje ni en sangre" ("Do you know what comforts me? What Rampín, my servant, said: people can beat me in money and riches, but not in lineage or bloodlines"; 418). Sagüeso pursues his goal by saying that, although he agrees with her, "será menester sangrar a todas dos, para ver cuál es mejor sangre" ("it will be necessary to bleed both of you, to see which one has the best blood"; 418).[15] In other words, he would have to sleep with both women in order to be absolutely sure. Rather than falling for this bait, Lozana goes on to declare herself superior to Celestina herself, stating that Celidonia ought to suffer the same fate that the Romans imposed on the people of Jerusalem.

The story to which she alludes goes as follows: In reply to the Romans' demand, when they first conquered the Levant, for twelve first-born sons as tribute—an obvious reference to the twelve tribes of Israel—the Jews had sent opulently dressed boys bearing a placard that read: "*Quis mayor unquam Israel?*" ("Who is greater than Israel?"; 419). Seeing this, the Romans sent their children with a banner inherited from Constantine that displayed a white cross on a red field, under which were three letters, SPQ. The Roman

The Holy Trinity and the Annunciation

children replied to those from Jerusalem: "*Senatus Populusque Romanus*" ("The Roman Senate and the people of Rome"; 419). Lozana adapts the story to the situation by simultaneously asking and replying: "—¿Quién mayor que Celidonia?—Lozana y Rampín en Roma" ("Who is greater than Celidonia? Lozana and Rampín in Rome"; 419).

This episode begins with a derisive commentary on blood and lineage that reflects the attitude of many conversos toward the Old Christian concept of "limpieza de sangre," that invisible but very much real barrier that separated Old Christians from New Christians. The juxtaposition of Rome and Jerusalem, of course, alludes to the victory of Christianity over Judaism and the continuing rivalry between the two faiths. Even in their defeat, however, the Jews believed that their religion was superior (i.e., the only true one). Hence the apparently quixotic question of the defeated Jewish children whom the Romans demanded as tribute: *Quis mayor unquam Israel*? ("Who is greater than Israel?")

The allusion to Constantine recalls the role of that Roman emperor in the eventual triumph of Christianity, which he adopted as the official religion of the empire. The fact that it was Pompey who conquered Jerusalem in 63 BC, long before Rome became Christian, suggests a deliberate anachronism. Clearly, Delicado was thinking in spiritual, rather than in historical terms. Although the placement of the three letters under the cross carried by the Roman children is meant to indicate the superiority of the people and senate of their city, their number brings to mind the Holy Trinity that constitutes the basis for the faith that the cross represents. The elimination of the fourth letter in the Roman abbreviation—the standard form was SPQR—shows that Delicado also used the number three deliberately in this instance. The replication of the Roman motto in a comparison between two whores, Lozana and Celidonia, with three corresponding nouns, "Lozana y Rampín en Roma" ("Lozana and Rampín in Rome") suggests yet another mockery of the dogma of the Holy Trinity, for Lozana's and Rampín's careers in Rome and the bond that united them were far from pious.

In support of this last interpretation one might note that Delicado entitles the *mamotreto* that follows (liii)—one including three interlocutors: Lozana, a prostitute; Divicia, a still unsatisfied old whore; and Sagüeso, the rogue whose main endeavor in life is to gamble and "cabalgar de balde" ("to get laid for free")—"Lo que pasa entre todos *tres*" ("What happened among all three"; 420). This indicates that the number three was indeed prominent in his mind, and in a very base context, at that. Note that, although there are three mottos, the one proffered by the children from Jerusalem does not have anything to do with the number three. It must also be observed here that, together with the three letters used to abbreviate the Roman motto and the

Chapter Seven

three nouns in Lozana's final reply, this last reference to the number three makes this renewed attack on Trinitarianism tripartite, thus matching the structure found in the previous examples.

Delicado returns to the attack on Trinitarianism shortly afterward, in Coridón's intercalated novella, where Lozana advises the young Coridón to disguise himself as a peasant woman and feign insanity in order to see the girl that he loves. (The latter had married an old man who was about to travel to another city.) Coridón accepts the advice, but not without remarking that Lozana really lives from *arte et ingenio* ("guile and ingenuity"). She replies: "¡Coridón, mira que quiere un loco ser sabio! Que cuanto dijeres e hicieres sea sin seso y bien pensado porque, a mi ver, más seso quiere *un* loco que no *tres* cuerdos, porque los locos son los que dicen las verdades. Di poco y verdadero y acaba riendo, y suelta siempre *una* ventosidad, y si soltares *dos*, serán sanidad, y si *tres*, asinidad" ("Coridón, beware that a madman needs to be wise! Let everything you say be brainless and well thought out, for, the way I see it, *one* madman requires more wisdom than *three* sane men, because fools are the ones who tell the truth. Speak little, truthfully, end up laughing, and always fart *once*; *two* farts in a row are healthy, but *three* are just plain stupid"; 437). Lozana concludes this advice by asking Coridón, who is Italian, to say three Spanish words without stuttering: *celestial, alcatara*, and *arrofaldada* (437–39).[16]

Once again, the author clearly gives the number three special emphasis. *One* madman is superior to *three* wise men because madmen usually tell the truth. Once again, one is contrasted with three. The madman, who is only one, stands for the one God, the God of the Old Testament, and that madman happens to be the only truthful character. The three opposing wise men, who represent the Holy Trinity, are obviously false.

To add insult to injury, Lozana advises Coridón to fart after telling the truth, but only once, perhaps twice at the most; three farts in a row are simply asinine. As if this were not yet enough, Lozana then asks her interlocutor to say exactly three words without stuttering, the first of which happens to be *celestial*.

Coridón tries very hard, but is unable to comply. This second instance of three successive references to the number three clearly constitutes a vulgar, deliberate mockery of the dogma of the Holy Trinity.

The idea that Coridón should disguise himself and feign madness in order to achieve what he wants brings to mind the ship of fools in the frontispiece of *La Lozana andaluza* and the literature of folly that became so popular during the late Middle Ages and Renaissance. This type of literature, which played such an important part in the works of northern European humanists seeking to reform Christianity, developed in Spain in a special manner because of the presence of many recent converts from Judaism. These New

Christians were far from being fully accepted by Old Christians who, in most instances, continued to regard them as Jews. By assuming the role of the court buffoon, New Christians were able to realize their need to express what they felt concerning the circumstances in which they had to live. Indeed, Márquez Villanueva has shown that virtually all the fifteenth-century Spanish court jesters were conversos (1982, 404). Through a systematized language of madness that availed itself of obscure allusions, these conversos were able to touch upon subjects "vedados a la expresión cuerda" ("barred from sane speech"; Márquez Villanueva 1985–86, 505) while making their listeners laugh. As Márquez Villanueva remarks of three sixteenth-century individuals—Don Francesillo de Zúñiga, a court jester; Francisco López de Villalobos, a royal physician; and Fray Antonio de Guevara, a man of the Church—who expressed themselves in that vein: "Just as their predecessors, all three had Jewish blood and, through the discovery of the liberating power of laughter, found in literature the only avenue for the affirmation of human dignity and intellectual freedom" (1982, 408).[17]

There is no question that Delicado also avails himself of this tradition. On the surface, Lozana's apparently disconnected discourse, in which she mentions the three things that Levantine Moors chided Christians for right after manifesting her disapproval of the manner in which some of her Roman customers squandered their husbands' hard-earned money, makes her seem a madwoman of sorts, for it does not make any sense. Since one item does not seem to be even remotely related to the other, she is in fact using the language of madness.

In Sagüeso's episode, it was obviously foolish, at least from an Old Christian point of view, for a conversa and prostitute like Lozana to take such great pride in her blood and lineage, not to mention the apparent idiocy of the people of Jerusalem in proclaiming the superiority of their city before their Roman conquerors as they submit to the Romans by sending to Rome the children demanded as tribute. At the literal level, Lozana's adaptation of the three words used by the Romans to assert their own superiority in a comparison between herself and a rival prostitute is obviously ridiculous.

Delicado makes his utilization of the discourse of folly even clearer when he has Lozana advise Coridón to feign madness in order to achieve his aim. Literary fools assume madness as a disguise, just as Coridón was supposed to do. That cover enables them to tell the truth with impunity, but they should take care to ensure that what they say is simultaneously foolish and thoroughly thought out, "sin seso y bien pensado" ("brainless and well thought out"; 437), its sting invariably cloaked with laughter and one or two unexpected farts, which would elicit even more laughter. Thus, besides availing himself of a technique widely used by other conversos to express themselves, Delicado has the daring to provide his readers with its recipe.[18]

Chapter Seven

When Lozana tells a doctor how she had earned one chicken and some eggs by repairing a skeleton key full of wax brought to her by an Italian couple, the doctor asks her how she had fixed it: "Pues decíme, señora Lozana, ¿qué hecistes a la llave, cualque *silogismo*, o qué?" ("Well, Lady Lozana, tell me: what did you do to the key? A syllogism or what?"; 461). As it stands, the word *syllogism* does not make any sense here. However, the term served as an allusion to the number three in itself, for a syllogism consists of three parts. Note that the popular *syllogism* used to "unbewitch" someone or something was—and still is—an incantation proffered while performing the sign of the cross, usually accompanied by the words "In the name of the Father, the Son, and the Holy Ghost." Used in this context, the term *syllogism* could also constitute a reference to the sign of the cross and the Holy Trinity that it represents.

This interpretation is reinforced when Lozana reveals that she had merely heated the key over the fire upstairs—her superstitious customers, who were waiting down below, could not see what she had done—describing the manner in which she had earned her present as follows: "y ganéme yo aquel presente sofísticamente" ("and so I won that present sophistically"; 461). In other words, the cunning Lozana profited through deception by using an apparently correct but admittedly false argument. Her evaluation of her own performance coincides with the doctor's, for Lozana's "sophism," besides echoing his "syllogism"—both are forms of argumentation—adds the concept of fallacy. Since the relationship between the two terms is undeniable, Lozana's choice of the word *sophism* represents an attack on the dogma of the Holy Trinity alluded to in the doctor's cryptic reference to *syllogism*, which is tripartite by definition. The implication is that those who believed in such a thing were nothing but simple, superstitious, ignorant people, like the Italian couple who had been so easily duped.

As we saw in Chapter 2 (pp. 60–61), this utilization of the word *syllogism* goes back to the fifteenth century, for Ferrant Manuel de Lando, a New Christian, uses it as a code for the Holy Trinity, stating that his adversary, Juan Alfonso de Baena, is an expert in the use of codes, and the latter, who is also a converso, takes care to include the word *sophism* in his reply.

As her conversation with the doctor continues, Lozana adds that, thanks to her verbal ingenuousness ("bien hablar"), that is, her ability to use such arguments, she had also received a small gold-plated silver goblet from a colonel. The doctor replies: "Ese bien hablar, adular incoñito le llamo yo" ("That smart talking is what I call 'adulating incognito'"; 461). The expression *adular incoñito* ("to adulate incognito"), besides alluding to the adulation of the unknown—the infinitive *adorar* ("to worship"), which sounds almost like *adular*, would have been too explicit—suggests a pornographic meaning, for the word *incoñito* (cf. *en coñito*, "in the little cunt") also refers

The Holy Trinity and the Annunciation

to the vagina. Lozana's reply, which acknowledges that the doctor was right on the mark twice in a row by calling him another Solomon, confirms this interpretation, as evidenced by the fourth of the items that she lists as being useless unless frequently shared: "Señor Salomón, sabé que cuatro cosas no valen nada, si no son participadas o comunicadas a menudo: el placer, y el saber, y el dinero, y el *coño de la mujer*, el cual no debe estar vacuo, según la filosofía natural" ("Sir Solomon, I'll have you know that four things are worthless unless they are shared or passed around frequently: pleasure, knowledge, money, and *a woman's cunt*, which, according to natural philosophy, should never be vacant"; 461). As we shall see, the simultaneous reference to the adulation of a vagina and the adulation of the unknown in such a context is yet another mockery of Catholic dogma.

In the next *mamotreto* (lxii), Lozana declares herself willing to allow the doctor "to irrigate" her "manantío" ("fount"; 465) whenever he wishes. Hearing this, her friend Imperia points out that she is better off with Rampín. Lozana agrees, but with the reservation that it would be good to find out for sure, that is, to compare the two men by sleeping with the doctor. She then goes on to state that there are *three* or *four* things that she would like to know, even though she lists only three at this point: "Vamos, señora, mas siempre es bueno saber. Que yo *tres* o *cuatro* cosas no sé que deseo conocer: la una, qué vía hacen, o qué color tienen los cuernos de los hombres; y la otra, querría leer lo que entiendo; y la otra, querría que en mi tiempo se perdiese el temor y la vergüenza, para que cada uno pida y haga lo que quisiere" ("Come on, Ma'am, it is always good to know, and I am ignorant of *three* or *four* things that I would like to find out: first, what man's horns look like and their color; another, I would like to be able to read what I understand; and another, I would like to see fear and shame disappear in my days, so that everyone could ask for and do what they want"; 465).

Lozana's queries are in fact statements. Only the first can be readily understood. It probably falls within the category of the discourse of folly, for people do not usually say these things with such frankness. The first item that arouses her curiosity is the color of the horns supposedly worn by cuckolded men. The answer is obvious: Since such men do not really grow any horns, her infidelity to Rampín would not matter, anyway. Of course Lozana was probably right as far as her consenting companion was concerned, but there is no doubt that most men and women would be violently opposed to her viewpoint.

Lozana's second statement is harder to decipher: She would like to be able to read what she claims to understand, whatever that might be. Coming from a prostitute, Lozana's third statement, where she expresses her hope to see fear and shame vanish during her lifetime so that everyone could ask for and do whatever he or she wanted, would seem to refer to uninhibited copulation. Lozana confirms this interpretation when she tells Imperia, who professed not to understand what she had meant, that "Cierto es que si yo no tuviese vergüenza, que cuantos hombres pasan querría que me besasen, y si no fuese el temor, cada uno entraría y pediría lo vedado" ("The truth is that, if I were not ashamed, I would want every man who passed by to kiss me, and, were it not for fear, each of them would come in and ask for what is forbidden"; 465).

Lozana then refers to the number three yet again by stating that "si yo supiese o viese estas *tres* cosas que arriba he dicho, sabría más que Juan d'Espera en Dios" ("if I knew or could see these *three* things I said above, I would know more than the Wandering Jew ["John Who Awaits God"]"; 465). Since the items in question constitute statements rather than questions, there was really nothing for her to find out, but Lozana modifies her original quest by adding the words *si viese*, "if I could see." Obviously, she would never be able to see any of them. It would be nothing less than extraordinary if the horns supposedly worn by cuckolded men became visible suddenly, if she could read everything that she thought she understood, and if people were able to shed their natural modesty completely from one moment to the next, behaving with the sexual freedom that she apparently craved. Thus, Lozana could be insinuating that she was as likely to see those three things as she was to see the Holy Trinity.

Given the manner in which the text has mocked the idea of three in one and one in three previously, the allusion to the legend of Juan d'Espera en Dios, the Wandering Jew, makes the attack on the dogma of the Holy Trinity suggested by Lozana's three statements even clearer. Briefly summarized, that legend, according to the version retold in Cristóbal de Villalón's *Crotalón* (ca. 1553), states that Christ passed by a shoemaker's house on his way to Calvary, and that the man, rather than taking pity on him, told him to move along. To which Christ replied, "I shall go, but you will stay forever to bear me witness."[19]

One possible implication of Lozana's words is that, despite the great knowledge often attributed to the long-lived and widely traveled Wandering Jew, who had seen Christ carrying the cross just before his crucifixion, the poor man still knew no more than she did concerning the Holy Trinity.[20] This interpretation is confirmed when Lozana finally poses the fourth query that she had mentioned earlier: "Y la cuarta que *penitus* iñoro es de quién me tengo de empreñar cuando alguno m'empreñe" ("And the fourth thing of which I am completely ignorant is by whom I ought to get pregnant when someone impregnates me"; 466).

Once again, this is more of a statement than a question. Because of the nature of her profession, a prostitute was not likely to know who had fathered her child if she happened to get pregnant. There is much more than this involved in Lozana's query, however, for, notwithstanding her profession, she also pretends not to know what a penis is with the double-meaning expression "*penitus* iñoro." There is no doubt that the Latinism is used salaciously here.[21] Obviously, any pregnant woman who made such an outrageous disclaimer could not possibly be telling the truth. Incredibly, Lozana's query echoes the Virgin Mary's famous question to the angel Gabriel when he told her that she was to conceive and bear a son: "How shall this happen, since I do not know man?" (Luke 1.34).[22] In the eyes of nonbelievers, who regarded the whole event in strictly human terms, the explanation that Mary had conceived, while remaining a virgin, by the grace of the Holy Spirit (Luke 1.35), was simply preposterous (see Lasker 1977, 153–59). In their eyes, a married woman who had a son by someone other than her husband was unfaithful and, therefore, a prostitute of sorts. Hence Delicado's attribution of the query to a whore.

This implication coincides with what, according to several inquisitorial documents, some conversos used to say about the Blessed Mother. In the trial against Catalina de Zamora in Ciudad Real in 1484, we recall, the defendant was accused of saying "que era Nuestra Señora vna puta judihuela" ("that Our Lady was a little Jewish whore"; Beinart 1974–77, 1: 389). We have also seen that in Oporto, the New Christian Tovar was reported to have said in reference to the Virgin Mary: "asy he ella vyrgem como he a may que me pario" ("she is as much a virgin as the mother who bore me"; Tavares 1987, 94), and in modern Sephardic versions of the ballad *El idólatra de María*, we recall, the Virgin Mary is still addressed as "Fedionda" ("stinking woman"), "puta María" ("Mary the Whore"), and "falsa y mentirosa" ("false and deceitful"; Armistead and Silverman 1982, 134; Catalán 1970, 271–73).[23]

At first glance, it is exceedingly funny for a prostitute like Lozana to claim that she does not know what a penis is and to wonder whom she should blame if she somehow gets pregnant. The principle of folly is operative here. At another level, the insinuation, mocking the dogma of the Incarnation of Christ as it does, constituted sheer madness in itself. Lozana continues to speak without bothering to wait for Imperia's obvious reply because such things could not be said with the freedom and impunity that she craved.

To a non-Christian, an understanding of Lozana's fourth query—what she is really asking is how a woman could possibly get pregnant without knowing a man in the biblical sense—would probably make the other *three* items that supposedly puzzle her more acceptable. By referring to the Incarnation in such a derisive manner right after mocking the Holy Trinity, Lozana could be insinuating that it is the birth of Christ that led to the creation of that doctrine, for Christ is the second person of the Holy Trinity. The attitude of the Jewish polemicists toward the Incarnation supports this deduction.[24]

Chapter Seven

Since Lozana perceives Christ as a man like any other, and an illegitimate child at that, the dogma of the Holy Trinity is nothing but a syllogism based on sheer sophistry. This interpretation is reinforced by the assignment of the number four to Lozana's query. Since it corresponds to the fourth of the items listed in the previous *mamotreto* as being useless unless frequently shared— a woman's vagina—Delicado is probably implying that the dogma of the Holy Trinity depends on a common woman.

Delicado has certainly made his point by now, but he is still unsatisfied. In the last *mamotreto*, that is, at the very end of Part III, Lozana tells Rampín that she dreamed about several mythological figures, including Mars, god of war, and that "navegando llegábamos a Venecia, donde Marte no puede estender su ira" ("we arrived by sea in Venice, where Mars cannot spread his anger"; 479). It was precisely in Venice that Delicado had sought refuge after the sack of Rome. Having told Rampín the rest of her dream, in which she also saw the tree of folly, Lozana remembers that an astrologer has said previously that either she or Rampín would go to paradise. Lozana decides that she will be the one to go. Since paradise has three doors, she says, she will enter through the one that she finds open, and then will find a way to get him in: "Yo quiero ir a paraíso, y entraré por la puerta que abierta hallare, pues tiene tres, y solicitaré que vais vos, que lo sabré hacer" ("I want to go to paradise, and I will enter through the gate I find open, since it has *three*, and I will ask for you to come, for I know how to do it"; 480). Lozana then enumerates "tres suertes de personas que acaban mal, como son: soldados y putanas y osurarios" ("three kinds of people who come to a bad end, such as soldiers, prostitutes, and usurers"; 480), and concludes by choosing to go the island of Lipari, where she will be free from "tanta fortuna pretérita, continua y futura" ("so much past, present, and future fortune"; 481).

Lozana sounds like a madwoman because she supposes that heaven has three doors and that she can serve as a go-between in heaven on behalf of Rampín. As she had told Coridón after advising him to disguise himself as a peasant woman and feign insanity in order to enter the house of a married young lady, however, "más seso quiere *un* loco que no *tres* cuerdos, porque los locos son los que dicen las verdades" ("*one* madman requires more wisdom than *three* sane men, because fools are the ones who tell the truth"; 214). Mad people can say what they wish and get away with it; indeed, there is a certain logic to Lozana's apparently mad reasoning. The three doors that she attributes to paradise could very well stand for the Holy Trinity: the Father, the Son, and the Holy Ghost.[25] The three sorts of persons who always meet a bad end, going straight to hell, could be those who are foolish enough to believe in that dogma. Lozana herself knows better; she is not about to fall into such a trap, for she chooses to go elsewhere instead. As far as she is concerned, her paradise will be in Lipari,[26] where, besides finding the peace

The Holy Trinity and the Annunciation

reported to have run away to the islands, she will also be free from the past, the present, and the future. Although these words could refer to God the Father, the Unitarian God of the Old Testament, for God always was, is, and will be, the context and the tripartite manner used to describe him points to the Trinitarian God of the New Testament. Moreover, as we have just seen, the expression in question constitutes the third of yet another series of references to the number three.

While speaking of the heaven with three doors, Lozana promises Rampín that, once in heaven, she will send him a letter telling him what to do for the sake of his soul through the first person who arrives afterward—provided anyone else does. Should she find peace in that same heaven, she will send it to him tied with a Solomonic knot. Anyone who wants it can untie it: "Si yo vo, os escriberé lo que por el alma habéis de hacer con el primero que venga, si viniere, y si veo la Paz, que allá está continua, la enviaré atada con este ñudo de Salomón, desátela quien la quisiere" ("If I get in, I will write to tell you what you must do for your soul through the first person who comes, if anyone does, and if I happen to see Peace, who is always there, I will send it to you bound with this knot of Solomon. Let whoever wants untie it"; 480).

Lozana does not really believe in a three-doored, Trinitarian Christian heaven, for she doubts that anyone will ever reach such a place.[27] The very idea of a Christian paradise is utterly meaningless to her. Consequently, the peace that she might encounter in a nonexistent heaven that she is not about to seek is no more real than that heaven. Should she find it, however, just in case, she will send it to Rampín, tied with a Solomonic knot. This enigmatic, cross-shaped knot, which also appears in an engraving (480), seems to constitute a challenge in itself. What could it possibly mean? It may not be unreasonable to surmise that Delicado names the knot after King Solomon in order to point to the Old Testament, thus providing his readers with another key. Anyone who wishes to know what he is really up to must understand his book, the meaning of which cannot be deciphered through a quick, superficial reading, as if untying a Gordian knot with a gentile sword, by brute force, but with the intellect suggested by the ironically cross-shaped knot named after a Jewish, Old Testament monarch whose wisdom had become proverbial.[28]

Having already said so much through his protagonist, the narrator begins to conclude the last *mamotreto* in his book with a clear reference to the Trinitarian God whom he has mocked: "Fenezca la historia compuesta en retrato, el más natural que el autor pudo, y acabóse hoy primo de diciembre, año de mil quinientos e veinte cuatro *a laude y honra de Dios trino y uno*" ("Let us finish the story written as a portrait, in the most faithful manner that the author was able to compose it. It was completed today, December 1, 1524, *in praise and honor of the one and triune God*"; 481). Once again,

225

three is one, and vice-versa. These hypocritical words constitute yet another act of derision and defiance, for Delicado pretends that he wrote his book in honor and praise of the God of the New Testament, when he did precisely the contrary.

In the exculpation ("escusa") placed after the last *mamotreto*, Delicado claims that his protagonist was a God-fearing woman who tried very hard to follow God's commandments; he then goes on to emphasize that she had a total of three names, one for each of the three places where she had lived:

> Y sin dubda en esto quiero dar gloria a la Lozana, que se guardaba muncho de hacer cosas que fuesen ofensa a Dios ni a sus mandamientos, porque, sin perjuicio de partes, procuraba comer y beber sin ofensión ninguna. La cual se apartó con tiempo, y se fue a vivir a la ínsula de Lípari, y allí se mudó el nombre, y se llamó la Vellida, de manera que gozó de tres nombres: en España, Aldonza, y en Roma, la Lozana, y en Lípari, la Vellida. (484 [57])

It is in the untitled *explicit* ("explanation") that follows that Delicado finally reveals that his protagonist's names, though apparently three different ones, are really one (487), three in one and one in three, thus mocking the doctrine of the Holy Trinity yet again by reference to the names of a prostitute. Since the third and last name given to the protagonist, La Vellida, was typically Jewish (Márquez Villanueva 1973, 93 and n12), its choice could very well signal Lozana's and Delicado's return to the Judaism of their ancestors (Macpherson and Mackay agree [1998, 221–22]). As we saw in the previous chapter, Lozana constitutes an alter ego for Francisco Delicado.

In the section entitled "Carta de excomunión contra una cruel doncella de sanidad" (Letter of excommunication against a cruel health maiden; 495), there is a cryptic allusion to "tres canominaciones" ("three co-names"; 497). This refers to a case brought before Cupid by a distraught lover against the cruel "doncella de sanidad" ("prostitute"; see Allaigre 1985b, 101) who had disdained him. Ugolini discovered that Delicado's source for the first part of this letter was Hernando de Ludueña's *Descomunión de amores fecha a su amiga* (Excommunication from Love to his mistress; 1974–75, 478–83; see also Dunn 1976a). The similarity between the two compositions ends with verse 32 of Delicado's letter, which continues with the condemnation of the cruel "maiden," excommunicated and thrown out of the temple of love (vv. 33–60), and with an elaborate curse of partial epic origins (vv. 61–76) that ends with a parody of the traditional description of the ideal feminine beauty (vv. 77–119).

The reference to the "tres canominaciones" ("three co-names"; v. 42), which appears in the lengthy section that Delicado appended to Ludueña's original, is found at the beginning of Cupid's judgment:

The Holy Trinity and the Annunciation

>   Capellanes y grandes curas
>   deste palacio real
>   de Amor y sus alturas
>   haced esta denunciación
> 40   porque no aclame cautela
>   desde agora apercibiendo
>   por *tres canominaciones*.
>
> (497 [58])

According to Allaigre, the word *canominaciones* is probably a misprint for *conominaciones*. Since it does not rhyme with *denunciación* (39) as it should, Delicado probably pluralizes the more appropriate singular found in an undetermined source in order to allude to Lozana's three names (p. 497 of his ed., n21). That could very well be the case. Since the expression being examined denotes three different names for the same person, however, Delicado is also deriding, once again, the idea of three in one and one in three. He also mocks the penalty that he himself risks, for, having been "denounced" by her spurned lover, the cruel "maiden" is thrown out of the temple and excommunicated "de nuestra ley tan bendita" ("from our blessed Law [Religion]"; 53). As indicated, Lozana, who had three names that were really one—"tres conominaciones"—is in fact Delicado's alter ego. Should he be denounced for what he did—the utilization of the charged word *denunciación* makes it clear that he is referring to the Inquisition—there is no question that the penalty that he faced would have been more severe than mere excommunication. Had he been caught in Spain, he would have been burned alive.

The very last appendix, the "Digresión que cuenta el autor en Venecia" (Digression written by the author in Venice), closes the book by listing three different items. The narrator asks his readers to pray for him; in his turn, he will pray to God for the Christians responsible for his second exile, from which he writes the following words: "quedo rogando a Dios por *buen fin* y *paz* y *sanidad* a todo el pueblo cristiano, amén" ("I remain praying to God for a *good end*, *peace*, and *health* for all the Christian people, amen"; 508). As Allaigre asks himself, "¿es esto una maldición o bendición?" ("is this a curse or a blessing?"; 508n12). Given what we know now, it sounds more like a tripartite curse.

Once again, there is no question that the corruption of sixteenth-century Rome, which was so well known that it became proverbial, served Delicado's purposes well. A great number of courtesans from almost every part of the known world (275) chose to settle in the Eternal City because of the flourishing business available thanks to the presence of what might be described as an army of unmarried, supposedly celibate clergymen. Delicado was a syphilitic priest, and, as one of his characters, Rampín, explicitly

Chapter Seven

points out, "Es la mayor parte de Roma burdel, y le dicen: Roma putana" ("Most of Rome is a bordello, and people call it 'Harlot Rome'"; 216).

On the other hand, although Delicado takes the misleading precaution of telling his readers that he is merely describing "lo que oí y vi, con menos culpa que Juvenal" ("what I heard and saw, with less guilt than Juvenal"; 169), his "realism" consists of much more than what meets the eye. He uses it to disguise several allegories, including a protest against his "voluntary" exile from his beloved Spain and an attack on the Holy Trinity.

As Delicado tells his readers with moving words, being able to live in one's own country "es una gran felicidad no estimada" ("is a great, unappreciated boon"; 486). Having resided for many years in Rome, which thus became his "segunda patria" ("second homeland"), he saw himself forced to go into another "voluntary" exile on February 10, 1528, "por no esperar las crueldades vindicativas de los naturales" ("so as to avoid the cruel revenge of the inhabitants"; 508). As we saw in the previous chapter, many Italians paradoxically blamed the Spanish marranos in their midst for the sack of Rome in the previous year by the combined armies of Charles V, even though those marranos had felt obliged to leave their country, the so-called "España mísera" ("wretched Spain"; 216) that did not really want them: "En 1527, cuando las tropas imperiales saquearon Roma, muchos italianos no dudaron en culpar de ello a los marranos españoles, con mucha injusticia además, puesto que el ejército, mandado por un general francés, el condestable de Borbón, contaba con soldados de varias nacionalidades" ("In 1527, when the imperial troops sacked Rome, many Italians did not hesitate to blame the Spanish marranos, and very unjustly at that, since the army, which was under the command of a French general, the Constable of Bourbon, consisted of soldiers of several nationalities"; Pérez 1981, 100).

As far as the marranos were concerned, peace was not to be found anywhere. Under the circumstances, it is not at all surprising that Delicado, besides protesting against his exiles—like his protagonist, he had lived in three different places, Spain, Rome, and Venice (Lipari)—should also have felt an irrepressible, understandable desire to attack the central doctrines of Christianity. Without the dogmas of the Incarnation and the Holy Trinity, the Catholicism that victimized him and his fellow conversos could not possibly have existed. And so he obliterated them through art, by creating a prostitute to serve as the incarnation of Rome, capital of Christendom, and of a religion which, in his opinion, was based on the ridiculous, illogical assumption that a woman who had never known a man could possibly bear any child, much less the Son of God. To him, such a woman was even worse than the syphilitic Lozana, the prostitute who constitutes his alter ego. Whereas the Blessed Mother had given birth to Christ, a Jew in whose name his people had suffered horrible atrocities, Lozana, a New Christian victim whose main

The Holy Trinity and the Annunciation

crime consisted of her Jewish background, was merely interested in surviving without causing harm to anyone: "sin perjuicio de partes, procuraba comer y beber sin ofensión ninguna" ("she tried to eat and drink without offense to anyone"; 484).

In Delicado's mind, Christianity had caused Spain to reject many of her children, forcing them to seek self-preservation in voluntary exile. Christianity had also led Rome to treat those poor orphans as would a cruel stepmother, forcing them to abandon their homes and to seek new ones elsewhere, yet another time, with the absurd accusation of committing a crime that would have been clearly against their self-interest. Delicado's anger was very great indeed. But since peace was not to be found anywhere, in the last analysis *La Lozana andaluza* is also a cry of anguish.

Delicado threw superficial readers off the scent with his apparently frank, "verisimilar," often hilarious vignettes. He did not express himself with a combination of hidden allegories, however, without yearning to share what he had to say with others. That is why he took care to admonish more discerning readers, those who could read in between the lines, at the end of the untitled *explicit*: "Por tanto, digo que para gozar d'este retrato y para murmurar del autor, que primero lo deben bien leer y entender, *sed non legatur in escolis*. No metí la tabla, aunque estaba hecha, porque esto basta por tabla" ("Therefore, I say that to enjoy this portrait and to backbite the author, you must first read and understand it well, *but let it not be read in schools*. I did not include the table of contents, although it was already made, because this is sufficient"; 487). An index was superfluous because this warning to read his book well and to understand it was enough of a guide in itself.

Those readers, intellectual conversos like Delicado himself who were aware of the fact that the discourse of folly constituted an ideal vehicle for free, albeit necessarily covert expression, had already been alerted by the ship of fools placed in the frontispiece (165). Named "Cavallo Venetiano" ("Venetian Horse"), this boat, which carried Lozana, Divicia, Celidonia, a rowing Rampín, and a few other "ladies" from Rome to Venice, is echoed by the tree of folly reportedly seen by Lozana in the dream that leads to her decision to retire in the very last *mamotreto* (lxvi). Although the prospective readers who could understand this aspect of *La Lozana andaluza* were already familiar with the requisite code, Delicado still hesitated to take any chances in this respect. He wanted to be understood. That is why he provided them with a key to the code in Coridón's intercalated novella.

To conclude, Delicado attacked the dogma of the Holy Trinity by giving his protagonist, a prostitute whom he created as an alter ego, three different names that are really one, and by repeatedly mocking the very idea of three in one and one in three in the third part and the appendices of a book that is itself divided into three parts. To him, the *peccadiglio di Spagna* ("the little sin from Spain") was far from being a "little sin," for he saw no sin at all in the uncompromising monotheism of the Old Testament. There is no need to recapitulate the other base manners in which Delicado often mocks this central dogma of Christianity, as well as the doctrine of the Incarnation. The examples upon which this chapter has focused demonstrate that all of this cannot be a matter of pure coincidence. Given the circumstances, it is certainly legitimate to ask whether a man who could do such a thing could possibly be a Christian. I think not.

Chapter Eight

Rojas, Delicado, and the Art of Subversion

Delicado's claim, on the very frontispiece of his book, that it contains "munchas mas cosas que la Celestina" ("many more things than *Celestina*"; 165), may have been an advertising gimmick, for *Celestina* was an extremely popular, bawdy work with the name of another woman on the title, but it is also a challenge, for *La Lozana andaluza* does indeed have much in common with *Celestina*. The two works are the most important precedents of the picaresque novel, and, although *La Lozana andaluza* was influenced by a variety of previous works and genres, its indebtedness to *Celestina* in both literary and ideological terms is much greater. As a converso, Delicado was able to understand *Celestina* in ways that most other readers could not, coinciding with and even at times exceeding Rojas in his covert criticism of Christian dogma.

According to Menéndez y Pelayo, Delicado's work is *sui generis*, a "libro inmundo y feo" ("filthy and ugly book"; 1961, 54) without any literary precedents (57), but the boat on the frontispiece immediately brings to mind the literature of folly that became extremely popular throughout Europe thanks to Sebastian Brant's *Ship of Fools* (1494) and Erasmus's *The Praise of Folly* (1509),[1] a genre whose main manifestation in Spain is Cervantes's immortal *Don Quixote* (1605; 1615).[2] The tradition of the court jester of the fifteenth century must also be taken into account (Márquez Villanueva 1979; 1982; 1985–86). Under the cover of madness, writers were able to deal more freely with certain religious and social subjects, since, after all, fools were not responsible for what they said.

As we have seen, Delicado's characters avail themselves frequently of this type of discourse. Significantly, the ship of fools found at the beginning (165) is matched by the "árbol de la locura" ("tree of folly"; 479), which, in the very last *mamotreto*, figures in a dream where Lozana also sees Mars, god of war, and how she and Rampín will eventually end up in Venice. Right after, in the first of the appendices, the narrator mentions the tree of folly again, informing his readers that, unlike many others, he was unable to pick

Chapter Eight

any leaves or branches from it because of his short stature (485). Thus, in a way, *La Lozana andaluza* is framed in the idea of folly.

Notwithstanding Menéndez y Pelayo's peremptory denial, Delicado uses several other literary sources. The second engraving testifies to the influence of Apuleius's *Golden Ass*, also known as *Metamorphosis*, which was very popular during the Middle Ages and the sixteenth century. In the *Golden Ass*, the narrator, a young man named Lucius Apuleius, who is identified with the author, is turned into an ass, has a series of adventures, including some bawdy ones, and regains his human form thanks to the intervention of Isis. The engraving in question, which, significantly, appears on the reverse of the title page, is presented as the second of a diptych, for the top portrays Lozana in a room, surrounded by various courtesans, while Rampín appears sitting in both corners. The bottom of this engraving is what brings to mind Apuleius's book, for it depicts a man standing next to an ass loaded with luggage, saying farewell to three women who look at him from two windows.[3] The man, then, is about to undertake a journey, and this echoes the voyage represented by the boat in the frontispiece.

Just in itself, this second engraving does not prove that Delicado had the *Golden Ass* in mind, but, right after, in the prologue, while explaining his reasons for writing his book, Delicado states mischievously that "los santos hombres por más saber, y otras veces por desenojarse, leían libros fabulosos y cogían entre las flores las mejores" ("holy men, at times to increase their knowledge and others to amuse themselves, read books of fiction and picked the best among the flowers"; 170).[4] As Hernández Ortiz demonstrated (1974, 46), these words are inspired in Diego López de Cortegana's introduction to his late-fifteenth-century translation of Apuleius: "pues que los santos doctores por más saber, e otras vezes por desenojarse, leyan libros de gentiles e los tenian por famillares" ("for the holy fathers, to increase their knowledge and at times to amuse themselves, read pagan books and were familiar with them"; 1915, 2).

There are additional reasons to believe that Delicado had Apuleius in mind. At the beginning of the *Golden Ass*, the protagonist travels to the province of Thessaly, in Greece (Apuleyo 1915, 4); Diomedes informs Lozana that this is one of the places that they have to visit in their travels throughout the Levant (184–85). Lozana's house in Rome is located "junto al río, pasada la vía Asinaria, más abajo" ("next to the river, a little past Asinaria [Asinine] Road"; 369), there are additional references to Apuleius throughout the book (see Joset 1997, 160–64; Juan Gil 1986), and, significantly, in the next to last *mamotreto* (lxv), Lozana agrees to help a recently arrived Italian gentleman, Micer Porfirio, who needed to teach his ass, named Robusto, how to read, because he had bet that "si venía a Roma con dinero, que ordenaba mi Robusto de bacalario" ("if I came to Rome with money, I could get my

Robusto to graduate with a bachelor's degree"; 476). The joke, of course, represents another example of the madness announced by the ship of fools at the beginning of *La Lozana andaluza*, and which is reflected in the tree of folly found right after Robusto's episode, in the very last *mamotreto*.

In Jacques Joset's opinion (1997, 160–61), this ass with a bachelor's degree also constitutes one of several indications of the rivalry that Delicado feels toward Rojas. In the very first of his appendices, where he excuses himself for having written such a book, Delicado takes care to point out that he is "iñorante y no bachiller" ("ignorant and not a Bachelor"; 485), thus taking a dig at Rojas, who refers to himself as "bachiller" ("Bachelor") in the acrostic verses of *Celestina*.

Clearly, Delicado is also calling Rojas an ass, but this literary war, as Joset calls it (1997, 161), is really a game, pretty much like the banter in which fifteenth-century conversos heaped insults about their Jewish background upon each other. At another level, by alluding to Apuleius at the very beginning of his book, Delicado could be signaling that the journey or story to follow is autobiographical. Note that Delicado insists on the need to read his book from beginning to end in the initial summary ("solamente gozará d'este retrato quien todo lo leyere" ["only those who read all of this portrait will enjoy it"; 171]), where he also asserts that this is crucial in order to understand the book properly: "lo que al principio falta se hallará al fin" ("what is missing in the beginning will be found at the end"; 173). Besides alerting readers, this emphasis on reading corresponds to the effort to teach Robusto how to read in the next to last of the sixty-six *mamotretos* that constitute the book.

After reminding us of the *Golden Ass* and its importance in this second strategic location, Delicado refers to it again in the first of the six appendices that follow with the words "yo confieso ser un asno, y no de oro" ("I confess I'm an ass, and not a golden one"; 486), thus apparently paraphrasing López de Cortegana's introduction to his Spanish translation: "Porque no se puede dudar sino que todos traemos a cuestas vn asno e no de oro, mas de piedra (y avn lo que peor es) de lodo" ("For it cannot be doubted that we all carry on our backs an ass which is not golden, but made of stone, and, what is even worse, of mud"; 1915, 2; see also Hernández Ortiz 1974, 46).

Thus, together with the ideas of folly and exile, the *Golden Ass* can also be said to frame *La Lozana andaluza*. The purpose, I repeat, is probably to signal that the journey that follows is autobiographic and encloses more than what meets the eye, for, whereas the real protagonist of the *Golden Ass* is Lucius Apuleius, albeit in the shape of an ass throughout most of the book, the real protagonist of *La Lozana andaluza* is Delicado, albeit as a "starred," syphilitic prostitute. At the end of the *Golden Ass,* Apuleius regains his human form; in the very last of the six appendices of *La Lozana andaluza*, it

Chapter Eight

is Delicado himself who writes from Venice, the city to which Lozana travels in the ship of fools that appears in the frontispiece. In addition, both books focus on a single hero.

Another source is Fernando del Pulgar, chronicler of the Catholic Monarchs. In the prologue, Delicado refers to his book as a *retrato*, a "portrait," and then mentions Pulgar, who was known for his *Claros varones de Castilla*, where he presented twenty-four brief portraits or biographies of personages in the court of Henry IV. In this book, Pulgar imitated the *Generaciones y semblanzas* of Fernán Pérez de Guzmán, whose work he admired. By mentioning him, Delicado gives an historical varnish to his portrait, characterizing it as a biography of sorts—and this brings the *Golden Ass* to mind once again—but, unlike his illustrious predecessor, he is going to concentrate on a single character. Since the first *mamotreto* opens with a description of Lozana's lineage, Delicado could be imitating the aforesaid portraits, which open with genealogies, even though the same technique is used in the *Golden Ass* and the contemporary romances of chivalry. Since the latter focused on only one hero, Delicado could well have also had the latter in mind as he began the story of his own, matchless antiheroine.[5]

In the prologue, Delicado suggests that he is not to blame for what follows, claiming: "solamente diré lo que oí y vi, con menos culpa que Juvenal, pues escribió lo que en su tiempo pasaba" ("I will only tell what I heard and saw, with less guilt than Juvenal, who wrote about what was happening in his time"; 169). Although he mentions Juvenal, the Roman satirist who vividly portrayed the vices of his age, these words bring to mind Alfonso Martínez de Toledo's *Arcipreste de Talavera o Corbacho* (1438), a misogynistic work where the author attacks women because, in his opinion, courtly love had caused them to replace God. Whenever he tells a story about the wiles of women that he witnessed directly, the archpriest likes to stress that he himself saw it (1992, 103, 107, 118, 198, etc.). Even more importantly, as he himself states, Delicado attempted to reproduce the language as it was spoken: "escribiendo para darme solacio y pasar mi fortuna, que en este tiempo el Señor me había dado, conformaba mi hablar al sonido de mis orejas" ("writing to give myself solace and to bear the fate that God had given me at this time, I tailored my speech to the sound of my ears"; 485). Although he fails to mention the Archpriest of Talavera, there is no question that the stories of the *Corbacho*, in which the characters seem to acquire an existence of their own, speaking with their own voices, constitute his most important precedent in this respect.

The critical disagreement as to whether, despite its bawdy subject matter, *La Lozana andaluza* is a Christian, moral work or not, brings to mind another clergyman, Juan Ruiz, Archpriest of Hita, and his *Libro de buen amor* (1330; 1343). Written in verse, the latter tells the adventures of the archpriest as he tries to conquer a series of women, and scholars continue to argue whether Juan Ruiz intended to teach about the love of God, as he professes, or carnal love, as he apparently does. The Archpriest definitely provides a good lesson in the literary uses of ambiguity. There may be another point of contact between both writers in the prologue of *La Lozana andaluza*, when the unreliable narrator warns readers not to take out or add one single word (171), only to change his mind in one of the appendices, where he asks readers to correct his work (492). This recalls the two lines in which Juan Ruiz, toward the end of his book, addresses his audience in similar terms: "Qualquier omne que l'oya, si bien trobar sopiere, / puede más añadir e emendar, si quisiere" ("Any man who hears it and knows how to make verses / can add and correct if he so wishes"; 1974, c. 1629*a*–*b*).

As we know, the "Auctor" figures as a character in his own work. He is portrayed in the act of writing, speaks with Rampín and with Lozana, and it is a friend of his, Silvano, who describes to the heroine Peña de Martos where he had been raised. At one point, when he decides to have a son, the "Auctor" even tries to engage Lozana's services in finding a widow for the task. Lozana offers to have the baby herself, to go to the city baths, presumably in order to get cleaned up, so that they can get started that very afternoon (379–80), and then the subject is dropped. Obviously, what we have here constitutes another example of folly, but, at a more serious level, the baby in question is probably the book that the "Auctor" is engaged in writing. The idea of making the "Auctor" a character in his own work, of course, is inspired in Diego de San Pedro's *Cárcel de amor*. In that novel, we recall, the "Auctor" and the protagonist, Leriano, constitute facets of San Pedro himself, and the book is a protest against the "Prison of Love" that Spain had become for him and other conversos. Also a converso, Delicado probably understood this aspect of San Pedro's work quite well. Besides appearing as the "Auctor" in a book that, in the last analysis, constitutes a protest against the injustice of exile, Delicado also created the figure of Lozana as an alter ego.

After telling Lozana about Peña de Martos, Silvano decides to leave because, hearing people coming, he does not wish to be in the way. Lozana asks him to return on Sunday, at supper time, and to be there on Monday as well, because she wishes him to read to her: "quiero que me leáis, vos que tenéis gracia, las coplas de Fajardo y la comedia Tinalaria y a Celestina, que huelgo de oír leer estas cosas muncho" ("I want you to read to me, since you have a flair for it, the verses of *Fajardo*, the play *Tinellaria*, and *Celestina*, for I greatly enjoy having these things read to me"; 399). The first two of these works had some influence in *La Lozana andaluza* as well. As Allegra pointed out (1983, 35), the *Coplas de Fajardo* are really the famous *Carajicomedia*, which is included in the *Cancionero de obras de burlas provocantes a risa* (Valencia, 1519).[6] The brothel-like language and environment in this work have much in common with Delicado's book, whose lengthy list of the nationalities of the whores found in Rome it may have inspired (Allegra 1983, 35). Written by Bartolomé de Torres Naharro, the *Tinellaria*, one of the six plays included in his *Propalladia* (Naples, 1517), also depicts the corruption of Rome, and the Italianisms and various languages used by the characters may have influenced Delicado as well (Allegra 1983, 34).

Another important source for Delicado was the anonymous *Comedia Thebayda*, printed in Valencia together with two other equally anonymous plays, *Seraphina* and *Hipólita* (1521). *Thebayda*'s lascivious Franquila constitutes a precedent for Lozana, and one of her lovers, the page Aminthas, could have served as a model for Rampín (Vilanova 1952b, xxxiii–xxxvi). A passage of the *Comedia Seraphina* inspired Lozana's lengthy list of the dishes she had learned to cook with her grandmother (xxxv). Vilanova attributes so much importance to the volume in which these three plays appeared that, in his opinion, it provided "el estímulo decisivo que decidió la creación literaria de Loçana" ("the decisive stimulus for the literary creation of *Lozana*"; xxxvi).

In sum, there is quite a variety of influences in *La Lozana andaluza*, and Delicado, who was obviously a well-read man, used the works that suited his needs, without favoring one genre over the other. As Hernández Ortiz pointed out, "cuando la novela y el teatro comenzaban a perfilarse y la poesía cobraba nuevos auges, Delicado evita la camisa de fuerza de los géneros literarios puesto que usa varios de ellos según le conviene" ("when the novel and the theater were beginning to take shape, and when poetry was reaching new heights, Delicado avoids the straitjacket of literary genres, for he uses several, depending on what is convenient for him"; 1974, 40). That is why *La Lozana andaluza* does not belong to any specific genre, pointing to a new one instead. Together with *Celestina*, whose genre has also been questioned, it is the most important precursor of the picaresque novel.

By giving such a prominent role to Celestina, Elicia, Areúsa, Calisto's servants, and Centurio, Rojas places in the center of the stage some of the lowest elements of society, bringing to the fore a picaresque underworld that, although not without some precedents, had not been deemed worthy of such attention in Spanish literature before. Within this underworld, Pármeno is the closest to the rogue or trickster that would eventually be known as "pícaro," for he is a young man of low extraction, an orphan, and, to some extent, his education and moral character reflect the society in which he lives.[7]

Besides depicting the same sort of world, *La Lozana andaluza* adds further picaresque elements. Lozana is an orphan of converso background who has no choice but to use her own resources in order to survive, and does so through her wits. Whereas the picaresque novel tells the story of a single character, *La Lozana andaluza* is "el primer relato biográfico de un personaje novelesco a lo largo de toda su vida tal como será concebido por la novela picaresca" ("the first biographic life story of a fictitious character in the manner that the picaresque novel will come to conceive it"; Vilanova 1952b, xxxvii). Until that time, the only thing similar were epic poems, romances of chivalry, or hagiographic stories, but these focused on the lives of heroes and saints, not rogues.

The parade of characters of different social backgrounds, including numerous clergymen, brings to mind the *Lazarillo*, where several of the boy's masters belong to the clergy. The structure of the *Lazarillo* is episodic, with the boy's sojourn with each master constituting an episode, and Lozana's numerous adventures, which are told one after the other, may be regarded as being roughly episodic. The heroine's apparent *joie de vivre* despite the kind of life that she has to live recalls the *humor negro* ("black humor") of the *pícaro* ("rogue"), whose ability to laugh at his own mishaps seems to ease the all too real harshness and sadness of his life, and the dedication to an unnamed patron recalls the equally unnamed *vuestra merced* ("Your Lordship") to whom the author of the *Lazarillo* dedicates his work. The depiction of a corrupt society with the concomitant social criticism are also characteristic of the picaresque novel. Last but not least, both *La Lozana andaluza* and the *Lazarillo* were published anonymously.[8]

Despite these important coincidences, however, there are several crucial differences as well. Whereas the picaresque novel is autobiographic, with the rogue telling the story of his or her life, Lozana speaks for herself only through dialogue, for the narration itself is in the third person. The *pícaro* suffers from hunger, goes from master to master, and travels from place to place, but Lozana is never hungry, and although she travels within Spain, in the Levant, and to Lipari/Venice, she spends most of her life in Rome, and takes care to live as her own mistress as soon as she arrives in that city. Whereas the *pícaro* starts out as an innocent child, changing and evolving as he learns from the corrupt world that surrounds him, Lozana is far from innocent from the very beginning. In fact, she is always the same, for her personality does not undergo any fundamental sort of change (Hernández Ortiz 1974, 150).

Although there are references to two picaresque characters, a "Rodriguillo español" ("little Spanish Rodrigo"; 216), a rogue who had lived in Rome before, and a folkloric character named Lazarillo, believed to have had an incestuous relationship with his grandmother ("el que cabalgó a su abuela" ["the one who mounted his grandmother"; 344]), these references are incidental, and, therefore, of little significance. The coincidences between

Chapter Eight

Rampín and the forthcoming *pícaro* are much greater and, therefore, ought to be pointed out. A converso like Lozana and most subsequent picaresque heroes, Rampín had at least two masters before meeting Lozana, a squire and a clergyman; became a consenting husband in order to make a living, just like Lázaro de Tormes; and experienced three adventures—the vomiting episode, the stolen eggplants, and the fall into the latrine—that are definitely picaresque in character (see Vilanova 1952b, xlvi–li).

Nevertheless, since it does not belong to a precise literary genre, *La Lozana andaluza* is best classified as a pre-picaresque work, constituting the closest precedent of the *Lazarillo de Tormes* (1554). Nicasio Salvador Miguel emphasized, and rightly so, that Delicado's book could hardly have served as a model for the *Lazarillo* or any of the other novels of the kind that followed; its circulation in Venice seems to have been drastically restricted, and there is nothing to indicate that anyone in Spain was even aware of its existence (1984, 439). This does not really matter, however. As Hernández Ortiz pointed out, Delicado's book indicates, earlier and better than any other literary work, that something new was in the air: "Independentemente del hecho de que la *Lozana* fuera, o no, conocida en los siglos posteriores a su publicación, las intenciones realistas de Delicado encuadran dentro de la evolución de la picaresca y apuntan hacia el futuro de la novela española y europea" ("Whether *Lozana* was known or not during the centuries that followed its publication, Delicado's realist purposes fit within the evolution of the picaresque, and point to the future of the Spanish and European novel"; 1974, 152). Stressing the importance of the converso element as well, Hughes expressed the same idea in rather eloquent terms:

> No se trata de influencia. No importa que haya leído o no el autor del *Lazarillo* la obra de Delicado, su mera existencia en Italia—ambiente relativamente libre, que servía como refugio para más de un autor converso—, en este momento histórico, y su perspectiva, que en mucho anticipa la perspectiva y el mundo picarescos, . . . descubren algo del fondo social e histórico que yacía detrás del contenido enajenado y el anonimato del *Lazarillo*. (1979, 332–33 [59])

Questions of genre aside, although *La Lozana andaluza* combines both prose and dialogue, without relying exclusively on the latter, as Rojas did, there is no doubt that *Celestina* was the main inspiration for Delicado. This can be seen in his numerous references and allusions to the title of Rojas's work and to the name of the old bawd (some of which disclose evidence of competition), in the manner in which he adapts and parodies the preliminary materials found in *Celestina*, in his derision of "limpieza de sangre," lack of respect for the Christian Scriptures, Christian prayer, and the saints, virtual omission of the names of Jesus and Mary, and in his covert attack against Christian dogma. Last but not least, although the two works depict an underworld of prostitution, both authors claim to have written them with edifying, moral purposes in mind.

Let us begin with the references and allusions to the old bawd. Having claimed that his book contains "munchas mas cosas que la Celestina" ("many more things than *Celestina*") in the frontispiece, Delicado alludes to it again right after, in the prologue, by saying that he is going to tell the story of a woman who, together with her servant, exercised in Rome "el arte de aquella mujer que fue en Salamanca en tiempo de Celestino segundo" ("the wiles of that woman who lived in Salamanca during the reign of Celestine II"; 169). Since Celestine II had been pope between 1143 and 1144, his name is mentioned in order to refer to Celestina, who was believed to have lived in Salamanca, even though that city lacked the port that the fleet attributed to Pleberio leads readers to imagine (see Deyermond 2001, 24–26), and probably also to suggest that both Celestina and the book to which she had given her name were already extremely old and perhaps even *passé*.

Lozana serves the Milanese ambassador "con una moza no virgen, sino apretada" ("with a girl who was no longer a virgin, but tight"; 289), which suggests that she was able to deceive him in order to get better paid. This echoes Celestina's ability to do the same with no less of an expert than the French ambassador, to whom she manages to sell the same girl as a virgin no fewer than three times (1987, 112). In the same *mamotreto*, when a man who sees Lozana enter into a house admires her and wonders who she is, another man laughs and says: "¡Hi, hi! Diré della como de la otra, que las piedras la conocién!" ("Hee-heeh! She is like what people said about the other one, 'that even the stones knew who she was'"; 290). This confirms that Delicado had *Celestina* in mind, for, while telling Calisto how everything and everyone calls the procuress an old whore, Pármeno claims that, when she goes by and a rock happens to hit another, "luego suena '¡Puta vieja!'" ("both cry out: 'Old whore'!"; 109). In other words, even the rocks knew her.

A deceased, renowned procuress known as La de los Ríos (the Rivers' Woman), who used to live in the same part of town as Lozana, earned good money by filling "la esponja llena de sangre de pichón para los virgos" ("sponges full of blood for [girls who wanted to look like] virgins"; 314). Her name brings to mind the location of Celestina's house "al cabo de la cibdad, allá cerca de las tenerías, en la cuesta del río" ("at the edge of town, near the tanneries along the river bank"; 110), and the virginity that the old bawd reconstructed with great expertise, even though her approach was slightly more prudent and thorough: "Esto de los virgos, unos hazía de

Chapter Eight

bexiga y otros curava de punto" ("Regarding maidenheads, some she made of bladder, others she sewed up"; 112). In fact, at one point Lozana compares La de los Ríos explicitly with Rojas's procuress: "si como me entremetí entre cortesanas, me entremetiera con romanas, mejor gallo me cantara que no me canta, como hizo la de los Ríos, que fue aquí a Roma peor que Celestina" ("if I had meddled with Roman women as I meddled with courtesans, I would have done much better. That is what that woman Los Ríos did. Here in Rome, she was worse than Celestina"; 324). Lozana herself has no desire to imitate either of these women, however: "Quiero vivir de mi sudor, yo no me empaché jamás con casadas ni con virgos, ni quise vender mozas ni llevar mensaje a quien no supiese yo cierto que era puta" ("I want to live by the sweat of my own brow, and I never encumbered myself with married women or virgins, nor did I want to sell girls or to take messages to anyone who I did not know for sure was a whore"; 324). Thus, Lozana places herself a notch above Celestina, even though the location of her house indicates that she is equally marginalized: "allí moro junto al río, pasada la Vía Asinaria, más abajo" ("I live over there, next to the river, a little past Asinaria [Asinine] Road"; 369).

The rivalry with *Celestina* reappears when a gentleman describes Lozana's house to the Neapolitan ambassador in the following terms: "Monseñor, ésta es Cárcel de Amor; aquí idolatró Calisto, aquí no se estima Melibea, aquí poco vale Celestina" ("Monsignor, this is the Prison of Love; Calisto idolized here, but Melibea is not valued and Celestina is not worth much"; 349). Celestina, then, would be utterly powerless in Lozana's house.

These words come at the very end of *mamotreto* 36. Significantly, the beginning of the *mamotreto* that follows includes an engraving used in the two editions of *Celestina* overseen by Delicado (Joset 1997, 151). It depicts Celestina (.CE.), Melibea (.ME.), Lucrecia (.LV.), Calisto (.CA.), and Sempronio (.SE.).[9] As Ronald Surtz pointed out, the placement of this engraving here points, once again, to Delicado's rivalry with *Celestina*: "Así que, si Delicado se propone superar el libro de Rojas, la inclusión de un grabado tomado de dicho libro sirve para recordar la jactancia de Delicado al mismo tiempo que invita al lector a averiguar la medida en que Delicado está cumpliendo su propósito" ("Therefore, if Delicado planned to surpass Rojas's book, the inclusion of an engraving taken from it serves to remind readers of his boasting while inviting them to ascertain the extent to which he is achieving his purpose"; 1992, 176). Note that the top half of the engraving on the reverse of the title page, with its depiction of Lozana, Rampín, Divicia, and several courtesans, with accompanying labels, probably constitutes a challenge as well, since it may be considered "una réplica visual del grabado tomado de *La Celestina*" ("a visual replica of the engraving taken from *Celestina*"; 176), and is strategically placed at the beginning of Part III as well. In the words of Surtz, "además de su evidente función de puntuación visual, el grabado repetido constituye una referencia a la obra que Delicado se propone superar" ("besides its clear function as visual punctuation, the repeated engraving constitutes a reference to the work that Delicado proposes to surpass"; 177).

Lozana's apparent rivalry with Celidonia refers to Celestina as well. According to Sagüeso, who is trying to get Lozana to sleep with him for free in order to prove the contrary, "no es nacida quien se le pueda comparar a Celidonia, porque Celestina la sacó de pila" ("no one can compare with Celidonia, because Celestina was her godmother"; 419). But Lozana believes herself to be far superior, for she replies: "—¿Quién mayor que Celidonia? —Lozana y Rampín en Roma" ("Who is greater than Celidonia? Lozana and Rampín in Rome"; 419). Later on, when she discovers that a maid whom she had refused to help in finding a customer for a poor girl "tanto estrecha que parece del todo virgen" ("so tight that she seems to be completely virgin"; 430) decided to seek Celidonia's assistance instead, Lozana says: "si todas las Celidonias o Celestinas que hay en Roma me diesen dos carlines al mes ... yo sería más rica que cuantas mujeres hay en la tierra" ("if all the Celidonias or Celestinas in Rome gave me two *carlines* per month ... I would be richer than all the women in this country"; 430). Besides placing Celidonia and Celestina at the same level—and note that the prefix of both women's names has to do with *caelum*, "heaven"—Lozana implies that she is superior to both. Thus, Celidonia seems to constitute a modern Celestina. But the rivalry with Rojas is friendly. The truth of the matter is that Delicado admires *Celestina*; as we have already seen, Lozana likes to have it read to her.

Obviously, it would be too much to expect this rivalry to be present whenever *La Lozana andaluza* echoes another character or situation from *Celestina*. When Aldonza elopes with Diomedes, her aunt complains: "El hombre deja el padre y la madre por la mujer, y la mujer olvida por el hombre su nido" ("Man leaves his father and his mother for a woman, and a woman forsakes her nest for a man"; 182). These words, which adapt a biblical passage ("For this reason a man leaves his father and mother and clings to his wife, and the two become one flesh"; Gen. 2.24),[10] echo Sempronio's complaint about the delirium that his master's sudden love for Melibea has induced: "Mandaste al hombre por la mujer dexar el padre y la madre" ("you commanded man to leave father and mother for the sake of a woman"; 94). Since the wording differs considerably in both texts and the biblical passage was widely known, what we have here is probably a mere coincidence. Lozana's berating of a courtesan, Angelica, by saying that she is really ugly and that her beauty is due to cosmetics ("su cara está en mudas cada noche. ... Por eso se dice que cada noche daba de cena a la cara" ["her face is covered with creams every night. ... That's why people say that she fed it

Chapter Eight

supper every night"; 357]) brings to mind Areúsa's indignation when Sempronio praises Melibea's beauty during the banquet held at Celestina's house with food stolen from Calisto ("Todo el año está encerrada con mudas de mil suziedades" ["She is locked in all year long, with creams made of all sorts of filthy things"; 226]), but the attack against cosmetics was a commonplace[11] and, once again, the lack of close textual correspondences indicates that Delicado did not have *Celestina* in mind at this point.

In fact, although Lozana and Celestina are prostitutes, exercise their profession in cities, dabble in cosmetics and medicine, have a diverse clientele, and worry about their honor or professional reputation, the two women are really quite different. Lozana begins her career at a very tender age and seems to take her own advice, according to which a whore ought to retire after twenty-eight years of service, for she appears to be in her middle years when she decides to move to Lipari.[12] An old woman, Celestina is at least sixty years old (273). Although she liked sex since she was little, Lozana is portrayed as a victim, for she is orphaned and then abandoned by Diomedes, acquiring syphilis in the process. Unlike the old bawd, Lozana does not corrupt and profit from innocent young girls, leading them into sin. She is not really a procuress, and her home cannot be characterized as a whorehouse. When she serves as an intermediary, as in the case of the Milanese ambassador, the girl involved is already a whore. And although she dabbles in folk spells, folk medicine, and is a bit of a quack, Lozana is not an evil, deceitful, mean witch like Celestina, and the thought of becoming involved with the devil does not even cross her mind.

There is no question, however, that Delicado was competing with *Celestina*, and further correspondences between his and Rojas's addenda (preliminary and postliminary materials) also reflect this rivalry. In *La Lozana andaluza*, the "Argumento" or summary that follows the prologue corresponds to *Celestina*'s much shorter "Argumento," which opens with general descriptions of Calisto's and Melibea's lineages: "Calisto fue de noble linage, de claro ingenio, de gentil disposición, de linda crianza dotado de muchas gracias, de stado mediano. Fue preso en el amor de Melibea, muger moça muy generosa, de alta y serenísima sangre, sublimada en próspero estado, una sola heredera a su padre Pleberio, y de su madre Alisa muy amada" ("Calisto was of noble lineage and of good intelligence. He was genteel and well bred, good-looking, and of medium rank. He fell in love with Melibea, a generous young lady of high noble rank, and very rich, for she was the sole heir to her father, Pleberio, and dearly loved by her mother, Alisa"; 82). In his own summary, Delicado starts by stating his book will begin with the same type of information, warning that it must be read *in toto*: "Decirse ha primero la cibdad, patria y linaje, ventura, desgracia y fortuna, su modo, manera y conversación, su trato, plática y fin, porque solamente gozará d'este retrato quien todo lo leyere" ("We will begin with the city and country of birth, fate, misfortunes and luck, ways, manners, speech, dealings, and end [purpose] of our protagonist, for only those who read all of this portrait will enjoy it"; 171). But since Delicado has only one main character, Lozana, this parallel may well have been inspired elsewhere. As already pointed out, the *Golden Ass* and the romances of chivalry are two good possibilities.

Still in this summary, after warning readers not to add or take off anything from his book, Delicado tells them that "si miran en ello, lo que al principio falta se hallará al fin" ("if you pay attention, you will see that what is missing at the beginning will be found at the end"; 173). These instructions echo the acrostic verses in which Rojas reminds his readers to do something similar: "buscad bien el fin de aquesto que escrivo, / o del principio leed su argumento" ("search well the end of this which I write / or read the opening argument from the beginning"; 73). But whereas Rojas goes on to claim, very seriously, that his book shows people how to free themselves from the chains of love ("leeldo y veréis que, aunque dulce cuento, / amantes, que os muestra salir de cativo" ["read it and you will see that though sweetly told, / lovers, the story shows you how to escape from captivity"; 73]), Delicado ends his instructions with a guffaw, for he curses his readers with the opposite if they should fail to do as he says: "y quien lo contrario hiciere, sea siempre enamorado y no querido amen" ("let whoever does otherwise be always in love and never loved back, amen"; 173). Clearly, Delicado has the preliminary verses of his illustrious predecessor in mind, and he is having fun with them.

Entitled "Cómo se escusa el autor" (How the author excuses himself; 482), Delicado's first appendix is probably inspired by the acrostic verses of *Celestina*, which bear a similar title "El autor, escusándose de su yerro en esta obra que escrivió" (The author, excusing himself for his error in this work which he wrote; 71). Among other excuses, Delicado defends his Andalusian Spanish and the spoken, colloquial style that he favors: "Y si quisieren reprehender que por qué no van munchas palabras en perfeta lengua castellana, digo que, siendo andaluz y no letrado, y escribiendo para darme solacio y pasar mi fortuna, que en este tiempo el Señor me había dado, conformaba mi hablar al sonido de mis orejas, que'es la lengua materna y su común hablar entre mujeres" ("And if people reprimand me because many words are not in perfect Castilian, my reply is that I am Andalusian and not learned, and that since I was writing to give myself solace and to bear the fate that God had given me at this time, I tailored my speech to the sound of my ears, for this is my mother's language [also: "mother tongue"], and the way in which women usually speak among themselves"; 484–85). These linguistic and stylistic remarks reflect a statement in Rojas's letter to a friend,

Chapter Eight

where he describes the "estilo elegante, jamás en nuestra castellana lengua visto ni oýdo" ("elegant style, never seen or heard in our Castilian language before"; 69) of the part of *Celestina* that he claims to have found already written. Since it is right after this that Delicado says that he is "iñorante y no bachiller" ("ignorant and not a Bachelor"; 485), thus jokingly recalling the bet about the ass with the bachelor's degree and the "Bachiller Fernando de Rojas" ("Bachelor Fernando de Rojas") in *Celestina*'s acrostic verses, the chances are that the parallel just noted is not a matter of coincidence.

Delicado's explanation for his apparent anonymity and his excuse for writing *La Lozana andaluza* were probably inspired by Rojas as well. Explaining his decision to remain anonymous, Rojas states that he is merely following the example of the author of Act 1 and that, like his predecessor, he does not wish to expose himself to malicious, unfounded criticism: "Y pues él con temor de detractores y nocibles lenguas más aparejadas a reprehender que a saber inventar, quiso celar e encubrir su nombre, no me culpéys si en el fin baxo que le pongo, no espresare el mío" ("And since he, fearing detractors and evil tongues, which are always quicker to criticize than to create, decided to hide and conceal his name, don't blame me if, given the poor conclusion that I added to his work, I prefer not to reveal mine as well"; 70). Another reason for him to remain anonymous is that people will think that writing *Celestina* was a waste of time for a lawyer like him, and that no one will believe that he completed it during a two-week vacation, as a pastime:

> Mayormente que, siendo jurista yo, aunque obra discreta, es ajena a mi facultad, y quien lo supiese diría que no por recreación de mi principal estudio, del qual yo más me precio, como es la verdad, lo fiziesse, antes distraýdo de los derechos, en esta nueva lavor me entremetiesse. Pero aunque no acierten, sería pago de mi osadía. Asimismo pensarían que no quinze días de unas vacaciones, mientra mis socios en sus tierras, en acabarlo me detoviesse, como es lo cierto. (70 [60])

If people might think that it was a bad thing for a lawyer to write a book like *Celestina*, one can just imagine what they would think about a priest writing a book such as *La Lozana andaluza*. That is probably why, without revealing his profession, Delicado gives it as an excuse for remaining anonymous: "Si me decís por qué en todo este retrato no puse mi nombre, digo que mi oficio me hizo noble, siendo de los mínimos de mis conterráneos, y por esto callé el nombre, por no vituperar el oficio escribiendo vanidades con menos culpa que otros que compusieron y no vieron como yo" ("If you ask me why I did not include my name anywhere in this portrait, I say that my profession made me noble, even though I was one of the least among my countrymen, and that I concealed my name so as not to disgrace my profession by writing trifles, albeit with less guilt than others who wrote and did not see things as well as I did"; 485). Like Rojas, Delicado also refers to those who might say that he wasted his time, and repeats that writing was a good distraction during a prolonged illness: "Y si dijeren que por qué perdí el tiempo retrayendo a la Lozana y a sus secaces, respondo que, siendo atormentado de una grande y prolija enfermedad, parecía que me espaciaba con estas vanidades" ("And if people ask why I wasted time portraying Lozana and her followers, my reply is that, suffering from a long and troublesome illness, it seemed that I amused myself with these trifles"; 485). Thus, both authors write their respective books as a pastime (Salvador Miguel 1984, 453). Since the illness to which the "priestly" Delicado refers is syphilis and *La Lozana andaluza* is the story of a syphilitic prostitute, Joset is definitely right in suspecting that all of this "parece ser un eco un tanto burlón" ("seems to be a somewhat mocking echo") of Rojas's two-week, lawyer's vacation (1997, 152). Obviously, Delicado's "vacation" in the hospital of San Giacomo degli Incurabili was a bit longer.

Rojas's anonymity has been attributed to fear, but Lida de Malkiel documented abundantly that, during the Middle Ages it was customary for an author to withhold his name from a work in which he imitated or continued another, and also when writing for a close-knit literary circle:

> el hecho de callar Fernando de Rojas su nombre y dejarlo asomar luego en el acróstico, lejos de constituir la ocurrencia insólita y casi siniestra que se ha antojado a los críticos de nuestros días, es una práctica medieval frecuente en imitadores y refundidores para dar a conocer su incompleta autoría, y frecuente también en autores que escriben para un estrecho círculo literario a quien su nombre no es desconocido, circunstancias ambas que cuadran notablemente con lo que se sabe de Rojas. (1962, 15 [61])

Rojas could certainly have been following a well-established custom, since, after all, he claimed that he was continuing something started, but, for unexplained reasons, left unfinished by another author. Rojas could also have been writing for a group of friends, but it is also important to note that neither of these two explanations excludes the possibility that his anonymity was also motivated by prudence. Although Rojas eventually unveiled his name in the acrostic verses, the caution and fear revealed by those verses and the three strophes appended at the end are undeniable.

Delicado imitates Rojas in the anonymity as well, but his constant bantering and scoffing suggest that he does not fear anything, and the hints he gives regarding his identity indicate that he is not serious about hiding it. As Salvador Miguel pointed out, in the text Delicado indicates where he was born, states that he had suffered from syphilis, gives the exact date of his departure from Rome to Venice, and refers to two of his books (1984, 451–52).

In addition, Delicado parodies the acrostic verses where Rojas eventually discloses his identity through one of his appendices, the burlesque "Carta de excomunión contra una cruel doncella de sanidad" (Letter of excommunication against a cruel health maiden; 495–501), also written in verse. Issued by Cupid, vicar of the god of love, this letter is really a verdict against a cruel prostitute who had been sued by a distraught lover for refusing him the remedy that he needed. The cruel "maiden" is excommunicated, thrown out of the temple of love, and cursed.

As suggested in the previous chapter, these verses enclose an attack on the dogma of the Holy Trinity as well. At the beginning of the poem, Cupid mentions "todas las tres edades" ("all the three ages"; v. 7) affected by the religion of love. These are probably the mythical ages of gold, silver, and iron, but the three refer to time, and, no matter how we divide it, time, of course, is one. There follows a cryptic allusion to "tres canominaciones" ("three co-names"; v. 42), i.e., "conominaciones" or three names for the same person, which, besides bringing up the idea of three in one and one in three, also recalls the fact that Lozana had three names that are really one. Note that these three "canominaciones" do not figure in Hernando Ludueña's *Descomunión de amores fecha a su amiga* (Excommunication from Love to his mistress; Ugolini 1974–75, 478–83), which served as a model for Delicado's poem.

The imitation, or, to be more precise, the parody of Rojas's acrostic verses becomes clear afterward. Like Ludueña, Delicado curses the maiden through an adaptation of the topos of the vertical description of the ideal beauty, but adds or modifies verses clearly designed to disclose his identity. For example, Ludueña's passages cursing the girl's eyebrows and nose are as follows:

> la ygualdad y negror,
> de sus çejas se despache;
> su nariz bien conpasada,
> 105 de todas tachas desnuda,
> la linda frente arrugada,
> se torne grande y quebrada,
> la barba luenga y aguda.
>
> (480–81 [62])

Delicado's corresponding verses take care to stress the "delicacy" of the two features under scrutiny:

> Y sus cejas *delicadas*,
> con la resplandeciente frente,
> se tornen tan espantables
> 84 como de un fiero serpiente.
> . . . .
> y su nariz *delicada*
> 90 con que todo el gesto arrea

se torne grande y quebrada
como de muy fea negra.

(499–500 [63])

Ludueña's vertical curse omits the girl's arms, but Delicado adds this feature, stressing, once again, their "delicacy":

> y sus brazos *delicados*,
> 110 codiciosos de abrazar,
> se le tornen consumidos,
> no hallen de qué tomar.

(500–01 [64])

As Joset has pointed out, there is no question that Delicado had in mind the acrostic verses where Rojas reveals his name (1997, 153–54). I would like to add that Delicado reveals his identity by alluding to himself no fewer than three times, with three forms of an adjective that is the same as his own name, and that, together with the previous "tres edades" ("three ages") and "tres canominaciones" ("three co-names"), we have no fewer than three successive references to the idea of three in one and one in three. As we saw in the previous chapter, Delicado enjoys mocking the tripartite concept in a tripartite manner, i.e., three times in a row.

This amounts to great daring, and, together with their burlesque character, these verses, which parody and mock the seriousness, caution, and timorousness found in Rojas's corresponding acrostic, denote anything but fear. Furthermore, through a sacrilegious parody of the excommunication ritual, Delicado probably also mocks both the Inquisition and the penalty he was risking. When Cupid urges the chaplains and the priests in the palace of the god of love to denounce the accused maiden at once ("haced esta denunciación"; v. 39), the word *denunciación* is enough in itself to conjure up the Inquisition. Cupid then urges the priests to excommunicate and cast the girl from the temple with the following words:

> Del templo luego la echéis
> como miembro disipado
> de nuestra ley tan bendita
> todos cubiertos de luto
> 55 con los versos acostumbrados
> que se cantan al defunto
> las campanas repicando,
> y el cura diga: muera
> su ánima en fuerte fragua,
> como esta lumbre de cera
> 60 veréis que muere en el agua,
> véngale luego a deshora

Chapter Eight

>la tan gran maldición
>de Sodoma y Gomorra
>y Atam y Abirón.
>
>(498–99 [65])

The ceremony was usually performed by twelve priests and a bishop, standing in a circle. The funeral dirges, the tolling bells, the curse of the officiating priest, and the candle all correspond to the ritual of excommunication,[13] in which the victim was cast from the body of Christ (the Church), and his soul consigned to Satan: "Candles were thrown to the floor, foot stamping, door closing, and spitting—common rites of separation—were used in anathema liturgies to signify . . . the excommunicate's delivery to Satan" (Vodola 1986, 46; see also Logan 1986, 537). Delicado changes the bishop into a parish priest and reduces the number of candles to one. Since this candle stands for the soul of the victim and is set in water, what we have here is probably a reversal of the ritual of baptism. If so, this constitutes yet another burlesque aspect of Delicado's parody, for the person excommunicated did not stop being a Christian: "The baptismal character is indelible and hence cannot be effaced by excommunication" (Hyland 1928, 7). In any case, there is more than a mere excommunication involved, for the girl's soul is to be thrown into a dire forge and cursed like Sodom and Gomorrah, which had been burned to the ground.[14] Given the times, there is no question that Delicado is thinking of the bonfires of the Inquisition. Rather than shaking with fear, he laughs by describing the affair in a burlesque manner; in so doing, besides parodying Rojas's acrostic verses, Delicado mocks the extraordinary precautions that he takes in those verses.

In sum, besides trying to compete with *Celestina*, Delicado includes a fair amount of banter with Rojas through his characters, miscellaneous references and allusions to his work, and even through some of his engravings. Although this recalls the banter observed between fifteenth-century converso poets, it differs in the sense that it is probably one-sided, for there is nothing to indicate that Rojas and Delicado knew each other, even though they were contemporaries, or that Delicado expected Rojas, who was still alive and well (he lived until 1541), to set eyes on *La Lozana andaluza*. On the other hand, since he is clearly teasing Rojas, the hypothesis cannot be summarily dismissed. Whatever the case may have been, Delicado understood *Celestina* and Rojas's extraordinary precautions better than most, and, except for his attack on "limpieza de sangre," showed it by imitating him in subversive ways that a select group of highly educated, intellectual conversos were more likely to apprehend.

Delicado's derision of the Old Christian concept of blood purity, we recall, is rather transparent. It occurs when Lozana, a conversa, boasts that

The Art of Subversion

no one is superior to her in lineage or bloodlines, and Sagüeso insists that it would be necessary to bleed her and Celidonia, another prostitute, in order to determine which of the two had the best blood. Rojas is far more ambiguous, for he perpetrates his attack through the use of the word *limpio*, "clean," which, although sufficient in itself to allude to blood purity, also meant "pure" and "chaste." More often than not, he uses the word in question in unexpected ways, associating it with deceit, with Celestina's and Claudina's professions as procuresses, with the alleged purity of Celestina's motives, and with the beds where two prostitutes, Areúsa and Elicia, earn their living. All of these examples could be dismissed as part of his technique, for antitheses abound in *Celestina*, but that is not the case when Calisto, while trying to get Melibea into bed, tells her that, given her blood purity, he can hardly believe his good luck. Since it would be ridiculous for a man to worry about a pretty girl's bloodlines before having sex with her, Rojas is clearly mocking "limpieza de sangre." He repeats the attack when Pleberio talks to Alisa about marrying off their daughter in order to preserve her "clean" reputation, and she includes a reference to his noble "blood" in her reply. Here Rojas is using a technique of disjunction also documented in *El Abencerraje* and the *Quijote*. In his last stanza at the end of *Celestina*, including the very last verse to issue from his pen, Rojas also uses the word *limpio* twice in order to reaffirm the moral purpose of his work. Other conversos could not fail to notice the irony of this charged word in such a context. Moreover, Alonso de Proaza's reference to the "clara nación" ("clear nation") of the author in the verses that follow denies that a converso is "unclean" by definition, for "clara nación" means both "illustrious" and "clean," as in the expression "clara sangre" ("illustrious blood"), which was also used in the sense of "claro linaje" ("illustrious lineage"; Covarrubias 1994, 321, s.v. "claro").

To judge from the manner in which they use them, Rojas and Delicado share a dislike for the Christian Scriptures and Christian prayer as well. Even the biblical material taken from the Old rather than from the New Testament is constantly misused. In *Celestina*, the most outrageous example is when Pármeno parodies Psalm 148, where everything in Creation praises the name of the Lord, in order to show how everyone and everything capable of making a sound called Celestina an old whore. As for the New Testament, Celestina tells Melibea that man shall not live by bread alone, paraphrasing the words of Christ to reject the temptation of the devil to turn a stone into a loaf of bread (Luke 4.4) as she herself was tempting the girl, and misapplies Jesus's teaching during the Sermon on the Mount when she tells Pármeno that his deceased mother, Claudina, who was a witch, must be in heaven because she had suffered persecution for justice's sake (Matt. 5.10). This systematic reversal of the Scriptures—there are several other examples—is

Chapter Eight

echoed, albeit less extensively, in *La Lozana andaluza*, where Lozana paraphrases the words of Christ by sending Rampín to inform the mace bearer and the letter carrier who seek her services as a prostitute that she cannot serve two masters at the same time (Matt. 6.24).

Christian prayer does not fare any better. Celestina's house is described as a shrine, and the prayers and rituals held there when the old bawd was younger are tantamount to various types of sexual activity. Throughout the whole work, prayer is systematically used as cover for illicit activities (Celestina spent much of her time in churches), to deceive others, and to seek help in sinning. Calisto asks God to lead Sempronio to Celestina's house as he had guided the Three Wise Men to Bethlehem and to Jesus with the star, and he even prays and kneels before the old bawd. Later he spends a whole day in church, before the altar of St. Mary Magdalene, no doubt because of her reputation as a sinner, praying for Celestina to succeed with Melibea. Hearing the good news, Calisto asks God not to let it be a dream, and later begs him to burn down the doors of Melibea's garden so that he can get in. When Melibea tells Calisto that she is committing a grave sin by meeting him, he replies that it cannot possibly be so, for God and his saints had granted him the favor in answer to his prayers. Whereas Calisto prays for illicit sex, Melibea begs God to help her to hide the true cause of her malady, which, of course, is also sacrilegious, for one should not ask God for assistance in deceiving others.

Although less extensively, Delicado mocks Christian prayer as well, but he favors the folkloric, paraliturgical incantations in which some people foolishly believed—and still do. He parodies those incantations, inventing one to cure Rampín's syphilis, one to cure a child from the evil eye, and another to cure a stableboy from the venereal disease that Lozana diagnoses after examining his erect penis. Since these are superstitious folk spells, it is possible to argue that Delicado is not really mocking Christian prayer here, but that is not the case when a bearded old woman claims to use the rosary that she carries every day, time and again, stating that she concludes each recitation with the *Gloria*. Since the rosary ends with the *Salve, Regina*, the old woman does not really know it, and this suggests that, like some conversos, the woman uses it as cover, and that the *Gloria* that she feels obliged to emphasize is the Christian prayer that bothers her most. The *Gloria* constitutes an affirmation of faith in the Holy Trinity, and it has been well documented that insincere conversos made every effort to avoid saying those brief words: "In the name of the Father, the Son, and the Holy Ghost."

This derision for Christian prayer is matched by lack of veneration and respect for the saints. As we saw, Calisto credits them, and St. Mary Magdalene in particular, for his success with Melibea. Celestina invokes the archangel St. Michael in order to bless a prostitute, Areúsa, and informs Melibea that, when armed, Calisto looks like another St. George. Besides belittling that saint, her statement encloses a pornographic connotation, for the word *armado* was also used as a metaphor for an erection. St. Appolonia, whose teeth were knocked out as she was being martyred during the reign of Decius, in Alexandria, figures in the folk spell that Melibea was supposed to provide for Calisto's grievous "toothache."[15] Since the spell was—and still is—for real toothaches, and Calisto's infirmity is a metaphor for sexual arousal, the manner in which the text deals with that poor saint is anything but respectful.

Delicado does not have much use for saints, either. In Martos, Mars, god of war, used to water his horses in what became the fountain named after St. Martha, patroness of the town, but, nevertheless, people believed that, thanks to the saint, the water was good for fevers. In the plaza, there was an altar dedicated to Martha's sister, St. Mary Magdalene, who is nicknamed "the hairy one," no doubt because she used her long hair to dry Christ's feet after washing them with her tears. She used to appear on the morning of St. John's (June 24), a day that, although dedicated by the Church to that saint, is still fraught with all sorts of pagan, pre-Christian superstitions having do to with rites of fertility. St. James, Patron of Spain, besides being associated with syphilis, is called "St. James of the Carts" because people with syphilis looked as if they had been run over by a cart. At one time Lozana swears by St. Arnold's ass, and the apocryphal Nefija appears as the saint who was so charitable that she gave alms by allowing herself to be mounted by everyone, until she eventually died of "sweet love."

In sum, Rojas and Delicado systematically turn upside down the Christian Scriptures, Christian prayer, and the saints, using them in a manner that is unquestionably sacrilegious and even heretical. Since there are no exceptions, this cannot be justified in literary terms. What we have here is not mere humor and irony, but shameless blasphemy in the guise of parody. Moreover, there is no doubt that Delicado understood this aspect of Rojas's work quite well.

The two writers also coincide in their dislike for the names of Jesus and Mary, for their rare appearance is both extraordinary and tantamount to a virtual absence. *Celestina*'s characters invoke God's name very often, but Jesus appears only five times and always as an expletive, being invariably placed in the mouth of women. Mary's name shows up only three times, and is always proffered by men: Pármeno uses it as an exclamation, Tristán includes it in a proverb in order to call Sosia an ass, and Calisto invokes it as he falls from the top of the ladder to his death, right after making love to Melibea in the *hortus conclusus* that also stands for Mary's perpetual virginity. Needless to say, there is no devotion here, either.

Like Rojas, Delicado invokes God time and again, and it is obvious that he also avoids the names of Jesus and Mary. Jesus appears twice when St. Martha is repeatedly designated as "Christ's hostess," but he is also

Chapter Eight

mentioned as "Savior" at the end of a folk spell, and as "Our Lord" when Delicado wishes health and prosperity to the captain of the imperial army to whom he dedicates his book. Since the last example is used to bless a captain in the army that had sacked Rome, the blessing in question could well be a disguised curse instead. Delicado also alludes to Christ indirectly twice by citing his words,[16] including Lozana's message to the two men who wanted to sleep with her that she could not serve two masters at the same time. Finally, Delicado may also allude to Our Lord twice through the expression "Body of God," for it was through Christ that God, who is pure spirit, acquired human flesh, becoming corporeal. The expression in question is applied to Rampín when he falls into a latrine and when he vomits after eating bacon.

Unless we count the "villa de Santa María" ("town of Holy Mary") reportedly located near Martos, the name of the Blessed Mother is never mentioned in *La Lozana andaluza*. The text alludes to her indirectly, however. When the letter carrier informs Lozana that, among the numerous types of whores found in Rome, there are "putas con virgo, putas sin virgo, putas el día del domingo, putas que guardan el sábado" ("virgin whores, whores without virginity, Sunday whores, and whores who keep the Sabbath until they have used the soap"; 271), there is no doubt that he has Mary in mind, for a whore could not possibly be a virgin, and some Jews and conversos said that the Virgin was really a prostitute. Besides distinguishing between Jewish and Christian whores, the references to Sundays and Saturdays make the blasphemy even clearer. Trujillo's designation of a bout with Lozana as a "visitación," we recall, alludes to the Blessed Mother indirectly through the Annunciation, and so does Lozana when she wonders who the father of her child could be if she happened to get pregnant, since she did not know what a penis was.

In a nutshell, Rojas and Delicado shared an aversion to the very names of Mary and Jesus. This aversion, which brings to mind Maimonides's "¡borrado sea su nombre y su recuerdo!" ("May his name and his memory be erased!"),[17] the reluctance of many conversos in uttering them, and the manner in which Sephardic balladry continues to deal with them, is understandable in view of the tremendous suffering of Jews at the hands of bad Christians throughout the centuries. Notwithstanding their Hebrew origins, the names "Jesus" and "Mary" are either seldom or never found among Jews, and it is not difficult to understand why they do not care to give such names to their children.[18] The manner in which Joseph Jacobs describes their feelings regarding Christ's name is worth quoting:

> Owing to the behavior of many Christians, the name of Jesus is an anathema and a stumbling-block to the vast majority of Jews, even at

the present day. The crimes committed against the Jews in the name of Christ have left natural traces in the descendants of the victims of such inhumanity, the majority of whom indeed still suffer in one way or another from many who profess to follow Christ. (1925, 1 [Foreword])

Delicado probably did not fail to notice *Celestina*'s avoidance of the names of Mary and Jesus, but, although he earned a living as a Catholic priest, the chances are that he did not need any lessons from Rojas in this regard. That is not the case with Rojas's treatment of Christian dogma. Although most readers failed to understand what he was up to, Delicado did not, and, as the manner in which *La Lozana andaluza* deals with Christian dogma demonstrates, he set out to surpass *Celestina* in this as well.

As we saw in Chapter 4, Rojas created the old bawd and procuress Celestina as a covert antithesis of the Blessed Mother. Her very name means "little Celestial one." On three occasions she is described as if she were a goddess, bringing to mind a charge that even some devout Catholics made because of the proportions that the cult of the Blessed Mother had reached. Everyone calls Celestina "mother," she is depicted with a rosary, and her main purpose in life is to ensure that every virgin in town is deflowered. Parodying the Virgin's role as Mediatrix, with the help of the devil, whom she conjures through a Black Mass, Celestina leads her followers to a carnal paradise where they achieve their "glory." People often address her with the same names given to Our Lady in her litany. At one point, Sempronio even calls her "madre bendita," which means precisely Blessed Mother. Many of these parallelisms (and others) have to be deciphered and brought together into a meaningful whole for the extent of Rojas's parody to become clear. By creating Celestina, whom he also characterizes as an insatiable whore, as a covert antithesis of the Blessed Mother, Rojas is also suggesting that the Virgin was a prostitute, transforming into art a charge made by many converts, some of whom paid with their lives for declaring openly that Our Lady was a bad woman whose son had not been fathered by her husband. Although this denial of the virginity of Mary is the main thrust of *Celestina*, Rojas then goes on to attack other aspects of Christian dogma.

He does this by turning his two courtly protagonists, Calisto and Melibea, into another Adam and Eve. Their initial tryst occurs in Melibea's garden thanks to Celestina, a temptress who is linked with the devil in several ways. Calisto and Melibea pay for their transgression by falling to their deaths. Although any garden could represent paradise, this transforms Melibea's idyllic "huerto" into another Garden of Eden. At another level, Melibea's polysemous garden has much in common with the Christian heaven as well. The walls that surround it recall the *hortus conclusus* that is emblematic of the Virgin Mary, Queen of Heaven. The ladder that Calisto uses to scale and breach the

Chapter Eight

walls corresponds to the biblical Jacob's ladder, and the "glory" that he experiences after tasting the forbidden fruit corresponds to the glory of the redeemed in heaven. According to Catholic theology, the Garden of Eden represents the spiritual paradise, which Christ, as the New Adam, and the Virgin, as the New Eve, enabled humanity to regain, thereby reversing the effects of the Original Sin committed by our first parents. Since Melibea's garden stands for both paradises, this transforms the two lovers into a New Adam and a New Eve. As we saw, Calisto and Melibea are linked with Christ and Mary in other ways, and, just before making love to Melibea for the first time, Calisto refers to her as *buen puerto* ("good, safe harbor"), as if he were a sailor and she were *Maria maris stella*, i.e., Mary in her role as Patroness of Mariners. In her reply, Melibea reminds Calisto of the *buen pastor* ("good shepherd"). Notwithstanding the humor involved here, the blasphemy is irrefutable. It corresponds to Profit Duran's crude objection to the dogma of the Holy Trinity, according to which the Son would have to sleep with his mother in order to be the same as his own father, as well as to non-Christian objections to the doctrines of the Virgin Birth and the Incarnation, on which, in the last analysis, the dogma of the Holy Trinity depends. If the Son of God had not become flesh through the Incarnation, the Holy Trinity would not exist.

Celestina's Black Mass, of course, involves a parody of the dogma of Transubstantiation as well, for, whereas the priest turns bread and wine into the body and blood of Christ, making him present, Celestina conjures the devil with goat's blood. Since all Black Masses reverse the Christian Mass, this parody may be interpreted exclusively in artistic terms, but it is not possible to do so when Calisto plucks Melibea like a bird and refuses the drink that she offers him, saying that her body is all he wants, and refers to sex as food and drink before making love to her. Here it is Melibea who becomes the Host or sacrificial victim, and this sacrilegious comparison between coitus and Communion involves a mockery of the dogma of Transubstantiation as well.

The doctrine of the Annunciation comes under attack when Melibea, while making love with Calisto, addresses him as if he were either an angel or a god, saying that all the pleasure is hers, and thanks him for the incomparable favor that his visitation represents. Melibea's gratitude, of course, encloses an allusion to the *Magnificat*, the beautiful prayer with which the Blessed Mother thanks the Lord for having chosen her (Luke 1.46–55).

Besides imitating Rojas in his attack against Christian dogmas, Delicado encloses a protest against exile and an attack against the capital of Christendom. Lozana's sailing adventures in the Levant, we recall, are designed to establish her identity as a syphilitic prostitute and to place on her forehead the "star" that, besides bringing to mind the star of David, marginalizes her as effectively as if she were a leper. Her departure from her native Spain parallels the exile of the converso women she meets upon arriving in Rome. As the text points out, they and their families had left their country for fear of the Inquisition. Lozana's syphilis eats her nose away, making her "roma," "flat-nosed," and thus she comes to represent "Roma," the very city where she supposedly works as a prostitute despite her obvious illness. The fact that Rome was also known at the time as "Roma putana" ("Harlot Rome") served Delicado's purposes well. Although Lozana's Roman adventures have been described as being very realistic, no man in his right mind would pay to have relations with such a clearly diseased woman. Like the other marranos in Rome, Lozana is forced to undertake a second exile after the sack of that city by the imperial army of Charles V, fearing the wrath of the inhabitants, who blamed the marranos for their misfortune. Since the book begins and ends with exile, *La Lozana andaluza* is an allegory about the "voluntary" exile of many conversos, for, as stressed in one of the appendices, being able to live in one's own country "cierto es una grande felicidad no estimada" ("is certainly a great, unappreciated boon"; 486). In fact, Delicado is also writing about his own experience, since, like Lozana, he was a syphilitic converso from Córdoba who lived in Rome for many years, leaving the city in February of 1528. Delicado went to Venice. Although Lozana is reported to have gone to Lipari, the engraving in the frontispiece depicts her in a boat with the motto: "a Venetia" ("to Venice").

Besides protesting against his exile and that of many marranos from their native Spain and the city that had become a second home to them, Delicado encloses in his book—whose initial ship of fools and the tree of folly mentioned in the last *mamotreto* also frame it in the idea of folly—a dangerous, merciless attack against Christian dogma. As we saw, the virginity of the Blessed Mother comes under assault when the letter carrier tells Lozana that, among the numerous types of whores found in Rome, there are virgin whores and whores without virginity, and that some rest on Sunday and others on Saturday. The Annunciation is violently attacked when Trujillo refers to a bout with Lozana as a "visitación" and when Lozana, claiming not to know what a penis is, wonders who the father of her child would be if she happened to get pregnant. Incredibly, this question echoes the Virgin Mary's famous question to the Angel Gabriel when she asks: "How shall this happen, since I do not know man?" (Luke 1.34).

Delicado's most extensive and perhaps even more virulent attack is against the Holy Trinity, however. He does this through the idea of three in one and one in three because it was enough in itself to allude to the concept of the Trinity. Born Aldonza, the protagonist becomes known as Lozana, changes her name to La Vellida when she decides to retire, and, as the narrator points out, since Lozana is an anagram for Aldonza, and La Vellida

Chapter Eight

("Beautiful") means the same as Lozana, her names, though apparently three, are really one. Thus, the concept of three in one and one in three is illustrated through the name(s) of a prostitute, no doubt because, according to some Jews and some conversos, the woman who had given birth to Jesus, the Second Person of the Holy Trinity, was an unfaithful wife. The assault is repeated over and over, and more so in the third part of a book that is divided into three parts. The three friends of the courtesans in Rampín's spell against syphilis are in fact one—syphilis itself. Lozana's first customers in Rome are exactly three—three in one and one in three—and their names suggest that they, in turn, represent only one man. Since the chief waiter's job is to taste the food for his master, he is associated with the mouth, while the mace bearer and the letter carrier with his bag represent the penis and the testicles, respectively. Note that it is Trigo—who, like other Jews, swears by "el Dio" rather than the suspiciously plural "Dios" (God) because of his uncompromising monotheism—who brings to Lozana these three clients. Reflecting on how hard the husbands of some women work in order to support them, Lozana says that they make three needles out of one, whereas their wives do precisely the opposite. In reply to the placard carried by the twelve firstborn sons sent as tribute to Rome ("Quis mayor unquam Israel?" ["Who is greater than Israel?"; 419]), the Romans send their children with a banner that displays a cross and three letters, SPQ ("Senatus Populusque Romanus" ["The Roman Senate and the people of Rome"; 419]), thus shortening the standard SPQR in order to contrast one (Israel) and three (Rome). When Coridón asks Lozana for help, she advises him to feign madness because one madman is superior to three wise men, and madmen always tell the truth. To add insult to injury, she warns Coridón to fart only once and no more than twice after telling the truth, for three farts in a row are simply asinine. A doctor wonders whether Lozana used a syllogism in order to "unbewitch" a key full of wax because the tripartite syllogism, closely followed by the term *sophism*, was a code word for the Holy Trinity. According to Lozana, heaven, which is supposed to have only one door, has exactly three. In his excommunication of the cruel "health maiden" who had refused her services to a customer from the religion of love, Cupid mentions "tres edades" ("three ages"; 496); the maiden goes by no less than "tres canominaciones" ("three conames"; 497); and the three adjectives used to curse her "cejas delicadas" ("delicate eyebrows"; 499); "nariz delicada" ("delicate nose"; 500), and "brazos delicados" ("delicate arms"; 500) refer only to one person—Delicado himself. Although not completely summarized above, the attacks against the Holy Trinity, like the last one, are usually undertaken by mentioning or alluding to the number three three times, that is, in a tripartite manner. Given all of this, the words that Delicado uses to conclude his book, "quedo rogando a Dios por *buen fin* y *paz* y *sanidad* a todo el pueblo cristiano, amén" ("I remain praying to God for a *good end*, *peace*, and *health* for all the Christian people, amen"; 508), are really a curse.

Compared to Rojas, Delicado's invective is much easier to decipher. Delicado was probably aware of this, for he teases Rojas for his precautions in the "Carta de excomunión" (Letter of excommunication) in which he parodies the acrostic verses that the latter wrote "escusándose de su yerro en esta obra que escrivió" ("excusing himself for his error in this work which he wrote"), going to the point of mocking the penalty that he himself risked. But then he was an external exile, living in Italy. As a disaffected, internal exile living in Spain, where the fires of the Inquisition were raging, Rojas could not afford to take such chances; hence his extraordinary precautions. Besides insisting on the moral purpose of his book, he pointed out that it could be interpreted in contradictory, conflicting ways, and provided himself with deniability by making his attacks extremely ambiguous.

This peculiar type of writing, which arose because of repression, is addressed only to trustworthy, like-minded readers, and the requisite ambiguity makes it impossible to provide the explicit, foolproof evidence that rationalist thought demands (Strauss 1952, 25–27). As the writers involved prudently ensured, "such evidence cannot possibly be forthcoming" (27).

Nevertheless, it is still possible to demonstrate how, in order to express their extremely dangerous, subversive ideas, Rojas and Delicado used metaphor, irony, parody, allegory, and folly as cover. Because people are less likely to think when they laugh, humor was one of their most potent weapons. Although the interpretation of such writing necessarily involves a certain amount of subjectivity, the evidence presented in this book makes it clear that the situation of both authors as converts must be taken into account in order to gain a fuller understanding of their works.

To conclude, Delicado's attacks against Christian dogma show that, as an intellectual, like-minded converso, he understood the subversive aspect of Rojas's work quite well, and that, besides trying to make Lozana superior to Celestina as a character, he also set out to surpass him in this respect. Whether he succeeded or not is for other readers to decide. I am certain of one thing, however: since no true Christian could do such things, Rojas and Delicado were two subversive, "unconverted" Spanish conversos.

Appendix
English Translations

These English translations for the block quotations are keyed to the numbers in brackets in the text. For the translations not credited to a specific source, see the explanation in the Preface (p. *xii*).

Chapter One
The Converso Problem

1. Some clergymen, other religious persons, and laymen informed the King and the Queen that many Christians of Jewish extraction reverted to Judaism, performed Jewish rites secretly in their homes, and did not believe in Christianity or behave as Catholics. They entrusted their consciences with these matters by requesting them, as Catholic princes, to punish that atrocious error. Were it not punished and stopped, it would grow to such a scale that our Holy Catholic Faith would suffer great detriment.

2. And those masses of people who were converted with swords over their heads, their homes sacked, burning behind them, and facing ruin: how could they possibly be sincere Christians? This generation was never able to forget how it had to embrace that new faith and, therefore, it could hardly have inculcated it in its children. That first generation had to be completely Jewish, and, within the home, the children were immersed in Judaism as soon as they were born.

3. In the first week of July . . . they took the route for quitting their native land, great and small, young and old, on foot or on horses, in carts, each continuing his journey to his destined port. They experienced great trouble and suffered indescribable misfortunes on the road, some falling, others rising, some dying, others being born, some fainting, others being attacked by illness. There was not a Christian but that pitied them and pleaded with them to be baptized. Some from misery were converted, but they were the few. The rabbis encouraged them and made the young people and women sing and play on pipes and tambours to enliven them and keep up their spirits and thus they left Castile and arrived at the ports where some embarked for Portugal. (Bernáldez 1962, trans. in Raphael 1992, 71–72; qtd. in Gerber 1992, 140)

English Translations to Pages 54–56

Chapter Two
Repression and Artistic Expression

4 Distinguished Teacher, subtle graduate
in the high sciences, prudent jurist,
the great depths of this secret
I would like you to explain to me:
5 if before the world was created,
when everything was darkness and confusion,
God already existed as a Trinity,
since the Son had not yet been incarnated.

And, should you tell me that together
10 as a Trinity and as one the Lord always was,
how was he able to become human,
and for the other two to leave him apart?

5 My Lord and Teacher, I would like to ask you:
since the Trinity is indivisible,
how was the Son able to incarnate
and to become human,
5 for the Creator to become created,
for the Redeemer to issue from the other two,
and for the three to remain equal, none greater or smaller,
all of one substance, without becoming separate?

6 25 And since Adam lost Paradise
by his own fault and was taken to hell,
why should God for this reason be
for his sake so basely crucified?
Moreover, it seems quite impossible
30 for God to suffer, being impassive.

7 As the Church commands us to believe,
I accept all of this unquestionably;
35 in disturbing you, my intention
was only to test your fine mettle.

8 10 Stay away from theology,
for it is much deeper than poetry,
its name is chaos, a profound abyss;
watch out, do not follow the steps of the king
who, with the subtlety of his heart,
15 made a mess out of the Three Persons,
beginning a great schism in part of the world.

9 My Lord, we hold that a married woman
10 with a husband, no matter how pitiful,

English Translations to Pages 56–58

             who lives with him very unsatisfied,
             sins if she desires to take another.
             On this account, I have imagined
             that she would neither sin nor fall in error,
15   since God Our Lord did the same thing
             to St. Joseph, who was married

             to the Holy Mary, as you well know,
             for it can be read in the story,
             and you, noble Lord, always explain it so
20   while commenting on the Holy Scripture.
             And since it pleased God and He decided
             to make His Son in somebody else's wife,
             it does not seem to me that one who sins
             in such a way deserves punishment.

10   And so I conclude that no one
             ought to stick to any single woman,
             but rather leave one and then take another,
40   making children wherever he can.

11   He bequests to the Trinity
             one of those worthless new coins,
             a couple of eggs to the Crusade,
20   as signs of being a Christian,
             and, to be more charitable,
             he leaves a hundred *maravedís*
             to the Jews, with the warning
             not to work on Saturdays.
25   He orders the cross to be placed
             by his feet—see what madness!—
             and the Koran, a stupid scripture,
             on his treacherous breast.
             The Torah, which was his life and light,
30   he wants on top of his head.
             Of these religions let the most powerful one
             take [the soul of] this hypocrite.

12   5   But deliver me from the cursed,
             dirty-tongued, vile, and damned
             Davihuelo, for he howls
             and yells many depravities,
             like one who has been condemned to hell.

13   He does not fear God, nor do I think
             that he believes in His Gospels;
30   he longs for gluttony and lust
             and never loses this craving,

English Translations to Pages 58–62

           This dirty, vile Hebrew,
           son of a filthy Hebrew woman.

14   Fernand Manuel, you scare those from the Çadique
           or Açuaica, over there in Seville,
           or some Galicians from Costanilla
           with that rattling of yours,
     5   but my tongue, made of iron from Vic,
           polished, graceful, and so overwhelms you,
           your talk of feats won't infuse it
           with so great a fear as to cause it terror.

15   To the noble, polished, valiant, and steadfast,
           bathed in the water of holy baptism,
           to the profound sage, who, through a syllogism,
           penetrates the centers of the motionless circle,
     5   to the pure jurist whose formation
           endowed him with the perfections of an able prophet,
           to the one worthy of a high and rich planet,
           I present my answer and reply.

16   Genteel nobleman, in a waning moon
           you read poets, from what I can fathom;
           for that reason, guide yourself by the aphorism
           of the great rhetorical poet, Dante,
     5   and you will then see that you wander,
           like a shining comet goes,
           when it turns toward the sun
           in order to subdue and equal its rays.

17   Pray tell me, gentlemen, by your wisdom,
    10 if the art of poetry is the product of science,
           or genius or enthusiasm,
           or audacity or prudence,
           or if the art of poetry verges upon madness,
           or if the one who practices it is in danger
    15 of having his body destroyed by a paroxysm,
           if the Creator of Nature does not protect him.

18   The Angel Lucifer in his pride
    10 wished to be like three in essence,
           but he could not be suffered with patience,
           and at once he was cast into the depths;
           and your face shows well
           that you follow in the steps of that hound
    15 with fury and stones, talking very loud
           and raving with fever.

English Translations to Pages 62–65

19   I will apply every punishment
    10 if you fail to show in my court,
        to you, who have no faith,
        an apostate with a soft tongue:
        jailed for life under my lock,
        you will no doubt be sentenced, Lord Bueso;
    15 then you will learn how I flog
        your waist with my cat-o'-nine-tails.

20   look, it is in jest
    15 that I address these verses to you,
        for my poems carry a fire
        that is even worse than tar
        and will burn you right away.

21   Good loyal knight
        without any blemish
        and of pure royal blood:
        What do you think of the suffering
    85 of these converted people?
        You're worthy of a thousand lordships,
        thanks to the valor of your heart and hands,
        and they, given their inconstancy,
        would have been better off as Jews
    90   than as Christians

22   30 For, Queen of great worth,
        who promotes the holy faith,
        Our Lord does not want
            with fury
        the death of sinners,
    35 but for them to live and repent.
        For, high-ranking Queen,
        daughter of an angelic mother,
        that crucified God,
        whose side was wounded,
    40 laced with insults,
            his head inclined,
        said: "Forgive them, Father."
        And so, powerful Queen,
        let this unceasing death
    45 end by your mercy
            and kindness,
        until Christmas time,
        when the fire feels good.

English Translations to Pages 65–80

23 Oh bitter, sad Ropero,
you can't even feel your grief!
Each and every one of your seventy years
you always said
5 *"Pure you remained,"*
and never used the Lord's name in vain.
I prayed the *Creed* and worshiped
stew pots of thick salt pork,
half-cooked rashers of bacon,
10 hearing masses and praying,
crossing myself over and over,
and I could never get rid
of this converso scent.
My knees bent
15 with great devotion
on holy days
I devoutly counted
and recited
the knots of the Passion,
20 worshiping God and Man,
as my Lord Most High,
who wiped clean my guilt,
but I still couldn't lose the reputation
of an old Jewish fag.

24 for I have children and grandchildren
65 and a poor, old father,
and a mother, Lady Jamila,
a young daughter and her sister
who never saw the baptismal font.

25 Regarding Jewish women, Abraham's wife, Sarah, while a prisoner of Pharaoh, defended her chastity using prayer as a weapon, and begged Our Lord to deliver her from him. And when Pharaoh tried to seduce her, Sarah's prayer was heard in Heaven and he fell ill. Discovering that his evil intentions had caused his illness, he had her freed without blemish.

Chapter Three
The Idea of "Limpieza" in *Celestina, La Lozana andaluza,* and Other Literary Works

26 They were extremely arrogant, thought that they were the best, most prudent, sharpest, and most illustrious people in the world, because they belonged to the lineage of the tribes of Israel. They were very diligent in obtaining honors, royal positions, and favors from kings and lords. Thanks to their excessive wealth, some mingled through marriage with the sons and daughters of

English Translations to Pages 80–96

Christian nobles and were very fortunate, since, for this reason, the Inquisition regarded them as good, highly honored Christians.

27 Illustrious and most reverend sir: You have probably learned about that new statute passed in Guipúzcoa which ordered us not to go there in order to marry or take up residence, etc., as if there were nothing better to do than to settle that fertile tableland and abundant farmland. It is not unlike that ordinance issued by the stonecutters of Toledo, which forbade their members to teach their craft to any convert. May the Lord preserve me, sir, but on careful consideration I have never seen a more ridiculous thing for one who knows the quality of that land and the character of its inhabitants. Isn't it laughable that all or almost all of them send their sons here to serve us, many of them as grooms, and yet are unwilling to become related through marriage to the very people they would serve? I certainly do not understand, my lord, how one can justify such behavior: to reject us as relatives but to choose us as masters. And I understand even less how they can accept on the one hand an ordinance prohibiting contact with us, while on the other they fill the homes of [converso] merchants and notaries here with their sons. At the same time, these very fathers formulate offensive laws against those who raise their sons for them and instruct them in trades and sources of income as they did for them when they were young. As for me, sir, I have seen more of these [Guipúzcoan] young men in the court clerk's house, learning to write, than at the Marquis Iñigo López's residence, learning how to joust. I also assure your worship that there are more Guipúzcoans living at the homes of the secretaries Fernand Alvares and Alfonso de Avila than at your home or at the Constable's even though you are from their land. By my faith, sir, I'm bringing up four of them in my own home, while their fathers pass laws like those I've mentioned. And more than forty honored and married men, whom I raised and educated, but certainly not to make such ordinances, are living in the region now. (Pulgar 1958, trans. Silverman 1976, 150–51).

28 If you wish to see my pure [*clean*] motive,
search well the end of this that I write,
. . . .
or read the opening argument from the beginning.

29 And so judge me not unchaste for that reason,
but rather zealous of a pure [*clean*] life . . .
put aside the jests, which are straw and chaff,
gleaning very *clean* from them the grain.

30 The lords of this world are very different from the Lord of Heaven. To hire a servant, the former first *scrutinize his lineage*, test his skill, take a good look at his appearance, and even want to know what kind of clothes he has. To enter God's service, however, the poorest is the richest, the humblest, the one with *the best lineage*. As long as he is willing to serve with PURITY [not of blood, but] *of the heart*, he is placed on the payroll at once, and his wages are so great that they surpass his wildest dreams.

265

English Translations to Pages 102–19

Chapter Four
Celestina as an Antithesis of the Blessed Mother

31 and so do not judge me unchaste for that reason,
but rather zealous of a *pure* [clean] life,
zealous to love, fear, and serve
the high, sovereign Lord and God.
And if my hand seems confused to you,
mixing turbid with clear reasoning,
put aside the jests, they are straw and chaff,
and glean very *clean* the grain from them.

32 What are you doing, key to my life? Oh Pármeno, I already see her. I am whole again, I am alive! Don't you see what a reverend person she is, and such dignity? . . . Oh glorious hope of my desired goal! Oh goal of my delighting hope! Oh cure of my passion, repair of my torment, my regeneration, renewal of my life, resurrection of my death! I wish to approach you, and covet to kiss those healing hands, but the unworthiness of my person prevents me from doing so, and so I worship the ground you tread on from here, and I will kiss it in reverence for you.

33 When she has something to gnaw on, she leaves the saints alone. When she goes to church with the beads in her hands, there isn't much to eat in the house. Although she raised you, I know her and her ways better than you. What she prays for with her beads is the number of virgins in her charge, how many lovers there are in the city, and how many girls are entrusted to her, how many stewards give her provisions and which one is the most generous, what their names are, so that if she happens to run into them she won't talk to them like a stranger, and which canon is the youngest and freest with his purse strings.

34 When I went to church, hats were doffed in my honor, as if I were a duchess. He who had the fewest dealings with me thought himself the worst off. When they spotted me half a league away, they put aside their missals. One by one and two by two, they came where I was, to see if I wanted anything, and to ask about their respective lasses. There were some who, being in the middle of saying Mass, became so nervous when they saw me come in that they didn't do or say anything right. Some called me "madam," others "aunt," others "love," and others "honorable woman." There we arranged their visits to my house and visits to theirs. There they offered me money, made me promises, and gave me other presents, kissing the hem of my cloak, and some even kissed me on the face to make me happier.

35 If she is with a hundred women and someone says "Old whore," she turns her head without any shame and replies with a happy countenance. Men spend time with her in get-togethers, parties, weddings, brotherhoods, and funerals. If she passes by dogs, they bark out "Old whore"; the birds do not sing any-

English Translations to Pages 123–57

thing else when she is nearby; if she is close to herds of sheep, they bleat it out; if next to horses and asses, they neigh "Old whore!" The frogs in the ponds do not croak anything else. If she goes among farriers, their hammers say the same thing. This also goes for carpenters, makers of armor, blacksmiths, tinkers, and wool-beaters; every type of tool sounds out her name. Carpenters sing her name, hairdressers comb to it, and weavers weave to it. Farmers in gardens and fields, vineyards, and harvests pass their daily toil with her. When gamblers lose at the gambling tables, her praises start ringing. Wherever she is, everything that makes a sound cries out her name. Oh, how many roasted bull's testicles her husband had to eat! What else can I tell you? Even when a rock strikes another, both cry out: "Old whore!"

36   Since the Glorious Virgin   is full of blessings,
full of grace   and free to speak,
none of her petitions   would ever be turned down,
for such a Son   would not deny such a Mother.

37   Behold the moon, and how clear it is. Behold the clouds, and how they move. Hear the rippling water of this little fountain, and its soft murmur and buzz as it goes through the green grass. Listen to the tall cypresses, and how some of their branches kiss each other thanks to the soft breeze that sways them. Behold their silent shades, how dark and fit they are to conceal our pleasure.

38   Hail, holy Queen, Mother of mercy; hail, our life, our sweetness and our hope. To thee we cry, poor banished children of Eve. To thee do we send up our sighs, mourning and weeping in this vale of tears. Turn then, most gracious advocate, thine eyes of mercy towards us. And after this our exile, show unto us the blessed fruit of thy womb, Jesus. O clement, O loving, O sweet Virgin Mary. Pray for us, O holy Mother of God. That we may be worthy of the promises of Christ. (*Saint Andrew Daily Missal* [1953], 942)

Chapter Five
Christian Prayer and Dogma in
Celestina: **The Polemic Continues**

39   Oh Sovereign God, Thou on whom all those who suffer call, from whom the passionate seek remedy, and the wounded medicine, to Thou, whom the Heavens, the seas, the earth, and the regions of hell obey, to Thou, who granted mankind dominion over all created things, I humbly plead: please give my heart the patience and strength to conceal my terrible passion, and to prevent the veil of chastity that covers my longing from being tarnished, pretending that my pain is another than the one that torments me.

40   Those of us who because of Eve   fell into perdition,
through her [the Virgin] recover   our lost ancestral home;
were it not for her   we would lay dead,
but her holy fruit   has redeemed us.

English Translations to Pages 157–60

By the holy fruit that she conceived,
who for the sake of the world suffered Passion and death,
we left the pit that Adam opened for us,
when despite the prohibition he took that bad bite.

41 *Between Ave and Eva*
lies a great difference.

For Eva took from us
Paradise and God,
and Ave returned them to us.
That is why, my friends,
between Ave and Eva
there lies a great difference.

42 Reward me for the news, lads,
for there has been born
the most beautiful baby boy
10 in our town.
The one who comes to free
imprisoned humankind,
and this is the Paradise
of the *Second Adam*.
15 He is the strong soldier,
the skillful captain
who over the abysses,
will triumph after death.
He is the one who caused
20 *Eva to change into Ave.*

43 Be silent, my light and counsel,
for your Father wanted
you to be of paradise
a *flower* that never *deflowers* [loses its petals]
and cries.

44 You look fair and rosy,
Holy Virgin.
In Bethlehem, town of love,
the rose gave birth to a *flower,*
Holy Virgin.
In Bethlehem, town of love,
the rose sprung from the rosebush,
Holy Virgin.
The rose gave birth to a *flower*
to be our Savior,
Holy Virgin.
The rose sprung from the rosebush,

and it was both God and mortal man,
Holy Virgin.

45 *Flower* born without being seeded,
why do you come to light in that manger?
Do you want those animals
to graze upon you, newly born?

46 You are the *daughter*, you are the *mother*,
of the same One who created you.
He is both your *son* and *father*,
and as a mother he gave you to us.

Chapter Six
"Sailing," Renaissance Rome, and Exile in
La Lozana andaluza: An Allegorical Reading

47 Mother, I saw
the boats in the sea
I die of love.

48 the sea is very calm;
to the oars, oarsmen,
this is the ship of love.

49 The ships are already leaving, mother;
they sail to the Levant.

50 Down the seas
go my eyes;
I want to go with them,
so they won't be all alone.

51 Down the seas
goes Catalina,
with her legs naked,
and a monk on top.

52 On the thighs of ivory, Tarquin
embarked his desire and, in a sea storm
he went for Lucrece's gulf;
a king always finds his way.

53 And the fourth sense is to see   when the boat raises its sails;
I passed my hand over her bosom   and put my body close to hers.
The fifth sense is to see   when the boat is put to sea.

English Translations to Pages 188–226

"Miss, pray raise your sails, I want to sail off now."
I sailed all night long, was never able to sleep;
when morning came I could hardly stand.

54 No, Madam, they come from all nations. The Spanish ones are from Castile, the Basque country, La Montaña, Galicia, Asturias, Toledo, Andalusia, Granada, Portugal, Navarre, Catalonia, Valencia, Aragon, and Majorca. Then there are women from Sardinia, Corsica, Sicily, Naples, Abruzzi, Pula, Calabria, Rome, Aquila, Siena, Florence, Pisa, Lucera, Bologna, Venice, Milan, Lombardy, Ferrara, Modena, Brescia, Mantua, Ravenna, Pesara, Urbino, Padua, Verona, Vicenza, Perugia, Novara, Cremona, Alexandria, Vercelli, Bergamo, Treviso, Piedmont, Savoy, Provence, Brittany, Gascony, France, Burgundy, England, Flanders, Germany, Slavic and Albanian women, as well as women from Crete, Bohemia, Hungary, Poland, from the other side of the mountains,[1] and Greece.

Chapter Seven
The Holy Trinity and
the Annunciation in *La Lozana andaluza*

55   There were three courtesans
              and they had three friends
              who were pages of Franquilano.
              One has hers publicly,
    5   another very secretly.
              The third's returns with each moon.
              May the one who says this prayer
              three times in a row
              be healthy when it is born.

56 I remember hearing Christian captives [?] in the Levant say how the Moors reproached Christians for *three* things: first, knowing how to write, they paid money to secretaries and others to write down their secrets; second, they deposited their money, which made the moneychangers rich; third, they feasted a third of the year, and all of this is enough to keep people in poverty and to enrich those who laugh because they profit from what belongs to others.

57 I have no doubt I want to praise Lozana for this, since she took great care not to do things to offend God or His commandments. She tried to eat and drink without offense to anyone. She retired in time, and went to live on this island of Lipari, where she changed her name, calling herself La Vellida. Thus, she enjoyed three names: Aldonza in Spain, Lozana in Rome, and La Vellida in Lipari.

English Translations to Pages 227–46

58 Chaplains and great priests
of this royal palace
of Love and his heights,
make this denunciation
40 so that caution won't applaud,
cautioning from this moment
through *three co-names*.

Chapter Eight
Rojas, Delicado, and the Art of Subversion

59 It is not a matter of influence. It does not matter whether the author of the *Lazarillo* read Delicado's work or not. *Lozana*'s mere existence in Italy—where a relatively free environment served as refuge for more than one converso writer—in that historical moment, together with its perspective, which foreshadows the perspective and the world of the picaresque considerably... uncovers something about the social and historical background that forms the backdrop for the alienated content and the anonymity of the *Lazarillo*.

60 Moreover, I am a lawyer and, although the original is an ingenious work, it is quite out of my field. If people knew who I was, they would not say that I wrote it as a distraction from my main area of study, in which I take the most pride—as I truly do—but that I allowed myself to be diverted from my legal studies and became involved in this new pursuit. Although they would be off the mark, they would chastise me for my daring. Likewise, they would not think that I spent only two weeks to finish it, during vacation, while my fellow students had gone home, even though this is the truth.

61 the fact that Rojas withholds his name and then allows it to show later in the acrostics is far from being the unusual and almost sinister occurrence that today's critics have imagined. On the contrary, it was a frequent medieval practice on the part of imitators and those who reworked a text, who used it in order to acknowledge their partial authorship. This practice was also followed by authors who wrote for a close-knit literary circle where their name was known, and both of these circumstances fit quite well with what we know about Rojas.

62 may the evenness and blackness
of her eyebrows be gone,
her well-proportioned nose
105 have all blemishes bared,
her pretty brow wrinkle
and turn big and broken,
and her chin long and sharp.

English Translations to Pages 246–48

63   And may her delicate eyebrows,
              together with her gleaming brow,
              become as frightful
    84   as those of a fierce snake.
              . . . .
              and her delicate nose,
    90   which adorns all her countenance,
              turn big and broken,
              like a very ugly black woman's.

64   and may her delicate arms,
    110   eager to embrace,
              waste away
              and find nothing to hold.

65 50 Throw her at once from the temple
              as a dissipated member
              of our so blessed religion,
              everyone covered in mourning,
              with the accustomed verses
    55   sung for the dead,
              with tolling bells,
              and those present will say:
                 "May her soul perish in a dire forge,
              as you see this light of wax
    60   die in the water.
              May then suddenly come to her
              as great a curse
              as that of Sodom and Gomorrah
              and Dathan and Abiram."

Notes

Preface

1. They are Burton Raffel's translation of *Don Quijote* (Cervantes 1999), Lesley Simpson's *Exemplary Stories* (1998), and Dawn L. Smith's *Eight Interludes* (1996).

2. Chapter 3 uses portions of "The Idea of 'Limpieza' in *La Celestina*," *Hispanic Studies in Honor of Joseph H. Silverman*, ed. Joseph V. Ricapito (Newark, DE: Juan de la Cuesta, 1988), 23–35. Chapter 4 is based on "Celestina as an Antithesis of the Virgin Mary," *JHP* 14.1 (1990–91): 7–41. Chapter 5 includes "Adam and Eve Imagery in *Celestina*: A Reinterpretation," *JHP* 17.2–3 (1993): 155–90. Chapter 6 conflates and expands "The 'Art of Sailing' in *La Lozana andaluza*," *HR* 66 (1998): 433–45, "The Idea of Exile in *La Lozana andaluza*: An Allegorical Reading," *Jewish Culture and the Hispanic World: Essays in Memory of Joseph H. Silverman*, ed. S. G. Armistead and M. M. Caspi, in collaboration with M. Baumgarten (Newark, DE: Juan de la Cuesta, 2001), 145–60, and also adapts portions of "'Un engaño a los ojos': Sex and Allegory in *La Lozana andaluza*," *Marriage and Sexuality in Medieval and Early Modern Iberia*, ed. Eukene Lacarra Lanz (New York and London: Routledge, 2002), 133–57. Copyright (© 2002). Reproduced by permission of Routledge/Taylor & Francis Books, Inc. Chapter 7 is based on "Anti-Trinitarianism and the Virgin Birth in *La Lozana andaluza*," published previously in *Hispania* 76.2 (1993): 197–203, and "The Holy Trinity in *La Lozana andaluza*," *HR* 62 (1994–95): 249–66. Chapter 8 includes an excerpt from "Imitation, Banter, and Competition: Francisco Delicado and *Celestina*," *RPh* 56 (2002–03): 293–305. I would like to thank the publishers of these studies for their permission to use them in this book.

Chapter One
The Converso Problem

1. It is important to note here that the conquering Muslim army commanded by Tariq was relatively small (18,000 men); that a faction of the Visigoths—Spain, which had been a Gothic monarchy since the beginning of the fifth century, was divided by a war of succession—collaborated with the invaders; that the Jews, who were being persecuted, also welcomed them; and that thousands of Christians converted to Islam (Barkaï 1994b, 16–17; Russell et al. 1982, 56–59). Among the population, religious tolerance was so great that "to the great distress of the Muslim clergy, Hispano-Muslims joyously joined their Christian neighbors in celebrating various non-Muslim holidays" such as New Year's, St. John's, and Christmas (Armistead 2000, 282n13).

2. As Márquez Villanueva recently pointed out, Christians and Jews fraternized "by attendance at weddings, circumcisions, baptisms and funerals, the visits to the sick, and the exchange of food and medicines, not to mention sexual intercourse or even proximity of genders" (2000a, 19). Note that, after Alfonso VI (1072–1109), some Castilian monarchs took pride in using the title "Rey de las tres religiones" ("King of the Three Religions"; Del Río 1963, 1: 29).

3. J. S. Gil 1985; Márquez Villanueva 1994b, 73–93, 171–82; 1994d.

4. Menéndez Pidal 1956; Menocal 1987; 1988; Millás Vallicrosa 1942; Ricapito 1996a; Steinschneider 1956; Watt 1972, 297–312.

5. Partly inspired by the fact that Jews, Muslims, and Christians also live together in present-day Israel, several collective works have examined the phenomenon recently, no doubt in the hope of bringing about the same religious and cultural tolerance in that country (Barkaï 1994a; Carrete Parrondo et al. 2000; Mann et al. 1992).

6. Note that, to some extent, Christian tolerance was a matter of expediency, since the skills of Jews and Muslims were needed; there were not yet enough Christians trained to replace them (Valdeón Baruque 1994, 39).

7. In the opinion of Gerber, contrary to what is often stated, these activities were not monopolized by Jews: "the historical stereotype that Jews were the sole, or even the principal, group of state financiers in this period is belied by the facts. Most finance officials, tax farmers, and moneylenders were Christian, and the Jews who assumed these roles were being assimilated into, rather than differentiated from, this mainstream endeavor" (1992, 96).

8. Suárez puts it as follows: "los primeros arrendatarios de los impuestos no eran otra cosa que instrumentos que endurecían las condiciones de los impuestos, mientras sus amos aparecían con las manos limpias y recogían los resultados" ("the first tax contractors were nothing but tools who made the tax conditions seem even harsher, and their masters appeared to be blameless even though they kept the profits for themselves"; 1992, 169). Kamen pointed out that between 1440 and1469 only 15 percent of the tax farmers serving the crown of Castile were Jews (1998, 11), but this figure ignores the great number of people who were either forced or felt compelled to convert shortly before (1391–1416). Many of them were no doubt civil servants who continued to occupy the same positions, and the Old Christian majority still regarded them as Jews.

9. The Jews of Aragon fought back, sending representatives to Rome in order to ask the Pope to condemn the calumnies (Gerber 1992, 112).

10. Hebrew and Arabic sources have been posited for the term. See Corominas 1954, 3: 272–75; Malkiel 1948; Netanyahu 1999, 59n153; Roth 1995, 3–6. As Corominas pointed out, the word "es indubitablemente aplicación figurada de *marrano*, 'cerdo,' vituperio aplicado, por sarcasmo, a los judíos y moros convertidos, a causa de la repugnancia que mostraban por la carne de ese animal" ("is no doubt a personification of *marrano*, 'pig,' an insult applied to converted Jews and Moors because of their repugnance to pork"; 1954, 3: 272).

11. As Barkaï pointed out, there had previously existed a tradition of erudite dialogue among Christian, Jewish, and Muslim scholars, but the Disputation of Tortosa put an end to such cordial exchanges: "À partir de là se fermèrent toutes les voies de dialogue interculturel dans la péninsule Ibérique" ("Afterward, all the opportunities for intercultural dialogue within the Iberian Peninsula were closed"; 1994c, 249).

12. According to Américo Castro, this concept is of Jewish origins, and was subsequently adopted by the Christians (1971, 44–48). Most scholars disagree (see Caro Baroja 1986, 1: 65; Netanyahu 1979–80, 397–408; 1995, 975–80).

13. Probably for fear of conflict with the papacy, no attempt was made to implement these statutes until 1437.

14. The most extensive research on this monastery was conducted by Sicroff (1965), who also devoted an article to Fray Diego's trial (1966).

15. Incidentally, Fray Diego had never been baptized, which means that he was still a Jew. Hoping to mitigate his punishment, he asked for the sacrament of baptism, and this is what enabled the Inquisition, whose jurisdiction did not usually extend to Jews, to have him burned (Sicroff 2000, 598).

16. This book, which is fundamental for all questions regarding "limpieza de sangre," has been translated into Spanish (Sicroff 1985), and the author is now working on an expanded English translation (personal communication).

17. For a fuller discussion of this passage, see Sicroff 1960, 264–65.

18. Costa Fontes 1990–93, 71–77; 1999, 28–29, 37. In the church of Argozelo (District of Bragança), Old Christians and New Christians used to be separated by a rope (Paulo 1985, 28). Until recently, crypto-Jews still existed in Ibiza as well (Mound 1984).

19. In our own time, some Jewish refugees from the Nazis were so traumatized that they did the same. One good example is that of Madeleine Albright, who did not discover that her Czechoslovakian family was Jewish until she became Secretary of State during the Clinton administration.

20. Toward the end of the sixteenth century, this led to the creation of a new profession, the *linajudos*, "whose principal occupation was to scrutinize lineages to discover traces of converso ancestry" (Pike 2000, xi). Candidates for certificates had to pay them off. These *linajudos* (some of converso extraction themselves) operated all over Spain, but were more numerous in Seville, where they lasted until the end of the seventeenth century (154).

21. The author had already expressed similar ideas ten years before (Kamen 1986).

22. One notable exception was Fernán Pérez de Guzmán, uncle of the Marquis of Santillana, who wrote short biographies of his contemporaries in *Generaciones y semblanzas* (1450–55). In his portrait of Pablo de Santa María, the former Salomon ha-Levi, who became bishop of Burgos after his conversion in 1390, Pérez de Guzmán reminds his contemporaries that, since many of the New Christians had been converted by force, it was not surprising that there should be false Catholics (i.e., Judaizers) among them. But he also points out that there were numerous exceptions, including devout monks and men such as Pablo de Santa María and his son, Alfonso, who had also become bishop of Burgos. They had done much for the faith. Consequently, it was absolutely wrong to claim that all conversos were bad Christians: "Por ende, a mi ver, no ansi preçisa e absolutamente se deue condenar toda una naçion, e non negando que las plantas nueuas e enxertos tyernos han menester mucha lauor e gran diligençia" ("Therefore, in my opinion it is not necessary to condemn a whole people, even though I must concede that new plants and fragile grafts need much work and great diligence"; 1965, 93). Being a man of his times, he suggests that the children of converts from Judaism ought to be taken away from their parents, but believes that, with proper indoctrination, the second- and third-generations of conversos will be truly Christian, and he concludes: "E ansi, a mi ver, en todas aquestas cosas son de dexar los estremos e tener modos e limites en los juyçios; o si de algunos saben que non guardan la ley, acusenlos ante los perlados en manera que la pena sea a ellos castigo e a otros enxenplo: mas condenar a todos e non acusar a ninguno, mas pareçe voluntad de dizir mal que zelo de correction" ("And so, the way I see it, extremes ought to be avoided in these matters, and opinions must be formulated with caution. And if it is discovered that some do not observe the faith, let them be accused before the prelates, so that the penalty will constitute a punishment for them and a lesson to others. But to condemn all without accusing anyone looks more like a propensity to gossip than a zeal to correct"; 94). Note that Pérez de Guzmán was writing these words around 1450, long before the establishment of the Inquisition (1478).

23. Beinart does not have any doubts (1981, 9), but Netanyahu disputes this (1995, 818–20).

24. Torquemada's uncle, Cardinal Juan de Torquemada, was a converso, but his brother, Tomás de Torquemada's father, may have had a different mother (Netanyahu 1995, 1249–50n60).

25. On Torquemada, see now also Huerga Criado's important study (1987).

26. Regarding these edicts, see Villa Calleja 1987.

27. For an example of the numerous printed or manuscript primers that were used in order to detect crypto-Jews, see Blázquez Miguel 1988, 91–93.

28. The word is apparently inspired on the large, scapular-like garment that Benedictine monks wore over their habits (Castro 1972, 3: 235–38).

29. This did not work in the case of Fray Luis de León. Angry because they did not approve of their daughter's marriage, Fray Luis's maternal grandparents sued to have the sanbenito of their son-in-law's family moved from Cuenca to Belmonte, where the couple resided. Fray Luis was nineteen years old at the time (Sicroff 1996, 279–80).

30. Regarding the crucial role played by crypto-Jewish women, see now Melammed 1999.

31. Bataillon 1982a, 166–76; Kamen 1998, 86–89; Selke 1980. For Valencia, see Haliczer's chapter on Illuminism, Erasmianism, and Protestantism (1990, 273–94).

32. See also Kamen 1998, 269–76. The standard work on the subject, of course, is Caro Baroja 1997; see also Caro Baroja 1996, 155–268.

33. See Caro Baroja 1986, 1: 359–69, 474–80; Domínguez Ortiz 1992, 85–94; Costa Fontes 1990–93, 68–69.

34. See Domínguez Ortiz 1992, 100–02; Braunstein 1936; Selke 1972.

35. For specific studies on these *familiares*, see now Bravo Lozano 1980; Coronas Tejada 1980; and García Cárcel 1980.

36. In two of his plays, Lope de Vega, who was himself a *familiar*, used variants of a contemporary story that illustrates this fear. In *Mirad a quién alabáis* (c. 1620), an inquisitor sends a page to a Jew's home, asking him for a plate of pears from a tree that he had, and the Jew is so frightened that he burns the tree and sends it to him. In *En los indicios la culpa*, written around the same time, the Jew is replaced by a nobleman, the pear tree becomes an orange tree, and the inquisitor sends a *familiar* who leaves a message asking the absent nobleman for some orange flowers. The nobleman sends the whole tree in order to keep the *familiar* from ever coming back. Juan de Luna also used a variant of the same story in his *Segunda parte de la vida de Lazarillo de Tormes*, published in Paris (1620). Here, the terrified victim is a farmer (Silverman 1983).

37. Cohen 1982; Kamen 1998; Netanyahu 1995; 1999; Rivkin 1982; Roth 1995.

38. Israel S. Révah, who had taken the time to read numerous inquisitorial trials very carefully, disagreed strongly with these ideas. The polemic that ensued is brought together in the fifth edition of Saraiva (1985, 211–91).

39. Although most Jews were pious, many members of the elite subscribed to a philosophical or rationalist current that, by emphasizing reason, had corroding effects upon faith and revelation, leading to religious skepticism. The ultimate source for this philosophy was Aristotle, as modified by Averroes (1126–98), the Muslim philosopher from Córdoba who wrote a series of commentaries on Aristotle's works, and Maimonides (1135–1204), the greatest Jewish philosopher of the Middle Ages, also born in Córdoba, who proposed a more rational philosophy of Judaism. During the fifteenth century, pious Jews denounced the intellectuals in their midst for alleging that the Scriptures were not literally true but allegorical, for claiming that Divine Providence did not play a role in human affairs, replacing it with fate, for denying the immortality of the soul, and for placing natural law and natural morality above the laws of the Torah and the traditional religious commandments (Baer 1992, 2: 253–59). The denial of the immortality of the soul, of course, also meant that paradise did not exist, and that, therefore, it was not true that God rewarded or punished people for their actions (Márquez Villanueva 1994c; see also Fraker 1966, 20–30).

40. Faur dedicates a whole chapter to an examination of the various types of conversos (1992, 41–52).

41. According to Netanyahu, "'the overwhelming majority of the 'marranos' at the time of the establishment of the Inquisition were not Jews, but 'detached from Judaism,' or rather, to put it more clearly, Christians" (1999, 3; Span. ed.: 1994).

42. It is interesting to note that, in the Amsterdam community, which was started at the beginning of the sixteenth century, mainly by refugees from Portugal, the two Iberian countries were referred to as "terras de idolatria" ("lands of idolatry"; Y. Kaplan 2000, 44).

43. See also Gitlitz and Davidson's prize-winning book on the recipes of Spain's secret Jews, which were culled from various inquisitorial trials (1999). Concerning *adafina*, which corresponds to Ashkenazic *cholent*, see Alvar 1971, 38 and n42.

44. For abundant evidence of the manners in which Jews helped conversos to observe the tenets of Jewish faith, see Melammed 1999, 16–30.

45. For full translations of the Edict of Expulsion, see Beinart 1992c, 28–31; Constable 1997, 353–56.

46. The story of the "Niño de La Guardia," which provoked great indignation throughout the country, probably influenced the opinion of the masses considerably. In 1490, in La Guardia, a small town near Toledo, several Jews and conversos were accused of crucifying a little Christian boy on Good Friday, in order to use his heart and blood, together with a stolen consecrated Host, in a satanic ritual designed to destroy all Christians. The accused were tried by the Inquisition and burned in Avila on November 16, 1491. This obviously false story of ritual murder provided much material for writers, including Lope de Vega, who took it to the stage and published it as *El santo niño de La Guardia*, and with the variant title of *El niño inocente de La Guardia* as well (1617; see Barkaï 1994b, 32; Beinart 1992c, 25–26; Caro Baroja 1986, 1: 181–88; J. Edwards 1999; Sicroff 1980, 701–03). Lope's play was re-edited in 1985.

47. Attempting to keep out Spanish refugees, supposedly in fear of their competition, the Jews of Rome offered the Pope 1,000 ducats. Alexander VI allowed them to settle in the city anyway and punished the Roman Jews by fining them for the same amount as the bribe. Moreover, he also forced them to give lodgings to the Spaniards (Allegra 1983, 24). So much for consistency.

48. The baptism was held in a sanctuary built to honor the Virgin Mary, reported to have appeared to a shepherd on the margins of the Guadalupe River at the beginning of the fourteenth century. As the town grew, it attracted many Jews, some of whose converso descendants became monks in the Jeronimite monastery previously discussed. The sanctuary was one of the Monarchs' favorite pilgrimage sites (S. García 1995).

49. According to the anti-Semitic Bernáldez, however, they managed to take out plenty of money by swallowing it: "Enpero es verdad que sacaron infinito oro e plata escondidamente, e en especial muchos cruzados e ducados abollados, en los vientres, que los tragavan e sacavan en el vientre, en los pasos donde avían de ser buscados e en los puertos de la tierra e del mar; e en especial las mugeres tragavan más, ca a persona acaescía tragar treinta ducados de una vez" ("However, it is true that they took out much hidden gold and silver, and especially many folded *cruzados* and ducats in their bellies, for they swallowed and thus got them through the places where they were to be searched, and in mountain passes and seaports. The women swallowed even more, for some gulped down thirty ducats at a time"; 1962, 256). Note that this statement reflects the love of money attributed to Jews, the medieval idea regarding the avarice of women, and the thirty coins reputedly paid to Judas for betraying Christ.

50. One of the extant manuscripts says "primera."

Chapter Two
Repression and Artistic Expression

1. After Whinnom 1980, most scholars have preferred to omit the article from the title.

2. All quotations from Delicado, *Lozana*, will be taken from the 1985 edtion.

3. Gilman 1972, 35–39. The family tree and the accompanying comments, which Gilman and Gonzálvez had published previously (1966, 19–23), are reproduced on pp. 498–504.

4. For a transcription of his trial, see Serrano y Sanz 1902, 260–80; the date of 1480 was chosen because the "crimes" that he confessed dated back to that year (277, 279).

5. Fernando Valle Lersundi, who descended from Rojas, published a full transcription in 1929.

6. Gilman's pathfinding biography is enriched by so many extensive commentaries, pertinent asides, and interesting insights that it is difficult to bring the essential facts together. For two excellent and succinct biographies where this is done, drawing much of their information from Gilman himself, see Dunn 1975, 13–19, 23–25, 29–31 and Lacarra 1990, 11–17.

7. Allegra hypothesized that Delicado was still alive at the time, surmising that the book would have been difficult to publish "sin la presencia y el acicate del que lo había escrito" ("without the presence and the pressure of the one who had written it";1983, 48), but it could also have been published posthumously. As we will see, there is no trace of Delicado after 1534.

8. See, for example, the prologues to his editions of *Celestina*, the *Amadís*, and *Primaleón* (rpt. in Gallina 1962, 79–80).

9. The first date makes more sense, however. Since we know that Delicado became syphilitic in 1502 or 1503, he would have to be only twelve or thirteen years old if he had been born in 1489.

10. For a fuller description of this engraving, see Ugolini 1974–75, 462–64.

11. De Voragine 1993, 2: 23–24; for a detailed study of the legend and its metamorphoses, see Delpech 1986; 1994; C. Vega 1995.

12. Regarding the custom of reading books out loud during the sixteenth and seventeenth centuries—Delicado himself refers to "letores y audientes" ("readers and listeners"; 492)—see Frenk 1997. For Delicado's text, which is rather short, see now Joset 1998, 302–04.

13. On *humilitas* and the related technique of *captatio benevolentiae*, see Curtius 1963, 407–13.

14. In 1534, in his introduction to Book III of *Primaleón*, Delicado reveals his authorship of *La Lozana andaluza*, which he had written "en el común hablar de la polida Andaluzía" ("in the common speech of polished Andalusia"; E. Asensio 1960–63, 1: 110), and praises the form of Castilian that was spoken there, while recognizing that the language is best spoken in Old Castile. Asensio argued that, in his *Diálogo de la lengua*, Juan de Valdés mistreats Nebrija, who was also Andalusian, in order to get at Delicado, but Guitarte disagreed. In his opinion, Valdés does not have Delicado in mind, and what he really criticizes is Nebrija's tendency to treat Castilian as a classical language (Guitarte 1979, 162).

15. Ugolini (1974–75, 484–91) and Allegra (1976) hypothesized that he was the same as the Francisco Delgado who was named bishop of Lugo in 1561 and transferred to Jaén in 1566, where he died in 1576, but D. Villanueva argued convincingly that this was a case of mere homonymity (1980).

16. See Castro 1971, 326–406. The saint was believed to appear, mounted on a white horse, in order to help Christians in their battles against Muslims; hence his title of "Santiago matamoros" ("St. James, killer of Moors").

17. In Portugal, the expressions "gente de nação" ("people of nation") and "homens de negócios" ("businessmen") were practically synonymous (Saraiva 1985, 127–40). Note that, already in 1450, Fernán Pérez de Guzmán referred to conversos as "una naçion" ("a nation [people]"; 1965, 93).

18. On the use of the apostle's name as part of a battle cry, see Castro 1971, 350–52.

19. Failing to see this, Allegra deduced that the author must have been a good Christian, since a crypto-Jew would not care to invoke the saint (1983, 52), but the irony involved here suggests precisely the opposite.

20. In *El cerco de Numancia*, a play that he wrote in the 1580s, Cervantes suggests precisely the same by naming Attila as one of the avengers of the Numantines, portrayed as brave Spaniards who commit collective suicide so as not to surrender to the Romans. But Attila did not allow his Huns to enter and sack Rome. Since the sack of 1527 is mentioned right after, the implication is clear:

Estas injurias vengará la mano	These injuries will be avenged by the hand
del fiero Atila en tiempos venideros,	of the fierce Attila in coming times,
poniendo al pueblo tan feroz romano	subjecting the cruel Roman people
sujeto a obedecer todos sus fueros.	to obey all of his laws.
Y portillos abriendo en Vaticano,	And tearing breaches in the Vatican,

tus bravos hijos, y otros estranjeros,   your brave children, with other
                                                                foreigners,
harán que para huir vuelva la planta   will make the great pilot of the
                                                                Holy Ship
el gran piloto de la nave santa.   show the soles of his feet and run.
     (Cervantes 1984, 56)

(For a perceptive examination of the telling ambiguities in this play, see Johnson 1981).

21. His 1531 edition of *La Celestina*, which was reprinted in 1534, retains the earlier essay on Spanish pronunciation, but deletes the earlier reference to his role as proofreader. This may indicate that he was no longer living. The parish archives of Venice for this period could probably confirm or refute this hypothesis, but they no longer exist (Ugolini 1974–75, 488–89).

22. The research to which we owe these findings is widely dispersed; Domínguez Ortiz brings much of it together in a chapter entitled "Los conversos y la cultura española" (1992, 205–40).

23. On Alvarez Gato, see Márquez Villanueva 1960, 43–79; Antón de Montoro: Gerli 1994–95; Rodríguez Puértolas 1990; Roncero López 1996; Scholberg 1971, 310–27; Juan de Mena: Lida de Malkiel 1941; 1950, 92–94 (E. Asensio 1967, 344–51, Carballo Picazo 1952, 273, and Street 1953, 151–52, disputed that he was a converso, however); Rodrigo Cota: Cantera Burgos 1970; Scholberg 1971, 320–26; Fray Iñigo de Mendoza: Rodríguez Puértolas 1968a, 13–65; 1968b, 325–28 (Fray Iñigo was a great-grandson of Pablo de Santa María); Mosén Diego de Valera: Gerli 1996–97; Rodríguez Puértolas 1998, 194–97; Diego de San Pedro: little is known about his life, including the dates of his birth and death (see Alborg 1992, 454n35; Parrilla 1995, xxxvii–xl; Whinnom 1974, 17–28); for summaries of the evidence regarding his converso background and overviews of the bibliography on the subject, see Whinnom 1974, 19–21; 1985, 17–21; Parrilla 1995, xl.

24. On Fray Luis, see Lázaro Carreter 1986, 19–27; Sicroff 1996. Tomás Álvarez (1995) and Toft (1995) present good syntheses regarding the background of St. Theresa and St. John of the Cross, respectively. For additional religious and mystic sixteenth-century writers of Jewish extraction, see Gómez-Menor 1995.

25. In reference to this early generation, Américo Castro pointed out: "El teatro español no hubiera nacido de no haber sido conversos, *judíos de casta*, Juan del Encina, Lucas Fernández, Torres Naharro y Diego Sánchez de Badajoz" ("Spanish theater would not have come into existence if Juan del Encina, Lucas Fernández, Torres Naharro, and Diego Sánchez de Badajoz had not been converts of Jewish extraction"; 1963, 272). Regarding Juan del Encina, see now Márquez Villanueva 1987; 2001.

26. On Ruiz de Alarcón, see King 1989, 17–36, and Márquez Villanueva's review of this book (1991). Constance H. Rose has written extensively on Antonio Enríquez Gómez (1973; 1977; 1987; 2000). On the latter, see also Lázaro Cebrián 1994 and Rica 1994.

27. See Bataillon 1964a; C. Rose 1971; 1983.

28. See McGrady 1968, 13–14. Márquez Villanueva (1983) identified Mateo Alemán with the Perlícaro of Jewish extraction who in 1605 is insulted by the protagonist of López de Úbeda's *La pícara Justina* (1982, 83–100) for his scandalous life and for delving into "astronomy" (read "astrology") and mathematics. Justina also threatens him with the only jail where he had not yet been: the jail of the Inquisition. Alemán hurriedly decided to emigrate to Mexico, even though he had already reached the age of sixty (see Márquez Villanueva 1994a).

29. On Buero Vallejo, see Halsey 1994 and Willis-Altamirano 2001; on Casona, see Moon 1985.

30. For additional examples, see Scholberg 1971, 338–44.

31. In their edition of the *Cancionero*, Dutton and González Cuenca indicate that the Costanilla is a street in Seville (Baena 1993, 640), but the euphemistic allusion to its inhabitants as "gallegos" makes it more likely to be the proverbial Costanilla de Valladolid, which, as we shall see in Chapter 3, is later linked with the squire in the third treatise of *Lazarillo de Tormes*.

32. Known as typology, this relationship has been defined as "the practice in the New Testament and the early church whereby a person or a series of events occurring in the Old Testament is interpreted as a type of foreshadowing of some person (almost invariably Christ) or feature in the Christian dispensation" (Metzger and Coogan 1993, 783–84). Thus, Christ is also known as "the New Adam." For a splendid application of typology to Berceo's *Milagros de Nuestra Señora*, see Gerli 1985; 1987, 35–48.

33. For a similar use of the words *syllogism* and *sophism* in *La Lozana andaluza*, see Chapter 7 (pp. 220, 256).

34. In 1492, "450 Jews of Málaga were designated as *Judíos moriscos* ('Morisco Jews') in the records of the conquerors" (Shepard 1982, 82) and "the Moor, in the vocabulary of the Spanish Golden Age, is often a Jewish converso" (81).

35. Rodrigo Cota (died after 1504), on the other hand, lived long enough to see his own brother Alonso burned (1486) and a nephew reconciled (1493; see Scholberg 1971, 326).

36. In other words, since Christ had forgiven the Jews, who, according to popular belief, were the ones who had crucified him, the Queen ought to forgive and protect the conversos.

37. As Ciceri pointed out, what we have here is "un'atroce burla" ("a horrible joke"): "Quando farà freddo, saranno più tollerabili gli incendi" ("The fires will be more tolerable / when it gets cold"; 1989, 446–47).

38. Somehow, circumcision came to be connected with castration and then with both impotence and homosexuality (Ciceri 1980, 34). According to the violently anti-Semitic *Libro llamado el Alboraique* (1488), sodomy was first practiced by Jews, who passed it on to the Moors; these, in their turn, taught it to bad Christians (Ciceri 1980, 34). The libel was so widespread that the exiles who went to Portugal in 1492 were accused of introducing homosexuality into that country (S. E. Rose 1983, 5).

39. Incest was another favorite accusation, and Jews were also supposedly cuckolds, since their wives were wont to cheat on them (S. E. Rose 1983, 3; see also Shepard 1982, 71). The reasoning, I imagine, is that, having been rendered impotent through circumcision, Jews were unable to satisfy their wives.

40. Jamila = "beautiful" in Arabic. The Arabism's implication would not be lost on readers. No Christian woman would have such a name, but Jews would have, just as they continue to have them in Morocco down to the present day: Alegría > Freha; Estrella > Nejma; Fortunée > Mes°oda. I would like to thank one of the anonymous readers for these observations.

41. On occasion, even Valera himself had to confront his past (see Rodríguez Puértolas 1998, 194–97).

42. Despite all the evidence to the contrary, Gregory Kaplan believes that such a code could not possibly exist: "My use of the term 'code' is not meant to imply that the writers I study created a secret discourse that was only comprehensible to *conversos*" (2002, 37).

43. Regarding his complex role, see Dunn 1979; Gerli 1989b; Mandrell 1983–84; Wardropper 1952.

44. All the quotations from San Pedro, *Cárcel*, will be taken from the 1984 edition.

45. I would like to thank Jack Weiner and Rabbi Javier E. Cattapan for bringing this to my attention.

46. Regarding this passage, see also Márquez Villanueva 1966, 193–94.

47. See Gerli 1981; Lida de Malkiel 1946; Tillier 1985.

48. The English translation of the *Holy Bible* just quoted follows the Vulgate: "vocavitque Pharao Abram et dixit ei quidnam est quod fecisti mihi quare non indicasti quod uxor tua esset quam ob causam dixisti esse sororem tuam ut tollerem eam mihi in uxorem nunc igitur ecce coniux tua accipe eam et vade" (Gen. 12.18–19; all Latin quotations from the Vulgate are taken from *Biblia Sacra* 1994). Pharaoh also marries Sarah in all the early Spanish Bibles that I was able to consult (*Biblias medievales romanceadas*; *Biblia medieval romanceada*; *Escorial Bible I..I.7*; *Escorial Bible I..ii.19*; *Biblia ladinada*; *Ladino Bible of Ferrara*). Since Pharaoh always marries Sarah, it seems reasonable to surmise that they slept together. To Samuel G. Armistead, my gratitude for enabling me to consult all of these Bibles. Incredibly, my modern Spanish *Santa Biblia* (1983) does not take matters as far. Since Pharaoh complains to Abraham that "yo pude haberla tomado por esposa," the marriage does not seem to take place.

49. In Alfonso X's *General estoria* Sarah also manages to escape from Pharaoh, but there is no prayer and God is always called "Dios" (1930, 111–12).

50. For a general introduction, see Strauss 1952, 22–37. Carrasco 1995, Márquez Villanueva 1998, and Surtz 1995 are useful for medieval and Golden Age Spain; for Franco's Spain, see Halsey 1994 and Ilie 1994. Nepaulsingh 1995 focuses on the Golden Age, but his arguments are not always convincing.

Chapter Three
The Idea of "Limpieza" in *Celestina*, *La Lozana andaluza*, and Other Literary Works

1. Unfortunately, Pablo de Santa María also became a great hater of the Jews. In his *Scrutinium Scripturarum*, he defines them as criminals and justifies the massacres of 1391 as divine punishment (Netanyhau 1995, 199–200).

2. Bernáldez penned his book in the form of *Memorias*, pretty much as the events that he witnessed were unfolding, and chap. 43, where he writes these words, focuses on the origins of the Inquisition. What we know for certain about the author is what he himself tells us in his work, but, early in the seventeenth century, Rodrigo Caro saw baptismal certificates signed by Bernáldez in Palacios between 1488 and 1513, and pointed out that the priest also served as chaplain to the infamous archbishop Diego de Deza (Bernáldez 1962, xviii–xxi).

3. For an extensive examination of this *Discurso*, see Sicroff 1960, 186–209; Domínguez Ortiz (1955, 94–97) discusses Salucio as well.

4. The 16th edition of the *Diccionario* of the Real Academia offers a "slightly" expanded definition: "Aplícase a las personas o familias que no tienen mezcla ni

raza de moros, judíos, herejes o penitenciados" ("It is applied to families without any mixture or blood of Moors, Jews, heretics, or people penanced by the Inquisition").

5. Allaigre, who, somehow, insisted on regarding *La Lozana andaluza* as an anti-Semitic work, pointed out that the emphasis here may lie on Sagüeso's proposal to bleed both women, because the word *sangrar* ("to bleed") was a euphemism for *desvirgar* ("to deflower"): "me pregunto si la dimensión erótica del juego sobre *sangre* y *sangrar* no es aquí el elemento que prevalece" ("I wonder if the element that prevails here is not the erotic dimension of the wordplay on *blood* and *to bleed*"; 1995, 44). As we have just seen, the emphasis in on lineage and, since all blood looks the same, Sagüeso's proposal entails a mockery of blood purity as well.

6. For bibliography on both points of view, see Snow 1985, nos. 57, 105–06, 123, 195, 211, 306, 344, 349, 684, 763, 833. Cardiel has reviewed the main arguments in some detail (1981, 153–56).

7. For the five passages not discussed in this chapter, see pp. 136, 233, 261, 293, and 298 of Severin's 1987 edition. There is a double meaning when Calisto orders his servants to take good care in preparing him a horse, because he could just happen to pass by Melibea's house: "Saquen un cavallo; límpienle mucho; aprieten bien la cincha, por si passare por casa de mi señora y mi Dios" ("Let them bring me a horse, groom [*clean*] him down well, tighten up his bellyband, just in case I should pass by the house of my lady and my God"; 136). As confirmed by the fact that Pármeno wonders if the horse is neighing on account of Melibea ("¿No basta un celoso en casa, o baruntas a Melibea?" ["Isn't an aroused man in the house enough? Or do you also sniff Melibea?"; 137]), the horse that Calisto wants "cleaned" symbolizes lust, the very infirmity that afflicts him. Another level of humor lies in Calisto's admonition that the horse be tightly cinched, as if he feared falling off while passing by Melibea's house. In other words, he was afraid that he might not be able to control his passion, looking ridiculous in the process.

8. There may be a hint of lesbianism earlier (see Severin 1997, 418–19), when Celestina emphasized her friendship with Claudina to Sempronio with these words: "Juntas comiémos, juntas durmiémos, juntas aviémos nuestros solazes, nuestros plazeres, nuestros consejos y conciertos" ("We ate together, we slept together, we had our good times and fun [pleasure] together, and we took counsel and made our plans together"; 142).

9. For some unfathomable reason, there are critics who still feel uncomfortable with the paradoxically vital role played by the stifling institution of "limpieza de sangre" in Spanish literature. This is reflected in three translations of *Celestina* where Calisto's reference to "the awkward matter of purity of blood" is rendered as "your pure intentions" and "your sincerity" (see Silverman 1976, 157n20).

10. This word is missing in the Zaragoza 1507 edition (Rojas 1987), but Severin includes it in her previous edition (1983, 205), and it appears in other editions of Rojas as well: i.e., Cejador 1968, 2: 146; Lacarra 1995, 118; Marciales 1985, 2: 241.

11. In the *Guzmán de Alfarache*, the hero's "levantisco" (Levantine, i.e., Eastern) father uses the same trick: "Tenía mi padre un largo rosario entero de quince dieces en que se enseñó a rezar —en lengua castellana hablo—, las cuentas gruesas más que avellanas. Éste se lo dio mi madre, que lo heredó de la suya. Nunca se le caía de las manos" ("My father had a long, whole rosary with fifteen decades of Ave Marias, with which he taught himself to pray—in Spanish, that is—and the beads were thicker than hazelnuts. My mother, who had inherited it from hers, gave it to him. It never left his hands"; Alemán 1981, 1: 107–08).

12. For other aspects of *Lazarillo de Tormes* as a converso work—the author's anonymity, the caustic, semi-outsider's view of contemporary society, the studious avoidance of the names of Jesus and Mary, and so on—see Castro 1967, 118–66; Gitlitz 2000; Lázaro Carreter 1972, 185–86; 1986, 27–35. Deyermond lists additional bibliography (1975, 26–27).

13. Barkaï 1994b, 34; as Barkaï pointed out, the expulsion of the Moriscos in 1609 and 1614 was even more cruel, for, whereas the Jews had been given the opportunity to convert in order to remain in their country, all the Moriscos were forced to leave (36).

14. As we shall see, the possibility of a Morisco author must be discarded. The book includes additional, oblique references to conversos of Jewish extraction, and the works penned by Moriscos did not circulate among the general population.

15. See also Guillén 1966, 35–47; 1971, 167–215; Holzinger 1978; Shipley 1977–78.

16. This brings to mind *La española inglesa*, an exemplary novel where Cervantes, instead of contrasting two different periods implicitly, compares two countries instead, for he makes his readers think about the situation of Iberian crypto-Jews by focusing on their crypto-Catholic counterparts in England. See Costa Fontes 1975; García Gómez 1990–93; Ricapito 1996b, 39–68.

17. In this splendid paper, Vasvari (1995) studies a fifteenth-century Flemish triptych that depicts the couple who commissioned the painting in a kneeling position, the Annunciation, and St. Joseph. St. Joseph is ironically engaged in building mousetraps at the very moment that the Angel Gabriel announces to the Blessed Mother that she is about to conceive and bear a son. Prof. Vasvari goes on to document the phallic significance of the mice that St. Joseph is trying to keep out of his home through numerous examples in various languages.

18. Don Juan Manuel had already given literary form to this tale during the fourteenth century (1991, no. 32). See also Goldberg 1998, K445 and X502.

19. Regarding the glorification of peasants in Golden Age or "early modern" theater in general, and their conflicts with the nobles, who were not believed to be as "pure," see also Salomon's fundamental book (1985, 685–705).

20. For other readings of this playlet as an attack on "limpieza de sangre," see E. Asensio 1973, 188–91; Bataillon 1964c, 260–62; Kirschner 1981; Lerner 1971; Moner 1981; Reed 1993, 150–75; Salomon 1985, 114–15; Wardropper 1984.

21. Cervantes 1982, 3: 258. I have transcribed Silverman's quotation of this passage from "Saber vidas ajenas" (1978, 202) because of the manner in which key expressions are emphasized, as well as for the laconic but revealing commentary inserted in brackets.

22. Cannavagio's summation of the problem reflects the views of many scholars: "Did Cervantes want to be the defender of established values? Or was he, on the contrary, out of tune with his epoch? Whatever his choices may have been, to insist that they were dictated to him by his membership in one of the two castes is to fall into the trap of superficial determinism. In Cervantes, let us not forget, the doctrinaire never takes precedence over the artist, and the subversive power of his *oeuvre* transcends the design from which it seems, at first sight, to proceed. To know that the most illustrious writer of the Golden Age, the very symbol of Spain's universal genius, was a *converso* forced to conceal his origins may perhaps throw light on certain aspects of his mental universe, but it will never provide us with a key to its creation" (1990, 20). This is very true. Unfortunately, some scholars prefer to ignore or deny this aspect of Cervantes's works as if, somehow, it detracted from his literary achievements, rather than adding to their richness and complexity.

23. This passage came to my attention thanks to Silverman 1971a, 701n30, where it is used to document the great hatred that Alemán had for peasants in general, partly because they felt themselves inherently superior to certain *hidalgos* ("nobles") by virtue of their proclaimed *limpieza* ("purity").

24. As we have seen, Jews and some converts thought that she was anything but pure; obviously, it is impossible to demonstrate that Alemán also had this in mind.

25. This also recalls the "limpieza" of the bed of a postitute, Areúsa, in *Celestina*.

26. As far as I know, no one has yet demonstrated that Alonso de Proaza (see McPheeters 1961), a humanist apparently born in Asturias, which was supposedly free from Jewish or Moorish contamination, was a New Christian, but, as we know, many converts tried to escape prejudice by claiming that their ancestors were either from Asturias or La Montaña (Castro 1963, 97–98; Gilman 1972, 46–47; Glaser 1954, 49–50; Silverman 1961, 289–301). Moreover, Proaza did write, and, as Marciales pointed out while trying to demonstrate—mistakenly, I think—that Rojas had nothing to fear from the Inquisition, "casi todos los que escribían lo eran" ("almost all of those who were writing were [New Christians]"; 1985, 1: 37).

Chapter Four
Celestina as an Antithesis of the Blessed Mother

1. The first edition, entitled *Comedia de Calisto y Melibea* (Burgos, 1499), consists of sixteen acts. The single copy that has reached us lacks the title page and begins with the general summary that precedes Act 1. The next two editions (Toledo, 1500; Seville, 1501) include essentially all the preliminary materials—title and subtitle, letter from the author to a friend, eleven acrostic stanzas of eight verses each (a twelfth was added subsequently), an *incipit*, the general summary—sixteen acts, and six stanzas in which the *corrector* ("editor") Alonso de Proaza tells readers how to figure out the acrostic, which reads "El bachjller Fernando de Roias acabo la comedia de Calysto y Melybea y fve nascjdo en la Pvebla de Montalvan" ("The Bachelor Fernando de Rojas finished the comedy of Calisto and Melibea and was born in Puebla de Montalbán"). In 1502 there appeared in Seville a new edition that added the prologue found after the preliminary verses, five new acts, known as "Tratado de Centurio" ("Centurio's Treatise"), and the three postliminary stanzas placed just before those written by Alonso de Proaza. Although the title was changed from *Comedia* to *Tragicomedia*, the author himself continues to use both in the *incipit*: "Síguese la Comedia o Tragicomedia de Calisto y Melibea" ("There follows the Comedy or Tragicomedy of Calisto and Melibea"; 82). The first example of this edition, which has been lost, is an Italian translation (Rome 1506). The first integral Spanish version appeared a year later (Zaragoza 1507).

2. Gilman examined these summaries in an article (1954–55) that he appended to his *The Art of "La Celestina"* (1956, 212–16; trans. into Span. 1974, 327–35). According to Gilman, Rojas was responsible for the summaries of the five new acts, revising the one for Act 14 as well. As McGrady convincingly argued, Rojas probably also wrote the general summary, in order "to fill in for the lacuna created by the missing folios" (1994, 39).

3. For a succinct summary of authorship theories, see Snow 1991, iv; this is a prologue to a book that offers yet another theory (Sánchez Sánchez-Serrano and

Prieto de la Iglesia 1991). Faulhaber's discovery of an early sixteenth-century ms. with a good portion of Act 1 (1990), which may constitute a copy of Rojas's holograph ms. (Faulhaber 1991), has led to much discussion. For bibliography and summaries of the arguments presented thus far, see Botta 1993, 1997; Conde 1997; and Orduna 1999.

4. If that was indeed the case, Cota is a far more likely candidate (Russell 1991, 27–31).

5. See Russell 1991, 37–55 and Stern 1996, 190–200. After reviewing previous arguments, both scholars concluded that it is a play.

6. Fortunately, Snow provided us with a magnificent critical bibliography (1985), which he has continued to update in *Celestinesca*.

7. For succinct summaries of both positions, see Cardiel Sanz 1981; Sánchez Sánchez-Serrano and Prieto de la Iglesia 1991, 41–42.

8. The main parallel that comes to mind is Juan Ruiz's *Libro de buen amor*, but everyone would agree that its ambiguity was intentional.

9. I will return to the subject in this chapter.

10. Note that these words were of special meaning to conversos. Although Christ had died for them as well, Old Christians did not accept them as equals.

11. Melibea's *cordón* used to be rendered into English as "girdle," but "rope belt" is a much better translation.

12. Gerli 1983; Seniff 1985, 45. For the use of this imagery in balladry, see Armistead and Silverman 1971, 245–46n6; Rogers 1980, 6–40.

13. In a "glosa de amores" ("gloss about love") written by Juan del Encina, who, incidentally, was a priest, the poet begins by asking the lady to get ready for the joust ("Pues por vos crece mi pena, / quiero, señora, rogaros / que queráis aparejaros / a la justa que se ordena"; ["Since my suffering for you grows, / Madam, I would like to beg you / to get ready / for the required joust"]), and then asks her to put the "fabric" at his service with these words: "Que de mi dolor crecido / la tela será remedio" ("For my great suffering / the fabric will be remedy"; Alzieu et al. 1984, 9). As Lacarra pointed out, "la petición de amor que Calisto hace a Melibea es mucho más explícita que la ambigua piedad que los amadores sentimentales requieren de sus amadas como el primero de los escalonados favores que esperan recibir" ("the proposition that Calisto makes to Melibea is much more explicit than the ambiguous pity that sentimental lovers ask their mistresses as the first of the gradual favors that they hope to receive"; 1990, 53).

14. As the verses that follow indicate, books were written with audiences in mind, for they were usually read out loud in front of groups of people (see Frenk 1997):

Si amas y quieres a mucha atención	If you are in love and want much attention
leyendo a Calisto mover los oyentes,	when you read Calisto's story, and to move your audience,
cumple que sepas hablar entre dientes;	you need to be able to mumble,
a vezes con gozo, esperança y passión,	at times with pleasure, hope, and passion,
a vezes ayrado con gran turbación;	at times angrily, with great confusion.
finge leyendo mil artes y modos;	While reading feign a thousand guises,

pregunta y responde por boca de todos,	ask and reply through everyone's mouth,
llorando o riyendo en tiempo y sazón. (345)	crying or laughing when appropriate.

15. See Costa Fontes 1997a, and now Costa Fontes 2000, 27–34, 51.

16. When Sempronio goes to Celestina's house, Elicia hides the client she is with in a broom closet, but Sempronio hears a noise. When Celestina says that it is a girl that a monk had ordered, he asks to see her, and Elicia, pretending to be jealous, becomes very angry. Sempronio calms her down as follows: "Calla, dios mío; ¿y enójaste? Que no la quiero ver a ella ni a mujer nascida" ("Be silent, my God! Why are you angry? I didn't want to see her or any other woman"; 106).

17. The expression, which is a translation of "amour courtois," was popularized by Gaston Paris at the end of the nineteenth century (Whinnom 1984, 15–16).

18. This title, which was soon popular among common readers, is first used in the Italian translation of 1519 (for an example from a will from 1511, see Kirby 1989), but it took much longer for it to be adopted in Spanish editions. For a thorough survey and discussion of the subject, see Kelley's study (1985).

19. As Gurza (1997) acknowledges, this idea had already been put forth by Correa (1962, 11n14).

20. For additional interpretations, see the entry for "Characterizations: Celestina" in the index to Snow's indispensable bibliography (1985, 100*b*).

21. The sixteenth-century glossator of the *Celestina comentada* interpreted Celestina's name in the same manner (Corfis 1998, 45–46).

22. Besides providing a useful summary of the various hypotheses, Abrams (1972–73) advances a new one of his own.

23. See Gurza 1977, 166; according to this author, the suffix *-ina* diminishes the qualities implied by "celeste" to a certain extent.

24. In the words of Cherchi, "un nombre como Celestina evoca mundos celestiales, angélicos, puros, es decir todo lo contrario de lo que la alcahueta es" ("a name like Celestina evokes celestial, angelical, pure worlds, that is to say, the complete opposite of what the procuress represents"; 1997, 84).

25. I added the exclamation and the accent on "dexó."

26. Zaragoza 1507 says "acerro," but Severin's previous edition (1983, 163) and others make it clear that the word in question ought to be "acorro": see Rojas 1968, 2: 67 (Cejador); 1985, 2: 188 (Marciales); 1995, 89 (Lacarra).

27. I refer to the Litany of Loreto, which, although used at that shrine only since the middle of the sixteenth century, is traceable to the early Middle Ages, when there were several other Marian litanies as well. Rojas was probably familiar with one or more litanies similar to that of Loreto, but I am unable to determine which. In the pages that follow, I omit the six titles (nos. 12, 45–49) added to that litany after its approval by Pius V in 1587. For a brief but instructive article concerning the litany in question, see the *New Catholic Encyclopedia* 1967, 8: 790–91 (I refer to its articles by volume and page number rather than by title because the other entries that I used are relatively lengthy). My source for the Latin titles is the *Saint Andrew Daily Missal* (1953), but they can be easily found in most missals.

28. Morón Arroyo understood this aspect of Celestina's figure clearly, for he states that Calisto addresses her "como el más devoto católico pudiera decir a la Virgen" ("as the most devout Catholic could address the Virgin"; 1984, 103), but he justifies this as an example of literary irony. That is indeed the case, but only when viewed in isolation, without being put together with everything else that follows; then it becomes an allegory.

29. Love was the cause of lovesickness ("mal de amores"), which, as we know, was regarded as a real sickness in the Middle Ages. Contemporary medical treatises dealt with the subject seriously. See Cátedra 1989; Macpherson and Mackay 1998, 188–95; Shipley 1975; Wack 1990; Whinnom 1984, 13–14.

30. Adams 1982, 154; these and other euphemisms and metaphors in *Celestina* are studied in Costa Fontes 1984; 1985; 1992, 86–92; 2000, 55–79; R. Ferré 1983; Gerli 1983; Handy 1983; Herrero 1984; 1986; Lacarra 1990, 45–50; 1996; Weinberg 1971; Weiner 1969; West 1979.

31. The expression "en tiempo honesto" ("at a decent hour"; 110) is used maliciously, in an ironic manner, for the middle of the night was far from being an appropriate time for any women, much less nuns, to leave their homes, and the "devotions" that they attend in Celestina's house are anything but legitimate.

32. Marciales also agrees that the apparent religious ceremonies take place in Celestina's house for, noting that the second part of the passage under scrutiny lacks a verb, he edits the text as follows: "Subió su hecho a más: que por medio de aquellas comunicaba con las más encerradas, hasta traer a execución su propósito. Y aquestas en tiempo onesto, como estaciones, processiones de noche, missas del gallo, missas del alva y otras secretas devociones, *muchas encubiertas vi entrar en su casa*" (1985, 2: 36).

33. As Lacarra pointed out, here the word *llorar* ("to weep") is a euphemism for *eyacular* ("to ejaculate"; 1996, 426).

34. In her analysis of the passage under scrutiny, Severin comes very close to this interpretation, for she suggests that Celestina's hovel is being turned into a convent (1980, 696). In other words, that critic also sees these activities as occurring in Celestina's house.

35. "One obvious corollary of the doctrine of the virgin birth was the emphasis on virginity and on clerical celibacy. 'Because the Lord's body grew together in the temple of the Virgin Mary's womb, he now requires of his ministers the purity of sexual continence.' Christ had not only remained a virgin himself and chosen to be born of a Virgin, but he had even selected as his guardian and putative father one who was also a virgin" (Pelikan 1978, 163–64).

36. Although it could be argued that this is where Celestina "seduces" nuns, not in her house, it goes without saying that the affairs that she arranges were less likely to be consummated in those places of worship.

37. As Castro suggested, this passage is probably inspired by *La misa de amor* (1965, 96–97), a ballad that still survives in the modern Castilian, Catalán, Galician, Portuguese, Spanish-American, and Sephardic traditions, and which is also known as *La bella en misa* (see Armistead et al. 1978, S7; Costa Fontes 1997b, S4).

38. The present edition (1987, based on Zaragoza 1507) has "Assí" here, but the other editions consulted confirm that "allí" is the correct word. See Rojas 1968, 2: 45 (Cejador); 1983, 151 (Severin); 1985, 2: 171 (Marciales); 1995, 80 (Lacarra).

39. Since Calisto speaks in earnest, his words cannot be regarded as mere hypocrisy. Although some irony is involved here—Calisto regards Celestina as a "savior"—the fact remains that one does not pray to God for such things. There may be yet another level of heresy. According to Morón Arroyo, this prayer imitates those found in missals and, therefore, it ought to conclude with a reference to Christ and the Holy Spirit. In that scholar's opinion, the omission "se debe probablemente al respecto de Rojas, sincero católico, por el misterio de la Santísima Trinidad. La Trinidad, punto crucial de la lucha entre cristianos y judíos, no debía ser mencionada en una obra de entretenimiento y menos en sentido paródico" ("is probably due to Rojas's respect, as a sincere Catholic, for the mystery of the Holy Trinity. The Trinity, a crucial point in the struggle between Christians and Jews, should not be mentioned in a work of entertainment, and much less as part of a parody"; 1984, 44). As we will see in the next chapter, however, Rojas probably attacked the Holy Trinity as well.

40. As Garci-Gómez suggested on the basis of ample documentation (1981), and as Kish and Ritzenhoff confirmed subsequently (1981), these "huevos asados" do indeed refer to bull's testicles, a folkloric aphrodisiac euphemistically designated as "mountain oysters" in some parts of the United States. According to the glossator of the *Celestina comentada*, the expression also meant *cornudo* ("cuckold") (Fernández-Rivera 1993).

41. This word is missing in Zaragoza 1507, but Severin includes it in her previous edition (Rojas 1983, 165).

42. Zaragoza 1507 says "a quien tú das dinero," but the present reading appears in Dr. Severin's previous edition (Rojas 1983, 166) and others (i.e., Lacarra's [1995, 90] and Russell's [1991, 449].)

43. The fact that Celestina also wishes to make a very good impression on Calisto in order to profit as much as possible from him does not detract from this interpretation.

44. See Costa Fontes 1985 and the bibliography in note 30, above.

45. For another, interesting evaluation of Alisa's role, see Gerli 1995a.

46. Celestina's request for the prayer of Saint Appolonia, which Melibea promises to write down and give her the day after, involves yet another level of humor, for it is a folk spell for real, not metaphorical toothaches. Since contemporary readers and listeners understood this, the passage must have made them laugh their heads off. For an example of the spell in question, see Costa Fontes 1995, 97n2.

47. Some scholars still debate the power of the spell (i.e., Lima 1998) and whether Celestina was a demonic witch or a mere sorceress, but what matters here is what the characters themselves think. Vian Herrero puts it as follows in her useful review of the previous scholarship on the subject: "La eficacia de los hechizos celestinescos, dudosa para algunos críticos literarios, no lo es para varios personajes de la obra, que están convencidos de la pericia de la alcahueta" ("Some literary critics doubt the effectiveness of Celestina's witchcraft, but that is not the case with several characters in the work, for they are convinced of the bawd's skill in those matters"; 1990, 65). Severin investigates the subject in detail as well (1995). See also Corfis 1998, 53–54; Severin 1997 (on Pármeno's mother, Claudina, as another witch); Vian Herrero 1997.

48. This idyllic description embodies foreboding signs of doom, however. As Shipley pointed out, the clouds have negative connotations, and so do the cypresses, which were usually associated with cemeteries (1973–74, 292–93).

49. According to Ruggerio, the enclosed garden stands for Mary's Immaculate Conception (1970, 57n7), but this is very unlikely here. That dogma, which was not officially proclaimed by the Catholic Church until 1854 even though it was believed much earlier (see Recio 1955), proclaims that the Blessed Mother was born without the stain of the Original Sin bequeathed by Adam and Eve to their descendants. Since it is impossible to relate this dogma to the idea of the enclosed garden, it seems that Prof. Ruggerio, in his otherwise excellent article, is confusing Mary's perpetual virginity with her Immaculate Conception.

50. At another level, this parallels the association of love with war in courtly poetry, where the lady is at times portrayed as a fortress that the lover must conquer by breaching its walls (Macpherson and Mackay 1998, 202–03; Maurizi 1998).

51. Blay Manzanera 1996; see also Blay Manzanera and Severin 1999, 43 (s.v. "Serpent / snake"; "Viper").

52. People who had sex in front of others were denounced for behaving like dogs, and, by encouraging such voyeurism, "Calisto seeks to lower himself and Melibea to the level of beasts" (England 2000, 80). England lists additional examples of voyeurism in *Celestina*.

53. Concerning the use of this type of language in the *cancioneros*, see also Mackay 1989 (= Macpherson and Mackay 1998, 140–56); Macpherson 1985 (= Macpherson and Mackay 1998, 82–98); and Tillier 1985.

54. There was another example of voyeurism here, for Celestina watched the event. This involves a parody of the custom of having witnesses during the first night of the weddings of important nobles and royal couples, in order to prevent future claims, during divorce proceedings, that the marriages had not been consummated (Castro 1965, 163–66). But the custom could have undesired effects; some modern historians apparently take seriously "the idea that the performance of the future Enrique IV was impaired by the inhibiting presence of witnesses on the night of his marriage to Blanca de Navarra in 1440" (England 2000, 84). Whatever the case may have been, Ferdinand of Aragon, who married Henry IV's sister, Isabella, did not seem to have any problems. The witnesses took the precaution to examine the bloody sheet, and the result was apparently celebrated right after with trumpets and other high-pitched instruments: "El arçobispo los desposó y veló, e aquel dia todo se consumió en fiestas y danças e mucha alegria; e la noche venida, el prinçipe e la princesa consumieron el matrimonio y estavan a la puerta de la cámara çiertos testigos puestos delante, los quales sacaron la sábana que en tales casos suelen mostrar, demás de aver visto la cámara do se ençerraron; la qual en sacándola, tocaron todas las tronpetas y atabales y menistriles altos" ("The archbishop married and watched over them, and that day was spent in parties, dances, and much merriment. When night came, the prince and the princess consummated their marriage. In front of the door of the room there were certain witnesses, who, besides inspecting the chamber, took out that sheet that is usually displayed in such cases. Upon taking it out, all the trumpets, timbrels, and high-pitched instruments were played"; Mosén Diego de Valera, *Memorial de diversas hazañas*, qtd. in Real de la Riva 1962, 384).

55. Contrary to Calisto, who fell by accident, Melibea jumps from the tower willingly, but, nevertheless, her death also results from a fall. Unlike Eve, Melibea "left" of her own volition, but this small difference does not detract from the analogy.

56. After pointing out that this shows that Calisto's last-minute "confession" was insincere, Morón Arroyo observed: "¿hubiera escrito Rojas esas palabras si no hubiera concebido su obra en un contexto cristiano?" ("would Rojas have written these words if he had not conceived his work within a Christian context?"; 1984, 45). This is true, but, as we will see, it does not mean that Rojas could not be subverting Christianity as well.

57. This applies equally to Celestina, who also shouts for confession as she is about to die, even though, as a witch, she had made a pact with the devil, and, therefore, her soul belonged to him: "lo habitual es que cuando un ser humano establece un pacto con el demonio, los términos de acuerdo son que el diablo favorece al mago en vida, y el mago entrega a cambio su alma" ("the usual thing is that when a human being makes a pact with the devil, the terms of the agreement are that the devil helps the conjurer who, in exchange, gives him his soul"; Vian Herrero 1990, 61–62).

58. Since Celestina boasts at one point that here clients included "abades de todas dignidades, desde obispos hasta sacristanes" ("clergymen of all ranks, from bishops to sextons"; 235), "Rojas procuró dejar muy en claro . . . que los clientes de Celestina eran primordialmente hombres de iglesia" ("Rojas tried to make it very clear . . . that Celestina's clients were mostly men of the Church"; Márquez Villanueva 1993, 58).

59. Robbins 1959, 471, qtd. in Ruggerio 1966, 7; see also Maravall 1986, 150.

60. It must be noted here that the opposite seems to occur in *Celestina*; in a passage full of humor, the old bawd threatens to punish the devil if he does not obey her summons "con presto movimiento" ("quickly"; 148).

61. Here I exclude the references and allusions to the name of Christ in the prefatory and concluding verses because, at that point, Rojas is cautiously attempting to justify himself for having written *Celestina*, while addressing the reader in a more direct manner.

62. I am thinking of some of the Latin poems of the goliards (see Waddell 1934) and the *Carmina Burana* (see Parlett 1986). Concerning the Peninsular languages, in one of Alfonso X's *cantigas d'escarnho e de mal dizer* ("songs of mockery and slander"), a *soldadeira* ("camp follower") who feels that she must refuse a suitor because he approaches her at the hour in which Christ died, clearly compares her "suffering" with His Passion (Rodrigues Lapa 1995, no. 14; see also Costa Fontes 2000, 27–34, and note 50, above). There are two well-known examples in Juan Ruiz's *Libro de Buen Amor*: the song about "Cruz cruzada, panadera" ("Crossed Cross, baker woman" [cc. 114–20]. For the meaning of *panadera* and abundant bibliography, see Armistead 1992, 87; Márquez Villanueva 1988; Vasvari 1983) and the parody of the canonical hours (cc. 372–87; see Vasvari 1983–84). Eisenberg provides a succinct, profusely documented summary of this type of religious parody (1976, 164–65). María Rosa Lida's study (1946), of course, remains essential.

63. It is true that the "secret" language of the *cancioneros* ("songbooks"; Whinnom 1981b) included religious terms that were used in an erotic and even pornographic manner, but the code was familiar to a great number of people.

64. For these and other heresies attributed to specific conversos in inquisitorial trials, see Chapter 1, pp. 26–27.

65. As we have seen, the title page of *La Lozana andaluza* claims: "contiene munchas mas cosas que la Celestina" ("[it] contains many more things than *Celestina*"; Delicado 1985, 165).

66. "quomodo fiet istud quoniam virum non cognosco."

67. Although many Jews left Portugal in 1497, the Portuguese "expulsion" which bears that date did not really take place, because King Manuel I did not want to lose one of the most educated and productive sectors of the population; for a brief survey of the situation, see Costa Fontes 1990–93, 67–71.

68. On this ballad, see also Costa Fontes 1994–95a.

69. As Lapesa observed, these words do not indicate any devotion for the Blessed Mother: "Aunque sean palabras de la Salve, no van dirigidas a una intercesora Madre del Dios-Hombre, sino a una hija cuya pérdida ha dejado a su viejo padre en irremediable desamparo" ("Although these words are from the *Salve*, they are not addressed to the interceding Mother of the Man-God, but to a daughter whose loss has left her old father irremediably helpless"; 1997, 109).

70. As Snow aptly summarized, the world depicted in *Celestina* "is a world with few signs of redemption, a true *lachrymarum valle* as heard in Pleberio's text-closing lamentations" (1995, 254). Elsewhere, Snow makes it clear that, in his opinion, the use of religion does not correspond to real faith: "The closure of the *Tragicomedia* is hugely powerful. I see this in the resonating echoes that leave us with a sense of incompletion, and of issues unresolved. It is a work in which one senses that the frequent references to God, to confession, to mass, churches and more, are probably devoid of any sincere religious feeling" (1997, 453–54). According to Ruggerio, this is tantamount to an attack on Christianity: "it is difficult not seeing in the lament the idea that the promises of religion are hollow and, even more specifically that those of Christianity, represented by the hope of salvation in Christ through the mystery of transubstantiation, lead us down the primrose path and give us in return for our faith nothing but meaningless suffering" (1977, 77–78). Responding to the critics who interpret Pleberio's lament as existentialist, Márquez Villanueva, on the other hand, relates Rojas's attitude to the rationalism that was current among learned Jews during the Middle Ages: "Por supuesto que Rojas no tiene nada de 'existencialista,' pero algo viene, en cambio, de una tradición averroísta cuyo Dios es un despersonalizado supuesto metafísico, un *Deus otiosus* ajeno a toda idea de Providencia por su inadecuación para interferir en el mecanismo de causas segundas que rige el mundo sublunar" ("Clearly, Rojas is not an existentialist at all, but on the other hand there is something derived from the Averroist tradition, where God is an impersonal, metaphysical hypothesis, an apathetic God who is foreign to any idea of Divine Providence because of His inadequacy to interfere in the mechanism of secondary causes which governs the earth"; 1994c, 282).

71. As Castro, Gilman, and other scholars who understood that Rojas incorporated a corrosive, systematic attack on the social, religious, and literary values of his time previously suggested, the man who was capable of writing such a work could not have been a true Christian. For additional, extensive bibliography on this subject, see the entry for "Converso sentiment in LC" in Snow 1985, 101*b*; as already mentioned (note 7, above), Cardiel Sanz (1981) provides a useful summary of the main views on both sides of this argument. The two most recent surveys of the converso question in *Celestina* were undertaken by Salvador Miguel (1989) and Kirby (1987).

Chapter Five
Christian Prayer and Dogma in *Celestina*: The Polemic Continues

1. *Encyclopedia Judaica* 1974, 15: 1208–09; Schlichting 1982.

2. "viro qui corripientem dura cervice contemnit repentinus superveniet interitus et eum sanitas non sequitur."

3. "dic ad eos vivo ego dicit Dominus Deus nolo mortem impii sed ut revertatur impius a via sua et vivat."

4. "Intrantes autem in domum salutate eam et siquidem fuerit domus digna veniat pax vestra super eam."

5. "non in pane solo vivet homo sed in omni verbo quod procedit de ore Dei" (Matt. 4.4). Repeated in Luke 4.4.

6. "anima quae peccaverit ipsa morietur filius non portabit iniquitatem patris et pater non portabit iniquitatem filii."

7. "Milites ergo cum crucifixissent eum acceperunt vestimenta eius et feccerunt quattuor partes unicuique militi partem et tunicam erat autem tunica inconsutilis desuper contexta per totum dixerunt ergo ad invicem non scindamus eam sed sortiamur de illa cuius sit."

8. Pármeno had lived with Celestina when he was a little boy, we recall. When the old woman reminds him that he used to sleep by her feet, he replies that "aunque era niño, me subías a la cabecera y me apretavas contigo, y porque olías a vieja, me huýa de ti" ("although I was little, sometimes you'd haul me up to the head of the bed and squeeze me against you, and, since you smelled like an old woman, I would get away from you"; 120). Severin sees a hint of child molestation in these words (1997, 418). Interestingly, Pármeno says that he also spent nine years with the Jeronimite monks of Guadalupe (264). Since Sempronio mentions right after that he had worked for Mollejas the gardener before (265), and Rojas owned a piece of land known as the garden of Mollejas, Gilman hypothesized that the author may have studied with those monks in his youth (1972, 216–17n19).

9. "beati pacifici quoniam filii Dei vocabuntur."

10. "beati qui persecutionem patiuntur propter iustitiam quoniam ipsorum est regnum caelorum."

11. And this, of course, invalidates the interpretation that the episode embodies a criticism of the Inquisition (see Gilman 1972, 131–32).

12. See also Covarrubias 1994, 686, s.v. "Juan" (Severin quotes the pertinent passage in Rojas 1987, 217n25).

13. The neutral inclusion of St. John's name in a proverb does not constitute an exception.

14. Another level of irony is involved here, for Sempronio is also referring to a "third," phallic "foot."

15. "quam ob rem relinquet homo patrem suum et matrem et adherebit uxori suae et erunt duo in carne una" (Gen. 2.24).

16. See note 5, above.

17. For additional examples, see Costa Fontes 1987, nos. 692–98, 700–02, 704–06.

18. Since, given its shape, the tower is also a phallic image, the blasphemy that its placement in the *hortus conclusus* implies ought to be obvious.

19. "ecce ancilla Domini fiat mihi secundum verbum tuum."

20. As Rodríguez Puértolas pointed out (Rojas 1996, 220n23), these words may echo the angel's announcement of Jesus's birth to the sherpherds: "for today in the town of David a Savior has been born to you, who is Christ the Lord" ("quia natus est vobis hodie salvator qui est Christus Dominus in civitate David"; Luke 2.11).

21. The example that follows is from Shakespeare's *Passionate Pilgrim*:

> See in my thigh, quoth she, here was the sore:
> She showed hers; he saw more *wounds* that one,
> And blushing fled, and left her all alone.
> (Shakespeare 1937, 1275a [stanza 7])

As noted by Partridge, the pudenda is clearly implied (1968, 222). For more examples of the word *llaga* in *Celestina*, see Costa Fontes 2000, 64–68.

22. Since *pena* was a euphemism for the penis, these words may involve yet another level of heresy.

23. Concerning the images of the lover as "sailor" or "swimmer," which are frequent in both traditional and erotic poetry, see Morales 1981, 87–89, 107; Alzieu et al. 1984, 214, 229, 236, 269, 284; and Chapter 6, pp. 176–79.

24. It goes without saying that, since the Good Shepherd should not "shear" his flock, Rojas could have been suggesting that either Christ or his ministers deceive those who follow him. Concerning the image of the lover as "shepherd," see also Morales 1981, 71, 96, 149, 290; Olinger 1985, 108–16.

25. The Moriscos also mocked Christians for eating their God and then disposing of Him "Por aquel postigo viejo / que nunca fuera cerrado" ("Through that old wicket / that was never shut"; Cardaillac 1977, 321). These verses belong to an epic ballad, *El entierro de Fernandarias* (Armistead et al. 1978, A7; for the existence of this and other Christian ballads among the Moriscos, see Armistead 1978).

26. "Spiritus Sanctus superveniet in te et virtus Altissimi obumbrabit tibi ideoque et quod nascetur sanctum vocabitur Filius Dei."

27. For the full text of this letter, in another translation, see Kobler 1978, 1: 276–82.

28. "Calisto" means "hermosísimo" ("very handsome") and "Melibea" means "la de voz suave, dulce" ("the one with a soft, sweet voice"; Rojas 1968, 31–32n22).

29. I am grateful to a former student, Robert Sitler, for bringing this to my attention.

30. Juan del Encina was a priest, an apparently convinced converso. Why did he call attention to such logical inconsistencies, though? The matter certainly deserves further study. One important step would be to determine whether this type of poetry was also being written in other countries.

31. The latest *Catechism of the Catholic Church*, approved by John Paul II in 1992 (Eng. trans., 1995), allows for mitigating factors ("Grave psychological disturbances, anguish, or grave fear of hardship, suffering, or torture can diminish the responsibility of the one committing suicide"; 609 [no. 2282]), but this was not the case before.

32. "propterea sicut per unum hominem in hunc mundum peccatum intravit et per peccatum mors et ita in omnes homines mors pertransiit in quo omnes peccaverunt" (Rom. 5.12).

Chapter Six
"Sailing," Renaissance Rome, and Exile in *La Lozana andaluza*:
An Allegorical Reading

1. Allegra (1973) suggested that this was the Prince of Orange, who replaced Charles de Bourbon, who had been killed as the assault began, because, in one of the appendices, Delicado addresses him as "señor Capitán del felicísimo ejército imperial" ("Lord Captain of the victorious imperial army"; 491).

2. All quotations from Delicado, *Lozana*, we recall, are from the 1985 edition.

3. Note that the word *natural* has more than one meaning in this sentence. The girl's beauty comes to her either by nature or from her bearing, but it could also come from her "nature"—i.e., her private parts.

4. In my opinion (see Chapter 2, pp. 45, 47), this is probably a literary trick designed to present the sack as the result of a prophecy.

5. Although *La Lozana andaluza* used to be practically ignored, much has been written on it during the last few decades. Despite its lack of author or subject indexes, Damiani and Imperiale's bibliography (1998) is extremely useful.

6. Brakhage 1986; Damiani 1970; Díez Borque 1972, 463; Espantoso-Foley 1977, 7, 20; Ferrara de Orduna 1973.

7. Comparing *Celestina* with *Lozana*, Damiani writes that "ambas obras ofrecen cierta tesis moral: en la *Celestina*, el implícito propósito predicador, visto a través de la 'caída' de los 'locos enamorados'; en la *Lozana*, el castigo providencial del gran saco de Roma" ("both works offer a certain moral thesis: in *Celestina*, the implicit preaching purpose is seen through the 'fall' of 'unchaste lovers'; in *Lozana*, through the divine punishment that the great sack of Rome represents"; 1970, 242; also in Damiani 1969a, 14).

8. Many critics also focused on Delicado's innovative narrative (Allaigre 1980a; Díez Borque 1972; Espantoso-Foley 1980; E. Friedman 1987; Goytisolo 1977, 53–57; Imperiale 1991), linguistic (Bubnova 1990–93; Criado de Val 1960–63; Gella Iturriaga 1978; Gómez Sierra 1996; Porto Bucciarelli 1990) techniques, and his possible influence on Cervantes and López de Úbeda (Bubnova 1990; Vilanova 1952a).

9. See, for example, Espantoso-Foley 1980, 258–60.

10. Dunn refuted this thesis (1976a). He pointed out that, though written in prose, the appended "Carta de excomunión contra una cruel doncella de sanidad" (Letter of excommunication against a cruel health maiden) on which Damiani based his theory is really in verse, that the sentence is passed on the "doncella" ("maiden") by Cupid, not by the author, and that, rather than being personal, the "denunciation" "begins a mock-legal style into which is inserted a ferocious malediction which is clearly another comic parody, this time of those extensive curses in epic ballads and chivalresque romance" (357). The fact that the verses in question are adapted from a "Descomunión de amores fecha a su amiga" (Excommunication from Love to his mistress) attributed to a Comendador Ludueña (see Ugolini 1974–75, 478–83) reinforces even further Dunn's contention that "there is no reason to suppose that Delicado himself is addressing a real woman" (357). It is only fair to point out, however, that the unreliable narrator suggests that he is basing himself on a real person (172). Thus, he begins to amuse himself with his readers from the very beginning.

11. Since Allaigre 1985b summarizes his groundbreaking *Sémantique* (1980b), which is not as easily available, I refer to the latter only when it includes information not found in the former.

12. Regarding the symbolism of the fountain, see Costa Fontes 1998a, 12–14.

13. For a more easily available edition of the whole poem, see Bell 1967, no. 13; Nunes 1959, 369–70; or Reckert and Macedo n.d., no. 21. For a list of early variants, see Frenk 1987, no. 536A.

14. For a list of variants, see Frenk 1987, no. 945.

15. Pharies argued that the Sp. *singar* and *chingar*, meaning "to coit," are ultimately related to the OFr *singler*, "to navigate," a term that "was applied to sculling, or rowing with one oar at the stern of a boat, whence the secondary meanings 'to sway' and 'to coit,' the latter with typical tertiary meanings as well" (1994, 317). Since "the ship and seafaring served as the vehicle for various . . . types of sexual metaphors in Greek and Latin" (Adams 1982, 25), the phenomenon is probably of Indo-European, perhaps even universal, character. For Latin and Greek examples of the boat metaphorically used for the womb or vagina, and the rower or passenger as the male, see Adams 1982, 89, 167. For one Italian example, see Boccaccio 1992, 409–17 (Vasvari 1994 studies a similar aspect of Boccaccio's work). A French popular ballad, *Les filles de la Rochelle*, uses several sailing metaphors (see Bénichou 1970, 190, 229–32; Doncieux 1904, 419–20; Roy 1954, 269–70). For English examples drawn from Shakespeare, see Partridge 1968, 68 ("board," "board a land carack," "boarding"). John Donne uses sailing metaphors as well (see Allen 1961; Corthell 1989, 32 and 41nn56–57; Dane 1979, 203). These metaphors also appear in the anonymous "When first Amintas sued for a kiss," a poem included in the miscellany *Comes amoris* (9), printed in 1687, and in a modern English folksong, "O Come All Ye Little Streamers" (Hodgart 1962, 167–68). Allen, who traces the image of the boat of love to Ovid's *Ars amatoria* and *Remedia amoris*, refers to additional Italian, French, and English examples. As witnessed by the popular American television program *The Love Boat* and the cruise ship with the same name—from what I understand, it is berthed in Long Beach, California—the image is still alive and well.

16. Other versions: Braga 1906–09, 1: 596–97; Costa 1961, 322; Costa Fontes 1979, no. 567; Dos Santos 1897–99, 166; Ferré et al. 1982, no. 53; Galhoz 1987–88, no. 824; Leite de Vasconcellos 1958–60, no. 932; Purcell 1987, no. 8.2.

17. It was recited in Taunton, MA, by Guilherme Alexandre da Silveira, a septuagenarian from the Island of Flores, Azores, on January 14, 1978.

18. The modern folk tradition also refers to these constant moves of prostitutes. Having recorded an early story about a prostitute (see Costa Fontes 1990 and now 2000, 9–26), Guilherme Alexandre da Silveira (see note 17, above) attributed the "sailing" story summarized in this paper to the same woman, saying: "Ela mudou-se. Pa tornar ali, era conhecida, qu'ela era muito linda" ("She moved. She couldn't go back there, because everyone knew her. She was very pretty").

19. In this context, it is interesting to note that in Juan Ruiz's *Libro de Buen Amor* (1974), Pitas Pajas, the artist who, in order to ensure his wife's chastity, paints a small sheep under her bellybutton before leaving on a journey, tells her that he is going to Flanders with the following words: "yo volo ir a Frandes, portaré muyta dona" ("I want to go to Flanders, and I will bring many presents"; 475*b*). The painter's name is metaphorical as well (see Vasvari 1992).

20. Once in Leghorn, Lozana sells her ring, and, somehow, still manages to keep it until she arrives in Rome. Once in Rome, she sells it again, for she informs a shirtmaker who wonders how she has managed to survive: "he vendido el anillo en nueve ducados" ("I have sold my ring for nine ducats"; 201). As we will see, later she shows the very same ring to a Jew named Trigo. For a convenient list of the numerous sexual metaphors used in *La Lozana andaluza*, see Criado de Val 1960–63.

21. Caro Baroja 1986, 1: 102–03; Castro 1967, 161; Shepard 1982, 129.

22. As these words indicate, the popularity of Lozana's grandmother with the clothes merchants did not depend completely on her culinary expertise.

23. The turnips can also be phallic. See Alzieu et al. 1984, nos. 75, v. 6 and n2; 85, v. 5; 121, v. 11; 137, v. 14.

24. Joly shows that the list has much in common with Moorish cooking (1988–89), but this does not justify the conclusion that Lozana is being portrayed as a descendant of Moriscos at this point. Since she was from Córdoba, it is only natural that her cooking should be similar to Moorish cuisine, which also excluded pork. After all, the region had been under Muslim control for nearly eight centuries. It should be kept in mind, however, that the grandmother who had taught Lozana to cook is associated with Jews, and that the protagonist's Jewish background is firmly established elsewhere in the text.

25. As we saw in Chapter 3 (pp. 83–84), Lozana also mocks "limpieza de sangre."

26. "Water" may be a euphemism for "lard" here.

27. As we saw, the Spanish Inquisition was approved by Sixtus IV in 1478, but the Catholic Monarchs did not implement it until 1480, when the first inquisitors arrived in Seville (Domínguez Ortiz 1992, 24). The first auto-da-fé was held in that city on February 6 of the following year (Kamen 1998, 47).

28. For an excellent analysis of the metaphors involved in this scene, see Damiani and Imperiale 1991, 24–27.

29. See Quevedo 1988, 16n5. Even today, the crypto-Jews of northeastern Portugal are described as being frequently red-headed. This characterization is a valid one for, while conducting field work in the area in 1980, I had the opportunity to verify that the number of red-headed individuals seemed to increase substantially in the so-called "Jewish villages" (see Costa Fontes 1990–93). Concerning the Spanish prejudice against red hair—a prejudice that is paralleled in other European countries—see Gillet 1925 and Monroe 1985–86, 787–88.

30. A former colleague of mine, Dr. Herbert Hochhauser, who is Jewish, told me that, while in the service, he reacted in exactly the same manner upon finding out that he had just eaten pork.

31. Note how the choice of his name, "little prick," besides fitting his mischievous action, also embodies an authorial condemnation of what he had done.

32. See pp. 255 (Rampín mentions their forthcoming wedding), 440 (Ovidio refers to him as her husband), and 447 (Lozana informs a rogue that she is a married woman).

33. Although I am perfectly aware of the important distinction between author and narrator—and in *La Lozana andaluza* there is an additional complication, for the "Auctor" is depicted as one of the characters, while in the very act of writing—I use the terms in question interchangeably. The individual ultimately responsible for the book is Delicado himself and, notwithstanding their importance, those distinctions do not have a bearing on the present study.

34. The majority of the moral comments—albeit ambiguous—are relegated to the appendices.

35. This is based on the well-known joke according to which a boy will do anything for a jackknife. The motif is also presented in *Celestina* (see Bershas 1978).

36. On the hierarchy among prostitutes, see Allaigre 1985a, 285–87.

37. In Naples it was also known as "il mal franzoso" ("the French disease"), a compliment that the French returned by naming it "le mal de Naples" ("the Neapolitan disease"); when Spain was England's greatest enemy, the English called it "the Spanish disease" (Delicado 1970–71, 251). At one time, the French also referred to syphilis as "the Spanish disease," and some Spaniards said that it was "el mal de las Indias" ("the disease from the Indies [American disease]"; Damiani 1972, 189). For a brief historical survey of this disease during the fifteenth and sixteenth centuries, see García-Verdugo 1994, 99–107 and Michael 2001. For the word *greñimón* ("grunting [?]"), see Weiner 1973.

38. The image, of course, comes from the Old Testament, which compares faithless Israel to a harlot or a faithless wife. Since Lozana is a New Christian, it is also important to note that, after the mass conversions that took place in Burgos and Barcelona during the pogroms of 1391, a Jewish writer referred to both cities in similar terms (Shepard 1975, 365–67; see also Salstad 1982, 32). According to Shepard, this also contributed to the characterization of Lozana as a whore, for, being a conversa, in a way she was also a faithless Jew (1975, 368–69). Note that the "star" on her forehead connects her to Israel as well. It disfigures and marginalizes her, just as their Jewish background marginalized her fellow conversos.

39. The little that we know about Delicado has been gleaned from his works. Concerning the passage of *La Lozana andaluza* where this information is put forth, see Damiani 1974, 13, and Hernández Ortiz 1974, 15.

40. For other examinations of this engraving, see Ugolini 1974–75, 474–76, and Bubnova 1987, 85–87.

41. Ugolini 1974–75, 474–75; Bubnova 1987, 86n12. In his edition, however, Allaigre associated Venice with Lipari (Delicado 1985, 166).

42. Surtz came to the same conclusion, but, in his opinion, Delicado did not get the idea until after his arrival in Venice, where he presumably introduced some changes to the text: "Es como si, al releer y retocar su manuscrito en el puerto seguro de Venecia, Delicado viera en Lozana un *alter ego*" ("It is as if, upon reading and touching up his manuscript in the safe harbor of Venice, Delicado saw Lozana as an alter ego"; 1992, 182).

43. I could not find this expression in his writings, and Mackay reports that he was also unable to find it (1992, 235n15).

44. These words would seem to refute Wardropper's thesis (1953b, 477) that Delicado's intended audience was restricted to the Spaniards who, like him, had seen themselves forced to leave Rome.

45. For a good overview of the role played by conversos in the picaresque novel, see Lee 1979, 8–9.

46. See also the discussion in Chapter 2, pp. 45–47.

47. As García-Verdugo indicated, the degeneration of the nose constitutes a late, advanced stage of syphilis (1994, 87), but Lozana's nose is already affected when she arrives in Rome, soon after acquiring the disease in Marseilles. Once again, so much for the supposed "realism" of her character.

48. Here I disagree with Imperiale, who suggested that Lozana escapes from her aunt (1995, 154). This aunt had not mistreated Lozana, and upon discovering that she had eloped with Diomedes, to whom she had introduced her, the woman protests and curses her: "¡Ay, sobrina! Y si mirara bien en vos, viera que me habiedes de burlar, mas no tenéis el eslabón. ¡Mirá qué pago, que si miro en ello, ella misma me hizo alcagüeta! ¡Va, va, que en tal pararás!" ("Oh, niece, if I had seen through you well, I would have realized that you would eventually deceive me, but you do not have a reason to do it. Look at the thanks I get! Come to think of it, she has turned me into a bawd! Well, you will become one yourself!"; 182–83).

Chapter Seven
The Holy Trinity and the Annunciation in *La Lozana andaluza*

1. See Chapter 5, note 4. Celestina, we recall, also uses these words when she first visits Melibea's house in order to corrupt her.

2. "Nemo potest duobus dominis servire."

3. I added this comma.

4. If he were a Jew, he would not have had to eat it.

5. Incredibly, Joset still doubts that Rampín is portrayed as a converso. He argues that Christian bread, which, unlike unleavened bread, is made with yeast, does not cause him any revulsion (!), that he fails to show any respect for Jewish traditions, such as Easter, despises Jews (1990–93, 545), and that the famous scene where he vomits the bacon can also be interpreted as follows: "el criado, borracho lamentable, actúa como un judío sin serlo" ("the servant, who is a hopeless drunk, acts like a Jew without being one"; 546). For a good examination of the various names used to designate Rampín, see the sequel to this article (Joset 1996).

6. According to Damiani, the expression "por el paraíso de quien acá os dejó" ("by the Paradise of the one who left you here"; 198), which also appears as "¡Buen paraíso haya quien acá os dejó!" ("May the one who left you here have a good Paradise!"; 450), constitutes a Jewish allusion to Christ (Delicado 1969, 52n53), but, although I suspect that he is probably right, I cannot explain why.

7. "quae cum vidisset turbata est in sermone eius."

8. Allaigre (Delicado 1985, 410n4) cites an erotic poem in order to show that this type of sacrilege was not unique to Delicado, but such poems are extremely rare—the other two examples that he mentions are quite different—and good Christians were not likely to make such comparisons. In the poem cited, a girl asks her mother not to speak ill of Fray Antón, because she is devoted to him, and concludes:

Cuando quiere entrar	When he wants to enter,
viene muy honesto,	he comes very chastely,
mesurado el gesto	with a restrained expression,
por disimular:	in order to pretend:
háceme turbar	His Visitation
su Visitación;	confuses me.
no me le digáis mal,	*Don't speak ill of him,*
que le tengo en devoción.	*for I'm devoted to him.*
(Alzieu et al. 1984, 107)	

As we can see, when the monk "enters" the girl, his "visitation" troubles her, pretty much like Gabriel's salutation troubled the Blessed Mother.

In my opinion, the author of this poem was probably a converso, but, in order to be more certain, it would be necessary to see if poems mocking the Annunciation in a similar manner are found in other European literatures of the time, and that is beyond the scope of the present book.

9. The name may derive from the Latin *ne fissa*, meaning "without a fissure" or a "cranny" (Allaigre 1995, 45).

10. Note, however, that the Disputation of Tortosa concentrated on the question of the coming of the Messiah, and that "the problems of the Trinity and the Incarnation were never once introduced into this great debate" (Baer 1992, 2: 187).

11. Delicado could also have been aware of an incipient Italian anti-Trinitarianism (see Williams 1962, 20–26). It eventually crystallized in the two major forms of Italian Anabaptism, a movement that claimed that Jesus was born of the seed of Joseph, thus denying Mary's virginity as well as the dogmas of the Incarnation and the Holy Trinity (see Williams 1972). Note that Williams makes a strong case concerning the probable influence of converso refugees in Italy on the development of Anabaptism in that country (1972, 161–66, 175–80).

12. Like Doña Garoza in *LBA*, v. 1346*a*, Aloroza corresponds to Classical Ar. *al-ᶜarūs* or *al-ᶜarūsa*; the latter form preferred in Colloquial Hispano-Arabic (as also in Mod. Moroccan Colloquial). Di Stefano (1999, 711–12n1346*a*), in his new ed. of *LBA*, has an important note, bringing in additional evidence from Sicilian, which also borrowed the word from Arabic: *garrusa, iarrusa, arrusa* 'donna facile a concedersi.' I am grateful to one of the anonymous readers for these valuable observations.

13. I cite the prayer in verse form rather than in prose, as Delicado printed it, so as better to show its irregular rhyme (assonance in *á–o*) and its relationship to similar folk spells and folk prayers, which often exhibit variants of the concluding formula (vv. 7–9). For numerous examples of such spells, see Pedrosa 1992a; 1992b; 1993; 1997; 1998; 2000, 63–206.

14. For several examples of such spells, see Costa Fontes 1987, nos. 1508–33. No.1526 is a variant of the "Oración de Santa Apolonia," the prayer that Celestina seeks from Melibea in order to cure Calisto's grievous "toothache."

15. As we have already seen, these words enclose a mocking reference to blood purity as well.

16. According to Allaigre, these terms are variants of the names given to prostitutes (Delicado 1985, 443n22).

17. See also Márquez Villanueva 1979. There are several examples from the fifteenth century in Chapter 2 (pp. 57–67).

18. Although this formula was used in other countries by non-converso fiction writers such as Rabelais and Shakespeare, the aims of those authors (see Kaiser 1963, esp. 1–16) were completely different.

19. For the original on which this summary is based, see Bataillon 1964b, 107. Gillet (1931, 28–30) and Anderson (1965, 107–08) also study the manifestations of this story in Spain. Aarne and Thompson classify it as a folktale (1973, no. 777); Robe lists a Mexican version collected in Austin, Texas (1973, no. 777).

20. Interestingly enough, Antonio Ruiz (or Rodríguez), an Old Christian imprisoned by the Inquisition for impersonating Juan d'Espera en Dios (1557), used to tell his victims that, to save their souls, they had to commission three novenas, one in Bethlehem, one in Rome, and another in Santiago. Antonio would then promise to take care of the matter, pocketing the cost of the novenas (Bataillon 1964b, 109–17). Although this happened about three decades after the publication of *La Lozana andaluza*, the hoax itself could certainly be much older, and Delicado's familiarity with a similar swindle could very well have inspired his association of the number three with the Wandering Jew.

21. Although Corominas (1954) does not document the word *pene* until the second half of the eighteenth century, the term was already used during the fifteenth century, as witnessed by a double entendre in the already cited poem where Juan del Encina challenges a certain "donzella": "Justa de amores hecha por Juan del Enzina a una donzella que mucho le penava, la qual de su pena quiso dolerse" (Joust of Love composed by Juan del Encina to a maiden who made him suffer much, and who felt sorry for his suffering):

Pues por vós crece mi *pena*,	Since my suffering for you grows,
quiero, señora, rogaros	Madam, I would like to beg you
que queráys aparejaros	to get ready
a la justa que se ordena.	for the required joust.

(Qtd. in MacPherson 1985, 60; for the full text, with the variant title "Comienza la justa de amores" ["The joust of love begins"], see Alzieu et al. 1984, 9–10).

The term in question reappears, in an equally euphemistic way, during the early seventeenth century. In *Don Quijote*, the innkeeper's wife demands the return of an ox tail that the barber used in a disguise with the following words: "Para mi santiguada, que no se ha aún de aprovechar más de mi *rabo* para su *barba*, y que me ha de volver mi *cola*; que anda *lo de* mi marido por esos suelos, que es *vergüenza*; digo, el *peine*, que solía yo *colgar* de mi buena *cola*" ("By my faith, you are not going to use my *tail* for a *beard* anymore, and you must give me my *tail* back. My husband's *thing* is dragging on the ground, which is a *shameful thing* ["sex organs"]. I mean, my *comb*, which I used to *hang* on that *tail* of mine"; Cervantes 1978, 1: 392; I have emphasized several key words to call attention to their double meaning, as it helps to understand the euphemistic utilization of term *peine*).

22. See Chapter 4, note 66.

23. For additional examples of this aversion to the Virgin Mary, see Chapter 4, pp. 137–39.

24. Although the medieval polemicists focused their criticisms especially on the Holy Trinity, "The chief reason for this Jewish reaction lay in the Christian doctrine of incarnation, which was professed to be a concomitant of the belief in the Trinity. . . . While Jewish theologians might accept the notion that God has a number of aspects, they totally rejected the possibility that one such aspect did, or even could, become human" (Lasker 1977, 105). Since "it was the doctrine of the incarnation that most truly set apart the Jewish and Christian concepts of God" (105), one might ask why the Jewish polemicists chose to concentrate on the Holy Trinity instead. The answer could very well be that such a focus would not be as offensive to the Christians among whom they lived. The acceptance of a messiah was easier, but only if the dogma of incarnation were not involved.

25. Obviously, the three doors could also be an allusion to the three major religions that used to coexist in Spain, Christianity, Judaism, and Islam, but, since Delicado refers to the number three no less than three times in a row, he is really thinking about the Holy Trinity.

26. As already indicated, however, the engraving on the frontispiece depicts Lozana on her way to Venice.

27. Although this attitude could also echo the inherited scepticism of many conversos concerning the possibility of an afterlife (see Márquez Villanueva 1973, 94 and n15), it seems to me that it is very unlikely to constitute an indication of religious indifference as well. If that were the case, the corrosive attack on the central dogma of Christianity would have been pointless.

28. And it goes without saying that the wise Solomon had never heard a thing about the Holy Trinity. For a splendid, profusely documented article on the complex symbolism of this knot, which incorporates both Jewish and Christian elements, see Macpherson and Mackay 1998, 205–22.

Chapter Eight
Rojas, Delicado, and the Art of Subversion

1. For easily available editions, see Brant 1962 and Erasmus 1979.

2. See Márquez Villanueva 1980.

3. See the facsimile edition (Delicado 1950). In his edition (1985), Allaigre reproduces only the second half of the diptych on the reverse of the title page (168), placing the top at the end of Part II (371). Damiani, however, reproduces the complete diptych in the beginning (1969, 32).

4. Note that the word *coger* ("to fetch, gather, collect") could also be read as *joder* ("to fuck").

5. Note that one of the women depicted in the engraving on the reverse of the title page is the same as Amadís's beloved (and faithless) Oriana.

6. It was reedited in 1978. For the *Carajicomedia*, see pp. 139–84.

7. See Snow's incisive article (1989). For a survey of the critical views on Pármeno, see also Russell 2001, 4–8.

8. As we will see, Delicado reveals his identity in the text, but this is far from being obvious.

9. See p. 350 of Allaigre's splendid edition (Delicado 1985). Although it reproduces the engravings, their placement in relation to the text can be best observed in the facsimile published in 1950.

10. See Chapter 5, note 15.

11. See, for example, Martínez de Toledo 1992, 157–59; as the author himself indicates, his source his Boccaccio.

12. When a captain asks Lozana how long a woman can work as a prostitute, she replies: "Dende doce años hasta cuarenta" ("From the age of twelve until forty"; 367).

13. I am grateful to Jerry Craddock for bringing this to my attention.

14. As for Dathan and Abiram, they rebelled against Moses, and, as punishment, God caused the ground beneath them to split open and to swallow them and their families (Num. 16.31–34).

15. For an extensive examination of St. Appolonia's legend, see now Beresford 2001.

16. Rojas's utilization of words attributed to Christ, of course, also constitutes an indirect way of alluding to him.

17. Maimonides, we recall, was referring only to Christ.

18. Note that the name "Jesús" is often used in Spanish.

Appendix: English Translations

1. Damiani's rendition of *tramontanas* as "Transylvanian" (Delicado 1987, 94) could very well be right, but I was unable to find documentation.

Abbreviations

Acme	*Acme: Annali della Facoltà di Lettere e Filosofia dell'Università degli Studi di Milano*, Milano.
AEM	*Anuario de Estudios Medievales*, Barcelona.
AHisp	*Archivo Hispalense: Revista Histórica, Literaria y Artística*, Barcelona.
AIA	*Archivo Ibero-Americano*, Madrid.
AION-SR	*Annali dell'Istituto Universitario Orientale, Napoli: Sezione Romanza*, Napoli.
AMed	*Anuario Medieval*, Jamaica, NY.
AO	*Archivum*, Oviedo.
BBMP	*Boletín de la Biblioteca Menéndez Pelayo*, Santander.
BHi	*Bulletin Hispanique*, Bordeaux.
BHS	*Bulletin of Hispanic Studies*, Liverpool / Glasgow.
BRAE	*Boletín de la Real Academia Española*, Madrid.
Brigantia	*Brigantia: Revista de Cultura*, Bragança.
Celestinesca	*Celestinesca*, East Lansing, MI.
Cervantes	*Cervantes: Bulletin of the Hispanic Society of America*, New York.
CH	*Crítica Hispánica*, Pittsburgh, PA.
Clavileño	*Clavileño*, Madrid.
CN	*Cultura Neolatina*, Modena.
CuA	*Cuadernos Americanos*, México, DF.
Donaire	*Donaire*, London.
Exemplaria	*Exemplaria: A Journal of Theory in Medieval and Renaissance Studies*, Asheville, NC.
FI	*Forum Italicum: A Journal of Italian Studies*, Stony Brook, NY.
FMLS	*Forum for Modern Language Studies*, St. Andrews, Scot.
Habis	*Habis*, Sevilla.
Hispania	*Hispania*, American Association of Teachers of Spanish and Portuguese, Washington, DC.
Hispanófila	*Hispanófila*, Chapel Hill, NC.
HR	*Hispanic Review*, Philadelphia, PA.
Iberoromania	*Iberoromania*, München.
IJHL	*Indiana Journal of Hispanic Literatures*, Bloomington, IN.
Il Vasari	*Il Vasari: Rivista d'Arte e di Studi Vasariani*, Bologna.
Ínsula	*Ínsula*, Madrid.
Italica	*Italica*, Columbus, OH.
JAOS	*Journal of the American Oriental Society*, Boulder, CO.
JFR	*Journal of Folklore Research*, Bloomington, IN.
JHP	*Journal of Hispanic Philology*, Hammond, IN.
KRQ	*Kentucky Romance Quarterly*, Lexington, KY.
La Corónica	*La Corónica*, Williamsburg, VA.
La Torre	*La Torre*, Río Piedras, PR.
LBR	*Luso-Brazilian Review*, Madison, WI.
Mediaevalia	*Mediaevalia: A Journal of Medieval Studies*, Binghamton, NY.

Abbreviations

MedLR	*Mediterranean Language Review*, Tel Aviv / Beer-Sheva.
Mélanges	*Mélanges de la Casa Velázquez*, Paris.
MLN	*Modern Language Notes*, Baltimore, MD.
MLR	*Modern Language Review*, London.
MR	*Monographic Review/Revista Monográfica*, Odessa, TX.
Neohelicon	*Neohelicon: Acta Comparationis Litterarum Universarum*, Dordrecht, Neth.
Neophilologus	*Neophilologus*, Amsterdam.
NRFH	*Nueva Revista de Filología Hispánica*, México, DF.
PAAJR	*Proceedings—American Academy for Jewish Research*, Philadelphia, PA.
PhQ	*Philological Quarterly*, Iowa City, IA.
PLL	*Papers of Language & Literature*, Edwardsville, IL.
PMLA	*Publications of the Modern Language Association*, New York.
Prohemio	*Prohemio*, Madrid–Pisa.
PSA	*Papeles de San Armadans*, Palma de Mallorca.
QIA	*Quaderni Ibero-Americani*, Torino.
Quimera	*Quimera*, Barcelona.
RABM	*Revista de Archivos, Bibliotecas y Museos*, Madrid.
RCEH	*Revista Canadiense de Estudios Hispánicos*, Toronto.
RDTP	*Revista de Dialectología y Tradiciones Populares*, Madrid.
Realidad	*Realidad*, Santiago de Chile.
REH	*Revista de Estudios Hispánicos*, St. Louis, MO.
REI	*Revue des Études Islamiques*, Paris.
REJ	*Revue des Études Juives*, Paris.
RF	*Romanische Forschungen*, Köln (Cologne).
RFE	*Revista de Filología Española*, Madrid.
RFH	*Revista de Filología Hispánica*, Buenos Aires.
RFolk	*Revista de Folklore*, Valladolid.
RHi	*Revue Hispanique*, Paris.
RHM	*Revista Hispánica Moderna*, New York.
RL	*Revista Lusitana*, Porto and Lisboa.
RLit	*Revista de Literatura*, Madrid.
RLNS	*Revista Lusitana* (Nova Série), Lisboa.
Ro	*Romania*, Paris.
ROcc	*Revista de Occidente*, Madrid.
RoN	*Romance Notes*, Chapel Hill, NC.
RoY	*Romanistisches Yahrbuch*, Berlin, New York.
RPh	*Romance Philology*, Berkeley.
RR	*The Romanic Review*, New York.
Saber Leer	*Saber Leer: Revista Crítica de Libros*, Madrid.
Sefarad	*Sefarad*, Madrid.
Segismundo	*Segismundo: Revista Hispánica de Teatro*, Madrid.
SI	*Studi Ispanici*, Pisa.
Sin Nombre	*Sin Nombre: Revista Trimestral Literaria*, San Juan, PR.
SRLI	*Southern Review: Literary and Interdisciplinary Essays*, Churchill, VIC, Austral.

Works Cited

Aarne, Antti, and Stith Thompson. 1973. *The Types of the Folktale: A Classification and Bibliography*. 2nd rev. ed. Folklore Fellows Commications 3. Helsinki: Academia Scientiarum Fennica.

El Abencerraje (novela y romancero). 1987. Ed. Francisco López Estrada. 5th ed. Madrid: Cátedra.

Abrams, Fred. 1972–73 "The Name 'Celestina': Why Did Fernando de Rojas Choose It?" *MLN* 14: 165–67.

Adams, J. N. 1982. *The Latin Sexual Vocabulary*. Baltimore, MD: Johns Hopkins UP.

Alberti, Giuseppe. 1941. "Le cortigiane, le stufe e la lue nella Roma del primo cinquecento." *Il Vasari* 3: 64–73.

Albó, Joseph. 1946. *Sefer Ha-'Ikkarim: Book of Principles*. Ed. and trans. Isaac Husik. 4 vols. in 5. Philadelphia: Jewish Publication Society of America.

Alborg, Juan Luis. 1992. *Historia de la literatura española*, 1: *Edad Media y Renacimiento*. 2nd ed. Madrid: Gredos.

Alcalá, Angel. 1987a. "Inquisitorial Control of Humanists and Writers." Alcalá, *The Spanish Inquisition and the Inquisitorial Mind* 321–59.

———, ed. 1987b. *The Spanish Inquisition and the Inquisitorial Mind*. Boulder, CO: Social Science Monographs.

———, ed. 1995. *Judíos. Sefarditas. Conversos: La expulsión de 1492 y sus consecuencias, ponencias del Congreso Internacional celebrado en Nueva York en noviembre de 1992*. Valladolid: Ámbito.

Alemán, Mateo. 1981. *Guzmán de Alfarache*. Ed. Benito Brancaforte. 2nd ed. 2 vols. Madrid: Cátedra.

Alfonso X, El Sabio. 1930. *General estoria: primera parte*. Ed. Antonio G. Solalinde. Madrid: Junta para Ampliación de Estudios e Investigaciones Científicas, Centro de Estudios Históricos.

———. 1986–89. *Cantigas de Santa Maria*. Ed. Walter Mettmann. 3 vols. Madrid: Castalia.

Allaigre, Claude. 1980a. "A propos des dialogues de la *Lozana andaluza*: La Pelegrina du mamotreto LXIII." *Essays sur le dialogue*. Introd. Jean Lavédrine. Grenoble: L'Université des Langues et Lettres. 102–14.

———. 1980b. *Sémantique et littérature: Le "Retrato de la Loçana andaluza" de Francisco Delicado*. Grenoble: Ministère des Universités.

———. 1985a. "Amours et prostitution dans le *Retrato de la Lozana Andaluza*." *Amours légitimes-Amours illégitimes en Espagne (XVIe–XVIIe siècles), Colloque internacional (Sorbonne, 3, 4, 5 et 6 octobre, 1984)*. Ed. Augustin Redondo. Paris: La Sorbonne. 285–99.

———. 1985b. Introducción. Delicado, *Retrato de La Lozana andaluza* 17–164.

Works Cited

Allaigre, Claude. 1995. "Sobre judíos y conversos en *La Lozana andaluza*." *Las dos grandes minorías étnico-religiosas en la literatura española del Siglo de Oro: los judeo-conversos y los moriscos: Actas del "Grand Séminaire" de Neuchâtel, Neuchâtel, 26 a 27 de mayo de 1994.* Annales Littéraires de l'Université de Besançon 588. Paris: Diffusion Les Belles Lettres. 37–50.

Allegra, Giovanni. 1973. "Breve nota acerca del 'Ilustre Señor' de *La Lozana andaluza*." *BRAE* 53: 391–97.

———. 1976. "Sobre una nueva hipótesis en la biografía de F. Delicado." *BRAE* 56: 523–35.

———. 1983. Estudio preliminar. Delicado, *La Lozana andaluza* 7–54.

Allen, D. C. 1961. "Donne and the Ship Metaphor." *MLN* 76: 308–14.

Alvar, Manuel. 1971. *Cantos de boda judeo-españoles*. Madrid: Consejo Superior de Investigaciones Científicas.

Alzieu, Pierre, Robert Jammes, and Yvan Lissorgues, eds. 1984. *Poesía erótica del Siglo de Oro*. Barcelona: Crítica.

Anderson, George K. 1965. *The Legend of the Wandering Jew*. Providence, RI: Brown UP.

Anderson Imbert, Enrique. 1949. "Comedia de Calisto y Melibea." *Realidad* 3: 301–08.

Apuleyo, Lucio. 1915. *Lucio Apuleyo del Asno de Oro*. Trans. Diego López de Cortegana. *Orígenes de la novela*. By Marcelino Menéndez y Pelayo. Ed. A. Bonilla y San Martín. 4 vols. Madrid: Bailly / Baillière. 4: 1–103.

Arbós, Cristina. 1985. "Los cancioneros castellanos del siglo XV como fuente para la historia de los judíos españoles." *Jews and Conversos: Studies in Society and the Inquisition: Proceedings of the Eighth World Congress of Jewish Studies Held at the Hebrew University of Jerusalem, August 16–21, 1981.* Ed. Yosef Kaplan. Jerusalem: World Union of Jewish Studies, Magnes, Hebrew U. 74–82.

Arellano, I[gnacio], M. C. Pinillos, F. Serralta, and M. Vitse, eds. 1996. *Studia aurea: Actas del III Congreso de la AISO (Toulouse, 1993)*. 3 vols. Pamplona–Toulouse: Grupo de Investigación Siglo de Oro, Universidad de Navarra, Literatura Española Medieval y del Siglo de Oro, Université de Toulouse.

Armistead, Samuel G. 1978. "¿Existió un romancero de tradición oral entre los moriscos?" *Actas del Coloquio Internacional sobre Literatura Aljamiada y Morisca*. Ed. Alvaro Galmés de Fuentes. Madrid: Gredos, 1978. 211–36.

———. 1992. *The Spanish Tradition in Louisiana*. Vol. 1. *Isleño Folkliterature*. Newark, DE: Juan de la Cuesta.

———. 2000. "The Memory of Tri-Religious Spain in the Sephardic *Romancero*." Carrete Parrondo et al. 265–86.

Armistead, Samuel G., and Mishael M. Caspi, eds., in collaboration with Murray Baumgarten. 2001. *Jewish Culture and the Hispanic World: Essays in Memory of Joseph H. Silverman*. Newark, DE: Juan de la Cuesta.

Works Cited

Armistead, Samuel G., in collaboration with Selma Margaretten, Paloma Montero, and Ana Valenciano. 1978. Musical transcriptions ed. Israel J. Katz. *El romancero judeo-español en el Archivo Menéndez Pidal (Catálogo-índice de romances y canciones)*. 3 vols. Madrid: Cátedra–Seminario Menéndez Pidal.

Armistead, Samuel G., and Joseph H. Silverman. 1971. *The Judeo-Spanish Ballad Chapbooks of Yacob Abraham Yoná*. Folk Literature of the Sephardic Jews 1. Berkeley and Los Angeles: U of California P.

———. 1982. "El sustrato cristiano del Romancero sefardí." *En torno al Romancero sefardí (Hispanismo y balcanismo de la tradición judeo-española)*. Madrid: Seminario Menéndez Pidal. 127–48. First published as "Christian Elements and De-Christianization in the Sephardic 'Romancero.'" *Collected Studies in Honour of Américo Castro's Eightieth Year*. Ed. Marcel P. Hornik. Oxford, Eng.: Lincombe Lodge Research Library, 1965. 21–38.

Asensio, Eugenio. 1960–63. "Juan de Valdés contra Delicado: fondo de una polémica." *Serta Philologica: Homenaje ofrecido a Dámaso Alonso por sus amigos y discípulos con ocasión de su 60.º aniversario*. 3 vols. Madrid: Gredos. 1: 101–13.

———. 1967. "La peculiaridad literaria de los conversos." *AEM* 4: 327–51.

———. 1973. "Entremeses." *Suma cervantina*. Ed. J. B. Avalle-Arce and E. C. Riley. London: Tamesis. 171–97.

Asensio, Manuel J. 1959. "La intención religiosa del *Lazarillo de Tormes* y Juan de Valdés." *HR* 27: 78–102.

Ayerbe-Chaux, Reynaldo. 1978. "La triple tentación de Melibea." *Celestinesca* 2.2: 3–11.

Baena, Juan Alfonso de. 1993. *Cancionero de Juan Alfonso de Baena*. Ed. Brian Dutton and Joaquín González Cuenca. Madrid: Visor.

Baer, Yitzhak. 1992. *A History of the Jews in Christian Spain*. Trans. Louis Schoffman. Introd. Benjamin R. Gampel. 2nd ed. 2 vols. Philadelphia and Jerusalem: Jewish Publication Society of America.

Bainton, Roland H. 1962. *Early and Medieval Christianity*. Boston: Beacon.

Barbera, Raymond E. 1970. "Medieval Iconography in the *Celestina*." *RR* 61: 5–13.

Barkaï, Ron, ed. 1994a. *Chrétiens, musulmans et juifs dans l'Espagne médievale*. Paris: Cerf.

———. 1994b. Introduction. Barkaï, *Chrétiens, musulmans et juifs* 9–38.

———. 1994c. "Les trois cultures ibériques entre dialogue et polémique." Barkaï, *Chrétiens, musulmans et juifs* 227–51.

Barrick, Mac E. 1977. "Celestina's Black Mass." *Celestinesca* 1.2: 11–14.

Bataillon, Marcel. 1964a. "Alonso Núñez de Reinoso y los marranos portugueses en Italia." Bataillon, *Varia lección de clásicos españoles* 55–80.

Bataillon, Marcel. 1964b. "Pérégrinations espagnoles du juif errant." *BHi* 43 (1941): 81–122. Trans. into Span. as "Peregrinaciones españolas del Judío errante." Bataillon, *Varia lección de clásicos españoles* 81–132.

———. 1964c. "*Ulenspiegel* y el *Retablo de las maravillas* de Cervantes." Bataillon, *Varia lección de clásicos españoles* 260–67.

———. 1964d. *Varia lección de clásicos españoles*. Madrid: Gredos.

———. 1982a. *Erasmo y España: estudios sobre la historia espiritual del siglo XVI*. 2nd ed. México, DF: Fondo de Cultura Económica.

———. 1982b. *Pícaros y picaresca: "La pícara Justina."* Trans. Francisco Rodríguez Vadillo. Madrid: Taurus.

Beinart, Haim, ed. 1974–77. *Records of the Trials of the Spanish Inquisition in Ciudad Real*. 2 vols. Jerusalem: Israel National Academy of Sciences and Humanities.

———. 1981. *Conversos on Trial: The Inquisition in Ciudad Real*. Hispania Judaica 3. Jerusalem: Magnes, Hebrew U.

———, ed. 1992a. *Moreshet Sepharad: The Sephardi Legacy*. 2 vols. Jerusalem: Magnes, Hebrew U.

———. 1992b. "The Conversos in Spain and Portugal in the 16th to the 18th Centuries." Beinart, *Moreshet Sepharad* 2: 43–67.

———. 1992c. "The Expulsion from Spain: Causes and Results." Beinart, *Moreshet Sepharad* 2: 11–42.

———. 1992d. "The Great Conversion and the Converso Problem." Beinart, *Moreshet Sepharad* 1: 346–82.

———. 1993. *Los judíos en España*. 2nd ed. Madrid: Mapfre.

Bell, Audrey F. G. 1967. *The Oxford Book of Portuguese Verse: XIIth Century–XXth Century*. 2nd ed. Ed. B. Vidigal. Oxford: Clarendon.

Beltrán, Rafael, and José Luis Canet, eds. 1997. *Cinco siglos de "Celestina": aportaciones interpretativas*. Valencia: Universitat.

Bennassar, Bartolomé. 1987. "Patterns of the Inquisitorial Mind as the Basis for a Pedagogy of Fear." Alcalá, *The Spanish Inquisition and the Inquisitorial Mind* 177–84.

———. 1994. "La Inquisición y los conversos según investigaciones recientes." López Alvarez et al., *Inquisición y conversos* 21–33.

Bénichou, Paul. 1970. *Nerval et la chanson folklorique*. Paris: José Corti.

Berceo, Gonzalo de. 1987. *Milagros de Nuestra Señora*. Ed. E. Michael Gerli. 2nd ed. Madrid: Cátedra.

Beresford, Andrew M. 2001. "'Una oración, señora, que le dixeron que sabías, de Sancta Polonia para el dolor de las muelas': *Celestina* and the Legend of St. Appolonia." Michael and Pattison 39–57.

Bernáldez, Andrés. 1962. *Memorias del reinado de los Reyes Católicos*. Ed. M. Gómez-Moreno and Juan de M. Carriazo. Madrid: Real Academia de la Historia.

Works Cited

Bershas, Henry N. 1978. "'Testigo es el cuchillo de tu abuelo' (*Celestina*, I)." *Celestinesca* 2.1: 7–11.

Biblia Ladinada. Escorial I.J.3. 1995. Vol. 1. Ed. Moshe Lazar. Madison, WI: Hispanic Seminary of Medieval Studies.

Biblia medieval romanceada según los manuscritos escurialenses I–j–3, I–j–8 y I–j–6. I:Pentateuco. 1927. Ed. Américo Castro, Agustín Millares Carlo, and Angel J. Battistessa. Buenos Aires: Jacobo Peuser.

Biblias medievales romanceadas. Biblia medieval romanceada judeo-cristiana. Versión del Antiguo Testamento en el siglo XIV, sobre los textos hebreo y latino. 1950. Vol. 1. Ed. P. José Llamas. Madrid: Instituto Francisco Suárez.

Biblia Sacra Iuxta Vulgatam Versionem. 1994. Stuttgart: Deutsche Bibelgesellschaft.

Blay Manzanera, Vicenta. 1996. "Más datos sobre la metáfora de la serpiente-cupiditas en *Celestina*." *Celestinesca* 20.1–2: 129–54.

Blay Manzanera, Vicenta, and Dorothy S. Severin. 1999. *Animals in Celestina.* Papers of the Medieval Hispanic Research Seminar 18. London: Dept. of Hispanic Studies, Queen Mary and Westfield College.

Blázquez Miguel, Juan. 1988. *Inquisición y criptojudaísmo.* Madrid: Kaydeda.

Blecua, José Manuel. 1984–87. *Poesía de la Edad de Oro.* 2 vols. Madrid: Castalia.

Boccaccio, Giovanni. 1992. *Il Corbaccio.* Ed. Julia Natali. Milan: Mursia.

Bodian, Miriam. 1997. *Hebrews of the Portuguese Nation: Conversos and Community in Early Amsterdam.* Bloomington: Indiana UP.

Bonilla y San Martín, Adolfo. 1906. "Antecedentes del tipo celestinesco en la literatura latina." *RHi* 15: 372–86.

Botta, Patrizia. 1993. "La *Celestina* de Palacio en sus aspectos materiales." *BRAE* 73: 347–66.

———. 1997. "El texto en movimiento (De la *Celestina* de Palacio a la *Celestina* Posterior)." Beltrán and Canet 135–59.

Braga, Teófilo. 1906–09. *Romanceiro Geral Português.* 2nd ed. 3 vols. Lisboa: Manuel Gomes; J. A. Rodrigues.

Brakhage, Pamela S. 1986. *The Theology of La Lozana andaluza.* Potomac, MD: Scripta Humanistica.

Brant, Sebastian. [1944] 1962. *The Ship of Fools.* Trans., introd., and commentary Edwin H. Zeydel. New York: Dover.

Braunstein, Baruch. 1936. *The Chuetas of Majorca: Conversos and the Inquisition of Majorca.* Scottdale, PA: Mennonite Publishing.

Bravo Lozano, Jesús. 1980. "Testamentos de familiares del Santo Oficio: algunos problemas." Pérez Villanueva 285–92.

Bubnova, Tatiana. 1987. *F. Delicado puesto en diálogo: las claves bajtinianas de "La Lozana andaluza."* México, DF: Universidad Nacional Autónoma.

———. 1990. "Cervantes y Delicado." *NRFH* 38: 567–90.

Works Cited

Bubnova, Tatiana. 1990–93. "La 'malicia malencónica' de Francisco Delicado." García Martín et al. 1: 195–202.

———. 1995. *"La lozana andaluza* como literatura erótica." López-Baralt and Márquez Villanueva 17–31.

Buendía López, José Luis. 1994. "La prostitución a través de la literatura española: de Francisco Delicado a los años 1920." Carrasco, *La prostitution en Espagne* 373–85.

Cancionero de obras de burlas provocantes a risa. 1978. Ed. Frank Domínguez. Valencia: Albatros Ediciones–Hispanófila.

Cannavagio, Jean. 1990. *Cervantes*. Trans. J. R. Jones. New York–London: Norton.

Cantera Burgos, Francisco. 1967. "El *Cancionero de Baena*: judíos y conversos en él." *Sefarad* 27: 71–111.

———. 1970. *El poeta Ruy Sánchez Cota (Rodrigo Cota) y su familia de judíos conversos*. Madrid: Universidad de Madrid, Facultad de Filosofía y Letras.

Carballo Picazo, Alfredo. 1952. "Juan de Mena: un documento inédito y una obra atribuida." *RLit* 1: 269–99.

Cardaillac, Louis. 1977. *Morisques et chrétiens: Un affrontement polémique (1492–1640)*. Pref. Fernand Braudel. Paris: Klincksieck.

Cardiel Sanz, Estrella. 1981. "La cuestión judía en *La Celestina*." *Actas de las Jornadas de Estudios Sefardíes*. Ed. Antonio Viudas Camarasa. Cáceres: Universidad de Extremadura. 151–59.

Caro Baroja, Julio. 1986. *Los judíos en la España moderna y contemporánea*. 3 vols. Madrid: Istmo.

———. 1996. *Inquisición, brujería y criptojudaísmo*. Barcelona: Galaxia Guttenberg, Círculo de Lectores.

———. 1997. *Las brujas y su mundo*. 2nd ed. Prólogo y álbum de Francisco J. Flores Arroyelo. Madrid: Alianza.

Carrasco, Raphaël, ed. 1994. *La prostitution en Espagne de l'époche des Rois Catholiques a la IIe République*. Centre de Recherches sur l'Espagne Moderne 2. Paris: Annales Littéraires de l'Université de Besançon, Diffusion les Belles Lettres.

———. 1995. "Historia y literatura: sobre minorías del Siglo de Oro." *Las dos grandes minorías étnico-religiosas en la literatura española del Siglo de Oro: los judeo-conversos y los moriscos: Actas del "Grand Séminaire" de Neuchâtel, Neuchâtel, 26 a 27 de mayo de 1994*. Annales Littéraires de l'Université de Besançon 588. Paris: Diffusion les Belles Lettres. 15–36.

Carrete Parrondo, Carlos. 1992. *El judaísmo español y la Inquisición*. Madrid: Mapfre.

Carrete Parrondo, Carlos, Marcelo Dascal, Francisco Márquez Villanueva, and Angel Sáenz Badillos, eds. 2000. *"Encuentros" and "Desencuentros": Spanish-Jewish Cultural Interaction throughout History*. Tel Aviv: U Publishing Projects.

Castro, Américo. [1963]. *De la edad conflictiva, 1: El drama de la honra en España y en su literatura*. 2nd ed. Madrid: Taurus.

———. 1965. *"La Celestina" como contienda literaria (castas y casticismos)*. Madrid: Revista de Occidente.

———. 1967. *Hacia Cervantes*. 3rd ed. Madrid: Taurus.

———. 1971. *La realidad histórica de España*. 4th ed. México, DF: Porrúa.

———. 1972. *De la España que aún no conocía*. Colección Perspectivas Españolas 6–8. 3 vols. México, DF: Finisterre.

———. 1974a. *Cervantes y los casticismos españoles*. Nota preliminar de Paulino Garagorri. Madrid: Alianza.

———. 1974b. "Sentido histórico-literario del jamón y del tocino." Castro, *Cervantes y los casticismos españoles* 25–32.

Catalán, Diego. 1970. *Por campos del Romancero: estudios sobre la tradición oral moderna*. Madrid: Gredos.

Catechism of the Catholic Church, with Modifications from the Editio Typica. 1995. An Image Book. New York and London: Doubleday.

Cátedra, Pedro M. 1989. *Amor y pedagogía en la Edad Media*. Salamanca: Universidad de Salamanca.

Cervantes Saavedra, Miguel de. 1976. *Entremeses*. Ed. Eugenio Asensio. Madrid: Castalia.

———. 1978. *El ingenioso hidalgo don Quijote de la Mancha*. 2 vols. Ed. Luis Andrés Murillo. Madrid: Castalia.

———. 1982. *Novelas ejemplares*. Ed. Juan Bautista Avalle-Arce. 2nd ed. 3 vols. Madrid: Castalia.

———. 1984. *El cerco de Numancia*. Ed. Robert Marrast. Madrid: Cátedra.

———. 1996. *Eight Interludes*. Trans. and ed. Dawn L. Smith. London–Rutland, VT: Everyman.

———. 1998. *Exemplary Stories*. Trans. Lesley Simpson. Oxford–New York: Oxford UP.

———. 1999. *Don Quijote*. Trans. Burton Raffel. Ed. Diana de Armas Wilson. New York and London: Norton.

Chastel, André. 1983. *The Sack of Rome, 1527*. Trans. Beth Archer. Princeton, NJ: Princeton UP.

Cherchi, Paolo. 1997. "Onomástica celestinesca y la tragedia del saber inútil." Beltrán and Canet 77–90.

Chiclana, Angel. 1988. Introducción. Delicado, *La Lozana andaluza* 15–62.

Ciceri, Marcella. 1980. "Livelli di trasgressione (dal riso all'insulto) nei canzonieri spagnoli." *Codici della trasgressività in area ispanica: Atti del Convegno di Verona, 12–13–14 giugno 1980*. Verona: Università degli Studi di Padova, Facoltà di Economia e Commercio, Istituto di Lingue e Letterature Straniere di Verona. 19–35.

Works Cited

Ciceri, Marcella. 1989. "Lo smascheramento del 'converso' e i suoi stereotipi nei canzonieri spagnoli." *Miscellanea di studi in onore di Aurelio Roncaglia a cinquant'anni dalla sua laurea*. 2 vols. Modena: Mucchi. 1: 435–50.

———, ed. 1990. *Montoro*.

Cirlot, J. E. 1972. *A Dictionary of Symbols*. Trans. Jack Sage. 2nd ed. New York: Philosophical Library.

Cohen, Martin A. 1982. "Toward a New Comprehension of the Marranos." Solà-Solé 1: 23–35.

Collera, Ana María, and Victoriano Roncero López, eds. 1996. *Nunca fue pena mayor (Estudios de literatura española en homenaje a Brian Dutton)*. Cuenca: Universidad de Castilla–La Mancha.

Comes amoris, or The Companion of Love. Being a choice collection of the newest songs now in use. With a thorow bass for each song for the harpsichord, theorbo, or bass-viol. 1687. London: Printed by Nat. Thompson for John Carr and Sam. Scott.

Conde, Juan Carlos. 1997. "El manuscrito II–520 de la Biblioteca de Palacio y la *Celestina*: balance y estado de la cuestión." Beltrán and Canet 161–85.

Constable, Olivia Remie, ed. 1997. *Medieval Iberia: Readings from Christian, Muslim, and Jewish Sources*. Philadelphia: U of Pennsylvania P.

Corfis, Ivy A. 1998. "Naming in *Celestina*." *Celestinesca* 22.1: 43–56.

Corominas, Joan. 1954. *Diccionario crítico etimológico de la lengua castellana*. 4 vols. Berne: Francke.

Coronas Tejada, Luis. 1980. "Estudio social de los familiares del Santo Oficio en Jaén a mediados del siglo XVII." Pérez Villanueva, *La Inquisición española* 293–302.

Correa, Gustavo. 1962. "Naturaleza, religión y honra en *La Celestina*." *PMLA* 77: 8–17.

Correas, Gonzalo. 1992. *Vocabulario de refranes y frases proverbiales*. Prol. Miguel Mir. Ed. Víctor Infantes. Madrid: Visor.

Corthell, Ronald J. 1989. "Donne's 'Disparitie': Inversion, Gender, and the Subject of Love in Some Songs and Sonnets." *Exemplaria* 1.1: 17–42.

Costa, Maria Rosa Dias. 1961. *Murteira, uma Povoação do Concelho de Loures: Etnografia, Linguagem, Folclore*. Lisboa: Junta Distrital de Lisboa.

Costa Fontes, Manuel da. 1975. "Love as an Equalizer in *La española inglesa*." *RoN* 16: 742–48.

———. 1979. *Romanceiro Português do Canadá*. Pref. Samuel G. Armistead and Joseph H. Silverman. Acta Universitatis Conimbrigensis. Coimbra: Universidade.

———. 1983. *Romanceiro da Ilha de S. Jorge*. Pref. Samuel G. Armistead and Joseph H. Silverman. Musical transcriptions by Halim El-Dabh. Acta Universitatis Conimbrigensis. Coimbra: Universidade.

———. 1984. "Celestina's *Hilado* and Related Symbols." *Celestinesca* 8.1: 3–13.

———. 1985. "Celestina's *Hilado* and Related Symbols: A Supplement." *Celestinesca* 9.1: 33–38.

———. 1987. *Romanceiro da Província de Trás-os-Montes (Distrito de Bragança)*. Collected with Maria-João Câmara Fontes. Pref. Samuel G. Armistead and Joseph H. Silverman. Musical transcriptions by Israel J. Katz. 2 vols. Acta Universitatis Conimbrigensis. Coimbra: Universidade.

———. 1988. "The Idea of 'Limpieza' in *La Celestina*." Ricapito, *Hispanic Studies* 23–35.

———. 1990. "A Portuguese Folk Story and Its Early Congeners." *HR* 58: 73–88.

———. 1990–91. "Celestina as an Antithesis of the Virgin Mary." *JHP* 14: 7–41.

———. 1990–93. "Four Portuguese Crypto-Jewish Prayers and Their 'Inquisitorial' Counterparts." *MedLR* 6–7: 67–104.

———. 1992. "Fernando de Rojas, Cervantes, and Two Portuguese Folk Stories." *Hispanic Medieval Studies in Honor of Samuel G. Armistead*. Ed. E. Michael Gerli and Harvey L. Sharrer. Madison, WI: Hispanic Seminary of Medieval Studies. 85–96.

———. 1993a. "Adam and Eve Imagery in *Celestina*: A Reinterpretation." *JHP* 17.2-3: 155–90.

———. 1993b. "Anti-Trinitarianism and the Virgin Birth in *La Lozana andaluza*." *Hispania* 76.2: 197–203.

———. 1994. "Between Oral and Written Transmission: *O Sacrifício de Isaac* in the Portuguese Oral Tradition." *JFR* 31: 57–96.

———. 1994–95a. "*El idólatra de María*: An Anti-Christian Jewish Ballad?" *RPh* 48: 255–64.

———. 1994–95b. "The Holy Trinity in *La Lozana andaluza*." *HR* 62: 249–66.

———. 1995. "Female Empowerment and Witchcraft in *Celestina*." *Celestinesca* 19.1–2: 93–104.

———. 1997a. "On Alfonso X's 'Interrupted' Encounter with a *Soldadeira*." *REH* 31: 93–101.

———. 1997b. *O Romanceiro Português e Brasileiro: Índice Temático e Bibliográfico (com uma bibliografia pan-hispânica e resumos de cada romance em inglês) / Portuguese and Brazilian Balladry: A Thematic and Bibliographic Index (with a Pan-Hispanic bibliography and English summaries for each text-type)*. Selection and commentary of the musical transcriptions by Israel J. Katz. Pan-European correlation by Samuel G. Armistead. Madison, WI: Hispanic Seminary of Medieval Studies.

———. 1998a. "Early Motifs and Metaphors in a Modern Traditional Poem: *A Fonte do Salgueirinho*." *LBR* 35: 11–23.

———. 1998b. "The 'Art of Sailing' in *La Lozana andaluza*." *HR* 66: 433–45.

———. 1999. "Duas Novas Orações Criptojudaicas de Rebordelo." *Ecos de uma Viagem: Em Honra de Eduardo M. Dias*. Ed. Francisco Cota Fagundes. Providence, RI: Gávea-Brown. 26–53.

Works Cited

Costa Fontes, Manuel da. 2000. *Folklore and Literature: Studies in the Portuguese, Brazilian, Sephardic, and Hispanic Oral Traditions*. Albany: State U of New York P.

———. 2001. "The Idea of Exile in *La Lozana andaluza*: An Allegorical Reading." Armistead et al., *Jewish Culture* 145–60.

———. 2002. "'Un engaño a los ojos': Sex and Allegory in *La Lozana andaluza*." *Marriage and Sexuality in Medieval and Early Modern Iberia*. Ed. Eukene Lacarra Lanz. Hispanic Issues 26. New York and London: Routledge. 133–57.

Covarrubias, Sebastián de. 1994. *Tesoro de la lengua castellana o española*. Ed. Felipe C. R. Maldonado. Rev. Manuel Camarero. Madrid: Castalia.

Crescas, Hasdai. 1992. *The Refutation of Christian Principles*. Trans. Daniel J. Lasker. Albany: State U of New York P.

Criado de Val, M[anuel]. 1960–63. "Antífrasis y contaminaciones de sentido erótico en *La Lozana andaluza*." *Studia Philologica: homenaje ofrecido a Dámaso Alonso*. 3 vols. Madrid: Gredos. 1: 431–57.

———. 1981. *Cervantes: su obra y su mundo*. Ed. Criado de Val. Madrid: EDI–6.

Cruz, Anne J. 1989. "Sexual Enclosure, Textual Escape: The *Pícara* as Prostitute in the Spanish Female Picaresque Novel." *Seeking the Woman in Late Medieval and Renaissance Writers: Essays in Feminist Contextual Criticism*. Ed. Sheila Fisher and Janet E. Halley. Knoxville: U of Tennessee P. 135–59.

Curtius, Ernst Robert. 1963. *European Literature and the Latin Middle Ages*. Trans. Willard R. Trask. New York and Evanston: Harper.

Damiani, Bruno M. 1969a. Introducción biográfica y crítica. Delicado, *La Lozana andaluza* 9–25.

———. 1969b. "Some Observations on Delicado's *El modo de adoperare el legno de India Occidentale*." *QIA* 37: 13–17.

———. 1970. "*La Lozana andaluza*: tradición literaria y sentido moral." *Actas del Tercer Congreso Internacional de Hispanistas*. Ed. Carlos H. Magis. México, DF: Colegio de México. 241–48.

———. 1972. "Un aspecto histórico de *La Lozana andaluza*." *MLN* 87: 178–92.

———. 1974. *Francisco Delicado*. New York: Twayne.

Damiani, Bruno M., and Louis Imperiale. 1991. "El erotismo en la literatura del Siglo de Oro." *MR* 7: 9–22.

———. 1998. *La Lozana andaluza a través de los siglos*. San Francisco and London: International Scholars.

Dane, Peter. 1979. "The Figure of the Pinnace in 'Aire and Angels.'" *SRLI* 12: 195–208.

Darst, David H. 1983. "The Literariness of *El Abencerraje*." González 265–73.

De Voragine, Jacobus. 1993. *The Golden Legend: Readings on the Saints*. Trans. William Granger Ryan. 2 vols. Princeton, NJ: Princeton UP.

Del Monte, Alberto. 1970. "Il giardino, la scala, la notte." *Acme* 23: 109–15.

Del Río, Angel. 1963. *Historia de la literatura española*. Rev. ed. 2 vols. New York: Holt.

Del Valle Rodríguez, Carlos, ed. 1992. *Polémica judeo-cristiana: estudios*. España Judía, Serie A. Madrid: Aben Ezra.

Delicado, Francisco. 1950. *Retrato de la Loçana andaluza: en lengua española: muy clarissima, cõpuesto en Roma*. Ed. Antonio Pérez Gómez. Valencia: Tipografía Moderna.

———. 1952. *La Loçana andaluza*. Ed. Antonio Vilanova. Barcelona: Selecciones Bibliófilas.

———. 1969. *La Lozana andaluza*. Ed. Bruno M. Damiani. Madrid: Castalia.

———. 1970–71. *El modo de adoperare el legno de India Occidentale*. Ed. Bruno M. Damiani. *RHM* 36: 251–71.

———. 1975. *Retrato de la Loçana andaluza*. Ed. Bruno M. Damiani and Giovanni Allegra. Madrid: José Porrúa Turanzas.

———. 1983. *La Lozana andaluza*. Ed. Giovanni Allegra. Madrid: Taurus.

———. 1985. *Retrato de la Lozana andaluza*. Ed. Claude Allaigre. Madrid: Cátedra.

———. 1987. *Portrait of Lozana, the Lusty Andalusian Woman*. Trans. Bruno M. Damiani. Potomac, MD: Scripta Humanistica.

———. 1988. *La Lozana andaluza*. Ed. Angel Chiclana. Colección Austral. Madrid: Espasa-Calpe.

Delpech, François. 1986. "De Marthe à Martha ou des mutations d'une identité transculturelle." *Culturas populares: diferencias, divergencias, conflictos: Actas del Coloquio celebrado en la Casa de Velázquez, los días 30 de noviembre y 1–2 de diciembre de 1983*. Ed. Yves-René Fonquerne and Alfonso Esteban. Madrid: Casa Velázquez–Universidad Complutense. 55–92.

———. 1994. "'Habla Marta, responde Justa; una puta a otra busca.' Notes de folklore caniculaire." Carrasco, *La prostitution en Espagne* 192–227.

Deyermond, Alan D. 1975. *Lazarillo de Tormes: A Critical Guide*. London: Grant & Cutler–Tamesis.

———. 1977. "Hilado-Cordón-Cadena: Symbolic Equivalence in *La Celestina*." *Celestinesca* 1.1: 6–12.

———. 1984. "'¡Muerto soy! ¡Confesión!': Celestina y el arrepentimiento a última hora." *De los romances-villancico a la poesía de Claudio Rodríguez: 22 ensayos sobre las literaturas española e hispano-americana en homenaje a Gustav Ziebenmann*. Ed. J. M. López de Abiada and A. López Bernasocchi. Madrid: J. Esteban. 129–40.

———. 1991. "Notes on Sentimental Romance: 2. On Text and Interpretation in *Grisel y Mirabella*: The Missing Tower and Other Difficulties." *AMed* 3: 101–13.

———. 2001. "Readers in, Readers of, *Celestina*." Michael and Pattison 13–37.

Deyermond, Alan D., and Ian Macpherson, eds. 1989. *The Age of the Catholic Monarchs, 1474–1516: Literary Studies in Memory of Keith Whinnom*. Liverpool, Eng.: Liverpool UP.

Díez Borque, José María. 1972. "Francisco Delicado, autor y personaje de 'La Lozana andaluza.'" *Prohemio* 3: 455–66.

Domínguez Ortiz, Antonio. [1955]. *Los conversos de origen judío después de la expulsión* [*La clase social de los conversos en Castilla en la Edad Moderna* on cover]. Monografías Histórico-Sociales 3. [Madrid]: Instituto Balmés de Sociología, Departamento de Historia Social, Consejo Superior de Investigaciones Científicas.

———. 1992. *Los judeoconversos en la España moderna*. Madrid: Mafre.

Doncieux, George. 1904. *Le romancéro populaire de la France: Choix de chansons populaires françaises*. Paris: Emile Bouillon.

Dos Santos, Felício. 1897–99. "Linguagem Popular de Trancoso (Notas para o Estudo dos Dialectos Beirões)." *RL* 5: 161–74.

Dunn, Peter N. 1975. *Fernando de Rojas*. Boston: Twayne.

———. 1976a. "A Postscript to *La Lozana andaluza*: Life and Poetry." *RF* 88: 355–60.

———. 1976b. "Pleberio's World." *PMLA* 91: 406–19.

———. 1979. "Narrator as Character in the *Cárcel de amor*." *MLN* 94: 187–99.

Edwards, John. 1996. "Spanish Jews and *Conversos* in Renaissance Rome: *La Lozana andaluza*." *Donaire* no. 6 (Apr.): 31–36.

———. 1999. "Ritual Murder in the Siglo de Oro: Lope de Vega's *El niño inocente de La Guardia*." *Proceedings of the Tenth British Conference on Judeo-Spanish Studies, 29 June–1 July 1997*. Ed. Annette Benaim. London: Dept. of Hispanic Studies, Queen Mary and Westfield College. 73–88.

Eesley, Anne. 1983. "Four Instances of '¡Confessión!' in *Celestina*." *Celestinesca* 7.2: 17–19.

Eisenberg, Daniel. 1976. "Two Problems of Identification in a Parody of Juan de Mena." *Oelschläger Festschrift*. [Chapel Hill, NC]: Estudios de Hispanófila. 157–70.

———. 1987. *A Study of "Don Quixote."* Pref. Richard Bjornson. Newark, DE: Juan de la Cuesta.

Encina, Juan del. 1972. *Poesía lírica y cancionero musical*. Ed. R. O. Jones and Carolyn R. Lee. Madrid: Castalia.

Encyclopædia Judaica. 1974. 16 vols. Jerusalem: Keter Publishing.

England, John. 2000. "'Testigos de mi gloria': Calisto's Bestial Behavior." *La Corónica* 28.2: 81–90.

Erasmus, Desiderius. 1979. *The Praise of Folly*. Trans., introd., and commentary by Clarence H. Miller. New Haven, CT: Yale UP.

Escorial Bible I..ii.19. 1992. Ed. Mark G. Littlefield. Madison, WI. Hispanic Seminary of Medieval Studies.

Escorial Bible I..I.7. 1996. Ed. Mark G. Littlefield. Madison, WI. Hispanic Seminary of Medieval Studies.

Espantoso-Foley, Augusta. 1977. *Delicado: "La Lozana andaluza."* London: Grant & Cutler–Tamesis.

———. 1980. "Técnica audio-visual del diálogo y retrato de *La Lozana andaluza*." Gordon and Rugg 258–60.

Faulhaber, Charles B. 1990. "*Celestina* de Palacio: Madrid, Biblioteca de Palacio, MS 1520." *Celestinesca* 14.2: 3–39.

———. 1991. "*Celestina* de Palacio: Rojas's Holograph Manuscript." *Celestinesca* 15.1: 3–52.

Faur, José. 1992. *In the Shadow of History: Jews and "Conversos" at the Dawn of Modernity*. Albany: State U of New York P.

Fernández-Rivera, Enrique J. 1993. "*Huevos asados*: nota marginal." *Celestinesca* 17.1: 57–60.

Ferrara de Orduna, Lilia. 1973. "Algunas observaciones sobre *La Lozana andaluza*." *AO* 23: 105–15.

Ferré, Pere, Vanda Anastácio, José Joaquim Dias Marques, and Ana Maria Martins. 1982. *Romances Tradicionais*. [Funchal]: Câmara Municipal.

Ferré, Rosario. 1983. "Celestina en el tejido de la 'cupiditas.'" *Celestinesca* 7.1: 3–16.

Ferrer Chivite, Manuel. 1996. "El escudero del *Lazarillo*, cristiano nuevo." Arellano et al. 3: 177–84.

Fraker, Charles F. 1966. "Judaism in the *Cancionero de Baena*." *Studies on the "Cancionero de Baena."* Chapel Hill: U of North Carolina P. 9–62.

Frenk, Margit. 1987. *Corpus de la antigua lírica popular hispánica (siglos XV a XVII)*. Madrid: Castalia.

———. 1997. *Entre la voz y el silencio*. Alcalá de Henares: Centro de Estudios Cervantinos.

Friedman, Edward H. 1987. *The Antiheroine's Voice: Narrative Discourse and Transformations of the Picaresque*. Columbia: U of Missouri P.

Friedman, Jerome. 1978. *Michael Servetus: A Case Study in Total Heresy*. Geneva: Droz.

Galhoz, Maria Aliete Dores. 1987–88. *Romanceiro Popular Português*. 2 vols. Lisboa: Instituto Nacional de Investigação Científica.

Gallina, Annamaria. 1962. "L'attività editoriali di due spagnoli a Venezia nella prima metà del '500." *SI* 1: 69–91.

García, Fray Sebastián. [1995]. "Los judíos en Guadalupe: Abrahán Senneor y su famoso bautismo el 15 de junio de 1492." *Jornadas extremeñas de estudios judaicos: raíces hebreas en Extremadura: del candelabro a la encina, Hervás, 16, 17, 18 y 19 de marzo de 1995: Actas*. Ed. Fernando Cortés Cortés and Lucía Castellano Barrios. Badajoz: Diputación–Revista de Estudios Extremeños–Junta de Extremadura, Consejería de Cultura y Patrimonio. 49–76.

García Cárcel, Ricardo. 1980. "Número y sociología de los familiares de la Inquisición valenciana." Pérez Villanueva 271–83.

García de la Concha, Víctor. 1972. "La intención religiosa del *Lazarillo*." *RFE* 55: 243–47.

García Gómez, Angel M. 1990–93. "Una historia sefardí como posible fuente de *La española inglesa* de Cervantes." *Actas del II Coloquio de la Asociación Internacional de Cervantistas, Alcalá de Henares, 6–9 noviembre 1989.* 3 vols. Barcelona: Anthropos. 621–28.

Garci-Gómez, Miguel. 1981. "'Huevos asados': afrodisíaco para el marido de Celestina." *Celestinesca* 5.1: 23–34.

García Martín, Manuel, Ignacio Arellano, Javier Blasco, and Marc Vitse, eds. 1990–93. *Estado actual de los estudios sobre el Siglo de Oro: Actas del II Congreso Internacional de Hispanistas del Siglo de Oro.* 2 vols. Salamanca: Universidad.

García-Verdugo, María Luisa. 1994. *"La Lozana andaluza" y la literatura del siglo XVI: la sífilis como enfermedad y metáfora.* Madrid: Pliegos.

Gella Iturriaga, José. 1978. "Los refranes de *La lozana andaluza*." *Libro-Homenaje a Antonio Pérez Gómez.* 2 vols. Cieza (Murcia): ". . . la fonte que mana y corre . . . ." 1: 255–68.

Gerber, Jane S. 1992. *The Jews of Spain: A History of the Sephardic Experience.* New York: Free Press.

Gerli, E. Michael. 1981. "Leriano's Libation: Notes on the *Cancionero* Lyric, *Ars Moriendi*, and the Probable Debt to Boccaccio." *MLN* 96: 414–20.

———. 1983. "Calisto's Hawk and the Image of a Medieval Tradition." *Ro* 104: 83–101.

———. 1985. "La tipología bíblica y la Introducción de los *Milagros de Nuestra Señora*." *BHS* 62: 7–14.

———. 1987. Introducción. Berceo 11–66.

———. 1989a. "*El retablo de las maravillas*: Cervantes' *Arte nuevo de deshacer comedias*." *HR* 57: 477–92.

———. 1989b. "Metafiction in Spanish Sentimental Romances." Deyermond and Macpherson 57–63.

———, ed. 1994. *Poesía cancioneril castellana.* Madrid: Akal.

———. 1994–95. "Antón de Montoro and the Wages of Eloquence: Poverty, Patronage, and Poetry in 15th-c. Castile." *RPh* 48: 265–76.

———. 1995a. "Complicitous Laughter: Hilarity and Seduction in *Celestina*." *HR* 16: 19–38.

———. 1995b. *Refiguring Authority: Reading, Writing, and Rewriting in Cervantes.* Lexington: UP of Kentucky.

———. 1996–97. "Performing Nobility: Mosén Diego de Valera and the Poetics of *Converso* Identity." *La Corónica* 25.1: 19–36.

Works Cited

Gil, José S. 1985. *La escuela de traductores de Toledo y sus colaboradores judíos.* Toledo: Instituto Provincial de Investigaciones y Estudios Toledanos, Diputación Provincial.

Gil, Juan. 1986. "Apuleyo y Delicado: el influjo de 'El asno de oro' en 'La Lozana andaluza.'" *Habis* 17: 209–19.

Gili Gaya, Samuel. 1967. Prólogo. *Obras.* By Diego de San Pedro, Clásicos Castellanos 133. Madrid: Espasa-Calpe. vii–xxxvii.

Gillet, Joseph E. 1925. "Traces of the Judas Legend in Spain." *RHi* 65: 316–41.

———. 1931. "Traces of the Wandering Jew in Spain." *RR* 22: 16–27.

Gilman, Stephen. 1954–55. "The Arguments to *La Celestina.*" *RPh* 8: 71–78.

———. 1956. *The Art of "La Celestina."* Madison, WI: U of Wisconsin P.

———. 1966. "The Death of Lazarillo de Tormes." *PMLA* 81: 149–66.

———. 1972. *The Spain of Fernando de Rojas: The Intellectual and Social Landscape of "La Celestina."* Princeton, NJ: Princeton UP.

———. 1974. *"La Celestina": arte y estructura.* Trans. Margit Frenk. Madrid: Taurus, 1982.

Gilman, Stephen, and Ramón Gonzálvez. 1966. "The Family of Fernando de Rojas." *RF* 78: 1–26.

Ginio, Alisa Meyuhas. 1996. "The Fortress of Faith—At the End of the West: Alonso de Espina and His *Fortalitium Fidei.*" Limor and Stroumsa 215–37.

Ginzberg, Louis. 1967–69. *The Legends of the Jews.* 7 vols. Philadelphia: Jewish Publication Society of America.

Gitlitz, David M. 1996. *Secrecy and Deceit: The Religion of the Crypto-Jews.* Philadelphia and Jerusalem: Jewish Publication Society.

———. 1996–97. Letter on "Inflecting the *Converso* Voice." *La Corónica* 25.2: 163–66.

———. 2000. "Inquisition Confessions and *Lazarillo de Tormes.*" *HR* 68: 53–74.

Gitlitz, David, and Linda Kay Davidson. 1999. *A Drizzle of Honey: The Lives and Recipes of Spain's Secret Jews.* New York: St. Martin's.

Glaser, Edward. 1954. "Referencias anti-semitas en la literatura española de la Edad de Oro." *NRFH* 8: 39–62.

Goldberg, Harriet. 1998. *Motif-Index of Medieval Spanish Folk Narratives.* Tempe, AZ: Medieval & Renaissance Texts & Studies.

Gómez-Menor, José Carlos. 1995. "Linaje judío de escritores religiosos y místicos españoles del siglo XVI." Alcalá, *Judíos. Sefarditas. Conversos* 587–600.

Gómez Sierra, Esther. 1996. "Aprender y saber latín: *Marta la Piadosa* vista desde *La Lozana andaluza.*" Arellano et al. 2: 159–67.

González, Angel, Tamara Hozapfel, and Alfred Rodríguez, eds. 1983. *Estudios sobre el Siglo de Oro en homenaje a Raymond R. MacCurdy.* Albuquerque and Madrid: U of New Mexico, Dept. of Modern and Classical Languages, and Cátedra.

Works Cited

Gordon, M., and Evelyn Rugg, eds. 1980. *Actas del sexto congreso internacional de hispanistas*. Toronto: Dept. of Spanish and Portuguese, U of Toronto.

Goytisolo, Juan. 1977. "Notas sobre *La Lozana andaluza*." *Disidencias*. Barcelona: Seix Barral. 37–61.

Green, Otis H. 1953. "La furia de Melibea." *Clavileño* 4 (Mar.–Apr.): 1–3.

Guillén, Claudio. 1966. Introduction. *"Lazarillo de Tormes" and "El Abencerraje."* Laurel Language Library. New York: Dell. 9–49.

———. 1971. *Literature as System: Essays toward the Theory of Literary History*. Princeton, NJ: Princeton UP.

———. 1988. *El primer Siglo de Oro: estudios sobre géneros y modelos*. Barcelona: Crítica.

Guitarte, Guillermo L. 1979. "¿Valdés contra Delicado?" *Homenaje a Fernando Antonio Martínez: estudios de lingüística, filología, literatura e historia cultural*. Bogotá: Instituto Caro y Cuervo. 147–67.

Gurza, Esperanza. 1977. *Lectura existencialista de "La Celestina."* Madrid: Gredos.

Gutwirth, E[leazar]. 1996. "Gender, History, and the Judeo-Christian Polemic." Limor and Stroumsa 257–78.

Haliczer, Stephen. 1990. *Inquisition and Society in the Kingdom of Valencia, 1478–1834*. Berkeley and Los Angeles: U of California P.

Halsey, Martha T. 1994. *From Dictatorship to Democracy: The Recent Plays of Buero Vallejo (from "La Fundación" to "Música cercana")*. Ottawa Hispanic Studies 17. Ottawa, Canada: Dovehouse.

Handy, Otis. 1983. "The Rhetorical and Psychological Defloration of Melibea." *Celestinesca* 7.1: 17–27.

Hawking, Jane. 1967. "Madre Celestina." *AION-SR* 9: 177–90.

Henningsen, Gustav. 1987. "The Eloquence of Figures: Statistics of the Spanish and Portuguese Inquisition and Prospects for Social History." Alcalá, *The Spanish Inquisition and the Inquisitorial Mind* 217–35.

Hernández Ortiz, José A. 1974. *La génesis artística de "La Lozana andaluza": el realismo literario de Francisco Delicado*. Prol. Juan Goytisolo. Madrid: Aguilera.

Herrero, Javier. 1984. "Celestina's Craft: The Devil in the Skein." *BHS* 61: 343–51.

———. 1986. "The Stubborn Text: Calisto's Toothache and Melibea's Girdle." *Literature among Discourses: The Spanish Golden Age*. Ed. W. Godzich and N. Spadaccini. Minneapolis, MN: U of Minnesota P. 132–47, 166–68.

Hesse, Everett W. 1966. "La función simbólica de *La Celestina*." *BBMP* 42: 87–95.

Hodgart, M[atthew] J[ohn] C[aldwell] 1962. *The Ballads*. 2nd ed. London: Hutchinson UP.

Holy Bible. 1961. New American Catholic Ed. New York: Benziger.

Holzinger, Walter. 1978. "The Militia of Love, War, and Virtue in the *Abencerraje y la hermosa Jarifa*: A Structural and Sociological Reassessment." *RCEH* 2: 227–38.

Hook, David. 1978. "'¿Para quién edifiqué torres?': A Footnote to Pleberio's Lament." *FMLS* 14: 25–31.

Hook, Judith. 1972. *The Sack of Rome, 1527*. London: Macmillan.

Huerga Criado, Pilar. 1987. "El inquisidor general Fray Tomás de Torquemada: una Inquisición nueva." *Nuevas aproximaciones* 7–51.

Hughes, John B. 1979. "Orígenes de la novela picaresca: *La Celestina* y *La Lozana andaluza*." *La picaresca: orígenes, textos y estructuras: Actas del I Congreso Internacional sobre la picaresca organizado por el patronato "Arcipreste de Hita*." Ed. M. Criado de Val. Madrid: Fundación Universitaria Española. 327–34.

Hyland, Francis Edward. 1928. *Excommunication: Its Nature, Historical Development and Effects*. Washington, DC: Catholic U of America.

Ilie, Paul. 1994. *Literature and Inner Exile: Authoritarian Spain, 1939–1975*. Baltimore and London: Johns Hopkins UP.

Imperiale, Louis. 1989. "Captación auditiva e imagen visual en la Roma de Francisco Delicado y Pietro Aretino." *Italo-Hispanic Literary Relations*. Ed. J. Helí Hernández. Potomac, MD: Scripta Humanistica. 71–81.

———. 1991. *El contexto dramático de "La Lozana andaluza."* Potomac, MD: Scripta Humanistica.

———. 1994. "Discurso autoral y anti-lenguaje en *La Lozana andaluza*." *CH* 16.2: 321–32.

———. 1995. "La quiebra de la voluntad patriarco-femenina en *La Lozana andaluza*." *Selected Proceedings of the Pennsylvania Foreign Language Conference (1991–1992)*. Ed. Gregorio C. Martín. Pittsburgh, PA: Duquesne U. 151–59.

———. 1997. *La Roma clandestina de Francisco Delicado y Pietro Aretino*. Studies on Cervantes and His Times 6. Prol. Tatiana Bubnova. New York: Lang.

Jacobs, Joseph. 1925. *Jesus as Others Saw Him: A Retrospect A. D. 54*. New York: Bernard G. Richards.

Johnson, Carroll B. 1981. "*La Numancia* y la estructura de la ambigüedad cervantina." Criado de Val, *Cervantes* 309–16.

Joly, Monique. 1988–89. "A propósito del tema culinario en *La Lozana andaluza*." *JHP* 13: 125–33.

Joset, Jacques. 1990–93. "De los nombres de Rampín." García Martín et al. 2: 543–48.

———. 1996. "De los nombres de Rampín (II)." Arellano et al. 3: 273–78.

———. 1997. ". . . y contiene munchas más cosas que la Celestina." *CN* 57.1–2: 147–66.

Works Cited

Joset, Jacques. 1998. "Muestra el Delicado a pronunciar la lengua española." *Estudios en honor del Profesor Josse de Kock*. Ed. N. Delbecque and C. De Paepe. Louvain, Belg.: Leuven UP. 297–310.

Kaiser, Walter. 1963. *Praisers of Folly: Erasmus, Rabelais, Shakespeare*. Cambridge, MA: Harvard UP.

Kamen, Henry. 1986. "Una crisis de conciencia en la Edad de Oro: Inquisición contra 'limpieza de sangre.'" *BHi* 88: 321–56.

———. 1996. "Limpieza and the Ghost of Américo Castro: Racism as a Tool of Literary Analysis." *HR* 64: 19–29.

———. 1998. *The Spanish Inquisition: A Historical Revision*. New Haven and London: Yale UP.

Kaplan, Gregory B. 2002. *The Evolution of "Converso" Literature: The Writings of the Converted Jews of Medieval Spain*. Gainesville: UP of Florida.

Kaplan, Yosef. 2000. "El vínculo prohibido: las relaciones de la 'nación sefardí' occidental con Iberia en el siglo XVII." Carrete Parrondo et al. 39–50.

Kasten, Lloyd A., and Frank J. Cody. 2001. *Tentative Dictionary of Medieval Spanish*. 2nd ed. New York: Hispanic Seminary of Medieval Studies.

Kelley, Erna Berndt. 1985. "Peripecias de un título: en torno al nombre de la obra de Fernando de Rojas." *Celestinesca* 9.2: 3–45.

King, Willard F. 1989. *Juan Ruiz de Alarcón, letrado y dramaturgo: su mundo mexicano y español*. México, DF: Colegio de México.

Kirby, Steven D. 1987. "Observaciones pragmáticas sobre tres aspectos de la crítica celestinesca." *Studia Hispanica Medievalia*. Ed. L. Teresa Valdivieso and Jorge H. Valdivieso. Buenos Aires: Universidad Católica Argentina. 71–79.

———. 1989. "¿Cuándo empezó a conocerse la obra de Fernando de Rojas como *Celestina*?" *Celestinesca* 13.1: 59–62.

Kirschner, Teresa J. 1981. "*El retablo de las maravillas*, de Cervantes, o la dramatización del miedo." Criado de Val, *Cervantes* 819–27.

Kish, Kathleen V., and Ursula Ritzenhoff. 1981. "On Translating 'Huevos Asados': Clues from Christof Wirsung." *Celestinesca* 5.2: 19–31.

Kobler, Franz, ed. 1978. *Letters of the Jews through the Ages: From Biblical Times to the Middle of the Eighteenth Century*. 2 vols. New York: East and West Library.

Lacarra, María Eugenia. 1990. *Cómo leer "La Celestina."* Madrid: Júcar.

———. 1996. "Sobre los 'dichos lascivos y rientes' en *Celestina*." Collera and Roncero López 419–33.

The Ladino Bible of Ferrara [1553]. 1992. Ed. Moshe Lazar. N.p.: Labyrinthos.

Lapesa, Rafael. 1987. Introducción. *El Abencerraje* 11–100.

———. 1997. "El vivir problemático en *La Celestina*." *De Berceo a Jorge Guillén*. Madrid: Gredos. 98–109.

Lasker, Daniel J. 1977. *Jewish Philosophical Polemics against Christianity in the Middle Ages.* New York: Ktav and Anti-defamation League of B'nai B'rith.

———. 1992. Foreword to the English Translation. Crescas 1–15.

Lazar, Moshe. 2000. "Rabbí Moses Arragel as Servant of Two Masters: A Call for Tolerance in a Century of Turmoil." Carrete Parrondo et al. 431–78.

Lázaro Carreter, Fernando. 1972. *"Lazarillo de Tormes" en la picaresca.* Barcelona: Ariel.

———. 1986. *La fuga del mundo como exilio interior (Fray Luis de León y el anónimo del Lazarillo).* Salamanca: Ediciones de la Universidad.

Lázaro Cebrián, Antonio. 1994. "Antonio Enríquez Gómez: el poder político-religioso de su tiempo." López Alvarez et al. 139–45.

Lea, Henry Charles. 1922. *A History of the Inquisition in Spain.* 4 vols. New York: Macmillan.

Lee, Ann Adele. 1979. *"Portrait of Lozana: The Lusty Andalusian Woman," by Francisco Delicado. Translated, Introduction, and Notes.* Diss. Columbia: U of South Carolina.

Leite de Vasconcellos, José. 1958–60. *Romanceiro Português.* 2 vols. Acta Universitatis Conimbrigensis. Coimbra: Universidade.

León, Fray Luis de. 1966–69. *De los nombres de Cristo.* 4th ed. 3 vols. Clásicos Castellanos 28, 33, 41. Madrid: Espasa-Calpe.

Lerner, Isaías. 1971. "Notas para el 'Entremés del retablo de las maravillas': fuente y recreación." *Estudios de literatura ofrecidos a Marcos A. Morínigo, Urbana, Illinois, 14–15 de mayo 1970.* Madrid: Ínsula. 37–55.

Lida [de Malkiel], María Rosa. 1941. "Para la biografía de Juan de Mena." *RFH* 3: 150–54.

———. 1946. "La hipérbole sacroprofana en la poesía castellana del siglo XV." *RFH* 8: 121–30.

———. 1950. *Juan de Mena, poeta del prerrenacimiento español.* México, DF: Colegio de México.

———. 1962. *La originalidad artística de "La Celestina."* Buenos Aires: Universitaria.

Lima, Robert. 1998. "The Arcane Paganism of Celestina: Platonic Magic Versus Satanic Witchcraft in *Tragicomedia de Calixto y Melibea.*" *Neophilologus* 82: 221–33.

Limor, Ora, and Guy G. Stroumsa, eds. 1996. *Contra Iudaeos: Ancient and Medieval Polemics between Christians and Jews.* Tübingen: Mohr.

Lindo, E. H. [1848] 1970. *The History of the Jews of Spain and Portugal.* New York: Burt Franklin.

Logan, F. Donald. 1986. "Excommunication." *Dictionary of the Middle Ages.* Ed. Joseph R. Strayer. New York: Scribner. 4: 536–38.

Works Cited

López Alvarez, Ana María, María Luisa Menéndez Robles, Ricardo Izquierdo Benito, and Santiago Palomero Plaza, eds. 1994. *Inquisición y conversos: conferencias pronunciadas en el III Curso de Cultura Hispano-Judía y Sefardí de la Universidad de Castilla–La Mancha celebrado en Toledo del 6 al 9 de septiembre de 1993.* Madrid: Asociación de Amigos del Museo Sefardí, Caja de Castilla–La Mancha.

López-Baralt, Luce, and Francisco Márquez Villanueva, eds. 1995. *Erotismo en las letras hispánicas: aspectos, modos y fronteras.* México, DF: Colegio de México.

López de Cortegana, Diego. 1915. Prohemio. *Apuleyo* 4: 1–3.

López de Úbeda, Francisco. 1982. *La pícara Justina.* Ed. Bruno Mario Damiani. Potomac, MD: Studia Humanitatis.

Maccoby, Hyam, ed. 1993. *Judaism on Trial: Jewish-Christian Disputations in the Middle Ages.* London and Washington: Littman Library of Jewish Civilization.

Mackay, Angus. 1989. "Courtly Love and Lust in Lioja." Deyermond and Macpherson 83–94.

———. 1992. "A Lost Generation: Francisco Delicado, Fernando del Pulgar, and the *Conversas* of Andalusia." *Circa 1492: Proceedings of the Jerusalem Colloquium: Litterae Judaeorum in Terra Hispanica.* Ed. Isaac Benabu. Jerusalem: Hebrew U, Faculty of Humanities–Misgav Yerushalayim Institute for Research on Sephardi and Oriental Jewish Heritage. 224–35.

Macpherson, Ian. 1985. "Secret Language in the *Cancioneros*: Some Courtly Codes." *BHS* 62: 51–63.

Macpherson, Ian, and Angus Mackay. 1998. *Love, Religion and Politics in Fifteenth Century Spain.* Leiden: Brill.

Macpherson, Ian, and Ralph Penny, eds. 1997. *The Medieval Mind: Hispanic Studies in Honour of Alan Deyermond.* London: Tamesis.

Malkiel, Yakov. 1948. "Hispano-Arabic *Marrano* and Its Hispano-Latin Homophone." *JAOS* 68: 175–84.

Mancing, Howard. 1976. "Fernando de Rojas, *La Celestina*, and *Lazarillo de Tormes*." *KRQ* 23: 47–61.

Mandrell, James. 1983–84. "Author and Authority in *Cárcel de amor*: The Role of El Auctor." *JHP* 8: 99–102.

Mann, Vivian B., Thomas F. Glick, and Jerrylinn D. Dodds, eds. 1992. *Convivencia: Jews, Muslims, and Christians in Medieval Spain.* New York: George Braziller and the Jewish Museum.

Manuel, Don Juan. 1991. *Libro de los enxiemplos del Conde Lucanor e de Patronio.* Madrid: Cátedra.

Maravall, José Antonio. 1986. *El mundo social de "La Celestina."* 3rd ed. Madrid: Gredos.

Works Cited

Marciales, Miguel. 1985. Introduction and critical ed. *Celestina: tragicomedia de Calisto y Melibea*. By Fernando de Rojas. Ed. Brian Dutton and Joseph T. Snow. 2 vols. Illinois Medieval Monographs 1. Urbana and Chicago: U of Illinois P.

Márquez Villanueva, Francisco. 1960. *Investigaciones sobre Juan Álvarez Gato: contribución al conocimiento de la literatura castellana del siglo XV*. Madrid: Anejos del Boletín de la Real Academia Española 4.

———. 1966. "'Cárcel de amor,' Novela Política." *ROcc* 14.2: 185–200. Rpt. in *Relecciones de literatura medieval*. Sevilla: Universidad de Sevilla, 1977. 75–94.

———. 1968. "Santa Teresa y el linaje." *Espiritualidad y literatura en el siglo XVI*. Madrid and Barcelona: Alfaguara. 139–205.

———. 1973. "El mundo converso de *La Lozana andaluza*." *AHisp* nos. 171–73: 87–97.

———. 1976. "Historia cultural e historia literaria: el caso de *Cárcel de amor*." *The Analysis of Hispanic Texts: Current Trends in Methodology: First York College Colloquium*. 2 vols. Vol. 1: Ed. Mary Ann Beck et al. Vol. 2: Ed. Lina E. Davis and Isabel C. Tarán. New York: Bilingual. 2: 145–57.

———. 1979. "Un aspect de la littérature du fou en Espagne." *L'humanisme dans les lettres espagnoles*. Ed. Augustin Redondo. Paris: J. Vrin. 233–50. Span. trans.: "Planteamiento de la literatura del 'loco' en España." *Sin Nombre* 10.4 (1979–80): 7–25.

———. 1980. "La locura emblemática en la segunda parte del *Quijote*." *Cervantes and the Renaissance: Papers of the Pomona College Cervantes Symposium, November 16–18, 1978*. Ed. Michael D. McGaha. Newark, DE: Juan de la Cuesta. 87–112.

———. 1982. "Jewish 'Fools' of the Spanish Fifteenth Century." *HR* 50: 385–409.

———. 1983. "La idendidad de Perlícaro." *Homenaje a José Manuel Blecua, ofrecido por sus discípulos, colegas y amigos*. Madrid: Gredos. 423–32.

———. 1985–86. "Literatura bufonesca o del loco." *NRFH* 34: 501–28.

———. 1987. "La *Trivagia* y el problema de la conciencia religiosa de Juan del Encina." *La Torre* 1: 473–500.

———. 1988. "Pan 'pudendum muliebris' y *Los españoles en Flandes*." Ricapito, *Hispanic Studies* 247–69.

———. 1991. "Juan Ruiz de Alarcón, al fin sin secretos." *Saber Leer* no. 43 (Mar.): 8–9.

———. 1993. *Orígenes y sociología del tema celestinesco*. Barcelona: Anthropos.

———. 1994a. "El canto de cisne de Mateo Alemán: los sucesos de d. frai García Guerra (1613)." López Alvarez et al. 241–60.

———. 1994b. *El concepto cultural alfonsí*. Madrid: Mapfre.

Works Cited

Márquez Villanueva, Francisco. 1994c. "'Nasçer e morir como bestias' (criptojudaísmo y averroísmo)." *Los judaizantes en Europa y la literatura castellana del Siglo de Oro.* Ed. Fernando Díaz Esteban. Madrid: Letrúmero. 273–93.

———. 1994d. "Nueva visión de la Escuela de Traductores toledanos." *The Heritage of the Jews of Spain: Proceedings of the First International Congress (Tel-Aviv, 1–4 July 1991).* Ed. Aviva Dorón. Tel-Aviv: Levinsky College of Education Publishing. 123–46.

———. 1996–97. Letter on "Inflecting the *Converso* Voice." *La Corónica* 25.2: 168–79.

———. 1998. "El problema con nuestros clásicos." *Quimera* no. 169 (June): 32–41.

———. 2000a. "Hispano-Jewish Cultural Interactions: A Conceptual Framework." Carrete Parrondo et al. 13–25.

———. 2000b. "Sobre el concepto de judaizante." Carrete Parrondo et al. 519–42.

———. 2001. "El mundo poético de los *Disparates* de Juan del Encina." Armistead et al. 351–79.

Martínez de Toledo, Alfonso. 1992. *Arcipreste de Talavera o Corbacho.* Ed. Michael Gerli. 4th ed. Madrid: Cátedra.

Martínez López, Enrique. 1992. "Mezclar berzas con capachos: armonía y guerra de castas en el *Entremés del Retablo de las Maravillas de Cervantes.*" *BRAE* 72: 67–171.

Martínez Torrón, Diego. 1979. "Erotismo en *La Lozana andaluza.*" *Erotismos.* Madrid: Espiral/Revista 6. 59–122.

Martins, Mário. 1978. *O Riso, o Sorriso, e a Paródia na Literatura Portuguesa de Quatrocentos.* Biblioteca Breve 15. Lisboa: Instituto de Cultura Portuguesa.

Maurizi, Françoise. 1998. "La escala de amor de Calisto." *Celestinesca* 22.2: 49–60.

McGrady, Donald. 1968. *Mateo Alemán.* New York: Twayne.

———. 1970. "Social Irony in the *Lazarillo de Tormes* and Its Implications for Authorship." *RPh* 23: 557–67.

———. 1994. "The Problematic Beginning of *Celestina.*" *Celestinesca* 18.2: 31–51.

McPheeters, D. W. 1961. *El humanista español Alonso de Proaza.* Madrid: Castalia.

Melammed, Renée Levine. 1999. *Heretics or Daughters of Israel? The Crypto-Jewish Women of Castile.* New York and Oxford: Oxford UP.

Menéndez y Pelayo, Marcelino. 1961. *Orígenes de la novela.* 4 vols. Obras Completas 16. 2nd ed. Madrid: Consejo Superior de Investigaciones Científicas. 4: 45–67.

Menéndez Pidal, Ramón. 1956. "España y la introducción de la ciencia árabe en Occidente." *España, eslabón entre la Cristiandad y el Islam.* Colección Austral 1280. Madrid: Espasa-Calpe. 33–60.

Menocal, María Rosa. 1987. *The Arabic Role in Medieval Literary History.* Philadelphia: U of Pennsylvania P.

———. 1988. "And How 'Western' Was the Rest of Europe?" Surtz 183–89.

Metzger, Bruce M., and Michael D. Coogan, eds. 1993. *The Oxford Companion to the Bible*. New York and Oxford: Oxford UP.

Michael, Ian. 2001. "*Celestina* and the Great Pox." Michael and Pattison 103–38.

Michael, Ian, and David G. Pattison, eds. 2001. *Context, Meaning and Reception of "Celestina": A Fifth Centenary Symposium*. Spec. issue of *BHS* 78.1: 1–176 pp. Also Abingdon: Carfax Publ. (Taylor & Francis Group); [Glasgow]: U of Glasgow, 2000.

Miguel Martínez, Emilio de. 1996. *"La Celestina" de Rojas*. Madrid: Gredos.

Millás Vallicrosa, José M. 1942. *Nuevas aportaciones para la transmisión de la ciencia a Europa a través de España*. Barcelona: Real Academia de Buenas Letras.

Moner, Michel. 1981. "Las maravillosas figuras de *El retablo de las maravillas*." Criado de Val, *Cervantes* 809–17.

Monroe, James T. 1985–86. "Prolegómenos al estudio de Ibn Quzmān: el poeta como bufón." *NRFH* 34: 769–99.

Montoro, Antón de. 1990. *Cancionero*. Ed. Marcella Ciceri. Introd. and notes by Julio Rodríguez Puértolas. Salamanca: Universidad.

Moon, Harold K. 1985. *Alejandro Casona*. Boston: Twayne.

Morales Blouin, Egla. 1981. *El ciervo y la fuente: mito y folklore del agua en la lírica tradicional*. Studia Humanitatis. Madrid: José Porrúa Turanzas.

Morón Arroyo, Ciriaco. 1974. *Sentido y forma de La Celestina*. Madrid: Cátedra.

———. 1984. *Sentido y forma de La Celestina*. 2nd rev. ed. Madrid: Cátedra.

———. 1994. *Celestina and Castilian Humanism at the End of the Fifteenth Century*. Occasional Papers 3. Binghamton, NY: Medieval and Renaissance Texts and Studies.

Mound, Gloria. 1984. "The Hitherto Unknown Jews of Ibiza and Formentera." *Glasgow 1984: Abstracts of Papers*. Ed. Nicholas G. Round. Glasgow: U of Glasgow, Dept. of Hispanic Studies. 19–20.

Nepaulsingh, Colbert I. 1995. *Apples of Gold in Filigrees of Silver: Jewish Writing in the Eyes of the Inquisition*. New York and London: Holmes & Meier.

Netanyahu, B. 1979–80. "Américo Castro and His View of the Origins of the Pureza de Sangre." *PAAJR* 46–47: 397–457.

———. 1994. *Los marranos españoles desde fines del siglo XIV a principios del XVI según las fuentes hebreas de la época*. Trans. Ciriaco Morón Arroyo. N.p.: Junta de Castilla y León, Consejería de Cultura y Turismo.

———. 1995. *The Origins of the Inquisition in Fifteenth-Century Spain*. New York: Random. A second edition (New York: New York Review of Books, 2001) appeared when the present book was already in final form; since the revisions and alterations do not seem to be extensive, I continued to follow the first edition.

Works Cited

Netanyahu, B. 1999. *The Marranos of Spain from the Late 14th to the Early 16th Century according to Contemporary Hebrew Sources.* 3rd ed. Ithaca and London: Cornell UP.

———. 2000. "The Old-New Controversy about Spanish Marranism." Carrete Parrondo et al. 545–78.

New Catholic Encyclopedia. 1967. Prepared by an Editorial Staff at Catholic University of America. 16 vols. New York: McGraw-Hill.

Nuevas aproximaciones: Inquisición española. 1987. Madrid: Centro de Estudios Inquisitoriales.

Nunes, José Joaquim. 1926–28. *Cantigas d'Amigo dos Trovadores Galego-Portugueses: Edição Crítica acompanhada de Introdução, Comentário, Variantes e Glossário.* 3 vols. Coimbra: Universidade. (Vol. 2 is from 1926; vols. 1 and 3 appeared in 1928).

———. [1959]. *Crestomatia Arcaica: Excertos da Literatura Portuguesa desde o que mais antigo se conhece até ao século XVI, acompanhada de Introdução Gramatical, Notas e Glossário.* 5th ed. Lisboa: Livraria Clássica.

Olinger, Paula. 1985. *Images of Transformation in Traditional Hispanic Poetry.* Newark, DE: Juan de la Cuesta.

Orduna, Germán. 1999. "El original del manuscrito de la *Comedia* de Fernando de Rojas: una conjetura." *Celestinesca* 23.1–2: 3–10.

Orozco, Beato Alonso de. 1966. "De nueve nombres de Cristo." Appendix to León 1: 257–77.

Paglialunga de Tuma, Mercedes. 1973. "Erotismo y parodia social en 'La Lozana andaluza.'" *La idea del cuerpo en las letras españolas (Siglos XIII a XVII).* Ed. Dinko Cvitanovic et al. Bahia Blanca, Arg.: Instituto de Humanidades, Universidad del Sur. 118–53.

Papo, Joseph M. 1987. *Sephardim in Twentieth Century America: In Search of Unity.* San Jose and Berkeley: Pelé Yoetz Books–Judah L. Magnes Museum.

Parlett, David. 1986. *Selections from the "Carmina Burana": A Verse Translation.* New York: Penguin.

Parrilla, Carmen. 1995. Prólogo. San Pedro, *Cárcel de amor* xxxvii–lxxxi.

Partridge, Eric. 1968. *Shakespeare's Bawdy: A Literary & Psychological Essay and a Comprehensive Glossary.* Rev. and enlarged. London: Routledge.

Paulo, Amílcar. 1971. *Os Criptojudeus.* Porto: Athena.

———. 1985. *Os Judeus Secretos em Portugal.* Porto: Labirinto.

Pedrosa, José Manuel. 1992a. "Correspondencias judías y cristianas de la oración de *Las cuatro esquinas.*" *Brigantia* 12: 19–39.

———. 1992b. "Oraciones y conjuros tradicionales de Logrosán (Cáceres)." *RFolk* no. 137: 159–63.

———. 1993. "Conjuros y ritos mágicos sobre la dentición infantil." *RDTP* 48: 155–67.

Works Cited

———. 1997. "El culto y la *Oración de San Onofre* en la tradición hispano-luso-brasileña." *RLNS* no. 16: 11–22.

———. 1998. "*Las tres llaves* y *Los huevos sin sal*: versiones hispano-cristianas y sefardíes de dos ensalmos mágicos tradicionales." *Sefarad* 58: 153–65.

———. 2000. *Entre la magia y la religión: oraciones, conjuros, ensalmos*. Biblioteca Mítica 2. Oiartzun, Gipuzkoa: Sendoa.

Pelikan, Jaroslav. 1978. *The Growth of Medieval Theology (600–1300)*. The Christian Tradition: A History of the Development of Doctrine 3. Chicago and London: U of Chicago P.

Pérez, Joseph. 1981. "La unidad religiosa en la España del siglo XVI." *Seis lecciones sobre la España de los Siglos de Oro (literatura e historia): homenaje a Marcel Bataillon*. Ed. Pedro M. Piñero Ramírez and Rogelio Reyes Cano. Sevilla: Universidad de Sevilla–Université de Bordeaux. 95–110.

Pérez de Guzmán, Fernando. 1965. *Generaciones y semblanzas*. Ed. J. Domínguez Bordona. Clásicos Castellanos 61. Madrid: Espasa-Calpe.

Pérez Villanueva, Joaquín, ed. 1980. *La Inquisición española: nueva visión, nuevos horizontes*. Madrid: Siglo Veintiuno.

Pharies, David. 1994. "The Derivation of Ibero-Romance *sing(l)ar, cing(l)ar, ching(l)ar*, etc." *BHS* 71: 301–28.

Pike, Ruth. 1969. "The *Conversos* in *La Lozana andaluza*." *MLN* 84: 304–08.

———. 2000. *"Linajudos" and "Conversos" in Seville: Greed and Prejudice in Sixteenth- and Seventeenth-Century Spain*. New York and Bern: Lang.

Pinto, Virgilio. 1987. "Censorship: A System of Control and an Instrument of Action." Alcalá, *The Spanish Inquisition and the Inquisitorial Mind* 303–20.

Porto Bucciarelli, Lucrecia Beatriz. 1990. "La paremiología, lo erótico y lo hampesco en *La Lozana andaluza*." *Marginalismo-S (Actas del 3.º Symposium Internacional del Departamento de Español de la Universidad de Groningen, 15, 16, y 17 de octubre de 1984)*. Ed. J. L. Alonso Hernández. Groningen: Rijksuniversiteit Groningen. 129–42.

Prieto, Antonio. 1975. *Morfología de la novela*. Barcelona: Planeta.

Pulgar, Fernando del. 1953. *Crónica de los muy altos e muy poderosos don Fernando e doña Isabel*. Ed. Cayetano Rosell. Biblioteca de Autores Españoles 70. Madrid: Atlas. 229–511.

———. 1958. *Letras: glosa a las Coplas de Mingo Revulgo*. Ed. J. Domínguez Bordona. Clásicos Castellanos 99. Madrid: Espasa-Calpe.

Purcell, Joanne B. 1987. *Novo Romanceiro Português das Ilhas Atlânticas, 1*. Ed. Isabel Rodríguez-García and João A. das Pedras Saramago. Fuentes para el Estudio del Romancero: Serie Luso-Brasileira 4. Madrid: Seminario Menéndez Pidal–Universidad Complutense.

Quevedo, Francisco de. 1988. *La vida del Buscón llamado don Pablos*. Ed. James Iffland. Newark, DE: Juan de la Cuesta.

Rank, Jerry R. 1980–81. "The Uses of 'Dios' and the Concept of God in *La Celestina*." *RCEH* 5: 75–91.

Raphael, David, ed. 1992. *The Expulsion 1492 Chronicles*. North Hollywood, CA: Carmi House.

Real Academia Española. 1939. *Diccionario de la lengua española*. 16th ed. Madrid: Espasa-Calpe.

Real de la Riva, César. 1962. "Notas a *La Celestina*." *Strenae: estudios de filología e historia dedicados al profesor Manuel García Blanco*. Filosofía y Letras 16. Salamanca: Acta Salmanticensia. 383–92.

Recio, P. Alejandro. 1955. "La Inmaculada en la predicación franciscano-española." *AIA* (2nd Series) 15: 105–200.

Reckert, Stephen, and Hélder Macedo. N.d. *Do Cancionero de Amigo*. 2nd ed. Lisboa: Assírio & Alvim.

Redondo, Agustín. 1965. "Fernando de Rojas y la Inquisición." *Mélanges* 1: 345–47.

Reed, Cory A. 1993. *The Novelist as Playwright: Cervantes and the "Entremés nuevo."* New York and Bern: Lang.

Resende, Garcia de. 1973. *Cancioneiro Geral*. Ed. Álvaro Júlio da Costa Pimpão and Aida Fernandes Dias. 2 vols. Coimbra: Centro de Estudos Românicos, Instituto de Alta Cultura.

Reyes, Alfonso. 1945. "La Garza Montesina." *Capítulos de literatura española (segunda serie)*. México, DF: Colegio de México. 89–99.

———. 1960–63. "Un enigma de *La Lozana andaluza*." *Serta Philologica: homenaje ofrecido a Dámaso Alonso por sus amigos y discípulos con ocasión de su 60.º aniversario*. 3 vols. Madrid: Gredos. 3: 151–54.

Rica, Carlos de la. 1994. "Antonio Enríquez Gómez: un nombre para la libertad." López Alvarez et al. 131–37.

Ricapito, Joseph V., ed. 1988. *Hispanic Studies in Honor of Joseph H. Silverman*. Newark, DE: Juan de la Cuesta.

———. 1996a. "Al-Andalus and the Origins of the Renaissance in Europe." *IJHL* 8: 55–74.

———. 1996b. *Cervantes's "Novelas ejemplares": Between History and Creativity*. Purdue Studies in Romance Literatures 10. West Lafayette, IN: Purdue UP.

Rivera, Olga. 2002. "La leche maternal y el sujeto de los descendientes en *La perfecta casada*." *HR* 70: 207–17.

Rivkin, Ellis. 1982. "How Jewish Were the New Christians?" Solà-Solé et al. 1: 105–15.

Robbins, Rossell Hope. 1959. *The Encyclopedia of Witchcraft and Demonology*. New York: Crown.

Robe, Stanley L. 1973. *Index of Mexican Folktales*. Folklore Studies 26. Berkeley: U of California P.

Rodrigues Lapa, Manuel, ed. 1995. *Cantigas d'escarnho e de mal dizer dos cancioneiros medievais galego-portugueses.* 3rd ed. Vigo and Lisboa: Ir Indo–João Sá da Costa.

Rodríguez Puértolas, Julio. 1968a. *Fray Iñigo de Mendoza y sus "Coplas de Vita Christi."* Madrid: Gredos.

———. 1968b. *Poesía de protesta en la Edad Media castellana: historia y antología.* Madrid: Gredos.

———. 1986. "Copleros y 'juglares' en el *Cancionero de Baena.*" *La juglaresca: Actas del I Congreso Internacional sobre la Juglaresca.* Ed. Manuel Criado de Val. Madrid: EDI-6. 101–09.

———. 1990. "Antón de Montoro y su poesía." Montoro 11–32.

———. 1996. Estudio preliminar. Rojas, *La Celestina* 5–96.

———. 1998. "Jews and *Conversos* in Fifteenth-Century Castilian *Cancioneros*: Texts and Contexts." *Poetry at Court in Trastamaran Spain: From the "Cancionero de Baena" to the "Cancionero General."* Ed. E. Michael Gerli and Julian Weiss. Tempe, AZ: Medieval & Renaissance Texts & Studies. 187–97.

Rogers, Edith. 1980. *The Perilous Hunt: Symbols in Hispanic and European Balladry.* Lexington: UP of Kentucky.

Rojas, Fernando de. [1958] 1975. *Celestina: A Play in Twenty-One Acts attributed to Fernando de Rojas.* Trans. Mack Hendricks Singleton. Madison: U of Wisconsin P.

———. 1968. *La Celestina.* Ed. Julio Cejador y Frauca. 2 vols. 6th ed. Clásicos Castellanos 20, 23. Madrid: Espasa-Calpe.

———. 1983. *La Celestina.* Ed. Dorothy S. Severin. 10th ed. Madrid: Alianza.

———. 1985. *Celestina: tragicomedia de Calisto y Melibea.* Introd. and critical ed. Miguel Marciales. Ed. Brian Dutton and Joseph T. Snow. 2 vols. Illinois Medieval Monographs 1. Urbana and Chicago: U of Illinois P.

———. 1987. *La Celestina.* Ed. Dorothy S. Severin. Notas en colaboración con Maite Cabello. Madrid: Cátedra.

———. 1991. *Comedia o tragicomedia de Calisto y Melibea.* Ed. Peter E. Russell. Madrid: Castalia.

———. 1995. *La Celestina.* Ed. María Eugenia Lacarra. 2nd ed. Madison, WI: Hispanic Seminary of Medieval Studies.

———. 1996. *La Celestina.* Ed. Julio Rodríguez Puértolas. Madrid: Akal.

Roncero López, Victoriano. 1996. "Algunos temas de la poesía humorística de Antón de Montoro." Collera and Roncero López 567–80.

Rose, Constance Hubbard. 1971. *Alonso Núñez de Reinoso: The Lament of a Sixteenth-Century Exile.* Rutherford, NJ: Dickinson UP.

———. 1973. "Antonio Enríquez Gómez and the Literature of Exile." *RF* 85: 63–77.

Works Cited

Rose, Constance Hubbard. 1977. "Antonio Enríquez Gómez et Manuel Fernandes de Villareal: Deux destins parallèles, une vision politique commune." *REJ* 136: 368–86.

———. 1983. "Alonso Núñez de Reinoso's Contribution to the Creation of the Novel." *Creation and Recreation: Experiments in Literary Form in Early Modern Spain: Studies in Honor of Stephen Gilman*. Ed. Ronald Surtz and Nora Weinerth. Newark, DE: Juan de la Cuesta. 89–103.

———. 1987. "The Marranos of the Seventeenth Century and the Case of the Merchant Writer Antonio Enríquez Gómez." Alcalá, *The Spanish Inquisition and the Inquisitorial Mind* 53–71.

———. 2000. "Antonio Enríquez Gómez y el templo de Salomón." Carrete Parrondo et al. 413–29.

Rose, Stanley E. 1983. "Anti-Semitism in the *Cancioneros* of the Fifteenth Century: The Accusation of Sexual Indiscretions." *Hispanófila* 26.3 [78] (May): 1–10.

Roth, Norman. 1995. *Conversos, Inquisition, and the Expulsion of the Jews from Spain*. Madison: U of Wisconsin P.

Roy, Claude. 1954. *Trésor de la poésie populaire française*. Textes choisis avec la collaboration de Claire Vervin. Paris: Seghers.

Ruggerio, Michael J. 1966. *The Evolution of the Go-Between in Spanish Literature through the Sixteenth Century*. University of California Publications in Modern Philology 78. Berkeley and Los Angeles: U of California P.

———. 1970. "*La Celestina*: Didacticism Once More." *RF* 82: 56–64.

———. 1977. "The Religious Message of *La Celestina*." *Studies in the Literature of Spain: Sixteenth and Seventeenth Centuries*. Ed. Ruggerio. Folio Papers on Foreign Languages and Literatures 10. Brockport, NY: Dept. of Foreign Languages, State U of New York. 69–81.

Ruiz, Juan. 1974. *Libro de buen amor*. Ed. Jacques Joset. 2 vols. Clásicos Castellanos 14, 17. Madrid: Espasa-Calpe.

———. 1999. *Libro del buon amore*. Trans. Vincenzo la Gioia. Ed. and notes by Giuseppe di Stefano. Milan: Rizzoli.

Russell, Peter E. 1978. "La magia como tema integral de la *Tragicomedia de Calisto y Melibea*." *Studia Philologica: homenaje a Dámaso Alonso*. 3 vols. Madrid: Gredos, 1961–63. 3: 337–54. Rpt. in his *Temas de "La Celestina" y otros estudios: del Cid al Quijote*. Barcelona: Ariel. 241–76.

———. 1991. Introducción. Rojas, *Comedia o tragicomedia de Calisto y Melibea* 11–173.

———. 2001. "The *Celestina* Then and Now." Michael and Pattison 1–11.

Russell, Peter E., et al., eds. 1982. *Introducción a la cultura hispánica, I. Historia, arte, música*. Trans. Josep María Portella. Barcelona: Crítica.

Saint Andrew Daily Missal with Vespers for Sundays and Feasts. [1953]. Ed. Dom Gaspar Lefebvre. Bruges, Belg. and Saint Paul, MN: Abbey of St. André and E. M. Lohmann.

Works Cited

Salomon, Noël. 1985. *Lo villano en el teatro del Siglo de Oro.* Trans. Beatriz Chenot. Madrid: Castalia.

Salstad, Mary Louise. 1982. "Biblical Parody in *La Lozana andaluza.*" *Iberoromania* 15: 21–36.

Salucio, Fray Agustín. 1975. *Discurso sobre los estatutos de limpieza de sangre (s.l.n.a. ¿1600?).* Introd. Antonio Pérez and Gómez Cid. Cieza (Murcia): ". . . la fonte que mana y corre . . . ."

Salvador Miguel, Nicasio. 1984. "Huellas de 'La Celestina' en 'La Lozana andaluza.'" *Estudios sobre el Siglo de Oro: homenaje a Francisco Ynduráin.* Madrid: Nacional. 431–59.

———. 1989. "El presunto judaísmo de *La Celestina.*" Deyermond and Macpherson 162–77.

San Pedro, Diego de. 1984. *Cárcel de amor.* Ed. Keith Whinnom. 2nd ed. Obras completas 2. Madrid: Castalia.

———. 1985. *Tractado de amores de Arnalte y Lucenda; Sermón.* Ed. Keith Whinnom. 2nd ed. Obras completas 1. Madrid: Castalia.

———. 1995. *Cárcel de amor: con la continuación de Nicolás Núñez.* Ed. Carmen Parrilla. Estudio preliminar de Alan Deyermond. Barcelona: Crítica.

Sancha, Justo de, ed. 1950. *Cancionero y romancero sagrados.* Biblioteca de Autores Españoles 35. Madrid: Atlas.

Sánchez Sánchez-Serrano, Antonio, and María Remedios Prieto de la Iglesia. 1991. *Fernando de Rojas y "La Celestina."* Barcelona: Teide.

Santa Biblia, con Deuterocanónicos. 1983. Versión popular. 2nd ed. Consejo Episcopal Latinoamericano. Nueva York: Sociedad Bíblica Americana.

Saraiva, António José. 1956. *A Inquisição Portuguesa.* Lisboa: Europa-América.

———. 1969. *Inquisição e Cristãos-Novos.* Porto: Inova.

———. 1985. *Inquisição e Cristãos-Novos.* 5th ed.: Lisboa: Estampa.

Schlichting, Günter. 1982. *Ein jüdisches Leben Jesu: die verschollene Toledot-Jeschu-Fassung Tam ⁻u-m⁻uʿad. Einleitung, Text, Übersetzung, Kommentar, Motivsynopse, Bibliographie.* Tübingen: J. C. B. Mohr (Paul Siebeck).

Scholberg, Kenneth R. 1971. *Sátira e invectiva en la España medieval.* Madrid: Gredos.

Selke, Angela. 1972. *Los chuetas y la Inquisición: vida y muerte en el ghetto de Mallorca.* Madrid: Taurus.

———. 1980. "El iluminismo de los conversos y la Inquisición: cristianismo interior de los 'alumbrados': resentimiento y sublimación." Pérez Villanueva 617–36.

Seniff, Dennis P. 1985. "'El falso boezuelo con su blando cencerrar': or, the Pantomime Ox Revisited." *Celestinesca* 9.1: 43–45.

Serrano Poncela, Segundo. 1962. "Aldonza la andaluza Lozana en Roma." *CuA* 122: 117–32.

Works Cited

Serrano y Sanz, M. 1902. "Noticias biográficas de Fernando de Rojas, autor de *La Celestina*, y del impresor Juan de Lucena." *RABM* 6: 245–99.

Severin, Dorothy S. 1980. "Parodia y sátira en *La Celestina*." Gordon and Rugg 695–97.

———. 1987. Introducción. Rojas, *La Celestina* 11–64.

———. 1995. *Witchcraft in "Celestina."* Papers of the Medieval Hispanic Research Seminar 1. London: Dept. of Hispanic Studies, Queen Mary and Westfield College.

———. 1997. "Was Celestina's Claudina Executed as a Witch?" Macpherson and Penny 417–24.

Shakespeare, William. 1937. *The Passionate Pilgrim*. In *Complete Works*. Roslyn, NY: Walter J. Black.

Shepard, Sanford. 1975. "Prostitutes and Pícaros in Inquisitional Spain." *Neohelicon* 3: 365–72.

———. 1982. *Lost Lexicon: Secret Meanings in the Vocabulary for Spanish Literature during the Inquisition*. Miami: Universal.

Shipley, George A. 1973–74. "'Non erat hic locus': The Disconcerted Reader in Melibea's Garden." *RPh* 27: 288–308.

———. 1975. "Concerting through Deceit: Unconventional Uses of Conventional Sickness Images in *La Celestina*." *MLR* 70: 324–32.

———. 1977–78. "La obra literaria como monumento histórico: el caso de *El Abencerraje*." *JHP* 2: 103–20.

Sicroff, Albert A. 1960. *Les controverses des statuts de "pureté de sang" en Espagne du XVe au XVIe siècle*. Paris: Didier.

———. 1965. "Clandestine Judaism in the Hieronymite Monastery of Nuestra Señora de Guadalupe." *Studies in Honor of M. J. Benardete*. Ed. Izaak A. Langnas and Barton Sholod. New York: Las Américas. 89–125.

———. 1966. "El caso del judaizante Jerónimo Fray Diego de Marchena." *Homenaje a Rodríguez-Moñino; estudios de erudición que le ofrecen sus amigos o discípulos hispanistas norteamericanos*. 2 vols. Madrid: Castalia. 2: 227–33.

———. 1980. "Notas equívocas en dos dramatizaciones de Lope del problema judaico: *El niño inocente de la Guardia* y *La hermosa Ester*." Gordon and Rugg 701–05.

———. 1985. *Los estatutos de limpieza de sangre: controversias entre los siglos XV y XVI*. Madrid: Taurus.

———. 1988. "The Arragel Bible: A Fifteenth-Century Rabbi Translates and Glosses the Bible for His Christian Master." Surtz et al. 173–82.

———. 1996. "La huida poética de fray Luis de León." *San Juan de la Cruz and Fray Luis de León: A Commemorative International Symposium, November 14–16, 1991, Hilles Library at Harvard University*. Ed. Mary Malcolm Gaylord and Francisco Márquez Villanueva. Newark, DE: Juan de la Cuesta. 275–88.

———. 2000. "Spanish Anti-Judaism: A Case of Religious Racism." Carrete Parrondo et al. 589–613.

Silverman, Joseph H. 1961. "Judíos y conversos en el *Libro de chistes* de Luis de Pinedo." *PSA* no. 69: 289–301.

———. 1971a. "Los 'hidalgos cansados' de Lope de Vega." *Homenaje a William L. Fichter: estudios sobre el teatro antiguo hispánico y otros ensayos.* Ed. A. David Kossoff and José Amor y Vásquez. Madrid: Castalia. 693–711.

———. 1971b. "Some Aspects of Literature and Life in the Golden Age of Spain." *Estudios de literatura ofrecidos a Marcos A. Morínigo, Urbana, Illinois, 14–15 de mayo de 1970.* Madrid: Ínsula. 131–70.

———. 1976. "The Spanish Jews: Early References and Later Effects." *Américo Castro and the Meaning of Spanish Civilization.* Ed. José Rubia Barcia and Selma Margaretten. Berkeley and Los Angeles: U of California P. 137–65.

———. 1978. "Saber vidas ajenas: un tema de vida y literatura y sus variantes cervantinas." *PSA* 267: 197–212.

———. 1983. "Una anécdota de Lope de Vega y Juan de Luna: *Mirad a quién alabáis, En los indicios la culpa* y la *Segunda parte de la vida de Lazarillo de Tormes.*" González et al. 103–08.

Snow, Joseph T. 1985. *Celestina by Fernando de Rojas: An Annotated Bibliography of World Interest 1930–1985.* Madison, WI: Hispanic Seminary of Medieval Studies.

———. 1989. "'¿Con qué pagaré esto?': The Life and Death of Pármeno." Deyermond and Macpherson 185–92.

———. 1991. Prólogo. Sánchez Sánchez-Serrano and Prieto de la Iglesia iii–vi.

———. 1995. "Fernando de Rojas as First Reader: Reader-Response Criticism and *Celestina.*" Vaquero and Deyermond 245–58.

———. 1997. "Reading the Silences of Fernando de Rojas." Macpherson and Penny 445–56.

Solà-Solé, Josep M., Samuel G. Armistead, and Joseph H. Silverman, eds. 1982. *Hispania Judaica: Studies on the History, Language, and Literature of the Jews of the Hispanic World.* 2 vols. Barcelona: Puvill.

Solà-Solé, Joseph M., and S. E. Rose. 1976–77. "Judíos y conversos en la poesía cortesana del siglo XV: el estilo políglota de Fray Diego de Valencia." *HR* 44: 371–85.

Spector, Norman. 1956. "The Procuress and Religious Hypocrisy." *Italica* 33: 52–59.

Steinschneider, Moritz. [1893] 1956. *Die hebraeischen Übersetzungen des Mittelalters und die Juden als Dolmetscher.* Graz: Akademische Druck- u. Verlagsanstalt.

Stern, Charlotte. 1996. *The Medieval Theater in Castile.* Medieval and Renaissance Studies 156. Binghamton, NY: Center for Medieval and Early Renaissance Studies.

Strauss, Leo. 1952. *Persecution and the Art of Writing.* Glencoe, IL: Free Press.

Works Cited

Street, Florence. 1953. "La vida de Juan de Mena." *BHi* 55: 149–73.

Suárez, Luis. 1992. *La expulsión de los judíos de España*. 2nd ed. Madrid: Mapfre.

Surtz, Ronald E. 1982. "'Sancta Lozana, ora pro nobis': Hagiography and Parody in Delicado's *Lozana andaluza*." *RoY* 33: 286–92.

———. 1992. "Texto e imagen en el *Retrato de la Lozana andaluza*." *NRFH* 40: 169–85.

———. 1995. "Características principales de la literatura escrita por conversos: algunos problemas de definición." Alcalá, *Judíos. Sefarditas. Conversos* 547–56.

Surtz, Ronald E., Jaime Ferrán, and Daniel P. Testa, eds. 1988. *Américo Castro: The Impact of His Thought: Essays to Mark the Centenary of His Birth*. Madison, WI: Hispanic Seminary of Medieval Studies.

Tavares, Maria José Pimenta Ferro. 1987. *Judaísmo e Inquisição: Estudos*. Lisboa: Presença.

Tillier, Jane Yvonne. 1985. "Passion Poetry in the *Cancioneros*." *BHS* 62: 65–78.

Toft, Evelyn. 1995. "La ascendencia judía de San Juan de la Cruz: huellas en su biografía y sus escritos." Alcalá, *Judíos. Sefarditas. Conversos* 601–08.

Tomás Álvarez, P. 1995. "Santa Teresa de Ávila en el drama de los judeo-conversos castellanos." Alcalá, *Judíos. Sefarditas. Conversos* 609–30.

Ugolini, Francesco A. 1974–75. *Nuovi dati intorno alla biografia di Francisco Delicado desunti da una sua sconosciuta operetta*. Estratto dagli Annali della Facoltà di Lettere e Filosofia della Università degli Studi di Perugia 12. Perugia: Di Salvi.

Valdeón Baruque, Julio. 1994. "Los orígenes de la Inquisición en Castilla." López Alvarez et al. 35–45.

Valle Lersundi, Fernando. 1929. "Testamento de Fernando de Rojas, autor de *La Celestina*, otorgado en la villa de Talavera, el 3 de abril de 1541." *RFE* 16: 366–88.

van Beysterveldt, Antony. 1977. "Nueva interpretación de *La Celestina*." *Segismundo* 11: 87–116.

Vaquero, Mercedes, and Alan Deyermond, eds. 1995. *Studies on Medieval Spanish Literature in Honor of Charles F. Fraker*. Madison, WI: Hispanic Seminary of Medieval Studies.

Vasvari, Louise O. 1983. "La semiología de la connotación: lectura polisémica de 'Cruz cruzada panadera.'" *NRFH* 32: 299–324.

———. 1983–84. "An Example of 'Parodia Sacra' in the *Libro de Buen Amor*: '*Quoniam*' '*Pudenda*.'" *La Corónica* 12: 195–203.

———. 1992. "Pitas Pajas: Popular Phonosymbolism." *REH* 26: 135–62.

———. 1994. "'L'usignuolo in gabbia': Popular Tradition and Pornographic Parody in the *Decameron*." *FI* 28: 224–51.

———. 1995 [for 1992]. "Joseph on the Margin: The Mérode Tryptic and Medieval Spectacle." *Mediaevalia* 18: 164–89.

Vega, Carlos Alberto. 1995. "Erotismo y ascetismo: imagen y texto en un incunable hagiográfico." López-Baralt and Márquez Villanueva 479–97.

Vega Carpio, Lope de. 1985. *El niño inocente de La Guardia.* Ed. Anthony J. Farrell. London: Tamesis.

Vian Herrero, Ana. 1990. "El pensamiento mágico en *Celestina,* 'instrumento de lid o contienda.'" *Celestinesca* 14.2: 41–91.

———. 1997. "Transformaciones del pensamiento mágico: el conjuro amatorio en la *Celestina* y en su linaje literario." Beltrán and Canet 209–38.

Vicente, Gil. [1979]. "Auto da Feira." *Obras completas de Gil Vicente.* Ed. Álvaro Júlio da Costa Pimpão. Porto: Livraria Civilização. 126–38.

La vida de Lazarillo de Tormes y de sus fortunas y adversidades. 1976. Ed. Joseph V. Ricapito. Madrid: Cátedra.

Vilanova, Antonio. 1952a. "Cervantes y *La Lozana andaluza.*" *Ínsula* no. 77 (May): 5.

———. 1952b. "La vida de Francisco Delgado." Delicado, *La Loçana andaluza* xi–lx.

Villa Calleja, Ignacio. 1987. "Investigación histórica de los 'Edictos de Fe' en la Inquisición Española (siglos XV–XIX)." *Nuevas aproximaciones* 233–56.

Villanueva, Darío. 1980. "Sobre Francisco Delicado, obispo de Lugo y Jaén." *BRAE* 90: 135–42.

Vodola, Elisabeth. 1986. *Excommunication in the Middle Ages.* Berkeley and Los Angeles: U of California P.

Wack, Mary Frances. 1990. *Lovesickness in the Middle Ages: The Viaticum and Its Commentaries.* Philadelphia: U of Pennsylvania P.

Waddell, Helen. 1934. *The Wandering Scholars.* 7th ed. London and New York: Constable–Barnes and Noble, 1966.

Wardropper, Bruce W. 1952. "Allegory and the Role of the Author in the *Cárcel de amor.*" *PhQ* 31: 39–44.

———. 1953a. "El mundo sentimental de la 'Cárcel de amor.'" *RFE* 37: 168–93.

———. 1953b. "La novela como retrato: el arte de Francisco Delicado." *NRFH* 7: 475–88.

———. 1984. "The Butt of Satire in *El retablo de las maravillas.*" *Cervantes* 4.1: 25–33.

Watt, W. Montgomery. 1972. "L'influence de l'Islam sur l'Europe médievale." *REI* 40: 297–327.

Weinberg, F. M. 1971. "Aspects of Symbolism in *La Celestina.*" *MLN* 86: 136–53.

Weiner, Jack. 1969. "Adam and Eve Imagery in *La Celestina.*" *PLL* 5: 389–96.

———. 1973. "El 'Santo Grillimón' en un poema del cancionero de Sebastián de Horozco." *Hispanófila* 47–49: 11–16.

West, Geoffrey. 1979. "The Unseemliness of Calisto's Toothache." *Celestinesca* 3.1: 3–10.

Works Cited

Whinnom, Keith. 1974. *Diego de San Pedro*. New York: Twayne.

———. 1980. "'La Celestina,' 'The Celestina,' and L2 Interference in L1." *Celestinesca* 4.2: 19–21.

———. 1981a. "Interpreting *La Celestina*: The Motives and the Personality of Fernando de Rojas." *Mediaeval and Renaissance Studies on Spain and Portugal in Honour of P. E. Russell*. Ed. F. W. Hodcroft et al. Oxford: Society for the Study of Mediaeval Languages and Literature. 53–68.

———. 1981b. *La poesía amatoria de la época de los Reyes Católicos*. Durham, Eng.: U of Durham.

———. 1984. Introducción crítica. San Pedro, *Cárcel de amor* 7–70.

———. 1985. Introducción biográfica y crítica. San Pedro, *Tractado de amores de Arnalte y Lucenda* 9–69.

Williams, George Hunston. 1962. *The Radical Reformation*. Philadelphia: Westminster.

———. 1972. "The Two Social Strands in Italian Anabaptism, ca. 1526–ca. 1565." *The Social History of the Reformation*. Ed. Lawrence P. Buck and Jonathan W. Zophy. Columbus: Ohio State UP. 156–207.

Willis-Altamirano, Susan. 2001. *Buero Vallejo's Theatre: Coded Resistance Models of Enlightment*. Frankfurt and New York: Lang.

Index

Aarne, Antti, and Stith Thompson, 300n19
Abencerraje y la hermosa Jarifa, El, 52–53, 88, 92–94, 97, 99
Abiram, and Dathan, 302n14
Abrabanel, Isaac, 29, 31
Abraham, 1, 75–76
Abrams, J. N., 287n22
adafina (*cholent*), 25, 277n43
Adam, 54–55, 59, 128–29. *See also* Adam and Eve
Adam and Eve, 60, 127, 151–70, 253, 289–90n49. *See also* Adam; Eve
Aguilar, Alonso de, 64
Alarcón, Juan Ruiz de, 52, 280n26
Alaroza, 212, 299n12
Albó, Joseph, 168, 210
Albright, Madeleine, 275n19
Alcalá de Henares, University, 48
Alemán, Mateo, 280n28, 285nn23–24
  Guzmán de Alfarache, 52, 97, 283–84n11
Alexander VI, Pope, 8, 29, 277n47
Alfonso VI, king of Leon and Castile, 273n2ch1
Alfonso X, "The Wise," king of Castile, 6, 111, 291n62
  Cantigas de Santa María, 111, 157, 162
  General estoria, 282n49
  Siete partidas, 6
Alfonso XI, king of Castile, 2
aljamas (*juderías*), 1, 24
Allaigre, Claude, *xii*, 180, 205–06, 213–14, 227, 283n5, 295n11, 298n41, 299n8, 300n16, 301n3, 302n9
Allegra, Giovanni, 43, 47, 49, 195, 212, 278n7, 279nn15 and 19, 294n1
Allen, D. C., 296n15
alumbrados (Illuminists), 17, 19, 135, 276n31
Alvarez, Leonor, 36
Alvarez Gato, Juan, 52, 68, 280n23
Amadís de Gaula, 47–48
American disease, 297n37. *See also* syphilis
Anabaptism (Italian), 299n11
Anaya, Diego de, 7
Anderson, George K., 300n19
Andrew, St., cross of,16
Annunciation, 156, 165, 167, 202, 206, 252, 254–55, 284n17, 299n8

anusim (forced converts), 23–24
Apple of Discord, 153
Appolonia, St., 104, 150, 251, 289n46, 300n14, 302n15
Apuleius, Lucius, *Golden Ass*, 232–33
Arana, Rodrigo de, 61–62
Aranda, Pedro de, bishop of Calahorra, 16
Arbués, Pedro de, 19
Aretino, Pietro, 174
  I ragionenti, 199
Arianism, 55
Aristotle, 142, 277n39
Armistead, Samuel G., *xii*, 282n48
  and Joseph H. Silverman, 139
Arnold, St., ass of (oath), 207, 251
Arragel de Guadalajara, Rabbi Mosé, 79
  Biblia del Alba, 79
Asensio, Eugenio, 279n14
Attila, 50, 279n20
Augustinians, 10
auto-da-fé, 14–15, 19, 36, 39, 93, 297n27
Averroes, 210, 277n39

Babylon, 73, 77
Baena, Juan Alfonso de, 51, 58–62, 67–68, 220
Baltanás, Fray Domingo de, 10–11
  Apologías sobre ciertas materias morales en que hay opinión, 10
banter, 57–58, 61, 63, 67–69, 233, 245, 248
baptism, 3–4, 7, 31, 36, 59–60, 132, 142, 169, 205, 248, 275n15
barcarolas ("boat songs"), 176
Barkaï, Ron, 274n11, 284n13
Barrick, Mac, 124
Beatitudes, 146–47
Beinart, Haim, 23, 25, 276n23
bella en misa, La, 288n37
Benedict XIII, Pope, 4–5
Berceo, Gonzalo de, 123, 162
  Milagros de Nuestra Señora, 157, 281n32
Bernáldez, Andrés, 23, 30–31, 278n49, 282n2
  Memorias del reinado de los Reyes Católicos, 80
Berrong, Richard M., *xii*
Black Mass, 124, 127, 131, 145, 254
Black Plague, 2
Blázquez Miguel, Juan, 19, 22, 25, 27–28

339

Index

blood purity. *See limpieza de sangre*
boat of folly, 193. *See also* folly; ship of fools
boat of love. *See* love boat
Boccaccio, Giovanni, 295n15, 302n11
Bonilla, Alonso de, 160
Bourbon, Charles de, 294n1
Brakhage, Pamela, 173
Brant, Sebastian, *Ship of Fools*, 231
Bubnova, Tatiana, 39, 45, 47, 174, 198
Buero Vallejo, Antonio, 53, 281n29
buffoon. *See* court jesters

Cancionero de Baena, x, 51–62, 69, 76, 138, 211
Cancionero de obras de burlas provocantes a risa, 235–36
Cannavagio, Jean, 284–85n22
cannibalism. *See* Eucharist: and cannibalism
cantigas de amigo, 176
cantigas d'escarnho e de mal dizer, 106, 291n62
captatio benevolentiae, 279n13
Carajicomedia, 235, 302n6
Cárcel de amor. *See* San Pedro, Diego de
Cardiel Sanz, Estrella, 292n71
Carmina Burana, 291n62
Caro, Rodrigo, 282n2
Cartagena, Alonso de, 81
Casona, Alejandro, 53, 281n29
Castro, Américo, xi, 52, 79, 84, 100, 103, 135, 274n12, 280n25, 288n37, 292n71
Catholic Monarchs, 8, 13–14, 20–21, 28–31, 68–69, 71, 77, 195, 234, 278n48, 290n54, 297n27
Cattapan, Javier E., Rabbi, *xii*, 282n45
Celestina (Rojas), *x*, 33, 37, 51, 84–90, 99–170, 231, 238–54, 257
Celestine II, Pope, 239
censorship, *xi*, 53, 69, 78, 135, 257, 281n29, 282n50
Cepeda, Alonso de, 12
Cervantes, Juan de, 35
Cervantes, Miguel de, *xii*, 53, 88, 94, 295n8
  El cerco de Numancia, 279–80n20
  El coloquio de los perros, 96
  Don Quijote, 11, 96–97, 273n1Pref, 300–01n21
  La española inglesa, 284n16
  El retablo de las maravillas, 94–95

Charles III, king of Navarre, 3
Charles V, Holy Roman Emperor, *x*, 9, 12, 35, 44, 172–73, 228, 255
Cherchi, Paolo, 287n24
Chiclana, Angel, 49, 174
Chirino, Alonso, 68
cholent, 277n43. *See also adafina*
Clement VII, Pope, 41, 48
Comedia Hipólita, 236
Comedia Seraphina, 236
Comedia Thebayda, 236
Comes amoris, 296n15
Commisso, Rosa, *xii*
Communion. *See* Eucharist
confession, 129–30, 130, 169, 290–91nn56–57, 292n70
Constantine, Roman emperor, 216–17
Contreras, Jaime, 17
convivencia, 1, 273nn1–2ch1, 274n6
Coplas de Fajardo, 235
Corominas, Joan, 110, 274n10
Correa, Gustavo, 119, 287n19
Cortés, Hernán, 35
Costanilla de Valladolid, 59, 91
Cota, Rodrigo, 52, 101, 280n23, 281n35, 286n4
courtesans, 213, 227–28
court jesters, 57–67, 219, 231
courtly love, 71, 73–74, 77, 105–07, 287n17, 290n50
Covarrubias, Sebastián de, 83, 109, 113, 144
Craddock, Jerry, *xii*, 302n13
Crescas, Hasdai Ben Judah, 210
  The Refutation of Christian Principles, 142, 166
Cruz, Anne, 198–99
crypto-Catholics, 284n16
crypto-Judaism, 14–15, 17, 20–22, 24–28, 35, 51, 77, 92, 108, 136, 141, 195, 275n18, 276nn27 and 30, 279n19, 284n16, 297n29. *See also* Judaize

Damiani, Bruno M., *xii*, 49, 173–75, 195, 212, 295n7, 299n6, 301n3
  and Louis Imperiale, 294n5
Darias Davila, Juan, bishop of Segovia, 16
Darst, David, 94
Dathan and Abiram, 302n14
Davidson, Linda Kay, David Gitlitz and, 277n43
Davihuelo, 58

Index

Decius, Roman emperor, 251
Delicado, Francisco, 38–50. *See also Lozana andaluza, La*
De consolatione infirmorum, 38, 44, 194
El modo de adoperare el legno de India Occidentale, 38, 41–44, 50, 191, 194, 202, 208
Spechio vulgare per li Sacerdoti, 38–40, 43, 191–92
Deyermond, Alan, 125
Deza, Diego de, 18, 68, 282n2
Disputation of Tortosa, 5–6, 60, 168, 210, 274n11, 299n10
Di Stefano, Giuseppe, 299–300n12
Divine Providence, 102, 189, 277n39, 292n70
Domínguez Ortiz, Antonio, 6, 18, 31–32, 280n22
Dominicans, 10, 14
Donne, John, 296n15
du Guesclin, Bertrand, 2, 59
Dunn, Peter, 173–74, 278n6, 295n10
Duran, Profit, 60, 167–68, 254
Duran, Simon, 210
d'Urbina, Gian, 50

Edict of Grace, 35–36
Edward, "the Black Prince," 2
Edwards, John, 174
Eesley, Anne, 130
Egypt, 25, 75
Egypt, St. Mary of, 174
Ehrman, Radd, *xii*
Eisenberg, Daniel, *xii*
Elizabeth, St., 165
Encina, Juan del, 41, 52, 168, 280n25, 286n13, 294n30, 300n21
Enríquez, Juana, 12
Enríquez Gómez, Antonio, 52, 280n26
entierro de Fernandarias, El, 294n25
Erasmus, *The Praise of Folly*, 118
Espantoso-Foley, Augusta, 173–75
Espina, Alonso de, *Fortalitium Fidei*, 14
Eucharist, 124, 164–66, 204–05, 254
and cannibalism, 164–65, 204
Eve, 128, 139. *See also* Adam and Eve
excommunication, 247–48

familiar, 20, 276nn35–36
Faulhaber, Charles B., 286n3

Faur, José, 277n40
Ferdinand III, of Castile, 1
Ferdinand, "the Catholic," 12, 19, 22, 29, 35. *See also* Catholic Monarchs
Fernández, Lucas, 280n25
Ferrara de Orduna, Lilia, 45
Ferrer, St. Vincent, 4–6
Ferrer Chivite, Manuel, 92
filles de la Rochelle, Les, 295n15
Fogaça, Diogo, 178
folk spells, 104, 150, 202, 208–09, 220, 250–51, 256, 289n46, 300nn13–14
folly, 214, 218–19, 229, 231, 255. *See also* boat of folly; ship of fools
Fraker, Charles, 54, 168, 211
Francis, St., 37, 141
Franciscans, 9
French disease, 180–82, 189, 208, 297n37. *See also* American disease; Neapolitan disease; Spanish disease; syphilis
Friedman, Edward, 174, 197

García de la Concha, Víctor, 135
García-Verdugo, María Luisa, 197, 298n47
Garci-Gómez, Miguel, 289n40
Garden of Eden, 55, 126, 128–29, 152, 154–55, 158, 169–70, 253–54
Genseric, 50
George, St., 250
Gerber, Jane S., 6, 29, 274n7
Gerli, E. Michael, 128, 157, 289n45
Gillet, Joseph E., 300n19
Gilman, Stephen, *xi*, 34, 84, 87, 99–100, 136, 278n6, 285n2, 292n71, 293n8
Gitlitz, David M., and Linda Kay Davidson, 277n43
Gloria, 209, 250
Gómez Barroso, Pedro, 2
González, William H., *xii*
González de Mendoza, Pedro, Cardinal of Spain, 81
González de Rojas, Garcí, 34
Good Shepherd, 162–63, 294n24
Goytisolo, Juan, 174, 198
Great Mother, 107–08
Guadalupe
    Jeronimite monastery, 8, 82, 167, 293n8
    Santa María sanctuary, 30, 277–78n48
Guevara, Fray Antonio de, 219

341

Index

Guillén, Claudio, 93
Guitarte, Guillermo L., 279n14
Gurza, Esperanza, 122, 287nn19 and 23
Gutwirth, Eleazar, 142
Guzmán, Leonor de, 2
Guzmán, Luis de, 79

ha-Levi, Salomon. *See* Santa María, Pablo de
Haliczer, Stephen, 16
ha-Lorqui, Joshua. *See* Santa Fe, Jerónimo de
Hawking, Jane, 110
Helen, St., 208
Henningsen, Gustav, 17
Henry II, king of Castile, 2–3
Henry III, king of Castile, 3–4
Henry IV, king of Castile, 14, 52, 68, 234, 290n54
Hernández, Diego, 72, 78
Hernández Ortiz, José, 47, 173, 232, 236, 238
Herrero, Vian, 289n47
Hochhauser, Herbert, 297n30
Holy Office. *See* Inquisition
Holy Trinity, x, 37–38, 53–55, 60–62, 76–77, 140, 142–43, 151, 165, 167–68, 170, 202, 209–30, 246–47, 250, 254–56, 299nn10–11, 301nn24, 25, 28
hortus conclusus ("enclosed garden"), 126–29, 134, 155–56, 158, 161, 168–69, 253, 293n18
Hughes, John B., 174, 238
humilitas, 279n13
Hundred Years' War, 2

idólatra de María, El, 27, 138–39, 223
Ignatius, St., 9–10
Ilie, Paul, *Literature and Inner Exile*, 53
Illuminists. *See alumbrados*
images, veneration of, 142, 151
Immaculate Conception, 289–90n49
Imperiale, Louis, 174, 185, 198–99, 298n48
  and Bruno M. Damiani, 294n5
incantation. *See* folk spells
Incarnation, x, 26, 142–43, 166, 168, 170, 209, 223, 228, 230, 254, 299nn10–11, 301n24
Inquisition, 9–10, 12–28, 35–36, 38–39, 50–53, 63–69, 71–72, 77–78, 80, 82, 84, 93, 103, 137–38, 140–41, 147, 174–75, 184, 195–96, 201, 227, 247–48, 255, 257, 275n15, 277n46, 280–81n28, 282n2, 283n4, 293n11, 297n27

Isaac, 1
Isabella, "the Catholic," 22, 52, 64, 281n36.
  See also Catholic Monarchs
Ishmael, 1
Isis, 232

Jacobs, Joseph, 252–53
Jacob's ladder. *See* Ladder of Jacob
James, St. *See* Santiago
Jeronimites, 8, 16, 82, 293n8
Jesuits, 9, 19
Jesus. *See* name of Jesus
Jiménez de Enbún, Jerónimo, 93
John I, king of Castile, 6
John II, king of Castile, 7–8, 19, 51–52, 68
John, St., the Baptist, 150, 153, 165, 207, 251
John of the Cross, St., x, 52, 280n24
John Paul II, Pope, 294n31
Joly, Monique, 296n24
Joseph, St., 56, 166–67, 203, 284n17
Joset, Jacques, 233, 245, 247, 298–99n5
Juan d'Espera en Dios. *See* Wandering Jew
Judaize, 11, 16–18, 20, 22–25, 29, 34, 275n22. *See also* crypto-Judaism
Judas, 145, 185
juderías (aljamas), 1
Julius II, Pope, 40
Juvenal, 234

Kamen, Henry, 5, 12, 18, 31–32, 274n8
Kaplan, Gregory, 74, 282n42
King's New Clothes, The, 95
Kirby, Steven D., 292n71
Kish, Kathleen V., and Ursula Ritzenhoff, 289n40
Koran, 1

Labrador, José, *xii*
Lacarra, María Eugenia, *xii*, 107, 163–64, 278n6, 286n13, 288n33
Ladder of Jacob, 155–56, 254
Laínez, Diego, 9
La Montaña, 12, 98, 285n26
  montañés, 59
Lancaster, Catalina of, 4
Lando, Ferrant Manuel de, 52–53, 58–59, 61, 76–77, 220
Lando, Pedro de, 59
Lapesa, Rafael, 94, 291–92n69
Larson, Jennifer, *xii*
Lasker, Daniel J., 167

Index

Lazarillo de Tormes. See *vida del Lazarillo de Tormes, La*
Lázaro Carreter, Fernando, 69
lena ("procuress"), 132
Leo X, Pope, 39, 184
León, Fray Luis de, 52, 159, 276n29, 280n24
 De los nombres de Cristo, 10–11
Leonisio de Salamanca, 139
Libro llamado el Alboraique, 281n38
Lida de Malkiel, María Rosa, 132, 245
limpieza de sangre ("blood purity"), 7–12, 18, 32, 34, 39, 71–73, 77, 79–100, 192, 217, 219, 238, 248–49, 275n16, 283nn5 and 9, 284n20, 285n23, 296n25, 300n15
linajudos, 275n20
Litany of Loreto, 287n27
literatura de cordel ("chapbook literature"), 179
locus amoenus, 126, 152
López de Cortegana, Diego, 232–33
López de Úbeda, Francisco, 295n8
 La pícara Justina, 98, 280–81n28
López de Villalobos, Francisco, 35, 219
love boat, 193, 295–96n15
lovesickness, 288n29
Lozana andaluza, La (Delicado), x, 33–34, 38, 40–41, 44–47, 49–51, 83–84, 171–257
Lucero, Diego Rodríguez, 27
Lucrece, 178
Ludueña, Hernando de, *Descomunión de amores fecha a su amiga*, 226, 246, 295n10
Luna, Alvaro de, 7
Luna, Juan de, *Segunda parte de la vida de Lazarillo de Tormes*, 276n36
Luna, Pedro de, Cardinal, 4

Mackay, Angus, 174, 207, 298n43
Magdalene, St. Mary, 43, 147–50, 202, 207–08, 250–51
Magnificat, 165, 254
Maimonides, Moses, 135, 210, 252, 277n39, 302n17
Maldonado de Silva, Francisco, 26
malsines ("back biters"), 18
mamotreto ("bundle of papers"), 33, 171–72
Manuel, Don Juan, 284n18

Manuel I, king of Portugal, 291n67
Marchena, Diego, 8, 274n14, 275n15
Marciales, Miguel, 34–35, 148, 285n26, 288n32
Maria maris stella, 162, 254
Mariana, Juan de, 19, 31
marinas ("sailing songs"), 176
Mariolatry, 131
Mariology, 131
Marmolejo, Juan, 67
Márquez Villanueva, Francisco, *xii*, 24, 38, 68, 71, 174, 183, 219, 273n2ch1, 280n28, 292n70
marranos, 1, 3, 6–7, 20, 59, 201, 228, 255
Martha, St., 42–43, 202–03, 207–08, 251
Martínez, Ferrant, 2–3
Martínez, Miguel, 151
Martínez de Toledo, Alfonso, 132, 302n11
 Arcipreste de Talavera o Corbacho, 234
Martínez Guijeño, Juan. See Silíceo
Martínez Torrón, Diego, 198
Martins, Mário, 178
Mary, Virgin. See name of Mary
Matthew, St., gospel of 147
McGrady, Donald, 91, 285n2
Melammed, Renée Levine, 4, 23–24
Mena, Juan de, 52, 101, 280n23
Mendoza, Fray Iñigo de, 52, 68, 280n23
Menéndez y Pelayo, Marcelino, 41, 186, 231–32
meshumadim ("renegades"), 24
Messiah, 5, 26, 38, 53, 108, 118, 130, 135–36, 142, 209, 299n10, 301n24
metaphors, sexual, 288n30, 296n20, 297n28
Michael, St., 150–51, 250
misa de amor, La, 288n37
Monçón, Iñigo de, 37
Monja, Fray Alfonso de la, 53
Montalbán, Alvaro de, 36–37
Montalbán, Pero de, 36
Montesino, Fray Ambrosio de, 160
Montoro, Antón de ("El Ropero"; "Clothes Merchant"), *x*, 52, 63–68, 78, 183, 280n23
Moors. See Muslims
Moriah, Mount, 1
Moriscos, 19, 40, 50, 93–94, 284nn13–14, 294n25, 296n24
Morón Arroyo, Ciriaco, 102, 107–09, 112, 126, 136, 164–65, 287–88n28, 288–89n39, 290n56

343

Index

Muslims, 1, 6, 12, 16, 28, 37, 63–64, 83, 92, 99, 139, 209, 216, 273n1ch1, 274nn5–6 and 10–11, 277n39, 285n26, 296n24

Nahmanides, 210
name of Jesus, avoidance of, 26–27, 134–37, 145, 151, 202–05, 239, 251–53, 284n12, 291n61
name of Mary, avoidance of, 27, 134–35, 137, 145, 151, 202, 205–07, 239, 251–53, 284n12
Narboni, Moses, 210
Navarra, Blanca de, 290n54
Neapolitan disease, 297n37. *See also* syphilis
Nebrija, Antonio de, 48–49, 279n14
Nefija, St., 207, 251
Netanyahu, B., 6–7, 24, 31, 276n23, 277n41
New Adam, 128, 140, 156–59, 161, 169–70, 254, 281n32
New Christians, *ix, x*, 3–4, 7–12, 17–19, 22, 26, 29, 36, 39, 51, 68–69, 73–74, 80–81, 83, 96–97, 100, 137, 174, 183, 192, 201, 211, 217–20, 223, 228, 275nn18 and 22, 285n26, 297n38
New Eve, 127–28, 140, 156–58, 161, 169–70, 254
Nicholas V, Pope, 8
niña de Gómez Arias, La, 206
Niño de La Guardia, 277n46
Nula, St., 207
Núñez, Costanza, 36
Núñez Coronel, Fernán. *See* Seneor, Abraham
Núñez de Reinoso, Alonso, *Historia de los amores de Clareo y Florisea*, 52

"O Come All Ye Little Streamers," 296n15
Old Christians, *ix*, 7, 9–10, 12, 18–21, 24–26, 50, 57, 59, 68–69, 76, 80, 82–84, 92, 95–97, 99, 137, 143, 151, 182, 192, 201–02, 217, 219, 248, 274n8, 275n18, 286n10, 300n20
Orange, Prince of, Filisberto de Chalôns, 294n1
Original Sin, 54–55, 59, 142, 170, 254, 289–90n49
Oropesa, Diego de, 36
Orozco, Alonso de, 159

Ovid
  Ars amatoria, 296n15
  Remedia amoris, 296n15

Paglialunga de Tuma, Mercedes, 198
Partridge, Eric, 293n21, 295–96n15
Passion of Christ, 54–55, 59, 75, 156, 291n62
Paul, St., 10, 27, 169
Pederzano, Giovan Battista, 47
Pérez de Guzmán, Fernán, 279n17
  Generaciones y semblanzas, 234, 275–76n22
Peter, St., 73–74, 77, 150–51
Peter I, of Castile, 2
Pharaoh, 25, 75–76, 282nn48–49
Pharies, David, 295n15
Philip II, of Spain, 9, 12–13, 17
Piçario de Palacios, Alvaro, 11
Pike, Ruth, 174
Pompey, 217
Portugal, 11, 15, 17, 21, 27, 31, 137, 195, 277n42, 279n17, 281n38, 291n67, 297n29
Portugal, María de, 2
Prado, Pérez de, 80
Primaleón, 33, 47–49
Prince of Orange, Filisberto de Chalôns, 294n1
princesa y el segador, La, 155
Prison of Love, 73, 77, 235, 240
Proaza, Alonso de, 99–100, 106, 249, 285nn1 and 26
prostitution in Rome, 188–89, 297n36
Protestantism, 17, 19, 69
Pulgar, Fernando del, 19–20, 22, 80–81, 174, 194–96, 201, 234
purity of the blood. *See* limpieza de sangre

Questión de amor de dos enamorados, 47
Quevedo, Francisco de, 11
Quitsland, Beth, *xii*

Rabelais, François, 300n18
Raffel, Burton, 273n1Pref
Red Sea, parting of, 121, 131
Resende, Garcia de, *Cancioneiro Geral*, 178
Révah, Israel S., 276n38
Reyes, Alfonso, 41, 174
Rhone River, 43, 202

344

Index

Ricapito, Joseph V., *xii*
Ritzenhoff, Ursula, Kathleen V. Kish and, 289n40
Robe, Stanley L., 300n19
Rocafort, Frances, *xii*
Rodríguez-Puértolas, Julio, 64
Rojas, Fernando de, 34–38. *See also* Celestina
Román, 63–64
Rose, Constance H., 280n26
Ruggerio, Michael J., 113, 132, 289–90n49, 292n70
Ruiz, Alonso, 37
Ruiz, Juan, *Libro de buen amor*, 106, 234–35, 286n8, 291n62, 296n19
Russell, Peter E., 302n7

saints, veneration of, 17, 142, 149–51, 202, 207–08, 238, 250–51
Salamanca, University, 7, 9–10, 35, 48
Salomon, Noël, 284n19
Salucio, Agustín, 82, 282n3
Salvador Miguel, Nicasio, 238, 245, 292n71
Salve, Regina, 139–40, 209, 250, 291–92n69
San Bartolomé, College of, 7, 9
sanbenito, 15–16, 18–19, 23, 37, 276n29
Sánchez Calavera, Ferrant, 52, 54–55, 76–77
Sánchez de Badajoz, Diego, 280n25
Sánchez de Cepeda, Juan, 12
Sánchez de Toledo, Juan. *See* Sánchez de Cepeda, Juan
San Pedro, Diego de, 52, 280n23
  Cárcel de amor, 47, 52–53, 70–78, 235
Santa Fe, Francisco de, 19
Santa Fe, Jerónimo de, 5–6, 18–19
Santa María, Pablo de, 79, 81, 275n22
  Scrutinium Scripturarum, 282n1
Santangel, Luis, 19
Santiago, 41–44, 49–50, 202, 208, 251, 279nn16 and 18
Santillana, Marquis of, 81, 275n22
Sarah (Abraham's wife), 75–76, 282nn48–49
Saraiva, Antonio José, 20
Sarmiento, Pedro, 7
Scholberg, Kenneth, 52, 67, 69
Seneor, Abraham (Fernán Núñez Coronel), 30
Sentencia-Estatuto ("Judgment and Statute"), 7–8
Sephardim, 27, 39, 138–39, 192, 223, 252, 288n37

Sermon on the Mount, 146, 204, 215, 249
Serrano Poncela, Segundo, 174
Severin, Dorothy S., *xi*, 103, 165, 288n34, 289nn41–42 and 47, 293n8, 302n7
Shadis, Miriam T., *xii*
Shakespeare, William, 295n15, 300n18
  Passionate Pilgrim, 293n21
Shem Tov, Joseph ben, 60, 168, 210
Shepard, Sanford, 28, 174, 297n38
Shipley, George, 289n48
ship of faith, 162
ship of fools, 214, 218, 229, 231. *See also* boat of folly; folly
Sicroff, Albert A., *xii*, 11, 31, 274n14
Silíceo (Juan Martínez Guijeño), 9, 12
Silverman, Joseph H., xi–xii, 96, 284n21
  and Samuel G. Armistead, 139
Simpson, Lesley, 273n1Pref
Singleton, Mack Hendricks, *xii*
Sitler, Robert, *xii*, 294n29
Sixtus IV, Pope, 14, 16, 297n27
Smith, Dawn L., 273n1Pref
Snow, Joseph T., *xii*, 102–03, 170, 285n3, 286n6, 287n20, 292nn70–71
Sodom and Gomorrah, 248
Solomon, 143, 221, 225, 301n28
Solomon, Moses ben, 210
sophism, 61, 220, 256, 281n33
Spanish disease, 297n37. *See also* syphilis
Spector, Norman, 132
star of David, 182, 200, 254, 297–98n38
Stern, Charlotte M., *xii*
St. James. *See* Santiago
Strbik, Elizabeth, *xii*
Suárez, Luis, 5, 274n8
Suárez Franco, Hernán, 34
Surtz, Ronald, 173, 240–41, 298n42
syllogism, 60–61, 167, 220, 256, 281
syphilis, 38–43, 51, 83, 175, 180, 182, 186–87, 189, 192, 194, 198–200, 202, 206, 208, 213, 227–28, 233, 242, 245, 250–51, 254–56, 278n9, 297n37, 298n47. *See also* American disease; French disease; Neapolitan disease; Spanish disease

Talavera, Fray Hernando de, bishop of Granada, 21, 27, 40
Tarascon (town), 43, 202
Tarascurus (Tarasconus; dragon), 43

345

Index

Tariq, 273n1ch1
Tarquin, 178
Tesalia (Thessaly), 180
Theresa of Avila, St., *ix*, 12, 34, 38, 52, 280n24
Thompson, Stith, Antti Aarne and, 300n19
Toledot Yeshu (Heb. "The Life of Jesus"), 142
toothache, 144, 251
tornadizos ("turncoats"), 6
Torquemada, Juan de, Cardinal, 68, 276n24
Torquemada, Tomás de, 14, 18, 28, 68, 276n24
Torres Naharro, Bartolomé de, 52, 280n25
  Propalladia, 135, 236
  Tinellaria (Tinalaria), 235–36
Transubstantiation, 28, 124, 142, 164, 168, 170, 254, 292n70
Trastámara, Henry, Count of, 2
"Tratado de Centurio," 285n1
tree of folly, 224, 229, 231, 255
Tree of the Knowledge of Good and Evil, 154, 156
trial by ordeal, 70
typology, 281n32

Ugolini, Francesco A., 41, 43, 47–49, 226, 279n15

Valdés, Juan de
  Diálogo de la lengua, 279n14
  Diálogo de las cosas ocurridas en Roma, 174
Valdés index, 69
Valencia, Nicolás de, *x*, 55–56, 68, 138
Valera, Fray Diego de, 54–55
Valera, Mosén Diego de, 52, 280n23, 281n41
  Ceremonial de príncipes, 68

Espejo de verdadera nobleza, 68
Memorial de diversas hazañas, 290n54
Valladolid, Juan de ("Juan Poeta"), 63
Valle Lersundi, Fernando, 278n5
Vaquero, Mercedes, *xii*
Vasvari, Louise O., *xii*, 284n17
Vega, Lope de, 95
  En los indicios la culpa, 276n36
  El niño inocente de La Guardia, 277n46
  El santo niño de La Guardia, 277n46
  Mirad a quién alabáis, 276n36
Vicente, Gil
  Auto da Feira, 160
  Nau de Amores, 177
vida del Lazarillo de Tormes, La, 53, 90–92, 135, 237–38, 281n31, 284n12
Vilanova, Antonio, 175, 236
Villalón, Cristóbal de, *Crotalón*, 222
Villanueva, Darío, 279n15
Virgin Birth, *x*, 28, 142, 151, 155, 166, 168, 170, 254, 288n35
Virgin Mary. *See* name of Mary
voyeurism, 290nn52 and 54

Wandering Jew (Juan d'Espera en Dios), 222, 300n20
Wardropper, Bruce, 175, 187, 194, 298n44
Weinberg, F. M., 107
Weiner, Jack, *xii*, 129, 152, 282n45
Williams, George Hunston, 299n11
witch trials, 17, 20
Wolf, Ferdinand J., 34

Ximénez, Hernán, 9

Zúñiga, Don Francesillo de, 219

About the Author

Manuel da Costa Fontes is a professor of Spanish and Portuguese at Kent State University. The author and editor of several books, he has published widely on the Portuguese ballad, crypto-Judaism, and medieval and Renaissance Spanish literature. His most recent book is *Folklore and Literature: Studies in the Portuguese, Brazilian, Sephardic, and Hispanic Oral Traditions.*

www.ingramcontent.com/pod-product-compliance
Lightning Source LLC
Chambersburg PA
CBHW022008300426
44117CB00005B/87